Teacher-Made Aids
FOR ELEMENTARY SCHOOL MATHEMATICS

Volume 3

*R*EADINGS FROM *ARITHMETIC TEACHER* & *TEACHING CHILDREN MATHEMATICS*

Edited by

Carole J. Reesink

Bemidji State University
Bemidji, Minnesota

National Council of Teachers of Mathematics

Library of Congress Cataloging-in-Publication Data:

Printed in the United States of America

Contents

Introduction 1

1. Computational Skills

a. Sets and Number Relationships

Bring On the Buttons 7
David J. Whitin
Arithmetic Teacher, January 1989

Making Mathematics Meaningful with M&M's 10
Paul S. Knecht
Arithmetic Teacher, May 1991

Humanumerals 12
Caroline Hollingsworth
Arithmetic Teacher, October 1985

From the File: Writing about the Importance of
Numbers 14
Bonnie V. Whitley
Arithmetic Teacher, January 1993

b. Place Value

Hole Math 17
Elisabeth Hanson
Teaching Children Mathematics, January 1996

A Language Arts Approach to Mathematics 21
Mary Lou Nevin
Arithmetic Teacher, November 1992

How to Make a Million 26
William B. Harrison
Arithmetic Teacher, September 1985

Readers' Exchange: "Apartment House"
Place Value 28
Cheryl Cummins
Teaching Children Mathematics, April 1995

From the File: Place Value 29
Mary Godwin
Arithmetic Teacher, November 1987

Readers' Dialogue: Keeping Tabs on a Million 30
Harry Bohan and Peggy Bohan
Arithmetic Teacher, April 1989

c. Computation—Whole Numbers

Let's Do It: Partitioning Sets for Number Concepts,
Place Value, and Long Division 35
John Van de Walle and Charles S. Thompson
Arithmetic Teacher, January 1985

72 Addition Facts Can Be Mastered
by Mid–Grade 1 41
Pamela S. Rightsel and Carol A. Thornton
Arithmetic Teacher, November 1985

Folder Electric Boards 44
Virginia R. Harvin and Ronald C. Welch
Arithmetic Teacher, December 1985

The Number Line and Mental Arithmetic 46
Theodore E. Kurland
Arithmetic Teacher, December 1990

"Equals" Means "Is the Same As" 49
Paul Shoecraft
Arithmetic Teacher, April 1989

Making Connections with Two-Digit
Multiplication 54
Gail R. Englert and Rose Sinicrope
Arithmetic Teacher, April 1994

Hands-On Addition and Subtraction with
the Three Pigs 57
Mary Marron Bartek
Teaching Children Mathematics, October 1997

Transition Boards: A Good Idea Made Better 60
John T. Sutton and Tonya D. Urbatsch
Arithmetic Teacher, January 1991

Let's Do It: The Power of 10 64
Charles S. Thompson and John Van de Walle
Arithmetic Teacher, November 1984

d. Rational Numbers

Multiplication of Fractions through Paper Folding 73
Rose Sinicrope and Harold W. Mick
Arithmetic Teacher, October 1992

From the File: Fraction Mobiles 78
Doris H. Gluck
Arithmetic Teacher, September 1989

IDEAS: Fraction Wheel 79
Alan Barson and Lois Barson
Arithmetic Teacher, January 1988

Fractions and Panes 81
Douglas Edge
Arithmetic Teacher, April 1987

Divide and Conquer: Unit Strips to the Rescue 84
*Frances R. Curcio, Francine Sicklick, and
Susan B. Turkel*
Arithmetic Teacher, December 1987

Two-Sided Pies: Help for Improper Fractions and
Mixed Numbers 90
Jocelyn Marie Rees
Arithmetic Teacher, December 1987

A Common-Cents Approach to Fractions 94
Judy Rocke
Teaching Children Mathematics, December 1995

2. Geometry

Flexible Straws 99
Gerard Prentice
Arithmetic Teacher, November 1989

Build a City 101
Jean A. Reynolds
Arithmetic Teacher, September 1985

Developing Spatial Skills with Three-Dimensional
Puzzles. 104
John Izard
Arithmetic Teacher, February 1990

The Art of Tessellation 107
Paul Giganti, Jr., and Mary Jo Cittadino
Arithmetic Teacher, March 1990

From the File: Predicting Rotations. 116
William Juraschek
Arithmetic Teacher, March 1989

The Inside-Out Box: An Analysis of Structures and
Space. 117
Marilyn L. Fowler
Teaching Children Mathematics, October 1996

Using Reflections to Find Symmetric and
Asymmetric Patterns 120
James R. Bidwell
Arithmetic Teacher, March 1987

Projective Geometry in the Elementary School 125
Helen Mansfield
Arithmetic Teacher, March 1985

Origami: Paper Folding—the Algorithmic Way. 130
Pamela Beth Heukerott
Arithmetic Teacher, January 1988

A Fifth-Grade Similarity Unit 134
*Ernest Woodward, Virginia Gibbs, and
Michael Shoulders*
Arithmetic Teacher, April 1992

From the File: Remove a Pretzel 138
Edward Arnsdorf
Arithmetic Teacher, May 1985

An Invitation to Topology 139
Jeanlee M. Poggi
Arithmetic Teacher, December 1985

Making and Exploring Tangrams 143
Andrejs Dunkels
Arithmetic Teacher, February 1990

Folded Fashions: Symmetry in Clothing Design. 147
Lisa J. Evered
Arithmetic Teacher, December 1992

Investigating Flags: A Multicultural Approach 149
Linda Dolinko
Teaching Children Mathematics, December 1996

Cross Sections of Clay Solids 154
William M. Carroll
Arithmetic Teacher, March 1988

Symmetry the Trademark Way 160
Barbara S. Renshaw
Arithmetic Teacher, September 1986

Symmetry in American Folk Art 164
Claudia Zaslavsky
Arithmetic Teacher, September 1990

3. Measurement

a. Metrics and English

Body Measurement 175
K. Allen Neufeld
Arithmetic Teacher, May 1989

IDEAS: Measurement Scavenger Hunt. 179
Robert Sovchik and L. J. Meconi
Arithmetic Teacher, January 1994

Multilevel Metric Games 181
Rosalie Jensen
Arithmetic Teacher, October 1984

Using a Metric Unit to Help Preservice Teachers
Appreciate the Value of Manipulative Materials . . . 184
Gretchen L. Johnson
Arithmetic Teacher, October 1987

From the File: Teaching Pi and Charity. 189
Jerry Silverman
Arithmetic Teacher, April 1992

b. Money

From the File: Money Bags. 193
Donald E. Van Ostrand
Arithmetic Teacher, November 1988

Teaching Money with Grids 194
Cathy L. Stevenson
Arithmetic Teacher, April 1990

From the File: Math That Rubs You Right. 196
Donna Colwell Rosser
Arithmetic Teacher, March 1991

From the File: Money Dominoes 197
Jean Christian Brewer
Arithmetic Teacher, January 1992

Mathematical Connections: Making It Happen in
Your Classroom 198
Ray T. Robicheaux
Arithmetic Teacher, April 1993

May I Take Your Order? 200
Linda Kulas
Teaching Children Mathematics, January 1997

The 5 and 3 Store. 204
Bonnie Harvey
Arithmetic Teacher, March 1994

c. Time

Readers' Dialogue: Calendar Mathematics. 209
Mary Ann Starkey
Arithmetic Teacher, March 1991

Teaching Students to Tell Time 210
Gloria S. Andrade
Arithmetic Teacher, April 1992

d. Angle

See It, Change It, Reason It Out 217
Jean M. Shaw
Arithmetic Teacher, April 1993

4. Graphs and Charts

Elementary School Activity: Graphing the
Stock Market 223
Margaret Kelly
Arithmetic Teacher, March 1986

Pictures, Tables, Graphs, and Questions:
Statistical Processes 226
Andrew C. Isaacs and Catherine Randall Kelso
Teaching Children Mathematics, February 1996

IDEAS: Which Flavor Wins the Taste Test? 231
*Daniel J. Brahier, Anne F. Brahier, and
William R. Speer*
Arithmetic Teacher, November 1992

Coordinate Geometry—Art and Mathematics 234
Michael Terc
Arithmetic Teacher, October 1985

From the File: Taste That Graph. 236
Joy Glicksberg
Arithmetic Teacher, December 1990

Cemetery Mathematics 237
Ernest Woodward, Sandra Frost, and Anita Smith
Arithmetic Teacher, December 1991

5. Probability and Statistics

Sampling Treats from a School of Fish 245
Jeanne Vissa
Arithmetic Teacher, March 1987

From the File: Using Plastic Recycling Numbers. . . . 247
Jean M. Shaw and Debby A. Chessin
Arithmetic Teacher, May 1994

Gummy Bears in the White House 248
Martin Vern Bonsangue and David L. Pagni
Teaching Children Mathematics, February 1996

Hamster Math: Authentic Experiences in
Data Collection 251
Beth Jorgensen
Teaching Children Mathematics, February 1996

Problem Solving with Combinations 255
Lyn English
Arithmetic Teacher, October 1992

Investigations: It's the Berries 261
Martha H. Hopkins
Teaching Children Mathematics, September 1997

Investigations: Truth or Coincidence? 266
Daniel J. Brahier
Teaching Children Mathematics, December 1996

Investigations: Nuts about Mathematics 270
Daniel J. Brahier and William R. Speer
Teaching Children Mathematics, December 1995

6. Problem Solving

Multiple Strategies: Product of Reasoning and
Communication 277
Alice J. Gill
Arithmetic Teacher, March 1993

Let's Do It: Promoting Mathematical Thinking 283
John Van de Walle and Charles S. Thompson
Arithmetic Teacher, February 1985

Station Break: A Mathematics Game Using
Cooperative Learning and Role Playing. 289
Rebecca D. Rees
Arithmetic Teacher, April 1990

Creative Problem Solving and Red Yarn. 294
Barbara Wilmot
Arithmetic Teacher, December 1985

Celebrate with Mathematics. 296
Winnie J. Peterson
Teaching Children Mathematics, November 1994

Strategy Spotlight: Determining the Correct
Operation with the Slow or Handicapped
Learner 297
Carol A. Thornton
Arithmetic Teacher, October 1987

7. Everyday Applications

"Reality Math" 301
Linda K. Moniuszko
Arithmetic Teacher, September 1991

Math around the Clock 307
Jeane M. Joyner
Arithmetic Teacher, November 1985

Newspapers: Connecting the Mathematics
Classroom to the World 312
Susan R. O'Connell
Teaching Children Mathematics, January 1995

From the File: Record-Setting Word Problems 317
Robert J. Sovchik
Arithmetic Teacher, March 1994

From the File: If Only I Had a V-8 318
Winnie Peterson
Arithmetic Teacher, March 1994

From the File: Finding the Average
with Frisbee Tosses 319
Mary E. Soles
Arithmetic Teacher, January 1989

A Practical Experience in Problem Solving:
A "10 000" Display 320
Linda Bickerton-Ross
Arithmetic Teacher, December 1988

From the File: Bubble Gum Spheres. 322
Gloria Sanok
Arithmetic Teacher, September 1988

Food for Math 323
Mary Brickman
Arithmetic Teacher, September 1986

8. Estimation and Approximation

From the File: Munchie Measurements 327
  Barbara Disharoon
  Arithmetic Teacher, December 1986

Readers' Dialogue: Popcorn and Mathematics 328
  Kimberley Girard
  Arithmetic Teacher, April 1989

Estimation Is Mathematical Thinking 329
  Sandra W. Harte and Matthew J. Glover
  Arithmetic Teacher, October 1993

9. Calculators and Computers

Let Your Fingers Do the Counting 335
  Charles D. Watson and Judy Trowell
  Arithmetic Teacher, October 1988

10. Multipurpose Aids

The Hundred-Board 341
  Marvin C. Volpel
  Arithmetic Teacher, December 1959

Cards, a Good Deal to Offer 346
  Douglas H. Clements and Leroy G. Callahan
  Arithmetic Teacher, September 1986

Manipulatives for the Metal Chalkboard 350
  Janet M. Sharp
  Teaching Children Mathematics, January 1996

IDEAS: Sneaker Tread Prints 352
  Carne S. Barnett
  Arithmetic Teacher, January 1991

From the File: 31derful Ways to Use Math
at Halloween 355
  Cathy A. Barklay
  Arithmetic Teacher, October 1992

Young Students Investigate Number Cubes 356
  Alex Friedlander
  Teaching Children Mathematics, September 1997

Seasonal Crafts: Discovering Mathematical
Relationships and Solving Mathematical
Problems 361
  Sydney L. Schwartz
  Teaching Children Mathematics, December 1994

Jar Lids—an Unusual Math Manipulative 366
  Carol R. Langbort
  Arithmetic Teacher, November 1988

Teaching Mathematics with Technology:
Teacher-Made Overhead Manipulatives 370
  James H. Wiebe
  Arithmetic Teacher, March 1990

Landmark Mathematics 372
  Trudy B. Cunningham
  Arithmetic Teacher, September 1985

Cooking Up Mathematics in the Kindergarten 375
  *Elizabeth Partridge, Sue Austin,
    Elizabeth Wadlington, and Joe Bitner*
  Teaching Children Mathematics, April 1996

Introduction

It has been approximately thirteen years since the last update of the Teacher-Made Aids series. In the subsequent years, the emphasis on using concrete manipulatives in the elementary school classroom has increased, and so it was logical that another collection of journal articles be compiled into a usable resource for the classroom teacher, student teachers, and mathematics supervisors. This present collection covers the time frame of October 1984 to November 1997 and represents an attempt to compile the most usable articles from the last thirteen years, with one exception. That article, "The Hundred-Board," was resurrected from the out-of-print Volume 1 of the Teacher-Made Aids series, since it still has very relevant application to today's mathematics teaching. It is also one that my student teachers are constantly requesting for reference.

This volume, like Volume 2, emphasizes two different kinds of manipulatives and aids: (1) one type where the teacher actually constructs the manipulatives or aids using poster board, glue, and so on, and (2) another type where the teacher uses "easy to obtain" or inexpensive materials to complete the project. From direct experience, the author knows that school budgets for materials other than textbooks are very meager and that most of the time the teachers are forced to make materials or purchase them on their own to make the budget stretch. It is hoped that this book will help with that problem.

Like Volume 2, this book also uses the "Ten Basic Skill Areas" listed by NCTM in the October 1977 *Arithmetic Teacher*. Those original "basic skills" areas were reworked in 1989 into the NCTM *Curriculum and Evaluation Standards for School Mathematics,* which as a whole emphasizes using concrete manipulatives for teaching mathematics understanding. It was difficult to categorize the articles. For example, many of the probability articles, although officially assigned to the probability and statistics area, actually involved real-life applications. It will also be noted that although many more articles could be related to the ten basic skill areas, one area had no applicable activities—Reasonableness of Answers. Perhaps this is an area where more work needs to be done.

I hope that Volume 3 will prove to be as useful to elementary school teachers, student teachers, and mathematics supervisors as Volume 2 has been in my own methods classrooms and workshops. Again, the experience of compiling the articles proved to be difficult. Not all articles dealing with concrete manipulatives or aids could be included, because of space constraints and redundancy. It is my hope that this volume will be as successful as the two previous volumes.

Chapter 1

Computational Skills

a. Sets and Number Relationships

Bring On the Buttons

by

David J. Whitin

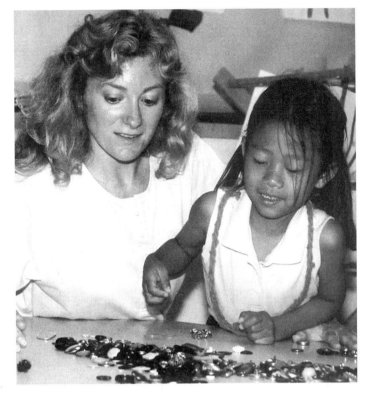

Have you ever entered an unfamiliar grocery store and had difficulty finding a particular item? I have. On what shelf is unsweetened cocoa? Some stores put it with flour and sugar because they consider it a baking product, whereas others place it beside coffee because it comes from a bean. And what about Worcestershire sauce? I have found it grouped with Chinese food in some stores and with condiments in other stores.

Why do I have trouble finding these items? The reason is that I do not know the store's classification system. Foods can be classified in innumerable ways. When I search one shelf and cannot find the needed item, I must devise another classification scheme; I am forced into becoming a more flexible thinker.

WHY CLASSIFICATION IS IMPORTANT

Children too must be given experiences that help them become flexible thinkers. Classifying objects in different ways encourages this kind of thinking. Classification is not only a basic operation in logic but also fundamental to learning about the physical world. We learn to distinguish between reptiles and mammals, oak leaves and maple leaves, blueberries and poisonous berries. Classification skills help us make some sense and order out of the vast number of things that surround us. Thank goodness that libraries, classified ads, and yes, even grocery stores are organized

in a way that allows us to access and use them efficiently. Classification is also a crucial concept for young children to understand before any meaningful number work can begin. Before children can group objects, they must know what a group is. Opportunities to sort and classify offer valuable experiences in helping children build this understanding. Buttons are a particularly useful material for sorting in the primary classroom.

CLASSIFICATION ACTIVITIES

Children can be engaged in numerous sorting activities with buttons. Initially they need to be given ample opportunity to sort and classify these objects in their own ways. As soon as buttons are tipped from the jar, children will not hesitate to share the distinguishing characteristics that they notice.

"Look at this big one!"

"I found one that is kind of rough."

"Mine has a design on it."

At this point your role as a teacher is to encourage children to talk about their discoveries and to share these observations with one another.

"John found a leather button. Has anyone else found a button like that?"

"Is this button the same as that one? How do you know?"

"Sarah, tell me about your buttons."

As children continue to describe their buttons, keep a list of the various attributes and post it on a nearby wall. Some of the characteristics that they notice might include the following:

holes—two holes, four holes, no holes

color—black, white, red, green, pink

size—big, small, tiny, medium

thickness—thin, thick

David Whitin teaches undergraduate and graduate courses at the University of South Carolina, Columbia, SC 29208. He is currently involved in a collaborative research study that focuses on creating a supportive literacy environment for young children.

texture—smooth, slick, groovy, bumpy

function—goes on a heavy coat, goes on a baby's dress

design—rings, bumps, flowers

sheen—shiny, bright, dull, faded

Write down the exact words that the children use. Some may seem more precise than others, but all are worthy contributions to this word bank of classification terms. Encourage children to describe buttons in various ways.

"Bill found this button and he called it shiny. How would you describe it?"

After allowing children several sessions to explore buttons in their own ways, the teacher may introduce the children to some of these classification games. This list of activities is not exhaustive, nor was it created solely by the author. Children devised many of these activities on their own and will continue to create some intriguing games if they are encouraged to do so.

Activity 1: Create a game

"Look at the buttons you have. Make up a game you could play with your buttons. It could be a guessing game, a matching game, or some other kind of game. It might be a game you play by yourself or with a friend. Be ready to share your game later with the class."

Activity 2: Show me

Each person in the group has a collection of buttons and takes a turn asking the group to "show me" a particular kind of button. For instance, one child might say, "Show me a red button," or another might refer to two attributes by saying, "Show me a smooth button with four holes." Each child who has a matching button can place it in the center of the table. The teacher can then ask, "How are these buttons the same? How are they different?" For instance, all the buttons may all be red but vary in size, texture, or number of holes. It is important for children to discuss these similarities and differences.

Activity 3: Making sets

"Sort your group of buttons into exactly two sets. Describe your sets to the rest of the class. Now combine your two button sets and make up a new rule for sorting them. How did you do it this time?" Children need opportunities to sort a given collection in various ways. These kinds of experiences help to demonstrate for children the arbitrary nature of our classification schemes.

A given collection can be sorted in many ways; each way is governed by a unique set of rules and each way is valid. People are always creating and reshuffling their own sets of classification rules as they reorganize a file cabinet, a workbench, or some kitchen shelves. The scheme that they ultimately decide on is the one that seems to be the most useful, convenient, and sensible. Flexible thinkers, however, know that their scheme is an arbitrary one and that they can rearrange their classification rules to meet their changing needs better. An activity such as the one previously described encourages children to be creative thinkers, prodding them to see that a given collection can be classified in

many ways. Whether the task is a classification exercise or a computational problem, good teachers know that it is more important for children to solve one problem in three different ways than three problems in the same way.

Activity 4: Which one is different?

The idea of this game is captured in a line from a song on "Sesame Street" that says, "One of these things is not like the others." One child sets out five buttons, all but one of which has something in common with the others. The partner tries to guess which one is different by giving a verbal explanation. Sometimes the guess may be based on a valid observation but may not be the rule that the first child chose. In this event, the partner needs to be praised for his or her reasoning and encouraged to try again until the secret rule is discovered.

Activity 5: Which one is gone?

Each pair of children takes out a set of three buttons. They study them for a short time and then one child looks away while the partner removes one button. The child looks back and tries to describe the button that is missing. When an adequate description is offered, the button is returned. Some children demand a fairly thorough accounting and request further details before relinquishing the button: "You haven't mentioned if it's shiny or if it has bumps on it. Tell me about that!" Children help each other use this language of attributes in meaningful ways.

Activity 6: Read my mind

Each pair of children selects five buttons. One child thinks of one of these buttons and the partner asks classification questions, trying to figure out which button it is. Only questions that can be answered "yes" or "no" should be asked. How many questions will it take? Can you make another set of five buttons that would be easier to use? Can you think of a set that would make the task more difficult? What happens if you start with a collection of ten buttons?

Activity 7: Put-away game

A group of buttons is placed before a pair of children. One child puts sets of buttons back in the jar according to the directions of the partner: "Put away all the buttons that are smooth" or "Put away all the buttons that have four holes and are not red." Children will monitor each other, making sure all the buttons of the required set are removed.

Activity 8: In my world

One child makes a set of buttons that remains hidden from the partner. The game begins when the first child takes a button from the set, places it on the table, and says, "This button is in my world." After selecting another button that is not part of the set, the child places it on the table also and says, "This button is not in my world." The partner must guess the classification rule by picking a button from the main pile and asking, "Is this button in your world?" After information is obtained from three more buttons, a guess can be made. Play continues until the rule is discovered.

Activity 9: Which loop?

Place two intersecting loops of yarn on the table. One child places buttons with a common attribute in one loop and buttons with a different attribute in the other loop. The overlapping area (or "shared" section, as children describe it) contains buttons with both attributes. As each button is placed into its corresponding loop, the partner tries to guess the classification rules. One such scheme is described in figure 1.

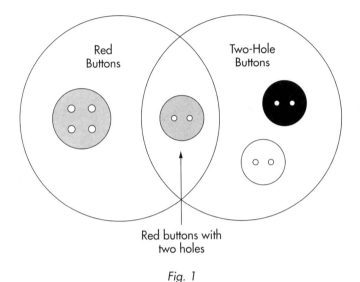

Red buttons with two holes

Fig. 1

Activity 10: Where does it go?

Make a series of cards with one attribute listed on each card. Pick two cards and place each one beside one of two overlapping loops of yarn. Figure 2 shows one example of this arrangement.

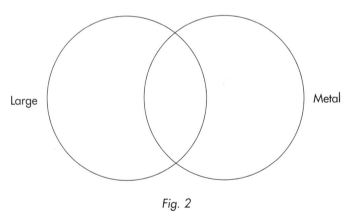

Fig. 2

Each partner takes a turn by closing his or her eyes, picking a button, and then placing it on one of the three sections or outside both strings if the button has neither attribute. To increase the complexity of the game, add a third loop, creating seven different regions, or use a combination of attributes for each loop, such as "large *and* thin" or "two holes *or* textured."

USING CHILDREN'S LITERATURE

Look for ways to integrate the study of buttons into other areas of the classroom. For example, buttons can be related to stories from children's literature. A beautiful classification story about buttons written by Arnold Lobel is entitled "The Lost Button," taken from *Frog and Toad Are Friends.* In this story Toad and Frog go for a walk. When they return, Toad notices that one of the buttons from his jacket is missing. When Frog tries to help his friend find the lost button, he uncovers many buttons in various locations but none possess the particular attributes of Toad's button. Toad finally finds his button lying on the floor in his own house. Onto his jacket Toad sews not only the button he lost but also all the buttons Frog found. Toad then presents Frog with his "new" jacket, covered with many different buttons.

How might this story be used in the classroom?

1. Look at the attributes that Toad describes. Do any children have a button that has four holes or is white, large, round, or thick? Find some of these and share them with the group.

2. The button that Toad was looking for was white, four-holed, big, round, and thick. Does anyone have a button like that?

3. Encourage children to use buttons from the class collection to act out the story. Can you act out the story using a different set of attributes for the buttons? Can you act out the story using a different set of objects, such as keys, shells, or rocks?

HOW TO BEGIN

Since buying new buttons for your classroom collection is expensive, be creative and search them out in other ways: (1) visit yard sales and local flea markets, where jars of buttons can often be purchased for a nominal fee; (2) cut buttons off old clothes that are to be discarded; (3) solicit the help of parents; and (4) ask local dry cleaners for some unclaimed buttons. Consult additional resources for other classification games and activities. Two excellent references include *Mathematics Their Way* by Mary Baratta-Lorton and *Mathematics ... a Way of Thinking* by Robert Baratta-Lorton.

Finally, the National Button Society, a nonprofit organization devoted to the promotion of collecting buttons, has a wealth of information on the history of buttons and disseminates guidelines for classifying certain kinds of buttons. This society also encourages the development of programs for junior collectors. Its address is 2733 Juno Place, Akron, OH 44313.

References

Baratta-Lorton, Mary. *Mathematics Their Way.* Menlo Park, Calif.: Addison-Wesley Publishing Co., 1976.

Baratta-Lorton, Robert. *Mathematics ... a Way of Thinking.* Menlo Park, Calif.: Addison-Wesley Publishing Co., 1977.

Lobel, Arnold. *Frog and Toad Are Friends.* New York: Harper & Row, 1970. ▲

Making Mathematics Meaningful with M&M's

by

Paul S. Knecht

Taking the last M&M from a tiny packet, three-and-one-half-year-old Jonathan observed plaintively, "There aren't much in it." And I began to wonder if M&M's might not just lend themselves to the development of prenumeration skills. Clearly the problem of too few M&M's is one of immediate relevance to children.

So I made a shopping trip. I bought a package of plain M&M's, found some large plastic bracelets that match the colors of M&M's, and added a blue bracelet to the set. I then scrounged some paper napkins and a miniature root-beer mug for a measuring device, and I was ready to try a brand new idea. My first "children," preservice teachers in my mathe-

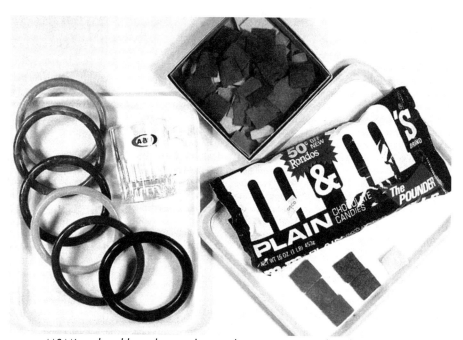

M&M's, colored bracelets, and a root-beer mug captured students' interest.

matics methods class, loved the activity. Next, I needed to see how my idea fared with the preschooler-kindergarten group. After several sessions with nieces and neighbors, I concluded that I was onto something good. One of the preservice teachers tried my plan with a nursery school group and later in her student teaching, and she was enthusiastic about the results. We have used it both to introduce and teach prenumeration skills and to assess students' mastery of these skills. Here is what we did.

We told six pupils that it was time for a mathematics lesson and seated them around a table. They were interested when we presented the colored bracelets and each got to choose one. They were even more interested when we opened the bag of M&M's and poured a root-beer-mug measure of them into a shallow tray on the table. Then we told the pupils that they could have all the M&M's that matched the color of their bracelet. Each bracelet was placed on a napkin and the pupils put the proper color of M&M's into the one they had chosen. They had no problems matching colors, but they exhibited varying degrees of dismay as they realized that some pupils had many M&M's and others had

few and that M&M's don't come in blue. We encouraged the pupils to talk about the situation—to tell how they felt and what they thought should be done. We made it very clear to them that it was up to them to find a way to divide the M&M's so that each pupil was happy with the outcome.

We then asked who had the most. When everyone agreed on the answer, the bracelet with the most was pushed to the center of the table. We then asked who had the next largest number. This pupil's bracelet was put next in order. When disagreement arose, we had to work out a strategy to determine which color went next. One pupil invariably applied the one-to-one-correspondence technique, and we made sure that each pupil could do that. The sets in question were aligned in two rows with each member matched side by side with one member of the set of the other color (fig. 1). This strategy was convincing to everyone. We placed the bracelets with equivalent sets side by side in the lineup and gave them the same ranking. Finally, we placed the blue one at the end of the line.

We talked about the *empty set* and introduced the term *zero* to describe how many M&M's it contained. We asked the pupils to show sets with *more than*, *less than*, and *the same as* a given set, and we practiced using these terms along with *most*, *least*, *next most*, and *equivalent sets* until everyone used them correctly.

Finally, we asked if the pupils would like to eat the M&M's. Interestingly enough, the activities held their attention, so we

Paul Knecht of Northern State College, Aberdeen, SD 57401, is developing a children's laboratory of science and mathematics for the instruction of elementary school teachers. He teaches science and science methods, building language in contexts of meaningful experience.

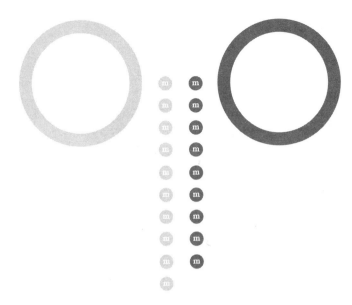

Fig. 1. Determining which set is larger

"fair" and if they were happy with it. One pupil was so concerned for everyone else that she wanted to give most of her M&M's away, keeping only two for herself. Each group with whom we have used this activity has come up with a workable solution. It is important to use a method proposed by the group.

Finally, when everyone agreed that the distribution was fair, the pupils ate the M&M's. We reminded them to rinse their mouths out afterwards, since sugar on the teeth feed the bacteria that create plaque and cause tooth decay!

Extensions of this lesson come readily: cardinal and ordinal numbers and the meaning of addition, subtraction, multiplication, and division are naturals. With one group, our culminating activity was to match the colors of the M&M's with squares of flannel and to build a histogram showing the distribution of colors of M&M's in several samples. We asked, "If you want the most M&M's, which color should you choose? Which color is next best? Do you think every sample of M&M's is like this one? How could we find out? Do you think every bag of M&M's is like this one? How could we find out? Who decides how many M&M's of each color are made? How do they decide? How could we find out?"

All of us enjoyed this experience. Surely one essential of effective mathematics teaching is finding problems that are real for the learner. This one certainly challenged my students to active learning.

Bibliography

Willoughby, Stephen. "How to Teach Mathematical Problem Solving." *Educational Leadership* 42 (April 1985): 90–91. ▲

had no problem delaying this most exciting part. We told them that they could eat the M&M's when everyone was happy with the way they were being shared. Their effusive response took me completely by surprise. They had been thinking about this problem from the outset. The strategies they proposed were both creative and practical. One was to put all the M&M's back into a pile and redistribute them one at a time around the circle. The remainder was to be given to the teacher. Another was to start evening up large and small sets until they were all about equal. We tried every suggestion and let the pupils decide if each was

Color-coordinated bracelets encompass M&M's arranged from most to least.

Humanumerals

by

Caroline Hollingsworth

Although tracing numerals on sandpaper or felt or in a sandbox is often recommended as a way of learning their shapes tactilely, children rarely use more than their fingers and eyes in such an activity. Why not get their whole body into the act? Use body language to transform little humans into *humanumerals!* (See photos 0–9.)

Just as recess often begins with calisthenics, mathematics can start with *numeralsthenics.* Each member of the class, standing next to his or her desk, can form physical representations of successive digits from 0 to 9.

After this warm-up, allow individual pupils to volunteer to play the role of the tens or units digits in whatever family of two-digit numbers are to be studied that day—multiples of 5 or 10, the twenties, the thirties, and so on.

Humanumerals provide an excellent opportunity for teachers to do something that is rarely done—merge two subject areas. Combine mathematics with physical education by shaping up with humanumerals! ▲

Caroline Hollingsworth is an associate professor of education in the Department of Early/Middle Childhood and Reading Education at Valdosta State College, Valdosta, GA 31698, where she prepares preservice and in-service teachers K–8 in mathematics education.

Photographic support was made possible by a Valdosta State College Faculty Research Grant.

From the File: Writing about the Importance of Numbers

by

Bonnie V. Whitley

Numbers

Writing about the Importance of Numbers

Objective: To show the importance of numbers

Materials: A section of newspaper for each student

Distribute a section of newspaper to each student. Have the students proceed as follows:

1. Find a number on one page of the newspaper and write it on a sheet of paper.
2. Write the headline or sentence that contains the number.
3. Rewrite the headline or sentence, leaving out the number.
4. What meaning does the number have? How does omitting the number change the meaning of the headline or sentence?
5. Is the number exact or an estimate? How can you tell?
6. Does a newspaper article always have at least one number in it? Can you find an article that does not have a number in it?
7. Show why numbers are important to a newspaper by giving five ways in which numbers are used in the newspaper.

My students and I were surprised to find only three very short articles without numbers in the forty pages of the newspaper we examined.

From the file of Bonnie V. Whitley, 3770 Knollwood Drive, Troutville, VA 24175 ▲

b. Place Value

Hole Math

by

Elisabeth Hanson

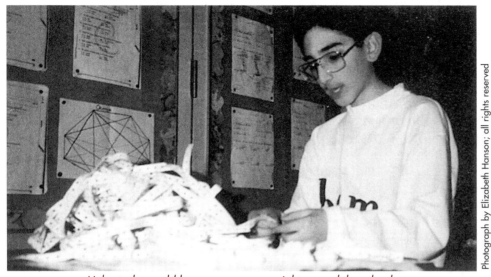

Hole stacks would become a common sight around the school.

"Holey cow! A million is a lot."

"Today we are going to work on *hole* numbers.

"There are a *hole* lot of ways to use your math manipulatives."

Students need concrete materials to manipulate in their study of mathematics. Teachers, therefore, need classroom sets of manipulatives that require limited storage space; are interesting to the students; require little time or energy to ensure that pieces are not lost, broken, or used in hazardous ways; and are flexible enough to be used in teaching many different mathematical concepts. School boards need to show concern for public money as they provide funding for such instructional materials.

Filling such a big order could be difficult, but our school has found a manipulative to do all those things and more, such as inspiring creative-writing activities, supplying material for art projects, and improving the environment by decreasing the amount of material sent to the local landfill.

This mathematics manipulative of the nineties was in the school computer laboratory waiting to be discovered. Once recognized, it spread throughout the K–6 building, leaving few curricular areas untouched. The material, in case the reader has not yet guessed, is the strip of holes that moves computer paper through a printer.

Students routinely remove these strips from the sides of their printouts before turning in assignments. By the end of a typical day, the computer laboratory trash can overflows with these strips of holes. Cleaning up at the end of one day sparked an idea.

When a fifth-grade mathematics class visited the laboratory to work on a spreadsheet assignment, the teacher began to muse aloud. "I wonder how many holes are thrown out on an average day in the laboratory? How long do you think it would take to collect a million holes? How much room would we need to store a million holes? Would they fill a shoe box? The hall showcase? The whole computer laboratory?"

The challenge had been issued. Energy immediately began to surge through the room. Charts were quickly drawn up to record random guesses on the various topics. Random guessing was soon set aside as data were collected. Calculating and serious estimating began. Cooperative groups formed naturally as students with similar ideas for conducting tests or similar hypotheses on results began discussions and research. The numbers of holes per sheet, students per class, and sheets per box of paper were used in calculations. Strips of holes were counted, stacked, and measured, as were shoe boxes, the showcase, and the room. Mathematical discussions, sometimes bordering on arguments, were impossible to contain in one room or class.

The project had begun! Students rapidly began using "holes" in these discussions to refer to the strips with holes in them—we will use their terminology throughout, when appropriate. A special "in" basket on a counter in the computer laboratory replaced the trash can when students began saving the holes from their work. As the basket filled, it was emptied into a plastic grocery bag. The plastic bags filled quickly, and shopping bags were found to hold more efficiently the growing collection of holes. While regular computer lessons went on in the laboratory, groups of students came to conduct further research, measuring or weighing the collection.

The computer-laboratory teacher met with teachers at different grade levels, and a plan was developed for counting the holes. The entire school was now involved—or was soon to be. Learning place-value concepts was the mathematical objective of the activities.

Elizabeth Hanson manages the computer laboratory at Asher Holmes Elementary School, Morganville, NJ 07751; ehanson@llnj.pppl.gov. She helps teachers integrate spreadsheets into their mathematics instruction.

COUNTING BEGINS

Counting began in earnest in March. First graders were the first to get involved. They practiced their counting skills by cutting the long strips of holes, many several pages long, into strips of ten. The ten-strips and any leftover holes were stored in separate containers labeled "tens" and "units," which were placed in each classroom. The "unit" strips were from one through nine holes long. How the counting was accomplished and how much counting was done were left up to the individual teacher. In some instances, the counting was a formal mathematics lesson in place value. In others, it was a playtime activity on rainy days or part of a mathematics station, which could be visited when other activities were complete.

Students discovered that accuracy could be checked by comparing lengths with a strip known to be correct. Spot checks were made. Some classes assigned "checkers." The number of "tens" and "units" grew in each room.

Interested teachers discovered ways to use the strips in their lessons. The boxes of unit strips contained different lengths, from one-strips through nine-strips. With a supply of these strips on each table, students in one class worked in cooperative groups to sort by length. The students then used two-strips to practice counting by 2s to 10 and stapled these ten strips—five two-strips—together. On other days, the size of strips changed and the target was raised. For example, students were asked to count to 100 using 5s, to 81 using 3s, or to 35 using 7s. Problem solving came into play when students became more familiar with the manipulative. "You can use only one kind of unit-strip at a time. Can you make exactly 100 holes? Will any other size of strip also work?"

Try counting to 81 using strips with three holes.

One teacher made a set of construction-paper place mats each with a target number. A numeral and its representation in holes were placed at the top; the mats were laminated for use at the mathematics center. Students then used strips from the units box to illustrate basic addition combinations for the target number. Sometimes only two addends were allowed. Sometimes the challenge was to find three strips that would add to the target. Sometimes the challenge was to find all possible combinations with no restriction on the number of strips used each time. The results were always recorded as equations on lined paper for later reference. Discussions on commutativity and number of families followed.

OTHER GRADES GET INTO THE ACT

The kindergarten students were the next to start counting. They heard the story *A Million Chameleons* by James Young (1990) and speculated on the size of a million things. Since kindergartners'

fine-motor skills are not as well developed as those of first graders, their teachers did not feel that accurately counting the tiny holes and cutting them into ten-strips would be possible. But it was now spring and they had been working with numbers for a while. They were ready to learn to count by 10s. The kindergarten teachers got the boxes of ten-strips that had been produced by the first graders, and the classes began counting them by 10s into 100-hole piles. Handling the ten-strips was not a dexterity problem, and no cutting was needed to form the stacks of 100 holes. With the help of a teaching assistant or parent, these stacks were then stapled together, and new, larger containers labeled "hundreds" were made for each kindergarten classroom.

Second- and third-grade teachers chose to reinforce place-value concepts by having students go through the entire process. They began with long lengths of holes, cut them into ten-strips, stapled the tens to make hundreds (hundred-bundles), and, as work progressed, bundled the hundreds with rubber bands to make thousands (thousand-bundles). While the counting process was going on, often as a free-time activity, manipulatives were being produced for mathematics classes.

Unit-strips were used to introduce the multiplication concepts of repeated addition and commutativity. They were a natural tool for producing arrays. Hundred-bundles, ten-strips, and unit-strips were used to teach or reinforce regrouping in addition and subtraction. Teachers found that activities originally developed for Cuisenaire rods and base-ten blocks could be used with the computer-hole strips produced during the counting process.

Students in grades 4, 5, and 6, although capable of going through the whole counting procedure, also had the ability to deal with the more tedious unit-strips. Students often worked in groups counting and stapling the units into groups of tens, then hundreds. The counted holes were sometimes placed in labeled envelopes when stapling was not practical. Periodically, fourth graders collected the finished thousand-bundles from the lower grades and tied them into ten thousand–packets using turquoise yarn. Unofficial contests evolved between upper-grade classes or groups of counters within classes. Counting in these grades was usually completed during students' free time.

How many shoe boxes are needed to hold one million holes?

In classes, estimation activities continued. How many shoe boxes would be needed to hold the million holes? The volume of shoe boxes was computed. Other measurements were taken. Averages were discussed when it was noticed that all shoe boxes are not the same. A feeling for large numbers began to grow. The holes also served as manipulatives for measurement lessons. "Estimate how many holes equal a gram." "Will 100 one-hole strips weigh the same as 10 ten-hole strips?"

THE "HOLE" SCHOOL IS INVOLVED

While various activities took place in classrooms throughout the school, students in the computer laboratory continued to save holes. The computer teachers in the middle school were enlisted, and their students also set aside the strips instead of trashing them. Although no official request for outside help was made, many students asked parents to save holes or saved their own holes at home and brought them to school, counted and bundled appropriately.

The showcase in the main hall next to the office was dedicated to the hole collection. Initially it was heaped with uncounted holes and decorated with a banner seeking an estimate of the number. As counting activities started, the showcase was transformed into a three-dimensional place-value chart. Different background colors showing ones, tens, hundreds, and thousands lined the back wall. The bundles and strips were piled appropriately on the shelf for storage, and teachers took whatever was needed for their planned lesson, returning to the showcase any remaining or rebundled holes. If some were lost, glued onto charts, or taken out of service in another way, it did not matter. A constant new supply came from the laboratory.

When we had finally collected and counted 10 ten thousand–packets, they were assembled with a band of pale-green butcher paper from the art room. As a few sixth graders created a place for them in the showcase, the morning's quiet was interrupted by the sound of rhythm instruments from the music room being played over the public-address system. The principal's voice was heard throughout the building: "We interrupt our morning's work with an important announcement. Asher students have just finished counting 100 000 holes! Good work and keep counting. I return you now to your regularly scheduled classes. Thank you." This same announcement was to become a milestone marker; by the time summer break rolled around in late June, it had been heard two more times.

PROGRESS TRACKED IN MAIN HALL

On the wall next to the showcase, bar graphs were added, one for each 100 000 holes counted. Bars were colored with a red marker in increments of 10 000 as the packets were placed in the showcase, thus making it easy for all to gauge the progress daily as they entered or left the building or went to the lunchroom.

Our counting results were continuously updated and displayed in the school's showcase.

Describing or categorizing the activities taking place around the building is difficult because of the number of ideas generated. Counting a million holes remained the schoolwide focus, but mathematics, art, and language activities took many forms.

One month, teachers were encouraged to plan a bulletin board somehow related to a million. Language-arts teachers chose expressions involving the word *million,* such as *one in a million* or *thanks a million,* for their theme. Students wrote stories using the expressions as their inspiration. A sixth-grade mathematics teacher had students research how ancient numeration systems indicated large numbers and displayed posters of the results. The computer teacher printed pages of asterisks to use as background paper and added the banner challenge, "Is This a Million *s?" A second grader successfully solved that challenge.

Stacks of ten-strips were stapled to make 100.

During the month of June, one teacher brought to school a "Puzzle of the Week" problem-solving contest each Tuesday morning for presentation during daily announcements. The questions were chosen to relate to large-number concepts, for example, if 2 toy soldiers take up six inches of space, how many feet will you need to line up 1 000 000 soldiers? An answer box was placed in the main hall near her classroom. Students wrote their answer and an explanation of their thinking and placed it in the box during the week. A lottery drawing was made from all the correct answers at the end of the week. The lucky winners received a tube of Life Saver Holes as a prize!

Sixth graders added facts with large numbers or posed simpler questions during their routine morning announcements. For example, an average human head grows about 100 000 hairs at one time. How many people would you need to have 1 000 000 hairs?

By summer vacation, hole mania had definitely set in! Students enjoyed the noisy "news breaks" whenever a hundred thousand–bundle was placed in the showcase. A few students begged to take home bags of holes over summer vacation so that they could keep counting! School ended with more than 300 000 holes in the showcase. Interest remained high.

ANOTHER HOLE YEAR

When school reopened in September, the showcase and bar graphs outlining our goal were still in place. Would we make our goal of one million this year? Five students appeared in the computer laboratory bearing the holes they had counted over the summer. One new kindergartner came in with a friend and with what was, for him, a large shoe box of holes in thousand-hole packets. They were from his older sister, who had graduated from our building the previous spring but spent the summer collecting and counting anyway. Throughout the new school year, holes were available for teachers to use as instructional manipulatives in their mathematics classes and for counting activities. Cartons that once held computers now sat along the wall of the laboratory labeled "tens," "hundreds," and "thousands." The units were stored in a fishbowl. Plastic grocery bags of uncounted holes were stacked in a nearby closet, waiting to be taken to classrooms. Teachers and students could take or leave holes at their convenience. The showcase display grew as hundred thousand–bundles were completed. Counting the unit-strips proved to be a task more tedious than educational and, except in the lowest grades where students worked on basic facts, few people bothered to count them. Not applying the little unit pieces toward the million meant that more of this popular manipulative was available for classroom use. The announcements continued as each new hundred thousand–bundle was completed. As visions of spring started to appear, we had counted approximately 700 000 holes. The staff decided to declare a whole day as "Hole Day"! Standardized testing was scheduled for one week in March before spring break. Everyone took tests for four days; on the fifth day, certain grades were tested in the morning. Friday afternoon, when all testing was completed, was an ideal time for a schoolwide count-in.

The computer-laboratory teacher enlisted the help of fourth-, fifth-, and sixth-grade representatives from the student council. Brown paper bags were labeled with place values appropriate for each class. A student-council representative was assigned to each classroom, with two in each primary-grade room. They helped the younger students with stapling or other tasks, served as runners keeping the classes supplied with the long strips for counting, and delivered completed thousands to the computer laboratory, where other helpers completed ten thousand—and hundred thousand—bundles.

At the appointed time, the entire school began counting together. Approximately fifty minutes later when counting stopped, two hundred thousand more holes had been added to the showcase—with accompanying fanfare. The helpers brought all work in progress to the laboratory and emptied the bags into the appropriate cartons. Although hundreds and thousands of holes were brought in to the laboratory, we had not met the goal of one million holes all in one place. This lack did not keep spirits from being high as students boarded the buses for home amid reminders that "Asher Students Really Count!" The main hall bulletin board also carried this slogan in large print.

Not long after students returned from spring vacation, the last hundred thousand–bundle was placed in the showcase for all to see. The questions were finally answered. Yes, we could save and count one million holes. Yes, we could fit one million holes in the showcase.

It took us almost one year of casual counting and one very busy afternoon. We did not even come close to counting all the saved holes. Months later, overlooked bags of uncounted holes occasionally emerged from the back of computer-room closets. We had had a year of mathematics activity on a budget of under $10, the cost of the Life Saver Hole prizes. We saw what a million of something looked like and experienced what it was like to count to a million.

The computer laboratory continues to generate this free manipulative, and teachers can request holes for their classroom anytime. Some students are still seen leaving the laboratory with handfuls of holes from their own printouts from time to time. Perhaps they are starting their own collection of a million holes!

Bibliography

National Council of Teachers of Mathematics. *Curriculum and Evaluation Standards for School Mathematics.* Reston, Va.: The Council, 1989.

Parker, Janet, and Connie Carroll Widmer. "Teaching Mathematics with Technology: How Big Is a Million?" *Arithmetic Teacher* 39 (September 1991): 38–41.

Ross, Rita, and Ray Kurtz. "Making Manipulatives Work: A Strategy for Success." *Arithmetic Teacher* 40 (January 1993): 254–57.

Schwartz, David M. *How Much Is a Million?* New York: Lothrop, Lee & Shepard, 1985.

———. *If You Made a Million.* New York: Lothrop, Lee & Shepard, 1987.

Young, James. *A Million Chameleons.* Boston: Little, Brown & Co., 1990. ▲

A Language Arts Approach to Mathematics

by

Mary Lou Nevin

© Stan Carstensen

"Getting the bugs out" of learning place-value concepts. Students dramatize the story with ladybugs grouped on paper flowers, then describe and record their results.

Mathematics involves more than just computational skills. Mathematics includes reasoning, thinking, communicating, and solving problems. It involves skills that children have experienced during their preschool years. Preschool children are actively involved in their own learning and through informal learning activities have experienced some of the processes expressed as verbs and listed in the *Curriculum and Evaluation Standards for School Mathematics* (NCTM 1989) as important for students to be able to communicate mathematically—explore, represent, solve, construct, discuss, use, investigate, describe, develop, and predict.

Teachers can help students communicate mathematically by giving them opportunities that reflect these processes. The teacher facilitates learning by starting with tasks that actively involve the students in reasoning, thinking, communicating, and solving problems.

Language is an important part of this active involvement. Language gives students the means to talk about mathematics, record mathematical sentences, and clarify their feelings about mathematics. Language enables students to label an object, describe it, and justify its inclusion. It helps connect the unknown with the known. When students are actively involved in learning a concept, they can discuss their actions and describe them mathematically.

The *Curriculum and Evaluation Standards* (NCTM 1989) focuses on a developmentally appropriate curriculum. The meaning of place value should grow out of the experience of grouping. Young students can begin with grouping small collections of objects and then working up to larger ones. This approach enables them to manipulate the materials easily and also helps to build visual images of the groupings. Once they can manipulate smaller groupings, they are ready to proceed to base-ten groupings. If students feel free to explore and investigate new groupings, they will not be afraid to group and regroup later on when they are introduced to the abstract place-value algorithm.

Literature is a natural way to introduce a new concept. Children love to listen to stories and are eager to become part of them. Stories require children to listen, interpret, and reflect on the content. Stories also help to explore concepts through active participation, to integrate new ideas, and to predict new outcomes. If a story is not available for a particular concept, the teacher can create one.

Grouping bugs helps students understand place value.

The following story was developed to introduce the concept of grouping, which is a prerequisite to understanding base ten. Although this story focuses on groupings of five, the teacher can adapt the story for groupings of ten if the class is developmentally ready.

Mary Lou Nevin teaches classes in mathematics education at California State University/Los Angeles, Los Angeles, CA 90032-8142. Photographs appear through the courtesy of Stan Carstensen and the cooperation of Jeff Ballarn's second-grade class at Monte Vista Elementary School in Los Angeles, whose principal is Marilyn Steuben.

Ladybugs, Take Your Place

Once upon a time some beautiful orange-and-black ladybugs were coming home from a long journey. They had been flying a long, long time and their wings were very tired. Each one kept saying, "Oh, I wish I could find a nice quiet flower garden full of beautiful flowers where I could rest for a while."

All the ladybugs were busy watching for a lovely garden. All of a sudden one ladybug screamed, "Look at that huge flower garden ahead of us!" Her scream frightened the other ladybugs for a moment, but they looked to where she was pointing. They said all together, "Let's fly down and take a closer look." As they flew closer to the flower garden, they said, "This garden is perfect." They loved the big flowers; the little flowers; the blue, red, yellow, orange, purple, and white flowers. Some of the flowers were tall, and some of the flowers were very short. The ladybugs were so excited! They all decided that they had found the perfect place to spend the night. They said, "We'll get a good night's sleep, and then tomorrow morning we shall fly home."

They had so many flowers from which to choose their beds that they had a hard time deciding which one they wanted for their own. As they were chattering and trying to make a decision, a booming voice yelled, "Quiet!" When they were quiet, the voice continued, "If you want to rest on my flowers, you must have five ladybugs on each flower—no more than five and no less than five." The frightened ladybugs said, "A-a-al-alright," and went about finding their beds.

Soon the garden was very quiet. All the ladybugs had fallen fast asleep and were dreaming of beautiful gardens when suddenly a booming voice yelled, "I thought I told you that each flower must have five ladybugs." Three scared little ladybugs answered, "Y-y-yes, but there were only three of us and we th-th-thought it would be OK to rest on this tiny little white flower."

The booming voice shouted, "I told you that you must have five on a flower and I meant five! Since there are only three of you, you will be called *extras* and you will have to rest on the ground until more ladybugs come!" The three sad ladybugs crept slowly down to the ground. They did not like the cold, dark ground, but they huddled together and were soon fast asleep dreaming of the beautiful flowers in the garden.

A classroom discussion in which the teacher asks probing questions can enable the teacher to determine if the students understand the story. Since students learn through talking and discussing ideas, the teacher has the opportunity to clarify any misconceptions they may have prior to proceeding to the next step.

The *Curriculum and Evaluation Standards* (NCTM 1989) states that students need to be actively involved in their learning; they need to construct, modify, and integrate ideas by interacting with the physical world, with materials, and with other students. Dramatizing the story actively involves all the students. They can reconstruct the story, modifying and integrating the various ideas. A successful experience enables them to use their problem-solving abilities to investigate groupings of different sizes, in particular, groups of ten.

Prior to acting out the story, the students can make the various props for the story, for instance, colored flowers and representations of ladybugs.

DRAMATIZING THE STORY

Vocabulary. The vocabulary introduced depends on the developmental level of the students and on their native language.

Materials. Large paper flowers and ladybug hats or paper-plate ladybugs

Directions. The students act out the story using the large flowers and the ladybug hats or the paper-plate representations. One student takes the role of the booming voice.

A discussion could follow of the ladybugs, their feelings, how the grouped ladybugs could make the sad ladybugs feel better, and what would happen if more ladybugs came or some went home.

After the students have dramatized the story several times and seem to understand the groupings, the story can be changed so that more ladybugs come to the garden or some fly home.

Dramatizing helps communicate mathematically.

DRAMATIZING ADDING AND SUBTRACTING LADYBUGS

Vocabulary. Add, subtract

Directions. The story should be retold with more ladybugs coming to visit the garden. Prior to retelling the story, the ladybugs should be identified. Then the class can predict the number of new flowers needed and the number of additional ladybugs. After dramatizing the story, the students can discuss their predictions.

Once the students have been successful with adding more ladybugs, the story can be changed so that some of the ladybugs fly home. The same procedures should be used as in adding ladybugs.

Once the students have dramatized the story and the teacher observes that they have an intuitive grasp of the concept of grouping, they can begin other activities related to the story. Their interpretation of the story enables them to explore groupings while constructing the flower garden; to investigate new groupings when ladybugs come to, or go from, the garden; to predict the number of flowers needed; and to discuss and describe their actions. These actions prepare them to use other materials that represent the actual dramatization.

READINESS

The dramatization of the story makes students active participants in their learning. They have opportunities to think, reason, and solve problems through their participation, which instills confidence in their abilities to group objects. As the students move from being the manipulatives to using ladybugs constructed from lima beans as the manipulative, they need a period of free play to explore the characteristics of the manipulative. I have found that placing the lima-bean ladybugs in a learning center for approximately a week before using them for instruction is adequate for their free play. During this period, the students are free to explore and investigate ways to use the ladybugs and flowers, satisfying their natural curiosity about the manipulative. Free play gives them the background information needed to begin to abstract the concept and helps them begin to build visualization skills, which are necessary at the abstract level.

Again, the students can make the materials used for the following activities. They can paint or cut out construction-paper flowers and ladybugs for the activity. An inexpensive ladybug can be made by spray-painting lima beans orange and letting the students make the ladybugs' spots with felt-tipped markers.

Comprehension check. The teacher should question the students about the story. If they have forgotten the events, the story should be retold.

The students are then ready to use the manipulative materials to develop new groupings, predict the outcomes of the groupings, validate their predictions, and discuss their findings.

LADYBUG ACTIVITIES
Activity 1: Ladybugs and flowers
Vocabulary. Greatest, least, extra

Materials. Ladybugs, flowers, chart (see fig. 1)

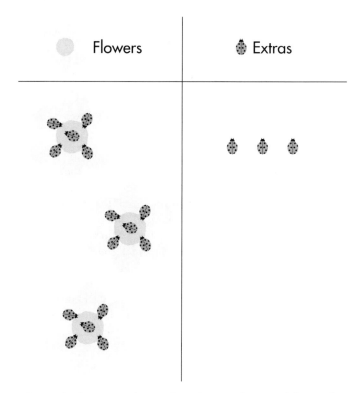

Fig. 1. Students record on a chart their predictions of the number of flowers needed and number of extra ladybugs if each flower holds five ladybugs.

Directions. Each student is given a handful of ladybugs and several flowers. The students investigate the number of ladybugs and predict the number of flowers needed to group five (ten) ladybugs on each flower. They then place the number of flowers needed on their desks and proceed to place five (ten) ladybugs on each flower. Each flower with five (ten) ladybugs is placed on the chart. The students validate their predictions, and the class discusses the results. After this discussion, a comparison of the number of flowers and the number of extra ladybugs can be made.

Learning-center activities. Place the materials in the learning center for further explorations. Small containers with various numbers of ladybugs and flowers should be used.

Optional flowers. Silk flowers can also be used for this activity. Magnets are placed on the ladybugs, and a piece of magnet is placed on the underside of the flower.

Activity 2: Show me
Vocabulary. Show me

Materials. Ladybugs, colored transparent flowers for use on the overhead projector, overhead projector

Directions. The teacher says, "Show me four flowers with five ladybugs on each flower and three extra ladybugs." All students model the grouping, and one is asked to model the grouping on the overhead projector, thus giving the students an immediate check of their work and the opportunity to correct their mistakes. The student demonstrating on the overhead projector describes the next grouping and chooses another student to model the grouping.

Extension. Grouping flowers and ladybugs on a bulletin board. Different numbers of ladybugs and flowers are placed on the bulletin board. The students group the ladybugs according to the teacher's directions. This activity could extend the concept of grouping to groupings of ten.

Activity 3: Imagine
Vocabulary. Imagine

Materials. Ladybugs, transparent flowers, overhead projector

Directions. The teacher tells about some ladybugs flying around looking for a flower bed. The teacher shows some ladybugs for a few seconds on the overhead projector, then turns off the projector. The students are asked to imagine how many flowers would be needed for groupings of five (ten) ladybugs. After several guesses, a student is asked to place the ladybugs on the flowers.

Activity 4: Adding or subtracting ladybugs
Vocabulary. Add, subtract

Materials. Ladybugs, flowers, charts

Directions. The teacher retells the story, with some ladybugs coming to the garden (or some flying away). The students rearrange the ladybugs on the flowers according to the teacher's story. The students can then describe the results, for instance, "I had four flowers and three extra ladybugs. Four more ladybugs came, and now I have five flowers and two extra ladybugs."

Activity 5: Rewrite the story

Vocabulary. Ten

Materials. Ladybugs, flowers, charts

Directions. Retell the story with ten ladybugs on each flower. Give the students small containers of ladybugs and have them place ten ladybugs on each flower then place the flowers and the extra ladybugs on their chart. After all the ladybugs have been placed on the charts, the teacher makes a large chart on the overhead projector or chalkboard and records each student's grouping. A comparison is then made of the numbers of flowers and of extra ladybugs.

Extension. The students are given numbers to represent the numbers of tens and ones they have. The students are then ordered from greatest to least.

Activity 6: Making connections

Materials. Ladybugs, recording devices (magic slates, individual chalkboards, or paper and pencil). (See fig. 2.)

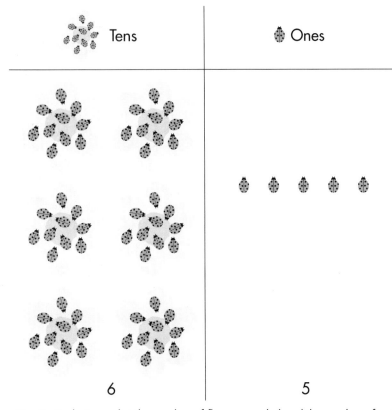

Fig. 2. Students predict the number of flowers needed and the number of extra ladybugs if each flower holds ten ladybugs. Recording devices are used to record the number of flowers and the number of extra ladybugs.

Directions. The teacher should ask the students to draw a large "T" on the recording device and then either to write the word *tens* or to draw a picture of a flower on the left side and either to write the word *ones* or to draw a ladybug on the right side. The teacher then places a grouping on the overhead projector and asks the students to represent the grouping numerically on their recording devices. For example, if the teacher places six flowers with ten ladybugs on each flower and five extra ladybugs, the student records "65."

Extension. The teacher records a number under the tens and the ones columns, and the students use their ladybugs and flowers to model the number. As a further check that the students are distinguishing between tens and ones, the teacher can write a number without using the chart. Students' responses often give a clue as to whether they are reading tens and ones or ones and tens.

Activity 7: Write a problem

Materials. Paper and pencil

Directions. The students should be asked to write problems about the ladybugs. If they cannot write the words, let them draw pictures to represent the ladybugs and flowers, dictate a problem to someone else, or use a tape recorder. Then place the problems in a learning center for other students to solve. Note: The students will also need to make containers of ladybugs to accompany their problems. The students' names are placed on the problems they created, and they are asked to correct all solutions for their problems.

REINFORCEMENT ACTIVITIES

Games enable students to reinforce concepts with their own peers and in a relaxed environment. Games can be varied according to the class's needs.

Activity 8: Ladybug collectors

Materials. Container of ladybugs, flowers, die

Directions. The students roll a die and collect the number of ladybugs indicated on the die. For every ten ladybugs a student collects, he or she is awarded a flower on which to place the group of ten ladybugs. Play continues until a student has a predetermined number of flowers.

Activity 9: Add a bug

Materials. Container of ladybugs, flowers, die, cards with directions (e.g., "You have six flowers with ten ladybugs on each flower.")

Directions. Each student draws a card to begin the game. To construct their flower beds, the students take turns rolling a die and adding the indicated number of ladybugs. When they have ten ladybugs, they must regroup and get another flower. The winner is the first one to get ninety-five (9 flowers and 5 ladybugs) or the student who can tell the number of tens and ones she or he has after an indicated period of time (e.g., 2 minutes). An added rule for the game is that if a student has ten ladybugs and does not place the ladybugs on a flower, any other player can take the ten ladybugs and place them on a flower to add to her or his collection.

Activity 10: The ladybug escape

Materials. Same as those for activity 9

Directions. The students begin with a predetermined number of flowers and ten ladybugs on each flower. A student rolls the die and takes away the number of ladybugs indicated by the die. If fewer than ten ladybugs remain on a flower, the student must discard the flower. The winner is the first person to discard all flowers and all ladybugs or the one who can tell the number of tens and ones remaining after an indicated period of time (e.g., 2 minutes). If a student discovers that another player has a flower with fewer than ten bugs on it, the player must add enough bugs to make ten, since all flowers must have ten bugs.

Activity 11: Ladybug concentration

Materials. Two sets of cards—one with flowers and extra ladybugs and the other with the corresponding numerals representing the numbers of flowers and extra ladybugs (see fig. 3).

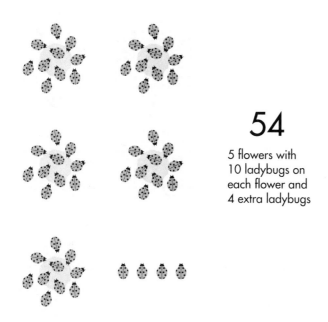

54

5 flowers with 10 ladybugs on each flower and 4 extra ladybugs

Fig. 3. Sample cards for "ladybug concentration"

Directions. Cards are spread out facedown. Students take turns selecting two cards at a time. The players keep those cards that form a pair and return facedown those that do not match. Play continues until all pairs have been matched. The winner is the player holding the most cards at the end of the game.

These activities take students from developing the concept of groupings to understanding base-ten groupings.

Although ladybugs and flowers have been used in these activities, many other materials can be substituted. Commercial products, such as numeration blocks, chain links, and Unifix cubes, or readily accessible materials, such as beans, plastic bags, paper clips, sticks, and rocks, can be used for these activities. The story would need to be changed to accommodate the material used.

CONCLUSION

Integrated language and mathematics activities can help students make sense of mathematics. These activities actively involve students in some of the processes expressed as verbs in the *Curriculum and Evaluation Standards for School Mathematics* (NCTM 1989). Students explore the concept of grouping by constructing groups of flowers and ladybugs, by predicting outcomes of groupings, by representing various groupings, by investigating regrouping, by discussing and describing their actions, and by using manipulatives to develop an understanding of the concept while building visual images.

These activities enable students to move from being a part of the story to using manipulatives to represent the story. Through these activities, students can develop an intuitive feeling for place value, not to mention improve their understanding of grouping and regrouping as they proceed to the abstract algorithms. Mathematics and language used effectively in the same lesson can foster success in mathematics.

Reference

National Council of Teachers of Mathematics. *Curriculum and Evaluation Standards for School Mathematics.* Reston, Va.: The Council, 1989. ▲

How to Make a Million

by

William B. Harrison

Every teacher at some time has heard a child use the words *million, billion,* and *trillion* to describe large numbers. Some rather enterprising students of mine who were bored with such "piddling" numbers as these came up with a *vigintillion.* (Have you heard of it? I hadn't!) A vigintillion is 10^{63} in the United States and France and 10^{120} in Germany and Great Britain.

This hideous number began appearing everywhere among my students: in conversations, in bets, and in written stories. Finally, in desperation, I banned the word from the class, threatening to destroy any paper that mentioned it. Before exorcising it completely, however, I asked, "How big *is* it?" Nobody could come up with any examples. So we talked about "smaller" numbers, and this led to the idea of making a model of 1 million.

Since I did not want the children to see the comparative sizes of 1 and 1 million until the model was completed, they were told only that we needed to build a cubic meter. They were familiar with this shape and its size. After it was built, I would show them how it could also be seen as 1 million.

The children decided to use lunch milk cartons as their building material, since these were available in reasonable quantities. After experimenting with different combinations, we found that if we glued two cartons together side by side, opened the tops, and then joined two sets of two by gluing the open tops together, they formed a sturdy rectangular "brick" that was approximately 12.7 cm × 18.4 cm × 4.4 cm. My students realized that we could not make an edge of exactly one meter with these bricks, but they estimated that by using five and one-half rows with eight bricks in each row, we could make a wall with edges slightly larger than a meter. Thus, one wall would take a total of 16 × 11 = 176 milk cartons.

We collected empty cartons from all the classes every day, washed them thoroughly (sour milk isn't pleasant!), and, after they had dried, glued them together to form the walls (fig. 1). It is important to stress to the students that you are *not* collecting 1 million cartons but are using those you do collect to make walls of a cube that will contain a million units. (An interesting

Fig. 1. Three sides glued together to approximate a cubic meter

related activity is to have the children figure how long it would take to collect a million cartons. My class would have needed around two hundred years!)

We used the students' estimates as guides and ended up with walls that were 101.2 cm × 101.6 cm. Since we started late in the year, we completed only three walls. The students then had to take into account the thickness of the bricks and figure out how much to trim the walls so that the final volume would be one cubic meter. You will have to choose your own method of construction according to the size and shape of your milk cartons and the masonry skills of your students.

When the walls were put together, the children covered each with a square meter of construction paper and drew 10 cm × 10 cm squares on the paper (fig. 2). Both activities were good measuring exercises. At one corner of the large cube, a 10-cm cube had the centimeters drawn in as well, and a face of the very corner centimeter cube was darkened (fig. 3). Finally, each student made a cubic centimeter and compared a face of it to the darkened face of this centimeter cube. The cubic meter contains 1 million of these cubic centimeters.

The model for a million is also useful in describing a billion. If you use a cubic millimeter to represent 1, then the cubic meter represents 1 billion cubic millimeters. However, since it is so difficult to imagine and to make a cubic millimeter, it is easier for

William Harrison is an elementary school teacher at Kyoto International School in Kyoto, Japan 602. Before going to Japan, he taught junior and senior high school mathematics in Massachusetts and Illinois.

Fig. 2. Measuring and drawing 10 cm × 10 cm squares on the sides of the cubic meter

the children to try to understand that it would take one thousand of the cubic meters to make a billion cubic centimeters.

Since all the gluing takes quite a while, I suggest you make this a long-term project that the students can work on in their free time. We took two-and-a-half months to build three sides, but the time was well spent, since the children enjoyed the project so much. They all brought their parents in on the last day of school to show them their million, explaining why we made it and how many of these cubes you would need for larger numbers. They were proud to say, "I made a million." ▲

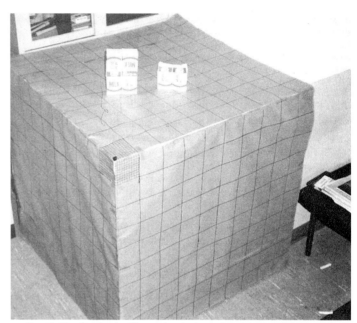
Fig. 3. The finished million. The darkened square on the upper front corner is the face of a cubic centimeter representing 1. On top of the "million" are the milk cartons that served as our building blocks.

Readers' Exchange: "Apartment House" Place Value

by

Cheryl Cummins

First-grade students enjoy learning the basics of place value using milk cartons, straws, and rubber bands. To prepare for a place-value unit, make two "apartment houses" from cafeteria milk cartons. After washing the cartons, open the top completely. Cover each with construction paper and label each as shown in figure 1.

Introduce the students to the "tenants," symbolized by the straws. As "landlord," I tell students the "house rules." A maximum of nine tenants can live in the "ones house," and only

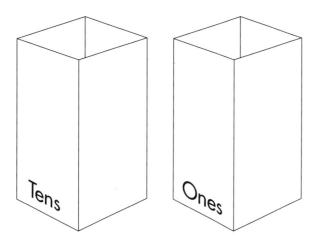

Fig. 1. Place-value apartment buildings

bundles of ten may live in the "tens house." When the tenth tenant tries to move into the ones house, all the ones must "bundle up" and move to the tens house. Model this scenario by putting various numbers of straws in the ones house as students count aloud. When the tenth stick is reached, bundle all ten together and move them to the tens house. To model how to count the tenants, remind students to count everyone in the tens house by ten because those tenants are really bundles of ten; those in the ones house are counted by ones. For example, if I have three bundles in the tens house and five single tenants in the ones house, students count 10, 20, 30, 31, 32, 33, 34, 35, and come up with thirty-five in all.

After some practice, students can make their own apartments, decorating them as they wish. Afterward, they can work in pairs and model bundling up and moving when that tenth tenant moves into the ones house. Also, by working with partners, children can practice counting the bundles of tens and ones, and those who are developmentally ready can write the numerals. This project can be a valuable learning experience for children. Teachers may find that it adds to their repertoire of ways to help children with the place-value concept.

Cheryl Cummins
1403 Brierwood Drive
Cleveland, MS 38732 ▲

From the File: Place Value

by

Mary Godwin

Numeration

Place Value

When teaching the concept of tens and ones, post each day's date using tens rods and ones cubes. (Attach the rods and cubes to oak tag with Fun Tack.) This approach not only reinforces the value of numerals up to 30 or 31 but also lays a groundwork for some mental mathematics activities, such as the following:

1. What date is left if I take away one ten? Two tens?

2. What would the date be if we add another ten? Another one?

3. What day would it be if I take away a one?

Today is
November

From the file of Mary Godwin, Eisenhower School, Piscataway, NJ 08854 ▲

Readers' Dialogue: Keeping Tabs on a Million

by

Harry Bohan

Peggy Bohan

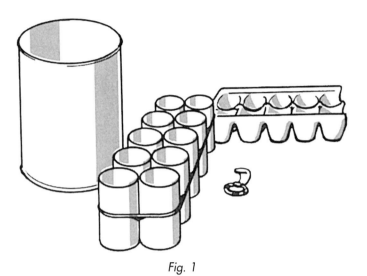

Fig. 1

Last year a third-grade class set out to collect a million tabs from soft-drink cans. Doing such a project periodically is helpful in pointing out to teacher and student alike just how big the number 1 million is. Although we have undertaken similar projects before, this time a new twist was added, leading to some interesting results.

Egg cartons were modified by removing two egg holders (see fig. 1). Incoming tabs were counted out one at a time, ten to an egg holder. Periodically we would stop and ask, "How many do we have now?" "How many tens?" (8), "How many ones?" (4), "What is 8 tens and 4 ones?" (84), "What would we need to have 96 tabs?" (9 full sections and 6 extra tabs).

Next I introduced ten small juice cans bound together with heavy rubber bands. Each can was just large enough to hold 100 tabs. When all ten holders in an egg carton were filled, the contents were poured into one of the juice cans as we repeated, "Ten tens make one hundred." Again we would periodically stop and ask, "How many do we have now? How many hundreds?" (4), "How many tens?" (6), "How many ones?" (8), "What is 4 hundreds, 6 tens, and 8 ones? What would it look like if we had 739 tabs?" Students began to question what we were going to do when all ten juice cans were full.

Ten coffee cans, each large enough to hold a thousand tabs, were introduced. One thousand took on a working definition as the ten full juice cans were poured into a waiting coffee can while we all recited, "Ten hundreds make a thousand." The same place-value-oriented questions were now applied to thousands, hundreds, tens, and ones. Certainly having reached a thousand, the goal of a million must be close at hand!

Soon parents were involved. They too needed help in understanding big numbers! At a PTA meeting several parents commented that we would probably reach our goal of a million in a week or so because they had started collecting tabs both at home and at the office!

We made a great event of the arrival of a large number of tabs. First, students were asked to estimate the number of tabs in the pile. It wasn't long before they began to overcome the third-grade disease of always estimating the number of a pile of anything to be

100! With such large quantities we would check estimates by pouring the tabs into containers of the appropriate size. Instead of counting out the tabs one at a time, we would say, "We had 3 459. Jack brought in 100! How does this contribution change our number? May brought a 1 000. How many do we have now?" The appropriate change was recorded on the bulletin board. (See fig. 2.)

Of course, the ongoing questions were, "Are we almost there? How many more to go? How many till we get to 5 000? Such questions led directly to addition and subtraction applications. The tabs were also useful in skip-counting activities.

Measurement, multiplication, and division applications were also abundant. The tabs were aluminum. Last year this metal was selling for $0.50 a pound. How much do 100 tabs weigh? Estimate and then use a scale to check. How does the weight of 1 000 tabs compare with that of 100 tabs? How could we find the value of 1 000 tabs without dumping them out of the coffee can? (The coffee cans were not made of aluminum.) How many pounds would we have to collect to make $20.00? How much are 10 000 tabs worth?

This activity presented many opportunities for graphing and problem solving. The price of aluminum has been rising. How about a line graph showing that? Should we sell now or hold out for a higher price? What facts do we need to consider when making this decision? How about a permanent graph showing our progress?

Excitement ruled when we first poured ten full coffee cans into one of the eagerly waiting five-gallon buckets! Even the teacher thought a million could not be far away! What a sobering thought to discover that we needed 100 of these ten thousands to reach our goal. Hope dwindled! Three months for 10 000. How many months for a million? How many years for a million?

millions	hundred thousands	ten thousands	thousands	hundreds	tens	ones
		7	8	3	6	5

Fig. 2. Keeping tabs

Now, 79 364 tabs later, a new year begins. Oops, 79 365—a fellow teacher just handed me another tab. Well, we didn't make our goal of a million tabs. However, we did accomplish the goal of having a better appreciation of how big a million really is. More important, no doubt exists that this group of students left my class with a better understanding of place value than any other group that has passed this way. We're starting over in my class, but the quest for a million has become a project of the entire elementary school. Aluminum is up to $0.55 a pound! Certainly a million is now within our grasp! Let's see now, a billion is only a thousand million! That means….

Harry Bohan
Sam Houston State University
Huntsville, TX 77340

Peggy Bohan
Stephen F. Austin Elementary School
Conroe, TX 77306

For other perspectives on a million see the following letters in "Readers' Dialogue": "A Million!?" (October 1987, 4); "How to See a Million" (September 1986, 4); and "How to Make a Million" (April 1986, 41).—Ed. ▲

c. Computation—Whole Numbers

Let's Do It: Partitioning Sets for Number Concepts, Place Value, and Long Division

by

John Van de Walle
Virginia Commonwealth University, Richmond, VA 23284

Charles S. Thompson
University of Louisville, Louisville, KY 40208

Partitioning, or separating objects into a given number of equal sets, is a natural activity for even the youngest schoolchild. We can use this easily understood notion to help develop simple number concepts, counting skills, and place-value concepts and even make long division a relatively painless activity.

WORKING WITH COUNTERS

Several worthwhile activities are possible with little more than such ordinary counters as lima beans, plastic chips, or wood cubes.

Give each child a handful of counters. Fifteen to twenty-five counters will do nicely, and children need not have the same amount. Also provide each child with six squares (15 cm × 15 cm) of construction paper or six small paper cups. These will be used to hold the counters as they are partitioned.

A simple story line will help motivate children for the activity, for example, "The friendly giant had a collection of golden eggs." (Refer to each child's set of counters.) "He wanted to share them among four friends." (Each child sets our four paper squares or cups.) "How many eggs did each friend get?" Assist the children in distributing their counters one at a time. Explain that since the giant is very fair, each friend will get the same amount. If any eggs are left, the giant will keep them for another time. When this process has been completed by all the children, ask a student the following: "Susan, how many eggs did each of your friends get? Did they all get the same amount? Did the giant have any left?" Repeat these same questions with other children, since their answers will vary. Note that the total number of counters need not be known. In fact, that number (the total) may be too large an amount for young children to understand.

Repeat the story several times but vary the number of the giant's friends from two to six. The children will be actively engaged in counting, in matching to see that each of their sets has the same number, and in making comparisons between their sets and those of a nearby classmate.

When children are ready to record what they have done, a record sheet like that in figure 1 can be used to create a more independent activity. It is an option to include the total number of counters at the top of the sheet. After the children separate their counters into two piles, they count the number in each and the number left over. These numbers are recorded on the first line. Next, the same counters are separated into three piles, and so on.

Modify these activities for use with other materials that are available to you. Blocks can be put in stacks, Unifix cubes in bars, and counting sticks in bundles, or rods

___ Beans		
Cups	Number of beans in each	Leftovers
2		
3		
4		
5		
6		

Fig. 1. A record sheet

can be formed into "trains." Changing the type of counters and the story lines will provide enough variation for you to repeat these activities many times.

Although division is usually delayed until third grade, even children in kindergarten can use counters and the partitioning concept to solve story problems involving division. "Mark wanted to put his books in three equal stacks. He had twelve books. How many books should he put in each stack?" Present problems like this orally and let children use counters to solve them. Also be sure to include simple addition, subtraction, and multiplication problems so that the partitioning process does not become mechanical.

PARTITIONING TWO TYPES OF OBJECTS

A simple yet significant step in these activities is to partition, or share, two types of objects. "Sarah was having a party for herself and four of her friends. She had some cookies and some candies, and she wanted to be sure that everyone got the same number of cookies and the same number of candies." For this story, give children different amounts of counters of two types (or colors). The children set out squares of paper as before and distribute the first type of counter, keeping any leftovers aside, and then the second kind of counter. As before, let children count and tell what each resulting set contains. For example, one child might note, "Each of my friends got three cookies and four candies."

The actual counters you use can realistically match the story line. For example, you could have the children partition pencils and crayons, reading books and mathematics books, round shells and curly shells, peanuts and walnuts, or red marbles and blue marbles. You can also begin to use two types of counters in word problems that initially specify how many of each type of object are to be shared. For example, "Margaret has nine pencils and thirteen erasers to share evenly among three people."

EXCHANGING AND TRADING NUMERICALLY RELATED SETS

Completing the previous activities is the first step leading to the *partitioning* of numerically related sets of objects. The second step is *exchanging and trading* numerically related sets, such as place-value pieces.

As a first activity, use beans and agree that a "cup" (of beans) will mean a small paper cup containing five beans. One way to develop this relationship is to start with a pile of beans and empty cups. Each child then counts out his or her own beans into "cups" (of five) and announces the result. "I have three cups (of beans) and two beans left over." This and similar activities can help establish the many-makes-one idea.

A reversal of the activity just described is to start with some cups and beans, with each cup already containing five beans. The children announce the total as "three cups and two." At your signal, each child dumps

out the beans from one cup and announces the result again, "two cups and seven." Then, "one cup and twelve," and finally, "no cups and seventeen." See figure 2.

These place-value, or place-value-readiness, activities can be done with any materials that can be easily counted and grouped. Bundles of craft sticks are popular, and Unifix cubes stuck together into bars are excellent for this purpose. Eventually you will find it advantageous to do these activities on a two-section mat, having children place loose beans or blocks on the right side and the grouped beans or blocks on the left side.

Similar activities involving materials that must be traded instead of grouped should also be completed. The activities are essentially the same, except that they involve trading instead of grouping or ungrouping. For example, centimeter grids can be cut into units, strips, and squares as shown in figure 3. Children can start with a small pile of unit pieces and count out five at a time. Each time they get five units, they trade for a strip. If they get five strips, they trade them for a square. When no more trades are possible, the result is announced or recorded, for example, as two squares, three strips, and four units.

To develop the reverse relationship, each child begins with a few squares, strips, and units. Then, starting with the squares, they trade them (one at a time) for five strips and then trade each strip for five units until only units remain on their playing mats.

Of course, strips and squares can also be cut into groups of three, four, or six. Sticks or Unifix cubes can be bundled and traded just like the strips and squares. On a more abstract level, colored chips or counters can be used as in the chip-trading activities. Then all

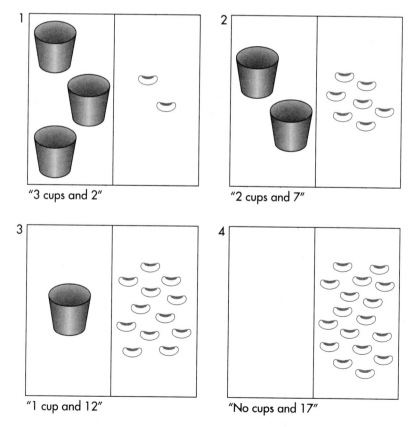

1   "3 cups and 2"

2   "2 cups and 7"

3   "1 cup and 12"

4   "No cups and 17"

Fig. 2. Exchanging and trading

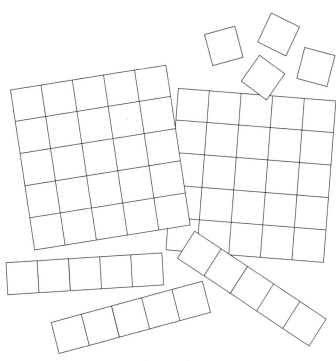

Fig. 3. Trading centimeter squares

Fig. 4. We can separate 7 cups (of 6 beans) and 2 loose beans into 3 equal sets with 2 left over.

children must agree that a certain number of red chips or counters, say five, is "worth" a yellow chip. For example, five reds can be traded for one yellow or one yellow for five reds. Coins (pennies, nickels, and quarters) can be used in the same way.

PARTITIONING NUMERICALLY RELATED SETS

Place-value-readiness activities, such as those done with the strips and squares, are certainly important in preparing children for place-value concepts in base ten. However, both place-value and division concepts are enhanced if numerically related sets are first used in partitioning activities similar to those discussed in the section on partitioning two types of sets.

For the purposes of illustration, we shall refer to cups and beans, although any of the materials discussed can be used. In this example we shall assume that each cup contains six beans. "Today let's pretend that we are in charge of sending out magic beans to our customers. We have five cups (of six beans) and two beans to send to two special customers." Have the children set out five cups and two beans. Set aside any extra cups and beans. The children use squares of construction paper for the "customers" and begin to partition the beans, starting first with the cups. In this case, when four cups have been distributed, ask the class, "Can each customer get another cup of beans?" (No) "So what can we do with the one cup we have left?" (Dump it out and pass out the single beans.) In this problem, each customer will receive two cups and four beans. Repeat the process using up to five "customers" and any number of cups and beans. Do not worry about remainders. Discuss these with the children and agree that if every set cannot get the same number of beans, then extra beans will be kept and called leftovers. Figure 4 shows the results of a similar problem involving leftovers.

The story line and the materials in the example can be changed often to add variety. Soon children should be able to complete the steps themselves, given only the problem statement. First they set out the required number of sets (squares of paper). Next they distribute the largest pieces (or groups), giving the same number to each set. Leftover pieces are then traded or broken apart into the next smaller unit until all materials have been distributed or until fewer units are left than sets. Using groups of six or fewer prevents the tedium that can easily result when groups of seven to ten are used.

Figure 5 shows the first few steps in distributing four squares, two strips, and five units among three sets. The strips and squares are in groups of six. The final result would be that each set contains one square, two strips, and five units, with two units left over.

PARTITIONING IN BASE TEN

The activities described so far are appropriate for first- and second-grade children preparing to learn place-value or division concepts. The activities can also be done by older children in preparation for long division. Any child who can master the type of task illustrated in figure 5 can proceed to the use of base-ten materials and learn to record the results in a structured way.

The first step is simply to repeat the previous partitioning activities using base-ten materials (i.e., cups of ten beans and some loose beans, or ones, tens, and hundreds grids like the units, strips, and squares). Continue posing the problems orally, or in written form, using place-value language: 6 tens and 8 ones separated into four sets. "How many in each set?" The results can be given orally or written in place-value terms: "1 T, 7 O." By third grade, children's use of hundreds in such problems is quite reasonable, for example, 6 hundreds, 2 tens, and 8 ones separated into four sets. Occasionally have children check the accuracy of their results by combining the equal sets they have made plus any leftovers to see that the total equals the initial amount. Besides clearly illustrating why multiplication (equal addition) checks division, the process strengthens place-value concepts and addition-with-regrouping concepts.

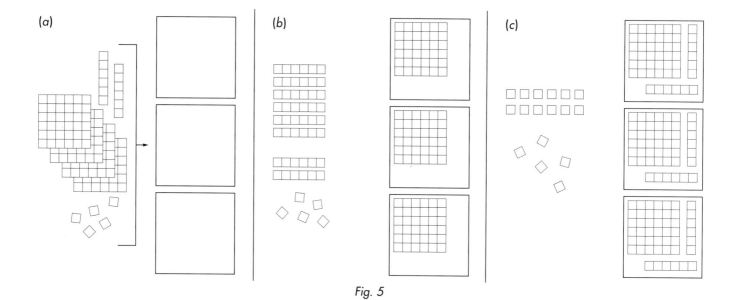

(a)   (b)   (c)

Fig. 5

Try to avoid posing problems requiring excessive counting of materials. Notice that 6 hundreds, 1 ten, and 4 ones separated into five sets requires trading 1 hundred for 10 tens and 1 ten for 10 ones. However, if you start with 4 hundreds instead of 6, the children will have to count out 40 tens, which can be tedious.

It is important for children to work at this strictly manipulative stage until they can routinely work problems without the teacher's direction and until they have developed a clear pattern of language. How many sets? Are there enough hundreds for each set? How many hundreds will each set get? How many hundreds will that be altogether? Are any hundreds left? Can you give more to each set? What do you do with the hundreds that are left over? How many tens should you get in trade? How many tens do you have in all? Are there enough tens for each set? These or similar questions should become so routine that the children are asking them of themselves as they work through the problems. We have found that children have a particular difficulty with the notion of the number "in each set" as opposed to the number "in all." Proceeding to a written level without clearly understanding this language is unnecessarily difficult.

RECORDING

The next step is to teach children to record with numerals what they are doing with the place-value pieces. On the chalkboard, present problems in the traditional format for division and discuss what the numbers mean, that is, the divisor tells how many sets are to be made and the dividend tells how many place-value pieces of each type are to be distributed. Have children use their squares of construction paper and their place-value pieces to set up the problem at their desks, as before (fig. 6(a)).

Work the problem together. After the hundreds have been distributed, stop and discuss how to record the amount distributed to each set. Emphasize that the numerals are written in the hundreds column because hundreds pieces were distributed (fig. 6(b)).

The next question, "How many hundreds were passed out in all?," is difficult because in the manipulative stage (no recording), this

issue is not important. The attention was always directed to the amount remaining. Explain, however, that in sports, in school, and in business, good recordkeeping is important. Thus, we want to keep track of everything so that when we are finished we will have a record of all that we did. The number of hundreds passed out is recorded under the hundreds digit so that we can easily subtract to find the number that are left. This last result should, of course, agree with the number of hundreds remaining to be distributed.

Manipulatively, the next step is to trade the leftover hundreds for tens. After this step is done, a new amount of tens is present, which should be recorded. Here, we would like to suggest a departure from the usual "bring down" process. We have found it easy simply to record exactly what actually has occurred: a change in the number of tens to be distributed. For the problem in figure 6(a), we no longer have five tens but rather twenty-five. Simply cross out the 2 (hundreds) and the 5 (tens) and record the 25 (tens) underneath. This procedure puts the entire numeral 25 in the tens column, which matches exactly the fact that 25 tens are to be distributed.

The next three numbers recorded are all in the tens column, and they parallel exactly the action in the hundreds column: the number of tens in each set (6), the number of tens passed out in all (24, or 6 × 4), and finally, the number of tens remaining (1). See fig. 6(c).

Next a trade is made, 1 ten for 10 ones, and it is recorded in the ones column (but no bring downs!). The ones column is then completed as were the other two.

Some comments on this rather unusual recording procedure are in order. First, note that it completely matches the manipulative procedure and the oral language developed in the very beginning. (See the last paragraph in the previous section.) Manipulatively, nothing is "brought down," and so this rather mysterious and totally symbolic procedure is completely avoided. Second, and most important, we have found that children in the third through sixth grades are able to understand this symbolism. Two months following instruction, one group of third graders was able to explain, in terms of units, strips, and squares, what every number

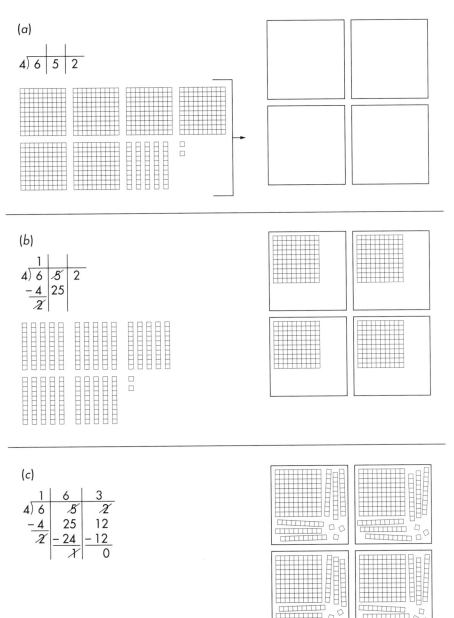

(a)

(b)

(c)

Fig. 6

When children have a problem with the symbolism, it is due to their immature handwriting. We strongly suggest that blank division worksheets be prepared with four division recording forms, like that shown in figure 7. The dividing lines between the placevalue columns are essential. Be sure to make the columns wide enough so that a child can easily write two-digit numerals.

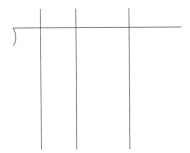

Fig. 7. A blank division recording form

SYMBOLIC WORK

When the children demonstrate that they completely understand the division and the recording processes, the place-value materials can be phased out. This step will be reached by different children at different times. Let those that need the reinforcement use the materials while others work without them.

Teach children to write problems on their own paper and draw place-value columns. If lined paper is turned sideways, two lines can be allotted for each column.

Give word problems frequently for the class to solve symbolically and then discuss the answers, especially the remainders. Once the symbolic procedure is understood, word problems that do not involve partitioning can also be presented, discussed, and then solved using the symbolic procedure already learned. An example of such a problem is the following: "The warehouse clerk had 235 glasses to ship to the department store. Each box would hold 8 glasses. How many boxes would be needed?" The answer to the computation is 29 with 3 left over. Thus, clearly the clerk will need 30 boxes to ship all the glasses.

With a totally symbolic mode, the activities need not be restricted to those involving three-digit dividends. As long as children understand that 1 thousand can be traded for 10 hundreds, such problems as $7104 \div 4$ are quite reasonable.

TWO-DIGIT DIVISORS

In the year 1985 we are a bit uncomfortable writing a paper on how to teach long division. Spending tedious hours drilling long division with two- and three-digit or decimal divisors is clearly an area that could be de-emphasized in favor of teaching problem

in a three-digit-by-one-digit division problem represented. We find no reason ever to change this recording technique to the bring-down version! Thus, no transitional algorithm is needed. Children learn to record what they already understand and continue to use that same symbolism and language long after the place-value materials have been removed.

To connect firmly the symbolism to the actions with the materials, place students in groups of three. Each group is given a set of problems to work, place-value pieces, and paper squares for making the sets. One child in the group is in charge of the materials and works the problem manipulatively. A second child records, with numerals, all the work that is being done manipulatively. The third child is the most important. He or she checks that trades, distributions, and recordings are correctly performed and that the other two workers are indeed working together. After each problem is completed, the three children change roles.

solving and other thinking skills. If long division is taught at all, it should be a meaningful process that can be learned and practiced by the student with minimal frustration.

The concept, the recording technique, and the language used to develop the algorithm with a one-digit divisor are all easily extended to two-digit divisors. To illustrate this point briefly, consider the problem in figure 8. In figure 8(a), two successive trades of place-value pieces have been recorded, producing 485 tens in the tens column. A conservative, or "safe," estimate was made that with this many tens, *at least* 5 tens could be distributed to each of the 67 sets. Multiplication indicates that 335 tens were distributed with 150 tens remaining. (Any number of tens from 3 to 7 could have been put in each set, but the operative phrase is "at least" 5 tens.) The fact that in this example enough tens remain to be distributed to each set presents no problem. Simply record in the tens column, above the 5, that 2 more tens are distributed (fig. 8(b)) and continue as before. When the problem is complete, it is clear that 7 tens and 2 ones were distributed with 32 ones left over.

If you follow the language of the place-value pieces exactly as was done in the manipulative activities, no new concept needs to be taught. Allowing children to make a second distribution in any column by stacking up the digits relieves the pressure and tedium frequently associated with long division.

We have used this approach and algorithm with children in the third through sixth grades. We see absolutely no reason to change the approach to introduce the "traditional" algorithm. A transition to any other form is not needed, ever! We have used it ourselves (in the absence of calculators). Why change it?

CONCLUSION

Certainly we are not the first to suggest using place-value pieces and partitioning to develop children's concepts of long division. We have tried to present a series of activities that will augment the development of number, counting, and place-value concepts in the earliest grades and to extend these concepts to a partitioning approach for long division in the third grade and up. Further, we have proposed some minor changes in the symbolic form of the algorithm for long division that we believe have a number of significant advantages, if indeed an algorithm for long division must be taught at all. Perhaps the algorithm we have illustrated will prove a little easier to live with until the day when long division with multidigit divisors is removed from the curriculum. ▲

(a)   (b)

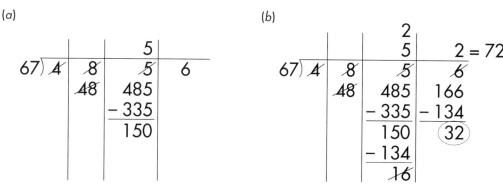

Fig. 8. Extending the approach to two-digit divisors

72 Addition Facts Can Be Mastered by Mid-Grade 1

by

Pamela S. Rightsel

Carol A. Thornton

We made it fun and made it work! Children in our first-grade classes mastered 72 of the 100 addition facts by the middle of first grade. The facts learned were of four types: "count ons" (facts having addends of 1, 2, or 3), "zero" facts, 10 sums, and doubles. Mastery was defined as a two-second response to a given addition fact. The school district also lent its support and gave permission to delay the formal teaching of subtraction until the second semester. The following sequence of activities serves as an outline of the approach that was taken.

1. *Count on.* At the beginning of the year, as part of early number work, the skill of counting on (1, 2, or 3) from any number (2–9) was developed and practiced.

2. *Circle the "bigger."* Early number work also focused on comparisons of numbers (to 10). At first, objects were used to illustrate the usual 1:1 matching procedure. Eventually, given two numbers, the children could circle the bigger.

3. *Frame and count on.* A deck of number cards (1–9), a small bucket, and chips were used. Cards were placed facedown in two piles: 1, 2, and 3 in the first pile; 4–9 in the second. Taking turns, the children drew a card from each pile and placed each on the ledge of the chalkboard for all to see. The children identified the "bigger" number and framed it with their hands. Then they counted on from the other number while the correct number of chips were dropped into the bucket (fig. 1). Children quickly learned to "read" cards like those in figure 1 as "frame 9, count on 2."

Fig. 1. Frame 9, count on 2.

4. *Circle the big one and count on.* Follow-up seat work involved sheets like that shown in figure 2. Children were asked to circle the bigger number, count on from it, and write the total. At first some children physically performed the framing and dropping movements as they circled numbers and counted on.

How Many in All?
1. 2, 7 _____
2. 5, 3 _____
3. 1, 8 _____
4. 2, 6 _____

Fig. 2. Circle the larger number, count on from there, and write the total.

5. 9 + 2: "9, count on 2." The term *addition* was then formally introduced: "We *add* when we put things together to find 'how many in all.'" Other situations involving addition, in and out of the classroom, were discussed and modeled. "When we add we can count on from the bigger number to find the total." So, at first, 9 + 2 was read as "9, *count on* 2." Later, the conventional term *plus* (used in our school district) was introduced, and the transition to 9 + 2 as "9 *plus* 2" was made.

6. *Turnarounds.* Next children explored the fact that "turnarounds" (commutatives) have the same answer. Two related activities were carried out.

    a. *Turn the paper around.* To start, children were asked to draw a picture of, and answer, an easy fact like 4 + 2 = __ (fig. 3(*a*)). Then they turned their paper 180° (fig. 3(*b*)) and wrote the fact to describe the picture.

    b. *Animal turnarounds.* The animal characters in figure 4(*a*) were used to reinforce the "turnaround" idea. Taking turns, children matched such turnarounds as 9 + 1 = 10 and 1 + 9 = 10, placed them together (fig. 4(*b*)), and turned the cards from front to back as they read the two related facts aloud.

Pam Rightsel teaches first grade in McLean County Unit District No. 5 at Hudson Grade School, Hudson, IL 61748. She has ten years of teaching experience at the primary level. Carol Thornton is a mathematics educator at Illinois State University, Normal, IL 61761, who currently is directing a federally funded, statewide project that, in 1983–84, focused on children's learning of number facts involving addition and subtraction.

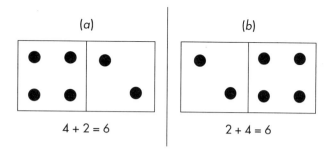

(a)

(b)

4 + 2 = 6

2 + 4 = 6

Fig. 3. "Turnarounds" have the same answers.

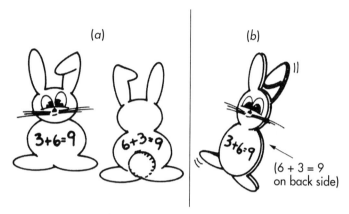

(a)

(b)

(6 + 3 = 9 on back side)

Fig. 4. Animal characters reinforce the turnaround idea.

7. *Zero facts.* Chips were used to illustrate such facts as 6 + 0 and 0 + 3. Besides the 6 and the 3, no extra chips are counted, so the nonzero number is the total.

8. *10 frame for "10 sums."* "What two numbers make 10?" This question was investigated next. At first children did a lot of work with Styrofoam chips on a 10 frame (fig. 5(a)). The teacher modeled the activity on the overhead projector using a 10-frame transparency and transparent chips. The children learned that the frame had ten spaces and practiced until they could quickly tell the number of spaces that were filled and empty in a 10 frame like that in figure 5(b). Later children wrote the number fact for given 10-frame pictures (see fig. 5(c)). They loved pages on which they only worked with number facts that had 10 as an answer (this idea was also used as a flash-card drill on "10" sums), and they liked the concentration game (using the 0–10 cards) in which any pair totaling 10 was a match.

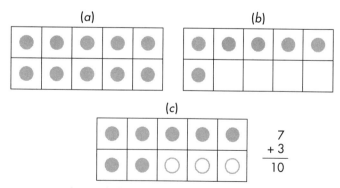

(a)

(b)

(c)

7
+ 3
___
10

Fig. 5. 10 frames helped students answer "What two numbers make 10?"

9. *Picture the double.* Pictures similar to those described for doubles by Thornton (1982) were used. Only three doubles were introduced in a session. Whenever possible, children were drawn into an activity as the picture for each double was presented. For 5 + 5, children traced each others' hands and marked "5" on each, "10" in all. For 7 + 7, they circled two full weeks on a calendar and counted the days in each week (7) and the total for both weeks (14). For 6 + 6, they dropped bottle caps of two colors into an egg carton and counted the total (12).

For 4 + 4, they drew a spider in the shape of an 8, "with a little head and big body," and four legs on each side (fig. 6). Then they traced over with their fingers the total number of legs (the "8" in the picture) before they wrote 4 + 4 = 8 underneath the picture.

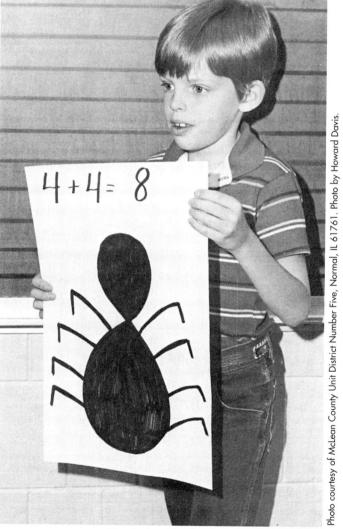

Photo courtesy of McLean County Unit District Number Five, Normal, IL 61761. Photo by Howard Davis.

Fig. 6. A spider for 8

10. *Stick and sum.* As follow-up work, children pasted pictures of each new double beside the corresponding written fact. From this point on, 5 + 5 was the "fingers fact," 7 + 7 was the "two-week fact," and so on. Thus, verbal as well as visual prompting was used. Children then completed exercises containing a mix of the facts studied to date. These exercises

often included special directions such as the following: "Use a green crayon. Circle all the two-week facts you can find on this page."

11. *Doubles concentration.* Following the introduction of all the doubles facts, a concentration game was constructed for each student. The doubles pictures were dittoed on one color of construction paper. On paper of another color, the doubles facts were dittoed. The children cut out the pieces on each paper and played doubles concentration with a partner and, later, with their parents.

12. *Speed drills.* Throughout this phase, *daily* fact drills of three to five minutes each were used once children had mastered two prerequisites:

   a. They could demonstrate their grasp of the addition *concept* by using counters to find or check answers to given facts.

   b. They could derive the answer to a given fact by using an appropriate strategy (e.g., counting on, thinking of the picture, or using the 10 frame).

One favorite game of this group was "race row." On a page with several rows of facts, *one* row was designated as the "race row." When all students were ready, a particular row was announced, and children circled it with a red crayon and raced to finish it. The goal was to see what row of students or team finished first.

Note. The progress of the children reported on here was paralleled by that of first graders and young special education students of 100 teachers throughout Illinois who recently participated in a project funded by the U.S. Department of Education's Division of Special Education and Rehabilitative Services (Grant No. G008301694, Project No. 029KH30133) to improve number-fact learning of developmentally immature and handicapped learners. Teachers in the project delayed work on subtraction until after Thanksgiving to focus early in the school year on counting skills, place value, and addition-concept work.

Reference

Thornton, Carol A. "Doubles Up—Easy!" *Arithmetic Teacher* 29 (April 1982): 20. ▲

Folder Electric Boards

by

Virginia R. Harvin

Ronald C. Welch

We know that immediate reinforcement of behavior facilitates learning. Teachers can easily make a device that provides immediate positive reinforcement—the electric board.

Electric boards have been available to teachers for many years; however, the older boards had serious limitations. They were cumbersome and usually had one wiring scheme, which was difficult to change. Once the students learned the pattern of the wiring scheme, they no longer benefited from matching questions and answers.

Flexible electric boards can be made by the teacher from manila folders, strips of foil, and a battery. The boards are lightweight, and the electrical pattern can be easily changed.

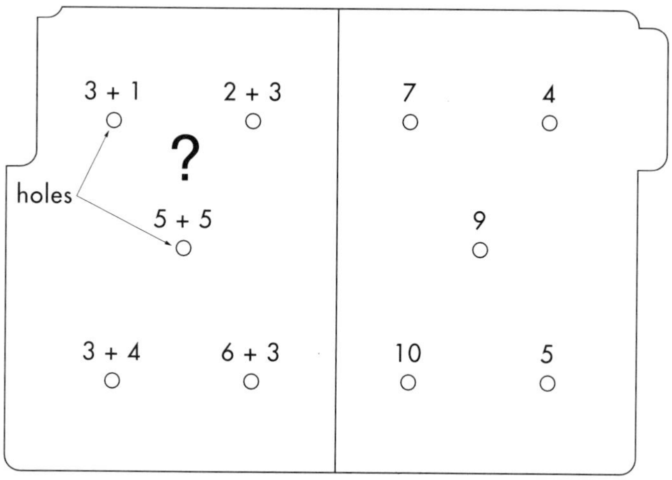

THE ELECTRIC BOARD

Making the electric board is easy. First, decide the skill to be practiced. Then write questions for the skill to be reviewed on one outer side of a manila folder and answers on the other. Cover the sides with clear adhesive paper or laminate them for durability. You may want to draw or paste some colorful pictures on the folder among the questions and answers to make the electric board more attractive for the user. After the folder is covered with questions and answers, use a paper punch to make a hole near each question and each answer. See figure 1.

The inside of the folder is now ready to be made into a series of circuits. Place a strip of aluminum foil from the hole for each question to the hole for the correct answer. Cover each piece of aluminum foil with masking tape as you place it on the back of the folder to keep the strips from shorting. See figure 2. After all the questions and answers have been connected, tape another folder to the back of the completed folder and seal the two together with tape. See figure 3.

Fig. 1. Punch holes near the questions and answers on a manila folder.

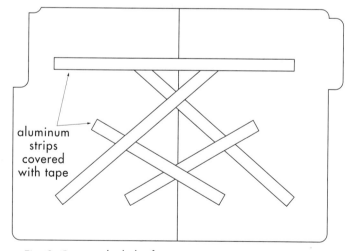

Fig. 2. Connect the holes from a question to its correct answer.

Virginia Harvin and Ronald Welch are professors of mathematics education in the School of Education at Indiana University, Marott Building, 902 North Meridian, Indianapolis, IN 46204. They both teach undergraduate and graduate courses in mathematics education and also serve as mathematics education consultants in public schools at the local, state, and national levels.

Now you are ready to connect the batteries. Attach one piece of light-gauge insulated wire about 60 cm long to the positive terminal of a 6-volt lantern battery (fig. 4). Attach another piece of light-gauge insulated wire about 5 cm long to the negative terminal of the battery. (Remember to trim the insulation from the wire before attaching it to the battery.) Connect the unattached

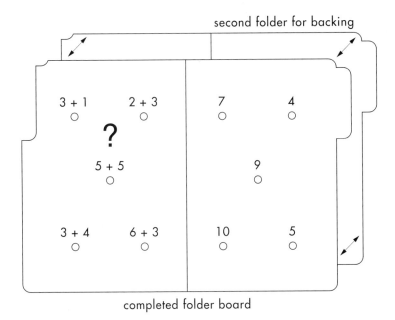

second folder for backing

3 + 1   2 + 3   7   4
  ○   ○   ○   ○

    ?

      5 + 5   9
        ○   ○

3 + 4   6 + 3   10   5
  ○   ○   ○   ○

completed folder board

Fig. 3. Cover the circuits with another folder.

end of the 5-cm piece of wire to a 6-volt light socket containing a bulb. On the other side of the light socket, attach a trimmed piece of insulated wire about 60 cm in length. Trim each end of the loose wires and attach alligator clips.

The battery can be placed in a margarine tub with a hole cut in the lid to allow the light bulb to stick through. The tub helps to hold the battery secure during use. The margarine lid can be decorated like a clown's face with the light for the nose. The child tests a match of a numeral with an equivalent expression by placing the two clips in the appropriate holes. If the answer is correct, the clown's nose will light up.

The electric board offers the students a novel reinforcement as they practice their skills. Some of the topics for which the board is helpful are basic facts, sets, measurement, time, money, and geometry. Students find electric boards challenging and fun. ▲

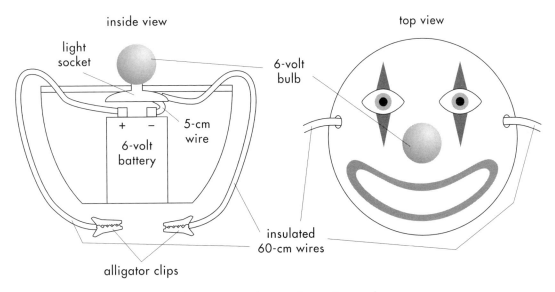

inside view   top view

light socket

6-volt bulb

5-cm wire

+ −
6-volt battery

insulated 60-cm wires

alligator clips

Fig. 4. The system used to match questions and answers

The Number Line and Mental Arithmetic

by

Theodore E. Kurland

Some students have easily recognized difficulties with addition and subtraction. Some have no trouble adding or subtracting single-digit numbers when the sums are less than ten (7 + 2, 5 + 4, etc.) but have to resort to their fingers for sums greater than ten (7 + 5, 8 + 6, etc.). Other students have no difficulty adding numbers whose sums are greater than ten, such as 7 + 5, but have difficulty determining their differences, like 12 – 7. Finally, some students have no difficulty adding 7 + 5 or 8 + 4 but cannot mentally add 17 + 5 or 18 + 4 or recognize the connection between the sum of single-digit numbers and numbers increased by orders of ten. Any one or a combination of these difficulties may appear when students compute; moreover, these problems will continue to plague them, curtailing their confidence and development in mathematics and mental arithmetic.

I have found an easy and effective method for correcting these persistent problems. This method takes adding and subtracting out of the realm of memorizing seemingly separate and unrelated facts and presents the procedures as an interrelated series of patterns. By using the number line, the student can observe at a glance several concepts pertaining to addition and subtraction, thus facilitating a mental picture of these concepts, their interrelatedness, and their transferability.

I start with a number line arranged as shown in figure 1. "Interval" cards, which correspond to the differences between the numbers on the number line, are used to display the intervals from two to ten. These interval cards are easily drawn on three-inch-by-five-inch cards like the one shown in figure 2. The interval cards demonstrate to the student that (1) addition on the number line proceeds from left to right, (2) subtraction proceeds from right to left, and (3) the difference between numbers can be viewed as a unique interval. At this level, the + and –

signs refer to addition and subtraction only and not to positive and negative integers. Thus, as shown in figure 3, the student would write 6 + 7 = 13 or 13 – 7 = 6.

By sliding the interval card along the number line, students can view all pairs of numbers with differences of seven and associate them simultaneously with the sum of the interval (seven) and the number on the number line to which it is being added. This addition and subtraction duality is very important for the students to see and understand, especially for those who have an easier time adding than subtracting (some students will count backward when subtracting). Taking time to let the student get familiar with the notion that this unique interval between pairs of numbers on the number line is both an addend and a difference is very rewarding, for the students will see that the subtraction process can be viewed as another addition process. In other words, instead of seeing subtraction as addition in reverse, as in "What is six from thirteen?" or "From thirteen subtract six," they will see it as just another addition problem by saying, "What must I add to six (in fig. 3) to get thirteen?"

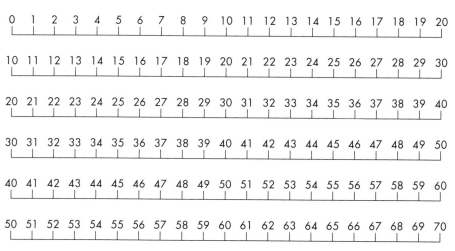

Fig. 1. My version of a number line

Several other relationships can be viewed on the number line and can help students form associations that will augment their arithmetic skills. Another such concept is demonstrated by moving the interval card down the series of number lines to show that if

Ted Kurland teaches eighth grade at Johnston Middle School, Houston, TX 77096. He is interested in developing manipulatives and visual aids that help students visualize and experience mathematical concepts.

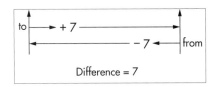

Fig. 2. The interval card

7 + 5 = 12, then 17 + 5 = 22, 27 + 5 = 32, and so on, as illustrated in figure 4. Students who fail to recognize this relationship have difficulty with 25 + 7 even though they know that 5 + 7 = 12. Here again, sliding the interval card along a vertical path that increases the sums by magnitudes of ten illustrates to the students that the facts they already know concerning sums and differences of single-digit numbers can be transferred to numbers throughout the number system.

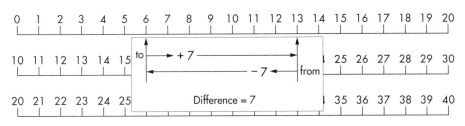

Fig. 3. The additive interval equals the difference.

With guided oral as well as written practice, students can develop a mental picture of the number line and the "difference intervals." An example of one activity sheet is shown in figure 5. Moreover, students use the cards and number line to explore other concepts, either independently or with guidance. For example, one excited fourth grader exclaimed, "Look! I can multiply with this." He then proceeded to explain while moving the 5-card along the line, as shown in figure 6, "See, three times five is fifteen."

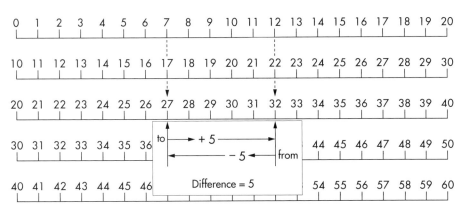

Fig. 4. Numbers increased by ten with a constant interval

The interval cards can also demonstrate what is meant by the *remainder* in division. This often-misunderstood concept is illustrated in figure 7 using the problem 13 ÷ 4. In figure 7a, we see that thirteen includes three groups of four with one unit (ones) remaining; whereas figure 7b shows that four can be divided into thirteen three whole times with an additional one of its four parts (1/4) *included*. In the second example, the term *remainder* is misleading, for the one-fourth represents not what remains but rather the additional portion that is "contained" in the answer.

Number Line
(to be filled out using the interval cards and number line)

Name _____

Interval Card	To or from =	Restate	Reverse Direction	Difference between
Add 6	to 7 = 13	7 + 6 = 13	13 − 6 = 7	13 and 7 is 6
Add 6	to 17 =			
Add 6	to 47 =			

⋮ ⋮ ⋮ ⋮

Subt 7	from 15 =			
Subt 7	from 25 =			
Subt 7	from 35 =			

⋮ ⋮ ⋮ ⋮

Fig. 5. Sample activity sheet

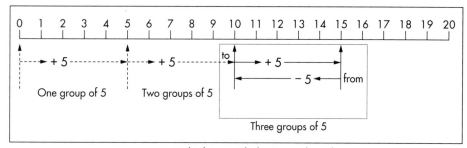

Fig. 6. Multiplying with the interval cards

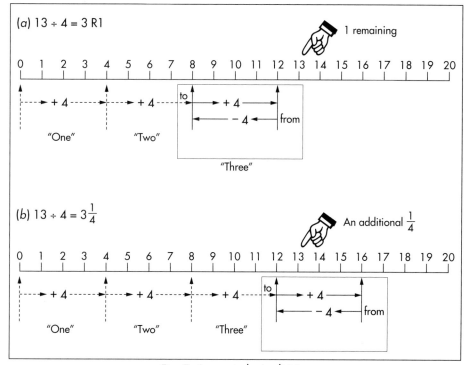

Fig. 7. A remainder in division

Finally, by developing a mental picture of the number line with its continuity and repetition of visual patterns, students will be able to find new strategies and insights that will greatly enhance their computational skills, as well as their understanding of the number system and its properties. ▲

"Equals" Means "Is the Same As"

Paul Shoecraft

Sister: "How are you doing in school?"

Brother: "Not good. Too many eagles."

Sister: "Eagles?"

Brother: "Yes. One plus one eagles two, two plus two eagles four, three plus three eagles six, ..."

"Equals" is a source of confusion for many children. Shown the following number sentences,

$$8 = 3 + 5,$$
$$6 = 6,$$

and

$$2 + 7 = 4 + 5,$$

many will alter the first to 3 + 5 = 8, the second to 6 + 0 = 6, and the third to 2 + 7 = 9 and 4 + 5 = 9 or 2 + 7 + 4 + 5 = 18. This inclination is particularly true of third graders; as many as 90 percent will reject 6 = 6.

Children exhibit a strong tendency to accept "equals" only when an operation sign such as "+" or "−" precedes it (Behr, Erlwanger, and Nichols 1980; Kieran 1981; Nibbelink 1981). They tend to think of it as an "operator," as an action signal like "find the answer," or as representing actions like "adds up to" (for addition sentences) or "produces" (for subtraction sentences) (Denmark 1976; Ginsburg 1982). Instead, they should interpret it as a relation, as a statement comparing two entities. It says in 8 = 3 + 5, for instance, that 8 "is the same as" 3 + 5.

Various factors, including the nature of present instruction, direct children's attention away from the correct meaning of "equals." Baroody and Ginsburg (1983, 200) state the following:

> Why ... do children seem to view "equals" as an operator rather than a relational symbol? One view is that this perception is an artifact of their early arithmetic training (Renwick 1932). Children are usually introduced to "equals" in the context of adding and in the 1 + 1 = ? format. Workbook and ditto exercises reinforce this format, and the child becomes accustomed to "equals" implying "adds up to" (cf. Van de Walle 1980). Indeed, Denmark, Barco, and Voran (1976) surveyed 10 elementary texts and found that "equals" as a relational symbol was generally not developed.

Thus from the very beginning of their schooling, children are predisposed to view or assimilate "equals" as an operator.

Ways to modify present instruction so as to draw attention to the relational meaning of "equals" include the following:

- Begin the use of the equal sign with equivalent and unequivalent numbers and sets of objects (e.g., 3 = 3, 4 ≠ 5,

$$\Box\Box\Box = {}_{\Box}\Box^{\Box}, \quad \Box\Box\Box\Box \neq {}^{\Box}\Box{}_{\Box}\Box^{\Box})$$

(Wynroth 1975). With kindergarten children, continue for three to four months before using the equal sign with addition and subtraction (Baroody and Ginsburg 1983).

- When first introducing addition and subtraction, avoid the use of the term "equals" and use instead phrases like "How much is

3 plus 4?" or "What is left if you subtract 3 from 5?" Parallel such instruction with nonstandard ways of representing "equals" (e.g.,

$$5$$
$$2 + 3$$

or $7 - 5 \rightarrow 2$) (Wynroth 1975).

- When speaking about number sentences, use phrases like "is the same as" or "is another name for" instead of "equals."

- Contrast "equals" with other relational terms such as "less" (or "shorter," "younger," etc.), "more" (or "longer," "older," etc.), and "unequal" (or "unlike," "different," etc.) (Behr, Erlwanger, and Nichols 1980).

- Have children work with different types of number sentences, including those of the form $c = a \times b$, $a = a$, and $a \times b = c \times d$ (Denmark 1976).

One way to model the relational view of "equals" is to have children use balances: teeter-totters, pan balances, and mathematical balances (Treadway 1977; Van de Walle and Thompson 1981; Yvon 1974). Teeter-totter activities, such as a small child balancing a large child or one child balancing several children, serve as kinesthetic models of "equals" as "balanced." If no teeter-totter is nearby, one can be made from scrap lumber (fig. 1). A four-by-four makes a good fulcrum, a two-by-six (or wider) a good balancing platform.

The pan balance is useful in introducing the solution of equations. When used with nonverbal activity cards like the ones in figures 2 and 3, it can be used with little teacher supervision. (A substitute for the "question box" containing an unknown number of blocks is an envelope with an unknown number of counters, golf tees, paper clips, or anything of uniform weight.) A strong point of a pan balance is that it is self-correcting: it balances for equalities and tilts for inequalities.

The mathematical balance differs from the pan balance in that it uses weights placed on pegs equidistant from a center point, as shown in figure 4. When used in conjunction with activity cards like the ones in figures 5 and 6, it allows for an easy transition from concrete to conceptual understanding (Denmark 1976). Like the pan balance, it is self-correcting.

A mathematics balance is easily made from the duplicating design in figure 7. See figure 8 for how to mount a copy of the design on a paper cup or an empty milk carton by using an unsharpened pencil. See figure 9 for how to bend paper clips to use as weights.

If mathematics consisted only of arithmetic, it might not matter if children ever acquired a relational view of "equals," but mathematics comprises more than arithmetic; and therein lies the problem. Fundamental to the study of algebra, for instance, are the following number properties for addition and multiplication:

Fig. 1. Exploring equality with a teeter-totter

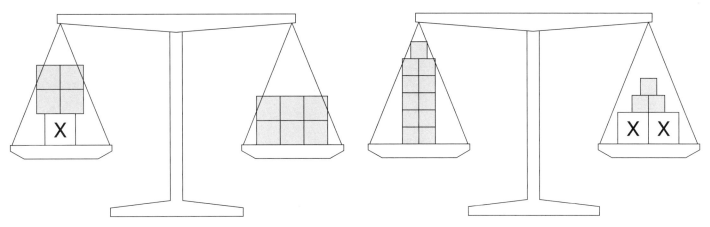

Fig. 2. Shows x + 4 = 6. To find x, remove four blocks from each side.

Fig. 3. Shows 11 = 2x + 3. To find x, remove three blocks from each side; then remove half the blocks from each side.

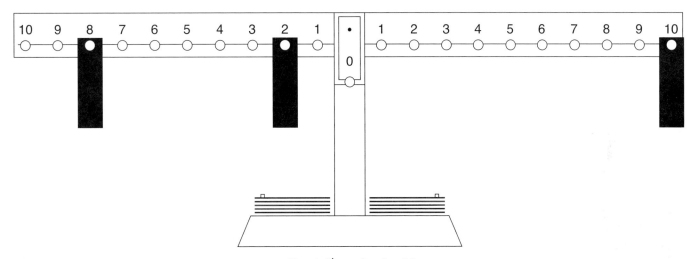

Fig. 4. Shows 8 + 2 = 10

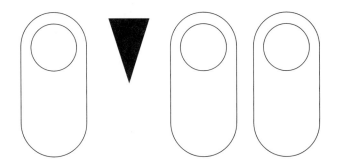

Fig. 5. Read "one on one (one weight on one peg) balanced by two on two" (two weights on two pegs). This pattern could show that 5 = 2 + 3, 7 = 1 + 6, or 10 = 2 + 8.

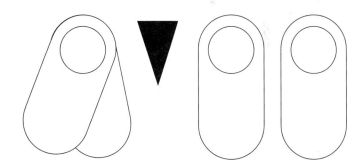

Fig. 6. Read "two on one (two weights on one peg) balanced by two on two." This pattern could show that $2 \times 3 = 1 + 5$, $2 \times 4 = 2 + 6$, or $2 \times 5 = 3 + 7$.

Associative properties:

$$(a + b) + c = a + (b + c),$$
$$(ab)c = a(bc)$$

Commutative properties:

$$a + b = b + a,$$
$$ab = ba$$

Distributive property:

$$a(b + c) = ab + ac$$

From the way they are written, we see that to understand them requires an understanding of number sentences like $2 + 7 = 4 + 5$, one that many children do not understand. Thus we have a clue as to why so many students do so poorly in algebra. Several researchers (e.g., Byers and Herscovics [1977]) have found that confusion

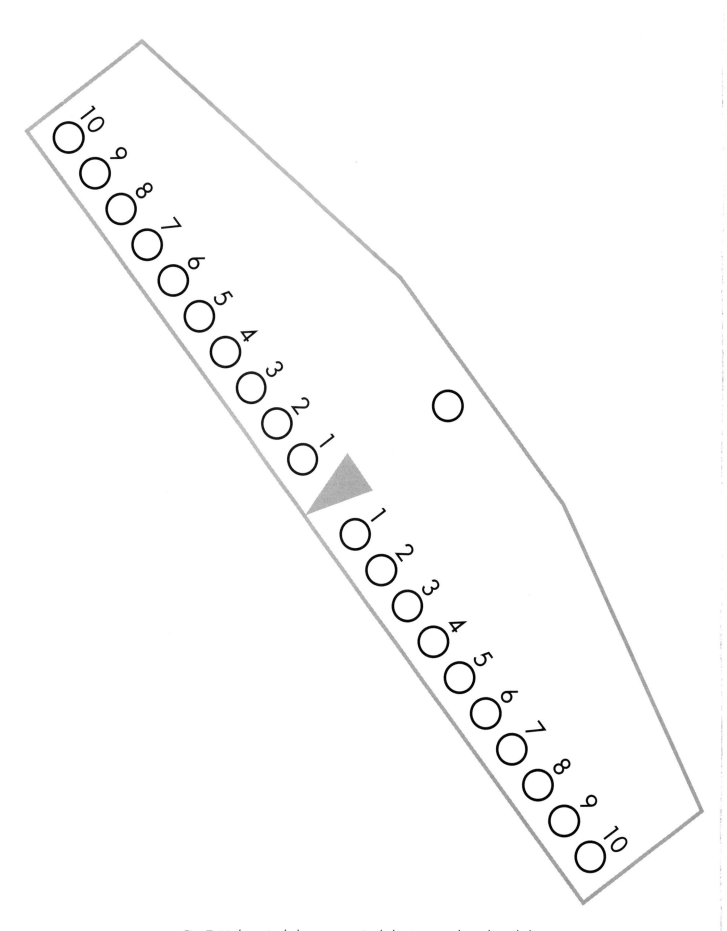

Fig. 7. Mathematics balance cutout. Back, laminate, and punch out holes.

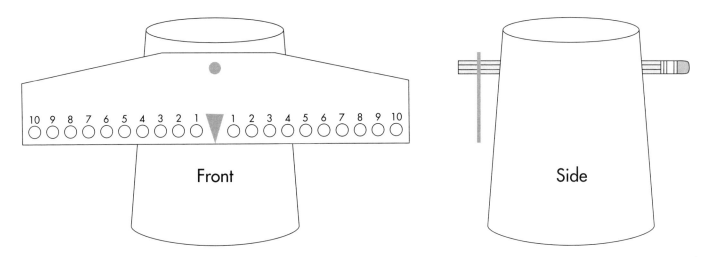

Fig. 8. Mount the design in figure 7 on a cup or empty milk carton using an unsharpened pencil.

about the equals sign persists into high school and college; also, it is likely that some algebra students are confused whenever it is used in an explanation. Imagine not understanding the relational meaning of the equals sign and being asked to solve $3x + 5 = 5x - 7$ or to complete

Fig. 9. A bent paper clip can be used as a weight.

$$(x + 3)^2 = x^2 + \underline{?}\,x + 9.$$

Psychologically it is probably neither possible nor desirable to attempt to eliminate totally an operator view of "equals" (Baroody and Ginsburg 1983). Although $4 + 3 = 7$ and $7 = 4 + 3$ are identical mathematically, they differ considerably in how we naturally think of them. The former is frequently and productively viewed as a *combining* process wherein the right-hand side represents the result, whereas the second implies a *decomposing* process wherein the right-hand side represents the parts of a whole. However, with the aim of preparing children for mathematics beyond arithmetic, what is wanted is instruction that broadens the operator view of "equals" to include a relational meaning.

References

Baroody, Arthur J., and Herbert P. Ginsburg. "The Effects of Instruction on Children's Understanding of the 'Equals' Sign." *Elementary School Journal* 84 (November 1983): 199–212.

Behr, Merlyn, Stanley H. Erlwanger, and Eugene Nichols. "How Children View the Equals Sign. "*Mathematics Teaching* 92 (September 1980): 13–15.

Byers, V., and N. Herscovics. "Understanding School Mathematics." *Mathematics Teaching* 81 (December 1977): 24–27.

Denmark, Tom. "Some Observations about the Mathematical Thinking of Young Children." Project for the Mathematical Development of Children. Tallahassee, Fla.: Florida State University, 1976.

Denmark, Tom, E. Barco, and J. Voran. *Final Report: A Teaching Experiment on Equality.* Project for the Mathematical Development of Children Technical Report No. 6. Florida State University, 1976. (ERIC Document Reproduction Service No. ED 144 805)

Ginsburg, Herbert P. *Children's Arithmetic: The Learning Process.* Rev. ed. New York: D. Van Nostrand Co., 1982.

Kieran, Carolyn. "Concepts Associated with the Equality Symbol." *Educational Studies in Mathematics* 12 (August 1981): 317–26.

Nibbelink, William H. "A Comparison of Vertical and Horizontal Forms for Open Sentences Relative to Performance by First Graders: Some Suggestions." *School Science and Mathematics* 81 (November 1981): 613–19.

Renwick, E. M. "Children's Misconceptions Concerning the Symbol for Mathematical Equality." *British Journal of Educational Psychology* 11 (1932): 173–83.

Treadway, Dan. "Out of Balance." *Arithmetic Teacher* 24 (January 1977): 14–16.

Van de Walle, John. "An Investigation of the Concepts of Equality and Mathematical Symbols Held by First-, Second-, and Third-Grade Children: An Informal Report." Paper presented at the annual meeting of the National Council of Teachers of Mathematics, Seattle, 1980.

Van de Walle, John, and Charles S. Thompson. "Let's Do It: A Poster-Board Balance Beam Helps Write Equations." *Arithmetic Teacher* 28 (May 1981): 4–8.

Wynroth, Lloyd Z. *Wynroth Math Program—the National Numbers Sequence.* Ithaca, N.Y.: L. Wynroth, 1975.

Yvon, Bernard R. "A Simple Balance Beam: Construction and Uses." *Arithmetic Teacher* 21 (November 1974): 584–87. ▲

Making Connections with Two-Digit Multiplication

by

Gail R. Englert

Rose Sinicrope

Students' observations indicated that they were analyzing the algorithm.

The mathematics curriculum in Norfolk Public Schools is arranged in a spiral, with concepts from twelve basic strands continually reviewed and developed. An emphasis is placed on connecting new ideas with previously studied concepts and on using models and manipulatives to understand the underlying operations.

This curriculum has furnished a good framework for my mathematics instruction. As the year progresses, my fourth-grade students are able to identify reasonable estimates before solving problems. They can confidently demonstrate solutions by using Dienes blocks and area models drawn on paper for multiplication problems involving two- and three-digit numbers by one-digit numbers.

The transition from multiplication by a one-digit number to that by a two-digit number is often assumed to be trivial. Previously, however, when we began to work exercises involving two-digit multipliers, the students became confused. Rather than using strategies that were based on their understanding of place value, they created nonsensical algorithms.

Having observed this missing connection in the curriculum in past years, I believed that we could bridge the gap by developing a solid base by using concrete representations before moving to the abstract algorithm. This belief is supported by Kennedy (1986, 6) who advocates the use of manipulatives: "Students who see and manipulate a variety of objects have clearer mental images and can represent abstract ideas more completely." Yet Heddens (1986, 14) warns, "Simply using manipulatives … is not sufficient; teachers must guide children to develop skills in thinking." To teach whole-number multiplication, Schultz (1991) recommends using an area model. Using this semiconcrete model enables students to develop the mental images necessary

to reason abstractly. Another advantage of this model is the frequency of real-world applications (Schultz 1991).

My students needed a concrete representation of the algorithm we were learning. We began by spending a class period reviewing our graphic area models of such problems as 2 × 14. Our drawings

(a) Rectangular representation of multiplication

(b) Multiplication of the ones digit

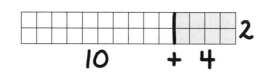

(c) Multiplication of the tens digit

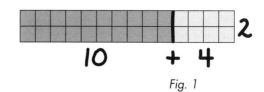

Fig. 1

Gail Englert is a fourth-grade teacher at Meadowbrook Elementary School, Norfolk, VA 23505. She is also a mathematics lead teacher for Norfolk Public Schools. She is interested in preparing her students to become independent problem solvers. Rose Sinicrope teaches at East Carolina University, Greenville, NC 27858. She is interested in children's conceptual development of number concepts and operations.

showed the partial products obtained by first multiplying 2 × 4 ones, then 2 × 1 ten (fig. 1(a)). We enhanced our models by using colors to represent the partial products; the first, 2 × 4 ones, we circled in red (fig. 1(b)), and the second, 2 × 1 ten, we circled in blue (fig. 1(c)).

We color-coded the digits and partial products used in the problem to the area model. Our partial products, 8 and 20, could be added to determine the solution. Students recalled that the area of the rectangle represented the product and that they could make estimates by using this concept. We practiced this method with several more pairs of numbers and recalled how we could add the partial products to end up with an answer in simplified form.

With the review completed, we investigated problems that involve two-digit multipliers. We drew the rectangular area to represent the problem, 12 × 14, on graph paper. The students noted that this rectangular shape looked almost like a square and that it was the same size along the top edge as was our first problem, 2 × 14. We subdivided the large rectangular area to show the place value of 12 (fig. 2(a)). Students looked at the other edge, 14, and decided to partition the rectangular area to show 10 + 4 (fig. 2(b)).

The large rectangular area was then subdivided into four smaller rectangular areas. We began with the lower-right-hand rectangular area, 2 × 4 ones, which we colored red. The students located the digits that corresponded to the diagram and noted that both digits were in the ones place. We recorded the partial product and continued (fig. 2(c)). Our next step used the rectangular area in the lower-left corner, 2 × 1 ten. We colored this rectangular area blue and located the digits needed for the problem (fig. 2(d)). One observant student pointed out that we had found this product when we solved 2 × 14.

With practice students could abstract.

My students need a concrete representation of the process.

We studied the problem and noticed that we had not used the tens digit in the multiplier, 12, yet. A common error that students make at this point is to multiply the tens digits together and skip the intermediate steps. By looking at our diagram we could see that two rectangular areas were left before our process was complete. The students realized that we would have to use the tens-place digit in 12 two times, just as we had used the ones digit two times. We located 1 ten × 4 ones, colored it green, and recorded

our product (fig. 2(e)). Only the largest partitioned rectangular region, 1 ten × 1 ten, was left. We colored that rectangular region purple and recorded our response (fig. 2(f)). There we had it—the solution to 12 × 14 written as four partial products: 8 + 20 + 40 + 100.

As we solved several more problems of increasing difficulty, students' observations indicated that they were analyzing the algorithm. One student stated, "We always do the largest rectangle last." Another student observed that the largest rectangle always had an area in the hundreds. Many students commented on the respective sizes of the four rectangular regions and on the pattern of steps we used to arrive at our final product. As they became increasingly excited over their discoveries, I pretended to be uncertain of their results. My lack of verification encouraged the students to support their statements with more connections among their drawings, the relationships of the partial products they recorded, and the structure of the abstract representation of multiplication.

Students began to see patterns.

After approximately four sessions, we were ready to begin modifying our recording system to show just two partial products. With additional practice the class discarded the concrete diagram and concentrated solely on the abstract representation.

Although the time spent in developing the multiplication algorithm using this visual approach is greater than the time needed to use a more traditional approach, less time is needed for review and reteaching. Students are able to attach meaning to the multiplication algorithm. Brownell (1986) stressed this meaningful approach to instruction as being important in learning mathematics. Because multiplication was meaningful, the students had a deeper and more permanent understanding.

Another advantage to this approach is being able to apply this model to more advanced mathematics. According to Skemp (1971), using models and manipulatives is necessary for children to abstract concepts into appropriate mathematical structures; these structures enable them to learn more mathematics and to solve problems. By using an area model for whole-number multiplication, students have a structure for multiplication that can make fraction multiplication and the multiplication of polynomials meaningful. Thus, the extra time invested in using this model for whole-number multiplication has both immediate and long-term benefits.

(a) Partition for the first factor

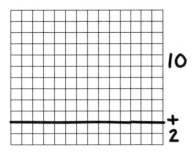

(b) Partition for the second factor

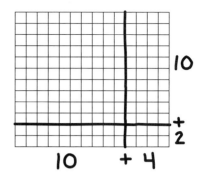

(c) First multiplication of the ones digit

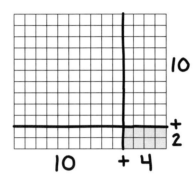

(d) First multiplication of the tens digit

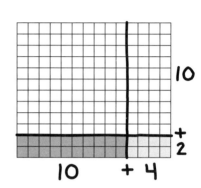

(e) Second multiplication of the ones digit

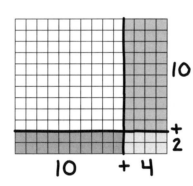

(f) Second multiplication of the tens digit

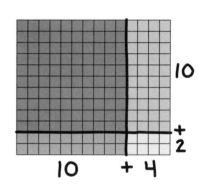

Fig. 2

Bibliography

Brownell, William A. "*AT* Classic: The Revolution in Arithmetic." *Arithmetic Teacher* 34 (October 1986): 38–42.

Heddens, James W. "Bridging the Gap between the Concrete and the Abstract." *Arithmetic Teacher* 33 (February 1986): 14–17.

Kennedy, Leonard M. "A Rationale." *Arithmetic Teacher* 33 (February 1986): 6–7.

May, Lola J. "Developing Multiplication Concepts." *Teaching PreK–8* 22 (November/December 1991): 16–17.

Moser, James M. "Curricular Issues." *Arithmetic Teacher* 33 (February 1986): 8–10.

National Council of Teachers of Mathematics. *Curriculum and Evaluation Standards for School Mathematics.* Reston, Va.: The Council, 1989.

Shultz, James E. "Area Models—Expanding the Mathematics of Grades 3–9." *Arithmetic Teacher* 39 (October 1991): 42–46.

Skemp, Richard S. *The Psychology of Learning Mathematics.* Hammondsworth, England: Penguin Books, 1971. ▲

Hands-On Addition and Subtraction with the Three Pigs

by

Mary Marron Bartek

Addition and subtraction with regrouping and across zeros can be difficult concepts for second and third graders. Although the traditional algorithms are not the only successful processes that students may use, they are commonly used in mathematics textbooks and, especially when zeros are involved, can be difficult processes to teach. I have found that several days spent with the Three Pigs can go a long way to increase students' understanding of the traditional algorithms.

I begin by telling the students that the Three Pigs, after their disastrous run-in with the wolf, have gone into the construction-supply business. Naturally, they specialize in bricks.

I seat my three volunteer "pigs" on chairs side by side in front of a chalkboard, hanging a sign with a pig face around each student's neck. The sign on the right also has the word "Ones"; the middle one shows the word "Tens"; and the left, the word "Hundreds." Throughout the activity, the place-value words will be visible.

I then give each pig a supply of bricks. Base-ten materials work well. Flats, longs, and units are needed. In addition, at least one set of ten longs bound by rubber bands and a group of ten units must be available. I cluster the ten units on a coffee-can lid. (Unifix supplies will work equally well if they are the type that can be joined to make 100s flats.) The first time we do the activity, I might give five flats to my Hundreds Pig, three longs to the Tens Pig, and six units to the Ones Pig. I ask each pig to tell what he or she has been given as I write the combined number on the chalkboard above.

When this activity is used for addition, the next step is for the brick suppliers to arrive. A volunteer supplier arrives at the Pigs' store with a tray (or wagonload or truckload) of bricks. We might begin with two hundreds, four tens, and one unit. The rules in this store, however, demand that all business begin with the Ones Pig, then the Tens Pig, and finally the big boss Hundreds Pig. The pigs receive their shipments in turn and take inventory of their bricks as they are received. The inventory process ensures that the Ones Pig never has ten bricks; nor the Tens Pig, ten tens; nor the Hundreds Pig, ten hundreds—another store rule. The students are told that if they get ten or more bricks, the set of ten must be sent to the next pig. I help them take inventory the first several times, verifying that each pig's total is nine or less.

Once the process has been practiced, it is time to introduce larger amounts. Our supplier may bring 473 bricks to our pigs, who already have 2 hundreds, 5 tens, and 8 units, respectively. When the Ones Pig inventories 11 bricks, we establish that he or she must deliver a stack of 10 to the Tens Pig. The 1 brick that remains is recorded on the chalkboard. When the 7 newly delivered longs are added to the original 5 and the long passed from the Ones Pig, the Tens Pig then has 13. Thus, he or she delivers one set of 10 tens to the Hundreds Pig before reporting an inventory of 3 tens remaining. Our Hundreds Pig then reports a total inventory of 7 hundreds.

Mary Bartek, TWGT@aol.com, is a teacher of gifted and enrichment students at Trails West Elementary School in Aurora, CO 80015. When this article was written, she was also teaching daily mathematics classes in grades 3–5 for the Littleton Public Schools in Littleton, Colorado.

It is important at this stage for some examples to include the number 0 in the supply or the solution. Assume that our Pigs begin with 5 hundreds, 0 tens, and 7 ones. When the supplier brings 243 bricks, the Ones Pig finds an inventory total of exactly 10. Unable to keep 10, the Ones Pig must pass the entire set to the Tens Pig, leaving the Ones Pig to report a 0. The Tens Pig has 0 to start with; the 1 ten from the Ones Pig's inventory plus 4 tens from the supplier makes a total of 5 tens. The Hundreds Pig reports a total of 7. The addition of 0 to the process is a natural one.

The students eventually take over recording activities on the chalkboard. A day or two into the simulation, I announce that the Pigs' expanding business requires that a bookkeeper be hired. The student bookkeeper replaces me at the chalkboard, recording the initial inventory, adding the new supply, and showing the final result. Students at their seats also join as bookkeepers at this stage. Using the "Three Pigs' Bricks" worksheet (see fig. 1), they fill in the transactions as they happen. This sheet gives me an immediate visible means to check students' understanding.

Three Pigs' Bricks

Hundreds   Tens   Ones

Fig. 1. The inventory is totaled by students.

The students can also help to create the scenarios. I may ask each pig how many bricks he or she would like to use to begin the simulation, then ask student volunteers to decide on the supply amounts. More thinking is involved if the student is asked to honor a specific teacher request, such as causing only the Tens Pig to pass bricks to the Hundreds Pig, or making the Ones Pig complete the transaction with an inventory of zero.

The Three Pigs activity can also be used to introduce subtraction. Instead of suppliers, a shopper comes for a specific number of bricks; this number is recorded on the chalkboard. Once again, all shoppers deal with the Ones Pig first. However, because it will be

essential for the Pigs to have "change" in their brick supplies before regrouping can begin, it is necessary to review the variety of ways in which the children can name a given amount. This task may be accomplished directly (e.g., In what ways can we show 235 with the base-ten blocks? Responses should include 2 hundreds, 3 tens, 5 ones; 1 hundred, 13 tens, 5 ones; 1 hundred, 12 tens, 15 ones; etc.) or within the context of the simulation. As the Pigs are getting their supplies, I may state that I wanted to give the Tens Pig a supply of 7 tens, but today only 6 tens are available. The students, recalling past experiences with numeration activities, say that using a group of 10 ones will produce the same amount. The 10 ones can be given to the Tens Pig on a coffee-can lid. When the same shortage occurs while supplying the Hundreds Pig, the students should offer that the same purpose will be served by 10 tens, which can be banded together into a group of 100.

Here is a subtraction scenario involving regrouping: The Hundreds Pig gets 5 ten-by-ten flats and a group of 10 longs bound with a rubber band, for a total of 6 hundreds. The Tens Pig receives 4 longs and a coffee-can lid with 10 ones, for a total of 5 tens; and the Ones Pig gets 3 ones. Next, a shopper approaches to buy 487 bricks; the shopper says to the Ones Pig, "I need seven bricks." The Ones Pig has only 3, so he or she goes to get more from the Tens Pig. The Ones Pig requests more bricks, but the Tens Pig can only give sets of 10, so the Tens Pig passes the coffee-can lid of 10 blocks. The Ones Pig can now complete the transaction with the shopper. When the buyer subsequently asks for 8 tens, the Tens Pig must obtain some from the Hundreds Pig.

Eventually, I give no bricks to the Tens Pig, as in the problem 407 – 268. The students naturally know to ask for some supplies from the Hundreds Pig. We record the subtraction with the regrouping on the chalkboard. The students have successfully subtracted across a zero. Early in the practice process, the student bookkeeper takes over as chalkboard recorder and the students record their answers on copies of the "Three Pigs' Bricks" subtraction worksheet (see fig. 2).

As in addition, the teacher and students can share the problem-creation duties. The teacher will want to include examples of problems that cover all the subtraction-with-zero "issues": regrouping for only the tens column, regrouping from both tens and hundreds to supply the ones, and so on. The following examples will help the teacher to include all the variations:

```
  407        503        570
- 246      - 247      - 461
-----      -----      -----


  400        300        700
- 217      - 150      - 408
-----      -----      -----
```

Three Pigs' Bricks

Hundreds Tens Ones

Fig. 2. Subtraction is used to answer the questions.

Student-made problems can be used to answer specific teacher requests. Student pigs may be asked to assign themselves a given number of bricks, or brick values may be assigned. Students in the class may then be asked to create a scenario so that the Tens Pig needs to ask the Hundreds Pig for more bricks, or so that both the Ones Pig and the Tens Pig need to request bricks.

The keys to the process at all stages are recording the information as it happens, asking lots of questions, and commenting on the action. "Tens Pig, how many do you have now?" "Hundreds Pig, how many sets of one hundred do you have now that you have given a set to the Tens Pig?" "Class, the Pigs had two hundreds, three tens, and eight ones before. Now that they have regrouped (or traded), the total number of bricks remains the same, but how many does each Pig have?" And always, so that regrouping is done for a purpose and not in a rote fashion, "Mr./Ms. Pig, do you have enough bricks to fill that order, or will you need to ask the pig next door for some supplies?"

Shopper

The class may eventually work in groups of four students, three as pigs and one as supplier or shopper, recording the additions or subtractions as they carry them out. Short, nightly homework assignments verify that the hands-on process can also be done with paper and pencil. In a matter of days, with all students having had the chance to be shoppers and sellers, the students have mastered the processes.

If the students enjoy the pigs simulation, extensions to other curricular areas are easy to include. The children will enjoy *The True Story of the Three Little Pigs* by Jon Scieszka (1989), which is an excellent introduction to a point of view. They may enjoy taking other well-known stories, or even nursery rhymes, and rewriting them from another viewpoint. (I have always thought that the giant in *Jack and the Beanstalk* was especially wronged!) A trip to the library is likely to elicit several versions of *The Three Pigs* as well. Some are funny; others are mean-spirited. These versions can be shared and compared. Another extension could be an investigation of the importance of pigs in American agriculture today. Does Iowa have more pigs or people? Now that the students are adept at subtracting, they may be able to investigate and arrive at the difference.

We have enjoyed this simulation thoroughly. Best of all, the students seemed to truly understand the process. Addition and subtraction were not just manipulations of numbers. They became something that the students could see and do when we enlisted the help of the Three Pigs.

SUPPLIES

- Three "Pig" signs with neck strings, labeled "Ones," "Tens," and "Hundreds"
- Trays on which to carry blocks (Styrofoam meat trays work well)
- Ten-by-ten flats of base-ten blocks
- Longs of base-ten blocks
- Base-ten unit blocks
- Ten longs bound together with rubber bands
- Ten ones collected on a coffee-can or other lid
- Unifix cubes arranged into ten-by-ten flats, ten sticks, and units can be substituted for the base-ten blocks.

Bibliography

Brenner, Barbara. *Walt Disney's Three Little Pigs*. New York: Random House, 1972.

Scieszka, Jon. *The True Story of the Three Little Pigs*. New York: Viking Penguin, 1989. ▲

Transition Boards: A Good Idea Made Better

by

John T. Sutton

Tonya D. Urbatsch

The *Curriculum and Evaluation Standards for School Mathematics* (NCTM 1989) recognizes that addition and subtraction computations remain an important part of the school mathematics curriculum and recommends that the emphasis be shifted to the understanding of concepts. Transition boards are simple devices to aid students' conceptual understanding.

For the past few years, teachers in Iowa, Illinois, and Missouri have attended our Activity Based Child-centered Mathematics (ABC Math) workshops and classes. As one component of these classes, Thompson and Van de Walle (1980) used their transition board to foster the linking level of addition and subtraction in base ten. As inevitably happens, teachers in each workshop offered suggestions for the improvement of the transition board. If every suggestion were adopted, the transition board would, at some point, be approximately the size of a roadside billboard. We have attempted to accept the suggestions that have increased the efficient use of the transition board while reducing its overall size.

CONSTRUCTING THE TRANSITION BOARDS

The revised transition boards (see fig. 1) can be made from any light-colored construction paper measuring 12 inches by 18 inches. The lines are drawn directly on the construction paper. The shaded areas indicate the use of construction paper of a contrasting color. The boards are then laminated or covered with clear plastic so that grease pencils, crayons, or overhead markers can be used for recording. The beauty of this board is that it can be used for addition or subtraction merely by reversing the board from top to bottom, which can be especially useful for "adding back" in subtraction proofs. Since the label areas remain blank, they can be used with any whole-number or decimal problem. Two boards can easily be overlapped to accommodate three place values (fig. 2).

John Sutton is the director of the Curriculum Consortium of North Central Iowa (CCNCI), Eldora, IA 50627. He enjoys using technology to teach others and teaching others to use technology, as well as creating different approaches to educational designs. Tonya Urbatsch is the coordinator of mathematics for the Davenport Community Schools in Davenport, IA 52803. She also organizes and teaches ABC Math classes for K–8 teachers.

GETTING READY TO USE THE BOARDS

Base-ten blocks, beans and bean sticks, bundles of sticks, or beans and cups can all serve as manipulatives to use for trading games and with the transition board. The authors caution against the use of colored chips, since they do not allow the student a proportional exchange of materials for an understanding of base ten.

To prepare the students for multidigit addition or subtraction, introduce the concept of regrouping, or fair trading. A number of trading games are recommended and can be used. These games are readily available and have been described by others (Willcutt, Spikell, and Greenes 1974; Laycock 1977; Thompson and Van de Walle 1981). We do, however, wish to emphasize that attempting to teach addition or subtraction without initially preparing the student with trading games would be counterproductive and could result in a lack of understanding due to lack of preparation. Manipulatives in and of themselves do not teach concepts; however, the use of manipulatives in a progressive developmental process does result in greater opportunities for conceptual understanding.

After building the concept of trading, some time should be spent exploring the concept of addition. The transition board links the concrete and the abstract representations of the problem, so only when the students are ready to learn a specific algorithm will they be ready to use the transition boards.

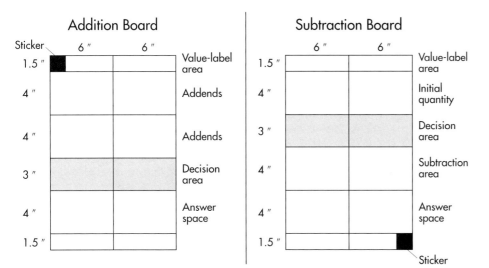

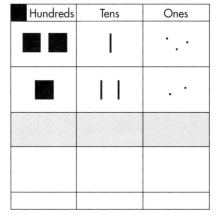

Fig. 1. Revised transition boards

Fig. 2. Overlapping boards

MULTIDIGIT ADDITION

To use the transition board as a link when teaching the multidigit-addition algorithm, make sure that the board correctly faces the student. One way to ensure that all students' boards are correctly oriented is to place a small sticker in the top corner of the board. Then when it is time to begin, merely tell students to "place the board so the sticker is at the top." The general strategy for teaching multidigit addition is to lead the students through the concrete, linking, and abstract levels. This path can be accomplished by having the students—

a) work only with the manipulatives on the transition board as the teacher orally states the problem while modeling on the overhead projector;

b) write the numbers on the chalkboard and use the manipulative pieces as they work with the materials on the transition board;

c) represent the numbers with pictorial models of the manipulatives on a small paper model of the transition board;

d) write the numbers in the spaces on a small paper model of the transition board; and

e) write the numbers on their paper.

Students should have mastered such necessary prerequisites as basic addition facts, the concept of addition, and the use of manipulatives to represent two-digit and three-digit numbers. Students can work independently with their own transition board; however, research indicates that a great learning advantage can be gained by working cooperatively in groups (Johnson and Johnson 1975).

TEACHING ADDITION

The addition process can begin with a real problem, preferably one that is interesting to the students. For example, suppose that our class has been invited to attend a movie to be presented in Mrs. Cahill's classroom. Our class has thirty-four students, and Mrs. Cahill's class has twenty-seven students. How many chairs will we need to seat everyone? Since the problem involves only tens and

ones, "TENS" and "ONES" need to be written in the top row. Then the students place the manipulative representation for the number 34 in the space for the first number on the transition board. Next the students place the manipulative representation for the number 27 in the space for the second number on the transition board (see the number-placement board in fig. 3*a*). The students then start at the top of the ones column and pull all the manipulatives in that column down to the decision area (see the decision-area board in fig. 3*b*). Once they get their pieces to the decision area, they must ask themselves, "Do we have enough for a fair trade?" Since in this example the answer is yes, the students trade in ten ones for one tens piece. The newly acquired tens piece is then placed at the top of the tens column. Any pieces left in the ones column are then transferred to the answer space on the transition board (see the ones answer board in fig. 3*c*).

The students are now ready to work in the tens column, moving all the pieces into the decision area. Once again, students ask themselves, "Do we have enough for a fair trade?" In this instance, the answer is no, so they scoop the pieces to the answer space. Since no more pieces can be moved, the teacher asks the students to look at the board (see the answer board in fig. 3*d*) and answer the original question: "How many chairs will we need for all the students to sit at the movie?" The students can look in the answer space and see that since six pieces are in the tens place and one piece is in the ones place, sixty-one chairs are needed.

It is recommended that the work initially focus only on manipulating the objects, not on recording each response. The purpose of working strictly at the concrete level using only manipulatives is to (*a*) learn the process of using the transition board to combine concrete objects for addition and (*b*) develop the concept of place value and trading from ones to tens and from tens to hundreds. Since this activity operates at the concrete level and students physically manipulate the objects, it is recommended that two-digit addition with and without regrouping be taught at the same time. The students can use a similar concrete developmental process with the transition board for two-digit addition with regrouping to hundreds (fig. 2).

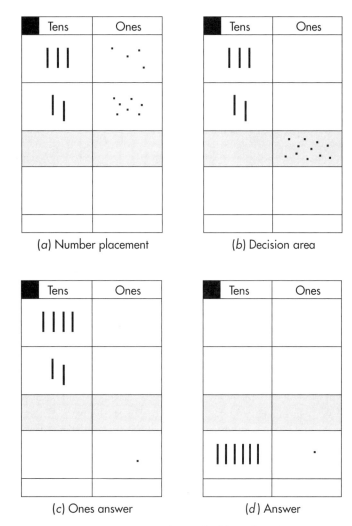

(a) Number placement   (b) Decision area

(c) Ones answer   (d) Answer

Fig. 3. Sequential use of addition board

Very often the question is asked, "How much time should be spent teaching at the concrete level?" The teacher is the only one who can answer that question. Since each student learns at a different pace, some students will need to spend more time working on problems at the concrete level than others. Students should be allowed to practice at this stage until they can easily perform the concrete operation. A reduction in the amount of time spent on working with manipulative materials may have a short-term payoff in students' computational facility, but it minimizes their potential for transfer (Beattie 1986).

The linking level can be taught at either the semiconcrete or the semiabstract level. In the semiconcrete mode, the students initially draw boxes, lines, and dots directly on the recording sheet (fig. 4) while actually manipulating the blocks. After many examples and applications at the semiconcrete level, the students begin drawing the problems on the recording sheet while the teacher exhibits the applications (examples) on the overhead projector. After a number of examples in this mode, the students enter the semiabstract stage in which they transfer examples of a problem that uses pictures of base-ten blocks (Madell and Stahl 1977) and write the numeral corresponding to the represented values on the recording sheet in the standard way (fig. 5). Also at the semiabstract level, students could represent their textbook problems with

either the blocks or the models and write the corresponding values on paper. The abstract level follows, with students writing the numbers of the problem as the teacher models with blocks on the overhead projector. The students are now ready to write with no aids whatsoever the numbers for problems given in a visual, an auditory, or a written form, similar to those in their textbooks.

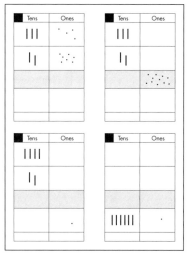

Fig. 4. Recording sheet   Fig. 5. Recording numerals

TEACHING SUBTRACTION

The transition board can be rotated 180 degrees to teach subtraction. "TENS" and "ONES" are written in the top row in the appropriate columns. Once again, the student can be prepared for the algorithm with the use of a story problem. For example, assume that out of thirty-seven students in the third grade, eighteen have not had the chicken pox. How many have already had the chicken pox? To use the board as a model, students model thirty-seven on the top row of the board with the blocks. Since eighteen are being taken away, small pieces of paper with the numbers 1 and 8 written on them are put in the third row of the board (see the subtraction-tickets board in fig. 6a. Some teachers call the numbered paper the "ticket for subtraction."

The students begin the problem by once again using the decision area to ask the question, "Does the ones column have enough blocks to take eight away?" Since it does not, one ten must be traded in for ten ones. These ones blocks are placed with the other seven (see the regrouping board in fig. 6b). Eight are then taken away by placing them on the ticket and removing the ticket from the board (see the ones-ticket board in fig. 6c). This step reinforces the part-part-whole concept of subtraction and sets up a situation in which checking the problem with addition becomes quite easy. After the blocks are removed, the ones blocks that are left are then moved down to the answer area. The next step, examining the tens column, is done in a similar manner (see the tens-ticket board in fig. 6d). The students once again use the decision area to ask the question, "Does the tens column contain enough blocks to take one away?" Since it does, one block is then placed on the ticket and removed from the board. The remaining block should be moved to the answer area. The students should be able to see that nineteen students have had the chicken pox. By turning the transition board 180 degrees, students can check

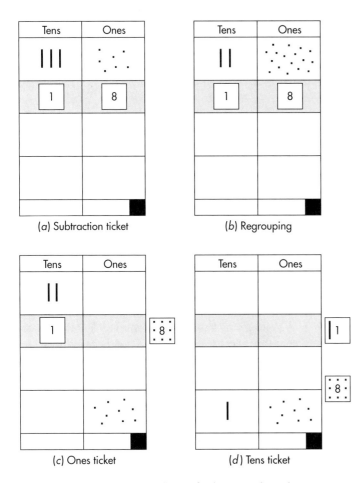

(a) Subtraction ticket

(b) Regrouping

(c) Ones ticket

(d) Tens ticket

Fig. 6. Sequential use of subtraction boards

USING THE TRANSITION BOARDS

Teachers have used the transition boards to make the link between the abstract and the concrete representation of addition and subtraction. Each teacher finds a unique way to use the boards; no one right way exists. Once the boards have been used for addition and subtraction of whole numbers, decimal addition and subtraction follow quite easily. Half a plastic or polystyrene egg or sphere could be used as a model of a decimal point. Students can see concretely what happens when decimals are added and subtracted. The goal in all the concrete manipulations is to develop independent learners. When students have trouble with an algorithm, they have a way of finding the answer—using either blocks or pictures to model the problem. They explain the problems to one another and through discussion gain a deeper understanding of the mathematical processes involved. If they have completed a set of problems, they can "prove" their answers by using the models. The teacher therefore is not the source of all the answers. The students begin to trust their own work and become more confident, self-sufficient learners.

References

Beattie, Ian D. "Modeling Operations and Algorithms." *Arithmetic Teacher* 33 (February 1986): 28.

Johnson, David W., and Roger T. Johnson. *Learning Together and Alone: Cooperation, Competition, and Individualization.* Englewood Cliffs, N.J.: Prentice Hall, 1975.

Laycock, Mary. *Base Ten Mathematics: Interludes for Every Math Text.* Hayward, Calif.: Activity Resources Co., 1976.

Madell, Robert, and Elizabeth Larkin Stahl. *Picturing Numeration: From Models to Symbols.* Palo Alto, Calif.: Creative Publications, 1977.

National Council of Teachers of Mathematics. *Curriculum and Evaluation Standards for School Mathematics.* Reston, Va.: The Council, 1989.

Thompson, Charles S., and John Van de Walle. "Let's Do It: Transition Boards: Moving from Materials to Symbols in Addition." *Arithmetic Teacher* 28 (December 1980): 4–8.

———. "Let's Do It: Transition Boards: Moving from Materials to Symbols in Subtraction." *Arithmetic Teacher* 28 (January 1981): 4–9.

Wilcutt, Robert E., Mark A. Spikell, and Carole E. Greenes. *Base Ten Activities.* Palo Alto, Calif.: Creative Publications, 1974. ▲

the subtraction with an addition problem by appropriately labeling the place values "TENS" and "ONES." Then they place materials representing the subtraction answer in the space for the first number and the tickets in the space for the second number (fig. 7) and follow the foregoing directions for addition.

As with the addition algorithm, the students advance through several steps: (*a*) working only with manipu-latives; (*b*) recording by drawing models of the blocks; (*c*) recording by writing the numerals; (*d*) modeling textbook problems with the blocks or models; and (*e*) solving the problems without any concrete aids.

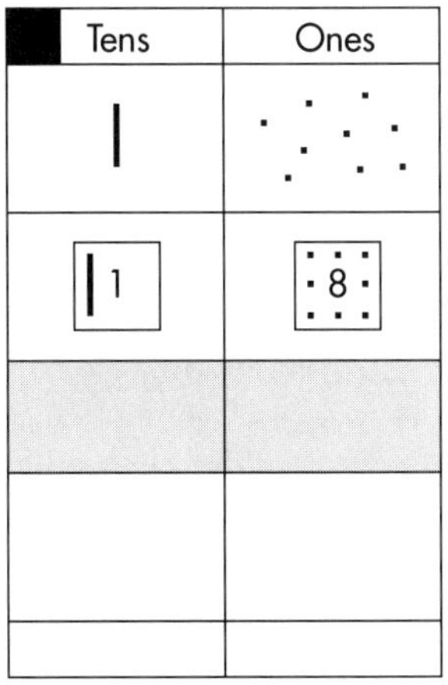

Fig. 7. Adding back

Let's Do It: The Power of 10

by

Charles S. Thompson
University of Louisville

John Van de Walle
Virginia Commonwealth University

Because 10 is the basis of our number system, children need to know the combinations of numbers that total 10. Knowing these combinations prepares children efficiently to solve addition problems that "bridge" 10. Examples of such problems are 8 + 5 = [ ], 27 + 4 = [ ], and 47 + 25 = [ ]. Knowing the number combinations for 10 also prepares children to learn the place-value nature of our number system.

Too often children learn about 10 by simply counting to and beyond 10 without ever thinking about 10 as a group or as having any special significance. In this way 9 is only the number after 8 and is not emphasized as 1 less than 10. Likewise, the number 14 is rarely thought of as a set of 10 and 4. Many other relationships are also overlooked.

We have used a simple manipulative aid called a "10 frame" and have found it to be particularly effective in teaching children the number combinations for 10, the addition facts that "bridge" 10, and the place-value nature of our number system. In this article we shall describe these "10 frames" and explain how they can be used to teach these numerical concepts and skills to children.

THE MODEL

The 10 frame was first shown to us by Robert Wirtz (1978) of Curriculum Development Associates. It consists of a simple 2 × 5 grid of squares as shown here:

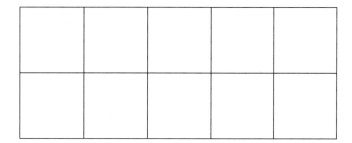

The frame itself can be drawn on a piece of tagboard (about 20 cm × 30 cm). Another idea is to use an egg carton with two end sections covered with masking tape or torn off. Counters are placed in the squares one at a time, beginning at the upper left and proceeding across until the first row is filled. The second row is then filled in the same manner. This model has several advantages.

One is that it encourages children to think of 10 as two 5s. Another is that every number displayed in the frame is automatically referenced to both 5 and 10. Note that on the frame, 7 is clearly 5 and 2 and also 3 less than 10. Four is 1 less than 5, and it takes 6 more to make 10. Every time a number is displayed in the frame a "10 fact" is clearly visible.

ACTIVITIES FOR LEARNING THE NUMBER COMBINATIONS FOR 10

1. In initial activities with the 10 frame, have children place counters in the squares, one at a time, and after they have placed each set of counters, have them orally describe the state of the 10 frame. Begin with the numbers 5 or less. For example, if you have children show 3 on their frames, they first place down three beans on the top row and then say "3 and 2." (The 2 refers to the counters needed to make a total of 5.) Later, when working with numbers from 0 to 10, children would say the two parts of 10 instead ("3 and 7" or "6 and 4").

2. A particularly good activity is for the teacher to call out numbers between 1 and 10 in a random order (draw cards, use a spinner, or just choose them). The children must then say "plus" or "minus" the amount needed to change their 10 frame so that it shows the number just called. For example, if the children's boards show 6 and you call 8, they would say "plus 2." Then they adjust the counters on their frame to represent the number called.

   Note. These two activities help children relate numerical quantities to one another and especially to the number 5. For example, they learn what has to be done to change seven counters to three counters. They also learn the various arrangements of the counters in the 10 frame, that is, the children learn that each number from 0 to 10 has a particular pattern. The next activity helps children to master these patterns.

3. Make a set of 10-frame dot cards, two each with zero through ten dots as shown in figure 1. These cards can be used for a variety of instant-recognition activities.

   One child (or the teacher) flashes a card to another child for an instant. The second child makes this number with counters on the 10 frame and then tells the number of dots or counters.

Fairly soon the children will be able to say the number of dots on the cards quite quickly, and the need for the counter version will diminish. Encourage the children to say the number of dots shown on the card as fast as they can.

The next step is to say the other part of 10, that is, the number of spaces on the card instead of the number of dots.

Finally, as the cards are shown, the children can say both parts of 10: "3 and 7." Children can then begin to use the cards and write complete number sentences for 10 (3 + 7 = 10).

A related use of the cards is to have the children say one more than the number of dots they see. Similarly, they can say two more or one or two less (remove the 1 and 0 cards for the "less" activities).

4. Similar activities can be done by holding up a set of fingers. To correlate fingers with the 10 frames, always show the numbers up to 5 on one hand and the numbers from 6 to 10 by adding (to a full hand) fingers from the other hand. The children tell the number of fingers that they see and how many more are needed to make 10. In fact all the activities involving cards can also be done with fingers.

5. After children have become quite competent with the parts of 10 using the 10 frames or fingers, the same activities should be repeated with materials that do *not* reflect 5s and 10. For example, if patterns of dots (e.g., patterns on dice or dominoes) for numbers up through 10 are flashed, have children say how many dots they see and also how many more are needed to make 10. The same activity should be done with simple numeral cards. These activities can be done orally or in written form. Number sentences can also be written.

6. A variation on the theme proves to be an intriguing activity for two children. One child takes ten counters and secretly puts some in one hand and the rest in the other. The first hand is then opened to show the number of counters. The second child then predicts how many counters remain in the closed hand.

7. Another enjoyable activity is derived from a game called Subtraction Race found in *Mathematics Their Way* (Baratta-Lorton 1976). In this game for two children, each child has a row of twenty to thirty counters. In turn, each child rolls a die with the numerals 4 through 9 on it. Then he or she removes not the number shown on the die, but

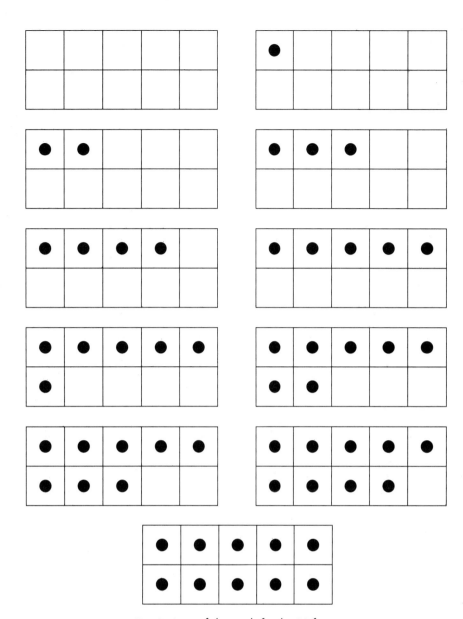

Fig. 1. A set of dot cards for the 10 frame

rather the number of counters needed to make 10. The goal is to be the first player to remove all the counters in the row.

PLACE-VALUE ACTIVITIES USING 10 FRAMES

Many of these activities are based on the Counting Game also found in *Mathematics Their Way*. These activities require a large collection of counters (we use lima beans) and a playing mat—a sheet of tagboard or construction paper placed horizontally on the child's desk. A line is drawn down the middle of the paper, and a 10 frame is drawn on the right-hand side (fig. 2).

8. In the initial activity the children place counters in their 10 frames one at a time and "read" the total after placing each counter. When the 10 frame is full the children "collect" all ten counters into a single group and place that group on the left side of their mats. They read the results as "one set of 10 and 0." Children continue placing counters on their mats

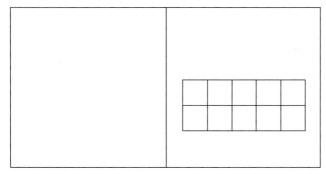

Fig. 2. A playing mat including a 10 frame

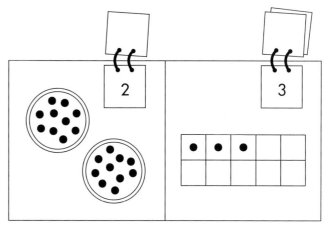

Fig. 3. Numeral cards record the total.

and announcing their totals—"one 10 and 1, one 10 and 2," and so forth—until forty or fifty counters have been played. Throughout this activity the children are periodically questioned regarding how many more counters are needed before a group of ten counters can be made. This question helps the children anticipate the grouping. (One easy form of collecting 10s is to place the counters into a small, shallow cup, available from restaurant supply stores.)

9. A subsequent activity involves removing counters from the playing mat one at a time and again announcing the results. This, of course, requires that the children break up groups of ten counters and transform them into ten individual units. (Dump the beans from the paper cup.)

   Note. Activities 9 and 10 focus on the essence of our place-value system. Children observe how numbers are built and how they are taken apart. Most important, they learn when to make the groups of 10 and how to count those groups separately from the leftovers. These concepts and skills are crucial for an understanding of the addition problems that "bridge" 10 as well as any computation with two-digit numbers.

10. Estimation activities make good use of 10 frames. A small jar of beans, peanuts, seeds, buttons, or other counters is shown to the children. The children estimate the total number of counters in terms of the number of sets of 10 that can be made and the number of leftovers. To check, the materials are placed one at a time in the 10 frames. The results are always announced in two ways: (1) as sets of 10 and leftovers and (2) as a standard number name (68).

11. Repeat activities 8, 9, and 10 but have children place numeral cards above the two sides of the playing mat. These cards are used to indicate the number of 10s and 1s present at any time (fig. 3). Using the numeral cards with the counters will help children connect the symbols to the place-value concepts represented. They can "see" how the 2 in 23 represents two 10s.

ACTIVITIES INVOLVING ADDITION PROBLEMS THAT "BRIDGE" 10

Initially children solve basic-fact exercises that "bridge" 10, such as 8 + 5 = [ ], by combining sets of eight and five objects and then counting the total to determine the sum. Other children count on from 8. The ultimate goal is that children will memorize these basic-fact combinations that bridge 10 and respond instantly with

the sums. But neither of the methods capitalizes on the power of 10. Consequently, both methods frequently prove fruitless as an aid to memorization.

Children can greatly benefit from knowing and using a more efficient intermediate computing strategy. We call the strategy "making 10." It is used when one addend is close to 10 and the sum is greater than 10. For example, to solve 8 + 5 = [ ], the idea is to shift 2 from the 5 to the 8, making 10, and then add on the remaining 3 to total 13. The problem in teaching this idea to children is not that it is too difficult but rather that finding a model to illustrate the idea concretely is difficult. A symbolic approach is nearly useless. The 10 frames work well.

12. For this activity, add a second 10-frame drawing to each playing mat as shown in figure 4. The activity is similar to the counting game described in activity 8 except that more than one counter can be added to the playing mat at one time. Usually a die is rolled or a spinner spun to indicate how many counters are to be added. On the first turn, counters are placed in the top frame. On the next turn, the counters are placed in the lower frame. At this point the two groups are combined by moving counters from the frame with the smaller number of counters to the other frame. Should either frame become filled in this process, the ten counters are made into a group and placed on the left side of the mat, as before. Then, the remaining counters, if any, are moved to the top frame. In this manner, at least one empty 10 frame is always available for the next turn. To reiterate, whenever two frames have counters, the counters are combined in the frame having the most counters.

Fig. 4. The playing mat can be modified to include two 10 frames.

For example, suppose that a child's mat has two groups of ten counters and seven counters remaining (fig. 5a). The child is asked to "add 6." These counters are placed in the lower frame (fig. 5b). Then three counters are moved to the upper frame to form a group of 10 and 3 (fig. 5c). The 10 frames enable the child to "see" how many of the new counters are needed to make another set of 10. Finally, the set of 10 is put into a cup, moved to the adjacent column, and the three remaining counters are moved to the top frame.

(a)

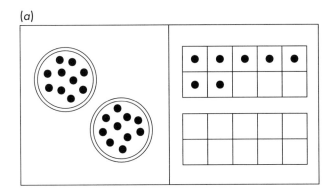

(b)

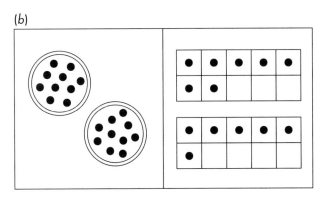

(c)

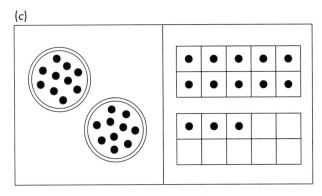

Fig. 5. 27 + 6 = 33.

The next series of activities focuses on concepts and skills that are very useful in helping children memorize most of the "hard" addition facts—those with sums greater than 10.

13. The first activity in the series emphasizes the numbers from 11 to 19 as a set of 10 plus another number. The child has a 10-frame card filled with ten dots ("10 card") and one each of the other 10-frame dot cards from 0 to 9. The 10 card is turned faceup on the desk, and the other cards are placed in a stack facedown. The top card is then turned over and placed to the right of the 10 card. The task is to name the total number of dots. Emphasis is placed on saying the total number of dots, for example, as "one 10 and 5" and as "15."

14. The following activity helps children "break off" a small amount (1, 2, or 3) from a number. Later the amount that was broken off will be used to "make 10." The activity requires a set of 10-frame cards with four or more dots on them and a die with the numbers 1, 2, 3, 1, 2, and 3. Initially the cards are placed facedown. To play, the child turns over a dot card and rolls the die. The number of dots shown by the die is mentally "removed" from the 10-frame card and the result announced. Children can take turns going through the deck, one rolling the die and the other turning the cards and saying the result. Encourage children to develop speed in this activity.

15. Follow up activity 14 with an oral drill. Point to one of the numerals 1, 2, or 3 that you have written on the chalkboard and say aloud a number from 4 to 10. Have the children give the difference of the two numbers. If they hesitate, remind them of the 10 frame (which you may want to have drawn on the board) and refer them to the previous activity.

16. Now the children are ready to solve any basic addition facts that lend themselves to "making 10," that is, all facts with 7, 8, or 9 as one of the addends and with sums greater than 10. Work on facts with 9 first. These facts require a mat with two 10 frames. The top frame has nine dots, and the bottom frame is blank. You will also need a deck of fact cards with all the basic addition facts involving 9. A fact card is turned faceup, and the child adds counters to the blank frame to model the fact (fig. 6). Note that 9 can be the top or the bottom number in the fact, or both. Once the fact is modeled, the child "makes 10" by sliding one counter from the bottom card to the top card, announces the equivalent 10 fact (such as 10 + 3), and says the total. The same process is repeated as described in activity 15 except that an 8 card (then a 7 card) is substituted for the 9 card and the corresponding fact cards are used.

17. A symbolic activity for making 10 but still with a cue for the student is indicated by the flash card shown in figure 7. A procedure similar to that in figure 6 is used. The child first tells what the equivalent 10 fact is and then gives the sum.

18. The strategy of "make 10" from two addends is profitably applied to teaching addition of two-digit numbers (fig. 8). The children show both addends with place-value materials on the mat. They slide counters from the 10 frame having the smaller number of loose counters to the other 10 frame. When a 10 is made they move that 10 over to the left-hand column as a group (or trade for a 10 stick, depending on which materials are being used). Next they count the number of 10s and 1s and record their answer.

After children can readily do these problems, they can also be taught to write the numerals that record the "regrouping" they do on the mat. This activity will help children "connect" those numerals to the concepts and processes already learned. Later they will be able to solve similar problems without using the

(a)

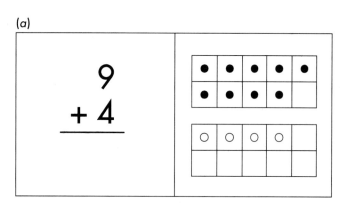

(b)

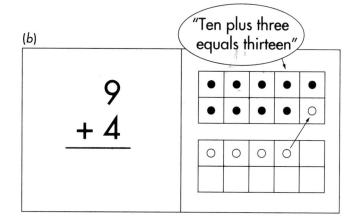

Fig. 6. Modeling the addition of one-digit numbers

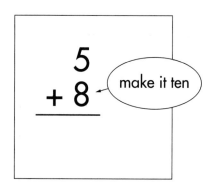

Fig. 7. A fact card with a clue

manipulative aids because a meaningful visual image of the action has been developed. A similar procedure can easily be developed for subtraction.

EXTENSIONS TO LARGER NUMBERS

The 10-frame model can easily be extended for use with larger numbers. One way to do this is to first have a centimeter grid copied onto sheets of heavy card stock. Then cut out about twenty 10 frames (each will be 2 cm × 5 cm) and twenty or more 100s. The 100s should be 10 cm × 10 cm. You will also need a large sheet of newsprint (at least 25 cm × 50 cm), some counters (beans or, even better, centimeter cubes), four sets of flip numeral cards as shown in figure 3, and some rubber bands. Lay the newsprint flat horizontally, draw three vertical lines to create place-value columns as shown in figure 9, and draw two large 10 frames in the "ones," column.

The activities, which use the cutout centimeter-grid pieces, involve placing them on the newsprint to create two-, three-, and four-digit numbers. Then the grids are either added or subtracted, and special attention is given to the processes involved and the results.

19. Initial activities should have children place counters one at a time on the 10 frame drawn on the newsprint and announce the results orally. When ten counters have been accumulated, they are traded for one of the 2 cm × 5 cm cutout 10 frames, which is placed in the tens column. When ten "10s" have been accumulated, they are traded for a 10 cm × 10 cm 100. Adding counters to the playing mat should continue until the number 300 is represented. (This may take several class sessions!) Emphasis should be given to the trading that occurs and to the verbalizing of total amounts. Note that no numerals have been used yet!

20. This activity reverses the steps of activity 19. Begin by representing 300 on the mats and have the children remove counters, again one at a time.

21. After children can perform activities 18 and 19 with ease—that is, they can anticipate the ensuing trades and verbalize the amounts readily—have them use the flip numeral cards above the place-value columns and verbalize the amounts.

22. Have the children place specified numbers of 1s, 10s, and 100s on their mats (e.g., three 1s, five 10s, four 100s) and determine the number represented. Then ask them to add 1s, 10s, or 100s one at a time and to verbalize the total after each addition. Later, have the children remove 1s, 10s, or 100s.

23. Extend activity 22 by adding 100s until ten 100s have been accumulated. Then, have students bundle them with a rubber band and place the bundle in the thousands column. If enough 100s are available, the class will be able to model numbers up to 9999 with these materials.

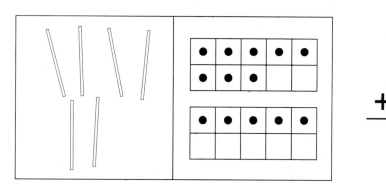

Fig. 8. Modeling the addition of two-digit numbers

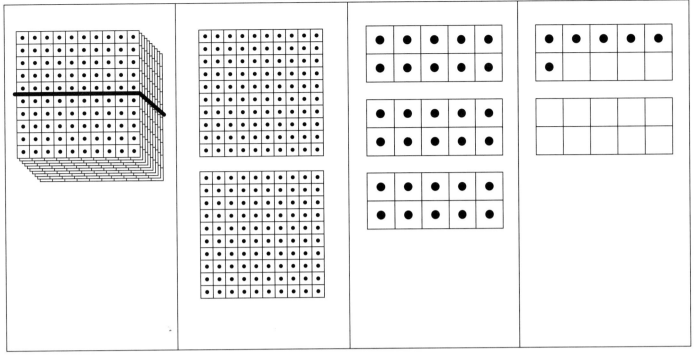

Fig. 9. A model of 1236

CONCLUSION

The 10 frame is not only a simple manipulative aid to make for your classroom but also a way to create an equally simple yet powerful image of 10 for the children. We have demonstrated how to use this aid and the corresponding "power of 10" to help with number concepts, addition facts, two-digit computation, and place-value concepts for three- and four-digit numbers. Perhaps you will find other ways to use 10 frames.

References

Baratta-Lorton, Mary. *Mathematics Their Way.* Menlo Park, Calif.: Addison-Wesley Publishing Co., 1976.

Wirtz, Robert. "An Elementary Mathematics Curriculum for All Children." Paper presented at the National Council of Supervisors of Mathematics meeting, San Diego, Calif., April 1978. ▲

d. Rational Numbers

Multiplication of Fractions through Paper Folding

by

Rose Sinicrope

Harold W. Mick

"One of the most well established facts in all mathematics education literature is that performance on fractions is undesirably low" (Hope and Owens 1987, 37). One example of that performance is that less than half of the seventh graders tested in the 1986 National Assessment of Educational Progress recognized that 5 1/4 equals 5 + 1/4 (Kouba et al. 1988)! We keep trying to comprehend why so many students and intelligent adults don't understand fractions.

Central to the complexity of rational numbers is the fraction symbol. This one symbol is used to represent many different concepts. Kieren (1980) has identified five very different concepts—part-holes, measures, divisions, operators, and ratios—that are represented by the fraction symbol. Other distinctions have been made. For example, in their analysis, Usiskin and Bell (1984) defined ten different uses of fractions: locations, ratio comparisons, counting units, variants of scientific notation, notations in algebra, scalars, multiplications acting across, division rates, division ratios, and powering growth. Unfortunately, many students and math-anxious adults view fractions as strictly part-wholes (Tobias 1978).

The fraction symbol represents many concepts.

When fractions are understood strictly as part-wholes, fraction multiplication, in which the product is smaller than a factor, is difficult to understand. This article presents a way to help all students understand a small but important portion of this complex topic. This instructional approach uses paper-folding activities. These activities can be represented by fraction-multiplication sentences. We use the operator concept of fraction and an extension of the union-of-equivalent-disjoint-sets concept of multiplication.

Almost all elementary curricula include good instruction on fractions as part-wholes and whole-number multiplication as the union of equivalent disjoint sets. Textbooks rarely present clear instruction on fractions as operators.

By *operator*, we mean the composition of whole-number multiplication and division. The numerator of a fraction represents multiplication and the denominator represents division. Usually, we do the division first; we partition a region, a line segment, or a set into congruent regions, congruent line segments, or equivalent subsets. Then we multiply; we replicate. For example, the operator "two-thirds" indicates (1) starting with the denominator, to divide into three equal parts and then take two of those equal parts or (2) starting with the numerator, to double in size and then divide into three equal parts.

Most students have a good understanding of multiplication of whole numbers as the union of equivalent disjoint sets. Students will explain that 3 × 5 is the same as 5 + 5 + 5. They are even able to create a story problem for a whole-number multiplication. As an example of 3 × 5, they tell a story about the number of sticks of chewing gum in three five-stick packs. Because of the emphasis in textbooks and curricula, students almost always associate multiplication with the union of equivalent sets that do not intersect.

Because of this focus, it is important that students be able to extend this meaning of multiplication of whole numbers to multiplication of fractions. We can help students develop this connection through paper-folding activities. The activities we describe meet our criteria of meaningful, uncontrived use of a manipulative to model the algorithm we want our students to learn.

NCTM's (1989) *Curriculum and Evaluation Standards for School Mathematics* presents the use of paper strips as a means to represent and teach equivalent fractions. Many teachers use circles to teach fraction concepts. Either representation can be meaningful. However, sheets of paper are easier to fold in various ways. Also, the use of sheets of paper enables students to see the connection between multiplication and area.

Rose Sinicrope teaches at East Carolina University, Greenville, NC 27858. She has been interested in teaching fractions since her beginning years as a teacher. Harold Mick teaches at Virginia Polytechnic Institute and State University, Blacksburg, VA 24061-0123. He is interested in the psychology of learning fractions, equations and graphs, and the use of technology in the mathematics curriculum.

WHOLE NUMBER OF WHOLE NUMBER

First, to help students extend the concept of whole-number multiplication to multiplication of fractions, we begin with such examples of whole-number multiplication as the three packs of five sticks of chewing gum. We emphasize the use of the word *of* by writing "3 groups of 5." Using empty gum packages with wrappers intact is a great technique for teaching the basic facts for multiplication by five. In discussing the representation, we have the students note that the first factor, 3, represents the number of packs and that the second factor, 5, represents the number of sticks.

Still building on the "three packs of five" meaning of multiplication, we teach the multiplication of fractions. The use of paper-folding activities is one type of representation that enables students to engage in an active, kinesthetic, tactile approach to learning. Harrison, Brindley, and Bye (1989) found that such an approach to instruction in fractions results in higher achievement and a better attitude toward the study of fractions.

To help students extend the concept of multiplication of whole numbers to the multiplication of fractions using paper folding, we start with stacks of two sheets of paper and ask the question, "May I have three of those stacks? How many sheets of paper are in three of those stacks?" Then we ask students to discuss the mathematics. "Can we write a multiplication sentence for what we did? Can we write a multiplication sentence for one of those stacks? For three stacks of five sheets? For two stacks of five sheets? For one stack of five sheets?" As we are discussing the multiplications, we record the action on the chalkboard, as shown in table 1.

Table 1. Whole-Number Multiplication

3 stacks of 2 sheets = 6 sheets	3 of 2 = 6
1 stack of 2 sheets = 2 sheets	1 of 2 = 2
3 stacks of 5 sheets = 15 sheets	3 of 5 = 15
2 stacks of 5 sheets = 10 sheets	2 of 5 = 10
1 stack of 5 sheets = 5 sheets	1 of 5 = 5

UNIT FRACTION OF WHOLE NUMBER WITH WHOLE NUMBER PRODUCT

At the next level of instruction, we explore one-half of a stack of two sheets, of four sheets, and of ten sheets. We begin with halves because halving is a common out-of-school experience for students. Even young children have an understanding of one-half used in this way (Kieren and Nelson 1978; Kieren and Southwell 1979). After discussing the symbol for one-half and the action involved, we explore one-fifth of five sheets, one-fifth of ten sheets, and one-fifth of thirty-five sheets. With each discussion, we record the multiplication sentence. From examples of this type, the students can generalize a rule for the multiplication of a unit fraction and a whole number that is a multiple of the denominator of the unit fraction.

UNIT FRACTION OF ONE

"May I have one-half of a sheet?" Instead of tearing the sheet into two pieces, we ask the students to fold, crease, and shade the portion. We record, "1/2 of 1 = 1/2." Then we ask, "If we have *one* sheet of paper, can we take one-third of it?" Discovering a way to fold the paper into three equal parts may be difficult for some students. It can be done by first wrapping the paper into a cylinder with one overlap. Next, gently flatten the cylinder without creasing to check for accuracy of overlap. To make a layer larger, gently relax your hold; to make a layer smaller, twist with a back-and-forth motion. When the overlap is aligned properly, tap the cylinder on a flat surface, flatten, and crease. Check for congruent regions by refolding in an accordion fashion. (Scott [1981] has thoroughly described this technique for folding paper into an odd number of pieces by varying the number of overlaps.) Again we have the students shade the portion and record, "1/3 of 1 = 1/3." At this time, reinforce the comparison of unit fractions. We ask, "Which is larger, one-third or one-half? One-fifth or one-twenty-sixth?"

Students can test their own hypotheses.

COMMON FRACTION OF ONE

Using another sheet of paper, we ask students how they can fold two-thirds of one. In the discussion, we emphasize dividing the paper into three equal parts and then shading two *of* those parts (see fig. 1). Students question whether division by 3 followed by multiplication by 2 is the same as multiplication by 2 followed by division by 3. We ask students to predict the result of first taking two sheets *of* paper and then dividing those two sheets by 3. We elicit demonstrations.

Two different methods are possible. One method is first to tape two sheets together and then after taping, fold the taped sheets into three equal parts vertically or horizontally (see fig. 2). The other method is to form a stack of two sheets and then fold the stack into three equal parts vertically or horizontally (see fig. 3). In this second method, students may need actually to see the stack torn into three parts and to examine the parts, comparing them to one sheet of paper. We have students confirm that the result is

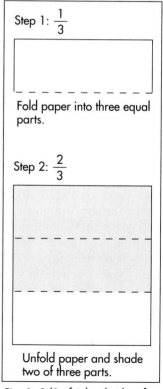

Step 1: $\frac{1}{3}$

Fold paper into three equal parts.

Step 2: $\frac{2}{3}$

Unfold paper and shade two of three parts.

Fig. 1. 2/3 of 1 by dividing first

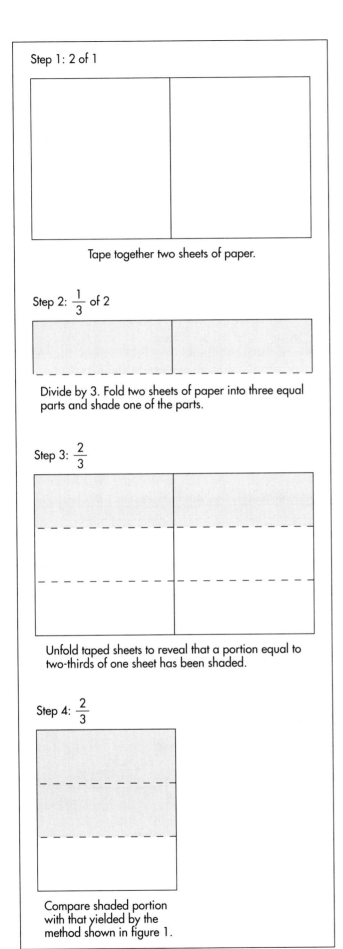

Step 1: 2 of 1

Tape together two sheets of paper.

Step 2: $\frac{1}{3}$ of 2

Divide by 3. Fold two sheets of paper into three equal parts and shade one of the parts.

Step 3: $\frac{2}{3}$

Unfold taped sheets to reveal that a portion equal to two-thirds of one sheet has been shaded.

Step 4: $\frac{2}{3}$

Compare shaded portion with that yielded by the method shown in figure 1.

Fig. 2. 2/3 of 1 by multiplying first

the same amount of paper. If the students fold in different directions, then the shapes are different. Tearing the paper and comparing it to some known value will be necessary to convince the students that the quantity is the same, although the shapes are different. By always using notebook-sized paper, the unit remains constant and is easily remembered.

FRACTION OF FRACTION

Next we ask students to fold one-fourth of one. We ask, "How did you determine one-fourth of one?" Students almost always respond, "Divide the paper in half and in half again." On the chalkboard, we write, "1/2 of 1/2 is 1/4." Scott's (1981) cylinder technique is another way to fold one-fourth of one. Next, we ask the students to predict, describe in words, and demonstrate how they can use paper folding to represent one-third of one-half. If the students have difficulty with this question, we ask them to show us one-sixth of a sheet.

Next the students are ready to develop an understanding of the multiplication of two fractions. Using the one-half shaded region (fold the unshaded region behind the shaded region), we ask students to take one-third of one-half. It is important that instruction focus on the process. The use of paper folding allows instruction to develop from the meaning. Students should be encouraged to explore different approaches to the same problem. For example, only horizontal folds can be used, only vertical folds can be used, or a horizontal fold can follow a vertical fold or a vertical fold can follow a horizontal fold.

Next, we have students take two-thirds of one-half. If the student first divides by 3 and then multiplies by 2, the model shows two-sixths (see fig. 4). We ask students to use a different color or a darker shading to screen the product. Shading helps the students keep track of the product without tearing and taping the paper. We can ask the students to multiply by 2 and then divide by 3. When this sequence is used, the model shows one-third (see fig. 5).

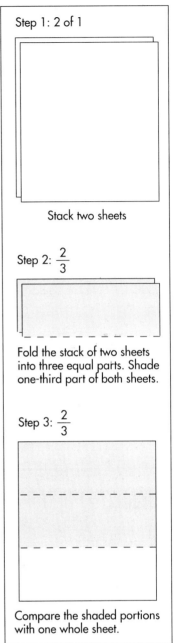

Step 1: 2 of 1

Stack two sheets

Step 2: $\frac{2}{3}$

Fold the stack of two sheets into three equal parts. Shade one-third part of both sheets.

Step 3: $\frac{2}{3}$

Compare the shaded portions with one whole sheet.

Fig. 3. 2/3 of 1 using another approach

Students' questions and comments will influence the selection of examples to be explored. Representations of many fractions with whole-number denominators less than fifteen can be folded with adequate accuracy. The following examples can be used: 1/2 of 1/3, 1/4 of 1/3, 1/3 of 2/3, 2/3 of 2/3 (see figs. 6–9). Students should be encouraged to explore different ways in which paper can be folded for a given problem. Paper-folding activities enable students to formulate and test their own hypotheses.

We think that oral expression is an important transition from the use of concrete materials to the use of symbols. We ask students if they can predict the product of two such fractions as one-fifth and three-fourths. We have students orally describe an appropriate paper-folding procedure. Next, we ask them to think about such a multiplication as four-fifths of three-sevenths. We ask, "Is the product less than, equal to, or greater than one? Is the product less than, equal to, or greater than three-sevenths?"

CONCLUSION

The examples discussed in this article illustrate how paper folding can be used to promote understandings related to multiplication of fractions. Future lessons may include the use of paper folding to develop cancellation properties. For other uses of paper folding to teach fractions, see Scott (1981). Another connection that is easy to build is the multiplication of fractions as Cartesian products (see Mick and Sinicrope [1989]).

The use of paper-folding activities to teach multiplication of fractions is practical, inexpensive (recycled paper can be used), and instructionally sound. Students are able to extend rational-number multiplication from whole-number multiplication. Students can understand why *of* means multiplication and why the multiplication of two proper fractions yields a smaller fraction. Discussion and framing the activities within a problem-solving format can help students connect the paper-folding activities with applications of multiplication of fractions. Instruction easily evolves as the students pose questions and discuss various approaches to the same problem. The students are doing mathematics. The instruction is very much in the spirit of the NCTM's *Curriculum and Evaluation Standards.* And it is fun!

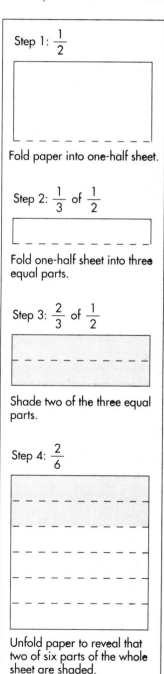

Fig. 4. 2/3 of 1/2

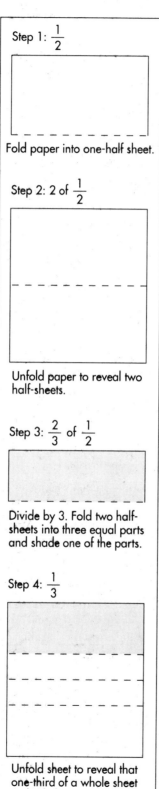

Fig. 5. 2/3 of 1/2

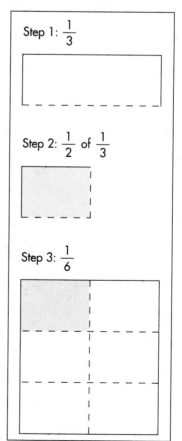
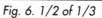

Fig. 6. 1/2 of 1/3

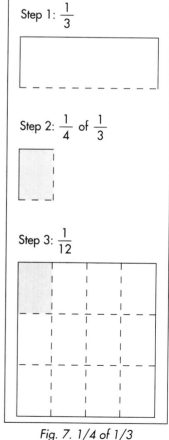

Fig. 7. 1/4 of 1/3

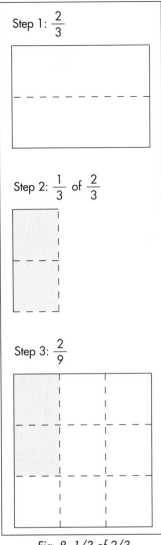

Fig. 8. 1/3 of 2/3

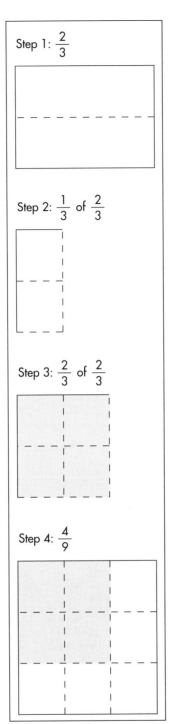

Fig. 9. 2/3 of 2/3

References

Harrison, Bruce, Selwyn Brindley, and Marshall P. Bye. "Allowing for Student Cognitive Levels in the Teaching of Fractions and Ratios." *Journal for Research in Mathematics Education* 20 (May 1989): 288–300.

Hope, Jack A., and Douglas T. Owens. "An Analysis of the Difficulty of Learning Fractions." *Focus on Learning Problems in Mathematics* 9 (Fall 1987): 25–40.

Kieren, Thomas E. "Knowing Rational Numbers: Ideas and Symbols." In *Selected Issues in Mathematics Education,* edited by Mary Montgomery Lindquist, 69–81. Reston, Va.: National Society for the Study of Education and National Council of Teachers of Mathematics, 1980.

Kieren, Thomas, and Doyal Nelson. "The Operator Construct of Rational Numbers in Children and Adolescents—an Exploratory Study." *Alberta Journal of Educational Psychology* 24 (March 1978): 22–30.

Kieren, Thomas E., and Beth Southwell. "The Development in Children and Adolescents of the Construct of Rational Numbers as Operators." *Alberta Journal of Educational Psychology* 25 (December 1979): 234–47.

Kouba, Vicky L., Catherine A. Brown, Thomas P. Carpenter, Mary M. Lindquist, Edward A. Silver, and Jane O. Swafford. "Results of the Fourth NAEP Assessment of Mathematics: Number, Operations, and Word Problems." *Arithmetic Teacher* 35 (April 1988): 14–19.

Mick, Harold W., and Rose Sinicrope. "Two Meanings of Fraction Multiplication." *School Science and Mathematics* 89 (December 1989): 632–39.

National Council of Teachers of Mathematics. *Curriculum and Evaluation Standards for School Mathematics.* Reston, Va.: The Council, 1989.

Scott, Wayne R. "Fractions Taught by Folding Paper Strips." *Arithmetic Teacher* 28 (January 1981): 18–22.

Tobias, Sheila. *Overcoming Math Anxiety.* New York: W. W. Norton & Co., 1978.

Usiskin, Zalman, and Max S. Bell. "Ten Often Ignored Applications of Rational-Number Concepts." *Arithmetic Teacher* 31 (February 1984): 48–50. ▲

From the File: Fraction Mobiles

by

Doris H. Gluck

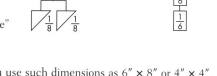

Fractions

Fraction Mobiles

Grade level: 3–8

Objective: Students will work with and become more familiar with equivalent fractions.

Materials: Each student or group of students will need:
- 1 metal hanger
- string (monofilament or dental floss)
- 6–8 bamboo skewers
- 1 fraction set (described below)

Fraction set: From oaktag, cardboard, or construction paper, make one fraction set for each student or group of students.

1 piece (square, rectangle, or equilateral triangle) to represent "1 whole"
3–4 1/2 pieces   4–6 1/4 pieces   6 1/3 pieces
8 1/8 pieces   6 1/6 pieces

Hints: These pieces can be cut fairly quickly with a paper cutter if you use such dimensions as 6″ × 8″ or 4″ × 4″. The fraction pieces, skewers, and string can be stored in manila envelopes labeled with the students' names.

Activity: Students are instructed to find the largest shape in their packet and label it "1." They should then label all the other pieces in their packets with the appropriate labels. Each student or group is to make a mobile using some or all the fraction pieces, bamboo skewers, string, and hanger (see illustration). The mobile must contain the "1" piece and at least two skewers set up with equivalent fractions. Students should be encouraged to make their equivalent skewers as complicated as possible, to use more than two skewers, and to make their mobiles visually pleasing.

From the file of Doris H. Gluck, Radnor Township School District, Wayne, PA 19087 ▲

IDEAS: Fraction Wheel

by

Alan Barson
School District of Philadelphia, Philadelphia, Pennsylvania

Lois Barson
School District of Philadelphia, Philadelphia, Pennsylvania

LEVELS 3, 4

Objective

To visualize and compare fractions

Directions

1. Reproduce a worksheet for every student.
2. Review directions 1, 2, and 3 on the worksheet with the class. Guide students in their completion.
3. Direct students to show several fractions, such as 1/4, 3/4, 2/5, 2/3, and so on.
4. Guide students through letter A at the bottom of the worksheet.
5. Instruct students to complete lettered items B through H by using their fraction wheels.
6. Review and correct the items.

Extension

Instruct students to use the fractions wheel often during their free time.

Answers

A. $\frac{1}{8} < \frac{1}{4}$ B. $\frac{5}{8} > \frac{1}{2}$ C. $\frac{2}{3} < \frac{5}{6}$

D. $\frac{1}{8} < \frac{1}{2}$ E. $\frac{2}{5} < \frac{3}{4}$ F. $\frac{7}{8} > \frac{4}{5}$

G. $\frac{3}{5} < \frac{5}{8}$ H. $\frac{5}{6} > \frac{3}{5}$

IDEAS: FRACTION WHEEL

Student Worksheet

Name _____

1. Cut out the two circles.
2. Cut along $\overline{AB}$ and $\overline{CD}$.
3. Fit the wheels together by inserting $\overline{CD}$ into $\overline{AB}$.
4. Move the shaded wheel around, and it will show you the size of each fraction on the dial.

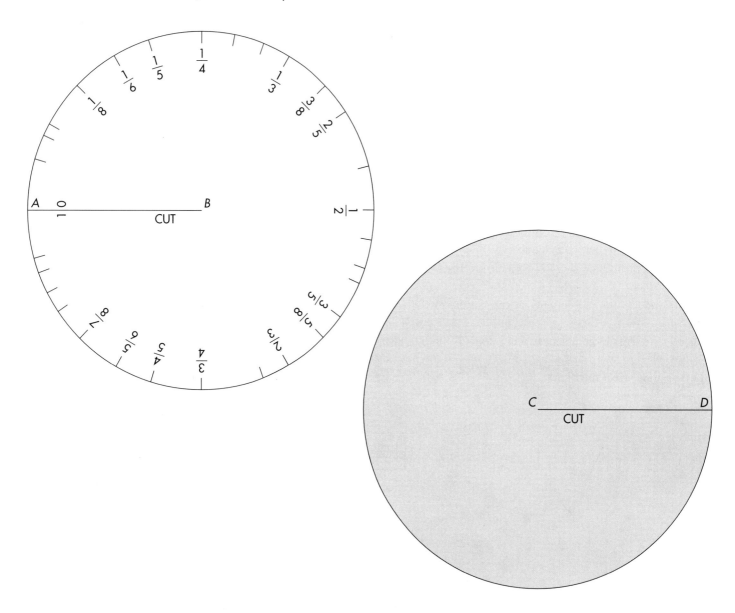

Complete the following expressions. Use symbols for greater than (>) or less than (<).

A. $\frac{1}{8}$ ☐ $\frac{1}{4}$ B. $\frac{5}{8}$ ☐ $\frac{1}{2}$ C. $\frac{2}{3}$ ☐ $\frac{5}{6}$ D. $\frac{1}{8}$ ☐ $\frac{1}{2}$

E. $\frac{2}{5}$ ☐ $\frac{3}{4}$ F. $\frac{7}{8}$ ☐ $\frac{4}{5}$ G. $\frac{3}{5}$ ☐ $\frac{5}{8}$ H. $\frac{5}{6}$ ☐ $\frac{3}{5}$

From *Teacher-Made Aids for Elementary School Mathematics, Vol. 3*

Fractions and Panes

by

Douglas Edge

Fig. 1. The panes that started it all

Recently I saw an interesting photograph of classroom windows that had been painted with colorful flowers by the children (fig. 1). One child had commented, "Now it always looks like spring outside."

Could classroom window panes be used to teach certain mathematics concepts? The following activities using panes were developed to help extend children's knowledge of fractional numbers.

ACTIVITY 1

First, select a window pane to serve as a basic unit. If real windows are not available, then you can construct a fake window on a bulletin board or wall. To develop the concept of one-fourth, you can divide each pane into fourths in different ways (see fig. 2 for suggestions). Ask the children to make sure each pane has been divided correctly by cutting and fitting newsprint onto one of the quarters. Then, by flipping or rotating if necessary, cover an adjoining section with the piece of newsprint. Each pane should be divided into four *equal* parts.

For a variation of this activity, window panes can be divided as shown in figure 3. Is each section a quarter of the whole? To investigate figure 3(a), fit a piece of newsprint onto one of the "long quarters"; cut it in half and then place the pieces side by side to fit onto one of the "square quarters." Although this does not reflect the standard part-whole meaning of one-quarter, each section covers one-quarter of the whole.

ACTIVITY 2

It is possible to compare quarters of different panes. Assuming that all the panes were originally the same size, shouldn't one-quarter of any one of them be equal to one-quarter of any

other? Children often think that one-quarter of figure 2(b) or figure 2(c) is definitely larger than one-quarter of figure 2(a). Measuring with the newsprint frequently helps them understand the equality of fractions.

ACTIVITY 3

Not all window panes are square. Consider the rectangular region shown in figure 4. Certainly the triangles formed by drawing the diagonals are not congruent. But do they have the same area? Do the upper and lower triangles seem larger? Fit newsprint to cover one of the regions. By cutting, attempt to cover an adjacent region. (Can one triangle be cut more than one way to fit the other?)

Yes, the triangles do have the same area, and although it is not suitable for primary children, a simple proof using the formula for the area of triangles does exist. The area of each triangle is one-quarter of the rectangular region.

The window panes must be cleaned and resectioned before continuing with the next activity. Incidentally, masking tape is very difficult to remove from windows. Poster paint works well and can be washed off easily.

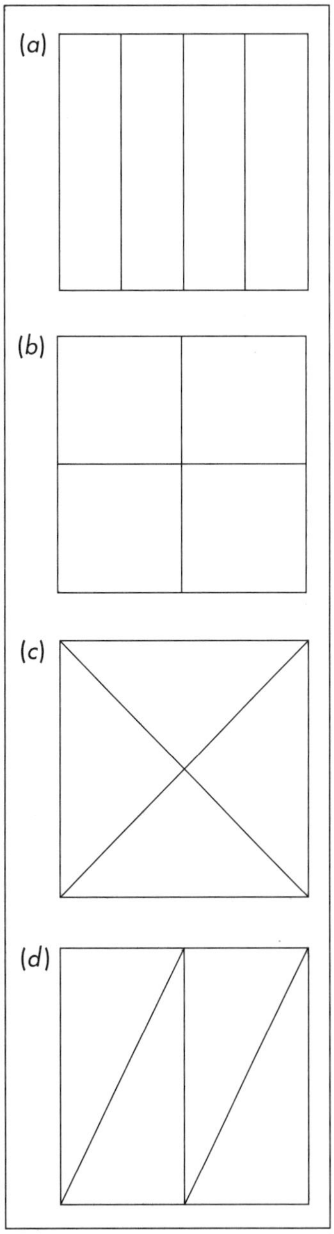

Fig. 2. Dividing a window pane into fourths

Douglas Edge teaches courses in elementary mathematics methods and in diagnosis and remediation at the University of Western Ontario, London, ON N6C 1G7.

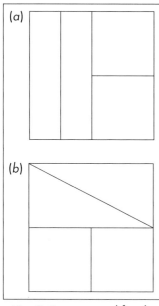
(a)

(b)

Fig. 3. Some unusual fourths

Fig. 4. Use newprint cutouts to show whether the triangles have the same area.

ACTIVITY 4

Section each pane to illustrate a different fraction. Divide the panes into halves, thirds, fourths, sixths, eighths, and twelfths as shown in figure 5. Aside from reviewing fraction names, you can conduct a whole set of investigations related to equivalent fractions. One-third of a pane is equivalent to how many sixths? (Use figs. 5(b) and 5(d).) How many twelfths? (Use figs. 5(b) and 5(f).)

It would be appropriate to design other activities to compare results from these window-pane investigations with those obtained from using such materials as Cuisenaire rods, fraction bars, and the fraction number line.

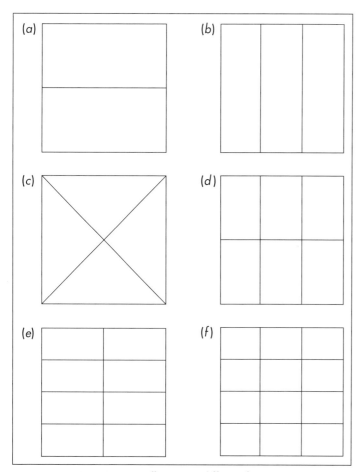

Fig. 5. Panes illustrating different fractions

As a follow-up to these activities, you might want to prepare a set of activity cards made from pictures of buildings or furniture having interesting arrangements of windows and window panes. Glue these pictures onto cards. Along with questions about symmetry and congruence, many questions about fractions can be asked:

- What fraction of the panes are square?
- What fraction of the panes are rectangular? (fig. 6(a))
- What fraction of the panes have rounded or curved edges? (figs. 6(b), 6(c))
- Look at the living-room windows. By estimation, what fraction of the larger pane is the smaller pane?
- Look at the windows on the house. Can you make up a fraction story for one-half and one-quarter? (fig. 6(d))

Photographs by Y. Morin-Grimard

Fig. 6. Questions can be asked about the windows in your town.

Many of these ideas can easily be adapted for teaching fractional concepts in the elementary grades. Early topics such as the meaning of fractions and equivalent fractions can be reviewed. Addition of the fractions 1/2 + 1/4 can be illustrated by covering a half and a quarter of a pane. If newsprint is used, it is possible to "see through" the newsprint to note that the covered half is equivalent to 2/4. The student can clearly see that the answer to 1/2 + 1/4 is the same as the answer to 2/4 + 1/4.

To illustrate the multiplication example of 1/2 × 3/4, divide the pane into halves and cover one half with tissue paper (fig. 7(a)). Then divide the pane into quarters and cover three of the four quarters with tissue paper of a different color (fig. 7(b)). The unit pane has thus been divided into eighths, and three of the eighths have been covered twice by the tissue paper. One-half of the three quarters is three-eighths!

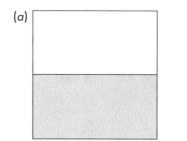 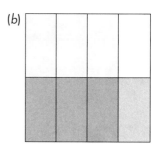

Fig. 7. Use tissue paper and window panes to show 1/2 × 3/4 = 3/8.

These types of activities can be extended to other parts of the classroom—bulletin boards, desk tips, and floor tiles, to name a few.

Do I dare mention that I hope all this hasn't been too paneful? ▲

Divide and Conquer: Unit Strips to the Rescue

by

Frances R. Curcio

Francine Sicklick

Susan B. Turkel

> Yours is not to reason why, just invert and multiply … that's the stuff of sterile instruction.
>
> —Steven J. Leinwand

Despite the years spent learning operations with fractions, many students approach some fraction operations with a bag-of-tricks perspective. This perspective leads many students to the invert-and-multiply rule for dividing fractions. Students who take the bag-of-tricks approach must rely on their memory, which often fails them. However, if meaning and understanding of concepts, nurtured with the use of concrete materials, were the basis for developing fraction operations, students would not have to remember meaningless rules. Conceptual understanding using concrete manipulative materials should precede intensive work on formal algorithms.

By the time students reach the division process in their fraction curriculum, they have often spent so much of their allotted time on related topics—equivalent fractions, least common denominator, greatest common factor, addition and subtraction of fractions, multiplication of fractions—that they tend to rush through this topic to make up time. It's tempting and easy to present the invert-and-multiply rule and follow that with a large amount of drill and practice. If only more time and care were given to the conceptual development of this delicate topic, the concepts learned would remain with students much longer.

The following activities develop the imagery and ideas necessary for a proper understanding of dividing fractions and the related computational algorithm. By enlarging, duplicating, cutting out, and using the unit strips in figure 1, the teacher is able to illustrate division ideas and provide a common base for a further understanding of division of fractions.

ACTIVITY 1A

Purpose: To illustrate division of a whole number by a unit fraction

Materials: At least two unit strips partitioned into thirds (see fig. 2)

The authors teach at Queens College of the City University of New York, Flushing, NY 11367. Curcio has been examining ways to use manipulatives to model the meaning of mathematics concepts in elementary instruction. Sicklick has a special interest in microcomputer applications. Turkel's special interest is in geometry and art.

Consider $1 \div 1/3$. The question we should ask relating to this expression is, How many one-thirds are in one whole? To illustrate this concept, use one unit strip that has been divided into three equivalent parts (i.e., thirds). How many thirds are in this unit strip? Three thirds are in one unit strip, so $1 \div 1/3 = 3$, which can also be written as 3/1. If we think $1 \div 1/3 = \square$ or $1 = \square \times 1/3$, then we can say $1 \div 1/3 = 3/1$ (or $1 = 3/1 \times 1/3$). Expressing this idea verbally, we have shown that one unit strip is equivalent to three groups of one third.

If three thirds are in one unit strip, how many thirds are in two unit strips?

We can show this idea with the strips. Use two of the unit strips that have been partitioned into thirds. How many thirds are in the two unit strips? Since three-thirds are in one unit strip, twice as many thirds must be in two unit strips, so that $2 \times 3 = 6$. Another way to look at this idea is the following:

$1 \div 1/3$ equals the number of thirds in one unit strip, and

$$1 \div \frac{1}{3} = \frac{3}{1} = 3.$$

We can substitute 3/1 for the expression $1 \div 1/3$ in $2 \div 1/3$ to get

$$2 \times \left(1 \div \frac{1}{3}\right) = 2 \times \frac{3}{1} = 6.$$

(Twice as many thirds are in two unit strips as are in one unit strip.)

Depending on students' readiness, continue with the unit strips as long as students have the need to "see" results. For example, use the strips and ask, How many thirds are in three unit strips? How many thirds are in four unit strips? and so on. Using both the concrete model and mathematical substitution, students can observe the following development. By ratios, we get

$$3 \div \frac{1}{3} = 9$$

and

$$3 \times \frac{3}{1} = 9,$$

so

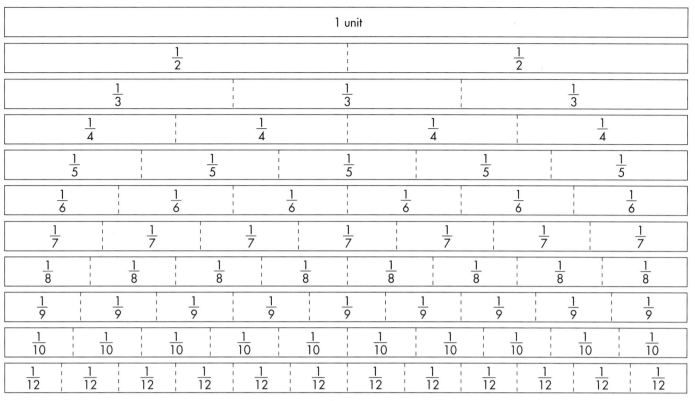

Fig. 1. A unit and equivalent fractional parts of a unit. Duplicate, laminate, and cut for students' use.

$\frac{1}{3}$	$\frac{1}{3}$	$\frac{1}{3}$

Fig. 2. Use these strips to determine 1 ÷ 1/3.

$$3 \div \frac{1}{3} = 3 \times \underline{\frac{3}{1}}$$

$$4 \div \frac{1}{3} = 12$$

and

$$4 \times \frac{3}{1} = 12,$$

so

$$4 \div \frac{1}{3} = 4 \times \underline{\frac{3}{1}}$$
$$\vdots$$

A pattern is evident. If we examine the underlined expressions, we can begin to see the development of the division algorithm (see part 1a of table 1). The teacher should record these results on the chalkboard and construct a table similar to table 1 by eliciting the information from the students.

ACTIVITY 1B

Purpose: To introduce and illustrate the concept of the "shifting unit" (Ellison 1972)

Materials: At least two unit strips partitioned into fifths (see fig. 3)

Consider 1 ÷ 3/5. The question we should ask relating to this expression is, How many groups of 3/5 are in one whole? To illustrate this concept, use one unit strip partitioned into fifths.

Consider three boxes (or 3/5) as the new unit. How many of these new units are in the original unit? Circle as many 3/5s as possible. What is left over? We see that one complete group of 3/5 and a part of another group of 3/5 are left. What part of 3/5 (three boxes) is the remaining piece? Two boxes are left (see fig. 4).

The remaining piece, containing two boxes, is 2/3 of the three-box unit. Originally the boxes had been named fifths because the original unit had been partitioned into five equal parts. However, the unit of reference shifted to 3/5 (or three boxes). Thus, 1 2/3 portions (or 5/3 portions) of the new unit called 3/5 are in the one unit strip. The question then arises, How many groups of 3/5 are in two unit strips? Since 1 2/3 are in one unit strip, twice as many

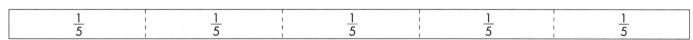

Fig. 3. Use these strips to determine 1 ÷ 3/5.

Table 1. Organized Results from Each Activity

	Activity	Results
1a	$1 \div \frac{1}{3} = 3$	
	$2 \div \frac{1}{3} = 6$ and $2 \times \frac{3}{1} = 6$	$2 \div \frac{1}{3} = 2 \times \frac{3}{1}$
	$3 \div \frac{1}{3} = 9$ and $3 \times \frac{3}{1} = 9$	$3 \div \frac{1}{3} = 3 \times \frac{3}{1}$
	$4 \div \frac{1}{3} = 12$ and $4 \times \frac{3}{1} = 12$	$4 \div \frac{1}{3} = 4 \times \frac{3}{1}$
1b	$1 \div \frac{3}{5} = \frac{5}{3}$	
	$2 \div \frac{3}{5} = \frac{10}{3}$ and $2 \times \frac{5}{3} = \frac{10}{3}$	$2 \div \frac{3}{5} = 2 \times \frac{5}{3}$
	$3 \div \frac{3}{5} = 5$ and $3 \times \frac{5}{3} = 5$	$3 \div \frac{3}{5} = 3 \times \frac{5}{3}$
	$4 \div \frac{3}{5} = \frac{20}{3}$ and $4 \times \frac{5}{3} = \frac{20}{3}$	$4 \div \frac{3}{5} = 4 \times \frac{5}{3}$
2a	$1 \div \frac{3}{8} = \frac{8}{3}$	
	$\frac{3}{4} \div \frac{3}{8} = 2$ and $\frac{3}{4} \times \frac{8}{3} = 2$	$\frac{3}{4} \div \frac{3}{8} = \frac{3}{4} \times \frac{8}{3}$
2b	$1 \div \frac{2}{3} = \frac{3}{2}$	
	$\frac{3}{4} \div \frac{2}{3} = \frac{9}{8}$ and $\frac{3}{4} \times \frac{3}{2} = \frac{9}{8}$	$\frac{3}{4} \div \frac{2}{3} = \frac{3}{4} \times \frac{3}{2}$
	$\frac{5}{6} \div \frac{2}{3} = \frac{5}{4}$ and $\frac{5}{6} \times \frac{3}{2} = \frac{5}{4}$	$\frac{5}{6} \div \frac{2}{3} = \frac{5}{6} \times \frac{3}{2}$

must be in two unit strips, so 2 × 1 2/3 = 2 × 5/3 = 10/3. Another way to look at this fact is the following:

1 ÷ 3/5 equals the number of 3/5 in one unit strip, and

$$1 \div \frac{3}{5} = 1\frac{2}{3} = \frac{5}{3}.$$

We can substitute 5/3 for the expression 1 ÷ 3/5 in 2 ÷ 3/5 to get

$$2 \times \left(1 \div \frac{3}{5}\right) = \frac{2}{1} \times \frac{5}{3} = \frac{10}{3} = 3\frac{1}{3}.$$

(Twice as many groups of 3/5 are in two unit strips as are in one unit strip.)

Note that it is convenient to rename 1 2/3 as 5/3 so that 2 × 1 2/3 becomes 2/1 × 5/3.

What does 2 ÷ 3/5 mean? We can illustrate by using the unit strips (see fig. 5). There are 3 1/3 portions of 3/5 in 2. Continuing in this same manner, since 1 ÷ 3/5 = 5/3 by ratios, we get the following:

$$3 \div \frac{3}{5} = 5$$

and

$$3 \times \frac{5}{3} = 5,$$

so

$$\underline{3 \div \frac{3}{5}} = \underline{3 \times \frac{5}{3}}$$

$$4 \div \frac{3}{5} = \frac{20}{3}$$

and

$$4 \times \frac{5}{3} = \frac{20}{3},$$

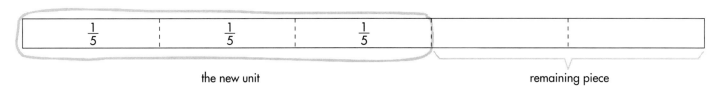

1/5
1/5
1/5
the new unit
remaining piece

Fig. 4. How many groups of 3/5 are in one unit? Answer: 1 and 2/3

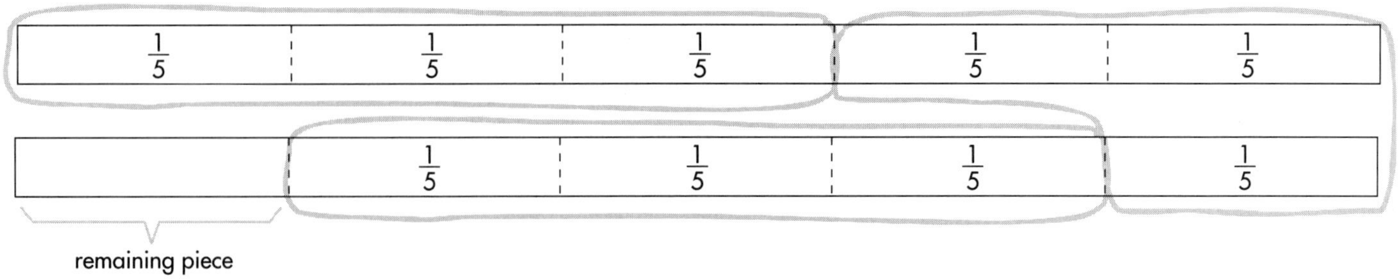

1/5
1/5
1/5
1/5
1/5
1/5
1/5
1/5
1/5
remaining piece

Fig. 5. How many groups of 3/5 are in two units? Answer: 3 and 1/3

so

$$4 \div \frac{3}{5} = 4 \times \frac{5}{3}.$$

And so the pattern continues. See part 1b in table 1.

ACTIVITY 2A

Purpose: To illustrate division of a fraction by a fraction when the divisor is a positive integral multiple of the dividend

Materials: One unit strip partitioned into eighths and one unit strip partitioned into fourths (see fig. 6)

Consider $3/4 \div 3/8$. Before we illustrate this example, we would like to examine $1 \div 3/8$ in preparation for the pattern work to follow. How many groups of 3/8 are in one unit? Two and a part of another 3/8 (see fig. 7).

What part of 3/8 is the remaining piece? This remaining piece contains two boxes and thus is 2/3 of the original three-box portion, named 3/8. Again, the unit of reference has been shifted and is now 3/8. Just as we can use this result to determine how many portions are in two unit strips, three unit strips, four unit strips, and so on, we can apply the same method to a part of a unit strip. How many groups of 3/8 are in 3/4 of a unit? Elicit from students that there is at least one. Here's a chance to help students observe that $3/8 < 3/4$.

Using a unit strip partitioned into eighths and a unit strip partitioned into fourths, have students identify that 6/8 is equivalent to 3/4. Now count the number of 3/8 portions in 3/4 of a unit strip (see fig. 8).

Two portions of 3/8 are in 3/4 of a unit. Also, this relationship can be expressed symbolically by using substitution. Since

$$1 \div \frac{3}{8} = 2\frac{2}{3}, \text{ or } \frac{8}{3},$$

then

$$\frac{3}{4} \div \frac{3}{8} = \frac{3}{4} \times \left(1 \div \frac{3}{8}\right) = \frac{3}{4} \times \frac{8}{3} = 2.$$

Let's review the meaning of all the parts of this division sentence. Before looking at 3/8 portions in part of one unit, we examined the number of 3/8 portions in one unit (i.e., $1 \div 3/8$); $1 \div 3/8$ was illustrated to determine how many portions of 3/8 exist in one unit, in a manner similar to the approach taken in activities 1a and 1b. We found that 2 2/3 portions (or 8/3 portions) of 3/8 are in one unit. To determine how many portions of 3/8 are in part of a unit, such as 3/4, we observe that 3/4 of the unit contains 3/4 of the number of portions of 3/8 contained in the unit. Here we are relying on students' understanding of multiplication in general and multiplication of fractions in particular.

Since the unit contains 2 2/3 portions of 3/8, then 3/4 of the unit contains $3/4 \times 2$ 2/3 portions of 3/8, or 2 portions of 3/8. Lining up the fourths and eighths visually depicts that two portions of 3/8 are in 3/4.

To help students observe the relationship between dividing by fractions and multiplying by the reciprocal, record the results in a table (see part 2a in table 1).

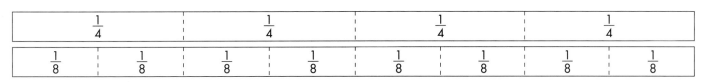

Fig. 6. Find 3/4 ÷ 3/8.

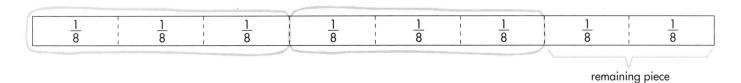

Fig. 7. How many groups of 3/8 are in one unit? Answer: 2 and 2/3

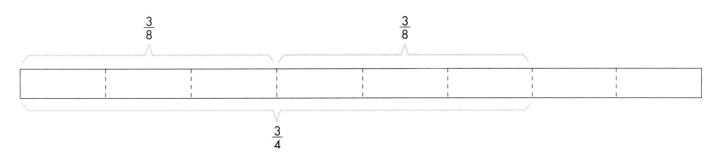

Fig. 8. How many groups of 3/8 are in 3/4? Answer: 2

ACTIVITY 2B

Purpose: To illustrate division of fractions when the divisor is not an integral multiple of the dividend

Materials: One unit partitioned into thirds, one unit partitioned into fourths (see fig. 9), one unit strip partitioned into thirds intact for cutting, and scissors

Consider 3/4 ÷ 2/3, which has been chosen for convenience to illustrate division of fractions when the divisor is not an integral multiple of the dividend. Before we illustrate this example, we would like to examine 1 ÷ 2/3 in preparation for the pattern work to follow.

How many groups of 2/3 are in one unit? One portion and a little more. What part of 2/3 is the leftover piece? It is 1/2 of the new reference unit, 2/3. Therefore, 1 1/2 portions (or 3/2 portions) of 2/3 are in one unit (see fig. 10).

Just as we can use this result to determine how many portions are in two unit strips, three unit strips, four unit strips, and so on, we can apply the same method to a part of a unit strip and rely on students' understanding of multiplication of fractions and substitution. Since

$$1 \div \frac{2}{3} = 1\frac{1}{2}, \text{ or } \frac{3}{2},$$

then

$$\frac{3}{4} \div \frac{2}{3} = \frac{3}{4} \times \left(1 \div \frac{2}{3}\right) = \frac{3}{4} \times \frac{3}{2} = \frac{9}{8}.$$

So

$$\frac{3}{4} \div \frac{2}{3} = \frac{9}{8}, \text{ or } 1\frac{1}{8}.$$

Since some students might not be comfortable with this numerical explanation, we return to our unit strips for verification. Look at the two unit strips in figure 9. How many groups of 2/3 are in 3/4 of a unit? Similar to our analysis in activity 2a, we can line up the 3/4 with 2/3 to find out how many portions of 2/3 are in 3/4 of a unit strip (see fig. 11). Elicit from students that there is at least one. Here's a chance to help students observe that 2/3 < 3/4.

Because the fractional divisor is not an integral multiple of the fractional dividend, we notice that the terminal line for 3/4 does not line up neatly with the terminal line for 2/3. Notice that one 2/3 portion and part of another 2/3 portion are in 3/4. To determine the portion of the 2/3 piece that is remaining, we will need to do some cutting.

After aligning the 3/4 pieces with the intact thirds unit strip, mark the terminal line of 3/4 on the thirds unit strip. Cut off the portion of the thirds unit strip not needed and discard it (see fig. 12).

Now cut off the remaining piece from the portion of 2/3 (see fig. 13). Using this remaining piece as a guide, mark off as many portions as possible in the 2/3 region. How many times does this remaining piece fit in the 2/3 portion? What is the fractional name for this little piece that is left? (See fig. 14.)

Count the number of pieces marked off in the 2/3 region. Since eight pieces are marked off, the remaining piece that was cut off to use as the guide is called 1/8. We have shown that 3/4 ÷ 2/3 = 1 1/8, which should be a reasonable result, since 1 ÷ 2/3 should be greater than 3/4 ÷ 2/3 and 1 1/2 > 1 1/8.

Let's review the meaning of all parts of the example, 3/4 ÷ 2/3. Before looking at 2/3 portions of part of one unit (3/4), we examined 1 ÷ 2/3 in a manner similar to the approach taken in the previous activities. We found 1 1/2 portions (or 3/2 portions) of 2/3 in one

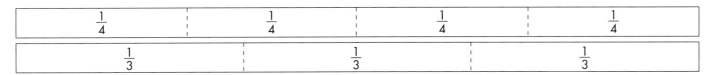

Fig. 9. Consider 3/4 ÷ 2/3

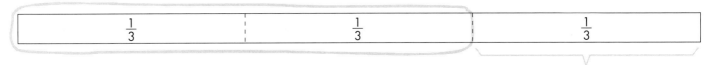

remaining piece

Fig. 10. One unit contains 1 1/2 portions of 2/3.

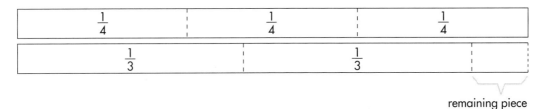

remaining piece

Fig. 11. How many groups of 2/3 are in 3/4?

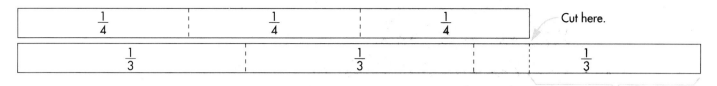

Fig. 12. Using the unit strip partitioned into thirds, align with 3/4 and cut off at the 3/4 mark. Discard the extra piece.

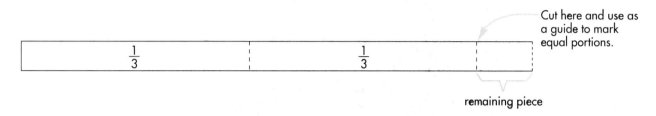

Fig. 13. Cut remaining piece and use it as a guide to mark off equal portions to determine what part of 2/3 it is.

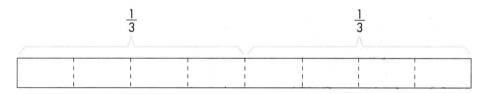

Fig. 14. Eight portions of the "remaing piece" are in 2/3. Therefore, it can be called "1/8."

unit. To determine how many portions of 2/3 are in part of a unit, such as 3/4, we observed that 3/4 of the unit contains 3/4 of the number of portions of 2/3 contained in the unit. Again, we are relying on students' understanding of multiplication of fractions. This result is included in table 1 (see part 2b).

Students can follow the same procedure for 5/6 ÷ 2/3. (The result has been included in table 1, part 2b.)

CONCLUDING REMARKS

We have used partitioned unit strips to begin to conceptualize what happens when we divide by common fractions. In each case, we began with a unit strip and explored the number of given portions (denoted by common fractions) in the unit. Using multiplication and substitution of equal values in the equalities, we have generated a pattern for multiples of this unit strip.

As the activities are completed over a period of several days, we recommend that the teacher organize all the results in a table, similar to table 1. Then, direct students' attention to the expressions underlined in each row. Using the concrete model, the symbolic expressions for the concrete manipulations, ratios, and the principle of substitution, students should be encouraged to formulate the invert-and-multiply rule.

The activities give students further insight into the division algorithm without relying on rote drill and memorization. The mathematical investigations presented develop a pattern that leads to a conceptual understanding of the division algorithm. We can now "reason why" when we invert and multiply!

References

Ellison, Alfred. "The Concept of the Shifting Unit." *Arithmetic Teacher* 19 (March 1972): 171–76.

Leinwand, Steven J. "5 Ways to Improve Your Math Teaching." *Learning* 85 14 (November/ December 1985): 85–88.

Bibliography

Arithmetic Teacher 31 (February 1984). Focus Issue: Rational Numbers.

Scott, Wayne R. "Fractions Taught by Folding Paper Strips." *Arithmetic Teacher* 28 (January 1981): 18–21.

Silvia, Evelyn M. "A Look at Division with Fractions." *Arithmetic Teacher* 30 (January 1983): 38–41.

Thompson, Charles. "Teaching Division of Fractions with Understanding." *Arithmetic Teacher* 27 (January 1979): 24–27.

Van de Walle, John, and Charles S. Thompson. "Let's Do It: Fractions with Fraction Strips." *Arithmetic Teacher* 32 (December 1984): 4–9.

Wiebe, James H. "Discovering Fractions on a 'Fraction Table.'" *Arithmetic Teacher* 33 (December 1985): 49–51. ▲

Two-Sided Pies: Help for Improper Fractions and Mixed Numbers

by

Jocelyn Marie Rees

Although emphasis on the development of fraction concepts is increasing, it occurs in the early grades when the discussion is limited to proper fractions. When improper fractions and mixed numbers are introduced, far less attention is given to the development of a sound conceptual base. It is not unusual to find a pupil who can draw a representation of five-sixths but not of seven-fourths. Even more infrequent is a youngster who can illustrate the equivalence of two and two-thirds to eight-thirds. Failure to acquire a clear understanding of fractions greater than one and their mixed-number equivalents severely limits pupils' meaningful use of these numbers and results in a weak background for the development of mixed numbers. This article suggests a model for improper fractions and mixed numbers and describes some activities for working with them at the precomputational level.

The model is based on one developed for proper fractions by Leutzinger and Nelson (1980). One of the model's strengths is the interlocking-circles design that allows the whole or unit to remain visible at all times while it still makes clear how many parts are being considered (fig. 1).

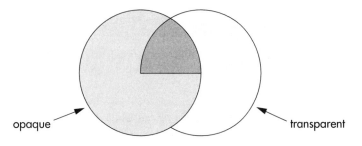

Fig. 1. Construction of the model

CONSTRUCTION

The model consists of one or more opaque circles and one transparent circle. A set of circles is made for each student. To construct the models you will need construction paper in as many colors as you choose to use and, for each color, a transparent sheet in a color that allows the fraction divisions to show through. About a dozen transparent circles can be made from one report cover. The color of the transparent sheet should change the color

of the opaque paper enough to make a visual difference between a covered and an uncovered section. If the markings to show fractional parts are done in black, transparent red over opaque tan and transparent yellow over opaque blue are good combinations. Many others are possible.

Each set of models should contain at least three opaque circles and one transparent circle for each denominator to be used (fig. 2). The opaque circles are marked (in black) on one side only to show fractional parts. The marked side will be referred to as the front. The transparent circles are not marked. One of the opaque circles for each denominator and its corresponding transparent circle should have one radius slashed so that these two pieces can be interlocked and rotated to represent each of the possible numerators.

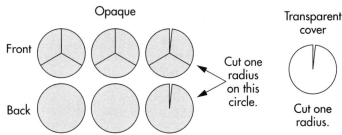

Fig. 2. A set of circles for representing fractions and mixed numbers

Since work with improper fractions and mixed numbers requires the use of several opaque circles marked for each denominator, use color coding of the denominators to make it easier to keep all the circles for one kind of fraction together. Care should be taken that pupils do not depend on color cues for identifying the fractional part. One way is to change the coding in each set. Set 1, for example, might have halves in yellow and thirds in red, but in set 2, the halves could be green and the thirds yellow. If pupils use different sets on successive days, they will not come to think of "halves" as synonymous with "red" or any other color. With this arrangement it is wise to keep all the pieces for each set in a separate envelope so that the pieces from the various sets do not become intermixed.

Figure 2 shows a set of circles for representing proper and improper thirds from one through nine. To represent ten or more thirds, additional opaque circles are needed.

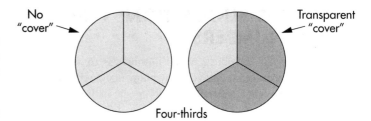

Fig. 4. A model of four-thirds

REPRESENTING PROPER FRACTIONS

To represent one-fourth, the pupil selects the opaque circle marked in fourths and interlocks it with a transparent "cover." He or she then rotates both, in opposite directions, until one-fourth of the opaque circle is uncovered.

Figure 3 shows how the model would appear when correctly used to represent one-fourth. Of course, the opposite convention can be adopted and pupils instructed to show the desired fractional part by covering it. However, pupils who used this model seemed automatically to select the uncovered portion to represent the part being considered. Perhaps they thought that they should hide the part that was not needed. It seemed wise to follow their lead.

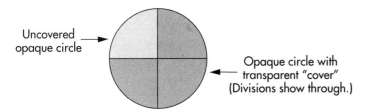

Fig. 3. A model of one-fourth

TEACHING SUGGESTIONS FOR IMPROPER FRACTIONS

When pupils are adept at using models such as these to show proper fractions, improper fractions can be introduced. Ask pupils to show one-third. They should respond by interlocking a transparent circle with an opaque one marked in thirds, and rotating the transparent circle so that one-third of the opaque one is uncovered. Review the interpretation of the model: a unit has been divided into three equal parts and we are considering one of those parts. Ask a pupil to write a numeral for this part on the chalkboard, and discuss the meaning of each of the terms: the denominator tells the number of equal-sized parts in the unit, and the numerator tells how many of those parts we are considering.

Follow the same sequence for two-thirds and three-thirds. Pupils will discover that they no longer need the transparent "cover," since all three of the equal-sized parts are being considered. Interpret, write, and discuss as before, but include in the discussion the fact that in showing three-thirds, one really shows the entire unit; that is, three-thirds is another name for one (whole).

When you ask pupils to show four-thirds, they will find it necessary to use a second unit with the transparent cover interlocked and rotated. (See fig. 4.) The discussion should emphasize the fact that four-thirds means more than one (whole). Continue in this way with each of the fractions through nine-thirds.

Repeat the sequence using the fractions one-fourth through twelve-fourths, then allow pupils to practice in pairs. One pupil can model an improper fraction having a denominator you have specified while the other writes the numeral for it. Then reverse the task by having the first pupil write a fractional numeral and the second pupil show a model for it. Since these activities focus attention on the numerator and on the use of the appropriate number of "units," later you can offer practice in which the denominator can also vary so that pupils must select the correctly marked circle for a given fraction.

Following these activities, pupils should compare improper fractions and develop generalizations about their results. Three categories require attention.

1. Pairs of fractions having the same denominator but different numerators (8/5 and 6/5)
2. Pairs having the same numerator but different denominators (8/5 and 8/6)
3. Pairs in which both the numerator and the denominator are different (8/5 and 7/4)

As before, pupils should represent the fractions with models and interpret the model orally before they encounter the written (abstract) notation. Even then, it is good practice to have the comparison written in the prose form before introducing the mathematical form. For example, the teacher might ask pupils to show eight-fifths and six-fifths and then to interpret their models by explaining, "Eight-fifths is more than six-fifths, but both are larger than one whole." The next step would be to have the comparison written in the form "Eight-fifths is greater than six-fifths." Finally pupils should learn to write the sentence "8/5 > 6/5."

As pupils indicate that they are assimilating these experiences, you can guide them to form generalizations about comparisons from the first two categories and perhaps from some examples in the third. With adequate experience, most pupils will come to realize that if the denominators of two fractions are the same (category 1), then the fraction having the larger numerator is the greater (8/3 > 7/3) and that if the numerators of two fractions are the same (category 2), then the one having the smaller denominator is the greater (7/3 > 7/4). More insight is required to compare fractions from the third category, in which both the numerators and the denominators are different, but in this way some pupils may discover that 9/5 is greater than 7/4. Both of these fractions are only one "piece" short of two (wholes), but the fifths "piece" is smaller, and therefore a smaller amount is "missing."

Pupils who have had adequate experiences in comparing proper fractions will easily move from a reliance on the concrete and semiconcrete models to accurate comparisons at the abstract level for the first two categories. Abstract work with most of the fractions in the third category requires the use of some computational procedure and should be delayed until readiness for these procedures is developed.

TEACHING SUGGESTIONS FOR MIXED NUMBERS

A possible way to introduce mixed numbers is to ask pupils to show eight-thirds and to tell you how many uncovered circles are in the model (two). Their work should appear as in figure 5, row 1 (3/3 + 3/3 + 2/3 = 8/3). Have them recall that three-thirds is another name for one (whole), and instruct them to turn one of the uncovered circles facedown so that the unmarked side is up. (See fig. 5, row 2.) Point out that turning the piece over is a way of showing that we are exchanging three-thirds for one whole. It may be helpful to liken this action to that of exchanging ten ones for one ten. After the exchange is made, ask whether or not it was a fair one, or ask whether the collection of circles still shows the same amount as at the start. Follow the same procedure with the second uncovered circle (see fig. 5, row 3), and question pupils about the meaning of the action. Next ask whether the last circle should be turned over. Pupils' responses will indicate their understanding (or lack of understanding). When it is agreed that turning over the two-thirds piece would not constitute a fair exchange, ask pupils to describe what the model now shows. They should respond that it represents two whole circles and two-thirds of another circle. If a pupil suggests "two and two-thirds," affirm the response but point out that this name is really a kind of "shorthand" for the longer form "two whole things and two-thirds of another." Thereafter, occasionally ask pupils to explain models and diagrams of mixed numbers in the long form as a check on their understanding.

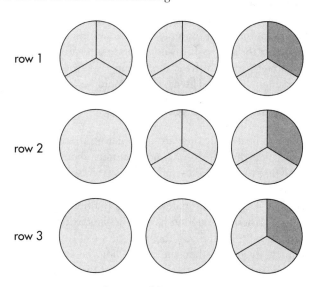

Fig. 5. "Fair" exchanges of fractional parts for one whole

Next give pupils practice in showing models for mixed numbers (given orally), and have them interpret each model. Tell the pupils that they will be making a model of three and five-eighths. Have each pupil select the circles marked in eighths in his or her set. Ask one pupil to tell in the long form what is meant by "three and five-eighths." A correct response will make the building of the model quite easy. Check the pupils' work to verify that their models show three circles with the unmarked sides turned up and one more circle with an interlocked transparent cover rotated to leave five of the eighths uncovered.

Extend the lesson by having pupils learn to write the appropriate numeral for each model and by discussing the meaning of the numeral. Offer some practice in translating the written numeral into a concrete form with the models and in explaining how the model represents the amount shown by the numeral.

COMPARING MIXED NUMBERS

Pupils can now be given experience in comparing mixed numbers. Have them use their "pies" to show two and two-thirds and also two and one-fourth, and ask which shows a greater amount. Help them to say that both models contain two wholes, but that the fractional part of the first (two-thirds) is greater than the fractional part of the second (one-fourth). Also have them write a prose sentence and a mathematical sentence that state the comparison ("Two and two-thirds is greater than two and one-fourth"; 2 2/3 > 2 1/4). Be sure to include comparisons in which the whole-number portions of the mixed numbers are different (1 5/6 < 2 1/3; 2 1/3 < 3 1/2; 3 1/5 > 2 4/5). This approach will make pupils aware that the relative sizes of the two fractions in such a comparison is irrelevant if one of the mixed numbers contains more "wholes" than the other.

EQUIVALENCE OF AN IMPROPER FRACTION AND A MIXED NUMBER

The equivalence of an improper fraction and a mixed number can be demonstrated by simply turning the "pies" faceup (marked side showing) or facedown (blank side showing). Begin by making a model for the mixed number (four and five-sixths in this example) as shown on the first row of figure 6. Ask pupils how many sixths are in one whole, and turn over the circle closest to the five-sixth model to verify their response. The model now appears as in row 2 of figure 6. Ask whether the model shows the same amount as at the start, and obtain agreement that it does. Continue with the other wholes and ask the same two questions. When completed the model will appear as in row 3 of figure 6.

You may wish to have pupils work in pairs, each using his or her own set of models. Name or write a mixed number and ask pupil A in each pair to model it. Pupil B then models its equivalent improper fraction and names the fraction. Pupil A should then make a statement expressing the equivalence of the two models, such as, "Four and five-sixths is the same amount as twenty-nine sixths." Also have pupils verbalize the meaning of each term in the improper fraction and of each part of the mixed number. Have pupils reverse roles and continue the practice. Be sure to include some exercises in which a whole number is expressed as an improper fraction (3 = 12/4).

Practicing these comparisons at the concrete and semiconcrete levels and discussing the meaning of the symbols will give pupils the necessary background for understanding the algorithms. As pupils represent these equivalences, help them to recognize what is counted in each of the two forms; that is, in the improper-fraction form we count the total number of pieces of a given fractional size, whereas in the mixed-number form we count pieces by groups to make as many wholes as possible and then name any remaining pieces as a proper fraction.

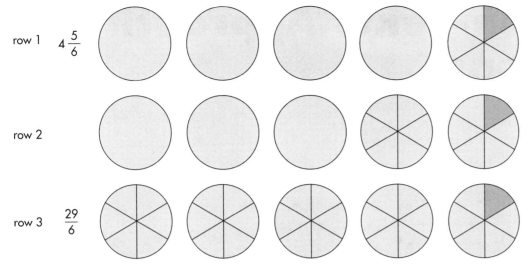

row 1 $4\frac{5}{6}$

row 2

row 3 $\frac{29}{6}$

Fig. 6. Expressing a mixed number as an improper fraction: 4 5/6 = 29/6

The procedure for expressing a mixed number as an improper fraction can be "discovered" from the previous work with models. Help pupils to see that in place of the four wholes are now four groups of six-sixths each. The number of sixths formed from the wholes can be found by adding (6/6 + 6/6 + 6/6 + 6/6) or by multiplying (4 × 6/6). (Note that the traditional instruction to multiply the whole number times the denominator is technically incorrect, since in the multiplication of fractions a whole number functions as a numerator. This may confuse some pupils.) Finally, have pupils add the number of sixths in the fractional part of the mixed number (5).

The use of the models to illustrate expressing an improper fraction as a mixed number is shown in figure 7. The first row represents the number as given (thirteen-fourths in this example). Ask pupils how many fourths they must exchange for a whole, that is, what size groups they must make; and turn over the leftmost circle to show the exchange. The model will now appear as in row 2. Verify that the model still represents the same amount as at the start, and repeat these questions as each of the other "whole" circles are turned over. Have pupils tell how many groups (wholes) have been made and identify the mixed number that the model now represents. Also have pupils make a statement expressing the equivalence, such as, "Thirteen-fourths is the same amount as three and one-fourth." You may then wish to have pupils work in pairs again as they did when learning to express a mixed number as an improper fraction.

An understanding of the procedure for expressing a mixed number as an improper fraction requires that the pupils see it as a multiplication situation (so many groups of a given size), and an understanding of the reverse procedure (expressing an improper fraction as a mixed number) requires that pupils recognize it as a division situation (How many groups of a given size can be formed from the given pieces?). When the model in figure 7 appears as in row 3, help pupils to recognize that they have found the number of groups, each four-fourths in size, that were contained in thirteen-fourths and that division is the appropriate operation. (Note that the division does not really involve a numerator and a denominator but rather both numerators. 13/4:4/4 = 13:4.)

SUMMARY

This article has attempted to show how a simple model can be used to represent improper fractions and mixed numbers, and the relationship between them. Such introductory lessons require the use of oral presentation of exercises and frequent opportunity for pupils to state orally the meaning of the actions performed with the models and of the symbols with which the actions are recorded.

Reference

Leutzinger, Larry P., and Glen Nelson. "Let's Do It: Fractions with Models." *Arithmetic Teacher* 27 (May 1980): 6–11. ▲

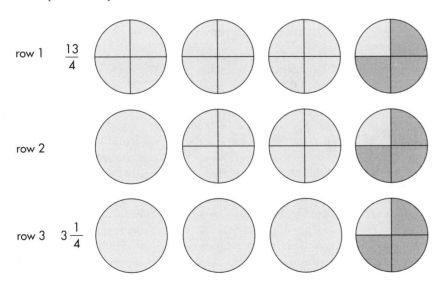

row 1 $\frac{13}{4}$

row 2

row 3 $3\frac{1}{4}$

Fig. 7. Expressing an improper fraction as a mixed number: 13/4 = 3 1/4

A Common-Cents Approach to Fractions

by

Judy Rocke

Students explore percent with 100 plastic worms.

Do students really understand what a school's speed-limit sign means? Does the 20 mph speed limit apply every school day, all day long, or does it apply only during the time the children are present in the school yard? Signs can be so confusing!

Mathematical signs and symbols can be just as confusing to students. For example, how can teachers help students recognize that 3/4, 75/100, 0.75, and 75 percent all represent the same portion of a whole? What do these signs and symbols really mean?

The NCTM's *Curriculum and Evaluation Standards for School Mathematics* (1989) for grades 5–8 emphasizes nurturing number relationships:

> In the middle school years, students come to recognize that numbers have multiple representations, so the development of concepts for fractions, ratios, decimals, and percents and the idea of multiple representations of these numbers need special attention and emphasis. (P. 87)

Consistent with the emphasis of the *Curriculum and Evaluation Standards,* this article shares activities that fourth, fifth, and sixth graders can enjoy as they discover relationships among fractions, decimals, and percents.

"100 THINGS"

One of the concepts usually explored in the intermediate grades is percents, which lends itself readily to a unit involving "100 things." The first step is to ask students to bring in individual collections

Judy Rocke teaches fifth grade at Danvers Elementary School, Danvers, IL 61732.

This article was prepared while the author was participating in staff-development activities sponsored by Project LINCS at Illinois State University, funded by the National Science Foundation through grant no. TPE-9150252. The views are those of the author, not necessarily of the funding agency.

of 100 things. This request has yielded such items as 100 birthday candles, 100 plastic fishing worms, and 100 rocks.

Students continue the unit by working in pairs, with one partner picking up "part" of a collection and the other noting both the percent that has been taken and the percent remaining. Later on students divide the items into groups by color, size, or shape and quiz each other about what percent is contained in each of these groups. They quickly realize that the divided groups must total 100 percent.

For example, Holly and Casey were working with candles. Casey divided his 100 candles into three disjoint groups, based on color. Holly said, "Twenty red candles—that's 20 percent. Thirty green candles, that's 30 percent. So that means there are fifty white candles, that has to be 50 percent. All the percents add up to 100 percent."

A "PENNY CHART"

On the third day of school, a penny chart can be introduced. To make the chart, poster board is divided into 100 squares, each large enough for a penny. On that day students tape three pennies to the chart, one for each day that they have been in school. They agree to add one penny to the chart each school day. When they have gone to school 100 days, 100 pennies, or $1, will be on the chart. On "dollar day," the class celebrates with a party.

Each student makes an individual penny chart using a ten-inch-by-ten-inch piece of graph paper. This chart is taped in the back of their mathematics books, along with a piece of notebook paper. Each day, as one student adds a penny to the class chart, the other students color in one square on their individual chart and decide how to record "progress" toward the dollar-day and class-party goal.

Students are challenged to represent this progress in as many different ways as possible. On the tenth day of the year, for example, Kelli volunteered, "We are 10/100 of the way toward our class party."

By brainstorming other *different ways,* students decided that 10/100 could also be written as 1/10, 10 percent, and 10-out-of-the-100 days needed for the class party. When Cody wondered if it could be written as 10 cents, students were asked to think of this amount in another way—as 10 out of the 100 cents needed for $1.00, or as the decimal 0.10.

FRINGE BENEFITS

The benefits of a daily-number activity have been extolled by Slovin (1992). Challenging students with the daily-number penny-chart activity can lead to several fringe benefits. For example, each year someone always asks how to figure out percent without using 100 items. This question presents an opportunity to introduce proportions.

To begin, the class considers only numbers that are factors of 100: 2, 4, 5, 10, 20, 25, and 50. By referring to the penny chart, students readily see that 1/10—one out of ten rows—equals 10/100, or 10 percent, 10 pennies out of 100 on the chart. Realizing that four quarters compose $1, they also see that 1/4 = 25/100, or 25 percent, or 25 pennies out of the 100 on the chart.

How do you figure out percent without using 100 things?

Students also typically ask how to find percents from numbers that are not factors of 100, such as 1/3. From earlier work, students recognize that one interpretation of the fraction 1/3 is 1 divided by 3, as in one candy bar shared among three people. Using a calculator, they carry out the division and round to the nearest 100th, which they can confidently change to a percent.

Another fringe benefit is that students discover for themselves how to simplify fractions. A search for different ways of recording has led them to understand, for example, that 10/100 = 1/10, that 1/4 equals 25/100, and so on, and soon they begin to generalize. Equivalent fractions become easy to understand as, day by day, students work with the penny chart.

A big breakthrough usually occurs around the eighteenth or twentieth day of school (see fig. 1). From then on, every time a fraction can be simplified, a method is found to justify students' thinking and that fraction is included on the chart. For example, on the twentieth day, Zachary wrote this information on the overhead-projector transparency: "20 out of 100 days, 20%, .20, 20/100."

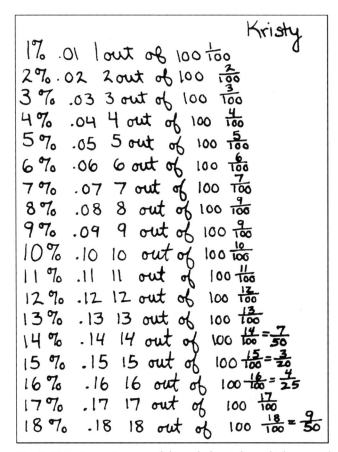

Fig. 1. Kristy's running record through the eighteenth day reveals when she started reducing to lowest terms.

Jenny said, "20/100 can be simplified to 2/10 because 10 is a factor of 20 and 100. Wait! Then you can go even smaller, 2/10 = 1/5." Jason said, "I got 1/5 right away because 20 is a factor of 20 and 100."

When the class was asked which way was correct, they decided that it did not matter, since both were correct. Matthew said, "In fact, you could start with 20/100 and use 4 as a factor and get 5/25. Then use 5 and you get 1/5. That's neat! It doesn't matter how you get to 1/5!"

Finally, students were asked how they knew when they were finished if a fraction could be simplified in so many ways. They discovered that a fraction is in lowest terms if the numerator and the denominator do not have any common factors other than 1.

DOLLAR-DAY CELEBRATION

When the 100th day arrives, special activities are planned to integrate other subjects:

- For reading, the class reads and discusses *The Hundred-Penny Box* by Sharon Bell Mathis (1986).

- During language arts, students begin a report about money. They research such questions as "Have we always had the coins we use today?" "What protection does paper money have to prevent counterfeiting?" Explain that material woven into large bills is visible only with ultraviolet light.

- In science, students work in groups to estimate and discover how many drops of water will fit on one side of a penny before the water rolls off the edge. They compare this number with that when using dimes and quarters. They also compare their results with those of others in the class.

- During mathematics, students work in groups of two or three. They estimate and determine how many dollars would be needed to frame the door of the classroom. They are given thirty minutes to discover which is the most and least "expensive" door in the school. After the half hour, they meet in the classroom and discuss their findings. Then they have another thirty minutes to estimate and measure the distance from one door to another, using a dollar bill as the unit of measure, and determine how expensive is the "trip." They conclude with a final activity by using the pennies from the penny chart and making a frequency chart and graph showing the years the pennies were made.

A student marks the fifty-fifth school day on a penny chart.

Students enjoy the challenge of finding different solutions.

During the day, students may choose to work on other activities, such as the following:

- If *a* is worth 1 cent, *b* is worth 2 cents, *c* is worth three cents, and so on, work with a partner to find words worth one dollar.

The word *telephone* is one example. Which classmate has the most expensive name?

- Estimate and then see how tall a tower can be built with pennies.

- Redesign the dollar bill.

NOT SO CONFUSING AFTER ALL

The 20 MPH speed-limit sign is not confusing if its meaning is clarified. Signs and symbols for percents, fractions, ratios, and decimals do not have to be confusing. In class, day by day, different ways of representing and recording decimals, fractions, and percents can become meaningful as they are discussed in relation to the penny chart and progress toward the goal of a class party. Important relationships are discovered and discussed, basic skills are learned, and students enjoy the challenge of searching for, and validating, different solutions. Dollar day is a much anticipated payoff.

References

Mathis, Sharon Bell. *The Hundred-Penny Box.* New York: Penguin Books, 1986.

National Council of Teachers of Mathematics. *Curriculum and Evaluation Standards for School Mathematics.* Reston, Va.: The Council, 1989.

Slovin, Hannah. "Number of the Day." *Arithmetic Teacher* 39 (March 1992): 20–31. ▲

Chapter 2

Geometry

Flexible Straws

by

Gerard Prentice

Using drinking straws to construct geometric figures has been a common activity for years. To join the straws many different materials have been used—plasticine, marshmallows, paper clips, pipe cleaners, and so on. Here is a new twist, or should I say "flex," to this topic.

Flexible straws have their own built-in fasteners! These plastic straws consist of two sections (about 5 cm and 14 cm in length) with a flexible section between them that allows the straws to be bent. To join straws simply cut along the length of the smaller section. After cutting, this section can be compressed to a smaller diameter, which can then be placed inside the longer section of a second straw (fig. 1).

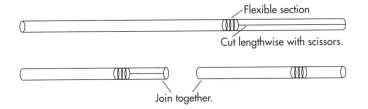

Fig. 1. Cut short end of straws prior to assembly.

By placing three straws together we can form an equilateral triangle. Four straws will produce a rhombus that can easily be adjusted to form a square. Adding more straws will produce other

regular two-dimensional shapes (fig. 2). These flexible creations can be used as a basis for the study of shapes and their properties; they can also be used as sorting hoops for a variety of activities.

Instead of using the full lengths of the straws, the longer ends can be cut to different lengths to study other figures as well, such as the parallelogram, rectangle, and trapezoid. With the exception of the triangle, which is a rigid figure, the shapes can be bent by pressing on one edge or vertex. This alteration of shapes can lead to the study of properties of figures and families of shapes. A rhombus and a square have the same dimensions; which has the largest area? What special figure can be formed by altering the shape, but not the dimensions, of a parallelogram?

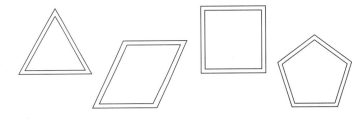

Fig. 2. Join straws to form polygons. No fasteners are needed.

To investigate the properties that relate to diagonals of figures, elastic thread found in most sewing departments can be used. After constructing a rectangle, use a needle and elastic thread to form the diagonals. Run the needle and thread through two opposite vertices and tie a knot at each end. Repeat for the other pair

Gerard Prentice is the mathematics consultant for the Lambton County Roman Catholic School Board, Sarnia, ON N7T 2N8. He has taught mathematics at the elementary and secondary school levels. His special interests are applications of geometry and the use of computers in education.

Geometry **99**

of opposite vertices. As the rectangle is then bent to form a parallelogram, the size of the diagonals will change, but they will still bisect each other (fig. 3).

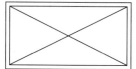 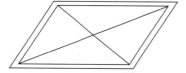

Fig. 3. Elastic thread for diagonals shows properties of figures.

Flexible straws can also be used to construct three-dimensional figures and then geometry mobiles for the classroom. Start by making the shapes of each of the faces of the figure as previously described. The edges of these faces can then be joined together using tape or twist-ties from trash bags. Each edge will consist of two straws. A good source of the twist-ties is telephone cable. It contains many strands of thin, plastic-coated wire that can easily be cut with scissors. If all straws used are the same length, a variety of regular polyhedrons can be constructed. By using different lengths one can form any type of figure—rectangular and triangular prisms and even complex shapes made up of a number of different figures (fig. 4).

After students have constructed a three-dimensional figure, they can be asked to make a net of the figure. Place the figure on a flat surface and then remove as few twist-ties as necessary to put each face on the same plane. The nets will vary depending on which twist-ties are removed. In a similar fashion the net of a figure can be constructed on a flat surface and then outer edges of the net joined using ties to construct the three-dimensional figure.

Some of the advantages of using flexible straws instead of regular straws and a variety of fasteners are these:

1. It is easy to assemble and disassemble two-dimensional shapes.
2. Two-dimensional shapes can be altered easily to show families of shapes (e.g., a rectangle is a special parallelogram).

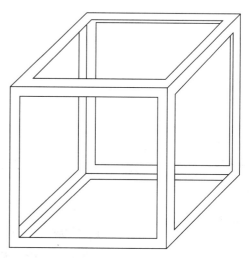

Fig. 4. Assemble three-dimensional figures using ties of thin, plastic-coated wire.

3. The figures are more durable. They do not easily break apart when dropped.
4. Fasteners are needed only for the construction of three-dimensional figures.
5. Fasteners are easy to install and remove.
6. Three-dimensional figures can be dismantled to show their nets.
7. Students can make the net of a three-dimensional figure and then join edges to form the figure.
8. Faces of three-dimensional figures can easily be seen, and individual faces can be removed for study without destroying the original figure. Simply remove the ties from each edge of the face to be removed.

Although flexible straws are more expensive than straight straws, the added cost is more than offset by the fact that fasteners do not need to be purchased. They can also be used over and over for a variety of new applications not possible with the other approaches. ▲

Build a City

by

Jean A. Reynolds

Could I find a new angle for the old geometry lesson? This thought crossed my mind as I prepared to teach a geometry unit to my class of fifth and sixth graders. The more I pored through old copies of teaching magazines and books, the more I became convinced that to give my students some tangible evidence that geometry is alive today in various careers, I would have to create the experience I sought for them. As a result, I designed a week-long build-a-city project to let my students become familiar with the history of the five Platonic solids and then use these solids to create a city.

The following materials are needed for this unit:

- Large white posterboard
- Polyhedral patterns and instructions
- Construction paper of various colors
- Tape or glue
- Rulers
- Crayons or paint
- Pencils
- Scissors

On Monday I introduced the build-a-city project. I gave a brief history of the only five regular polyhedra—the Platonic solids. As I related this history to the students, I showed models of the five solids (fig. 1) and defined a regular polyhedron—a solid comprising many faces that are the same regular polygon. Students were also shown how each solid was constructed.

Evidence of four of these solids—tetrahedron, octahedron, hexahedron (cube), and icosahedron—is found in ancient Egyptian architecture and artifacts. The Pythagoreans discovered the fifth regular polyhedron, the dodecahedron, before 400 B.C., when Plato independently discovered and studied all five solids. The

name "Platonic solids" is derived from this great philosopher and mathematician. Euclid's *Elements,* written around 300 B.C., gives an extensive treatment of the geometry of the Platonic solids. The Greeks believed the Platonic solids to be the essence of the four elemental substances: earth (hexahedron), air (octahedron), fire (tetrahedron), and water (icosahedron). The dodecahedron symbolized the combination of everything—the universe. Pictures of these solids, along with others, and directions for making them appear in the 1985 issues of the *Mathematics Teacher.*

The next step in the project was to discuss the emergence of cities: their components (transportation, education, economy, culture, housing, government, and recreation); the jobs engendered by their growth; and how the Platonic polyhedra began to be used in their architecture. The need to organize growing cities gave birth to the job of city planner. At this point in our discussion I divided the class into five groups, or "cities."

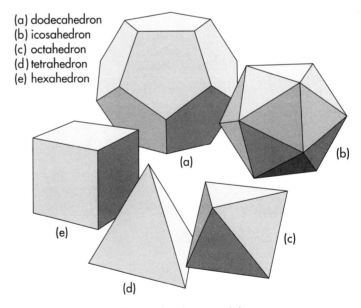

(a) dodecahedron
(b) icosahedron
(c) octahedron
(d) tetrahedron
(e) hexahedron

Fig. 1. The Platonic solids

Formerly a teacher at Churchill Road Elementary School in Fairfax, Virginia, Jean Reynolds is currently pursuing a Ph.D. in education at Stanford University, Stanford, CA 94305.

1. Cut the pieces out of sturdy cardboard.

2. Label each piece as indicated on the transfer sheet.

3. Place one set of six cardboard pattern pieces in each group's bag. The six pattern pieces are large square, triangle, pentagon, small square, triangle, pentagon.

4. On a note card write the following directions:
   To make a—

   (a) Dodecahedron—Cut twelve pentagonal pieces of the same size.
       Join three cut pentagonal pieces at each corner.
       Tape or glue the pieces together.

   (b) Icosahedron—Cut twenty triangular pieces of the same size.
       Join five cut triangular pieces at each corner.
       Tape or glue the pieces together.

   (c) Octahedron—Cut eight triangular pieces of the same size.
       Join four cut triangular pieces at each corner.
       Tape or glue the pieces together.

   (d) Tetrahedron—Cut four triangular pieces of the same size.
       Join three cut triangular pieces at each corner.
       Tape or glue the pieces together.

   (e) Hexahedron—Cut six square pieces of the same size.
       Join three cut square pieces at each corner.
       Tape or glue the pieces together.

5. Place one note card in each group's bag.

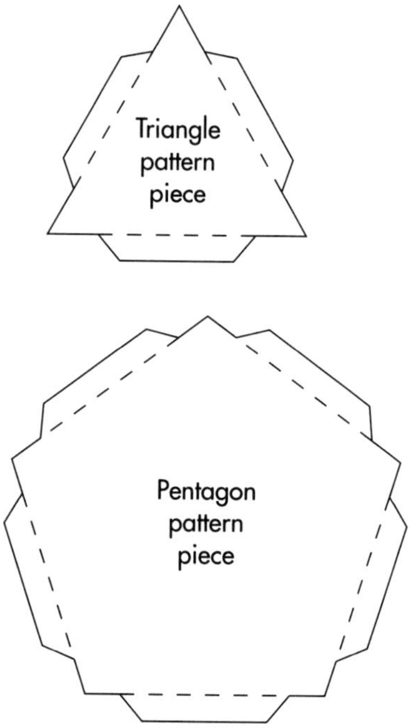

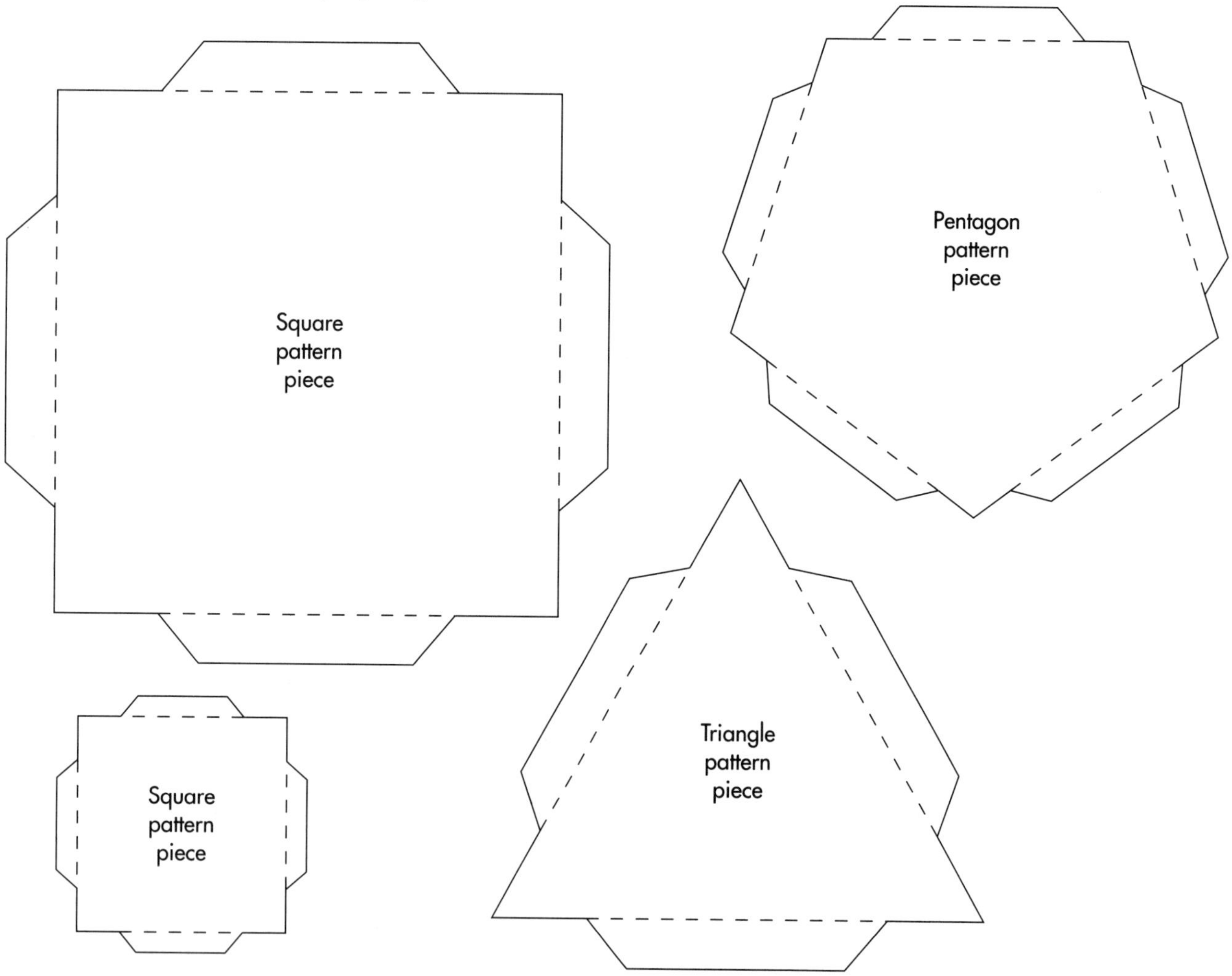

Triangle pattern piece

Pentagon pattern piece

Square pattern piece

Pentagon pattern piece

Square pattern piece

Triangle pattern piece

Fig. 2. How to use the pattern pieces

Each city elected a mayor to keep order during the meeting of the city council. In the council meeting the students discussed the particulars of their city—where it was located (land, sea, air); how they would include each component of a city (seven components were listed on the overhead projector); who would be city planners (at least two students); and who would be architect-builders (the remaining students). I set only three rules:

1. The buildings had to be constructed using only Platonic solids (more than two solids could be combined to form one building).

2. Each building had to be named in accordance with its polyhedral name (e.g., tetrahedron taxi station or cubic court).

3. Each city had to include the seven components of cities.

The cities slowly organized themselves. Soon, ideas began to flow to give substance to unique plans.

The following day, Tuesday, the cities' officials met. Using the overhead projector, I went over the day's tasks:

1. City planners were to section off their cities' sheets (large white posterboard) into districts, decide where each building was to be placed, and devise the transportation systems.

2. Architect-builders were to begin designing and constructing buildings according to assignments made during the previous day's council meeting and from advice offered by the city planners.

Each city received a paper bag containing six pattern pieces: one large and one small square, one large and one small regular pentagon, and one large and one small equilateral triangle. The directions for constructing each polyhedron were written on the large pattern pieces. Instead of giving the students polyhedral patterns that just needed to be cut and folded, I wanted them to see that regular polyhedra are constructed by joining regular polygons at each vertex. Thus, the patterns are regular polygons. See figure 2.

Architect-builders kept in mind the following questions while designing and building:

What is the purpose of my building?

What combinations of shapes will be most pleasing to see?

How large should my building be?

What can I name my building so that its shape is in its name?

Some students attempted to design their buildings according to the element symbolized by the polyhedron. For example, a large dodecahedron became a museum reflecting the accumulation of knowledge from all parts of the universe in one building.

The excitement of planning, designing, and building grew as the project spilled from the mathematics period into recess and free work time during the ensuing two days. Some students, usually quick to deplore mathematics, commented, "This is the most fun math we've had all year." The most reticent students began interacting in their cities, and natural leaders emerged to pacify unruly group members and aid the organization of the city. Students began helping each other cut pattern pieces while the glue on their own buildings was drying. Cooperation was necessary to achieve the desired results.

On the final working day, Friday, the excitement peaked as the last touches were placed on the buildings glued down on city sheets: color for the grounds and roads, name cards for each building, streetlights, windows and doors, and, finally, the city's name. Each mayor introduced the city by name and gave important facts pertaining to its history or purpose. Architect-builders then told the names and purposes of their buildings. City planners also commented on the overall planning of their city. See figure 3.

Fig. 3. A finished city

After all cities were introduced, the students went from city to city surveying their peers' handiwork and imagination. We voted by secret ballot for the first- and second-place cities. They would be displayed in a showcase for all the school to see. Then we discussed the hardships encountered in group work; specific difficulties in planning, designing, and building; and the overall lessons learned through this project.

I feel that by doing this project the students developed a keener eye for geometry in their worlds as well as a sense of belonging in a small group working toward a common goal. Perhaps far more important than the scholastic (history and mathematics) lessons were the group-interaction skills learned—listening, cooperating, and sharing—for these are paramount to becoming citizens in the global community. My goals for this unit were met.

"Let no one destitute of geometry enter my doors." I propose a slight modification of Plato's inscription as a motto for all elementary school teachers: "Let no one destitute of geometry leave my doors."

Bibliography

Hosken, Fran P. *The Language of Cities.* New York: Macmillan Co., 1968.

Ibe, Milagros D. "Mathematics and Art from One Shape." *Arithmetic Teacher* 18 (March 1971): 183–84.

Jacobs, Harold R. *Mathematics—a Human Endeavor.* San Francisco: W. H. Freeman & Co., 1970.

National Council of Teachers of Mathematics. *Historical Topics for the Mathematics Classroom.* Thirty-first Yearbook. Washington, D.C.: The Council, 1969.

Wenninger, Magnus J. *Polyhedron Models for the Classroom.* Reston, Va.: National Council of Teachers of Mathematics, 1979. ▲

Developing Spatial Skills with Three-Dimensional Puzzles

by

John Izard

Spatial skills are an important component of the mathematics curriculum. Both teachers and students have to make use of their spatial skills when using two-dimensional diagrams to represent three-dimensional objects and when interpreting photographs or television images (see, e.g., Pohl [1986]; Greenfield [1987]; Smith [1987]; Bright and Harvey [1988]; Carroll [1988]).

Although a high proportion of students appear to have an intuitive notion of volume, substantial numbers of students have difficulty in visualizing three-dimensional objects. Many are unable to identify how an object would look if viewed from another perspective (Kouba et al. 1988; Brown et al. 1988; Ben-Haim, Lappan, and Houang 1985).

Activities with solids can increase the proportion of students who are able to visualize (Izard 1987; Ben-Chaim, Lappan, and Houang 1988). This article gives plans for the construction of seven three-dimensional puzzle pieces from wooden cubes and gives details for their assembly into a series of solids as puzzle tasks. These puzzle tasks can be used in the classroom to develop spatial skills. The student is required to choose two or more puzzle pieces from the seven basic units and to assemble these pieces to match the solid.

The early puzzle tasks presented in this article are easy to accomplish, and the later ones gradually become more difflcult. From my experience in presenting these tasks to students in fourth through ninth grade, I have discovered that students require a wide variation in the time needed to achieve success, even with the initial two or three tasks. Some sixth-grade students can complete a task in less than a minute, whereas others in the same class cannot complete the same task in fifteen minutes. Although the relative difficulty has been established by using the puzzles in classrooms at the fourth-grade level and above, one needs to be aware that the order of difficulty probably varies according to the prior experience of the students. If students work in pairs to attempt each task, they will have many opportunities to discuss their successful and unsuccessful efforts and to suggest alternative strategies for the solution of each puzzle.

John Izard heads the Development and Training Division of the Australian Council for Educational Research, P.O. Box 210, Hawthorn, Victoria 3122, Australia.

The provision of hands-on experience for each student, rather than a demonstration by the teacher, is an essential part of the process. Each student should handle the puzzle pieces and have the opportunity to investigate the ways in which they can be rotated. Combining the pieces in different ways allows students to gain experience in the three-dimensional context before being required to tackle tasks that require a knowledge of one or more conventions for two-dimensional representation of three dimensions. It follows that the tasks should be presented, at least in the early stages, with actual solids rather than in diagrammatic form. After students are familiar with the pieces and can select and assemble the pieces to match the various solids, the same tasks can be presented in diagrammatic form so that experience can be gained in relating two-dimensional representations to the actual solids.

MAKING THE PUZZLE PIECES

The seven puzzle pieces used in the tasks are made from twenty-seven identical wooden cubes. (Wooden cubes with each side 2 centimeters [3/4 inch] can be handled easily and can be glued together without difficulty. The glue used to assemble the pieces needs to be able to stand up to frequent use.) Figure 1 shows a two-dimensional representation of each puzzle piece to be assembled, together with a pattern showing how to build that piece. Each pattern shows the number of cubes in each column.

For example, one puzzle piece looks like this when assembled:

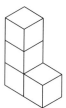

The pattern shown with this diagram,

3
1

,

indicates a tower of three cubes joined to one cube at "ground" level.

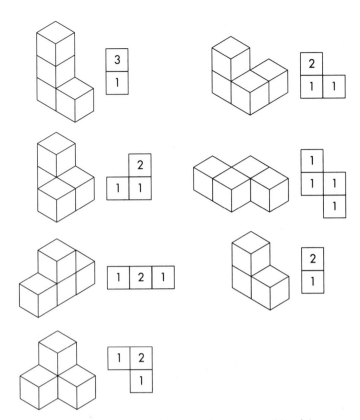

Fig. 1. Representations and patterns for the assembly of the seven puzzle pieces

MAKING THE PUZZLE TASKS

The puzzle tasks are presented in the form of solids assembled from cubes of the same size as those used in constructing the puzzle pieces. The first two puzzle tasks involve solids made from two of the seven puzzle pieces. Figure 2 shows a two-dimensional representation of each assembled solid for these first two puzzle tasks and the pattern for assembly of each puzzle task from the cubes, using the same format that was used to show how the puzzle pieces are to be assembled. Each pattern shows the number of cubes in each column.

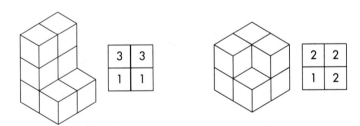

Fig. 2. Solids made from two of the seven puzzle pieces

Figure 3 shows four solids that are made from three of the seven puzzle pieces, but not necessarily the same three in each solid. Each of the solids shown in figure 4 requires four of the seven puzzle pieces. The solids shown in figure 5 require five, six, or all seven of the puzzle pieces. The solid using all seven pieces is a puzzle from Denmark known as the Soma cube. One set of possible solutions can be found in the Appendix.

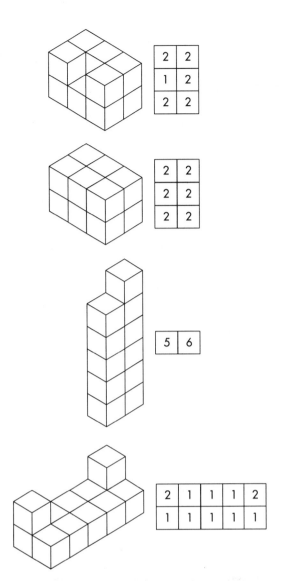

Fig. 3. Solids made from three of the seven puzzle pieces

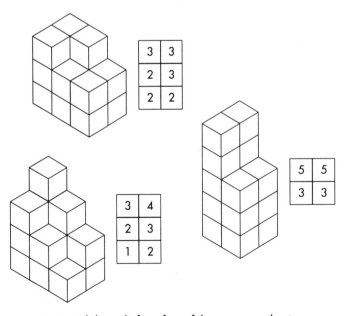

Fig. 4. Solids made from four of the seven puzzle pieces

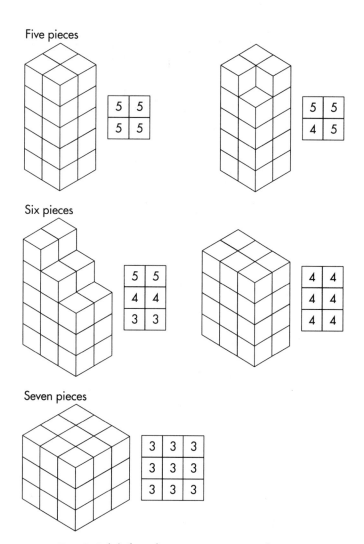

Fig. 5. Solids from five, six, or seven puzzle pieces

USING THE PUZZLES IN THE CLASSROOM

The puzzle tasks illustrated in figures 2–5 are in increasing order of difficulty. Of course, the students do not get to assemble the puzzle solids from unit cubes; they have to use a set of the seven puzzle pieces. Each student, or group of two students, to attempt a puzzle task will need the seven pieces, even though some pieces will not be used in their solution of the problem. Some puzzles may be solved in more than one way, and the strategies used will vary considerably. Some students reject particular pieces from consideration on valid grounds, whereas others reject pieces in inappropriate ways. Some students make a conscious attempt to imagine what a piece would look like if it were part of the solid being built, and this effort often gives clues to which other pieces will or will not fit.

Some "less able" mathematics students complete these tasks rapidly and accurately and derive a great deal of satisfaction from their success. Some "more able" mathematics students—and teachers—find the puzzle tasks a challenge that demands problem-solving strategies of a kind different from those they use elsewhere and, therefore, take longer to solve the puzzles. Students may be told the number of pieces required for a particular solid, but they should not be told which pieces are required.

Students who are proficient in completing the puzzles when given actual solids can be given the task of matching various two-dimensional representations with the appropriate actual puzzle pieces. If this assignment can be achieved without many errors, students can be given their puzzle task as a two-dimensional diagram rather than as a solid.

Puzzle tasks like those described in this article offer a challenge to students and teachers alike. The tasks lend an opportunity to develop geometric skills in an informal way, and they present both male and female students with problems that go beyond the traditional pencil-and-paper mathematics.

Appendix

If the seven representations in figure 1 are called a–g, respectively, some possible solutions for figures 2–5 are the following:

Figure 2: a, b; d, g

Figure 3: c, e, g; c, f, g; b, c, e

Figure 4: a, b, e, g; a, d, f, g; a, c, d, f

Figure 5: a, c, d, e, f; a, c, d, f, g; a, b, c, d, e, f; a, b, c, d, e, f, a, b, c, d, e, f, g

References

Ben-Chaim, David, Glenda Lappan, and Richard T. Houang. "The Effect of Instruction on Spatial Visualization Skills of Middle School Boys and Girls." *American Educational Research Journal* 25 (Spring 1988): 51–71.

Ben-Haim, David, Glenda Lappan, and Richard T. Houang. "Visualizing Rectangular Solids Made of Small Cubes: Analyzing and Effecting Students' Performance." *Educational Studies in Mathematics* 16 (1985): 389–409.

Bright, George W., and John G. Harvey. "Learning and Fun with Geometry Games." *Arithmetic Teacher* 35 (April 1988): 22–26.

Brown, Catherine A., Thomas P. Carpenter, Vicky L. Kouba, Mary M. Lindquist, Edward A. Silver, and Jane O. Swafford. "Secondary School Results for the Fourth NAEP Mathematics Assessment: Algebra, Geometry, Mathematical Methods, and Attitudes." *Mathematics Teacher* 81 (May 1988): 337–47, 397.

Carroll, William. "Cross Sections of Clay Solids." *Arithmetic Teacher* 35 (March 1988): 6–11.

Greenfield, Patricia M. "Electric Technologies, Education, and Cognitive Development." In *Applications of Cognitive Psychology*, edited by Dale E. Berger, Kathy Pezdek, and William P. Banks, 17–32. Hillsdale, N.J.: Lawrence Erlbaum Associates, 1987.

Izard, John F. "Acquisition of Spatial Skills under Various Conditions of Instruction." Paper delivered at the First Joint AARENZARE Conference, Christchurch, New Zealand, December 1987.

Kouba, Vicky L., Catherine A. Brown, Thomas P. Carpenter, Mary M. Lindquist, Edward A. Silver, and Jane O. Swafford. "Results of the Fourth NAEP Assessment of Mathematics: Measurement, Geometry, Data Interpretation, Attitudes, and Other Topics." *Arithmetic Teacher* 35 (May 1988): 10–16.

Pohl, Victoria. "Producing Curved Surfaces in the Octahedron: Enrichment for Junior High School Students." *Arithmetic Teacher* 34 (November 1986): 30–35.

Smith, Lyle R. "Discoveries with Rectangles and Rectangular Solids." *Mathematics Teacher* 80 (April 1987): 274–76. ▲

The Art of Tessellation

by

Paul Giganti, Jr.

Mary Jo Cittadino

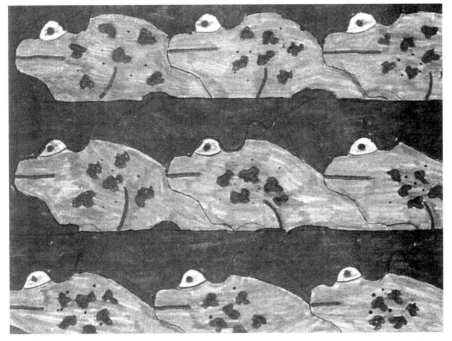

Students need to be encouraged to develop and explore their own artistic creativity and to exercise their spatial sense within mathematics. A project in student-designed tessellations can let students discover one aspect of mathematics that has fascinated creative persons throughout history. Leonardo da Vinci, M. C. Escher, and numerous others have used such mathematics in unique ways. Tessellation is a perfect example of how mathematics complements other disciplines.

Students in grade 3 through adult, with many different levels of ability in mathematics, can create tessellations. Tessellations do not depend heavily on numerical skills; all students have equal access and equal chances for success in creating beautiful artwork through tessellations. Many students become "experts" and "advisors" for the first time in the context of a mathematics class. This article relates our experience in presenting tessellations in both classrooms and teacher in-service workshops.

Students need to experience the excitement and beauty of mathematics beyond numerical calculations. Introduce your students to tessellations, a project that combines mathematics and art. A tessellation is a tiling, made up of the repeated use of polygons and other curved figures to completely fill a plane without gaps or overlapping, just like the tiles on a kitchen or bathroom floor. See figure 1.

PRELIMINARY ACTIVITIES

Several preliminary activities will help your students understand the concept and process of covering a flat surface, or tessellating, before the final tessellation project begins.

- Use geometric figures (square, rhombus, triangle, hexagon, rectangle) to clarify the concept of tessellations. Give each student several congruent pieces, such as Pattern Block pieces. A few are included on the master-pattern sheet. Encourage them to see how they can arrange their figures to cover a surface completely. Let them make and share arrangements that do not cover a surface. Next, give each student just one polygon; have

Fig. 1. A tessellation

Paul Giganti is a mathematics educator and teacher trainer at the Lawrence Hall of Science at the University of California at Berkeley. He is active in the California Mathematics Project, the EQUALS and Family Mathematics projects, and the California Mathematics Council. He is currently the editor of the Communicator, *the journal of the California Mathematics Council. Mary Jo Cittadino, FAMILY MATH Network Coordinator at Lawrence Hall of Science, University of California at Berkeley, is interested in ensuring that the beauty and excitement of mathematics is experienced by all students.*

them place this polygon in the middle of a blank piece of paper and trace around it. Lining the polygon up with any side of the traced image, have them trace their polygon again. Students should repeat this process until they see that they can cover the entire paper in this manner. The instructor or students can also demonstrate their arrangement using Pattern Blocks on an overhead projector.

- Talk about examples of differently shaped tiles that students have seen covering bathroom and kitchen floors, bricks they have seen covering patios, and tilelike patterns they have seen on wrapping paper, fabric, wallpaper, and so on. (See fig. 2.) Look through magazines to find examples of pictures of tiling or tessellations. Have students make a collage of the pictures.

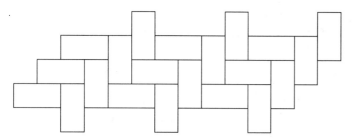

Fig. 2. Tessellations are everywhere—such as in the pattern of bricks on a patio.

- Use tessellations as an opportunity to introduce or review geometric terms, such as *polygon, opposite, slide, rotate, hexagon,* and *congruent*. The mathematical vocabulary will help students understand the process of tessellation. (See the Glossary.)

- Students should experiment using geometric shapes of their own choosing, such as pentagons, other types of quadrilaterals, irregular triangles, and so on, to discover which ones tessellate and which ones don't. Make a "will work/won't work" wall chart on which students can paste up examples of figures that will tessellate and ones that will not. Remind them that uncovered "holes" or overlapping figures are not permissible.

- Find as many of the M. C. Escher art books as you can and share them with your class. Ask them to look for basic geometric figures, as well as pick out some recurring irregular features that Escher used in his tessellations. (See the Bibliography.)

Many of these preliminary activities take only minutes of class time and can be done concurrently with the study of other mathematics subjects, such as geometry and measurement. After completion of these activities, students will have a clear understanding of tessellations and be ready and eager to tessellate.

THE "NIBBLE" TECHNIQUE

Many geometric shapes tessellate. Polygons that tessellate can be altered to create irregularly shaped pictures that also tessellate. Using a simple "nibble" technique, students can easily create irregularly shaped tiles that will become tessellating pictures.

The "nibble" technique permits learners to change the shapes of figures. One overall rule to follow when altering a geometric

shape to create a tessellation is that the shape must retain the same area as the original shape.

Translations or slides

This transformation is restricted to polygons—parallelograms and hexagons—whose opposite sides are parallel and congruent because an operation on one side always affects the opposite side.

- Using the master-patterns sheet provided, copy and cut from heavy card stock or old manila folders one of the shapes for each student. All students start with the square, which is the easiest shape to use, and experiment with the other shapes later.

- One side of this piece should first be colored completely with crayon to prevent students from inadvertently flipping the piece while moving or taping their "nibble."

- Demonstrate the "nibble" technique on the overhead projector. The technique that is easiest for beginners is to cut into one corner of a square, stressing that the choice is completely arbitrary and that you are starting and ending your cut at an adjacent corner. A "nibble" that is cut from adjacent corners will be easier to line up when matching sides. (See fig. 3.)

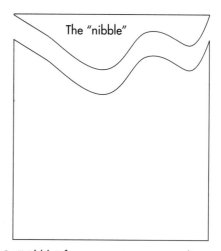

The "nibble"

Fig. 3. "Nibble" from one corner to an adjacent one.

- Warn students that once they begin "nibbling" their square, no scraps can be discarded. Every piece has to be accounted for!

- Next demonstrate how to slide the newly cut "nibble" across to the congruent and parallel side. It must match the straight edges and corners before being attached to the side. Tape the "nibble" carefully and securely in its new home. (See fig. 4.)

- Since a square has four sides, a second "nibble" can be cut from one of the other pair of parallel sides and slid to the opposite side, once again matching the straight edges very carefully and then taping it into place. Remember: no trimming to fit! (See fig. 5.)

When students have finished "nibbling" and taping the sides of their square, they are ready to tessellate with the resulting shape. We recommend that at this point you use scrap paper just large enough to allow tracing the shape several times (8.5″ × 11″ or 9″ × 12″).

Master-Pattern Sheet

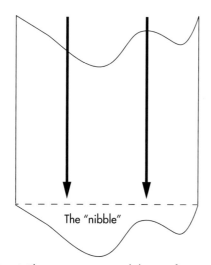

Fig. 4. This movement is a slide transformation.

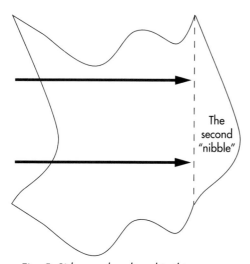

Fig. 5. Sides can be altered in this manner.

- Demonstrate again on the overhead projector how to tessellate by repeated tracing of a sample irregular tile. Stress that students must be very careful in lining up their shape with the sides of the shapes they have already traced. "Sliding" means the shape itself slides along the plane—up, down, left, or right. Care must also be taken not to flip the piece over or rotate it while tracing. Keeping the color side up at all times should help.

- Students can practice the nibble-and-slide technique for the other geometric shapes. The more sides, the more sides they can alter (e.g., the hexagon will allow them to modify three pairs of sides).

When they have created a favorite shape, they are ready for a fresh piece of paper on which to tessellate. Students complete their project by carefully adding detail and color to their tessellated design. It is very important that adequate time and emphasis be given to the artistic part of this mathematical lesson. Though certain rules must be followed to create a tessellation, students are limited only by their imaginations in its artistic design!

Once students find success in tessellating on a small scale, completing a larger, poster-sized tessellation project can give students a great deal of satisfaction.

Rotations or turns

This transformation is restricted to polygons—triangles, parallelograms, and hexagons—with adjacent sides that are congruent. Students should master the slide technique before trying rotations or turns.

- Begin again with the square. Give students another square cut from tagboard or a manila folder and have them color one side to distinguish a front and back. Using the "nibble" technique, students cut out a "nibble" from corner to corner of their square, but this time they rotate the "nibble" at its endpoint to an adjacent side of their square, not an opposite side. Again they tape the piece securely into place after carefully matching the straight edges. (See fig. 6.)

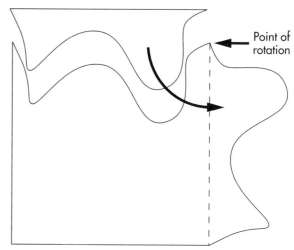

Fig. 6. This transformation is a rotation.

- The students alter another side of the square and rotate this "nibble" from its endpoint to the adjacent side of the square and tape. We strongly recommend that all the sides of the square be altered differently to avoid confusion when tessellating. (See fig. 7.)

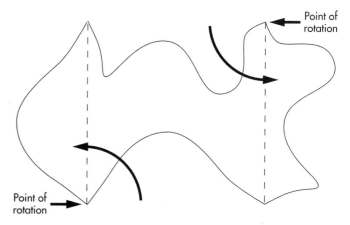

Fig. 7. All sides of the original shape have been altered.

- Students now rotate or turn the shape as they move and trace the tile to cover the plane.

- Students may need to experiment to tessellate shapes altered in this manner. For some shapes, flipping the pieces is necessary to tessellate the plane.

Rotation or turn at midpoints

Students use a ruler to mark the midpoint on each of the four sides of the square, then proceed to make a "nibble" from one corner to the marked midpoint of a side of a square. They rotate this piece about the side's midpoint onto the remaining half of this same side, then tape. They repeat this procedure for all four sides of the square. (See fig. 8.)

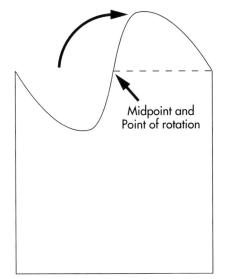

Fig. 8. A rotation around the midpoint of a side

Experimenting with variations

- Students can experiment with beginning their cut from one corner and terminating it at any point before reaching the other corner.

- Another variation is to avoid corners at the beginning and end of one's cut on a side. This approach requires using a ruler to determine exactly where to affix the piece on the opposite or adjacent side. For an altered shape to tessellate the plane, it is imperative that it match exactly the position from where it came.

THE ART IN TESSELLATIONS

To create a beautiful and interesting tessellation, students must understand that tessellation is a true combination of art and mathematics; both are equally important. To facilitate students' successful artistic tessellations, the teacher should stress the artistic part of tessellating as much as the mathematical part. The following suggestions will help your students think like artists.

- Share examples of your own tessellations. Nothing encourages students more than seeing projects their teachers have done themselves. See the tessellation by the author in figure 9.

- Advise your students that thought, care, and time are important ingredients in any good tessellation; careful work or a rushed job show up quite clearly in tessellations.

- Introduce the artistic side of tessellations by using blank irregular tessellations, such as those in figure 10, on the overhead projector. Put a single transparent sample tile on the projector and brainstorm with the whole class about objects or animals into which the tile could be transformed by adding lines, marks,

Fig. 9. Author's tessellation

or color. Try rotating the tile to see different things.

- Using the tessellation worksheets, have students add just the art work to make a finished tessellation. Make sure they share their results with the whole class. (See student worksheets A and B.)

- Explain to students that the irregular tessellation that they create may not look like anything recognizable at first. It is very difficult to create a specific object right from the beginning. Instead they must use their imagination and add the artwork to make their tile look like something. If students have difficulty seeing a design in their tiles, encourage them to get suggestions from classmates; a student will often see a wonderful possibility in someone else's shape.

Fig. 10. Many choices can be made for coloring this shape. One possibility is the tessellation in figure 1.

- As they trace and draw their own tessellation projects, students should make very light lines so that changes will be easy to make. After all the tracing is done—students may need to "fudge" a little here and there—have them go back over all the lines freehand to make them darker and to correct any errors in tracing.

- Color makes all the difference in successful tessellations, as it does in most artwork. Using contrasting colors for adjacent tiles, like on a checkerboard, is one very effective technique.

- Some students may wish to experiment by coloring each tile or a row of tiles with a different design. (See student illustrations in fig. 11.)

- Keep reminding your students that they are indeed creating a work of art!

Name _____

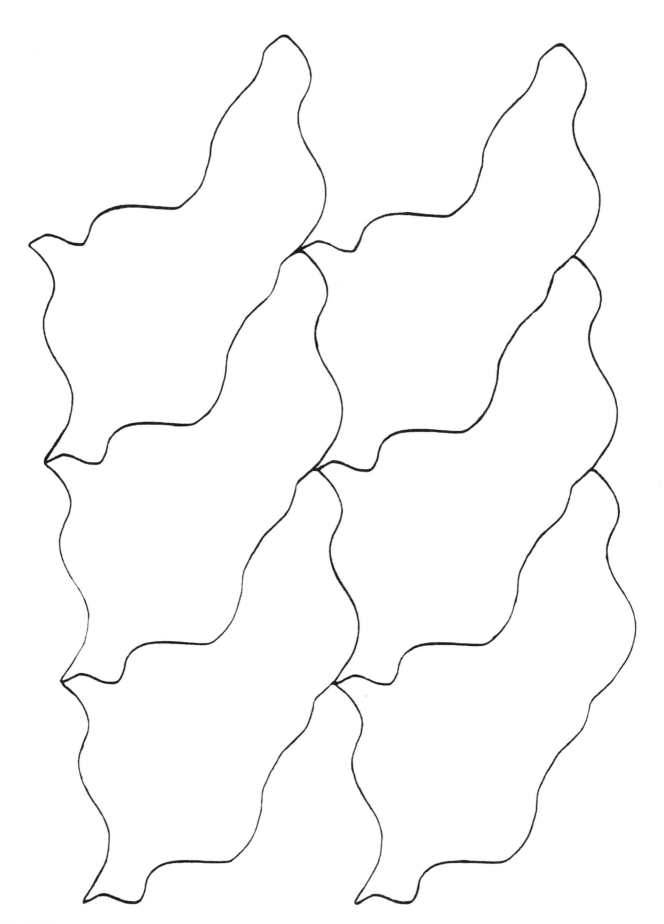

Name _____

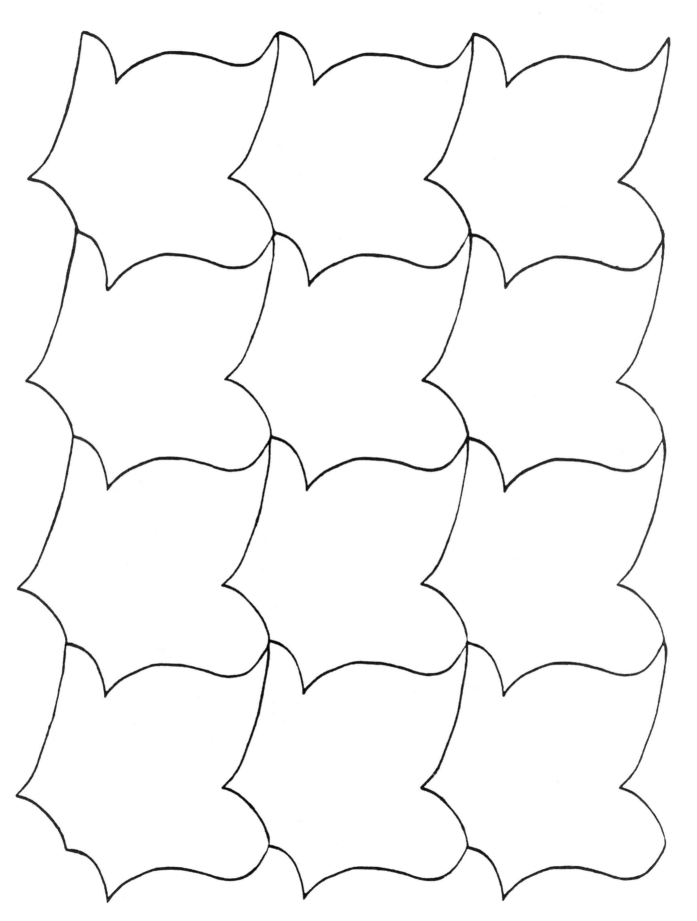

WHAT TO LOOK FOR WHEN SHAPES DON'T TESSELLATE

- Often students will inadvertently flip over the "nibble" piece before reattaching. This mistake can be avoided if students color one side of their shape first.
- Sometimes students do not tape their "nibble" piece directly opposite, or parallel to, the spot from which it was cut. This constraint is important when doing slides.
- If a "nibble" involves two sides at a corner and is rotated to an adjacent side, the tile will not tessellate.
- If students use too much tape, they will extend the area of the original shape, and it will not tessellate.

CONCLUSION

Students need to understand that not all mathematics activities take fifty minutes from start to finish. Tessellations represent an example of project-oriented mathematics. Though a complete tessellation project from preliminary activities to a final poster-sized tessellation can spread over several weeks while students are learning about tessellations, they will also be exploring many elements of the mathematics curriculum. Their spatial sense is cultivated and heightened as they explore figures, relationships in figures, and effects of changing figures. Working with tessellations is valuable and well worth the time spent.

GLOSSARY OF TESSELLATING TERMS

congruent
Same size and same shape

polygon
Closed figures formed by straight line segments

poly = many (Greek); *gon* = angle (Greek)

Fig. 11

regular polygon

Has all sides congruent and all angles congruent; that is, the length of each side of a polygon is the same and the measure of every angle is the same

quadrilateral

Any polygon with four sides

square

Two pairs of parallel sides, all sides congruent, four right angles

rectangle

Two pairs of parallel sides, opposite sides congruent, four right angles

rhombus

Two pairs of parallel sides, all sides congruent

parallelogram

Two pairs of parallel sides

kite

Two distinct pairs of adjacent sides congruent (note that flipping or reflecting a triangle will result in a kite), $AB = BC$ and $AD = CD$ (see fig. 12)

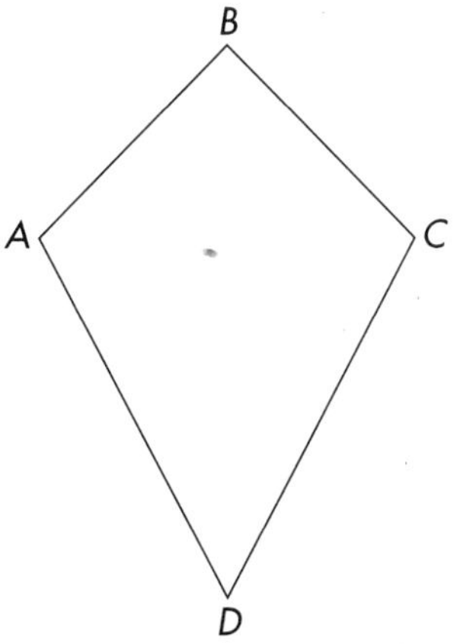

regular tessellation

Covers the plane with repetition of one particular regular polygon

side

Straight line segment of a polygon, for example, a dodecagon is a polygon with twelve sides

similar

Same shape but not necessarily the same size

transformation

Correspondence or matching between points of the plane, for instance, by rotation or reflection

trapezoid

One and only one pair of parallel sides

vertex

Point where two sides meet

Fig. 12

TESSELLATING MATERIALS

- Overhead projector
- Pattern Blocks or attribute blocks
- Tagboard, recycled manila folders, or other cardboard sheets
- Pencils, scissors, rulers, glue, tape, and construction paper
- Marking pens, colored pencils, crayons, and the like
- Scrap paper (8.5″ × 11″ or 8.5″ × 14″)
- Good-quality paper in many different sizes
- Pattern Blocks for overhead projector (optional)

Bibliography

Bezuszka, Stanley, Margaret Kenney, and Linda Silvey. *Tessellations: The Geometry of Patterns.* Palo Alto, Calif.: Creative Publications, 1977.

Billings, Karen, Carol Campbell, and Alice Schwandt. *Art 'n' Math.* Eugene, Oreg.: Action Math Associates, 1975.

Bolster, L. Carey. "Tessellations." *Mathematics Teacher* 66 (April 1973): 339–42.

Critchlow, Keith. *Islamic Patterns.* London: Thames and Hudson, 1976.

El-Said, Issam, and Ayse Parman. *Geometric Concepts in Islamic Art.* London: World of Islam Festival Publishing, 1976.

Ernst, Bruno. *The Magic Mirror of M. C. Escher,* translated by John E. Brigham. New York: Random House, 1976.

Escher, M. C. "The Graphic Work of M. C. Escher." In *Mathematical Carnival.* New York: Vintage Books, 1977.

Gardner, Martin. "The Art of M. C. Escher." In *Mathematical Carnival.* New York: Vintage Books, 1977.

———. "Mathematical Games." *Scientific American* 233 (July 1975): 112–17.

Haak, Sheila. "Transformation Geometry and the Artwork of M. C. Escher." *Mathematics Teacher* 69 (December 1976): 647–52.

Kaiser, Barbara. "Explorations with Tessellating Polygons." *Arithmetic Teacher* 36 (December 1988): 19–24.

Krause, Marina C. *Multicultural Mathematics Materials.* Reston, Va.: National Council of Teachers of Mathematics, 1983.

Locher, J. L., ed. *The World of M. C. Escher.* New York: Harry N. Abrams Publishers, 1971.

MacGillavry, Caroline H. *Symmetry Aspects of M. C. Escher's Periodic Drawings.* Utrecht: A. Oosthoek's Uitgeversmaatschappij NV, published for the International Union of Crystallography, 1965.

Maletsky, Evan M. "Designs with Tessellations." *Mathematics Teacher* 67 (April 1974): 335–38.

O'Daffer, Phares G., and Stanley R. Clemens. *Geometry: An Investigative Approach.* Menlo Park, Calif.: Addison-Wesley Publishing Co., 1976.

———. *Laboratory Investigations in Geometry.* Menlo Park, Calif.: Addison-Wesley Publishing Co., 1976.

Ranucci, Ernest R. "Master of Tessellations: M. C. Escher, 1898–1972." *Mathematics Teacher* 67 (April 1974): 229–306.

———. "Space Filling in Two Dimensions." *Mathematics Teacher* 64 (November 1971): 587–93.

———. "Tiny Treasury of Tessellations." *Mathematics Teacher* 61 (February 1968): 114–17.

Ranucci, Ernest R., and J. L. Teeters. *Creating Escher Type Drawings.* Palo Alto, Calif.: Creative Publications, 1977.

Seymour, Dale. *Tessellation Teaching Masters.* Palo Alto, Calif.: Dale Seymour Publications, 1988.

Seymour, Dale, and Jill Britton. *Introduction to Tessellations.* Palo Alto, Calif: Dale Seymour Publications, 1988.

Shubnikov, A. V. *Symmetry in Science and Art,* translated by David Harker. New York and London: Plenum Press, 1974.

Teeters, Joseph L. "How to Draw Tessellations of the Escher Type." *Mathematics Teacher* 67 (April 1974): 307–10.

Van de Walle, John, and Charles S. Thompson. "Let's Do It: Concepts, Art, and Fun from Simple Tiling Patterns." *Arithmetic Teacher* 28 (November 1980): 4–8.

Zurstadt, Betty K. "Tessellations and the Art of M. C. Escher." *Arithmetic Teacher* 31 (January 1984): 54–55. ▲

From the File: Predicting Rotations

by

William Juraschek
University of Colorado at Denver

Geometry

Predicting Rotations

Materials: A rotation board (a piece of stiff cardboard about 30 cm square), blank cards, colored transparency the same size as the cards, and an answer grid

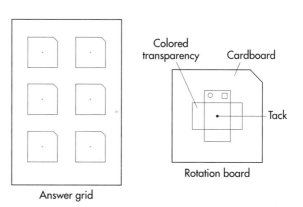

Answer grid

Rotation board

Procedures: On one of the blank cards draw a simple design like the one shown. Put the transparency on top of the card and affix both to the rotation board, which serves as a fixed reference. The notches on the board and transparency are also for reference. Rotate the transparency and then ask students to draw their predictions of how the card will appear when it is rotated to coincide with the transparency. Compare outcomes with predictions. Begin with simple designs using quarter, half, and three-quarter turns to the right. Follow with rotations to the left and cards with more complex designs. Do these activities occasionally throughout the year.

From the file of William Juraschek, University of Colorado at Denver, Denver, CO 80202 ▲

The Inside-Out Box: An Analysis of Structures and Space

by

Marilyn L. Fowler

Students analyze their boxes.

The NCTM's Standards address the need for children to develop spatial sense and explore the effects of transforming, combining, subdividing, and changing geometric figures (1989). Yet our students show weakness in these skills when compared with children of other nations (Stigler, Lee, and Stevenson 1990, quoted in Grouws 1992). The positive correlation between spatial abilities and mathematics achievement at all levels (Fennema and Sherman 1977; Fennema and Sherman 1978; and Guay and McDaniel 1977; all cited in Grouws 1992) shows that teachers need to present activities that can develop children's spatial abilities.

The following activity for children of any age is an interesting and practical spatial-manipulation lesson that will result in a useful product. Teachers who have presented this learning experience report that they are surprised at the ease with which some students can predict the shape of a box that has been opened and laid flat. In so doing, these students are providing authentic evidence of their spatial abilities.

MATERIALS

Students in kindergarten will need at least twenty construction-paper shapes cut into 16-cm-by-8-cm rectangles, 8-cm-by-8-cm squares, and miscellaneous triangles and other shapes. Students in grades 1–6 will need drawing paper; tape and tape dispensers; glue or paste; one sheet of butcher paper for each two-student team; and recycled containers, such as cereal, toothpaste, aspirin, cracker, and film boxes.

PREPARATION

The teacher should form two-student teams. Once the boxes are collected, prepare a box by gently separating it at the glued areas. Fold it again into its original box shape and lightly tape it back together. For kindergarten only, cut construction-paper pieces for the "box maps."

THE CONSTRUCTION BEGINS

To begin the activity, I place all the collected containers around the children's tables or on the floor. Children can hold and touch the containers and are encouraged to look inside. They discuss the containers and how they are used. Are containers made for certain purposes? How does a container protect the items inside? What purpose does the decoration on the outside serve? Are some containers unfit for the products inside that may break or get crushed? What is done to prevent these problems? From what materials are the containers made?

Students then observe the empty cereal box and see that its front face is a rectangular or a square shape. They are asked to guess the shape of the back of the box before it is shown to them, as well as of the sides and the bottom. Children are asked, "Why do you think that the back side will be a rectangle or square?" They talk together about their ideas and report back, and then all the faces and edges of the box are counted.

Students analyze how the box opens and closes. What has been designed to allow the box to reclose tightly and what makes it

---

Marilyn Fowler, fowler@tenet.edu, works for the Texas Statewide Systemic Initiative, the University of Texas at Austin, Austin, TX 78712. She is interested in ways that teachers can make elementary classrooms more interesting with design, invention, analysis of everyday objects, and the mathematics intrinsic to those processes. She codirects with engineers a teachers' institute called DTEACh, which is dedicated to those interests.

The author wishes to thank Mr. Lannon's fifth-grade class at Harris Elementary School in Austin, Texas, for its assistance during the preparation of this article.

work? The children describe the features of the closing mechanism. Sometimes this mechanism includes a tab that fits into a slot. However, if the box is to be thrown away after its first use, no closing mechanism is found.

Students then see that the box can be opened out flat because I have unfastened it at the seams. I ask students to close their eyes and imagine how the box will appear if it is opened and placed flat on the floor.

How many times did you change your minds?

The kindergarten student teams then use the cut-paper shapes to make a map of what they think the cereal box will look like when it is laid flat. Note that the boxes in this activity are peeled apart at the seams, and students should examine where those seams are before making predictions. If the box is *cut* down the sides, the predictions would be quite different. Children move the shapes around until they are arranged the way they should be. I ask older children to sketch how the flattened box will appear, indicating whether the decoration is facedown. Teams should be asked to place a special mark where the opening and closing mechanism will be found once the box is flattened. For an additional challenge, ask students to mark on their map where other features of the cereal box will be when the box is flat, such as the list of ingredients, the brand name, or a cartoon figure (see fig. 1 for a diagram of an opened-and-laid-flat cereal box).

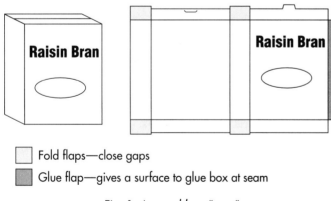

Fold flaps—close gaps

Glue flap—gives a surface to glue box at seam

Fig. 1. A cereal-box "map"

The group is then brought together to check its maps or sketches against the actual geometry of the opened-flat box. I carefully untape the cereal box then lay the box flat and ask the children to compare their maps and sketches with the flattened box. Students check their blueprints and see if they can find where their predictions differ from the actual box. These questions help guide their thinking:

• Did you fail to predict some sides or faces? What is the function of those parts? (Extra flaps provide surfaces for gluing and others form effective seals.)

• How many times did you change your minds about an arrangement of paper pieces before you settled on one?

• Did both team members present good ideas and listen to each other's ideas?

Student teams then choose one box to analyze. They look at the seams and glued edges and then make a map or sketch that predicts their opened-flat box. They can ask for help to peel the sides apart and match up their map or sketch with the actual flattened box (see figs. 2 and 3 for additional box maps).

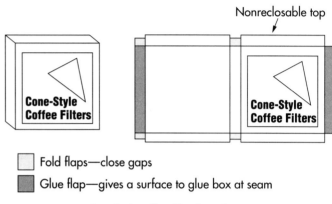

Fold flaps—close gaps

Glue flap—gives a surface to glue box at seam

Fig. 2. A coffee-filter-box "map"

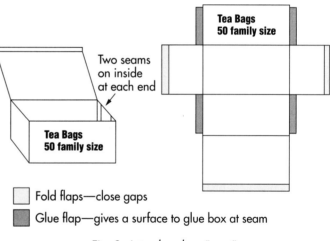

Fold flaps—close gaps

Glue flap—gives a surface to glue box at seam

Fig. 3. A tea-bag-box "map"

Later, I demonstrate that my original cereal box and others like it can be turned inside out and taped together to make a new box. Students then describe the new box, counting the number of faces as before. Is the new box more pleasing visually than the old box? The design and lettering are out of sight, which makes the box easier to decorate. How does the inside-out box open and shut, or how might one change it so that it does?

Students then help write a "design brief," or short challenge statement, to describe the assignment of making a nicely decorated inside-out box. It reads

Design Brief: Design and make a structure that....

Students might fill in the words to read "Design and make a structure that is a decorated inside-out box." Please note that the best use of this activity is in the context of a need from science, social studies, or literature. Remind students that the hamster needs a temporary home, the model town requires a set of sturdy buildings, or a story character needs extra storage. Then the design brief might read:

Design Brief: Design and make a structure that is a decorated inside-out box and will make a temporary home for our hamster.

The rules, or specifications for the project, can also be written with the children's help but should include the following:

• It should have six faces.
• It should be pleasing to look at.
• It should have one face that opens and shuts.

Students can then ask questions about the design brief and specifications; "wait time" allows each item to be discussed in depth.

Once students have made a plan, they select a box and unfasten the seams. When the teams have completed their structure by making an inside-out box, they evaluate the following:

• Was it difficult to turn the box inside out?
• How did partners help each other?
• Describe how the door opens and closes.
• Explain how you wish this box could be used by others.
• Show your blueprint. Explain how it looks like your inside-out box.

Teams write or dictate descriptions of their product, and the structure along with a written description is then placed in a design gallery (see fig. 4).

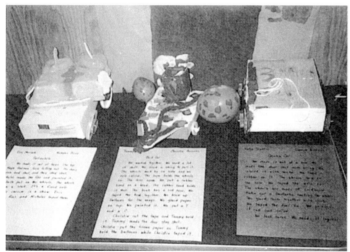

Fig. 4. Inside-out box "vehicles" adorn part of the display.

This use of common containers provides a link for children to connect school science with everyday technology. Also, the inside-out boxes can become sturdy mailing cartons and containers for gifts. My family especially enjoys finding bright graham-cracker advertising lining the inside of the box they receive!

Resources

Fowler, Marilyn. "Containers and Boxes," In *Beginning Lessons in Engineering Design.* Austin, Tex.: Bar-None Publishing, 1993.

This book details classroom lessons in design and engineering.

Williams, Pat, and David Jinx. *Design and Technology 5–12.* Philadelphia: Falmer Press, 1985.

This book presents an overview of the design and technology approach for curriculum writers and teachers.

References

Fennema, Elizabeth, and Julia A. Sherman. "Sex-Related Differences in Mathematics Achievement, Spatial Visualization, and Affective Factors." *American Educational Research Journal* 14 (Spring 1977): 51–71. Quoted in *Handbook of Research on Mathematics Teaching and Learning,* edited by Douglas A. Grouws. New York: Macmillan Publishing Co., and Reston, Va.: National Council of Teachers of Mathematics, 1992.

———. "Sex-Related Differences in Mathematics Achievement and Related Factors: A Further Study." *Journal for Research in Mathematics Education* 9 (May 1978): 189–203. Quoted in *Handbook of Research on Mathematics Teaching and Learning,* edited by Douglas A. Grouws. New York: Macmillan Publishing Co., and Reston, Va.: National Council of Teachers of Mathematics, 1992.

Grouws, Douglas A., ed. *Handbook of Research on Mathematics Teaching and Learning.* New York: Macmillan Publishing Co., and Reston, Va.: National Council of Teachers of Mathematics, 1992.

Guay, Roland B., and Ernest D. McDaniel. "The Relationship between Mathematics Achievement and Spatial Ability among Elementary School Children." *Journal for Research in Mathematics Education* 8 (May 1977): 211–15. Quoted in *Handbook of Research on Mathematics Teaching and Learning,* edited by Douglas A. Grouws. New York: Macmillan Publishing Co., and Reston, Va.: National Council of Teachers of Mathematics, 1992.

National Council of Teachers of Mathematics. *Curriculum and Evaluation Standards for School Mathematics.* Reston, Va.: The Council, 1989.

Stigler, James W., Shin-Ying Lee, and Harold W. Stevenson. *Mathematical Knowledge of Chinese, Japanese, and American Elementary School Children.* Reston, Va.: National Council of Teachers of Mathematics, 1990. Quoted in *Handbook of Research on Mathematics Teaching and Learning,* edited by Douglas A. Grouws. New York: Macmillan Publishing Co., and Reston, Va.: National Council of Teachers of Mathematics, 1992. ▲

Using Reflections to Find Symmetric and Asymmetric Patterns

by

James R. Bidwell

The concept of line symmetry is usually introduced in the elementary school by folding shapes, using mirrors, or drawing lines on a picture. Good follow-up activities are needed to give the student enough time to explore this concept of symmetry adequately. The activities presented here focus on

1. using a mirror to "move" a pattern;
2. finding patterns with one, two, or four lines of symmetry;
3. finding asymmetrical patterns;
4. deciding if patterns are different; and
5. solving the problem of finding all the patterns possible.

The problem-solving techniques include using a model, drawing patterns, considering every case, making a table, and discriminating among patterns (what is the same, what is different). The activities can be presented at a variety of grade levels, from about grade 3 to grade 7 depending on the depth desired.

To explore these activities, the student needs a 3 × 3 square grid, monochromatic squares that fit the grid, and a mirror or other reflecting surface, such as a Mira (fig. 1). To get more enjoyment and understanding from the discussion, make the grid and squares and use them.

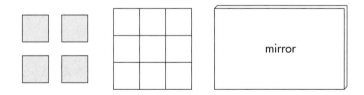

Fig. 1. Four colored squares, a grid, and a mirror are needed for this activity.

First, the lines of symmetry of the 3 × 3 grid need to be discovered. This can be done by using the mirror. The student will find four ways of placing the mirror so that the image is the same as what lies behind the mirror. Each of these lines along which the mirror

James Bidwell teaches at Central Michigan University, Mount Pleasant, MI 48859. He is most interested in elementary school mathematics education and the history of mathematics.

lies is a *line of symmetry* for the grid (fig. 2). Any line-symmetric pattern on the grid must use one or more of these four dashed lines as a line of symmetry.

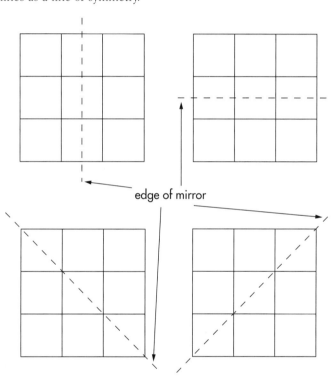

Fig. 2. The grid has four lines of symmetry.

USING A MIRROR TO "MOVE" A PATTERN

Once the student is sure of the four lines of symmetry (the reflecting lines), he or she can begin to use the squares on the grid. Place three of them as shown in the first part of figure 3 to make a pattern on the grid. For this activity, a *pattern on the grid* includes both the *squares* and the grid itself. Now using the mirror, reflect the pattern and move it on the grid (fig. 3). If part of the pattern is behind the mirror, reversing the mirror will show where it moves. By moving the three squares to their new position or by using a different reflection line or both, further moves can be found for the original pattern. Students should use this process to find eight different positions for the three squares shown in the first part of figure 3 (fig. 4).

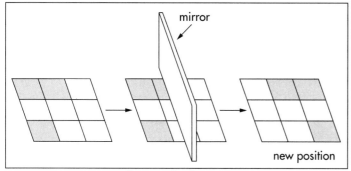

Fig. 3. A reflection of a three-square pattern

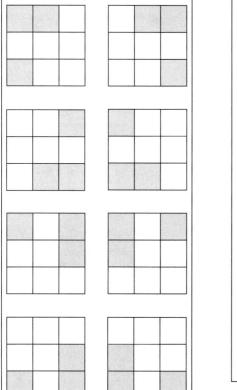

Fig. 4. The eight positions of the three-square pattern

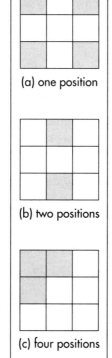

(a) one position

(b) two positions

(c) four positions

Fig. 5. Patterns with one, two, and four positions

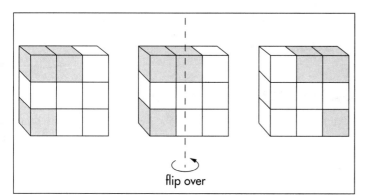

Fig. 6. Some students can see the patterns better with cubes.

Students should now try different patterns (using one to four squares) and move the pattern around the grid. They will find one, two, four, or eight different positions depending on the pattern chosen. (Sometimes the pattern moves into itself!) Figure 5 shows examples of the other three possibilities.

Students who have trouble "seeing" the moves as described (using a mirror) could use a physical model. Using Lego or Multilink cubes (or other devices), the student can make the desired pattern with cubes of two colors (it is better if one is white). Now a reflecting line becomes a "flip" line for the pattern of cubes. Figure 6 shows the same move as figure 3.

FINDING PATTERNS WITH ONE, TWO, OR FOUR LINES OF SYMMETRY

With sufficient experience "moving" patterns, students are ready for the next step. Some patterns that they attempted to move probably moved into themselves using one of the four reflecting lines. Whenever that happens, the reflecting line is a *line of symmetry* for the pattern. One of the four lines of symmetry for the grid must be used. Figure 7 shows the patterns of figure 5 with their lines of symmetry added. As students explore various patterns, they will find that patterns with one line of symmetry always can be moved to only four different positions; those with two lines, two positions; and those with four lines, one position. This is because the line of symmetry of the pattern moved the pattern into itself. Students can begin to collect patterns, grouping them by the number of lines of symmetry.

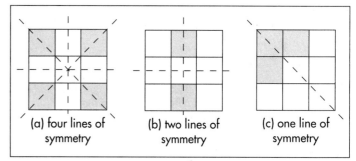

(a) four lines of symmetry

(b) two lines of symmetry

(c) one line of symmetry

Fig. 7. Lines of symmetry

FINDING ASYMMETRICAL PATTERNS

Among the various patterns, students will find many like the one with which we started (fig. 3). These patterns have eight possible positions and no line of symmetry. They are called *asymmetrical* patterns on the grid. Figure 8 shows three other asymmetrical patterns. Students can collect these patterns as well.

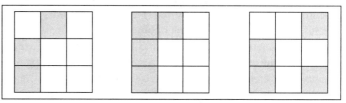

Fig. 8. Asymmetrical patterns

While searching for asymmetrical patterns, students may find one exceptional case—a pattern with no line of symmetry but only four possible positions on the grid. This *one* exception is shown in figure 9. Students can verify that each reflecting line moves the pattern, but no combination of moves and reflections will produce more than four positions. The pattern in figure 9 has another type of symmetry that causes this exception—point symmetry. A pattern has point symmetry if it is its own image through a central point. Because of this symmetry, four of the eight possible positions reflect back into themselves (using different lines of reflection) instead of making new positions. This pattern is the *only* exception to the development of the 3 × 3 grid.

Fig. 9. An assymetrical pattern with only four positions on the grid

DECIDING IF PATTERNS ARE DIFFERENT

As soon as students begin to collect different patterns, the question will arise whether two patterns are the same or not. Figure 10 shows two patterns. Are they the same or different? Many students will believe them to be different because the squares are placed differently *relative to positions outside the 3 × 3 grid itself.* That is, figure 10 shows two different *oriented* patterns. Let us call this oriented position case 1.

Some students will say that figure 10 shows the same pattern because one is the reflection of the other; that is, one can be moved to the other. They are the same *relative to the grid itself.* If the two patterns are made from Lego or Multilink blocks of the same colors and put in a sack, it is impossible to tell which one we draw out. Let us call this *unoriented* position case 2.

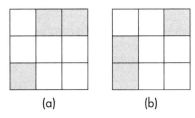

(a)   (b)

Fig. 10. Some students feel these patterns are different (oriented), whereas others see them as the same (unoriented).

In case 1, every grid square has a fixed position. Students may wish to number or label them. Whether each square is colored or not will help create *two* different patterns. Every time a colored square is added or removed, a new pattern is created. That is, we have two choices in coloring each of the nine squares. This creates $2^9 = 512$ different colorings, or patterns, for the 3 × 3 grid (from no colored pieces to all nine), when oriented patterns are concerned.

In case 2, because a pattern that is "moved" into another position is considered the same, many fewer different patterns can be found. In fact, only 102 different unoriented patterns exist. Recall that an asymmetrical pattern has eight different positions to which it can be moved. That is, each *unoriented* asymmetric pattern accounts for eight oriented asymmetric patterns. Similarly, each *unoriented* pattern with *one* line of symmetry accounts for four oriented patterns, and so on. Table 1 summarizes this situation.

Table 1

Number of lines of symmetry in unoriented patterns	Number of corresponding oriented patterns
0*	8
0**	4
1	4
2	2
4	1

* Asymmetric
** See figure 9.

Students should be allowed time to discuss whether or not patterns that are moved are the same. This decision is a matter of *definition*, not of *fact*. Students should be made comfortable with either decision. Under either definition, the activity that follows is helpful in finding *all* patterns (either 512 or 102).

FINDING ALL THE UNORIENTED PATTERNS

Suppose students wish to find all 102 unoriented patterns (case 2). Can any further help be found besides table 1? Yes, we can cut the work in half by studying figure 11. Pattern 11*a* can be obtained from 11*b* (or vice versa) by exchanging colored and uncolored squares. In this sense, every pattern with five to nine colored squares can be reduced to a corresponding pattern with only zero to four colored squares. Thus we really need to find only the 51 patterns using zero to four colored squares; the other 51 will be found by exchanging colored and uncolored squares.

By finding the 51 unoriented patterns using zero to four colored squares, students can account for the 102 patterns, and by using table 1, they can also account for all 512 oriented patterns or colorings of the 3 × 3 grid. Table 2 summarizes the number of patterns possible according to the number of lines of symmetry. Figure 12 shows the 51 patterns using zero to four colored squares arranged by lines of symmetry.

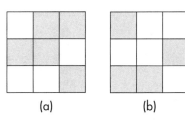

(a)   (b)

Fig. 11. Figure (a) can be obtained by interchanging colored and uncolored squares with (b).

EXTENSION ACTIVITIES

If your students have "solved" the 3 × 3 grid, they can move on to the 4 × 4 grid. As the reader will probably guess, the number of patterns is much greater: $2^{16} = 65\,536$ oriented patterns (number of possible colorings) are possible. A total of 4 274 different unoriented patterns (this number can be found using a theorem from group theory), symmetrical and asymmetrical, are possible

Table 2

Number of lines of symmetry	Number of unoriented patterns using 0 to 4 squares	Number of oriented patterns accounted for using 0 to 9 squares
0*	18	288
0**	1	8
1	24	192
2	4	16
4	4	8
Total	51	512

* Asymmetric
** See figure 9.

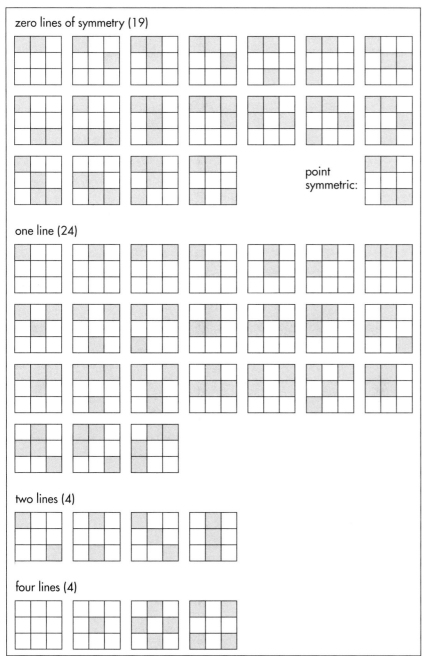

zero lines of symmetry (19)

point symmetric:

one line (24)

two lines (4)

four lines (4)

Fig. 12. Complete list of patterns using zero to four colored squares on a 3 × 3 grid

(compared to 102 for the 3 × 3 grid). I have found 68 symmetric patterns using from zero to four squares (up to eight squares can be used to make different patterns). Asymmetrical patterns can also be found. Obviously, students should not attempt to find *all* the patterns in the 4 × 4 grid. However, students might concentrate on finding patterns with, say, four lines of symmetry.

An easier alternative is to look at the 3 × 3 triangular grid (fig. 13(a)). This grid has three lines of symmetry, which can be discovered by using a mirror (fig. 13 (b)). The grid has nine small triangles, and so up to nine colored triangles can be placed to make patterns. Notice that any pattern using more than four colored triangles will match a pattern with four or fewer triangles. Three patterns on the grid are shown in figure 14. Each symmetric pattern will have no, one, or three lines of symmetry, as marked on these examples. Students can find both symmetric and asymmetric patterns. (*Note:* Point symmetry on this grid occurs *only* along with line symmetry and thus is not a problem.) Students may wish to predict how many different unoriented symmetric patterns they will be able to find. Will this be more or fewer than the number on the 3 × 3 square grid?

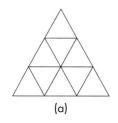

(a)

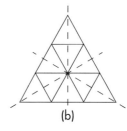

(b)

Fig. 13. Some students may find it easier to work with a triangular pattern.

Students should be able to find 32 unoriented symmetric patterns on the 3 × 3 triangular grid and 28 unoriented asymmetric patterns using from zero to four colored triangles. Students can discover that each unoriented asymmetric pattern accounts for 6 oriented patterns on the grid. An unoriented pattern with one line of symmetry accounts for 3 oriented patterns, whereas one with three lines of symmetry is unique. When the 60 patterns have been found, your students can verify that all the $2^9 = 512$ different oriented patterns for zero to nine colored triangles can

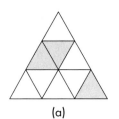 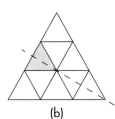 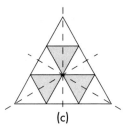

(a)　　　　　(b)　　　　　(c)

Fig. 14. Patterns with no line, one line, and three lines of symmetry

be accounted for by creating a table similar to table 2. A list of these triangular patterns has not been provided. Readers are encouraged to explore on their own.

These grid-pattern activities can be done at different levels of formality and can lead to interesting discussions on symmetry and counting problems. It certainly is not necessary to have your students be concerned with finding *all* patterns unless they are ready for such an activity. Younger students may be challenged enough to find and categorize the various unoriented patterns. Your students will have a deeper knowledge of symmetry and asymmetry after spending time looking for these simple patterns. ▲

Projective Geometry in the Elementary School

by

Helen Mansfield

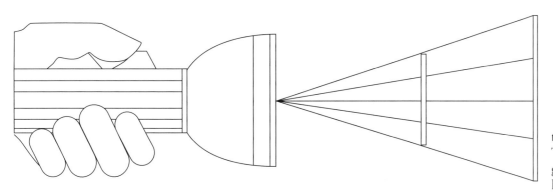

Simple ideas in projective geometry are rarely taught in elementary schools. This article suggests some reasons why such ideas should have a place in the curriculum and describes some lessons on projective geometry that were taught to a class of ten-year-olds.

It is important to teach geometry for many reasons. One of the most important reasons is to develop adequate spatial skills to enable children to solve problems. Spatial skills and understanding can only be developed through a program that affords a wide range of appropriate activities. These activities must be chosen not just to teach terminology and the properties of shapes but also to promote in children the ability to reason, to predict, and to represent their knowledge in appropriate ways.

It is difficult to decide which spatial relations to teach, which concepts are important, and which skills will help children to solve problems. It is also difficult to find practical, everyday problems for children to solve that match their level of cognitive development and, thus, enhance their understanding and skills. An extra difficulty that teachers face is deciding how much transformation geometry to include in the program. On the one hand, transformation geometry is advocated as providing enjoyable classroom activities for children, and yet its final value as an approach to geometry is not necessarily apparent to all teachers. On the other hand, it seems important to build up a strong background of knowledge about shapes and their properties, and transformation geometry is just one of the ways of doing this.

"PERCEPTUAL" AND "REPRESENTATIONAL" KNOWLEDGE

In his writings, Piaget distinguishes between the "perceptual" and the "representational" levels of knowledge in children. At the perceptual level, children derive their knowledge from direct contact with objects, whereas at the representational level, they are able to imagine new situations, draw inferences, and predict. Representational knowledge is, therefore, more sophisticated

than perceptual knowledge. Two examples of activities for geometry at the perceptual level are these:

1. The child is given some Plasticine models of a cube, cuts through them at various angles, and observes the shapes of the cut surfaces.
2. The child locates the lines of symmetry of an equilateral triangle by using a Mira.

Two examples of activities for geometry at the representational level are as follows:

1. The child predicts the shapes of the possible cross sections of a cube and experiments to prove the hypotheses.
2. The child hypothesizes that an equilateral triangle has three lines of symmetry on the basis of its congruent features and checks this hypothesis with a Mira.

These examples suggest that the same subject matter can be approached at either the perceptual or the representational level of knowledge. If this observation is correct, then any geometric topic for young children might be taught at either of these two levels, or indeed both. Activities at the perceptual level might be more appropriate for younger children or for older children at the beginning of a new section of work. Offering activities at the representational level, when appropriate, is important so that children are encouraged to use higher-order thought processes.

ORDER OF CONCEPTS

Since any type of geometric concept or skill can probably be approached at either the perceptual or representational level, it may be that the nature of geometry itself should determine where

Helen Mansfield is a teacher of mathematics and methods courses for pre-service and in-service primary school (K–7) teachers at Churchlands College, Perth, Western Australia. She served as a member of the Working Party, which developed the Western Australia Primary Mathematics Syllabus.

The author would like to thank Joy Scott of Churchlands College for her assistance in the preparation of the art for this manuscript.

it should be placed in the child's schooling. Piaget's study suggests that children develop geometric concepts in a particular order. First, topological concepts, then, projective concepts, and finally, Euclidean concepts appear. A good understanding of Euclidean concepts depends on the orderly development of the two previous groups of concepts.

In topology, shapes can be altered by bending, stretching, twisting, and compressing but not by tearing or joining. Some properties of the shape that stay the same while it is being changed in these ways include open, closed, simple, or nonsimple. An activity in which children can explore topological ideas is to have them sketch simple figures on a balloon and observe the figures as they stretch and pull the balloon.

Projective geometry can occur in two different kinds of situations. Either a point source of light is used, from which the rays of light are divergent, or sunlight is used, from which the rays of light are approximately parallel. This second kind of projective geometry is called *affine geometry*. The shadows that can be obtained from a shape are different in some respects in these two situations. In both kinds of projective geometry, a shape with straight sides will have a shadow with straight sides, although the lengths of the sides will be different. The number of sides will be the same, but the angles of the shadow may be different from those of the shape. In affine geometry, however, a shape with parallel sides will always cast a shadow with parallel sides, whereas in point-source projections this condition does not necessarily hold. The reader is invited to verify this difference. A particular case of projective geometry that should be mentioned occurs when a shape is held parallel to the surface on which its shadow is being cast. In this position, the shadow will be similar to the shape. An activity for children involving point-source projections is to compare a slide with its image on the screen. An affine activity is to use a shadow technique to find the height of an inaccessible object outdoors.

Euclidean geometry deals with the properties of shapes that stay the same as the shape is moved around through a reflection, rotation, or translation. As these transformations alter neither the size nor the shape of figures, such properties as lengths of sides and measures of angles remain unchanged. The ideas of congruence are studied in Euclidean geometry. Most teachers are very familiar with activities that use reflections, rotations, or translations. Quite a lot of the teaching of geometry draws to some extent on these ways of moving shapes. For example, lessons on line symmetry are common, and reflection is often taught through paper-folding or mirror techniques.

Significant changes have taken place over the past twenty years with respect to teaching both Euclidean geometry and topology. These changes have occurred as teachers have become more familiar with non-Euclidean geometry and have sought new approaches to the teaching of the traditional Euclidean curriculum. Many textbooks now include lessons on Euclidean transformations, and these lessons are interesting and attractive to children. Some textbooks now include activities to develop topological concepts, too. These activities might occur in lessons that deal with simple closed curves, with polygons as special cases of these. Such topics as networks or Möbius strips sometimes occur in extension activities.

In most textbooks, though, little attention is paid to activities that will enhance children's understanding of projective concepts. The notable exception is the inclusion in some texts of lessons on similar shapes. Activities to develop projective concepts may be difficult to find or difficult to teach, or they may not be seen as important activities in their own right. However, if Piaget's theory is correct in the order it suggests for the acquisition of geometric concepts by children, then activities to develop projective ideas do need to be presented to children in the elementary school to lay the foundations for the later orderly development of Euclidean concepts.

SOME LESSONS IN PROJECTIVE GEOMETRY

The lessons that follow have been designed to explore whether worthwhile activities in projective geometry can be found and taught successfully to children in elementary school. Although the lessons are mainly at the perceptual level, since they are introductory, some activities are included that require representational levels of thinking as described by Piaget. The children involved were all ten years old.

Lesson 1

Purpose: To introduce children to some intuitive ideas about projections from a point source of light. These ideas included the following:

1. The shadow of a shape can be altered in size by varying the distance of the shape from the light source.
2. The shape of a shadow can vary according to how the shape is tilted with respect to the screen.
3. Parallel edges on a shape do not necessarily yield parallel lines on its shadow.

The activities used to illustrate these concepts are simple and at the perceptual level. Have the children make shadow pictures with their hands, using a flashlight to produce the light (fig. 1). The shadow pictures, generally of bird or animal shapes, can be outlined with colors on white paper and superimposed on one another to give some attractive visual records of the activity. The children can then experiment with the shadows of a cardboard square, holding it at different angles to the screen. They will find that they can obtain squares of various sizes if they hold the square parallel to the screen, and they can obtain shadows with

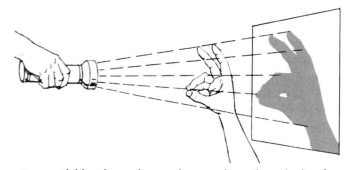

Fig. 1. Children begin their explorations by making shadow figures from a point source of light.

one or no pair of sides parallel by tilting it at an angle to the screen. They should note that the square always casts a quadrilateral as its shadow. Finally, this activity can be extended by investigating the shapes of shadows of other simple polygons. The children should conclude that since a triangle never has parallel sides, a triangle of any shape can produce a triangular shadow of any shape.

Lesson 2

Purpose: To introduce children to some intuitive ideas about projections from a distant source of light—the sun. The ideas for exploration include the following:

1. The sun's position in the sky determines the direction of shadows.
2. Blocking the sun's rays produces shadows.
3. Parallel sides on a shape cast parallel shadows.

Again, the activities are at the perceptual level and fun for the children to do. With their own shadows, have children make two-headed monsters, one-legged monsters, multibodied monsters, tall, short, and wide shadows (fig. 2). They will find that they can obtain bent shadows and curved shadows (using pipecleaners) only by casting the shadow onto a curved or bent surface, such as steps or tree trunks (fig. 3). One question that puzzles children is whether a shadow is darker where two shadows overlap (fig. 4). Cast shadows of a cardboard square onto paper taped to the ground, and record the shadows by outlining their edges. The children will find that a square can have any parallelogram as its shadow; the parallel sides of the square cast parallel shadows. Compare this result with the shadows obtained from the square in the previous lesson. Repeat the activity for other simple polygons.

Fig. 2. The children use the sun's rays to make monsters.

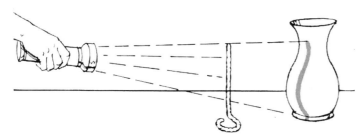

Fig. 3. Pipe cleaners make curved shadows if cast onto a curved surface.

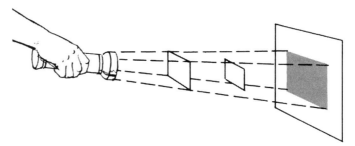

Fig. 4. Under some circumstances, two different objects can cast the same shadow.

Lesson 3

Purpose: To give children a problem-solving experience in projective geometry. Pose 2 problems to the children. Given shape A, make shadow B; use B to make shadow C. Then ask these questions:

1. Can shape A cast shadow C directly?
2. Can shadow B cast a shadow to match shape A?

These problems are the combinations and inverses of projections suggested by Dienes and Golding (1967) and require thinking beyond the perceptual level. Note that these problems are really asking whether projections are transitive and symmetric relations. Have the children attempt to solve these problems both in sunlight and with a flashlight by casting the shadows of cardboard polygons onto cardboard and marking and cutting out the shapes of the shadows. They should find that both tasks can be carried out quite easily in sunlight, although a lot of experimentation with the position and orientation of each shape may be necessary. However, it is only sometimes possible to accomplish the second task in point-source light. Some of the children may think that this problem can not be solved where B is similar to A and an enlargement of it. They may manage to show that in this case, the two shapes would have to be held parallel with the larger shape closer to the source of light. Although the smaller shape can be blocked out completely by the larger shape, it cannot be covered exactly.

Lesson 4

Purpose: To investigate the effect of the position of the point source of light on the shadow of a shape held parallel to the screen. This activity is at the perceptual level of thought.

Place a cardboard polygon on a cup on a white sheet of paper, and hence parallel to it (fig. 5). Clamp a flashlight above the shape. Allow the children to move the angle from which the flashlight shines on the shape, as well as its distance above the shape. In investigating the shadows obtained, the children should realize that no matter where the flashlight is located, the shadow is always similar to the original shape. Verify this finding by outlining the shadows and superimposing corresponding angles of the polygon to check congruence.

Lesson 5

Purpose: To investigate further the properties of similar figures obtained by a point-source projection. This activity is also at the perceptual level of thought.

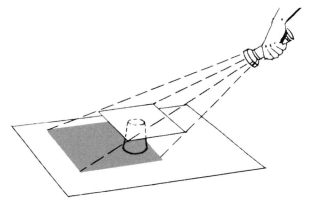

Fig. 5. The position of a point source of light has an effect on the size of the shadow the polygon casts.

In this lesson, the children make a string projection model of a point-source projection (fig. 6). A cardboard polygon is held parallel to a large sheet of cardboard and clamped in position. Strings are passed through small holes at each vertex of the polygon, tied at the top, and taped to a convenient support. Each of the strings is pulled taut and taped to the cardboard base. The shape defined by the ends of the strings represents the "shadow" of the polygon, and the knot at the top represents the point source of light.

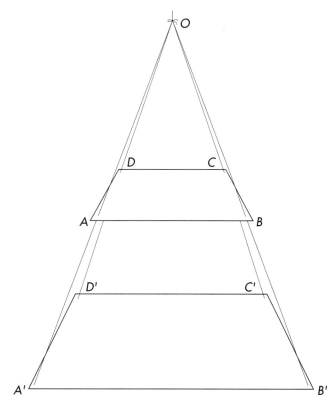

Fig. 6. A string-and-cardboard model of a point source of light shining against on object (ABCD), along with its shadow (A'B'C'D')

The children will find that as long as the polygon is held parallel to the floor, the "shadow" is similar to it. This finding is demonstrated by the superimposition of the angles. Measure corresponding lengths and compute corresponding ratios. Although it is difficult for the children to obtain a completely accurate model

(for example, it is difficult to ensure that the strings are absolutely straight), the values our students obtained for the following sets of ratios were remarkably close:

$$\frac{OA}{OA'}, \frac{OB}{OB'}, \frac{OC}{OC'}, \frac{OD}{OD'}$$

and

$$\frac{AB}{A'B'}, \frac{BC}{B'C'}, \frac{CD}{C'D'}, \frac{AD}{A'D'}.$$

Incidentally, since the actual measurements of the strings are not whole numbers, calculators can be used to compute these ratios. In this activity, the focus is on the possible generalizations about the ratios rather than on computation.

Lesson 6

Purpose: To investigate the effect of a change in perspective on the appearance of an object. Both perceptual and representational thought are required in this lesson.

The three edges meeting at one vertex of a cardboard box are each to be colored differently and the box placed on a bench outside (fig. 7). Ask the children to imagine themselves to be viewing the box from different positions and to draw the appearance of the colored corner as it appears to them. The children should be aware that the angles on the box might appear to vary, but they may be unable to predict in what ways this will happen. They should then view the box from different positions, varying their distance from the box and the angle from which they view it. Closing one eye, they should "match" the edges of the box with a pair of pencils and compare the angle formed by the pencils with the actual angle on the box. They should find that the pencils can form an acute, right, or obtuse angle, depending on the elevation from which it is viewed. However, moving out in a straight line from the box does not cause the angle to appear to change.

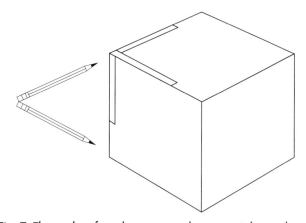

Fig. 7. The angles of a cube appear to be acute, right, or obtuse, depending on how they are viewed. The angles can be described with a pair of pencils.

Finally, have the children set up a vertical stick near a wall or straight path (to furnish horizontal, vertical, and parallel lines as referents) and photograph the stick from a variety of elevations and distances, which are to be written down and kept for the next lesson.

Lesson 7

Purpose: To examine the effect of changes in perspective on angles and on parallel, vertical, and horizontal lines.

Examine the photographs taken in the previous lesson together with the records that have been kept. The children will find that the distance from which they photographed the stick affects its apparent size. Its photographic image is smaller the further away the photograph was taken. The photographs enable the children to compare the angle the stick appears to make with, say, the edge of the path when viewed from different positions. Two photographs taken from the same distance but from different positions might look like figure 8, for example. Since the edge of the path and the top and bottom of the wall constituted parallel lines, the photographs recorded in quite a dramatic way that parallel lines appear to converge at a distance. Surprisingly, this last observation had not previously been made by some of the children in the group. When they were then asked to draw a long, straight road as it would appear to them if they were walking down it, some drew the lines the same distance apart for the length of the page, despite their discussion of the photographs they had taken. These children might benefit greatly from more activities in projective geometry.

These lessons by no means exhaust the range of appropriate activities from which teachers can draw to teach projective geometry. They may reveal some weaknesses in the children's grasp of concepts in projective geometry, but they also show that these activities are appropriate for this age level. They are worth trying in your classroom.

References

Dienes, Zoltan P., and E. W. Golding. *Geometry through Transformations.* Paris: E.S.A., 1967.

Piaget, Jean, and Barbel Inhelder. *The Child's Conception of Space.* London: Routledge & Kegan Paul, 1956. ▲

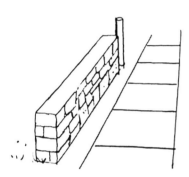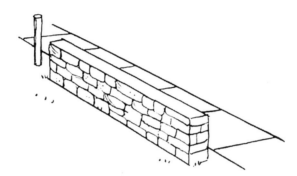

Fig. 8. A stick next to a wall was photographed from different directions.

Origami: Paper Folding— the Algorithmic Way

by

Pamela Beth Heukerott

Origami, the oriental art of paper folding, is simple, appealing, and economical. I have used this craft successfully to teach upper elementary students concepts and skills in geometry involving polygons, angles, measurement, symmetry, and congruence. This approach also serves as an example of a geometric algorithm, a sequence of steps to get a result, not unlike the rules for adding whole numbers and so on.

The only material needed is crisp, thin paper colored on one side and cut into squares of any dimension. Plain white duplicating paper that the students have colored on one side, wrapping paper, or packaged origami paper, which is available in art, crafts, and oriental stores, are equally suitable. However, construction paper is too soft and tears when it is repeatedly folded. It is also helpful to have origami instruction books available for reference. These can be borrowed from a library or purchased at a bookstore. Many are in paper and cost under five dollars. A list of titles is given at the end of this article.

GETTING STARTED

To prepare to present origami to a class, you should become familiar with origami symbols (see fig. 1), basic folds and bases,

instruction diagrams, and the format in which the instructions are given. This can be accomplished by reading books; however, it is more fun to attend a workshop to learn basic folding. These are often given at libraries, museums, or learning centers.

Instructions are given in both diagram and narrative form. Each step in the folding sequence is numbered. By looking at the next step each time, you can see how the paper should look when each fold is executed.

Symbol	Name	What It Means
↻	Turn over	Turn figure over
- - - - -	Valley fold	Fold resembling a V with the crease at the bottom center of a "valley"
⌒→	Directional arrow	Shows what direction to fold the paper
☐	White side or area of paper	White side of paper facing up
▨	Colored side or area of paper	Colored side of paper facing up

Fig. 1. Some standard origami symbols

Pamela Beth Heukerott, formerly a fifth-grade mathematics and science teacher, has presented origami demonstrations and workshops. She currently resides at 194 Garth Road, Scarsdale, NY 10583.

Origami creations range from very simple to complicated forms. Regardless of the form's complexity, a few guidelines will promote success. First, read the instructions carefully, since any mistake in folding will show. Second, test the folds for accuracy and congruence. Often the paper is folded in half. This can be accomplished by pinching corner points before making final folds. Third, press the paper into the line on which it is to be folded and toward the center of the square rather than toward the edges. This precaution prevents the paper from skewing or deviating from folds along lines of symmetry.

Although a complex figure may look more attractive, you will find it better to begin with the easier forms, such as the drinking cup, boats, the carp, flapping birds, rabbits, the house, and the balloon. The skill and confidence gained from earlier success will enable you to handle more advanced folding. You will also develop the ability to see where a series of folds will take you.

AN ORIGAMI LESSON

Before beginning with a group, I present a large model of what we will be making. In addition, guidelines for folding (see fig. 2), diagrams for first folds (see fig. 3), and standard bases (see fig. 4) are written on large charts or on the chalkboard. I explain that all forms begin with the same first folds, either diagonal or book. From then on, various angles are divided by folding the paper in different directions.

1. Understand directions thoroughly.
2. Test folds first.
3. Fold into crease.
4. Make sharp creases.

Fig. 2. Guidelines for folding

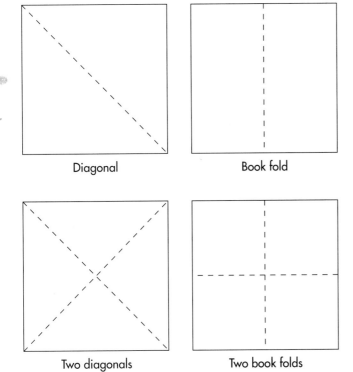

Fig. 3. Diagrams for first folds

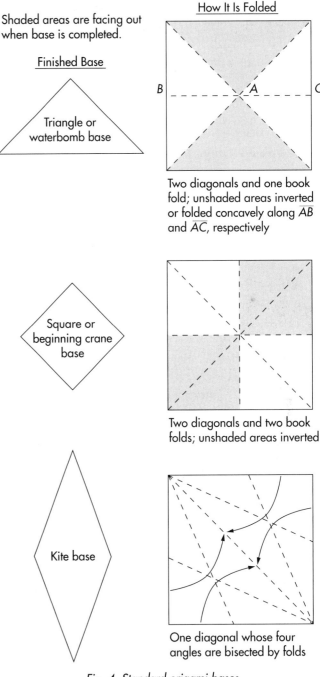

Fig. 4. Standard origami bases

Give directions orally. Sometimes this presentation is supplemented with written instructions. While presenting the steps, introduce geometry terms so that the students learn them in context and experience them concretely. Here is a partial list of terms: *length, width, depth, dimension, plane, square, triangle, rectangle, isosceles triangle, right triangle, angle, right angle, acute angle, diagonal, degree, bisect, congruent, symmetry, perpendicular, area, perimeter,* and *measurement.*

ANALYZING AN ORIGAMI FORM

During the lesson encourage divergent thinking by asking the question, "What can we say about the shape we see?" One student acts as the secretary and writes down the observations on the chalkboard.

Here's an example. Let's say that we are folding the carp (see fig. 5). We have just folded the two diagonals. The students have been asked to examine the paper. Some responses are as follows:

1. The square is divided into four triangles.
2. Each triangle is one-fourth of the square.
3. The triangles are the same size.
4. The triangles are congruent.
5. The three angles in each triangle equal 180 degrees.
6. Each triangle is a right triangle.
7. The triangles are isosceles triangles.
8. The angles in each triangle are 45 degrees, 45 degrees, and 90 degrees.
9. A diagonal divides the square into two triangles.
10. The diagonal bisects the right angles in the square.
11. The area of the four triangles is the same.
12. The perimeter of the four triangles is the same.
13. Each triangle has two equal angles.
14. Each triangle has two acute angles.

This open-ended-question approach encourages students to analyze the figure without the pressure of obtaining one right answer. It enables the teacher to assess what the class already knows about geometry concepts and vocabulary. The teacher can extend the folding lessons by focusing on methods of measuring length, angles, or area; testing congruence; and studying the attributes of plane and three-dimensional figures. Through origami the students also get experience in sequencing, following directions, reading diagrams, and developing vocabulary and concepts, in addition to having fun.

INCORPORATING ORIGAMI INTO A LEARNING CENTER

Many children express an enthusiastic interest in continuing origami once it has been introduced. It is easy and inexpensive to incorporate this craft into a classroom learning center or resource room. Just make origami books and paper available. Put up models and pictures of origami forms with clear, easy-to-follow instructions. Display completed forms on shelves, on bulletin boards, or in dioramas. Mobiles are an attractive way to show off completed figures.

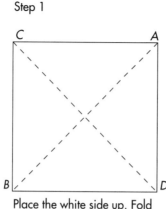

Step 1

Place the white side up. Fold along the diagonals $\overline{AB}$ and $\overline{CD}$. Then open flat.

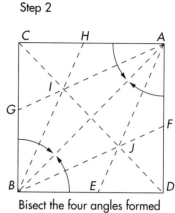

Step 2

Bisect the four angles formed by $\overline{AB}$, namely ∠CAB, ∠DAB, ∠DBA, and ∠CBA. Open flat.

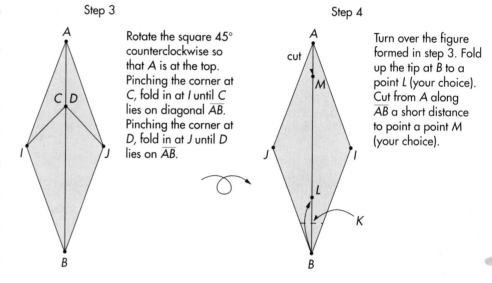

Step 3

Rotate the square 45° counterclockwise so that A is at the top. Pinching the corner at C, fold in at I until C lies on diagonal $\overline{AB}$. Pinching the corner at D, fold in at J until D lies on $\overline{AB}$.

Step 4

Turn over the figure formed in step 3. Fold up the tip at B to a point L (your choice). Cut from A along $\overline{AB}$ a short distance to point a point M (your choice).

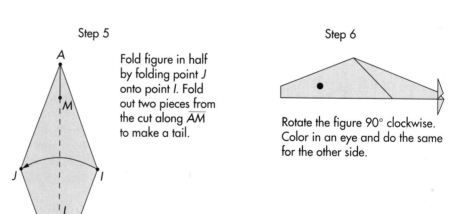

Step 5

Fold figure in half by folding point J onto point I. Fold out two pieces from the cut along $\overline{AM}$ to make a tail.

Step 6

Rotate the figure 90° clockwise. Color in an eye and do the same for the other side.

These directions are for the teacher, not the student. Once the teacher has mastered the approach, then the teacher should talk to the students and work with them to make the folds.

Fig. 5. How to fold the carp

Children should be encouraged to teach one another how to fold different forms. Students can have contests to see who can fold a form the smallest or the fastest or the best from memory. Students can also create their own forms. Successful ones should be written up in standard origami format.

SUMMING UP

Origami works quite effectively as a motivational device. I have been folding with children and adults in classes and workshops for a number of years. When someone asks, "What are we going to make today?" I produce a fan of brightly colored squares with a smile and say, "How about an owl or a snapdragon?"

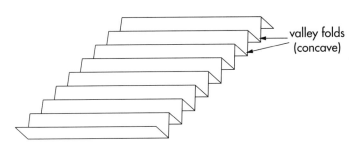

valley folds
(concave)

Example of valley folds

Bibliography

Below is a list of books on origami. All of them contain an introductory section on basic folds, origami symbols, and how to read diagrams. The clearest and most expensive book is *The World of Origami* by Isao Honda. This oversized paperback has large illustrations, attractive photographs, and figures grouped into categories according to the bases with which they begin. The other books are less expensive and have proved satisfactory in my classrooms. I have included the Sakoda book *Modern Origami f*or those who want to do more advanced folding.

Honda, Isao. *The World of Origami.* Toyko and San Francisco: Japan Publications U.S.A., 1976.

Kashara, Kunihiko. *Creative Origami.* Tokyo: Japan Publications U.S.A., 1977.

———. *Origami Made Easy.* Tokyo: Japan Publications, U.S.A., 1973.

Kawai, Toyoaki. *Colorful Origami.* New York: Barnes & Noble, 1984.

Murray, William D., and Francis J. Rigney. *Paper Folding for Beginners.* New York: Dover Publications, 1960.

Sakoda, James Minoru. *Modern Origami.* New York: Simon & Schuster, 1969. ▲

A Fifth-Grade Similarity Unit

by

Ernest Woodward

Virginia Gibbs

Michael Shoulders

Laminated strips hinged with paper fasteners serve to demonstrate the concept of similarity of triangles.

Similarity is certainly an important geometric, spatial-sense concept. Understanding similarity prepares the student for other topics in mathematics. For instance, the NCTM's (1989) *Curriculum and Evaluation Standards for School Mathematics* points out that similarity concepts can facilitate students' understanding of proportional reasoning. Also, numerous everyday applications of similarity involve such visual materials as blueprints, maps, graphs, models, and photographs. Despite the obvious importance of similarity, we have found that this topic does not receive appropriate consideration in the mathematics curriculum. Such omission is inappropriate because students will not gain the prerequisite informal geometry experiences for further study. As a result, we planned a similarity unit designed for fifth graders but probably appropriate for middle school students who have not had any significant experiences with similarity. The five-day unit was taught to a fifth-grade class at Byrns L. Darden Elementary School in Clarksville, Tennessee. A short description of the unit and a description of students' reactions to the individual lessons follow.

In preparation for the similarity unit we presented a short lesson on congruence. Students were given a handout, a blank transparency, and a transparency marking pen and asked which segments on the handout were congruent to a given segment also on the handout. They answered that question by tracing the given segment on the blank transparency and checking to see if the copy "matched" the other segments. A comparable approach was taken with angles, triangles, and quadrilaterals.

Ernest Woodward teaches mathematics and mathematics education courses at Austin Peay State University, Clarksville, TN 37044. He is particularly interested in the application of van Hiele learning levels to the teaching and learning of geometry. Virginia Gibbs is a fifth-grade teacher at Byrns L. Darden Elementary School, Clarksville, TN 37042. She is pursuing a master's degree at Austin Peay State University, where her thesis involves the application of van Hiele levels to teaching geometry. Michael Shoulders is a fifth-grade teacher at Minglewood Elementary School, Clarksville, TN 37042. He is interested in finding ways to improve elementary school mathematics instruction, particularly in geometry.

THE SIMILARITY UNIT

Lesson I

Each student was presented with cutout versions of the triangles pictured in figure 1. These cutout triangles were made from construction paper and were laminated. The students were told that the triangles were similar and that they were to try to find out what this term meant.

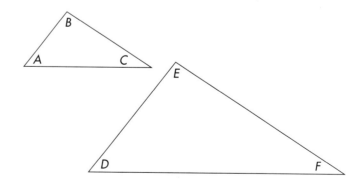

Fig. 1. Original similar triangles

Students immediately started examining and comparing the triangles. Very soon one student observed that the three angles of one triangle were congruent to the three angles of the other triangle.

Others agreed, and the teacher illustrated that property by matching up the corresponding angles. The teacher then suggested that it might be desirable to compare the sides of the two triangles. Several students mentioned that the sides of the larger triangle were twice as long as the sides of the smaller triangle. Others pointed out that the sides of the smaller triangle were half as long as the sides of the larger triangle. The teacher told them to check to see if this statement was really true. Eventually the teacher directed the students to place the small triangle on top of the large triangle so that vertex A covered vertex D. Then they were told to put on the large triangle a dot that corresponded to vertex C. Next the teacher said to "slide" the small triangle over so that vertex C covered vertex F. It was decided that this tactic clearly illustrated the twice-as-long (or half-as-long) relationship that had been suggested earlier. A comparable approach was taken with the other two sides. When this investigation was completed, each side of the large triangle was to have a dot at its midpoint. However, instead of just placing dots, a few students actually copied the entire small triangle successively (see fig. 2). One student remarked that since four copies of the small triangle covered the large triangle, the large triangle was actually four times as large as the small triangle. The teacher did not pursue this observation with the entire group.

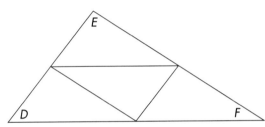

Fig. 2. A student has traced copies of the smaller triangle onto the larger triangle.

Next, each student was given laminated versions of the quadrilaterals illustrated in figure 3. They were told that the quadrilaterals were similar and were directed to compare these quadrilaterals. The students decided that the corresponding angles of the two quadrilaterals were congruent and that the corresponding sides of the smaller quadrilateral were half as long as those of the larger quadrilateral.

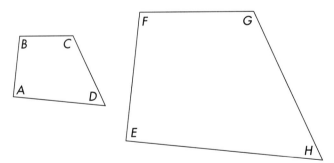

Fig. 3. The original similar quadrilaterals

Lesson 2

Lesson 2 began with a short review of what had been done in the previous lesson. Next the teacher distributed laminated versions of two triangles. One triangle was identical to the small triangle of

lesson 1, and the other triangle was similar to this small triangle. The students were told to investigate these similar triangles. They decided that again the corresponding angles were congruent and that this time each side of the small triangle was one-third as long as the corresponding side of the large triangle. They were told to place two dots on each side of the large triangle to show that a one-third relationship between corresponding sides did exist. Several students traced the entire small triangle repeatedly and decided that the small triangle was one-ninth the size of the large triangle. At this point the teacher discussed this situation with the entire class. Students were not bothered that a one-to-three ratio existed for lengths of corresponding sides and yet a one-to-nine ratio occurred between the areas of the two triangles.

Next the teacher distributed two similar quadrilaterals to each student. The smaller quadrilateral was identical to the small quadrilateral in lesson 1, and the larger quadrilateral was one in which the sides were three times as long as those of the small quadrilateral. The students investigated and made the appropriate generalizations about these similar quadrilaterals.

Then the teacher distributed laminated versions of the rectangles pictured in figure 4. The students were told that these rectangles were not similar and were asked to discover why they were not so. After a short time, a student mentioned that one of the shorter sides of the small rectangle was one-third as long as a shorter side of the large rectangle, whereas the ratio of the lengths of the longer sides was one-half.

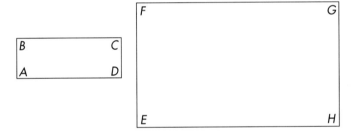

Fig. 4. Examples of nonsimilar rectangles

A lengthy discussion about similarity followed, and students decided that for figures to be similar, their corresponding sides did not have to be twice (half) as long but that the ratio of the lengths of corresponding sides had to be equal.

Next the students were presented with two worksheets and cutouts of a triangle and a quadrilateral. The first page included several pictures of quadrilaterals, and the students were asked to find which of these quadrilaterals were similar to the cutout version of the quadrilateral. The second page consisted of pictures of triangles, and the directions were to find which of the triangles were similar to the cutout version of the triangle. On both worksheets those figures that were similar to the original ones had sides in a one-to-two or one-to-three ratio. In general, the students were very successful with this activity.

Lesson 3

This lesson began with a short summary of what had happened in lesson 2. Then the teacher distributed eight paper fasteners together with eight laminated strips labeled *a, b, c, d, e, f, g,* and *h.* Each strip had a hole punched in each end. The students found that the strip labeled *a* was half as long as the strip labeled *e,* the strip labeled *b* was half as long as the strip labeled *f,* the strip labeled *c* was half as long as the strip labeled *g,* and the strip labeled *d* was half as long as the strip labeled *h.* The students were directed to use the fasteners to make one triangle with the strips labeled *a, b,* and *c* and another triangle with the strips labeled *e, f,* and *g.* Immediately several students said that the resulting triangles were similar, and the others quickly agreed. Next the teacher said to make a quadrilateral with the strips labeled *a, b, c,* and *d* and another quadrilateral with the strips labeled *e, f, g,* and *h.* We had hoped that the students would recognize that the quadrilaterals were not necessarily similar because of lack of rigidity. However, they were so fascinated with this lack of rigidity that it was difficult to get them to focus on the lack of similarity. It probably would have been better to have had them make different quadrilaterals with strips prior to the unit. (These strips can also be used in the development of other concepts.) The teacher did make the point that the two quadrilaterals were not necessarily similar.

Next the teacher distributed the large triangle and the large quadrilateral from lesson 1 and the large triangle and the large quadrilateral from lesson 2. With significant assistance from the teacher, the students decided that the two triangles were similar with a corresponding ratio of sides of two-to-three (three-to-two) and that the quadrilaterals were also similar with the corresponding ratio of sides of two-to-three (three-to-two). They were able to make this determination as a result of the dots that had been placed on the sides of these figures in lessons 2 and 3.

Lesson 4

This lesson began with a very brief review of similarity. Next the teacher reverted to dot-paper pictures of triangles given on a transparency and asked which of the pictured triangles were similar to a specific triangle. With the teacher's help, the students were able to complete this exercise. Next were drawn pictures of dot-paper segments that were twice, half, and two-thirds as long as a given dot-paper segment shown on a transparency. The directions on the next transparency were to draw a dot-paper picture of a triangle similar to a given dot-paper triangle. This task was accomplished after considerable discussion. One student asked whether two triangles of the same size (he meant congruent) would be similar. This question sparked a lengthy discussion concerning what it means for triangles to be similar, and finally it was decided that congruent triangles are actually similar. On the last transparency students were to draw a quadrilateral similar to a pictured quadrilateral; an appropriate quadrilateral was drawn.

Next the teacher distributed a worksheet that included the two problems in figure 5. Only about half the students were able to draw appropriate figures, but this was the first occasion on which they had been asked to draw dot-paper pictures.

Lesson 5

Prior to class we made copies of one page of a local elementary school yearbook. This page included rectangle-shaped pictures of

Draw a triangle that is similar to the one pictured.

Draw a rectangle that is similar to the one pictured. Each side of your rectangle should be half as long as the corresponding side of the rectangle pictured.

Fig. 5. Sample worksheet for dot-paper pictures

four different sizes. We also used the copying machine to make reduced-sized copies of this page. The sides of a smaller copy were half as long as the sides of an original copy. Each student was given one of each of these pages and asked to compare them. Several students predicted that these pages were similar, and this conjecture was verified. Almost immediately one student predicted that corresponding pictures on the two pages were similar. The teacher distributed scissors, and the students cut out pictures from the reduced copy and compared them to corresponding pictures on the full-sized copy. It was decided that indeed each picture on the reduced copy was similar to the corresponding picture on the full-sized copy and that the corresponding ratio was one-to-two (two-to-one). One student compared two of his cutouts from the reduced copy and decided (correctly) that two of the pictures were not similar.

The students were then given a handout that included the problems in figure 6. Over two-thirds of the students were able to construct the appropriate figures for the first two problems, and almost half the students drew appropriate figures for the last two problems.

Make figures similar to those pictured by using four copies of the figure.

Make figures similar to those pictured by using nine copies of the figure.

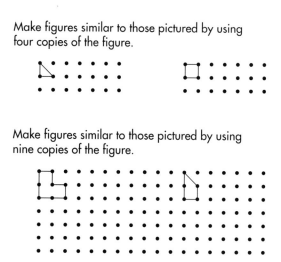

Fig. 6. Sample worksheet for enlargements

SUMMARY AND CONCLUSIONS

As mentioned earlier, in preparation for this unit a short lesson on congruence was taught. In retrospect, we think that it would have been desirable to have included in this lesson some examples wherein students were required to draw dot-paper figures congruent to given figures. This practice would have eased the transition to the situation wherein students were required to draw dot-paper figures similar to given figures. Also, prior to the unit it would have been desirable for students to have had some experiences making quadrilaterals with strips and fasteners.

In planning the unit, we decided that requiring students to use a ruler to measure the lengths of sides of similar figures would distract them from the focus of the unit. As a result, students were required to make comparisons by using the lengths of sides of initial figures as units. Also, we restricted the investigations to situations in which the ratio of similarity was one-half, one-third, and two-thirds because we believed that these fifth-grade students were very comfortable with these fractions. We tried to avoid situations involving difficult equivalent-fraction concepts, but we did include some dot-paper examples in which students needed to recognize simple equivalent fractions (4/6 = 2/3). These restrictions were probably wise choices.

We had decided to avoid any discussion of the relationship between similarity and congruence. However, as mentioned earlier, one student asked about this relationship, and the teacher felt compelled to respond. It appeared to us that most of the students were happy with the resulting discussion and explanation, which added to their understanding of similarity.

We had considered initiating the unit with cutouts of squares rather than triangles. We decided against this approach because we were afraid that the students would see that for squares, when the ratio of the lengths of sides is one-half, the ratio of the areas is one-fourth. In our naive opinion this discovery might be confusing to students. We wanted to be sure that students focused on the ratio of the lengths of sides. However, as mentioned earlier, on two separate occasions students pointed out situations in which the ratios of area and similarity were different. Eventually the teacher discussed this occurrence with the entire class, and it did not appear to confuse them. As a matter of fact, we think we could have expanded the unit to include a lesson in which the students would have generalized that if the ratio of similarity is a/b, then the ratio of area is $(a/b)^2$.

Our classroom-management approach was to distribute the cutouts or worksheets, allow the students to investigate individually, and complete the lesson with a large-group discussion of what had been learned. Occasionally, in the individual work sessions two students would compare results, and in that situation some dialogue took place between the teacher and individual students.

Concerning students' reactions to the unit, the two things that impressed us most were that—

1. the students enthusiastically attacked the investigations and

2. they made interpretations about similarity beyond our expectations of them.

This outcome illustrates the significance of approaching the teaching of elementary school mathematics topics with a sequence of lessons involving the use of concrete materials.

Bibliography

Lappan, Glenda, William Fitzgerald, Elizabeth Phillips, and Mary Jean Winter. *Similarity and Equivalent Fractions*. Middle Grades Mathematics Project. Reading, Mass.: Addison-Wesley Publishing Co., 1986.

National Council of Teachers of Mathematics. *Curriculum and Evaluation Standards for School Mathematics*. Reston, Va.: The Council, 1989. ▲

From the File: Remove a Pretzel

by

Edward Arnsdorf

Geometry

Remove a Pretzel

The following problems can be posed using toothpicks or short pretzel sticks on an overhead projector. Students copy the model and then solve the problem.

1. Start with
   (a) Remove two pretzels to get three triangles.
   (b) Remove two pretzels leaving two triangles.
   (c) Remove three pretzels leaving one triangle.
   (d) Remove three pretzels leaving two triangles.
   (e) Remove six pretzels leaving one triangle.

2. Start with
   (a) Remove two pretzels to leave three squares.
   (b) Remove two pretzels to leave two squares.
   (c) Remove one pretzel to leave three squares.
   (d) Remove four pretzels to leave one square.
   (e) Remove four pretzels to leave two squares.
   (f) Remove four pretzels to leave three squares.

Answers:

1. (a)   (b)   (c)   (d)   (e)

2. (a)   (b)   (c)   (d)   (e)   (f)

From the file of Edward Arnsdorf, California State University, Sacramento, CA 95819 ▲

An Invitation to Topology

by

Jeanlee M. Poggi

Topology—it's full of surprises! In this fascinating branch of mathematics, the inside becomes the ouside, a doughnut is equivalent to a coffe cup, and four colors are all you need to color a map.

Topology gives the classroom teacher many opportunities to foster students' higher-level thinking, as advocated by *An Agenda for Action* (NCTM 1980). Exploring patterns and relationships, defining vocabulary, developing spatial awareness, and classifying can all be brought into play. Moreover, explorations of topology encourage curiosity and flexible thinking and thus appeal to students who are not comfortable with algorithmic thinking.

The two sets of activities described in this article have been designed to stimulate thinking skills and to bring some topological fun into the mathematics curriculum. One set of activities explores Möbius strips; the other deals with tori. The activities can be presented separately or as a pair, can be scheduled consecutively or at intervals, and can be used effectively with students in the fourth through eighth grades.

Since concepts are strengthened by a variety of experiences, two or more activities should be used in each session. If your students work quickly, you may wish to incorporate additional suggestions from the lists of follow-up or alternative activities. If your group takes more time than expected, you can use the "pin down" activities in your next class meeting with them.

Additional ideas about topology can be found in the publications listed in the Bibliography.

SESSION 1: MÖBIUS STRIPS

Warm-up discussion. Tell students that this session is part of an exploration of topology—a special branch of mathematics that studies how geometric figures or surfaces can seem to be completely changed yet stay the same in some ways. Sound confusing? It is, at first, but exploring topology leads to some fascinating adventures in thinking.

Explain that the subject of this activity is Möbius strips, which were created more than 100 years ago by the mathematician August Ferdinand Möbius. Möbius was playing with objects to see what would happen when they were bent, stretched, or twisted.

He came up with a surprising discovery.

Activity 1. Each student will need scissors, two markers or crayons of contrasting colors, cellophane tape, and a strip of adding-machine tape about 2 in. wide by 2 1/2 ft. long. When these materials have been distributed, hold up a strip of adding-machine tape with the ends overlapping, so it makes a smooth circle. Ask the students what will happen if they tape the ends together and cut the strip down the middle the long way, around the circumference of the circle. (They'd have two narrower strips of tape.) Give the ends of the strip a half twist and ask, "Now what will happen if you tape the ends together and cut the strip down the middle?" (Most students will expect two tapes to result.) Next, have the students lay the strips flat and color the left and right ends (facing up) a different color. Demonstrate how to twist the strips so that the ends overlap, with the colored ends visible above and below (see fig. 1).

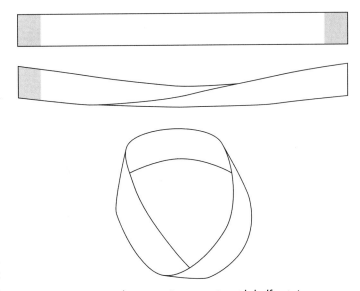

Fig. 1. Möbius strip (paper strip with half-twist)

Jeanlee Poggi teaches in the R.I.S.E. Program at C. W. Post College and is an educational consultant for the Child Development/Learning Diagnostic Program at Schneider Children's Hospital. She resides at 90 Valentine Avenue, Glen Cove, NY 11542.

The author wishes to thank Shirley Kunoff, assistant professor of mathematics at C. W. Post College, for reading this manuscript and offering valuable suggestions for its improvement.

Then have students firmly tape each strip, covering both colored bands with tape. Ask the students to draw a line from the colored band where the strips are joined, all the way around—the long way—and back to the starting point. Pique your students' curiosity by calling their attention to the fact that something odd happened. Why did the line they drew go all the way around the strip? Did they start making the line on the top of the strip? If so, where *is* the top? Where is the bottom? (A Möbius strip has no top or bottom, only one continuous surface.)

Tell your students to cut along the line they made. As they finish cutting, stimulate group discussion by asking both fact-finding and open-ended questions. What happened? Why did they end up with one long narrow strip instead of two? How did the strip of paper change when it was twisted? What didn't change? How did it change when it was cut?

Activity 2. Ask students to draw a line down the middle of the long paper strip formed from cutting the first strip in activity 1. Then have them cut along that line. Surprise! (Students will now have two narrow intertwined strips.)

Activity 3. Encourage the students to make other discoveries about the paper strips. What happens if they start with a new half-twist strip as in activity 1 but, instead of cutting the strip down the middle, cut it one-third of the way from the edge? What if they give another strip a full twist, so that one colored band shows and the other is hidden, and then cut it?

Develop a chart to organize your students' discoveries. Start with the framework shown in figure 2 and add to it as additional paper strips are completed. To keep the activity moving, accept a variety of responses. If some observations are questionable, you can discuss them when pinning down the group's findings.

Paper Strips	
Type of Strip	*Results of Different Cuts*
Half-twist	Cut down middle: one long strip
Long strip	Cut down middle: two intertwined strips
New half-twist strip	Cut one-third from edge: two intertwined strips
Full twist	Cut down middle: two intertwined strips again!

Fig. 2

Follow-up or alternative activities

- Have students make another half-twist Möbius strip. Tell them they can prove that a Möbius strip has only one surface if they try to follow these impossible directions: Color the strip, doing a section at a time and moving the strip as needed, so that the

top is one color and the bottom is another color. (It can't be done: the whole strip will be the same color.)

- Suggest that they start at the colored band joining the ends of the Möbius strip and write a "Möbius Strip Autobiography"—phrases or sentences about their past and current interests.

- How about writing the autobiography before twisting the strip? Tell students to lay the adding-machine tape flat on the desk, write on one side, turn it over, and then write on the other side. Finally, twist it into a Möbius strip and read it.

The pin-down. Review vocabulary terms such as *Möbius strip* and others that may have come up in this session, eliciting students' definitions. Discuss practical uses of the Möbius strip. For example, some fan belts used in cars and refrigerators and conveyor belts used in escalators and moving sidewalks are Möbius strips. They have only one surface so as to wear evenly. Film loops from the media center might also be Möbius strips. What would make students think so?

To complete the session, review the chart of findings and make a display of paper strips, labeling them as to how they were twisted and cut. Ask interested students to bring in a "Möbius fan belt" to show to the class or to do further research on topology and share their information with the group. Let students take home paper strips so they can show their discoveries to their families.

SESSION 2: BELIEVE IT OR NOT!— TORI AND GENUSES

Warm-up discussion. If you did the first session with your students, call their attention to the display of paper strips and tell them that today's activity will continue the exploration of topology. If you plan to do only session 2, begin with the comments about topology suggested at the beginning of session 1.

After introducing the activity, write this mathematical sentence on the board:

A doughnut is equivalent to a coffee cup.

Tell your students that to a topologist, a doughnut and a coffee cup are equivalent because one can be changed into the other without breaking. Show the class a doughnut and a coffee cup, pointing out that the hole in the coffee cup is in the handle (the cup part is an indentation, not a hole). Explain that topologists have a mathematical term for a doughnut shape: a *torus*.

Note: In planning this session, consider doing activity 4, then having small groups do alternative activities. You may wish to reserve activity 5 as a follow-up for advanced students or for groups that are especially interested in topology because it deals with a method of determining genus that is more complex than that described in activity 4.

Activity 4. Demonstrate how to make a torus by flattening clay and punching a hole in it. Give the students a rough idea of how the torus can be stretched into a coffee-cup shape by pushing the hole over to one side, pinching the rest of the clay, and gradually kneading and folding it into a cup shape. (See fig. 3.)

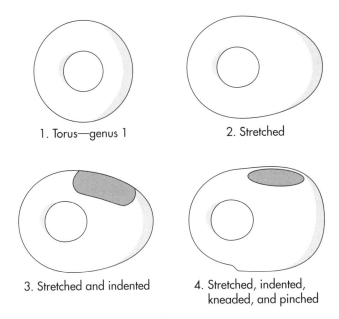

1. Torus—genus 1

2. Stretched

3. Stretched and indented

4. Stretched, indented, kneaded, and pinched

Fig. 3

Tell your students that topologists have names for various shapes that can be made from clay or other pliable materials. A shape that has no hole is called genus 0; a shape with one hole is genus 1; two holes, genus 2; and so on.

Distribute small amounts of clay to your students. Have some do the doughnut-and-coffee cup activity, but invite the others to make objects of various genuses. To get started, encourage students to generate a list of interesting objects, such as the following:

- Michael Jackson's glove
- Cookie jar
- Running shoe
- Cube, diamond, star
- Phonograph record
- T-shirt
- Floppy disk

Discussion. When students have completed making their shapes from clay, discuss the objects and classify them according to their genuses. On the preceding list, the cookie jar, cube, diamond, star, and glove are of genus 0 because they can be made from clay without having holes punched in them; the record and the floppy disk are of genus 1; other objects can be classified as "genus 2 and greater." If your students make objects that are not readily classified by this method, demonstrate the method used in activity 5 or follow up the next day, using that activity.

Activity 5. Remind your students that one way to explain the genus of a shape is to describe how many holes it has. Explain that a second method can be used to determine the genus of an object. Then write these directions on the board:

Find the largest number of successive closed-curve cuts that will leave the shape in one piece.

Next, ask a student to take a torus, draw a closed curve as shown in figure 4, and cut it. What happens? (The cut through the torus will open the surface and leave the torus in one piece. If the student makes another closed-curve cut, the torus will separate into two segments. Only one closed-curve cut can be made without breaking the torus into parts, so it is classified as a shape of genus 1.)

Now help your students draw closed curves around the objects they have made, then cut through them to test this method, and discuss their findings. For example, students may discover that any closed-curve cut through a sphere will result in two segments. Therefore, the sphere is classified as genus 0 (no cuts can be made that do not result in two separate pieces). See figure 4 for additional illustrations.

Note: be sure that students cut *around* and *through* the objects. Such items as a phonograph record or pretzel may cause some confusion unless students draw appropriate closed curves, keeping in mind that these objects should be cut torus-style. Some students will not want to cut up objects they have enjoyed making; let them work in teams with others, or have them make duplicates to cut.

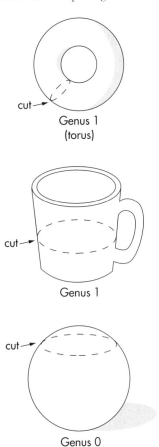

cut →

Genus 1 (torus)

cut →

Genus 1

cut →

Genus 0

Fig. 4. Second method to determine genus

Follow-up or alternative activities

- Give students pipe cleaners and have them make capital letters and numbers that are topologically equivalent. Provide a chart of letters and numbers as a starting point, demonstrating that 7 and *S* are topologically equivalent because each can be changed into the other without cutting the pipe cleaners. (Other topological equivalents include 7, *S*, 1, *L*, *M*, and 2; 8 and *B*; 0 and *D*; 6, 9, and *P*.)

- Provide bags of small objects and ask students to classify them and then mount them on posterboard according to their genuses.

- Invite students to draw creatures and objects from the imaginary planets Genus 0, Genus 1, and Genus 3. (Every being and object on the planet should be of the same genus.)

The pin-down. Write this definition of topology on the board:

Topology is a special kind of mathematics that studies the ways that surfaces can stay the same, even if they are bent, twisted, or punched into shapes that look completely different.

Then write other terms used with these activities and elicit the students' definitions (*equivalents, torus,* and *genus*). If the students also did session 1, review the term *Möbius strip* and note that it is studied in topology, though it is something that changes when it is twisted.

Survey the various topological projects your class has completed and make a display of them. Have students sign their work. Include definitions of terms in the display.

To conclude your exploration of topology, you and your students might like to have a party featuring topological snacks. Doughnuts (genus 1) and pretzels (genus 2 or greater) should, of course, be included. Before eating, ask students to classify the snacks according to their genuses.

Bibliography

Battista, Michael T. "Distortions: An Activity for Practice and Exploration." *Arithmetic Teacher* 29 (January 1982): 34–36.

Pencil-and-paper activities with distortions and geometric transformations

Bergamini, David. *Mathematics,* pp. 176–91. New York: Time-Life Books, 1963.

Elegantly illustrated article on various aspects of topology, including genuses and Möbius strips

Burns, Marilyn. *The I Hate Mathematics! Book.* Boston: Little, Brown & Co., 1975.

Ideas about topology will be found in the section entitled "A Topological Garden" and scattered throughout the book.

National Council of Teachers of Mathematics. *An Agenda for Action: Recommendations for School Mathematics of the 1980s.* Reston, Va.: The Council, 1980.

Slesnick, Twila. "Problem Solving: Some Thoughts and Activities." *Arithmetic Teacher* 31 (March 1984): 41–43.

Activities with networks

West, Beverly Henderson, et al. *The Prentice Hall Encyclopedia of Mathematics,* pp. 577–85.

The section on topology includes information about the recent solution of the four-color map problem, as well as clear explanations of other aspects of topology. ▲

Making and Exploring Tangrams

by

Andrejs Dunkels

Tangrams have been around for considerable time. Many of us have used them for activities to promote our students' sense of shapes. The most popular approach seems to be to use commercially produced cardboard or plastic tangram sets or alternatively a template from which the pupils cut out the pieces. Sometimes the pieces are numbered from 1 through 7 for reference. This article reports my experience of having pupils create their own tangrams. This activity offers pupils a rich experience in geometry and spatial sense.

I have avoided the ready-made tangram sets and have used the proper names of the figures rather than number them when talking about them. While producing the tangram pieces the pupils have taken the opportunity to discuss aspects of spatial sense: sizes, shapes, similarities, and differences. This approach focuses more on geometry than the standard approach.

Prior to the first lesson with tangrams the class would have done some paper-folding with squares and rectangles. The pupils would, therefore, have experienced the fact that a square can be folded and then cut in half in a variety of ways. They would have found that half a square plus half a square does not always make a square. They would also have tried to cut as large a square as possible from a rectangular sheet of paper. My first tangram lesson actually begins with a review of that procedure as shown in figure 1a–d.

In the past I had avoided having the pupils cut with scissors along paper folds because of the accuracy required of the tangram pieces. Now I realize that scissors are just fine for paper folds and that the imperfections are part of any practical activity.

Let's turn our attention to the square. I usually give a square to five- and six-year-olds rather than start with a rectangular sheet. We cut the square along the diagonal fold (fig. 2) and end up with two half squares. What do we call such shapes? (triangles) They can be put together in a variety of ways, producing other shapes. Do you know the names of those shapes? (See fig. 3.) ([a] parallelogram, [b] triangle, [c] no special name, [d] pentagon)

If we put one of the half-square triangles on top of the other we get a perfect covering, within the accuracy of the instruments, of course. Next we put one of the triangles to the side, fold the other in half, and cut along the fold line, as in figure 4. Doing so

produces two new pieces. What shape are they? (triangles) What can we say about their sizes? Can they be put together in ways other than along the last cut?

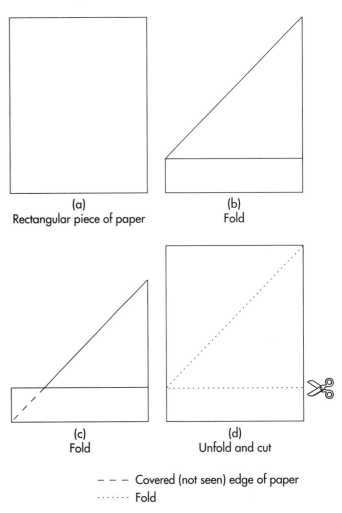

(a)
Rectangular piece of paper

(b)
Fold

(c)
Fold

(d)
Unfold and cut

– – – Covered (not seen) edge of paper
······ Fold

Fig. 1. Making a square from a rectangle

Andrejs Dunkels is an associate professor of mathematics at Lulea University, S-951 87 LULEA, Sweden. He devotes half his time to teaching engineering students and the other half to teaching prospective elementary school teachers. Concept formation has a high ranking among his interests.

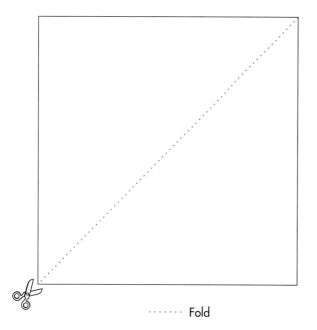

Fig. 2. The square is cut in half along the diagonal.

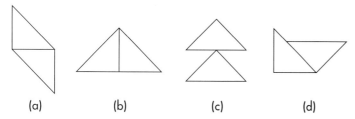

(a)   (b)   (c)   (d)

Fig. 3. Half a square plus half a square does not always make a square. (These are reduced.)

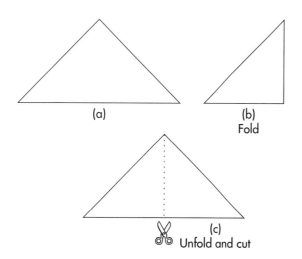

(a)   (b)
Fold

(c)
Unfold and cut

Fig. 4. The big triangle is cut into two equal triangles.

Compare our new triangles with the bigger one. We could put them together and hold them to the light. Figure 5 shows the result. In figure 5a we see that the smaller triangle is actually half the bigger. Therefore the clear strip in figure 5b must be half the bigger triangle, too. This relationship is interesting in that it defies first appearances. What about the size of the clear strip in figure 5c?

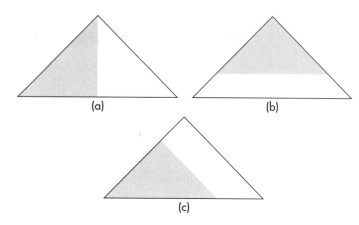

(a)   (b)

(c)

Fig. 5. The small triangle is exactly half the big triangle.

The pupils find many attributes and relationships to discover and discuss. The goal is to talk about mathematics, not just find the answer. It is a matter of exploring for the pleasure of an intellectual and aesthetic experience. Figure 6 shows one way of arranging the two smaller triangles and holding them to the light. Many pupils call this arrangement the "fox" or the "dog."

At this point we have three pieces— two smaller triangles (eventually even smaller triangles will be made) and one big triangle—all of the same shape. We put the small ones to the side and continue with the big one. The next fold needs special care. The purpose of the fold is to mark the midpoint of the longest side of the triangle, and so it is to be made in such a

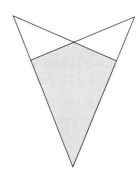

Fig. 6. The "fox" or "dog"

way that we do not get a fold through the whole triangle (see fig. 7). The midpoint is needed for the next fold. Bring the vertex opposite the midpoint to coincide with the midpoint, then fold, unfold, and cut, as shown in figure 8. The triangle we then cut off is to be compared with the other triangles in the same way as we have done before, and also with the remaining "strip," or trapezoid. During the entire folding and cutting procedure we

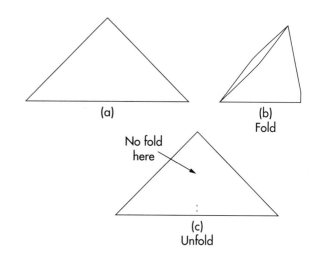

(a)   (b)
Fold

No fold
here

(c)
Unfold

Fig. 7. Fold the triangle just to mark the midpoint of the base.

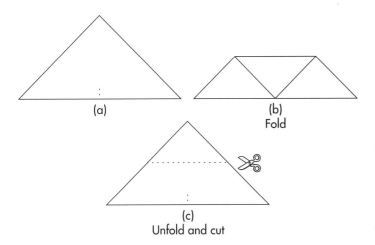

Fig. 8. The midpoint makes it possible to produce a fold parallel to the base.

use a lot of geometric terms to describe our actions and resulting shapes. No need arises for any numbering of the pieces as we produce them. It is advantageous to speak about them by either using their names or describing them.

Next we put our three triangles to the side. Note that the triangles that we formerly referred to as the "small triangles" will now be called the "big triangles." This transition happens more or less unconsciously. Continue cutting the fourth piece (the trapezoid). Bring one of the corners to the midpoint, as shown in figure 9, to produce a new triangle. More time is allotted for exploration. Since all triangles we produce are similar, we get the same patterns over and over again. They differ only in size. Encountering them is like meeting old friends.

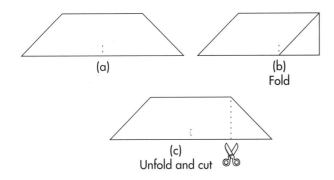

Fig. 9. A small triangle is cut off.

Next we cut off a square (see fig. 10) to compare with each of the previously produced pieces. As before, shapes, sizes, and patterns are explored and discussed. Ideas from the pupils are encouraged and tried. One fruitful investigation begins by allowing the right angle of each of the triangles to coincide with one of the right angles of the square. When we put one of the sides of the square symmetrically along the longest side of the big triangle, then the square sticks out a little. And if we do the same with the middle triangle, we see that the heights of the square and the triangle are the same. The remaining piece, which looks like a mouse, is exactly the same as the square and the smallest triangle. The square and the middle triangle are the same size.

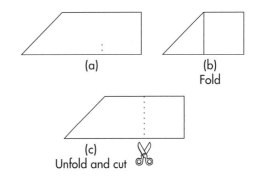

Fig. 10. This easy cut gives a square.

The last fold is the most exciting and the most difficult one. First we identify the two opposite corners indicated by arrows in figure 11. Next we grasp the trapezoid with one hand at each of these two corners. The corners are then brought together as shown in figures 11b and 11c. The result is one more triangle and a parallelogram. Once more we allow time for comparisons and explorations.

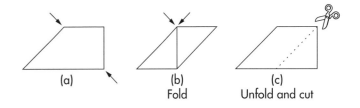

Fig. 11. Here's the hardest fold!

The cutting has come to a close, and we have our seven tangram pieces. Of course, the pupils next want to put their pieces together to make the square we began with (fig. 12). The teacher does not need to state the problem; it arises by itself quite naturally. Nobody questions the relevance of the task. Everybody is amazed, and many are amused, by the fact that it is far more difficult than expected to arrange the square. The pupils' conviction that making a square is possible is a definite advantage for the teacher.

When the square is completed, I tell the pupils the story about the Emperor Tan of China who dropped his square mirror on the

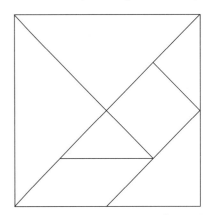

Fig. 12. The pieces arranged to form the starting square

stone floor one day 3000 years ago. The mirror broke into exactly those seven pieces that we have cut. Tan used them for entertainment, forming all kinds of pictures. Tan's rules were that all pieces must be used and that no overlapping is allowed. The pupils are given time for free play and exploration with their own tangram sets. They are not given any examples to copy or any silhouette figures to make. They get a chance to create by themselves without the limitation that examples tend to introduce. Later, much later, the teacher has opportunities to use examples, silhouettes, perhaps plastic tangram sets, and all the rest, if desired.

A big advantage of folding and cutting tangrams is that a class can produce tangram sets of different sizes. The pupils can then make pictures with tangram figures, for example, a man, a dog from a smaller set, and a bird from a still smaller set. (See fig. 13.) All these figures can then be glued onto a sheet of paper and colored with water colors. The pupils can then make their own tangram exhibition.

After using activities like those described in this article, teachers might find that the plastic tangram sets are not needed. Even books showing examples will often be superfluous; at least they need not be brought in immediately. The pupils produce enough examples themselves and can be sufficiently challenged by their classmates rather than by books or worksheets.

Bibliography

Bolster, L. Carey, and Evan M. Maletsky. "Activities: Tangram Geometry." *Mathematics Teacher* 70 (March 1977): 239–42.

———. "Activities: Tangram Mathematics." *Mathematics Teacher* 70 (February 1977): 143–45.

Dickoff, Steven S. "Paper Folding and Cutting a Set of Tangram Pieces." *Arithmetic Teacher* 18 (April 1971): 250–52.

Russell, Dorothy S., and Elaine M. Bologna. "Teaching Geometry with Tangrams." *Arithmetic Teacher* 30 (October 1982): 34–38. ▲

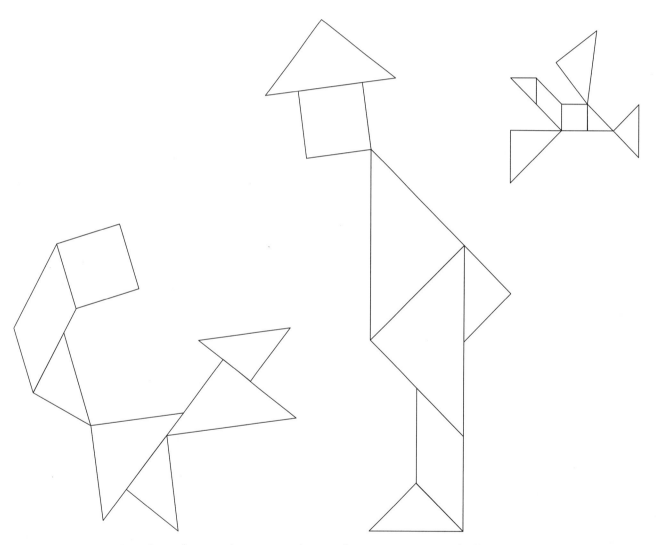

Fig. 13. Pupils can make pictures with pieces from starting squares of different sizes.

Folded Fashions: Symmetry in Clothing Design

by

Lisa J. Evered

Recent reports supported by research indicate the need to encourage girls as well as boys to continue the study of mathematics. Two reasons often given for the lack of females' interest in mathematics are its perception as a male domain and the scarcity of female role models. These influences appear to be active early in the mathematics curriculum. Despite the efforts of concerned teachers and textbook publishers, the majority of classroom applications of mathematics are oriented more toward males than females. Further, historical references to such female mathematicians as Hypatia, Kovalevsky, and Noether do little to encourage today's young women who may not wish to become mathematicians to choose vocations in which mathematics is important.

One field perceived as both a female and a male domain is fashion design. Chanel and the Fendi sisters are equally as famous as their male counterparts Dior and Cardin. Perhaps the greatest creator of the art of fashion was the French designer Madeleine Vionnet. Madame Vionnet often was referred to as the "Euclid of Fashion" (Demornex 1991). Many of her most successful designs were clearly geometric. Madame Vionnet was a feminist before anyone knew the meaning of the word. At the age of twenty she embarked on a career in fashion design and dominated haute couture until her death in 1975. She designed dresses for the most stylish women of her day, including the Duchess of Windsor and Marlene Dietrich. During her lifetime her salon on the Avenue Montaigne in Paris was the center of the fashion world.

Vionnet's gowns frequently employed patterns that exploited symmetry. Perhaps the most famous of her symmetric gowns was cut from a circular piece of silk folded twice to form a quarter sector, as illustrated in figure 1a. The two folds, or axes of symmetry, are indicated by segments *A* and *C*. This sector is then cut in the shape of a capital *M* as in figure 1b. When unfolded about axis *A*, the shape looks like that illustrated in figure 1c. When the silk is folded along axes *B* and *B'*, the result is the A-line gown illustrated in figure 1d. Because the silk has been cut on the bias—that is, diagonally to the threads of the fabric—the gown falls elegantly from the the shoulders and may be worn either without or with a belt, as illustrated in figure 1e. Gowns and coats of this unique symmetric style were copied by fashion houses throughout the world. Popular film stars, such as Audrey Hepburn, Doris Day, and Grace Kelly, were often pictured in Vionnet-inspired symmetric gowns.

(a) A gown cut from a circular piece of silk folded twice

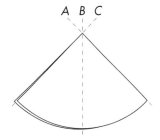

(b) Cuts made from the shape in (a)

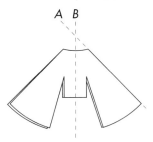

(c) Unfolding the shape in (b)

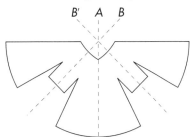

(d) Folding (c) along B and B'

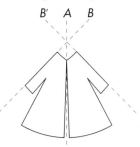

(e) The finished gown

Fig. 1

Your students can make a miniature gown of the Vionnet type using a paper napkin instead of fabric. Fold the napkin twice to make a square and then trim the napkin to form the quarter sector. Follow the steps in figures 1a, b, c, d, and e to create a paper Vionnet-typed A-line gown.

Lisa Evered teaches at Iona College, New Rochelle, NY 10801. With special interests in probability, statistics, and international mathematics education, she has served as a consultant to countries in Europe, Africa, and Latin America.

Other designs using symmetry much in the way Vionnet did are possible. Your students may enjoy attempting to create their own new designs. Vionnet experimented with her gowns by using small silk squares and miniature wooden mannequins. Paper napkins and male or female fashion dolls can serve the student designer equally well. Alternatively, students could make life-sized patterns from newspaper or cloth. You can demonstrate how to construct slacks and a loose-fitting shirt by using Vionnet's symmetric principles, always ensuring that when the napkin is folded and the cuts are made, the paper pattern remains in one piece. Seams can be simulated with staples or glue. Follow the steps in figures 2a, b, and c to create symmetric Vionnet-typed slacks and a shirt. Be sure to call your students' attention to each axis of symmetry. Ask how they can alter the pattern to reduce the number of seams required.

figures 3a, b, c, and d. Notice that the napkin and hence the material remain in one piece after cutting and that unfolding and folding always occur along axes of symmetry. Teachers can extend the activity by asking students to experiment with other ways of folding and cutting the napkin to obtain the same gown.

Use a fashion bulletin board to illustrate symmetry and asymmetry.

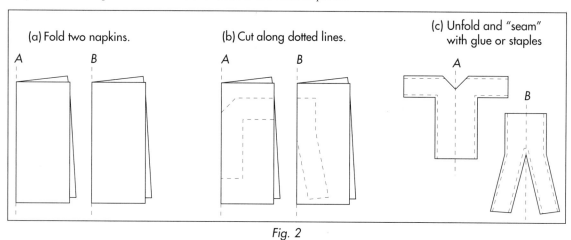

(a) Fold two napkins.   (b) Cut along dotted lines.   (c) Unfold and "seam" with glue or staples

Fig. 2

Students can create their own designs.

Once your students master the techniques of symmetric design à la Vionnet, the possibilities for exploration are endless. One project could be to collect illustrations of symmetric and asymmetric fashions for bulletin-board display. Encourage students to explore symmetry and asymmetry in this unusual way. In each design ask the student designer to identify any axes of symmetry and to explain how symmetry played a role in this creation. Perhaps one of your students may find that her or his creative abilities and mathematical knowledge will lead to a career in fashion design as distinguished as that of Madame Madeleine Vionnet, "the Euclid of Haute Couture."

A more challenging design requires a double fold that is then unfolded and refolded in a different way to create a dress with mantle sleeves. To recreate this Vionnet design, follow the sequence in

Reference

Demornex, Jacqueline. *Madeleine Vionnet*. New York: Rizzoli International Publications, 1991. ▲

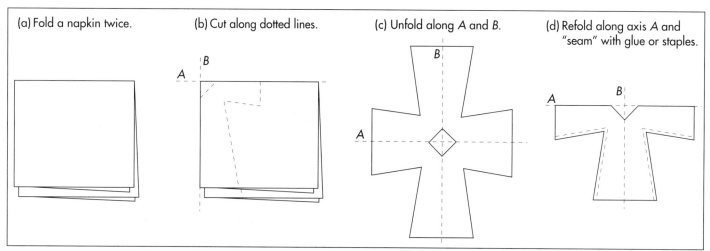

(a) Fold a napkin twice.   (b) Cut along dotted lines.   (c) Unfold along A and B.   (d) Refold along axis A and "seam" with glue or staples.

Fig. 3

Investigating Flags: A Multicultural Approach

by

Linda Dolinko

As potential designers, students see a flag and its stars from a new angle.

Hispanic Heritage month was approaching. I wanted to come up with a new and exciting activity for my fifth-grade class. An article in the newspaper discussing the impending statehood vote in Puerto Rico grabbed my attention. I immediately wondered about our present American flag. How could it be modified to accommodate a fifty-first star? What a great mathematical problem for my class! In this article, I describe how that idea led to a series of activities that involved my fifth-grade class in a meaningful and exciting multicultural and multidisciplinary investigation that incorporated a lot of mathematical thinking. To me, the activities that evolved reflect the rich connections inherent in the vision of the *Curriculum and Evaluation Standards for School Mathematics* (NCTM 1989).

The activity fostered a rich mathematical language.

Before presenting the problem, we had an extensive discussion about the varieties and uses of flags and what they symbolize. I distributed a copy of International Signal Flags (Silverman 1989) (see fig. 1). We examined the various designs of the flags and the deliberate way in which they are divided into regions. Similarities among the flags became obvious, and children noticed patterns in the arrangements of the colors within each individual flag. Geometric shapes were identified, and their sizes were compared. Rich mathematical language emerged throughout our investigation as we discussed the fractional parts that were formed. For example, the top piece (1/2) in flag E is equal to the two top pieces (1/4 + 1/4) in flag U and is also equal to the eight pieces on the upper two rows (1/16 + 1/16 + 1/16 + 1/16 + 1/16 + 1/16 + 1/16 + 1/16) in flag N. We made many such equivalent-fraction discoveries by using other denominators.

The students made predictions and were able to verify them. For example, they thought that the area of the center square of flag P was 1/9 the total area of the flag. To verify this idea, some students extended the lines to form nine squares and concluded that the center square number 1 was indeed 1/9 of the total flag. Others, however, needed more proof. These students cut out the square and traced it over the entire flag. They were able to see that nine of those squares covered the flag, and they, too, agreed that square 1 was 1/9 of the flag.

Next, we analyzed the American flag by studying its canton, the left-hand corner's blue field that is studded with stars; the space between the stars; and the width of the stripes. Observations were made, including the pattern of the stars (6, 5, 6, 5, 6, 5, 6, 5, 6), the thirteen stripes of equal width symbolizing the original colonies (the children thought that all stripes were equal so that no one state would seem more important than the others), and the shape of the canton as compared with the size and shape of the entire flag. (See fig. 2.)

Linda Dolinko teaches fifth grade at M. S. 181, Bronx, NY 10475. She believes that investigation and discovery empower students to become confident learners, with the ability to think and express themselves mathematically.

International Signal Flags

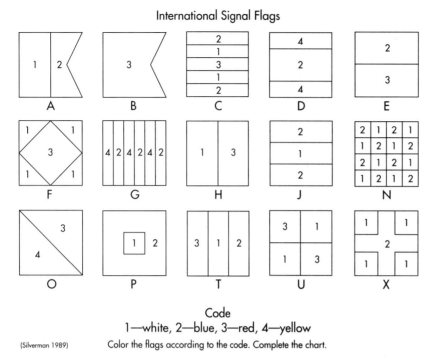

Code
1—white, 2—blue, 3—red, 4—yellow

(Silverman 1989) Color the flags according to the code. Complete the chart.

Fig. 1. Students realized the numerous areas of mathematics involved in flag design.

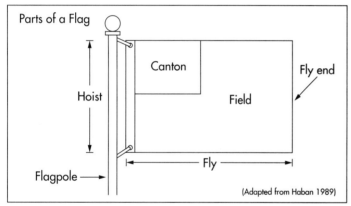

Fig. 2. This illustration helped students explore the relative sizes of the canton and the field. They then could apply this knowledge to their own designs.

We compared the flags of the United States and Puerto Rico by listing their characteristics. The list grew, and I introduced the Venn diagram as a way to organize the listed information to simplify understanding (fig. 3). The students had never heard of a Venn diagram. Using the lists and the Venn diagram to generate the elements in the union and intersection reinforced the similarities and differences clearly. Students could see the relationships almost instantly.

Students used Venn diagrams to see relationships.

On subsequent days, we talked about the Puerto Rican vote and explored the differences between a state and a commonwealth. The students shared their opinions and backed them up with facts. They cited the positives and negatives for each option—including independence—that would appear on the ballot.

The class was motivated to learn more about flags, so I extended the analysis to include the flags of the Hispanic countries. I compiled a booklet containing pictures of twenty flags and the stories behind the flags' creation (Devereaux 1992).

In groups of two, the children picked out of a hat slips of paper naming two countries. I had paired countries in such a way that similarities as well as differences could be noted between the countries' flags. Each group's task was to list the applicable characteristics, from which we created a class chart of the twenty flags and their various attributes. Stars marked the presence of these characteristics (fig. 4).

Comparison between Flags

United States	Puerto Rico
50 stars	One star
Stripes	Stripes
Rectangular canton	Triangular canton
Blue canton	Blue canton
Small stars	Large star
Colors are red, white, and blue.	Colors are red, white, and blue.

Venn Diagram Comparing United States and Puerto Rican Flags

50 stars — Stripes — One star

Rectangular canton — Colors are red, white, and blue. — Triangular canton

Small stars — Blue canton — Large star

Fig. 3. This Venn diagram introduced rich mathematical language and immediate observations.

	Without cantons	Stars	Cantons	Thin stripes	Thirds	Fourths	Red/white/blue	2 colors
1. Argentina	★				★		★	
2. Bolivia					★			
3. Chile		★	★			★		
4. Columbia				★		★		
5. Costa Rica				★		★		
6. Cuba		★	★	★				
7. Dominican Republic						★	★	
8. Equador								
9. El Salvador	★				★		★	
10. Guatemala					★		★	
11. Honduras			★		★		★	
12. Mexico		★			★			
13. Nicaragua		★			★		★	
14. Panama			★			★		
15. Paraguay		★			★		★	★
16. Peru					★		★	
17. Puerto Rico		★	★	★		★		
18. Spain				★			★	
19. Uruguay				★	★		★	
20. Venezuela		★	★		★			

Fig. 4. Class chart showing the characteristics of flags of Hispanic countries

We then transferred the data to a Venn diagram. Transferring the information from the chart was simple, and the Venn diagrams made the data more visual in nature. When we met to share information, I asked the class to describe the circles in the Venn diagrams. When one girl said, "The section in the middle is a part of both circles," I introduced intersection and union. We discussed the meaning of intersection and gave examples, including the intersection of two streets and of parallels of latitude and meridians of longitude. Students realized that an intersection was vital when describing map locations. Simply using either the latitude or longitude would not pinpoint a single location, nor would naming only one street in an intersection. However, identifying the intersection narrows many choices down to one. The class was then able to understand that in the current context, intersection meant "a part of both," a common thread. The location of the intersection is on both of the individual lines.

A flag center was needed to display our findings. We included the chart, Venn diagrams, and books and encyclopedias showing the flags and explaining the related stories. I also brought in miniflags for display, which stimulated a discussion on materials used to produce flags. Flags seemed to be everywhere and flowing into every curriculum area.

At this point, I brought up the challenge and related class project. Working under the assumption that Puerto Rico voted for statehood, the American flag would have to be altered to accommodate fifty-one stars. The students were to work either alone or with one other person to create a new American flag. The children were asked to be creative but had certain restrictions: all

flags must have thirteen stripes and fifty-one stars; and only the colors red, white, and blue could be used. The children were encouraged to use their imaginations but were to remember that a flag is a very important symbol. American citizens should be proud to wave this new flag.

To begin the project, we discussed the history of the United States flag, examining the first flag with its thirteen stripes and thirteen stars. An important history lesson evolved from learning about the events leading to its creation, including how Betsy Ross was chosen to sew the pieces of the flag. We talked about the colors of the flag and their significance: red for blood, white for purity, and blue for honor. Most important from a mathematical point of view, we examined the arrangement of the stars on the present flag.

We also discussed the fact that the number 51 is not prime; it is a composite number with factors of 1, 3, 17, and 51. Some obvious arrangements, for example, 3 rows of 17 stars or 17 rows of 3 stars, evolved from this discussion.

The next day the students chose a partner and began work. During the following week I met with each pair, examining the pair's sketches and making certain that they were able to explain each part of the flag, what it symbolized, and their reasons for its inclusion. The fifty-one stars were arranged on their cantons in a variety of ways, some incredibly creative, some just rearranged. (See fig. 5.)

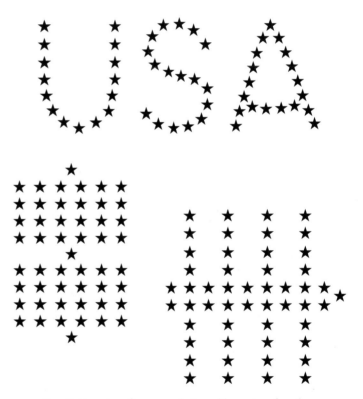

Fig. 5. Samples of cantons designed by pairs of students

Before the groups began to sketch, we reviewed the fact that the stars were not randomly placed on the canton. Each was equidistant from another in all directions. The students realized that they needed to design a specific arrangement and then work out the pattern. A great deal of trial and error was involved, but they finally seemed ready to turn their sketches into flags.

The transfer of the sketches onto 8 1/2-by-14-inch paper proved to be the most difficult part of the project but was a wonderful mathematical hands-on task.

Each flag had thirteen horizontal stripes, so we discussed how to figure out the width of each stripe. To divide the paper into thirteen stripes of equal width met with absolute failure, so we decided to estimate. I asked, "If the paper measures 8 1/2 inches and we need to make thirteen equal stripes, *about* how wide will each one be? More than one inch? Less than one inch? Give me reasons." The majority knew that the stripe had to be less than 1 inch wide, but just how much less was more difficult. "Will it be more than 1/2 inch?" I asked. One student reasoned that if each one was exactly 1/2 inch, then two stripes would equal 1 inch and counting by twos to twelve would total six. He needed to add 1/2 inch for the odd thirteenth stripe, so he ended up with 6 1/2 inches. Since we had 8 1/2 inches available for use, each had to be a little wider than 1/2 inch. The students knew that 3/4 inch was too wide because, as one girl explained, "3/4 × 13 = 39/4 = 9 3/4 inches, and we only have 8 1/2 inches."

By working with our calculators and rulers, we agreed to see how many inches we would have if each stripe was 10/16 inch wide. We punched 10/16 into the calculator as 10 divided by 16, multiplied by 13, then rounded the product to the nearest tenth, 8.1. We did the same for 11/16 and rounded to 8.9. The class decided that because 8 1/2, or 8.5, was exactly midway between the two, they would use 10/16 and, if necessary, trim down the bottom stripe. The class's motivation and enthusiasm enabled us to complete these complicated calculations.

The cantons on the original sketches varied in size and shape, so that after the stripes were finally penciled in, the students tested different sizes until they were happy with the look.

Positioning the stars proved to be an easier task. The students used stick-on stars and adjusted the distance between them by measuring with rulers.

I learned that the schoolwide Hispanic Heritage program would include a ceremony during which select fifth graders would march into the auditorium carrying twenty flags, each representing a country with Hispanic roots and language. When I mentioned my idea about creating a new American flag, my colleagues insisted that it should be incorporated into the program. After a lengthy discussion, we decided that my students would select four flags out of the class and those four would become finalists. We would create a class ballot, have each class vote, and announce the results at the assembly. The four finalists would recreate their masterpieces on fabric and march in the parade of flags.

When the flags were finished, they were displayed, and each student voted by secret ballot for two flags. I used the honor system and hoped that only one vote out of the two votes per child would be for his or her own flag.

After a lesson on tallying, one student recorded the votes on the chalkboard while another read the ballots. We declared the four winners and analyzed the vote. Thirty students were present that day, resulting in sixty votes. We discussed the fractional part of the whole vote that each flag received, for example, 15/60; then reviewed proper and improper fractions, reducing to lowest terms, equivalence, and comparing fractions.

I prepared a ballot so that students could vote for the flag of their choice. Along with a class ballot, each teacher received a letter explaining the voting process. The four flags were displayed outside our classroom, and teachers brought their classes to view them before the vote. (See fig. 6.) The entire school was involved, grades 5–8, and my fifth graders felt very special!

Fig. 6. Students display the four flags that were on the school-wide ballot.

During the week that the school was voting, the eight student winners from the four classes were busily working on their flags. They were transferring their "creations" onto pillowcases cut in half, which involved more estimating and measuring, but this time the process went more smoothly. When widths of stripes and sizes of cantons were agreed on, the designs were penciled onto the fabric. Permanent red and blue markers were used to color the flags. The colors ran through the fabric to the back, making the flag look factory made. We used yardsticks for the flagpoles. When viewing these flags, one would never know they were homemade!

By the time that we heard that Puerto Rican voters chose to remain in a commonwealth, we were too involved in our project for the news to dampen our spirits.

Election day arrived and the votes were counted The students carried their original flags in the parade of flags, following those of the Hispanic nations. The winner was the flag with the large star surrounded by clusters of small stars. The children were *all* thrilled, especially the flag finalists.

The theme extended far beyond the topic of flags. Several students brought in coins and stamps used in the Hispanic countries. Then we studied the United States, and state-flag explorations began immediately.

CONCLUDING COMMENTS

The extensions for this activity are numerous. Discussions on bilateral symmetry—vertical, horizontal, or diagonal—as well as rotational symmetry—as in flags F and X in figure 1—immediately come to mind. An investigation could also be conducted on possible arrangements and patterns of the stars with forty-eight states as well as fifty states.

Connections are still being made, and new ideas are emerging. A simple theme led to a wonderful variety of mathematical and nonmathematical topics. Interest, motivation, and hands-on activities spurred wonderful learning.

This experience supports whole-language and interdisciplinary learning. Through investigating and creating flags with a purpose, learning emerged that related to many areas of the mathematics curriculum. As the students explored patterns and relationships, they were involved in activities that related to geometry and spatial sense, linear and area measurement, fractions, and basic arithmetic operations. Venn diagrams became a powerful tool for communicating the similarities and differences they observed. As I reflected on this experience, I recognized that although this unit was planned initially for a social studies class, it became an effective way to teach important mathematical concepts in a meaningful context rather than in isolation.

References

Devereaux, Eve. *Flags of the World.* New York/New Jersey: Crescent Books, Publisher, 1992.

Haban, Rita D. *How Proudly They Wave: Flags of the United States.* Minneapolis, Minn.: Lerner Publications, 1989.

National Council of Teachers of Mathematics. *Curriculum and Evaluation Standards for School Mathematics.* Reston, Va.: The Council, 1989.

Silverman, Helene. "Ideas." *Arithmetic Teacher* 37 (November 1989): 26–30. ▲

Cross Sections of Clay Solids

by

William M. Carroll

This geometry exercise for intermediate and junior high school students has three goals for students: (1) to create three-dimensional clay figures; (2) to think in three dimensions; and (3) to develop vocabulary. Working individually from pictures, students first construct geometric solids out of clay. Second, they attempt to visualize what happens when a solid is sliced at a particular location and angle. The type of solid and how it is sliced will determine the plane figure that will result—trapezoid, ellipse, and so on (see fig. 1). Third, students develop a geometry vocabulary by naming the solids they construct. For example, a cube is identified as a hexahedron; a doughnut is a torus. More important, students are asked to name or describe the cross section formed. Since they are not given the correct vocabulary, they must seek it out or develop it on their own. They will find that the terms *rectangle* and *square* are not adequate to name all four-sided polygons.

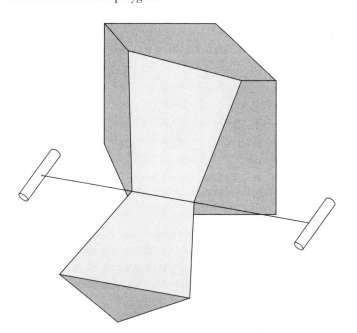

Fig. 1. The cube is sliced to produce a trapezoidal cross section.

William Carroll is a teacher of mathematics at Roosevelt High School in Chicago, IL 60657. He has previously taught at preschool and elementary school levels.

In addition to these three objectives, students are given experience in forming hypotheses and then testing the correctness of their ideas. They try to predict the plane figure that would be formed by sectioning a solid; then they test their predictions by slicing the solid and recording their hypotheses and conclusions in a table (see sheet 1).

MATERIALS

The only materials needed for the activity are some modeling clay, a tool for slicing the plane sections, and worksheets for students. Having tables or desks where the students can work individually would also help. Use an oil-based clay, like the colored clay sold at toy stores; water-based clay will dry out quickly if not stored correctly. For slicing the cross section, a clay slicer, sometimes called a piano wire, can be found at art supply stores for about a dollar. Otherwise, construct your own clay slicer by attaching a wire between two strips of wood or dowels (see fig. 1). Other cutting tools, like knives, tend to distort the shape of the clay as they move through it. When slicing the clay, hold the wire taut and pull it slowly and smoothly through the clay. Sheets 1, 2, and 3 present some sample activity worksheets.

INTRODUCING CROSS SECTIONS

Use the idea of cutting fruits and vegetables to introduce the concept of cross sections to students. Most students can visualize at least some of these cross sections. Imagine cutting a carrot. If the slice is straight down through the carrot widthwise, the cross section revealed is a circle, assuming it is a perfect carrot, not a lopsided one. If the cut is made on a slant instead of straight, the cross section will be a flattened circle—an ellipse. The more slanted the slice, the flatter the ellipse. If a carrot is cut lengthwise from tip to tip, the cross section will look something like a thin isosceles triangle with a semicircle at the base. Now imagine slicing an orange. The cross section will always be a circle, although the size of the circle will vary, depending on where the cut is made.

PREDICTING THE RESULTS

Next use the introductory worksheet (sheet 1) on an overhead projector or on the chalkboard. The figure at the top of sheet 1

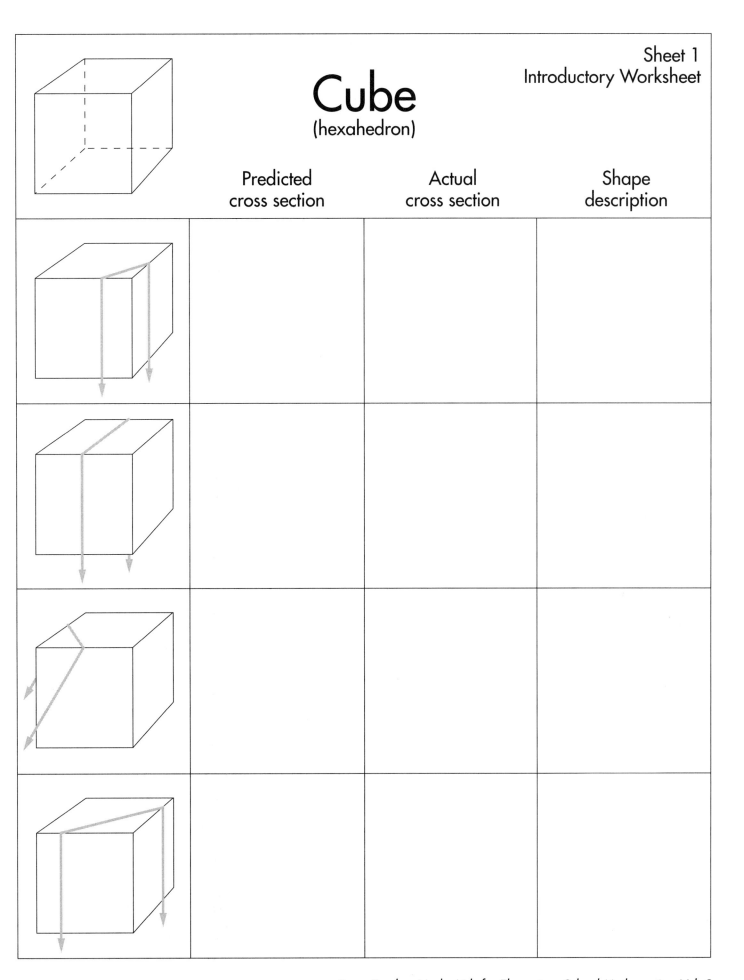

Cube
(hexahedron)

	Predicted cross section	Actual cross section	Shape description

Cylinder

	Predicted cross section	Actual cross section	Shape description

Cone

	Predicted cross section	Actual cross section	Shape description

Pyramid (with square base)   Torus (doughnut)   Triangular prism

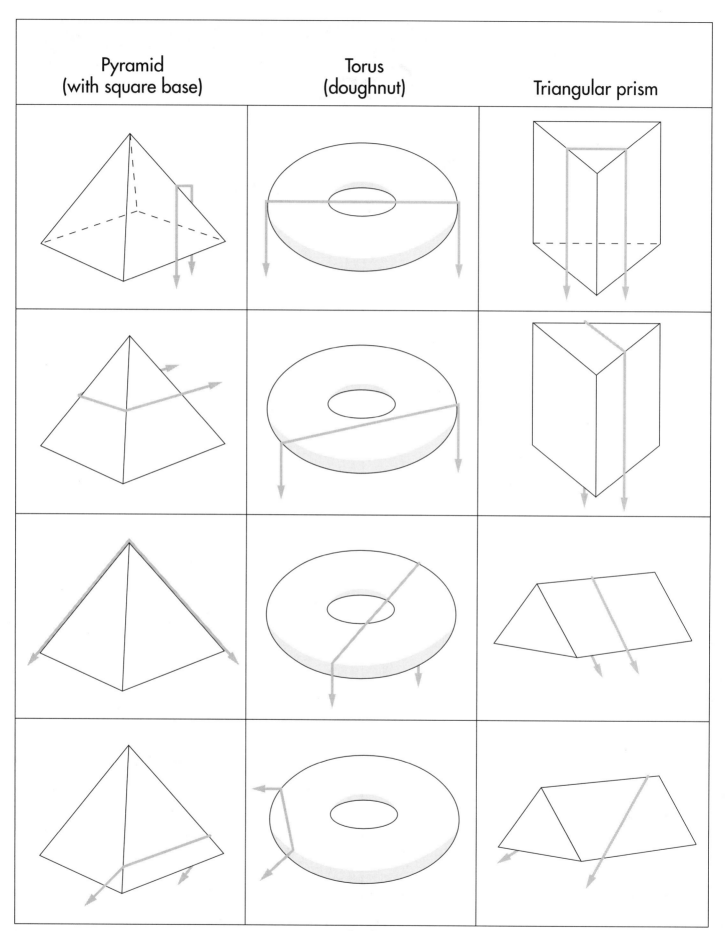

Fig. 2

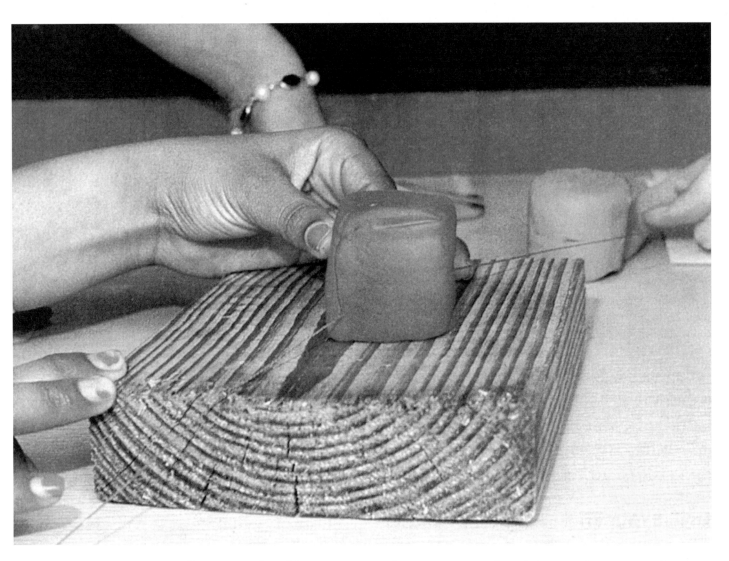

shows the solid that students will construct; dotted lines represent the hidden edges on the opposite side of the solid. The first column below the figure shows the solid again, with arrows indicating the direction and angle of the section. In the second column, the students make a drawing representing their predictions of the cross section. After the slicing, the actual cross section is drawn in the third column. In the last column, students write the name or description of the shape.

SLICING THE SOLIDS

Form a cube of clay large enough so that students can see it and you can work with it comfortably. Demonstrate how to do one or two of the cross sections, showing students how to read the diagram and how to cut through the figure evenly; follow the direction of the cut on the worksheet. Point out that for the predicted cross section, they should draw only the two-dimensional shape revealed by the cut, not the solid remaining behind it.

Let the students decide what the first cross section will be. Then make the cut and have them determine how the shape compares with their predictions. In the third column, name the cross section. They should have no trouble naming the first cross section

on sheet 1 as a rectangle and the second as a square. Let some of the students make the slices for the third and fourth examples. A little practice may be required to make a reasonably straight slice through clay. If the clay solid is put on a block of wood or some similar platform, making a clean cut will be easier.

By the time the four examples on sheet 1 are completed, students will probably be ready to try some cross sections on their own. If not, do another worksheet together. Sheets 2 and 3 are designed for students' use. Figure 2 illustrates a few more ideas from which more worksheets can be developed.

Students can work on this activity independently or in pairs. Working together, with one student holding the solid and another slicing it, facilitates the process and improves the results. Making an accurate conic section alone (sheet 3) can be a little awkward. Don't expect all students to come up with the correct answers, even after sectioning the solids. The degree of accuracy in visualizing the cross section, in forming and slicing the clay solid, and in naming the plane figure formed will depend on the students' abilities and interests. It is hoped that all students will improve their skills and gain new insights into geometry after doing these exercises. ▲

Symmetry the Trademark Way

by

Barbara S. Renshaw

Trademark 1:
Westinghouse Electric Corporation

Trademark 2:
Ralston Purina Company

Pepsi-Cola, Shell Oil, Chevrolet, Mattel, Westinghouse. What possible link could exist between these companies and the teaching of mathematics in the classroom? Interestingly enough, the trademark designs of these and other companies can provide a familiar yet innovative way for students to look at a number of mathematical concepts. These concepts include symmetry, mathematical curves, geometric shapes, similarity, angles, graphic representation of numerals, reflections, and translations. Though all these topics lend themselves to further analysis and interpretation, this discussion is limited to how two common types of symmetry— line and rotational—can be taught using some familiar trademarks. In particular, the article focuses on how trademarks and symmetry can be presented through the bulletin board.

Trademark 3:
Caterpillar Tractor Company

Trademark 4:
General Electric Company

Fig. 1. Some trademarks have line symmetry and others do not.

LINE SYMMETRY

Before students can examine the symmetrical properties of trademarks, they must clearly understand line and rotational symmetry. A figure with line symmetry can be thought of as having its own flip image about a certain line of symmetry. In such a figure, each point on one side of the line of symmetry corresponds to a point on the other side with both being the same distance from a given point of the line. Figure 1 shows that some figures have many lines of symmetry and others have none.

Some practical activities in tracing and folding, or with a Mira, can help reinforce this idea. To show by tracing that a figure has line symmetry, students can trace the figure onto a piece of tracing paper or clear plastic and then flip the tracing about the line of symmetry (fig. 2). If the tracing fits the original figure after being flipped, the figure has line symmetry. Folding (fig. 3) and Mira activities are two further methods for testing a figure for line symmetry. To test a figure by using the folding method, students can trace the figure and then experiment to see if the figure can be folded so that the two halves match exactly. If such a folding line can be found, then the figure has line symmetry and the fold is the line of symmetry. To test with a Mira (or a piece of

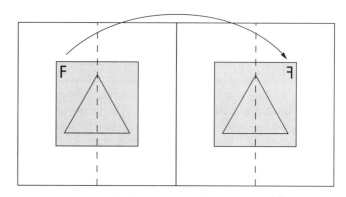

Fig. 2. Testing for line symmetry by tracing and flipping

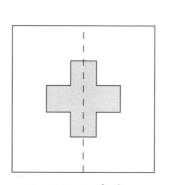
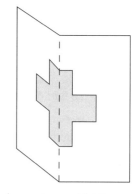

Fig. 3. Testing for line symmetry by tracing and folding

Barbara Renshaw teaches mathematics at Bedford Junior High School, Bedford, TX 76021. She seeks to make mathematics an enjoyable experience rather than a dreaded one for students at the junior high and middle school levels.

Plexiglas), students can position the Mira on the figure so that half the figure combined with its reflection in the Mira form the entire figure (fig. 4). Used together, the Mira and the folding methods can provide a check for one another.

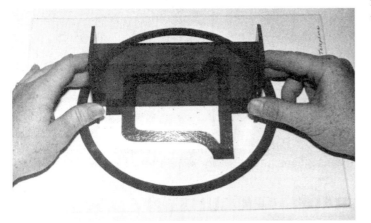

Fig. 4. Testing for line symmetry with a Mira

ROTATIONAL SYMMETRY

It is also important for students to have a clear understanding of rotational symmetry. A figure with rotational symmetry matches itself exactly when rotated or turned less than a full turn. A square is one example of such a figure. Figure 5 demonstrates how a square will match itself after a quarter turn (90°), a two-quarter turn (180°), and a three-quarter turn (270°). The angles given describe the angles of rotation for the square. It should be noted that since the tracing of any figure exactly matches the original figure after a complete rotation, full turns (360°) are not considered when speaking of rotational symmetry.

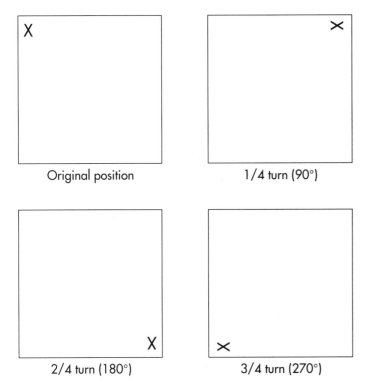

Original position   1/4 turn (90°)

2/4 turn (180°)   3/4 turn (270°)

Fig. 5. An example of rotational symmetry

Students can participate in hands-on experiences with rotational symmetry by tracing a figure with rotational symmetry as they did when testing figures for line symmetry. The tracing can then be placed directly on the original figure, and while one point (the figure's center of rotation) is held fixed, the tracing can be turned until it exactly fits the original (fig. 6).

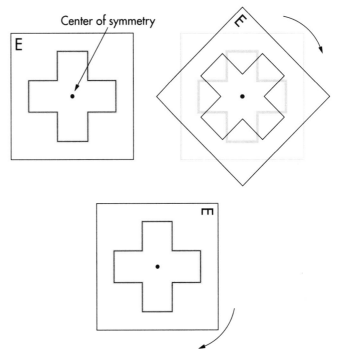

Center of symmetry

Fig. 6. Testing for rotational symmetry by tracing and turning

Point symmetry. Point symmetry is a special type of rotational symmetry—symmetry under a half-turn. A figure has point symmetry when the tracing of a figure exactly matches the original after a half-turn (180°) about the center of rotation. Many figures with rotational symmetry also have point symmetry.

SYMMETRY IN TRADEMARKS

After students have gained a clear understanding of line and rotational symmetry and have had some practical experiences working with these ideas, they can begin to consider the symmetrical properties of trademarks. Some of the trademarks mentioned earlier will be examined here. As an example, the trademark of the Shell Oil Company is one that displays line symmetry. This figure can be traced and folded in such a way that the two figures match exactly. The resulting fold corresponds to the line of symmetry depicted by the broken line in figure 7. Each point on the left side of the line of symmetry corresponds to a point on the right side that is the same distance from a given point of the line (e.g., A corresponds to A', B corresponds to B'). When the same tracing is rotated on top of the original figure, it does not exactly match the original figure at any point. Therefore, the figure does not have rotational symmetry.

When the trademark of the Chrysler Corporation is traced and folded, five fold lines are found such that the two figures fit exactly one on another. In other words, the trademark has five lines of

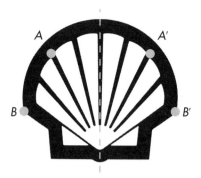

Fig. 7. Line symmetry but not rotational symmetry in the Shell trademark

symmetry. These are indicated by the broken lines in figure 8. When this figure is tested for rotational symmetry, four turns are found that will rotate the tracing back onto the original figure. These occur every one-fifth turn or, stated as angles of rotation, every 72 degrees.

The Chevrolet trademark (fig. 9) has point symmetry, a special type of rotational symmetry mentioned earlier. Though no line of symmetry can be found through the trace-and-fold method, the tracing exactly matches the original figure when it is turned a half-turn (180°). The figure therefore has point symmetry.

Thus far, trademarks with line, rotational, and point symmetry have been discussed and illustrated. One question that might be posed at this point is, Can *one* trademark have *all three* types of symmetry? Mattel's trademark, pictured in figure 10, can be examined to answer this question. By tracing this figure and testing it for line symmetry by the folding method, we can find

numerous lines of symmetry. By rotating the tracing, students can also discover numerous angles of rotation, one of these being through a half-turn (180°). This procedure confirms the existence of both point and rotational symmetry. Therefore, it is possible for a trademark to have all three types of symmetry—line, rotational, and point.

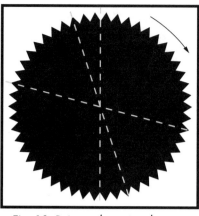

Fig. 10. Point and rotational symmetry with the Mattel trademark

TRADEMARK BULLETIN BOARD

Now that we see how symmetry can be taught and how symmetry is exhibited in some common trademarks, how can we help students become interested in looking at trademarks in terms of their symmetry? One way is through an active-involvement bulletin board.

To make the bulletin board, it is first necessary to select a variety of trademarks, preferably ones with which the students are familiar. The trademarks should demonstrate line, rotational, or point symmetry as well as combinations of these; some nonexamples might also be included. Magazines, newspapers, and especially the Yellow Pages are good places to search for trademarks. Some common symmetrical ones are shown in figure 11.

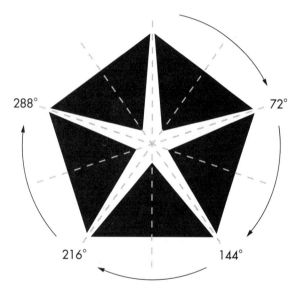

Fig. 8. Rotational symmetry with the Chrysler Corporation trademark

Fig. 11. Some trademarks for your bulletin board

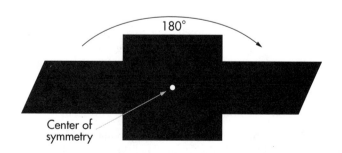

Fig. 9. Point symmetry with the Chevrolet trademark

After selecting the trademarks, you will need to draw or have them drawn on heavy paper and colored to resemble authentic ones. Figure 12 shows how the bulletin board might look.

It is highly recommended that packets of materials also be included to get the students actively involved with the symmetry

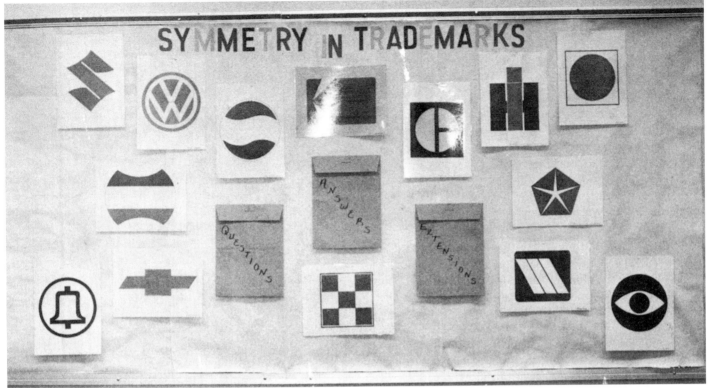

Fig. 12. A bulletin board with questions

of trademarks. One way to do this is to attach three envelopes to the bulletin board—the first containing sheets of questions about the trademarks and their properties of symmetry; the second, an answer key; and the third, extension or challenge problems. Some sample questions that can be used include the following:

1. Which trademarks have exactly one line of symmetry? Exactly two lines of symmetry?

2. Which trademarks have exactly three lines of symmetry? Do any have more than three lines of symmetry?

3. Which trademarks have rotational symmetry? Do any of these also have point symmetry? Which ones?

4. Do any of the trademarks have line symmetry but no rotational symmetry? Name them.

5. Must figures with rotational symmetry also have line symmetry? If not, name a trademark that is an example.

6. Do all the trademarks have either line or rotational symmetry? If not, give an example.

7. Consider the trademarks you found that have exactly two lines of symmetry. What relationship do you notice between the two lines?

8. Look through old newspapers, magazines, or the Yellow Pages. Cut out ten trademarks with symmetry. Glue them on a sheet of notebook paper and write beside each the kind of symmetry it has.

Some possible extension problems for the third envelope follow:

1. Using the trademarks with rotational symmetry, make a table showing how many different turns will rotate each figure onto itself. Give the angles of rotation for each figure. (*Hint:* 360° ÷ (number of rotations) = angle of rotation.)

2. Design your own trademark with either line symmetry, rotational symmetry, or both. Tell what kind of symmetry your trademark has.

As this article demonstrates, many things can be done with symmetry by using common trademark designs. Working with trademarks is one way to make the study of symmetry more fun, interesting, and real to students. Afterward, symmetry will no longer be just something they talk about in the classroom; it will be something they can see and recognize in the real world.

Bibliography

"Geometry and Visualization." Mathematics Resource Project. Eugene: University of Oregon, 1977.

Metz, James. "Mathematics Expressed in Trademarks." *Mathematics Teacher* 74 (September 1981): 437–40.

O'Daffer, Phares G., and Stanley R. Clemens. *Geometry: An Investigative Approach.* Menlo Park, Calif.: Addison-Wesley Publishing Co., 1976.

Permission to use the figures in this article was received from the following:

American Tourister	Mattel
P. A. Bergner & Co.	Maytag Co.
Caterpillar Tractor Co.	Pepsico
CBS	Ralston Purina Co.
Chrysler Corp.	Shell Oil Co.
General Electric Co.	U.S. Suzuki Motor Corp.
International Harvester Co.	Westinghouse Electric Corp. ▲

Symmetry in American Folk Art

by

Claudia Zaslavsky

Symmetrical designs and repeated patterns are important elements in the arts of many cultures—in fabrics, masks, pottery, and wood carvings, to mention just a few examples (Appleton 1971; Chatley 1986; Harris 1987; Krause 1983; Larsen and Gull 1977; Zaslavsky 1973, 1979, 1981, 1987). Many examples can be found in the textile arts alone. Symmetrical patterns in quilts and rugs, the subject of this article, often have symbolic meaning and play a role similar to writing in conveying ideas. The artist, who is usually anonymous, may introduce variations on the traditional themes or may boldly create new designs.

The analysis of symmetry in folk art can be a fascinating project involving mathematics, social studies, and fine arts. A study of folk art can also furnish the types of physical experiences that are essential for the development of spatial thinking. Geometric concepts have real meaning when they are presented in such a concrete and relevant form.

The first section of this article focuses on American quilts, and the second section features Navajo rugs, both fine examples of repeated motifs and symmetrical designs in American folk art. The teaching ideas in each of the two sections can be used independently of each other.

QUILTS

Symmetry of the square

The square is the basic shape for quilt making. To study the symmetry of a square, each student should have a paper square and should label the corners consecutively *A, B, C, D.*

To test for *line symmetry,* ask the students to fold the square so that one half matches the other half. This *fold line* is called an *axis of symmetry.* Along how many lines can the square be folded

so that one half matches the other half? The square has four axes of symmetry. In technical terms, the square has *line symmetry of order four* (fig. 1a).

To test for *rotational symmetry,* the student traces the square on a sheet of paper and labels the corners to match. Placing a pencil point or a fingertip on the center of both squares, the student rotates the free square until it matches the traced square. The process continues until the free square is back to the original position. The square has *turn,* or *rotational, symmetry of order four* because it matches the traced square in four different positions as it turns (fig. 1b).

(a)

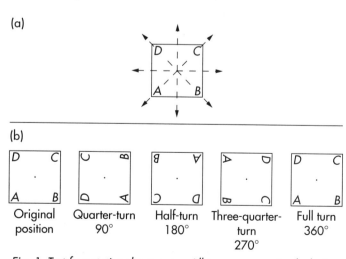

(b)

Original position	Quarter-turn 90°	Half-turn 180°	Three-quarter-turn 270°	Full turn 360°

Fig. 1. Test for rotational symmetry. All turns are counterclockwise.

Claudia Zaslavsky, a retired mathematics instructor, is an educational consultant and writer in New York, NY 10040. She is particularly interested in cultural applications of mathematics and equity issues in mathematics education.

I want to thank E. Sapadin, principal of Public School 189M, for his cooperation with the photography in his school, and Iris Mitchell for permitting Sam Zaslavsky to photograph her students.

Analysis of quilt patterns

An analysis of the design in each square of the coverlet (fig. 2) furnishes an excellent setting for the study of line and rotational symmetry.

Distribute a copy of the quilt to each student. For convenience, each small square in the quilt is identified by its position on the 5 × 5 grid (fig. 3). The first square in the upper-left corner is designated square A-1; the square below it, B-1, and so on.

For each small square in turn, ask the students to imagine that they are folding it on a line in such a way that one half of the design matches the other half. In how many ways can this matching be done, using a different imaginary line each time? Each such line is a *fold line*, or *axis of symmetry*. Another way to find an axis of symmetry is to place the edge of a mirror on the design so that the reflection in the mirror matches the half of the design hidden behind the mirror. When matching occurs, the edge of the mirror is on an axis of symmetry (Walter 1985).

Some students may claim, rightfully, that one half of the design *almost* matches the other half, but since the two halves are not exactly alike, the design is not symmetrical. This observation can lead into a stimulating discussion about the differences in appearance between factory-made and hand-crafted patterns. Hand-crafted textile art often has small design flaws that the factory

process can avoid. Usually we consider the intentions of the artist and overlook insignificant or unavoidable deviations from perfection. Of course, congruence is only an ideal and can never be achieved in the real world.

Students should be able to analyze each square for rotational symmetry by turning the photograph of the quilt. In how many positions does the square, along with the design it encloses, resemble the original? Remind students to include the original position when they consider the order of rotational symmetry.

As an example, examine square A-2 and its ten-vaned-pinwheel design. It is not possible to fold the square along any lines so that one half of the pinwheel matches the other half. However, when we give the quilt a half-turn—not a quarter-turn or a three-quarter-turn—the design looks the same as in the original position. Therefore, square A-2 has line symmetry of order zero and rotational symmetry of order two.

	1	2	3	4	5
A	A-1	A-2	A-3	A-4	A-5
B					
C					
D					
E					

Fig. 3

The class might be divided into groups, each assigned to analyze a different row of small squares. After discussing their analyses, the students can summarize their conclusions in tabular form. Table 1 summarizes row A. Of course, no square in the quilt can have symmetry of an order higher than four, the symmetry of the square itself.

Table 1

Square	Order of symmetry	
	Line	Rotational
A-1	4	4
A-2	0	2
A-3	4	4
A-4	4	4
A-5	0	1

For an additional challenge, have the students analyze a design element within each square of the quilt. For example, the seven-petaled flower in square A-1 has both line and turn symmetry of order seven. Table 2 is a summary of design elements in row A. Of course, the students might choose different design elements.

Fig. 2. Nineteenth-century American coverlet, embroidered and quilted

The Metropolitan Museum of Art, gift of Eliza Polhemus Cobb, through Mrs. Arthur Bunker, 1952 (52.103)

Table 2

Internal design		Order of symmetry	
		Line	Rotational
A–1 flower	✳	7	7
A–2 pinwheel	❁	0	10
A–3 leaf	🍃	1	1
A–4 center flower	❀	16	8
A–5 sprig	✿	0	1

Making quilt patterns

Students can create their own patchwork quilts, each contributing one square. The designs can be cut from folded paper and pasted to sheets of contrasting color, or they can be drawn with colored markers. Some students may like to embroider or appliqué on cloth. They should be encouraged to describe the elements of their patterns and the types of symmetry involved. These creations are their very own, and they might well be proud to display them.

On display in the lobby of my local elementary school are the beautiful hangings in figures 4 and 5, both based on the square as the motif. To make the tapestry in figure 4, a fifth-grade art class arranged felt squares of different sizes and colors in symmetrical patterns and glued them to larger squares. These, in turn, were fastened to a white backing.

Fig. 5. Patchwork hanging

Fig. 4. Felt hanging

Students in fifth-grade art class of I. Knesz, PS 189M, New York, New York

Each student in a fourth-grade class contributed one square to the patchwork quilt in figure 5. The thirty squares are identical in construction, consisting of small pieces of print or solid-colored cloth combined as in figure 6. By mixing and matching the colors and patterns of the fabrics as their fancy led them, these students were able to achieve a varied and pleasing effect. "I was an art major," said their teacher, "and I had them make the quilt so that they would get a feeling for life in colonial times. I like to combine social studies with art. Now we are doing Native American bead patterns." I added that the students also seemed to be doing very well in mathematics.

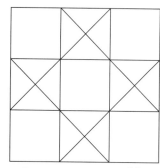

Fig. 6. One square of the patchwork hanging

History of American quilts

The art of quilting came to America with the Dutch and English settlers. Quilting bees, or parties, were a favorite activity of colonial women, restricted as they were to the home and the church. A wedding, a visit by a famous personage, and the arrival of a new minister were all occasions for making special "presentation" quilts. African-American women, too, contributed to this art form (Barry 1989). Beautiful quilt designs were developed and passed along from generation to generation, some examples ending up in museum collections, a celebration of women's contributions to the arts over the years.

Today quilting is both a popular hobby and a medium of expression for professional artists. A recent exhibit at the American Craft Museum in New York City featured pairs of quilts sharing similar themes. Each pair consisted of a modern example and a classic dating from the period from 1830 to 1930. The common theme for one pair was a square of solid-colored fabric, "the most basic form of quilt expression." An antique Amish composition of light and dark squares was contrasted with Debra Millard's contemporary computer-generated design based on shifting rotations of the square (Katz 1987).

NAVAJO RUGS

Women are weavers of rugs, as well as quilters. The intricate patterns and fine workmanship of Navajo rugs, sometimes called the "first American tapestries," earn for them a well-deserved place in museums. The geometric designs in the Navajo rugs in figures 7 and 8 are fairly simple, compared with the elaborate patterns found in museum pieces, and offer good models for young students. Both rugs were photographed as they hung on the wall; consequently, their rectangular shape appears somewhat distorted.

Symmetry of the rectangle

Although square rugs are not unusual, most Navajo rugs are rectangular. To study the symmetry of the rectangle, each student should have a paper rectangle and should label the corners A, B, C, D in consecutive order.

To test for *line symmetry*, the students fold the rectangle so that one half matches the other half. The rectangle has two fold

Fig. 8. Navajo rug

lines, or *axes of symmetry*, and is said to have *line symmetry of order two* (fig. 9a).

To test for *rotational symmetry*, the student traces the rectangle on a sheet of paper and labels the corners to match. Placing a fingertip or pencil point on the center of both rectangles, the student rotates the free rectangle until it matches the traced rectangle. This maneuver requires a half-turn, or 180-degree rotation. Another half-turn brings the rectangle back to its original position. The rectangle has *turn*, or *rotational, symmetry of order two* because it matches the traced rectangle in two different positions as it rotates (fig. 9b).

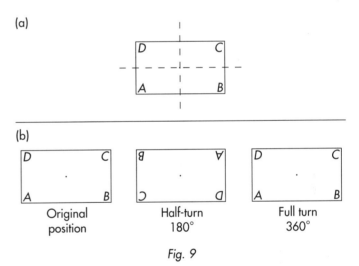

Fig. 9

Analysis of rug patterns

The rug in figure 7 has both line and rotational symmetry of order two, the type of symmetry in the rectangle that defines its shape. If we make allowance for an error, the Navajo rug in figure 8 also has both line and rotational symmetry of order two. To find the error, examine the design within the two squares in each corner of the rug. The lower-right corner is different from the other three. Sometimes weavers introduce errors on purpose to indicate that human beings are not perfect.

Challenge your students with these questions, using terminology suitable to their level of understanding:

1. Can a rectangular rug, viewed as a whole, have line symmetry or rotational symmetry of an order greater than two? (No)

Fig. 7. Navajo rug

2. Can a rectangular rug have just one line of symmetry? (Yes)

3. Can it have rotational symmetry of order one and line symmetry of order zero? (Yes)

4. Can it have exactly two lines of symmetry but rotational symmetry of an order other than two? Remember that the order of rotational symmetry of any figure must be at least one. (No)

5. Can it have rotational symmetry of order two but a different order of line symmetry? (Yes, line symmetry of order zero)

When students answer "yes" to any question, ask them to validate their assertions by making sketches or by finding appropriate examples in books, magazines, or newspaper advertisements.

Creating a rug border or strip pattern

Students can create simple borders or frieze patterns on grid paper, using the zigzag design, either as a symmetrical motif (fig. 10a) or as an asymmetrical motif (fig. 10b). To start them off, prepare a worksheet showing the beginning of several patterns, as in the examples (figs. 10c and 10d).

The student continues the given pattern by drawing or tracing the motif in each rectangle of the strip. The dimensions of the basic rectangle may vary from one band to the next: 3 × 3 (as in fig. 10c), 3 × 4 (as in fig. 10d), 3 × 5, 4 × 5, and so on. A different motif or rectangle of different dimensions can be assigned to each group of students. Encourage them to vary the given patterns and to invent their own. For students who are sophisticated in the ways of the computer, a challenging task is to devise a program that generates borders with repeated motifs (DeTemple 1986; Ryoti 1986; Zaslavsky 1973, 1979). After they have completed

and colored their borders, the students should display the works of art and explain the mathematics involved.

Designing a rug

To put all these ideas together, students might design their own symmetrical Navajo-style rugs on grid paper. The student sketches a geometric pattern in pencil in one quadrant of the rectangle, reflects the design in the three remaining quadrants, adds a border based on a repeated motif, and colors the rug. For a wonderful class project, students might describe in writing the relevant mathematics and put all the items together in a book.

CONCLUSION

The activities described in this article are adaptable to all age groups. Since they are open-ended, they are appropriate for slow, average, and gifted students. Students can pursue their individual interests according to their aptitudes. Even turned-off students respond to the challenge posed by informal hands-on work with geometric ideas. Some students may want to learn more about the mathematical aspects of the designs, whereas others may be more interested in artistic expression. Whichever emphasis they choose, they will have gained valuable mathematical experience.

Activities such as these may have special appeal for students who are not interested in mathematics for its own sake. Investigations into sex-role stereotyping reveal that boys are more likely than girls to receive exposure to such informal sources of mathematical learning as puzzles, sports, and construction toys, whereas girls are socialized to care more about people. By integrating

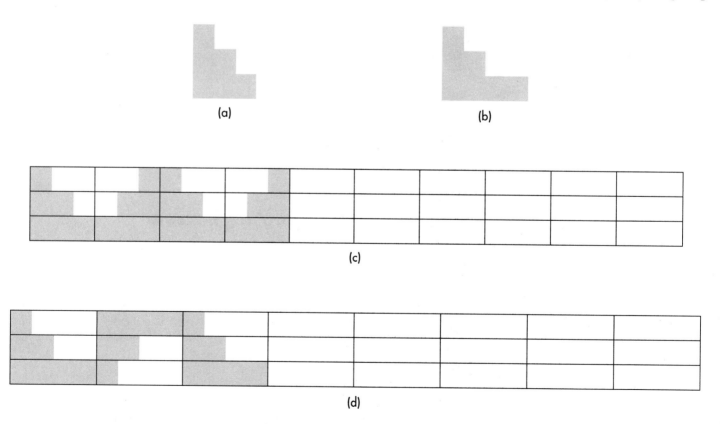

(a)

(b)

(c)

(d)

Fig. 10

Fig. 11. American folk art in U.S. postage stamps

mathematics education with the study of culture, art, and history, we may motivate more girls to become interested in mathematics.

Activities such as those described here help students to become aware of the role that mathematics plays in all societies—of the fact that mathematics is a dynamic, growing, changing area of human endeavor. At the same time they learn to appreciate the arts of people in all parts of the world. They can take pride in their own heritage as they become familiar with other cultures (fig. 11).

Bibliography

Appleton, LeRoy H. *American Indian Design and Decoration.* New York: Dover Publications, 1971.

Arizona Highways 50 (July 1974). Phoenix: Arizona Department of Transportation. Entire issue on Southwest Indian rugs and blankets.

Barry, Ann. "Quilting Has African Roots, a New Exhibition Suggests." *New York Times,* 16 November 1989, sec. C12.

Bidwell, James K. "Using Reflections to Find Symmetric and Asymmetric Patterns." *Arithmetic Teacher* 34 (March 1987): 10–15.

Chatley, Diana. "Sewing Mathematics." *Mathematics Teaching* 117 (December 1986): 24–25. Includes illustrations in color of traditional embroidery and patchwork patterns.

DeTemple, Duane. "Reflection Borders for Patchwork Quilts." *Mathematics Teacher* 79 (February 1986): 138–43.

Harris, Mary. "Mathematics and Fabrics." *Mathematics Teaching* 120 (1987): 43–45.

Katz, Ruth J. "Exhibition of Quilts Pairs Old with New." *New York Times,* 29 October 1987, sec. C3.

Krause, Marina C. *Multicultural Mathematics Materials.* Reston, Va.: National Council of Teachers of Mathematics, 1983.

Larsen, Judith LaBelle, and Carol Waugh Gull. *The Patchwork Quilt Design and Coloring Book.* New York: New Century, 1977.

Renshaw, Barbara S. "Symmetry the Trademark Way." *Arithmetic Teacher* 34 (September 1986): 6–12.

Ryoti, Don E. "Computer Corner: Using the Computer and Logo to Investigate Symmetry." *Arithmetic Teacher* 34 (November 1986): 36–37.

Sawada, Daiyo. "Symmetry and Tessellations from Rotational Transformations on Transparencies." *Arithmetic Teacher* 33 (December 1985): 12–13.

Walter, Marion. *The Mirror Puzzle Book.* New York: Parkwest Publications, 1985.

Willcutt, Bob. "Triangular Tiles for Your Patio." *Arithmetic Teacher* 34 (May 1987): 43–45.

Zaslavsky, Claudia. *Africa Counts: Number and Pattern in African Culture.* Boston: Prindle, Weber & Schmidt, 1973. Reprint. Westport, Conn.: Lawrence Hill Co., Publishers, 1979.

———. *Math Comes Alive: Activities from Many Cultures.* Portland, Maine: J. Weston Walch, 1987.

———. "The Shape of a Symbol, the Symbolism of a Shape." *Teacher* 99 (February 1981): 36–43.

———. "Symmetry Along with Other Mathematical Concepts and Applications in African Life." In *Applications in School Mathematics,* 1979 Yearbook of the National Council of Teachers of Mathematics, edited by Sidney Sharron and Robert E. Reys, 82–97. Reston, Va.: The Council, 1979. ▲

Chapter 3
Measurement

a. Metrics and English

Body Measurement

by

K. Allen Neufeld

In teaching the customary units of measure, the teacher risks offering too few activities that focus on measuring or on determining relationships among units. In the metric system, relationships among units are especially important and become clear to students when we offer them the opportunity to measure many familiar objects. The human body is made up of many parts that students measure with great interest. A student's knowledge of the measures of some of these body parts can be helpful in making estimates of the measures of other objects in his or her immediate environment.

Pagni (1979) describes a number of activities based on human variability. Discrete variables such as eye and hair color cannot be assigned numerical values, but students can benefit by constructing graphs that illustrate the classification according to each of these variables. Shaw (1984) presents a variety of activities based on estimates and measurements of the length of various parts of the body. A knowledge of one's own height is shown to be helpful in making an accurate estimate of the height of a door or a desk.

Such continuous variables as height and mass can easily be measured. From the measurement of height and other linear measures of different parts of the human body, one can calculate other such continuous variables as surface area and volume. An understanding of these variables can be applied to solving a number of problems relating mathematics and science.

MEASUREMENTS AND CALCULATIONS

The following activities have been tried successfully with students from grades 4 to 9 as well as with prospective teachers and teachers at in-service sessions. The first activity is to have the student lie on her or his back (legs together and arms held close to sides) on a large sheet of brown wrapping paper while the teacher or a classmate draws a line around the student as illustrated in figure 1. Next the student lies on her or his side with arms outstretched, and another sketch is made of the body in this position. Then the student kneels with the top of the head on the paper for a "headprint" drawing. Finally a drawing is made of one footprint. The pencil should be held at an inward slant to minimize error. Use a soft lead pencil to protect the student's clothing. The lines can be darkened with a felt-tip marking pen.

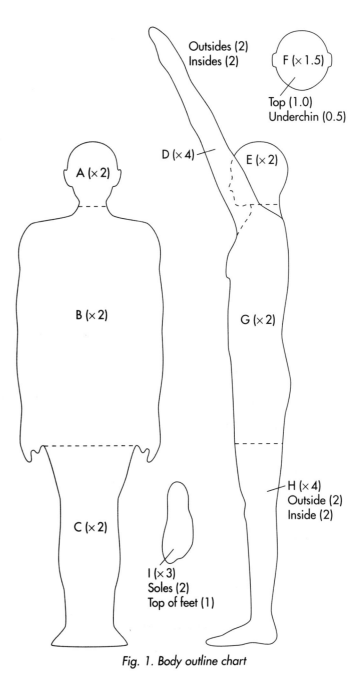

Fig. 1. Body outline chart

Allen Neufeld teaches curriculum and instruction courses in elementary mathematics and coordinates the practicum for the elementary education department at the University of Alberta, Edmonton, AB T6G 2E1. He conducts research relating mathematics and music at the kindergarten level.

Measurement **175**

The next step is to use a tape measure or meterstick to make a number of linear measures of the body outline. All measures should be recorded to the nearest decimeter rounded to one decimal place. For children who aren't ready for decimal calculations, measures can be recorded in centimeters. Even though most body lines are curved, each part of the body to be measured should be considered as a rectangle. The head (A in fig. 2) is shown to have a length of 2.3 dm and a width of 1.2 dm. It is important to rectangularize each body part, as has been done with the head in figure 2, so that one obtains an average measure, not a measure of the widest or narrowest place. Calculate the approximate surface area of the front of the head (the face) by multiplying the length by the width and rounding to the nearest tenth, in this example, 2.3 × 1.2 = 2.8 dm². This number has been recorded on the chart in table 1. The instruction to multiply this number by 2 is based on the fact that the approximate surface area of the front and the back of the head is the same, resulting in a total of 5.6 dm².

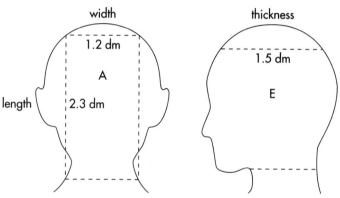

Fig. 2. Example of measures of length, width, and thickness

Table 1. Body Surface Area Chart

Body parts					Approximate surface area
Head, front and back (A)	2.8	×	2	=	5.6
Torso, front and back (B)		×	2	=	
Legs, front and back (C)		×	2	=	
Arms, sides (D)		×	4	=	
Head, sides (E)		×	2	=	
Head, top and underchin (F)		×	1.5	=	
Torso, sides (G)		×	2	=	
Legs, sides (H)		×	4	=	
Feet, top and bottom (I)		×	3	=	
The approximate total surface area is					dm².

The remaining surface-area calculations can be similarly completed for the torso and arms (B), legs (C), sides of the arms (D), sides of the head (E), top of the head (F), sides of the torso (G), sides of the legs (H), and feet (I). In some special situations the surface area is not multiplied by 2. For each of the sides of the arms (D) and the sides of the legs (H), it is necessary to multiply

by 4 because each of the two arms and legs has an "outside" and an "inside." The surface area of the top of the head should be multiplied by 1.5 to account for the area underneath the chin. The surface area of one footprint should be multiplied by 3 to account for the area of both soles and the tops of the feet between the toes and the ankles. When all these individual surface areas have been calculated, find the sum to get the total surface area.

CALCULATING VOLUME AND DENSITY

The volume of the human body can be calculated using the linear measurements already made. Imagine that a rectangular solid of each body part is being made. The surface area of the face (A in fig. 2) was calculated to be 2.8 dm². If the width, or thickness, of the side of the head (E) is 1.5 dm, then the volume of the head can be calculated to be 2.8 × 1.5 = 4.2 dm³, again rounded to the nearest tenth. The volume of the torso including arms (B and G) and legs (C and H) can be similarly calculated and recorded on the chart in table 2. When all the individual volumes have been calculated, find the sum to get the total volume for the body.

After the basic measurements of height and mass have been made and the surface area and volume of the student have been calculated, a number of interesting calculations can be made including density (mass/volume), surface area/volume, height minus mass, surface area/area of one footprint, and height/mass. The statistics for each student are unique and interesting to the student being measured. Of more general interest are number patterns indicated by the measurements and calculations for a group of students of the same age, a group of students of ages differing by one year, or a particular student at different ages. The data in table 3 illustrate the latter situation in which measurements of the author's daughter were taken at three-year intervals. The data suggest that whereas most numbers increase with the age of the person being measured, some remain nearly constant, and one set of data shows a decrease with age. Students can be asked to speculate on the reasons for the increase, stability, and decrease as indicated for particular variables.

Table 2. Body Volume Chart

Body part	Surface area		Thickness		Volume
Head (A)	2.8	×	1.5	=	4.2
Torso (B)		×		=	
Legs (C)		×		=	
The approximate total volume is					dm³.

PROBLEMS RELATED TO BODY MEASUREMENT

An understanding of density and surface area can lead to the solution of several problems relating mathematics and science. Why do babies float more easily than older children or adults? One of the students in a teacher-education course volunteered to do the series of measurements on her four-year-old child. The density of the child was calculated to be 0.52 (kg/dm³), considerably less than the densities of older children as indicated by the chart in table 3. It is generally accepted that the density of an adult peaks at approximately 0.95. Since the density of water is 1.0, anything with a density greater than 1.0 would sink in water.

Table 3. Data for One Child at Three Ages

Age (years)	10	13	16
Height (cm)	140	160	171
Mass (kg)	31	52	65
Surface area (dm^2)	110	150	175
Volume (dm^3)	41	67	79
Footprint area (dm^2)	1.4	1.7	2.0
Mass/volume (density)	0.76	0.78	0.82
Surface area/volume	2.7	2.2	2.2
Height – mass	109	108	106
Surface area/footprint area	78.6	88.2	87.5
Height/mass	4.5	3.1	2.6

The following problem was posed by Lange (1975): "Why can a fly sit on the surface of water in a pail while it would be drowned if it flew into a shower of water?" Since the fly has a density of approximately 0.25, it is very buoyant. The surface area of a fly is approximately 0.6 cm^3. Since the water covering the surface area of anything in a shower is approximately 0.05 cm in thickness, the amount of water surrounding the fly is 0.03 cm^3 and has a mass of 0.03 g. Since the mass of the fly itself is only one-third of the mass of water clinging to its body, little doubt remains about why the fly's life is in danger when it ventures into a shower of water. When one poses similar problems about a human walking on water or taking a shower, the results are completely opposite. A human has difficulty floating because the body's density is close to the density of water. A human is not affected adversely in a shower, however, because the mass of the water that clings to the body is approximately one-hundredth of the mass of the body.

Eicholz, O'Daffer, and Fleenor (1976) described another set of interesting relationships that exist between the lengths of the major bones of the body and the height of the body. Use the chart in figure 3 to determine the height of a student by measuring each of the following bones: humerus (upper arm), radius (lower arm), femur (upper leg), and tibia (lower leg). Compare each of the estimates of height with the actual height of the student. Anthropologists, using a single bone from a human skeleton, can estimate quite accurately the height of a man or woman who lived many centuries ago. It might be interesting to have students consider whether these relationships have changed from the time of the cave person to the present.

USING A NOMOGRAM

One of the first activities described was to find an approximate measure of the surface area of a human body. Medical doctors DuBois and DuBois (1916) used a nomogram like the one illustrated in figure 4 for finding the surface area of a body when treating burn victims. As an example, a line has been drawn joining a

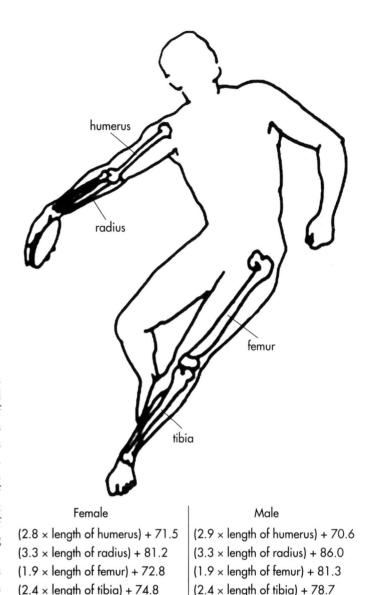

Female	Male
(2.8 × length of humerus) + 71.5	(2.9 × length of humerus) + 70.6
(3.3 × length of radius) + 81.2	(3.3 × length of radius) + 86.0
(1.9 × length of femur) + 72.8	(1.9 × length of femur) + 81.3
(2.4 × length of tibia) + 74.8	(2.4 × length of tibia) + 78.7

Fig. 3. Height based on the length of major bones

height of 150 cm on the left scale with a mass of 60 kg on the right scale. According to the place where the line crosses the middle scale, a person with this height and mass has a surface area of 1.55 m^2, which is equivalent to 155 dm^2. After finding the surface area of a student by measuring the area inside the body sketch on the large sheet of brown paper, compare the findings to the result obtained from using the nomogram. Usually the former procedure yields a larger surface area than the nomogram. The former method, however, has the advantage of offering much experience in relating linear measure to surface measure to volume measure.

Some students can benefit from the building of model bodies. Strips of brown paper tape usually used for wrapping parcels can be used to represent the circumference of the body at various points. For example, the paper tape wrapped around the head at the forehead can be made to form a loop by moistening and sticking together the ends. This loop can then be fastened to a dowel representing the backbone. Similarly, loops can be made to model the circumference of the body at the neck, chest, waistline, stomach, hips, and various points on the arms and legs. To

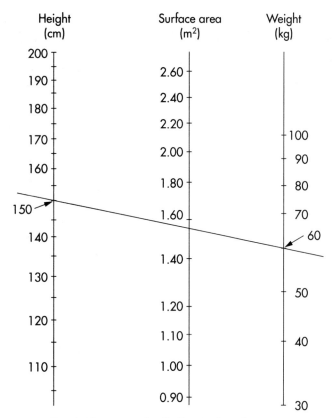

Fig. 4. Nomogram for finding body surface area

give some stability to the model, vertical strips of moistened tape can be used to connect the various horizontal loops. Since life-sized models require a large amount of tape, it may be desirable to introduce models constructed to a scale of 2:1, 5:1, or 10:1. If we use the latter scale, the circumference of a forehead that is actually 60 cm would be represented by a 6-cm tape.

Another type of body model can be constructed from centimeter cubes using the scale of 1 dm = 1 cm. The model illustrated in figure 5 is based on the measurements of the ten-year-old student that are given in table 3. The height of 14 dm is represented by a height of 14 cm. The width of the body from shoulder to shoulder, which is approximately 4 dm, is represented by four cubes having a total width of 4 cm.

SUMMARY

Students' measures of their own bodies can enhance the teaching of measurement. The activities described in this article are based on the concrete, pictorial, and abstract modes of instruction. The human body is translated into a sketch or picture that becomes the basis for a series of measures that are recorded as abstract numerical symbols. Relationships like the one expressed by the formula for density (mass/volume) are more readily understood when students are able to see the connections between the numerical symbols and the human bodies of themselves and their classmates that furnished the initial sources for the symbols.

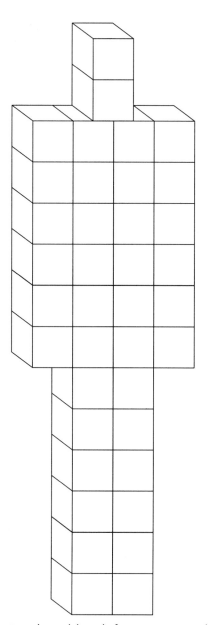

Fig. 5. Body model made from centimeter cubes

References

DuBois, Delafield, and Eugene F. DuBois. "A Formula to Estimate the Approximate Body Surface Area if Height and Weight Be Known." *Archives of Internal Medicine* 17 (June 1916): 865–71.

Eicholz, Robert E., Phares G. O'Daffer, and Charles R. Fleenor. *School Mathematics 1*. Reading, Mass.: Addison-Wesley Publishing Co., 1976.

Lange, Muriel. *Geometry in Modules, Book B*. Reading, Mass.: Addison-Wesley Publishing Co., 1975.

Pagni, David L. "Applications in School Mathematics: Human Variability." In *Applications in School Mathematics*, 1979 Yearbook of the National Council of Teachers of Mathematics, edited by Sidney Sharron and Robert E. Reys, 43–58. Reston, Va.: The Council, 1979.

Shaw, Jean M. "IDEAS." *Arithmetic Teacher* 32 (December 1984): 2–24. ▲

IDEAS: Measurement Scavenger Hunt

by

Robert Sovchik
University of Akron, Akron, Ohio

L. J. Meconi
Gonzaga University, Spokane, Washington

LEVELS K–3

Background

Young students can gain valuable experience using such fundamental measurement units as centimeters, meters, and grams, as well as nonstandard units, during a short walk near their school. A measurement scavenger hunt can help reinforce fundamental measurement units. Students can discover items that exemplify measurement attributes contained on a short list. Later, they can discuss their findings in class and develop valuable communication skills as they share results.

Objectives

To identify examples of items with predetermined measures; to communicate their findings by justifying to class members the reasons for selection

Directions

1. Duplicate the activity sheet "Measurement Scavenger Hunt" for each student.
2. Form groups of three to five students and give each group a list of items to find, such as those discussed on the "Measurement Scavenger Hunt" activity sheet. Have each team member measure the length of his or her thumbs, forefingers, and hands to provide an easy reference for the measurement tasks.
3. Lead the students on a short walk. Be sure the route takes them past trees, rocks, and twigs.
4. For younger students, discuss any possible measurement items you find along the route. Older students can record the findings on the activity sheet.
5. Have a follow-up discussion so that students can explain their results. Ask students to justify and explain their findings.

Extension

Repeat this activity using such customary units as inches, feet, and pounds. Use familiar items in the classroom as references. Also, consider scheduling this activity during another season, perhaps in the autumn when leaves have fallen. Leaf patterns could serve as source material for your list of scavenger items. For example, direct the students to find a leaf with more than three points or one that has a rounded design. Have students estimate the weight of a bag of leaves, using a see-saw and a student whose weight is known.

MEASUREMENT SCAVENGER HUNT

Name _____

Student Worksheet

My thumb is _____ centimeters long. My hand is _____ centimeters long. My forefinger is _____ centimeters long.

Find a twig, a leaf, a rock, and a blade of grass to match each of the following measurements. Indicate approximately how many centimeters long each item is.

Item	Longer than your hand (It is about this many centimeters long.)	Shorter than your thumb (It is about this many centimeters long.)	Longer than your forefinger but shorter than your hand (It is about this many centimeters long.)
Twig	_____ cm	_____ cm	_____ cm
Leaf	_____ cm	_____ cm	_____ cm
Blade of grass	_____ cm	_____ cm	_____ cm
A special item you found on your walk	_____ cm	_____ cm	_____ cm

How many hands long is the longest twig you found? _____ How many cm long is it? _____

How many hands long is the longest blade of grass? _____ How many cm long is it? _____

Which tree on your walk is the oldest? Why do you think so? _____

_____

Find two leaves, one twice as big as the other. Why do you think it is twice as big? _____

_____

_____

Multilevel Metric Games

by

Rosalie Jensen

The goal of the games described here is the improvement of skills in comparison, estimation, and linear measurement. Because children are motivated by their interest in the outcomes of the games, they do not associate the practice in them with the tedium of some drill problems. The materials needed are easy to make, and some of them can be made by the children themselves. Several sets of rules are given for each set of materials so that the games can be used on different levels. Children may wish to create their own rules once they have learned to play these games. They can be played alone or in small groups.

CATCH A METRIC FISH

Materials

Set of paper fish of different lengths from 4 centimeters to 10 or 12 centimeters with a paper clip attached to each fish (see fig. 1); wooden dowel "fishing pole" with a magnet at the end of the line; box to use as a "pond"; centimeter ruler or centimeter cubes (for some games)

Objectives

1. To compare objects with respect to length
2. To measure in centimeters

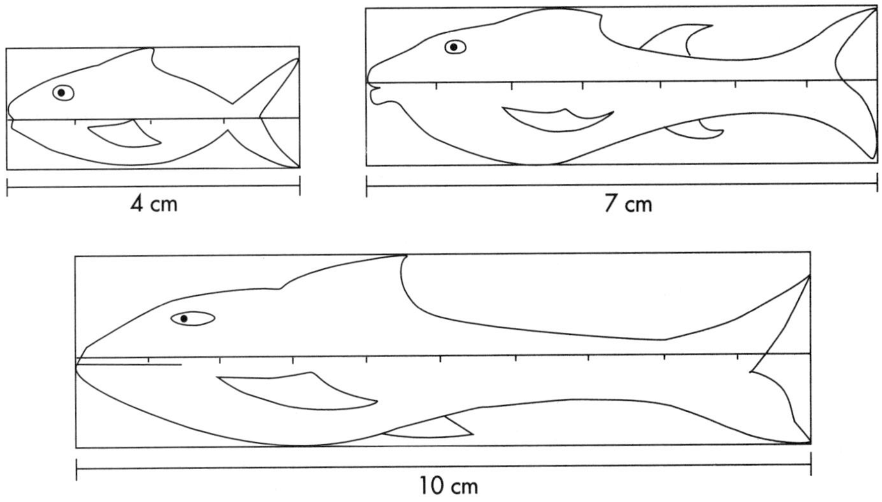

Fig. 1. Some metric fish

Directions

Game 1. Each player in a small group of children uses the fishing pole to catch one fish. The player with the longest fish takes all the fish caught in that round. After several rounds or when all the fish have been removed from the pond, each child counts his or her fish to determine who has the greatest number of fish.

Game 2. Each player in turn pulls out a fish. The game continues until one player has two fish of the same length. That player is the winner. All fish are placed back in the pond before a new game begins.

Game 3. Each player in turn pulls out a fish. After a given number of turns, say five, each player places his or her fish end to end. The player with the longest string of fish is the winner.

Game 4. Each player in turn pulls out one fish until all the fish have been caught. Players determine how many pairs (two fish of the same length) they have. The player with the most pairs is the winner.

Game 5. Each player in turn pulls out a fish. The first player to pull out a fish that has a specific measure, say 5 centimeters, is the winner. Place all fish back in the pond before beginning a new game.

Game 6. Each player in turn pulls out a fish. As each new fish is pulled out, the player places it at the tail of the preceding fish. The first player with a string of fish longer than a specified length, say 30 centimeters, is the winner. Players measure with a centimeter ruler or centimeter cubes.

Game 7. Each player in turn pulls out a fish. When all fish have been caught, players make pairs that consist of two fish with a certain combined length, such as 10 centimeters.

Rosalie Jensen is a professor at Georgia State University in Atlanta, GA 30303. She teaches undergraduate and graduate-level courses in mathematics education and serves as chairman of the Department of Curriculum and Instruction.

The player with the greatest number of qualifying pairs is the winner.

Note: All these games can be adapted to cooperative rather than competitive activities by having children cooperate in achieving the goals. For example, in game 7 children can cooperate to see how *many* pairs of fish of a given length the whole group can catch.

METRIC CAR PARK

Materials

A "parking lot" consisting of a board or file folder marked with spaces of lengths ranging from 5 to 15 centimeters (see fig. 2 for a sample layout [not actual size]); paper or cardboard cars with lengths corresponding to the lengths of the spaces; centimeter ruler (for some games); box or envelope for cars

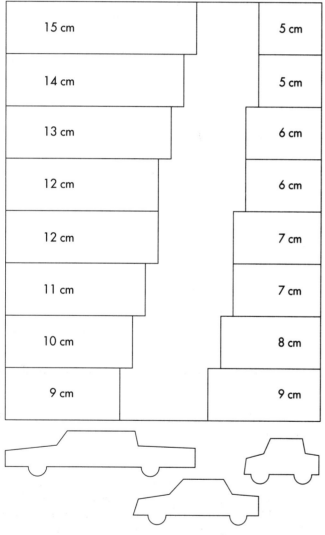

Fig. 2. A metric car park

Objectives

1. To match the length of a car to the length of a parking space
2. To measure in centimeters
3. To estimate which parking place will be suited to a given car

Directions

Game 1. Each player in turn reaches into the box, pulls out a car, and places the car in a parking space. If the car fits, the player receives 1 point. Younger children may be allowed to keep trying until a correct space is found. When all the cars have been parked, there should be no cars or spaces left over. Each player adds up individual points for a total score.

Game 2. Each player in turn reaches into the box, pulls out a car, measures it with a centimeter ruler or centimeter cubes, and puts it in an appropriate parking space. Each car correctly placed is worth 1 point for the player.

Game 3. Each player reaches into the box, takes out a car, estimates its length, and places it in a space. If the player is correct, the length of the car will match the length of the space. If the player is incorrect, he or she must place the car back in the box and wait for another turn. Each correct placement is worth 1 point.

MAKE-A-METER

Materials

About 60 cards (or small index cards) about 7 centimeters by 12 centimeters with line segments marked ranging from 2 centimeters to 12 centimeters (see sample cards in fig. 3); a metric tape or meterstick; a fairly large playing area on the floor or on a table.

Objectives

1. To learn that 10 centimeters have the same length as 1 decimeter and that 100 centimeters have the same length as 1 meter
2. To learn to group by tens in the metric system

Directions

One player shuffles the cards and gives one card to each player. The remaining cards are placed face down on the playing area. Each player in turn draws a card from the deck and arranges his or her cards in a line so that the end point on each card is at the edge of the next card, as illustrated in figure 4 (the cards are not drawn to actual size). A player may rearrange the cards at any time so as to group by tens for easier counting or, if permissible, may place the meterstick or metric tape next to the line to check the total length of the cards. Several goals are given below.

Game 1. The game ends when any player has a line longer than 1 meter.

Game 2. The game ends when any player has a line exactly 1 meter long. In this version, players may remove cards from their lines and replace them by new cards drawn from the deck on any turn. The cards removed are placed in a pile beside the player for possible future rearrangements during that game.

Game 3. The object of this version is to come closest to 1 meter in length. For example, suppose one player stops at 98 cm. Other players continue to draw until they wish to stop. If another player stops at 103 cm and another at 101 cm, the player with 101 cm is the winner of the game. No cards may be removed from a line at any time during the game.

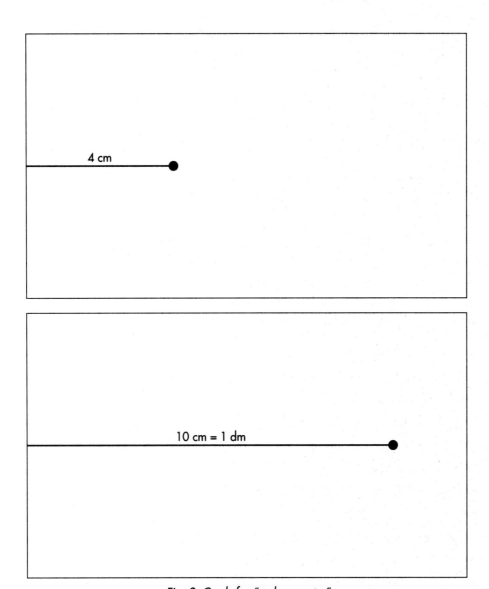

Fig. 3. Cards for "make-a-meter"

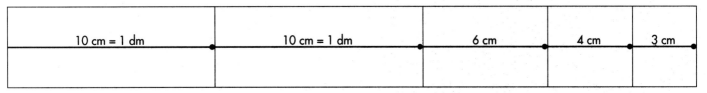

Fig. 4. Lining up the cards in "make-a-meter"

Game 4. The goal of this game is to come closest to 1 meter without going over 1 meter. Any player who draws a card that makes his or her line longer than 1 meter is out of the game for that round. Any player may stop drawing cards at any time but may not remove any cards from the line. At a later time the player may resume drawing cards if he or she has a chance to make a line closer to 1 meter than another player. Example: Player A stops at 93 cm but draws another card when Player B has 98 cm and Player C has 95 cm. If Player A draws a 6-cm card or a 7-cm card, Player A is closer than either of the other players to 1 meter. In this case they will each probably wish to draw another card. If Player A draws a card with 8 cm or longer on it, Player A is out of the game. (This version is similar to the card game blackjack.) ▲

Using a Metric Unit to Help Preservice Teachers Appreciate the Value of Manipulative Materials

by

Gretchen L. Johnson

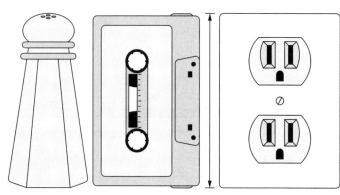

Preservice teachers in my elementary mathematics methods class often find it difficult to imagine how much help manipulative materials or an activity approach can be to a child in learning a new concept. To help them understand, I teach them the metric system—for many an intimidating subject—using the same materials and approaches that would be used with children, although covering the material in a shorter period of time. If these methods help the preservice teachers learn the metric system, then they should be convinced that the same approaches will work with children. In turn, they will be more likely to use manipulatives in their own classrooms in the future.

Over a six-week period, ten to fifteen minutes of each class are devoted to metrics. This approach gives the students time to internalize each metric unit of measure before we go on to the next one. It also provides a welcome change from the usual classroom activities.

LINEAR MEASUREMENT

We begin with the decimeter. Although it is not a commonly used unit, its size is commonly found and thus it helps to link metrics with students' daily lives. Each student works with a strip of paper one decimeter long and one centimeter wide (see fig. 1 a). The length of the strip is not identified. They are simply asked to find something about as long as this strip in their purse or briefcase, or on their clothing or body. They turn up an amazing variety of items: address books, photographs, lipsticks, eye liner, calculators, cough-drop boxes, pocket tissues, cigarette packages, hands (measured across the knuckles or the palm), thumbs (from tip of nail to base of hand), eyes (from outside corner to outside corner), pockets, and the space between buttons. Students are surprised at this handy

unit. At this point, they are told that the unit is a part of the metric system and is called a decimeter. For homework, they find four objects at home that are a decimeter wide, or long, or tall and draw a life-sized picture of each. My purpose is to link the decimeter with objects familiar to them so that they will develop a visual image not easily forgotten.

The objects they have found in their homes are listed on the chalkboard: soap dishes, light switch plates, thermostats, salt and pepper shakers, coffee mugs, vitamin bottles, ashtrays, crayon boxes, cans of tuna and sardines, slices of bread, and cassette tapes. They pass around their pictures, which later will be made into a decimeter poster. By now they are beginning to relax a bit about metrics.

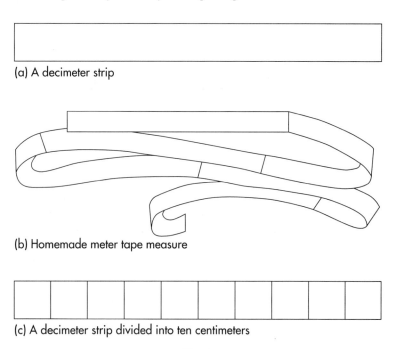

(a) A decimeter strip

(b) Homemade meter tape measure

(c) A decimeter strip divided into ten centimeters

Fig. 1

Gretchen Johnson teaches elementary mathematics methods and early childhood courses at the State University of New York/College at Old Westbury, Old Westbury, NY 11568. She is especially interested in how learning in methods classes transfers to later classroom instruction.

To explore the measurement skill of estimation, we go on to measuring larger objects. Using their decimeter strip as a pattern, they cut out several more strips of paper that are a decimeter long. On a worksheet (see fig. 2), they list three objects in the room that they would like to measure. Looking at the first of the objects, they estimate its size in decimeters and record their estimate on the worksheet. Then they measure the object by laying decimeter strips along the side of it and counting the number of strips. They enter the actual measurement on their worksheet and indicate if their estimate was too high or too low. Then they go on to the second object. Their goal should not be to estimate correctly on the first try but to improve their estimates with subsequent tries. It's important when they estimate to try to visualize the decimeter unit as clearly as possible. Everyone now has a good idea of a decimeter because they can relate it to a favorite possession or to a part of their own body or clothing. They know what it means to use estimation in measurement activities, and they have practiced the measurement skill of laying out multiple units and counting.

Next, the students tape ten decimeter strips together to make a *meter* (fig. 1b). Their homework assignment is to record on a worksheet (see fig. 2) estimates and actual measurements in meters for bathtubs, beds, and cars or bicycles. Students enjoy measuring familiar possessions. On their own initiatives, many of them use both meters and decimeters to get a more precise measurement.

I am measuring _____ with _____

| | | | My estimate was (check one) | |
Object	My estimate	My actual measurement	Too high	Too low

Fig. 2

Over the next week or so, we do several more measurement activities with meters. Once they are comfortable with this unit and have a visual sense of its size, I have them take their original decimeter strip and divide it into ten equal parts (fig. 1c). First they divide the strip in half by folding. Then they divide each half into five approximately equal parts (trial and error is acceptable). They search for items in their possession or in the room that are one centimeter long or wide. They find paper clips (one centimeter wide), finger nails (one centimeter wide), thumb tacks (one centimeter long and one centimeter in diameter at the head), buttons (one centimeter in diameter), and pencils (one centimeter in cross section). If they are not sure or just want to check, we line up ten of each item on the overhead projector next to a decimeter strip to see if ten of them equal a decimeter. In that way we find out that large paper clips are a centimeter in width but that those of regular size are a bit too small (see fig. 3).

As this point, the prefixes *centi* and *deci* are introduced and we discuss how centimeters and decimeters relate to a meter. The students lay out their homemade strips on the desk in front of them to see these relationships. Now they can use all three of these units together to measure several objects in the classroom and record the measurements in meters, decimeters, and centimeters. They're pleasantly surprised at how easy it is to record these metric measurements using decimals (table 1). They also learn how easy it is to read figures representing metric measurements. For example, 5.46 meters can be read 5 meters, 4 decimeters, and 6 centimeters or 5 meters and 46 centimeters or 54 decimeters and 6 centimeters or 546 centimeters.

Table 1

Object	Meters	Decimeters	Centimeters	In meters only
Width of teacher's desk	1	4	6	1.46
Height of door	2	2	3	2.23

THE HISTORY OF THE METRIC SYSTEM

Now that the students are gaining confidence in their ability to handle the metric system and have some sense of its ease and efficiency, we talk about why and when it was invented. If the history of the metric system had been introduced at the beginning of the unit, it would have been abstract and perhaps threatening to them. But now they are curious. We talk about the American and French revolutions and the growth of science (scientists, not merchants, invented metrics). They're surprised that it is almost 200 years old. They agree that it made sense for the French Academy to select units that are multiples of ten. They are challenged to think of a better way, and they can't. They're also amazed that a meter represents an actual fraction of the circumference of the earth, and they ask how in the eighteenth century scientists could ever have figured out the distance from the North

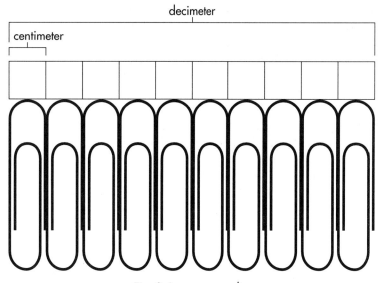

Fig. 3. Large paper clips

Pole to the equator. (A meter is one ten-millionth of this distance.) Many of them are puzzled (even angry) that so many people in the United States resist adopting a system of measurement that is used by 90 percent of the nations of the world.

MEASUREMENT OF AREA

A surprising number of preservice teachers are not clear on the meaning of the term *area*. Most of them remember the formula for area ($A = l \times w$), but since length and width are linear measurements, remembering this formula has not helped them to understand the meaning of area as a surface to be covered or a flat space to be filled in (as in planting a garden). In this class, they learn the concept of area by building on their knowledge of a decimeter. For homework they construct several squares out of cardboard that measure one decimeter on a side. In class, we use these square decimeters to measure the area of their chair seat, desk, notebook, and textbook. They cover each object with square decimeters and count.

On a worksheet (see fig. 2), they estimate the areas of three other objects in square decimeters and then measure each by covering it with square decimeters and counting. They work in groups, pooling their square decimeters and cutting more out of paper if necessary. Doing this activity several times gives them a feel for the meaning of area.

We move on to square meters, and for homework the students construct a square meter out of newspaper. They are usually surprised at its size. In class, we lay out one of these square meters and cover it with square decimeters. This pursuit leads to a discussion of why a linear meter is 10 times the size of a decimeter whereas a square meter is 100 times the size of a square decimeter. This activity graphically illustrates for them why the formula for area calls for measures of two dimensions—length and width.

Since most of our students come to school by car, they are asked to write the answers to two questions: Do you think all of the spaces in the parking lot are the same size? and How many square meters do you estimate will cover one of these spaces? Then in groups of seven or eight, they go to the lot, taking all of the thirty or so square meters with them. They select two spaces in different parts of the lot, cover each space with square meters, and count the square meters. (We try not to do this on a windy day.) The students usually find that many of the parking spaces are not the same size and that they greatly underestimated the area of the spaces. This exercise makes even more clear the meaning of the term *area* as a surface to be covered.

To practice measuring area with square centimeters, each of the students is given a sheet of square centimeter paper and asked to find the area of their hand in square centimeters. Afterward, we discuss their results, including the methods that they used. Students always come up with several ways to solve this problem, which also turns out to be a good lesson in problem solving. Most of them trace their hand on the paper, although some of them do it with the fingers spread apart (a legacy of the "turkeys" they made in elementary school by tracing their hand); others trace with their fingers together. Some number the squares and count, including the fractional parts. Others draw a rectangle around their hand, figure out the

area of the rectangle, and then subtract the square centimeters uncovered by their hand. Still others use estimation skills, figuring out the total number of square centimeters on the page and reasoning that their hand covers one-half or one-third of the page.

Students are often surprised at the ingenuity of their classmates' methods and often disappointed at what they perceive to be their own lack of imagination. They can't understand, for example, why it never occurred to them to close their fingers when tracing their hand—so as to present a more solid figure with which to work. They learn that many ways to solve a problem exist but that some ways may be more efficient than others. They learn a great deal from the thinking of their peers.

They repeat this activity for homework, selecting an object in their home or dormitory room to measure. This activity gives them a chance to try out some of their classmates' methods. It also helps them to develop a visual image of a square centimeter.

MEASUREMENT OF VOLUME AND CAPACITY

To introduce the concepts of volume and capacity and the metric units associated with these attributes, I ask the students to collect six cardboard square decimeters (now quite familiar to them). In class, we look at a square decimeter and discuss what we would have to do if we wanted to use it to hold two cups of sugar. They agree that it would have to have sides—not only length and width now, but height. They tape together five square decimeters, leaving the sixth one attached on only one side so that they have a box that can be open or closed (see fig. 4). We discuss the difference between the box when it is open and when it is closed, noting that when open it has a capacity of one cubic decimeter and when closed it takes up one cubic decimeter of space.

Working in small groups with the entire class's supply of cubic decimeters, they estimate the capacity in cubic decimeters of several shopping bags (see fig. 5). Using the same worksheet as in other measurement activities, they record their estimates, fill the bags with cubic decimeters, and count how many are required to fill each bag. We talk about the difference between surface area (measured in square units) and three-dimensional space (measured in cubic units).

For the next activity, they use patterns for closed and open cubic centimeter boxes (see fig. 6) and make several of each; cardboard from empty cereal boxes, milk containers, and so on can be used. At the next class session, each student works with a partner to figure out how many cubic centimeters will fill a cubic decimeter box. Since enough cubic centimeters are not available to fill the cubic decimeter box, the students have to use the few they have and figure out the answer. They are usually surprised that the answer is one thousand, a fact that leads to a discussion of how the number of dimensions affects the relationships among the centimeter, decimeter, and meter units. They have their homemade measuring instruments available for comparison. They review their decimeters and centimeters; their square decimeters and square centimeters; and their cubic decimeters and cubic centimeters; then they look for the differences. We make a chart on the chalkboard to record the pattern (see fig. 7).

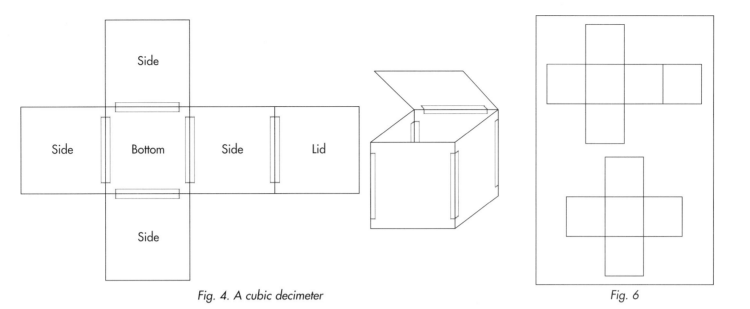

Fig. 4. A cubic decimeter

Fig. 6

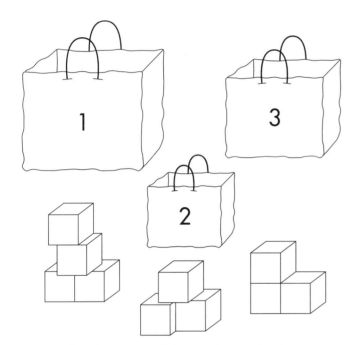

Fig. 5. Finding the capacity of shopping bags with cubic decimeters

MEASUREMENT OF LIQUIDS

For most students, learning about the unit for the measurement of liquid capacity is as much an eye-opener as their previous experiences with metrics. With their open cubic decimeter boxes in front of them, we review the meaning of capacity. Then they line their boxes with plastic bags, fill them to the top with water, close the bags with twisters, and remove the plastic bags from the boxes (see fig. 8). When they find that this is the elusive *liter* of their soda purchases, they're very pleased with themselves. They repeat this activity at home and compare a liter to a quart measure (a liter is a little more than a quart). At the next class session they reason that if we switched to liters for milk and juice, prices could justifiably be a bit higher than they are now for a quart. They think it's "neat" that metric measurements are related to each other in these ways.

MEASUREMENT OF WEIGHT

To show them just how cleverly the metric system fits together (unlike our own English system), we briefly discuss metric units for weight. Taking a liter bag of water out of a cubic decimeter box, we pass it around the room, this time paying attention to how heavy it feels. Using a balance scale, we compare its weight to a shoe, a sneaker, several notebooks, and a two-pound package of sugar. Only after we do several comparisons do they learn that this cubic decimeter of water has a weight of one kilogram and that in the metric system not only length and volume measures are related but liquid measure and weight as well. We balance our kilogram of water with an equal weight of clay. This way we have a more manageable material to work with and can subdivide it into one-half of a kilogram (500 grams), one-quarter of a kilogram (250 grams), and one-eighth of a kilogram (125 grams). If time permits, students can take turns weighing several objects with these homemade weights.

We talk about how a person could start with one unit, such as the decimeter (just as they did), and create the other units. By dividing the decimeter into ten equal parts, a person would have a centimeter. By attaching ten decimeters together, a person would have a meter. Using the decimeter as a guide, a person could make a square decimeter. By putting five square decimeters together, he or she could make a cubic decimeter box. Filling the box with a plastic liner and water, the person could produce a liter of water. The liter of water represents a kilogram in weight. I tell them that this is one of my favorite examination questions!

SUMMING UP

Having explored a variety of metric units and having made several homemade measuring instruments, my preservice teacher-students are now quite comfortable with the metric system. They have a visual image in their heads of the size of several units. They know how the units relate to each other. They know a little about the history of metrics. Only when they reach this stage of readiness do I give them several references so that they can further pursue metrics on their own.

Decimeter	What it measures	Dimensions	Size in centimeters
One decimeter	length (or width or height)	one	10 centimeters (1 × 10)
One square decimeter	area	two (length and width or side and side)	100 square centimeters (10 × 10)
One cubic decimeter	volume (or capacity)	three (length, width, and height or side, side, and side)	1000 cubic centimeters (10 × 10 × 10)

Fig. 7. The decimeter and centimeter connection

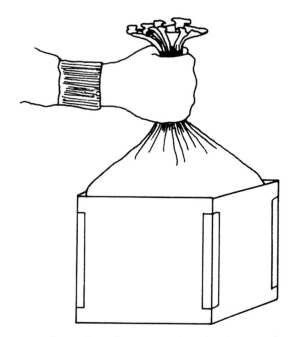

Fig. 8. Lifting a liter of water out of a cubic decimeter box

objects; and recognizing the differences among linear, area, and volume measurements.

But the main goals of teaching this hands-on metric unit have been to convince preservice teachers of the value of manipulative materials for learning new mathematics concepts and to help them understand the meaning of a manipulative approach to teaching mathematics. The activities described here are successful in achieving these goals. By the end of the unit, the student teachers have a repertoire of hands-on measurement activities that they can use in a classroom. They are also convinced that what has worked for them will work for children.

Bibliography

Hallerberg, Arthur. "The Metric System: Past, Present, Future?" *Arithmetic Teacher* 20 (April 1973): 247–55.

Jensen, Rosalie. "Multilevel Metric Games." *Arithmetic Teacher* 31 (October 1984): 36–39.

Keyser, Tamara J., and Randall J. Souviney. *Measurement and the Child's Environment.* Santa Monica, Calif.: Goodyear Publishing Co., 1980.

Kurtz, V. Ray. *Metrics for Elementary and Middle Schools.* Washington, D.C.: National Education Association, 1978.

Masat, Francis E., and Charles H. Page. *Teaching the Metric System with Activities.* Lincoln, Neb.: Professional Educators Publications, 1977.

Mathematics Education Task Force. *An Introduction to the SI Metric System: In-Service Guide for Teaching Measurement, Kindergarten through Grade Eight.* Sacramento, Calif.: California State Department of Education, 1975.

Michigan Council of Teachers of Mathematics. *Activities in Metric Measurement.* Monograph No. 11, Guidelines for Quality Mathematics Teaching Monograph Series. November 1976.

University of the State of New York, Bureau of Elementary Curriculum Development. "Let's Use the Metric System: A Supplement to Mathematics K–6." Albany, N.Y.: State Education Department, n.d.

University of the State of New York, Bureau of General Education Curriculum Development. "Suggestions for Teaching Mathematics Using Laboratory Approaches in Grades 1–3: The Metric System." Albany, N.Y.: State Education Department, 1977. ▲

We sum up what they have learned by making a chart of all the units they know. We indicate on the chart what each unit measures and a common object or two that can be used as a referent. For example, the kilogram measures weight (or mass) and is about as heavy as a two-pound box of sugar. The liter measures liquid capacity and is the amount of liquid that fits into a cubic decimeter box; it is also a little more than a quart.

We also review and record some general measurement skills and concepts that they have used in their metric activities, including the idea that these skills and concepts are applicable to all measurement systems, not just the metric system. Some of the items that we come up with are the following skills: laying down multiple copies of units and counting; iterating (using only one unit and moving it along, keeping track of the number as you go), estimating to form a mental image of a unit and to measure inaccessible

From the File:
Teaching Pi and Charity

by

Jerry Silverman

Geometry

Teaching Pi and Charity

Whenever I teach the ratio of circumference to diameter, I try to make it a memorable experience in more than one way:

1. I ask each student to bring in a can of food that has a paper label.

2. Students carefully slit vertically, remove, and measure the labels lengthwise (this length is actually the circumference of the cans).

3. Students measure the diameters of the cans and divide the result into the labels' lengths.

4. They record the quotients on the chalkboard to show that everyone, regardless of the size of can, gets something in the vicinity of 3.14.

5. They then tape the labels back onto their original cans.

6. We donate the cans to the home-school coordinator for distribution to a needy family or local food bank.

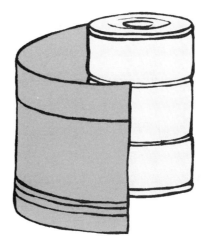

From the file of Jerry Silverman, Edward Bok Voc-Tech School, Philadelphia, PA 19148 ▲

b. Money

From the File: Money Bags

by
Donald E. Van Ostrand

Money

Money Bags

The teaching of concepts related to money requires the use of manipulatives, preferably the coins themselves. One way to give hands-on practice while preventing coins from rolling off the desks is to use resealable plastic 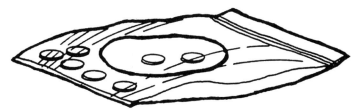 bags. On the outside of each bag draw a large circle. In the bag place the coins necessary for the particular lesson and seal the bag. Each child receives his or her own bag.

Instruct children to shake the bags to force all coins to the bottom. From this point questions can be asked, such as, "Show me a penny," and students move the coins with their fingers to the area inside the circle. The teacher can quickly scan the bags to ensure that all students have responded correctly. Other questions: "Show me one way to make six cents." "You have five cents to spend. Put five pennies inside the circle. You spend two cents. Move two cents out of the circle. How much do you have left?" Later, two bags can be used to compare quantities and values.

From the file of Donald E. Van Ostrand, Howard County Public Schools, Ellicott City, MD 21043 ▲

Teaching Money with Grids

by

Cathy L. Stevenson

Counting money and making change are often difficult concepts for students in the primary grades to grasp. Boys and girls often do not comprehend the relative values of the coins and how to combine these values to determine amounts of money. This problem often seems to exist even when students are able to give the names of the coins and their individual values by rote memory.

Monetary concepts can be taught using several rectangular shapes in varying sizes that represent values of coins to cover the squares of a hundred chart (Ginaitis 1978). In the construction of this manipulative, a 1 × 1 square of the same size as the squares on the hundred chart would represent one penny, whereas a 1 × 5 rectangle would represent a nickel; a 2 × 5 rectangle, a dime; a 5 × 5, a quarter; and a 10 × 5, a half-dollar. One side of each rectangular coin piece should have the smaller grid squares drawn on it (fig. 1), and the other side should have a picture of the respective coins (fig. 2). The limitation of this manipulative becomes evident, however, when one attempts to show $0.10, because the 2 × 5 rectangle would cover the numbers 1 through 5 and 11 through 15 on the hundred chart instead of 1 through 10.

Another difficulty results when teaching the concept of counting change. It is not possible to use the hundred chart to demonstrate the use of the fewest coins to make change. For example, if a student were asked to demonstrate how much change would result from spending $0.58 out of $1.00, the child would cover squares 1 to 58 with a piece of tagboard to represent the amount spent. The remaining area of the hundred chart would then be covered with the rectangular pieces to represent the change received. Normally, one would receive two pennies, a nickel, a dime, and a quarter in this situation, because this combination

would be the smallest number of coins to total $0.42, the change from $1.00. However, this amount cannot be demonstrated using the hundred chart, since the chart would not have a remaining area in the correct configuration to accommodate the 5 × 5 quarter shape.

To correct the limitations in this manipulative, some spatial adaptations can be made. The 10 × 10 square hundred chart can be replaced with a 20 × 5 grid that is then divided into four 5 × 5 squares. These 5 × 5 squares, each containing twenty-five smaller squares, should be numbered consecutively from 1 to 100 (see fig. 3). The rectangular pieces used to represent the coins can remain the same. The change in the chart makes it possible for a student to use the fewest possible coin pieces to demonstrate an amount of money without encountering the problem of having the wrong numbers covered on the grid.

The grid and the rectangular shapes that represent coin value are very adaptable for teaching several skills related to counting money. The activities that follow are only a few of the possible ones that may be beneficial to students. These activities proceed from easiest to hardest and from most concrete to least concrete.

Cathy Stevenson is a third-grade teacher at Selmaville School in Salem, IL 62881. She is also a former teacher of learning disabled students.

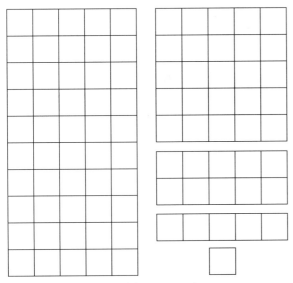

Fig. 1. Grid side of the rectangular coin pieces

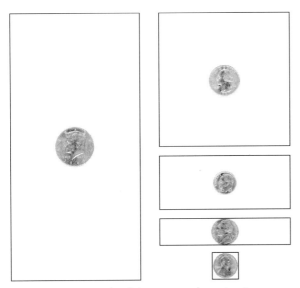

Fig. 2. Coin side of the rectangular coin pieces

ACTIVITIES FOR TEACHING THE COUNTING OF MONEY

1. Have the students cover various amounts using the fewest rectangular pieces possible. The biggest pieces should be used first, and then the others should be used in order of size. For example, to cover $0.82 the students should choose a 10 × 5, a 5 × 5, a 1 × 5, and two 1 × 1 pieces. Using the rectangular pieces with the grid side faceup first is a good way to begin because the students can visualize the activity as a jigsaw puzzle.

2. Have students replace large pieces with several smaller pieces of equal value. For instance, one 5 × 5 can be replaced by two 2 × 5 pieces and a 1 × 5. By replacing the larger pieces in as many ways as possible, the students have an opportunity to learn to make coin exchanges in several ways.

3. Have students find as many ways as possible to cover a given amount.

4. Gradually take the charts away and have the students use only the rectangles to make given amounts.

5. Have students determine the values of various combinations of the rectangular pieces.

6. The foregoing activities should then be repeated with the coin side of the rectangular pieces faceup.

7. Proceed to having the students use actual money to "fill" areas. For example, for $0.38 students would lay down a quarter to stand for boxes 1 through 25, a dime for 26 through 35, and three pennies for 36 through 38.

8. Tell students which coins to lay down on the chart and have them determine the value of those coins.

9. Have students count out given amounts using only coins.

10. Have students determine the value of given coin combinations without using the chart.

ACTIVITIES FOR MAKING CHANGE

1. Use tagboard pieces to cover an amount spent. Have the students decide which rectangular pieces will cover the remaining squares. For example, if $0.84 were spent, the child would use a 1 × 1, a 1 × 5, and a 2 × 5 piece to cover the boxes for change received from $1.00. In this example the smallest pieces should be used first, and the students should attempt to use as few pieces as possible.

2. Replace the rectangular pieces with real coins and repeat the previous activity.

3. As the students become more proficient, take the charts away.

In conclusion, the ability to use money correctly should be a vital objective for every mathematics program. Because this skill is necessary on a day-to-day basis throughout life, educators cannot ignore the need for teaching monetary skills. Many boys and girls will not learn these concepts incidentally but only through a concerted effort on the part of the teacher to develop the concepts through the use of manipulatives such as those described in this article.

1	2	3	4	5
6	7	8	9	10
11	12	13	14	15
16	17	18	19	20
21	22	23	24	25
26	27	28	29	30
31	32	33	34	35
36	37	38	39	40
41	42	43	44	45
46	47	48	49	50
51	52	53	54	55
56	57	58	59	60
61	62	63	64	65
66	67	68	69	70
71	72	73	74	75
76	77	78	79	80
81	82	83	84	85
86	87	88	89	90
91	92	93	94	95
96	97	98	99	100

Fig. 3. A 20 × 5 grid to replace the usual hundreds chart

Reference

Ginaitis, Stephen J. "Sense with Cents." *Arithmetic Teacher* 25 (January 1978): 43. ▲

From the File:
Math That Rubs You Right

by

Donna Colwell Rosser

Money

Math That Rubs You Right

If parents are interested in helping their child with coin recognition and problem solving, suggest that they help the child make rubbings as easy facsimiles of coins, then use the facsimiles to personalize and solve such problems as these:

1. If _____(your child)_____ got for his/her birthday, how much did she/he receive in all? _____

2. _____(your child)_____ was helping _____(adult)_____ to clean out _____(your child)_____ 's room. They found in a drawer. They found under the bed. They found in a little box. They found in a pocket of his/her pants.

(a) How many quarters were found? _____ How many cents does that equal? _____
(b) How many dimes were found? _____ How many cents does that equal? _____
(c) How many nickels were found? _____ How many cents does that equal? _____
(d) How many pennies were found? _____ How many cents does that equal? _____
(e) What is the total of the money _____(your child)_____ and _____(parent)_____ found in the room? _____

From the file of Donna Colwell Rosser, McKees Rocks, PA 15136 ▲

From the File: Money Dominoes

by

Jean Christian Brewer

Money

Money Dominoes

This activity teaches the recognition of equal values of sets of coins. The game is played like dominoes, except that instead of matching the number of dots on two playing pieces, the student matches equivalent values of coins (see the illustration). The game is recommended for students in grades 2–5. Used as a family game, it permits parents to participate in the learning process.

Preparing the game
Cut some old wall paneling into thirty-six three-inch-by-six-inch pieces. Spray-paint them black with a white line segment on each one to divide it in half. Glue pictures of coins onto the painted playing pieces and then varnish the tiles. No set number of playing pieces is required; fewer coins of lesser value can be used for younger students.

Rules of the game
The game can be played by two to four players. Two players take eight pieces each, three players take seven, and four players take five pieces. The game is played just like dominoes. The winner is the player whose unplayed pieces have the lowest total value of coins at the end of the game.

From the file of Jean Christian Brewer, Tunkhannock, PA 18657 ▲

Tile A—turned up to begin play; tile B—5 nickels are matched to the quarter on tile A; tile C—2 quarters are matched to 1 quarter, 2 dimes, 1 nickel on tile B; tile D—matches 1 dime, 3 nickels to the quarter on tile A

Mathematical Connections: Making It Happen in Your Classroom

by

Ray T. Robicheaux

Some years ago I heard past NCTM president Shirley M. Frye admonish her audience not to be "two-by-four teachers—stuck between two covers of the book and the four walls of the classroom." This statement seems to lie at the very heart of the *Curriculum and Evaluation Standards for School Mathematics* (NCTM 1989), for it seems that teachers' efforts are basically aimed at changing school mathematics to more closely approximate real-world mathematics.

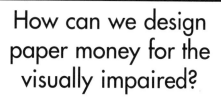

How can we design paper money for the visually impaired?

"The vision of the *Curriculum and Evaluation Standards* is that mathematical reasoning, problem solving, communication, and connections must be central" (NCTM 1991, 19). Thus validated against the curriculum standards, worthwhile mathematical tasks must possess one or more of the aforementioned ingredients. Problems that students perceive to be real are of greater interest to them than typical textbook problems. Students find them easier to talk about and more in need of solutions. This article relates an experience when the "teachable moment" afforded the opportunity to share such a problem. The premise is that you, acting as facilitator in your class, have many opportunities to create both the connections and the environment for the "teachable moment" to occur.

Ray Robicheaux teaches undergraduate mathematics and mathematics education courses at Louisiana State University at Eunice, Eunice, LA 70535. He is codirector of Science, Mathematics and Integrated Learning Experience (SMILE), a National Science Foundation–funded teacher-enhancement project.

A former student of mine related that she really liked the new directions she saw in the mathematics curriculum. Yet she still found it quite difficult to find or create activities for her sixth-grade class. In the course of the discussion, I accepted her invitation to do a demonstration lesson with her class. Fortunately, I was able to visit the classroom before the day of my scheduled lesson. I walked in on a social studies lesson near the end of a film about Helen Keller. After the film, the teacher had "blindfolded" some of the students and had them experience the difficulty of doing ordinary things when you cannot see. I thought she had really created a feeling of empathy in her students. The next day I began the demonstration lesson by reminding the students of the problems they had encountered while being blindfolded. I asked one student to close his eyes. I handed him a $10 bill and asked if he could identify it. He guessed incorrectly as the rest of the class watched. I then shared this problem with the class:

> Currently seven different denominations of paper currency are in circulation in the United States—the $1, $2, $5, $10, $20, $50, and $100 bills. Suppose, in an effort to assist visually impaired people, we attempt by a combination of corner-cutting to distinguish the different bills by touch. For uniformity, we agree that if a corner is cut from a bill, each "cut" will be the same—a right isosceles triangle with 1-centimeter legs. Is it possible to distinguish the bills in this manner? If so, use the play money supplied to model a solution. And remember, your overall purpose is to help visually impaired people.

The class was divided into cooperative groups, and play money was furnished. Some questions arose about the "cut." After illustrating the triangular cut and noting the congruency (same size and shape) of two triangles, we noted that in this situation estimation would serve well; one did not have to measure exactly for purposes of the problem.

Some groups chose to draw. Others bent or cut corners from the play money. In less than three minutes an enthusiastic group yelled, "We got it!" Figure 1 depicts its solution. I asked the group to check the $10 bill and $20 bill closely. I then instructed one of the members of the group to close her eyes and then identify which of the two bills I would hand her. I flipped the $20 bill to match the $10 bill and handed it to her. Other groups had quit working to watch. She identified the $20 bill as the $10 bill, opened her eyes, and immediately realized her error, exclaiming, "I forgot you can't tell the back from the front when you can't see!" A few other students made similar errors, but most were corrected by others within their group.

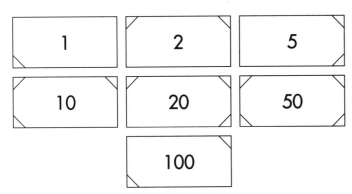

Fig. 1. An initial attempt at cutting corners to distinguish different denominations

The question then arose whether at least one corner must be cut. Asking the questioner to close his eyes, I gave him an uncut bill and one with a corner cut off. I asked if he could distinguish the bills. He answered that he could, and the group then reported they had a solution (fig. 2). Soon other groups had solutions.

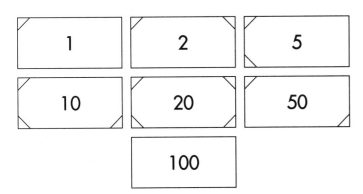

Fig. 2. A solution distinguishing the seven denominations

I checked with each group, noted their solutions, and congratulated them on their efforts. I then reminded them of our original intention—to help visually impaired people. I suggested that in our effort to help, we may have changed only the form of the problem. I went to the first group (fig. 2) and told them to study their bills because I was going to check them on recognition. All four closed their eyes; I snipped another corner from the $1 bill as the class watched (fig. 3). The group identified the bill as the $50 bill. Collective "Ahas" were heard, heads went down, chatter increased considerably—at this juncture students recognized the pattern.

Fig. 3. An example of converting a lower denomination to a higher value

Note that more than one solution is possible—the cuts for the $5, $10, and $20 bills can be interchanged. We rechecked our models and discussed the pattern. We noted that with a proper solution (see fig. 4), people who cut a corner would be foolish, since they would only defraud themselves.

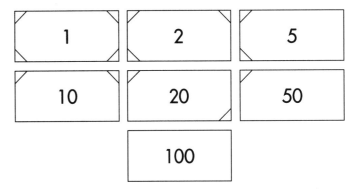

Fig. 4. An example of a proper solution

Next consider the problem. I selected this particular problem to espouse connections to a real-world situation for the teacher and also because she had enabled me to make the connection—she had given me the "teachable moment." Beyond connection, the problem lends itself to communication. It presents a reason to review and discuss congruency and right isosceles triangles and to consider estimation versus exactness in terms of the cut made. The students talked about "turns and flips"—transformation geometry. The problem required combinatorial logic and employed the problem-solving heuristic of pattern recognition.

Opportunities for real-world mathematics exist all about us. Suppose I also taught science and were to discuss recycling. I wonder how many bills I would have to cut before the "corners" would constitute enough recycled paper for a new bill? Let's see. First I would have to measure exactly, find the area of the "corner cut" and of the bill, and then…. Wonder if it makes a difference which bill is cut? Wonder if we should print equal numbers of each bill? Wonder if visually impaired people can distinguish between the different bills as they now are? If so, how do they do it (social studies connection)? I wonder if…. Don't be a "2 × 4" mathematics teacher. The teachable moment and the real-world connections are yours to make.

References

National Council of Teachers of Mathematics. *Curriculum and Evaluation Standards for School Mathematics.* Reston, Va.: The Council, 1989.

———. *Professional Standards for Teaching Mathematics.* Reston. Va.: The Council, 1991. ▲

May I Take Your Order?

by

Linda Kulas

Profits from a class project benefited the humane society—and the children.

Most third graders have enjoyed an occasignal foray to a fast-food establishment or, if they were lucky, to a more formal restaurant. I decided to build on this experience and to extend the mathematics learning in my classroom with a unit called "restaurant mathematics."

RESTAURANT MATHEMATICS

I began this unit by collecting menus from several local restaurants and letting each child select one menu to use. In addition, each child was given a set amount of play money to spend at the chosen restaurant and a recording sheet on which to list menu selections, prices, the bill's total, and any change received.

Linda Kulas teaches third and fourth grade at Guilford Central School, Guilford, VT 05301. She is interested in helping children make connections between classroom mathematics and real-life situations.

For the first activity, children selected a predetermined number of items from the menu and recorded them on the sheet. By applying the appropriate addition and subtraction skills already developed and practiced in class, they computed their bill and the change they would receive. They were encouraged to check the work with their calculators. A few practice sessions were required for all the children to master the basic concepts inherent in these restaurant transactions.

One beginning assignment had a side benefit of encouraging good nutritional practices:

> Buy a breakfast for yourself that includes a fruit, a grain, and a dairy choice. You have five dollars to spend. What will your bill total? What change will you get back from your five dollars?

To expand the complexity of the assignment, the students were given an increased amount of money over time and were encouraged to order any number of items from the menu. A later assignment involved spending twenty-five dollars to treat a friend to lunch. An example of a completed recording sheet is shown in figure 1. To personalize the activity even more, children could be given a budget of fifty dollars that could be used to take their entire family to dinner.

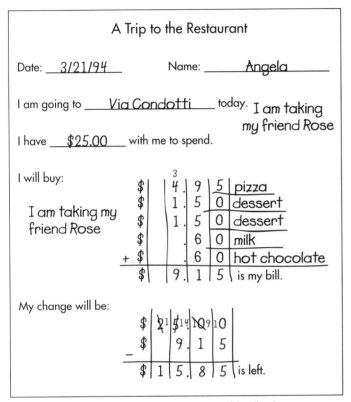

Fig. 1. This student did not exceed her budget.

Solving problems presented in this format soon became very comfortable for all the children in the class. This activity could easily be adapted to meet the individual skills of the children. The level of interest remained high as students chose which restaurant to visit and what to purchase.

It was only a matter of time before students asked if they could run their own restaurant. Because my teaching philosophy has evolved to emphasize student empowerment and participation in curriculum development, I found myself saying, "Why not?"

ORGANIZING A CLASSROOM RESTAURANT

In the week that followed, students participated in a wide range of activities and made many decisions. We began by writing a letter to their families, sharing with them our intentions and asking for their help with food donations. The children made all the decisions about the minirestaurant and soon realized the importance of dividing tasks among committees. They chose to open their restaurant to the primary wing of the school, which included kindergarten through third grade.

Eventually the children devised a system that split the class into three teams of seven or eight children. Each team supplied the

food for two visiting classes of children. Our menu, the product of a class vote, included fruit juice, fruits and vegetables, popcorn, cheese and crackers, cookies, and a "special of the day" that allowed for creativity at home when preparing donations. The three teams rotated the restaurant duties: for two shifts, each team assumed the role of server; food preparer; and cashier, host, and bus person. Each child took home a "food donation opportunity form," which listed the specific dates the food was needed, indicated the types of food wanted, and asked for a commitment from the child's family. (See fig. 2.)

Food Donation Opportunity Form

My team is responsible for providing food for our class restaurant on April _____.

I need to bring in one donation to serve approximately 20 children. Please select one from the following list of possibilities:

- fruit or vegetable (finger food and cut at home if needed)
- crackers and cheese (sliced)
- cookies
- fruit juice (2 cans)
- special of the day (finger food and simple)

- -

I will donate _____ for the class

restaurant to be sent to school on _____.

Thank you for your help—we couldn't do this without you!

Fig. 2. A donation form aids in communication with parents.

The children wanted to use their own money to buy paper products and some food. Recognizing an excellent opportunity to introduce the concept of stockholding, I helped them develop a system for selling stock to raise capital. By selling shares at twenty-five cents each, the children were able to acquire start-up funds to cover initial restaurant expenses. Each stock purchaser was limited to buying four shares and received a formal stock certificate to record the purchase (fig. 3). Purchasers were also informed that they would be repaid at the end of the project if the restaurant broke even. Participation in the stock plan was optional. Many children used their allowances or savings to buy from one to four shares of stock.

A committee presented to the class a list of possible ways to donate any restaurant profits, which was discussed and voted on. A discussion of the tie vote—to improve the school's baseball field or to donate funds to the county's humane society—became a fascinating study in children's values and ethical decision making. The final vote favored the humane society.

With organizational matters concluded, the children invited a parent who was also a professional restaurant-personnel trainer to present a thirty-minute training session on personal hygiene, social manners, and taking and serving orders. She introduced the children to the new word *waitron*, a nonsexist alternative to

This is to certify that

_____

purchased _____ share(s) of stock, 1 share @ 25¢ in the

_____ Restaurant

on _____

Signed _____

Fig. 3. A stock certificate was issued to those students interested in raising capital for the restaurant.

You Are Invited to the Third Grade Restaurant!

Thursday, April 29
9:30 a.m., 10:45 a.m., 2:00 p.m.

Fig. 4. The grand opening is advertised.

waiter and *waitress*, that the children decided to use in their restaurant. This presentation added a serious slant to the project to which the children responded by carrying out their different responsibilities very professionally.

The children used real restaurant ordering forms and practiced adding the orders in that format after reviewing a transparency of a restaurant's form on the overhead projector. The final step was to role-play the different jobs. Each child practiced preparing food, taking and serving orders, and being cashier for about one hour, which was time well spent.

THE GRAND OPENING

The actual two days of restaurant life in our classroom ran smoothly. We were open for business during two twenty-five-minute morning sessions and one afternoon session. Six classes were served. The children prepared invitations for special guests from the middle school, teachers and others in our school building, and parents (see fig. 4).

The classroom desks were pushed together to form large tables that could seat six customers. The restaurant's atmosphere was enhanced by covering the tables with borrowed tablecloths and decorating them with centerpieces. The waitrons continued the theme by wearing matching aprons.

The children set their price range from five cents to fifty cents so that all children could participate. The class composed and sent the following letter to primary students' families:

!Snacktime!

This Wednesday 4/28/93 and Thursday 4/29/93 Mrs. Kulas's class is having a little restaurant. The prices are low and the food is healthy. We would like you to give your kid, or kids some money to buy snacks. Some of the snacks will be:

fruit juice—10¢
fruit and vegetables—small 15¢, large 25¢
popcorn—10¢
cheese/crackers—5¢
cookies—15¢
special of the day—25¢–50¢

The third grade class

Classroom teachers brought extra nickels to ensure that all children could purchase a snack.

Profits would go to the humane society.

Customers were seated by the host and given a menu that had been handwritten by the class (fig. 5). Waitrons wrote orders and served food. Cashiers used calculators to figure larger bills more quickly. The bus persons were assigned the least popular job—cleaning up after customers.

Menu

1) Cheese/Crackers	5¢
2) Cookies	15¢
3) Fruit/Vegetables	15¢ small
	25¢ large
4) Popcorn	10¢
5) Juice	25¢
6) Special of the day	25¢
	50¢

Fig. 5

The response, in terms of both food donations from third-grade families and customer appreciation, was fantastic. The finance committee prepared the following final statement:

Dear Stockholders and Interested People.

The 3rd grade Snack bar was a smash. We made $89.00 dollars. We must give $21.50 back to our stockholders. The profit is $67.50 to go to the Windham County Humane Society.

Thanks for all your support.

Yours truly,
Andrew
Billy
Meghan

For the 3rd grade class.

PROJECT ACCOMPLISHMENTS AND EXTENSIONS

In addition to transferring basic mathematics skills to a real-life situation, this restaurant project helped children learn about committee work, economic principles of stocks and shareholding, concepts of profit and nonprofit work, costs and profits, and social graces and conventions in the workplace. The students' work with money helped them to figure bills, make change, and learn how to use a calculator quickly and accurately. Group decision making and designing a project from start to finish were also valuable experiences for these young children.

An extension of this project witnessed a small group of third graders making a shopping trip to the grocery store to buy supplies, offering the opportunity to view unit pricing and to comparison shop. One group also visited the bank to have adequate change on hand for the restaurant's cash-register drawer. A class trip was made to the county humane society to donate the proceeds from the project and to visit a local restaurant. Our donation furnished a six-month supply of food for the occupants of one dog cage and one cat cage.

The final assignment asked children to write an assessment of the class restaurant and to include what they had learned, what they disliked, and what should be changed the next time. This activity constituted a fine opportunity for reflection and an excellent connection between language arts and mathematics.

MODIFYING THE MODEL

The restaurant project could easily be modified to fit the particular needs and strengths of the children in a given classroom. It presupposes reasonably well developed social skills and previous experiences with problem-solving strategies. Spending several months working together as a group should precede implementing the project.

The restaurant activity could be simplified by reducing the number of classes served, limiting the menu choices, and preparing the food in school.

The project could be adapted to different socioeconomic settings by allocating a small part of the classroom budget to cover the initial costs of the restaurant or by seeking a loan or donation from a local community organization. The latter approach would strengthen ties between the school and the community. Since expenses are very low—about twenty dollars to serve 150 customers—and a profit is almost a certainty, being able to pay back any loans incurred is a reasonable expectation. Although the model assumes some food donations from the families of students, covering the increased costs for food prepared in school or purchased should be possible. If the classes come from a population of limited financial means, teachers could supply the children with play money or tickets if participating classes have a fund or classroom budget from which to draw.

This project could also be adapted to fit the skills and needs of a classroom of older students. Such an expanded restaurant might feed more customers; offer a more elaborate menu; or serve a full meal, such as breakfast or lunch. The project could also be an excellent fund-raising activity for a class trip.

The children's basic experience of applying their mathematics learning to a real-life situation and developing their own model for a classroom activity has the potential for being a powerful learning experience in a variety of settings.

The following journal entries sum up students' sentiments:

• "My thoughts about the restaurant: the best part was being a watron. The not so good part was bus person! Running the restaurant thoutht me that you have to go as fast as you can. I think that the restaurant went good! I wouldn't change any thing!"

• "The best part about the snack bar was being a waitron because you got [to take] orders and add up there bill. The hard part about being a waitron is balancing the tray. The bad part about the restaurant was the mess people made. Running a restaurant taught me that you have to be very clean."

• "The best part about the snack bar was being a watress. I realy felt likee I was working in a restaurant it was a lot of fun! I also licked working in the kichen. I would give people there order it was fun. What was cind of hard for me is that I couldn't get all of the orders down fast enef so the other people would not have to wait to long. Runing the restaurant tot me how to work with people and how to cuwoperrate better. I also lernd how to macke a costermer happy. By being clean and have a smiyle. I learned how to cory a trey and yoose checks. If I would change any thing I would have more tables and chars and I would have the uper grads come."

• "The best part about the snack bar [was] that we made so much money for the humains society…. Running the restaurant tought me about how to sell things at fair prices."

Bibliography

Moniuszko, Linda K. "'Reality Math.'" *Arithmetic Teacher* 39 (September 1991): 10–16.

National Council of Teachers of Mathematics. *Curriculum and Evaluation Standards for School Mathematics.* Reston, Va.: The Council, 1989. ▲

The 5 and 3 Store

by

Bonnie Harvey

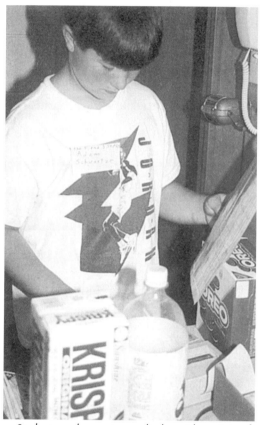

Students and parents supplied a wide variety of products.

"Lane two is open. Lane two is open." This statement was greeted with enthusiasm as students shopped in a "grocery store" set up to offer experience in money skills and management.

This unit was introduced during the first month of school when the fifth-grade students in Room 5-3 at Mayview Elementary in Mayview, Missouri, were asked to start saving empty food containers. Students were told that a grocery store would be set up in the room to present a lesson in consumer mathematics. Each student would be given fake currency by the teacher to gain experience in shopping and learning to work with money. The store was made to look as realistic as possible. Empty canned goods that had been opened from the bottom were placed on the table so they looked unused. Empty plastic bread and candy bags were stuffed with paper, and used cereal boxes and detergent containers were taped shut.

Spendthrift students learned the value of money.

By the end of November, enough items to use in the store had been collected to fill several large trash bags. This experience involved students in direct participation, which was planned. When students came back from their Thanksgiving break, they set up their "5 and 3 Grocery Store" (see fig. 1).

Bonnie Harvey teaches fifth grade in the Odessa R-7 School District, Mayview, MO 64071. She has sixteen years of teaching experience at the elementary and junior high school levels.

Students and parents supplied a wide variety of products. Everything from baby formula to soft-drink cartons and hair-care items lined the table. Props played an important role in setting up the 5 and 3 Grocery Store. Among the props used were several copies of the Missouri sales-tax sheet, four adding machines, grocery carts, a table for the groceries, calculators, twenty dollars in fake currency for each shopper, and enough fake money for the clerks to make change.

Before the grand opening and any time new items were brought in, students helped price merchandise by using felt-tipped markers to write the price on the box, sack, or can before stocking the table. The teacher helped students price items in comparison to what they would cost in the local grocery store. Pricing gave everyone an opportunity to think about the cost of each item.

The big day for the grand opening finally arrived. Students could go to the store when they were done with their work. They also had a forty-minute period each day for one month when they could visit the store. Each student started out with twenty dollars in fake currency with which to purchase goods. In the beginning, students could buy as many groceries as they wanted. Some students discovered that they did not have enough money to pay their grocery bill. The clerks at each of the four checkout lanes would use the adding machines to total each student's purchases, use the subtotal key before adding tax, and then total to find the final amount. At this point, the purchaser would hand the cashier enough money to cover the purchase. The cashier's responsibility was to give the correct change to the customer using the fake currency and coins.

After several days, the spendthrift students were encouraged to learn more about the value of money. At one point, they could have only five dollars to purchase their goods. They quickly learned that their five dollars did not buy very much. Sometimes

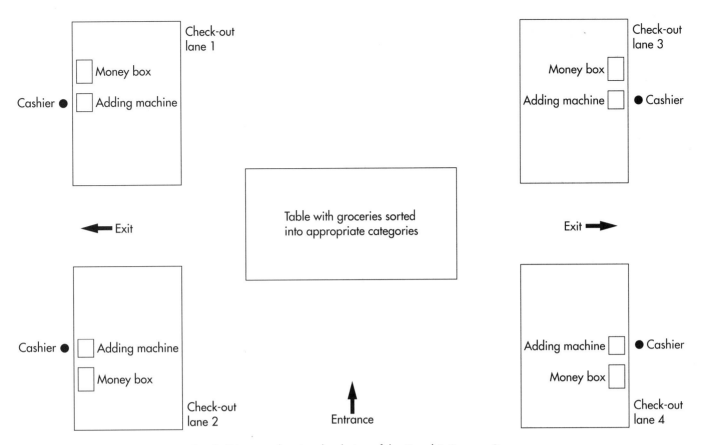

Fig. 1. Diagram showing the design of the 5 and 3 Grocery Store

they could not purchase an item they wanted because they were over their budget. They then had to decide which item or items they could do without. Some students made shopping lists at home and then realized they could not afford everything, so they learned to economize.

Calculator use can be incorporated into this activity. Students can add their purchases, calculate tax, and total their bill before going to one of the check-out lanes. In this way, they are more actively involved and can double check to see if the cashier is doing his or her job correctly. On a related note, cooperative learning evolved as students helped other students learn to use the adding machines and make correct change.

The big day for the grand opening finally arrived.

Estimation is a skill that students will use many times in their lives. One day a cart was filled with groceries that were distributed around the room with each student receiving four items. Students were to estimate the total amount of the four items so they would generally know what their bill would be. They did a great job of approximating the cost of their purchases.

As the closing day of the store approached, students reflected on the objectives achieved. The smiles, teamwork, and yes, even grocery lists, told that the time and effort spent had been a worthwhile experience.

Items were priced as they would be in the store.

The store accomplished several objectives. Students learned the following:

- to appreciate the value of money in relation to purchasing power
- to use a sales-tax sheet
- to make change
- to become better estimators

THE 5 AND 3 STORE

Students learned to appreciate the value of money in relation to purchasing power.

They saw the importance of estimation.

The following list of students' comments reveals their feelings about the store:

- "I like the store because I like estimating."
- "I did not like money; but now I really do, thanks to the store."

Estimation skills were honed.

- "I just wish it was real food. Even though it isn't, this store is still super fun."
- "I really enjoyed learning about shopping in the store and counting change."
- "I like the store because I learned to add tax and subtract change."
- "I think it shows you what it would be like when you grow up and how to spend your money."

The last comment sums up the real objective of the unit. Frequently money is taken for granted by students who do not comprehend how much money is needed to live. This lesson allowed students the opportunity to use skills of money management that will follow them into adulthood.

Changes that will be implemented in the next 5-and-3-Grocery-Store unit will include discussion about, and emphasis on, nutrition and the four basic food groups, along with proper meal planning and the effect of improper eating habits on the body.

Bibliography

Axelson, Sharon. "Supermarket Challenge." *Arithmetic Teacher* 40 (October 1992): 84–88.

Brickman, Mary. "Food for Math." *Arithmetic Teacher* 34 (September 1986): 48–49.

Burkett, Leonard, and Edie L. Whitfield. "Store-bought Mathematics." *Arithmetic Teacher* 33 (December 1985): 36–37.

Burzler, Donald R., Jr. "Be a Super Shopper!" *Arithmetic Teacher* 25 (March 1978): 40–44, 46.

Dahlquist, Joyce. "Playing Store for Real." *Arithmetic Teacher* 24 (March 1977): 208–10.

Dana, Marcia E., and Mary Montgomery Lindquist. "Food for Thought." *Arithmetic Teacher* 25 (April 1978): 6–11. ▲

c. Time

Readers' Dialogue: Calendar Mathematics

by

Mary Ann Starkey

The daily routine of marking the calendar is a real-world activity that meets many of the NCTM's curriculum standards. Students are encouraged to be problem solvers and mathematical thinkers other than just during mathematics class. Number sense, time communication, problem solving, and mathematical connections to the real world are all part of calendar mathematics.

Marking our classroom calendar has become a major event in our daily routine. Solving the system then locating the appropriate date is a total-class activity. Each month has a different system. The students soon discover the system to locate the day's date. Last year's systems were as follows:

September—Apple cutouts with little happy-face stickers. The apple with six happy faces represented 6 September.

October—Jack-o'-lantern cutouts with tally marks. The jack-o'-lantern with ||||| illustrated 6 October.

November—Turkey cutouts with mathematics problems on them. The turkey with the problem 3 + 3 depicted 6 November.

December—Tree cutouts with stars and gold balls. Each gold ball equaled 10 and each star equaled 1. The tree with one gold ball and one star denoted 11 December.

January—Student-made snowman cutouts with number words on them. The snowman with the word *five* represented 5 January.

February—Heart cutouts with letters of the alphabet. The heart with E, the fifth letter, depicted 5 February. (27 February = AA, 28 February = BB, 29 February = CC.)

March—Shamrock cutouts with combination mathematics problems. The shamrock with the problem 3 + 3 − 1 illustrated 5 March.

April—Umbrella cutouts with Roman numerals. The umbrella with one X represented 10 April.

May—Flower cutouts with paper money. The flower with a dime and two pennies depicted 12 May. May's format resulted in the most elaborate discussion periods. Students explained alternative ways to arrive at the date—even pulling their lunch money out of their pockets to prove a point.

June—Bear cutouts with ordinal words. The bear with the word *second* denoted 2 June.

As the year went by, students, parents, and fellow teachers soon suggested alternative calendar systems. I now have more ideas than months in a school year!

Mary Ann Starkey
1549 Hilltop Road
Downingtown, PA 19335 ▲

Teaching Students to Tell Time

by

Gloria S. Andrade

Recently I read that teaching the skill of telling time is unessential because, after all, "Is any adult unable to perform this task?" I can't agree with that reasoning because too many of my nine- and ten-year-old students are embarrassed by their inability to tell time.

Realizing this need, I've developed a sequence of activities beginning with concrete explorations that enables students to understand the concept of time and how analog clocks work.

I first presented the following lessons to second graders in February and have since used it with students in the third and fourth grades who are unable to tell time.

By communicating to parents the activities and objectives presented in this unit, this learning experience can be supported and extended to the students' daily lives.

The unit has the following objectives:

Cognitive: The students will be able to read an analog clock, as well as understand the reading of a digital clock with 100 percent accuracy.

Affective: (1) Students will be able to work cooperatively in small groups to solve problems presented in this unit. (2) Students will express enjoyment of mathematics and show improved self-concept.

Psychomotor: Students will manipulate a variety of materials and will engage in role-playing activities to master successfully the skill of telling time.

DAY 1

Objectives

Cognitive: Students will be able to skip-count the pattern 5, 10, 15, 20, … using kinesthetic movements and snap-clap rhythms after laying out sixty Unifix cubes in a circular pattern to simulate the face of a clock.

Affective: Students will be able to work cooperatively in small groups to construct a simulated analog clock.

Gloria Andrade teaches Chapter 1 mathematics at the Hyman Fine School in Attleboro, MA 02703. She has a special interest in designing developmental mathematics activities for elementary school children.

Psychomotor: Students, while role-playing various parts of a clock, will be able to simulate the passage of time in minutes on their analog clock.

Activities

The students work in groups of four. Each group is given a set of Unifix cubes, beans, counters, or plastic cubes. Their task is to count sixty objects, which most do by grouping them in sets of ten. Because of past experiences, most students are more comfortable working in base ten. This task could be accomplished in base five but would require more direction by the teacher.

Each group is assigned a floor space marked with a small circle. This location becomes the base from which students are to use their manipulatives to form a large circle. It is interesting to see how they work this out. Some use only their eyes, others use a yardstick to measure equal distances from the center, and still others use terms like "not straight lines, they have to curve the manipulatives." (See fig. 1.) After the circle is made, each team is given twelve two-inch-by-three-inch cards on which they are told to write the numbers 1 through 12.

Fig. 1. Working cooperatively, students use sixty Unifix cubes to form a circle.

At this point the students are gathered as a whole group to review their tasks and to predict what they are constructing. Some know that they are making a clock. Next they study their clocks and assign names to the parts (minute marks and hour numerals).

What is missing? They answer, "Hands!" and assume the role of the hands. Each team selects a "big hand" and a "little hand." Another person becomes a "caller" and the last, a "clapper." The task of the caller is to count to sixty slowly as "Big" walks around the clock; the clapper claps at each multiple of five. "Big" stops at each multiple of five, and "Little" then places, in sequence, the numbered cards at the sound of each clap (see fig. 2).

In reviewing this activity, the students come to the following conclusions:

1. A pattern emerges: the minute hand repeats the skip-counting pattern 5, 10, 15, ..., 60. This pattern is written on the chalkboard by one member from each team, and students circle the repeated pattern on the chalkboard. This exercise helps those who need additional experience in seeing pattern and sequence.

2. " Big" walks sixty beats.

3. The students note that the numbers 1–12 do not refer to "Big."

4. Someone usually asks if we are learning the five-times table. Another asks if we are dividing sixty by fives.

DAY 2

Objectives

Cognitive: Students will be able to tell that fifteen and thirty minutes past the hour are equal to a quarter hour and a half hour, respectively, and correctly position the hands of the clock by using kinesthetic movements and chanting the skip-counting pattern 5, 10, 15, ...

Affective: Students will be able to work cooperatively in small groups to simulate the movements of the hands on a clock.

Psychomotor: Students, while role-playing and chanting, will simulate the position of the minute and hour hands as at the half hour.

Activities

We set up our clocks as we do on day 1, but this time we stop at thirty and discover that thirty manipulatives are left; thus, we conclude that thirty minutes is a half-hour. We lay tape down to show that the clock can be divided in half by connecting between the 12 and the 6 (see fig. 3).

One team may note that we could divide the circle in half by connecting the 9 and the 3. The students discover that if we begin counting "Big's" passage at the 12, as we had done on the first day, then fifteen minutes and forty-five minutes of time pass when "Big" stands at 3 and 9, respectively.

The students also discover that the clockface is now divided in four equal parts. I explain that the fifteen-count position can be called *quarter past the hour* and the forty-five-count position can be referred to as *forty-five minutes past the hour,* or *fifteen minutes*

to the next hour. Using a variety of terms and expressions broadens the student's mathematical vocabulary and enriches the understanding of the language of mathematics for the young learner.

"Little" and "Big" start this day's journey at 12 o'clock. I record this time on the chalkboard in words and in its numerical form. Students decide that "Big" rests at this point; thus, its position is written as __:00 (its eyes are closed). The caller signals "Big" and "Little" to begin their hour's journey.

The caller and the clapper (student designated to signal 12:05, 12:10, etc.) continue keeping time until "Big" reaches thirty minutes past the hour. When the students are asked to recall what part of the circle has been covered, they chant, "Half." Half the journey is over; thus, the hour hand, "Little," which had been moving slowly to the next number, should be halfway to the destination and thereafter should move closer to the next hour as "Big" moves the remaining thirty beats to its on-the-hour position, or journey's end.

The students enjoy repeating this activity, taking the various roles in turn. Some students dramatize "Big" by clasping their hands over their head. Sometimes the clock ticks very slowly, and at times it breaks down. Nevertheless, the students share many

Fig. 2. "Big" walks around the clock stopping at multiples of 5; "Little" places the numbered cards 1–12 in sequence.

Fig. 3. Laying down tape to show that thirty cubes are equal to half the circle (half of "Big's" hour-long journey)

laughs, and when the clock runs perfectly, they put on a show for the entire group. (See fig. 4.) We call our acts the "Swiss Clock Makers"; some call their clocks the "Swatches."

DAY 3

Objectives

Cognitive: Shown cards with time written digitally and in words, students playing the role of the hands will position themselves correctly on a simulated clock.

Affective: Students will be able to work cooperatively to position the hands of a simulated clock correctly.

Psychomotor: While clapping, chanting, and role-playing the hands of a clock, students will simulate the passage of time on an analog clock in minutes and hours.

Activities

We repeat the activity for day 2, but this time the clapper holds up cards to display the time digitally, for example, 10:15 or 10:25, and in words, for example, ten twenty-five or twenty-five minutes after ten.

This connecting-level activity is the students' first experience of seeing the printed symbol. To reinforce the movements of the hour hand, known as "Little," the hour remains the same in each set of cards used by the cooperative groups.

Fig. 4. The audience looks on as "Big" and "Little" travel an hour's journey while the clapper and the caller assist them.

When the members of a cooperative group successfully complete an hour's passage, the students exchange roles and a new set of cards with a new hour is displayed.

This activity gives the students the opportunity to play each role and permits the students who learn more quickly to assist those who need more time and explanation. The students solve their own problems through cooperative-learning techniques.

DAY 4

Objectives

Cognitive: Shown cards written in digital time, students working individually will show the time correctly by using manipulatives to simulate a clockface.

Affective: At the completion of this activity, the students will demonstrate confidence in completing independent tasks.

Psychomotor: Students will be able to manipulate the various parts of a clock to show the time recorded on cards.

Activities

The students are each given sixty lima beans, twelve small circles on which they write the numbers 1–12, paper, and a brad to construct hands. On their desk, the students construct a clock similar to the one that had been made in the group but smaller. We repeat the activities from days 1, 2, and 3 using the paper hands. On this day, I hold up cards that sometimes change both the minutes and the hour, for example, 1:25, 12:30, 3:00, and 1:45. (See fig. 5.) I state the hour first and then the minutes, as well as the reverse. I explain that one can say twelve forty-five, fifteen minutes to one, or even forty-five minutes after twelve, as well as write 12:45.

Fig. 5. Working independently manipulating the hands of the clock to record time given

DAY 5

Objectives

Cognitive: After investigating a variety of timepieces, the students will (1) list the similarities of these clocks to those produced by the class and (2) be able to record the time appearing on commercially made clocks.

Affective: By exploring, investigating, and questioning, students will show an increased curiosity about various kinds of clocks and watches.

Activities

I begin the lesson by displaying a Judy Clock, a large, commercially made classroom clock whose parts are visible and easily manipulated by young learners. Each student has his or her own commercially made learning clock. We list all the similarities of this clock to our hand-made productions. We then explore the watches and clocks that I had brought in. We tour the school and look for all the different kinds of clocks. The students' homework is to see how many different timepieces they can find that night.

Then we divide into teams and using the miniature clocks, students take turns, one writing down a time, the other recording it on the clock. (If you haven't any commercially made clocks, students can make some from patterns or even paper plates.) See figure 6.

DAY 6

Objectives

Cognitive: Students will write a real or fanciful story that includes the times of events, which they will record on blank clockfaces on separate sheets of paper that will be compiled with their stories into a book.

Affective: Students will appreciate clocks and time as they appear in children's literature, specifically in Eric Carle's *The Grouchy Lady Bug* (1986).

Activities

This lesson is based on Eric Carle's book *The Grouchy Lady Bug* (1986). Using their individual clocks, the students record the time of each event in this story.

The story leads to a discussion of the number of hours in a day (24) and the repetition of the twelve-hour sequence on a clockface for morning and evening hours. The students discover that the hour hand makes two revolutions of the clockface in a day. Beginning with midnight, they record this pattern, which is then written on the chalkboard: 12 P.M., 1 A.M., 2 A.M., …, 12 noon, 1 P.M., 2 P.M.…."

The students then write a real or fanciful story about their own activities. I stamp a clockface on separate eight-inch-by-ten-inch pieces of paper, which the students include in their books. This activity requires a few days to complete.

While the students are writing their stories, I call on them individually to assess their progress. Strategies for formative and summative assessment include interviews and observations. From these questions and procedures, I determine at what level (concrete, connective, or symbolic) each student has achieved the objectives.

While working with or interviewing students during these lessons, I record the following observations:

1. Students articulate the relationship between the time shown on analog clocks and the digital expression of time, for example, "Oh, that '12:45' means the minute hand went forty-five minutes after twelve," or "In fifteen minutes it will be '1:00.'"

2. Even second graders want to tell time to the minute. They are even able to read 10:12.

3. "Mommy is so happy I can tell time now," reports one little girl.

4. "I love to tell time," says one of the boys.

Another important part of this unit is the station where the students work independently on activities that give them practice in "telling time."

The following materials are available at this station:

• A teacher-designed matching card

• Laminated worksheets taken from blackline masters

Fig. 6. Working with the Judy Clock and commercially made clocks

- A stamp of a clockface with which students make their own games
- Digital and analog clocks for investigation and discovery
- Trend® wipe-off cards
- Commercially prepared puzzle matching cards
- Game boards with teacher-designed cards
- The computer program Telling Time (1985) (See fig. 7.)

This learning series lasts two weeks, but the telling-time station remains available for the students to enjoy. Since the students determine which activity interests them, I continually add new, creative, open-ended activities related to telling time.

Now the students are constantly asking if I want to know what time it is. Instead of frustrated learners, I have a class full of engaged, on-task, happy explorers, eager to master a task. To be sure, as with using money, telling time is a skill that should be constantly reinforced at home and school. Therefore, the best possible program of learning will include a letter to parents describing the unit and asking for their support and commitment to help their children master this skill.

References

Carle, Eric. *The Grouchy Ladybug*. New York: Harper & Row, Publishers, 1977 (paperback). First Harper Trophy ed. (hardcover). New York: Thomas Y. Crowell Co., Publishers, 1986.

Telling Time. 1985, 48K Apple family. Gamco Indus., Box 1911, Big Spring, TX 79720-0211. ▲

Mark Stockwell

Fig. 7. Working on the Gamco Telling Time Program (At this level, students are asked to write time shown in numerals.)

d. Angle

See It, Change It, Reason It Out

by

Jean M. Shaw

When we attended the Smithsonian Institution's traveling exhibition on kaleidoscopes at our University Museum, several undergraduate students made an interesting discovery. Part of the exhibit featured a device with hinged mirrors and colored objects that could be arranged on a table; participants arranged the objects and explored the different effects that they could see reflected in the mirrors. When the students placed a colored strip between the ends of the mirrors and looked directly into the mirrors, which were positioned to create an angle with measure 90 degrees, they saw a square (fig. 1a). When they changed the angle of the mirrors, they saw a regular pentagon or hexagon.

The excited students shared their discovery with several classmates. Back in our classroom, we followed up on the discovery. Using pieces of paper with lines drawn on them, the students manipulated small plastic mirrors at various angles to show an equilateral triangle reflected in the mirrors (fig. 1b). By making the angle smaller by a few degrees, the students also made a square, regular pentagon, regular hexagon (fig. 1c), regular heptagon, regular octagon (fig. 1d), and so on. After some experimentation, the students made generalizations: the larger the angle of the mirrors, the fewer sides in the regular polygon they saw; the smaller the angle, the more sides each regular polygon had.

The students wondered exactly how large was each angle between the mirrors. Some arranged their mirrors and measured with a protractor. Their measurements generally varied by a degree or two but were close. We put some of their measurements in a chart

Jean Shaw teaches at the University of Mississippi, University, MS 38677. She is the author of various mathematics-education materials for children and adults.

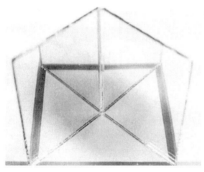

(a) Arranging the mirrors at approximately right angles lets us see a square.

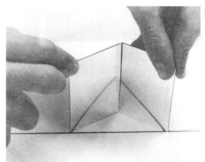

(b) An obtuse angle between the mirrors reveals an equilateral triangle.

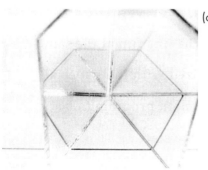

(c) The mirrors clearly show the six equilateral triangles that make up the regular hexagon.

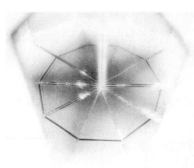

(d) A regular octagon is produced when the angle of the mirrors is about 45 degrees.

Fig. 1

(table 1) and looked for patterns. The students could see that their initial conclusion—the smaller the angle, the greater the number of sides—held true. But exactly how large were the angles?

A student pointed out that she actually saw five angles around the center of her regular pentagon. Other students tested this idea with their mirrors and papers and found that the number of angles was the same as the number of sides in the polygons they created by manipulating the mirrors. Another student stated that these central angles should be equal because the sides of the regular polygons were equal. She suggested that dividing 360 degrees, the number of degrees around the center point of each figure, by the number of sides would yield the number of degrees we were seeking. Different groups of students tried different figures and found that their calculations matched well with the measurements they had made. We added another column to the chart that we had made (table 2).

Table 1. Measures of central angles

Figure	Angle measures
Square	90°, 89°, 90°, 91°
Regular pentagon	70°, 72°, 71°, 73°
Regular hexagon	60°, 60°, 58.5°, 62°

Table 2. Measures of central angles

Figure	Angle measures	Number of central angles	Central angles
Square	90°, 89°, 90°, 91°	4	90°
Regular pentagon	70°, 72°, 71°, 73°	5	72°
Regular hexagon	60°, 60°, 58.5°, 62°	6	60°

Students then tried the idea of drawing an angle with a measure from the chart and arranging their mirrors on the rays of the angle. When they drew in a line segment to cross the sides of the angle, they saw a regular figure if the line segment intersected the mirrors. For example, if a student drew a 45-degree angle and drew a line segment, as shown in figure 2a, she saw a regular octagon.

The wider the angle of the mirrors, the ...

I raised the question of exactly where the line segment should be drawn to produce the most accurate figures. Some students suggested drawing a bisector of each angle and drawing the line segment perpendicular to the bisector; most students had already done this process "by eye." I reminded students that they could think of each polygon as a set of isosceles triangles with the same vertex; the mirrors reflected the same length and so sides $\overline{AB}$ and $\overline{AC}$ were the same length (fig. 2b). To demonstrate informally that the measures of the base angles of an isosceles triangle are equal, we folded a paper isosceles triangle from A to a point, D, midway between B and C (fig. 2c). The measures of angles B and C were then seen to be equal. Since we knew that the sum of the measures of angles A, B, and C was 180 degrees (the students had previously demonstrated this idea by tearing off the three corners of various paper triangles [fig. 3] and arranging these corners along a line segment), $m\angle B + m\angle C = 180 - m\angle A$. Since $m\angle B = m\angle C$, then $m\angle B = (180° - m\angle A)/2$ and $m\angle C = (180° - m\angle A)/2$.

This activity presented another method for students to draw angles on which to place their mirrors. For a regular decagon, for example,

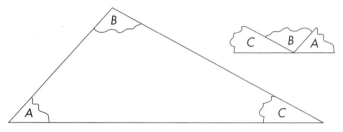

Fig. 3. Tearing off the angles of a triangle and repositioning the pieces to show that the sum of the measures of the angles is 180 degrees

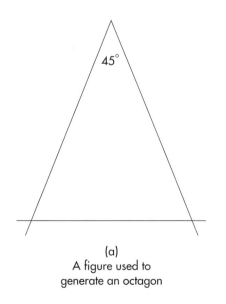

(a)
A figure used to generate an octagon

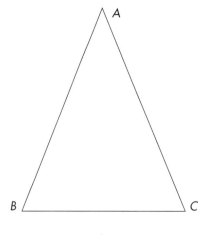

(b)
Isosceles triangles ($AB = AC$) produced the most accurate figures.

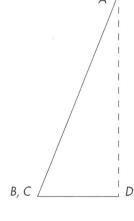

(c)
Folding shows that $\angle B \cong \angle C$.

Fig. 2

the central angles are 360° ÷ 10, or 36 degrees. The measures of angles *B* and *C* are each (180° − 36°)/2, or 72 degrees (fig. 4).

Students worked in groups carefully to draw line segments on which their mirrors could be placed to reflect several different regular polygons. They tested their drawings by arranging the mirrors and checking to see that they actually saw the figures that they intended. They labeled each pair of line segments with the name of the figure they saw (fig. 5). Several students commented that they could use a similar lesson with middle school students in the field work they would subsequently do. They later did so and were pleased with their guided-discovery lessons.

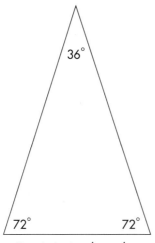

Fig. 4. A triangle used to generate a decagon

When we checked, the calculations were very close to the measurements.

This experience involved conjecture and experimentation; much communication; and building connections among science, geometry, and numbers. Both students and I posed problems and explained the reasoning that was involved as we worked. Readers might use a similar lesson with middle school students. Exploration and extensions of the ideas would make a good individual project for a mathematics or science fair. Teacher educators may also wish to build on the ideas in their elementary mathematics methods classes. ▲

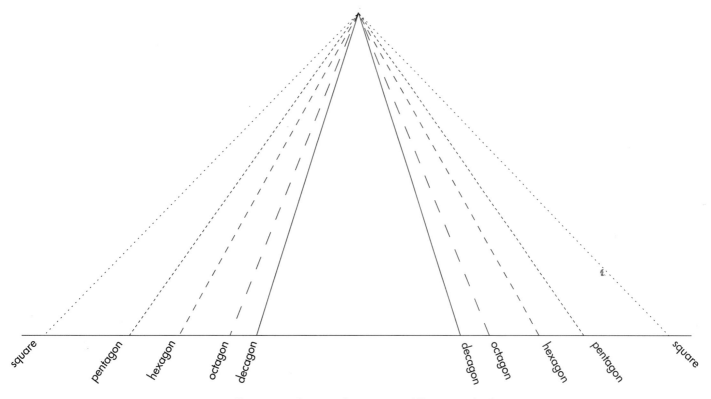

Fig. 5. Different isosceles triangles generate different regular figures.

Chapter 4
Graphs and Charts

Elementary School Activity: Graphing the Stock Market

by

Margaret Kelly

To most second-grade pupils, the Dow-Jones industrial average, as reported on the nightly news, might mean anything from a super-strength cleaner to an extra-large weight lifter. But I found that when McDonald's, Mattel Toys, and other familiar companies were mentioned, visions of hamburgers and toys made dealing with the complicated stock market more meaningful.

Cohen (1977), Holtan (1964), Lyda (1947), and others have stated that using realistic situations helps children develop problem-solving and related skills. Using data about companies with which children have firsthand experience seems to pique their interest and substantially increase their attention span in completing graphing activities. I have found these activities to be insightful and motivating for children in second through sixth grades. Since most local papers publish a report of the market values of stocks of at least those companies that directly affect local employment, some information is readily available.

READINESS

To succeed fully in graphing stock prices, children must be able to add and subtract with regrouping. Although the financial page often reports losses and gains in terms of fractions, I have found it unnecessary for the younger children to convert common fractions to decimal form. A simple developmental lesson on how the conversion is made, followed by the posting of a chart illustrating the conversions, is all that is necessary (fig. 1). The thousandths digits in the conversion for eighths have been dropped rather than rounded.

DEMONSTRATION

To begin the stock market project, the class selects one company whose stock reports appear in the local paper. As part of this activity, we discuss the long-term prospects of the companies. Many of my pupils do not realize that because the future is unknown, investments produce no guaranteed returns. Money can be lost as well as made when a risk is taken.

On the first day of the demonstration week, I present a recording sheet. The horizontal axis is labeled with the days of the week (fig. 2). But because the prices of the stocks listed in the newspaper vary widely, the labeling of the vertical axis has to wait until

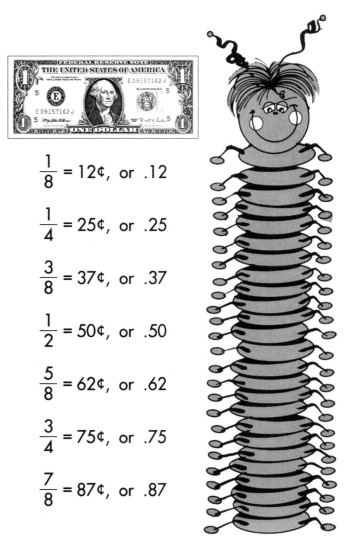

$$\frac{1}{8} = 12¢, \text{ or } .12$$

$$\frac{1}{4} = 25¢, \text{ or } .25$$

$$\frac{3}{8} = 37¢, \text{ or } .37$$

$$\frac{1}{2} = 50¢, \text{ or } .50$$

$$\frac{5}{8} = 62¢, \text{ or } .62$$

$$\frac{3}{4} = 75¢, \text{ or } .75$$

$$\frac{7}{8} = 87¢, \text{ or } .87$$

Fig. 1. Converting Fractions

the class chooses its stock. I find it best to plot the first day's price midway on the vertical axis to allow for either a rise or fall in the price as the week continues.

Peggy Kelly teaches a fifth- and sixth-grade split class at Lakeview Elementary School for the Weber School District, Eden, UT 84310. She is completing her doctorate at Utah State University and has special interest in mathematical problem-solving teaching techniques for both in-service and preservice teachers.

Graphs and Charts **223**

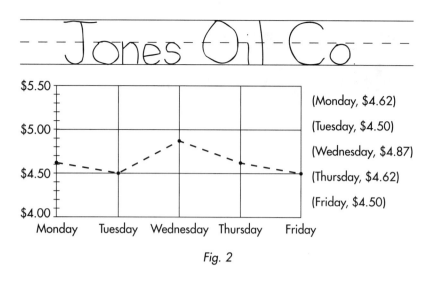

Jones Oil Co.

(Monday, $4.62)
(Tuesday, $4.50)
(Wednesday, $4.87)
(Thursday, $4.62)
(Friday, $4.50)

Fig. 2

The first time I plotted the beginning price midway on a prelabeled axis, the class was totally confused. Through experience, I've discovered that it saves time to explain why Monday's price is plotted midway on the vertical axis and then the remainder of the axis is labeled. A discussion of the need to allow for a possible rise and fall of the price further emphasizes the uncertainty of the market.

After presenting the recording sheet, I use play money to show the class the exact amount being spent. If the stock price is $4.62, I count out $4.62, which is then exchanged for a certificate of stock ownership. Then I graph the amount of the purchase above the day on which it is purchased. In an attempt to introduce ordered pairs, I have found that recording in parentheses at the side of the chart both the day and the amount helps pupils understand the relationship between ordered pairs and graphing.

The children became very interested in cumulative gains and losses when they were told that the stock would be sold on Friday and the paper certificate exchanged for the value of the stock as posted that day. It is not uncommon to see children gathering at the daily posting of the stock page, trying to locate the stock price and mentally calculating gains and losses.

On Friday, the share of stock is sold for the price posted in the most recent edition of the newspaper. The following are some questions that can be answered from the graph:

1. Did we gain or lose money? How do you know?

2. What was the price of the stock on Monday? Friday? Tuesday? On the other days of the week?

3. If we had chosen to sell the stock on Thursday, would the results have been the same? Why?

INDIVIDUAL PROJECTS

At this point, many of the children become interested in selecting their own stock. With some classes, working in small groups is best; in others, the pupils prefer to work individually. As they become increasingly adept at posting their own stock prices, the amount of time spent on the daily graphing decreases to about five minutes.

By glancing at the bulletin board of graphs, a teacher can quickly tell how well students are able to read the stock market report

and plot the prices. (It is unusual for the stock to take a drastic rise or fall during the week.)

Since the children decide when to sell their stocks, the economic concept of opportunity cost becomes appropriate for discussion. Their decision to sell is based on their belief that either they have made as much money as possible or have lost as much money as they can afford; what might be gained or lost by further participation in the market is the opportunity cost. To determine whether the decision to sell or retain their stock has been a good one, the children continue to plot their stock prices until the project is over. Comparisons are then made between the selling price and the current price. Again, all information is graphed and recorded (fig. 3).

DOW-JONES AVERAGE

At the end of the first week, the children calculate their gains or losses. Questions for discussion similar to those suggested as part of the demonstration aid individual comprehension of what has actually happened. It quickly becomes apparent that some stocks have been rising while others have been falling and that the starting value of a stock has little bearing on how much money is made. A discussion of the Dow-Jones industrial average becomes valuable after students have plotted two weeks of averages. I have found that the actual calculation of the average is of little interest to most children in the early grades; however, students at all levels enjoy plotting the points.

Inferences were made from the Dow average about the probable paths of individual stocks. Current world events are discussed because the stock market frequently reacts to them. Thus, children become interested in listening to the news as a way of making decisions about whether or not to sell their stock.

VARIATIONS AND EXTENSIONS

1. In my second-grade class two pupils entered their stock market project in the Weber School District Economics Fair (fig. 4). They wrote an impressive report on their project, justifying their decision to sell their stock and evaluating their gains.

2. One year an upper-grade class chose to "buy" several shares of one stock. Each student graphed his or her stocks by the unit price and by the total investment. With a large investment, the children began to see the multiplicative effect of gains and losses.

3. When given a specific amount of money, members of a fourth-grade class chose to diversify their individual portfolios. Graphs were then made of individual stocks as well as of the total investment. With a large investment, the children began to see the multiplicative effect of balancing gains and losses.

4. One of my fifth-grade classes extended its study of the Dow-Jones averages by selecting stock in proportion to the sixty-five stocks on which Dow-Jones averages are based

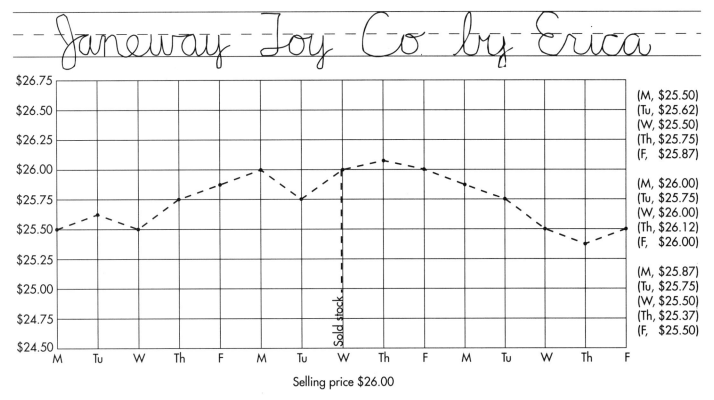

Janeway Toy Co by Erica

(M, $25.50)	
(Tu, $25.62)	
(W, $25.50)	
(Th, $25.75)	
(F, $25.87)	
(M, $26.00)	
(Tu, $25.75)	
(W, $26.00)	
(Th, $26.12)	
(F, $26.00)	
(M, $25.87)	
(Tu, $25.75)	
(W, $25.50)	
(Th, $25.37)	
(F, $25.50)	

Selling price $26.00

Fig. 3

(thirty industrial, fifteen utilities, and twenty transportation stocks). The same group became interested in other indicators and followed the Standard & Poor's 500 average (not always published in the local paper). This project motivated the students to investigate the *Wall Street Journal* and *Fortune*. A large number of creative problems can be devised with these publications.

Fig. 4

CONCLUSION

Stock-market information is readily available and can be used effectively in the mathematics classroom. Students seem to take a personal interest in their imaginary investments—they celebrate their gains and mourn their losses. Quite by surprise, the children discover how easy it is for them to interpret any graph. Understanding the methods involved in making their own graphs and easily extracting information from graphs become parts of their repertoire of mathematical skills.

Bibliography

Cohen, Martin P. "Interest and Its Relationship to Problem-solving Ability among Secondary School Mathematics Students." Ph.D. diss., University of Texas at Austin, 1976. *Dissertation Abstracts International* 37A (1977): 4929.

Holtan, Boyd. "Motivation and General Mathematics Students." *Mathematics Teacher* 57 (January 1964): 20–25.

Lyda, W. J. "Direct, Practical Experiences in Mathematics and Success in Solving Realistic Verbal 'Reasoning' Problems in Arithmetic." *Mathematics Teacher* 40 (April 1947): 166–67.

Trimble, Harold C., and Jon L. Higgins. "Problems, Applications, Interest and Motivation." In *Applied Mathematical Problem Solving,* edited by Richard Lesh, Diane Mierkiewicz, and Mary Kantowski, pp. 25–36. Columbus, Ohio: ERIC Clearinghouse for Science, Mathematics, and Environmental Education, 1979.

Walbourne, C. W., and M. V. Morphett. "Unfamiliar Situations as a Difficulty in Solving Arithmetic Problems." *Journal of Educational Research* 8 (1928): 220–24. ▲

Pictures, Tables, Graphs, and Questions: Statistical Processes

by

Andrew C. Isaacs

Catherine Randall Kelso

Predictions, explanations, and journal writing are all parts of the investigations.

In an address to the American Association for the Advancement of Science, John Dewey (1910) contrasted the *facts* of science with the *method* of science and argued that the method, rather than the facts, should be preeminent in the school curriculum. But what is that method? More particularly, how does that method appear when transformed to fall within the scope of children's lives? How can the fundamentally quantitative method of modern science be simplified as much as possible, but not too much, so that children can apply it to questions arising from their own experience?

This article outlines one approach to this problem by teaching science as a process of collecting, organizing, and analyzing data (Goldberg and Boulanger 1981; Goldberg and Wagreich 1989, 1990). We hope to show that this brand of science is naturally integrated with mathematics. We begin with a description of an investigation designed for the second grade called "Marshmallows and Containers."

MARSHMALLOWS AND CONTAINERS

As class begins, students sit together in groups of three with three different containers: a bowl, for instance, a disposable margarine tub; a 100-cc graduated cylinder; and a small paper cup. The teacher shows the class a bag of miniature marshmallows and asks, "Which container will hold the most marshmallows? Why do you think so?"

The teacher encourages the groups to discuss their predictions and explanations and to record their ideas in their journals. Many groups report to the class that they think that the graduated cylinder will hold the most because it is the tallest. One boy explains

Andy Isaacs is a writer for the teacher-development component of the University of Chicago School Mathematics Project (UCSMP), Chicago, IL 60637; aisaacs@uchicago.edu. He is interested in helping teachers implement standards-based curricula. Catherine Kelso develops curriculum at the Institute for Mathematics and Science Education, University of Chicago, Chicago, IL 60637; u20335@uicvm.uic.edu. She is currently working on a mathematics curriculum project for grades K–5.

that he thinks the cylinder will hold the most because even if he could stretch the plastic in the bowl to be tall like the cylinder, it still would not be as tall and would not hold as much. Other groups choose the bowl because it is wider than the other containers.

When the groups have recorded their predictions, the teacher asks the class how they could check them. She introduces the term *volume,* as a measure of the space inside the container. She asks, "How could you find out which container has the greatest volume?" This question leads naturally to an experiment: The students will fill each of the containers with marshmallows, count them, and record the numbers in a data table.

The teacher explains how they will collect the data then demonstrates the experimental procedure by filling the cylinder with miniature marshmallows and the bowl with larger marshmallows. The students immediately shout, "That's not fair!" The teacher then asks the class to describe a "fair" procedure. The class decides that the marshmallows must all be of the same size and that they should be dropped into the containers rather than tightly packed. To conclude the class, each student draws a picture of the experiment. Figure 1 shows three containers being filled and marshmallows being counted by tens in an egg carton.

The class discussed a "fair" procedure.

The next day, the children use their pictures to review the experiment before beginning the data collection. Each group receives

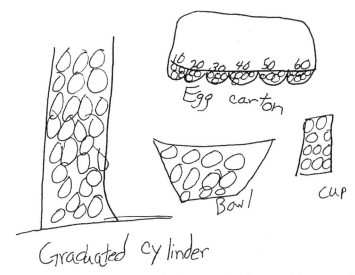

Fig. 1. One student's picture for the "Marshmallows and Containers" project

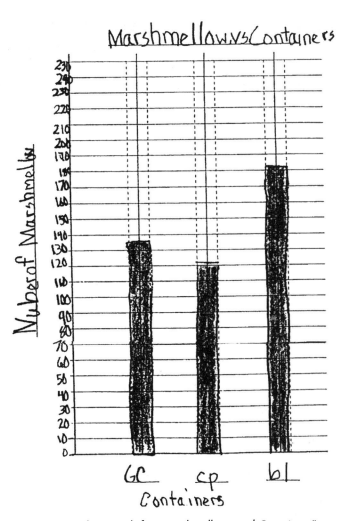

Fig. 3. A bar graph for "Marshmallows and Containers"

a two-column data table, completes the column headings, and writes the names or draws pictures of the containers in the first column. The teacher emphasizes the need for accuracy in counting, and the children discuss various methods for grouping and counting the marshmallows. As the students begin their work, the teacher circulates, coaches, and assesses.

After the children complete their data tables (fig. 2), the teacher leads a discussion in which the groups compare their results to find whether the results are reasonable. Most groups report that about 135 marshmallows are in the graduated cylinder and agree that numbers close to 135, but not exactly 135, are acceptable. A group that had recorded only 110 marshmallows for the cylinder decides to refill the cylinder and count again.

Container	Number of Marshmellow units (N)
Graduated cylinder	133
cup	121
bowl	181

Fig. 2. A data table for "Marshmallows and Containers"

On the third day, students graph the data on a bar graph and analyze the results. (See fig. 3.) These graphs will be useful in comparing results across groups, in supporting multiple solution methods, and in fostering number sense and estimation skills.

Differences and similarities across groups are then examined. Differences among groups are most apparent in the data tables. Students discuss reasons for these differences: variations in how the marshmallows were packed, differences in how completely the containers were filled, errors in counting. Uniformity of results across groups is more apparent in the graphs: although the graphs are not exactly the same, they are similar. On every student's

graph, the tallest bar is for the bowl. The class lists reasons for this basic agreement: all groups (1) used identical containers, (2) used the same-sized marshmallows, and (3) put the marshmallows in their containers the same way.

A lively discussion ensues about why the bowl holds the most—that is, because of its much greater width than the cylinder's—leading to verbalization of this reasoning by many of those students who had predicted that the graduated cylinder would hold the most.

Posing the questions is not trivial.

On the final day of the experiment, students work in groups to write answers to questions about the data: "Which container is the tallest?" "The shortest?" "Which held the most marshmallows?" Later questions ask for predictions and generalizations: "Will a taller container always have a bigger volume than a shorter one?" "Why?" Students also write about volume in their journals: "Volume is the space in something like a cup" and "Volume is like how big the space is, not [just] the height."

MATHEMATICS IN CONTEXT

Two principles underlie the children's version of the foregoing scientific method. First, an investigation should begin within the children's own experiences. In this laboratory, children use objects from their everyday lives to investigate a familiar situation. Children's everyday knowledge, like a scientist's theory, supplies a framework for interpreting the results of the investigation. Without that framework the investigation would remain hollow and meaningless.

The second principle is that an investigation should also transcend children's everyday experiences. The exploration must go somewhere; it must lead the children both to a better understanding of the immediate situation and to improved skills, understandings, habits, and attitudes.

Balancing these principles requires a teacher's judgment. Students must follow their own ideas but be guaranteed that those ideas will lead somewhere. The teacher must decide how much scaffolding to build and how best to guide students in directions that are fruitful rather than sterile. Students should advance not only in skill and understanding but also in autonomy and perseverance. A teacher's most important and difficult job is to decide just how much structure to furnish the way.

The "Marshmallows and Containers" involves several particular skills and concepts: measurement, graphing, number sense, problem solving in context, and communication. More important than these specific skills and concepts, however, is the overall approach the children take in the investigation. The children identify and work with variables; they collect, organize, and graph data; and they analyze the results.

These general techniques can be applied to other problems and comprise a child's version of a four-phase scientific method: (1) beginning the investigation, (2) collecting and organizing the data, (3) graphing the data, and (4) analyzing the experimental results. We discuss these four phases and illustrate our discussion with references both to "Marshmallows and Containers" and to a fifth-grade experiment called "Evaporation," in which children study the volume of water in an container over time.

BEGINNING THE INVESTIGATION

Most investigations begin with a question, does not have to be momentous or clever but must be meaningful to children. If the question connects with their experience, children will need no flashy inducements to want to find the answer. With "Marshmallows and Containers," the question was "Which container holds the most marshmallows?" Questions with an explicit quantitative aspect, something that children can count or measure, work well. Questions that can be recast quantitatively are also appropriate. For example, the question "What happens when water evaporates?" can be narrowed to "What happens to the volume of the water in an open container left standing out for several days?"

Once a suitable question has been posed, the many variables related to the question must be identified. In "Marshmallows and Containers" the variables involved include the type of container, the size of the marshmallows, how the marshmallows are packed, and the number of marshmallows that fit in the containers. In

"Evaporation," relevant variables are the type of liquid, the exposed surface area, the temperature, and time.

If too many variables change simultaneously, obtaining meaningful results can be difficult or impossible. In an ideal experiment, more easily realized in the laboratory than in the real world, a scientist focuses on only two variables and strives to hold all others constant. Thus, "Marshmallows and Containers" focuses on the kind of container—bowl, cylinder, cup—and the number of marshmallows while using one size of marshmallow and packing all the containers "fairly." In "Evaporation," students measure the volume of water in a container and the elapsed time while holding the location of the container, the exposed surface area, and the temperature fixed.

By the end of the investigation's first phase, the original question has been refined into a precise query about the relationship between two well-defined variables about which the children can gather information. Drawing a picture is an excellent way (1) to summarize and communicate this beginning phase, (2) to plan what is to come, (3) to help children understand and organize what they are to do, and (4) to help teachers assess whether students are ready to proceed. Figure 4 shows one student's "Evaporation" picture, indicating the two primary variables—V, volume, and t, time in days; two important controlled variables—the location of the jars on the window sill and the time of day for taking measurements; and the procedure—pouring water from the graduated cylinder into the jars and cleaning up with paper towels. The student who drew this picture is now ready to gather data.

Fig. 4. Picturing the "Evaporation" experiment

COLLECTING AND ORGANIZING THE DATA

The children gather the data and organize them in a table. A data table with two main columns is sufficient for most experiments. The name of a variable, including units if appropriate, heads each column. Figure 5 shows students' data tables for "Evaporation."

The data table is useful for preserving the data, controlling error, and identifying patterns. Children can detect blunders when a measurement deviates too much from established patterns, and

Container 1		Container 2	
t time in days	V Volume in c.c.	t time in days	V Volume in c.c.
0	100 c.c.	0	100 c.c.
2	91 c.c.	2	84 c.c.
5	80 c.c.	5	80 c.c.
7	74 c.c.	7	66 c.c.
9	67 c.c.	9	50 c.c.
13	52 c.c.	13	28 c.c.
15	44 c.c.	15	23 c.c.

Fig. 5. Data tables showing water loss over time

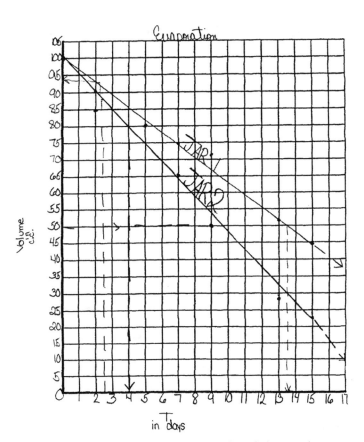

Fig. 6. An "Evaporation" graph showing best-fit lines and interpolations

they can control inevitable measurement error by averaging several trials.

Students almost always work in small groups to gather data. This organization makes managing the equipment easier, but it also helps in other ways. Complicated procedures may require that several students work together to gather the data. When measurements are difficult, multiple trials are easier for a group to complete than for an individual. Several students working together are more likely to notice when patterns begin to emerge in the data as a relationship between two key variables becomes evident.

GRAPHING THE DATA

Although the relationship between the variables may be evident in a data table, it is usually clearer in a graph. Accordingly, after data are gathered, a graph should be drawn. A bar graph is usually best when one of the variables is qualitative, as in the "Marshmallows and Containers" activity. When both variables are quantitative, as with the "Evaporation" project, a point graph is often, though not always, appropriate.

The data table can help identify patterns.

The basics of bar and point graphing are well known and are not discussed here, but one special point-graphing technique is worth noting. Often, as shown in figure 6, a line can be fit to the data points, not by using a complicated statistical procedure but simply by using the naked eye. The student uses a transparent ruler or a thread and moves it around until it fits the data points as closely as possible. This best-fit line is useful for controlling errors, identifying patterns, and making predictions.

ANALYZING THE EXPERIMENTAL RESULTS

The relationship between the variables has been displayed in (1) the physical materials, (2) the picture, (3) the data table, and (4) the graph. The last phase is an analysis of the entire situation.

Begin by asking a series of straightforward questions: "Did the tallest container hold the most marshmallows?" "When did your container have 80 cc of water in it?" More demanding questions require prediction: "How many marshmallows would two bowls hold?" "In how many days will all the water have evaporated?" Asking what would happen if one of the fixed variables is changed can build a broader understanding of the situation: "What would happen if we used large instead of miniature marshmallows?" "What would happen if we changed the temperature in our evaporation study?" Checking predictions by further experimentation is time-consuming but worthwhile because connections are reinforced between mathematical abstractions and the real world.

The end of the investigation may be a completely satisfying answer to the original question, but, more often than not, the end is another question that can lead to further investigations. The marshmallows activity, for example, might lead to an investigation of the liquid capacities of other short and tall containers. After the "Evaporation" experiment, children might design and carry out an investigation into the relationship between the exposed surface area of the water and how quickly it evaporates.

PICTURE, TABLE, GRAPH, QUESTIONS

Each of the foregoing phases usually requires one or more class periods in addition to time spent becoming familiar with the equipment and completing further experiments. Thus, a laboratory is an extended activity that may last a week or even longer, which is much longer than a typical mathematics or science lesson, but has significant benefits.

First, the four phases simplify the scientific method enough for children to use but not so much that it fails to resemble what scientists do: identify variables, draw pictures, measure, organize data in tables, graph data, and look for patterns. Whatever the scientific method—measure, analyze, generalize; hypothesize, test, repeat; or something else—this four-phase method captures a significant part of it. Students are thus inducted into the authentic practice of science.

They develop number sense and estimation skills.

The method fosters children's sense making. Children handle numbers they have generated themselves and that are meaningful to them by counting or measuring. Experimental errors help them develop number sense and estimation skills. Patterns in their tables and graphs assist them in making sense of the numbers. Mathematics in context is more understandable.

The approach is multimodal, which has benefits for both individual students and heterogeneous groups of students (Bruner 1964; Lesh, Post, and Behr 1987; Silver 1986; Hiebert 1988). The multiple representations of relationships among the variables permit problems to be solved in more than one way, allowing different students to approach the same content in ways they understand. The container that holds the most marshmallows, for example, can be found from the graph, the data table, or the marshmallows themselves. The number of days until all the water has evaporated can be predicted by extrapolating on the graph or by extending patterns in the data table and can then be verified using the apparatus. Students can compare these various approaches, thus helping them make connections within mathematics as well as between the informal mathematics of their everyday experience and more formal mathematics.

CONCLUSION

The four-phase method helps children connect their everyday experiences with formal mathematics. As they investigate everyday situations quantitatively, children handle variables, explore relationships between variables, master a few powerful techniques for representing these relationships, and use these multiple representations to generate a wide variety of problem solutions. By beginning and ending in familiar situations, the abstractions of mathematics are linked to children's everyday knowledge. As students master this method, they become increasingly autonomous and flexible in its application. Then we can truly say they have learned to think mathematically.

References

Bruner, Jerome S. "The Course of Cognitive Growth." *American Psychologist* 19 (January 1964): 1–15.

Dewey, John. "Science as Subject-Matter and as Method." *Science* 31 (January 1910): 121–27.

Goldberg, Howard, and F. David Boulanger. "Science for Elementary School Teachers: A Quantitative Approach." *American Journal of Physics* 49 (February 1981): 120–24.

Goldberg, Howard, and Philip Wagreich. "Focus on Integrating Science and Math." *Science and Children* 2 (February 1989): 22–24.

———. "A Model Integrated Mathematics and Science Program for the Elementary School." *International Journal of Educational Research* 14 (March-April 1990): 193–214.

Hiebert, James. "A Theory of Developing Competence with Written Mathematical Symbols." *Educational Studies in Mathematics* 19 (August 1988): 333–55.

Lesh, Richard, Thomas Post, and Merlyn Behr. "Representations and Translations among Representation in Mathematics Learning and Problem Solving." In *Problems of Representation in the Teaching and Learning of Mathematics,* edited by C. Janvier. Hillsdale, N.J.: Lawrence Erlbaum Associates, 1987.

Silver, Edward. "Using Conceptual and Procedural Knowledge: A Focus on Relationships." In *Conceptual and Procedural Knowledge: The Case of Mathematics,* edited by James Hiebert. Hillsdale, N.J.: Lawrence Erlbaum Associates, 1986. ▲

IDEAS: Which Flavor Wins the Taste Test?

by

Daniel J. Brahier
Catholic School Services, Toledo, Ohio

Anne F. Brahier
Mathematics Consultant/Tutor, Perrysburg, Ohio

William R. Speer
Bowling Green State University, Bowling Green, Ohio

LEVELS K–2

Background

Students are frequently exposed to television commercials and radio advertisements on which the results of taste tests of beverages and foods are used to promote various food items. In addition, students often encounter such statements as, "Four out of five doctors recommend [a certain health aid]." In this activity, students engage in a preference test and process results from the test.

Objective

To conduct an experiment that requires students to gather and record data. Students represent the data by making a concrete bar graph and a picture graph, and then analyze the data. The activity also enhances counting skills as students gather the information.

Directions

1. Begin a discussion by asking students to name their favorite cartoon character. Keep a list and a frequency count of their responses on the chalkboard. Point out that every person is unique and that not everyone likes the same things. Ask the class if they can think of any television commercials or radio advertisements that address the idea of a person's preferring one brand over another (e.g., students may respond that the two major cola manufacturers often claim that they are preferred over the others). Explain to the class that they will be conducting their own "taste test."

2. Out of sight of the students, prepare two pitchers of a powdered drink. For each pitcher, use a different flavor that can be distinguished by color (e.g., orange and lime). Label the pitchers "X" and "Y." Also prepare two *small* paper cups for each student and label them "X" and "Y." Making certain that the students do not see which flavor is in each lettered cup, pour a small quantity of each drink into the cups.

3. Put students in pairs. One student in each pair closes his or her eyes so that he or she cannot see the color of the drink or the letter on the cup. The other student gives the first one a taste of each of the flavors in any order. Each student votes for the flavor he or she prefers and records its letter. Repeat the process with the students' roles reversed.

4. When the class has finished the taste test, each student brings to the front of the room the empty cup that had contained his or her preferred flavor. By placing a small piece of construction paper or cardboard between cups, students stack the cups with like letters to form a concrete graph of the results of the taste test, as shown in figure 1.

Because a large number of cups are physically difficult to stack, it is convenient to use an object to represent several cups. For example, if more than ten students choose a particular flavor, then every ten cups should be traded for a large can from juice or other drink. That is, if twenty-three students chose flavor X, then the concrete graph would consist of two stacked cans and three stacked cups, each marked with the letter X. Using a can in place of ten cups not only allows teachers to introduce representative graphing but also supplies a real context for the study of grouping by tens and place value.

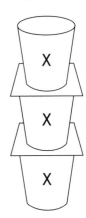

Fig. 1. A concrete graph of the results of the taste test

5. Have students look at the concrete graph. Ask such processing questions as "Which drink was the favorite for the class?" "Do you think the results would be the same if another class did the same test?" "Why or why not?" "Would the results be exactly the same if we ran the experiment in this class a year from now?" "Why or why not?" "What do

you think might happen if we added a third flavor to the taste test?" "How could we find out if the class liked another flavor better than the two flavors used in the taste test?" "Do television commercials that claim that people like one type of cola better than another necessarily mean that *you* will like it better, too?"

6. Using crayons or colored markers that match the drinks' colors, have students color in the cans and cups on the activity page to match the number of cans and cups in the stacks at the front of the room. The picture graphs now represent the results of the class's voting in the taste test. Have the class count the number of cans and cups in each stack and record that number on the activity page.

Answers

Answers will vary, depending on the flavors chosen and the individual preferences of a class.

Extensions

1. Apply the activity to another subject area that is being discussed. For example, if students are studying the seasons of the year, they can be asked to vote for their favorite season and use a snowflake, a flower, a sun, and a fall-colored leaf with which to cast their vote. Discuss the results and ask students to explain their choices. In literature, students can be asked to vote for their favorite character in a story and explain why they chose that person.

2. Analyzing preference votes can be incorporated into the mathematics class in a number of ways. For example, if the class is studying geometric shapes and their properties, the teacher might consider giving them a sheet with drawings of a triangle, a rectangle, and a hexagon, all of which are of about the same general size. Ask each student in the class to estimate which of the polygons has the greatest perimeter. Have each student color and cut out the polygon that represents her or his "vote." Make a concrete graph by gluing the polygons onto a piece of butcher paper to form a picture graph. Then give each student a new sheet and a piece of string or a ruler, as appropriate, and have the students measure the perimeters of the polygons to determine the correct answer. Some students may suspect that the triangle has the least perimeter because it has the fewest number of sides. Therefore, teachers may want to draw the diagram so that the triangle, though it has fewer sides, actually has the greatest perimeter.

3. Conduct the foregoing extension but have the students predict which shape has the greatest area instead of perimeter. Then have them cut out the three polygons, lay them on graph paper, and trace the shapes. Count the number of squares (complete and partial) within the shapes on the graph paper to compare approximate areas.

WHICH FLAVOR WINS THE TASTE TEST?   Name _____

Student Worksheet

1. Color the picture to match the cans and cups that you and your classmates stacked. Color one can for every ten votes given a flavor. Each cup stands for one vote.

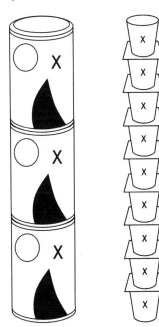  

2. Use the picture graph to fill in the table.

Flavor of drink	Number of cans	Number of cups	Total of votes
X			
Y			

3. Which flavor did the class like the most? _____

4. Which flavor did the class like least? _____

5. How many more votes did the favorite drink get than the second-choice drink? _____

From Teacher-Made Aids for Elementary School Mathematics, Vol. 3

Coordinate Geometry— Art and Mathematics

by

Michael Terc

Our students cry for self-expression, for a chance to see mathematics in action. Frequently, however, the structure of mathematics does not lend itself to individual style or variation. Problem solving can tend to be dull and monotonous rather than exciting and stimulating.

Not all mathematics can be fun and games, but teachers have an obligation to make the subject as enjoyable as possible. If we come upon a topic that nurtures students' involvement and enjoyment, we should capitalize on it.

One such topic that I recently taught has the potential to generate and foster students' involvement and lends itself to real individual effort. I hope this record of my experience and satisfaction will allow me to share my joy and excitement with my colleagues.

The topic is *coordinate geometry*. Basically, coordinate geometry is a combination of algebra and geometry. It is treated in high school mathematics courses, but fundamental concepts can be introduced to students at an earlier age. I hope to dispel the notion that it is inappropriate for the elementary school student.

My first encounter with teaching coordinate geometry was quite enlightening. I began by describing the coordinate axes and the method used to plot points on the graph. Many students were unable to appreciate the beauty of Descartes's invention. I decided to arrange my coordinates so that a familiar picture or geometric object would emerge. At first, my patterns were simple. For example, my initial designs were a horse's head (fig. 1), a boat, and a house, each consisting of no more than twenty pairs of coordinates.

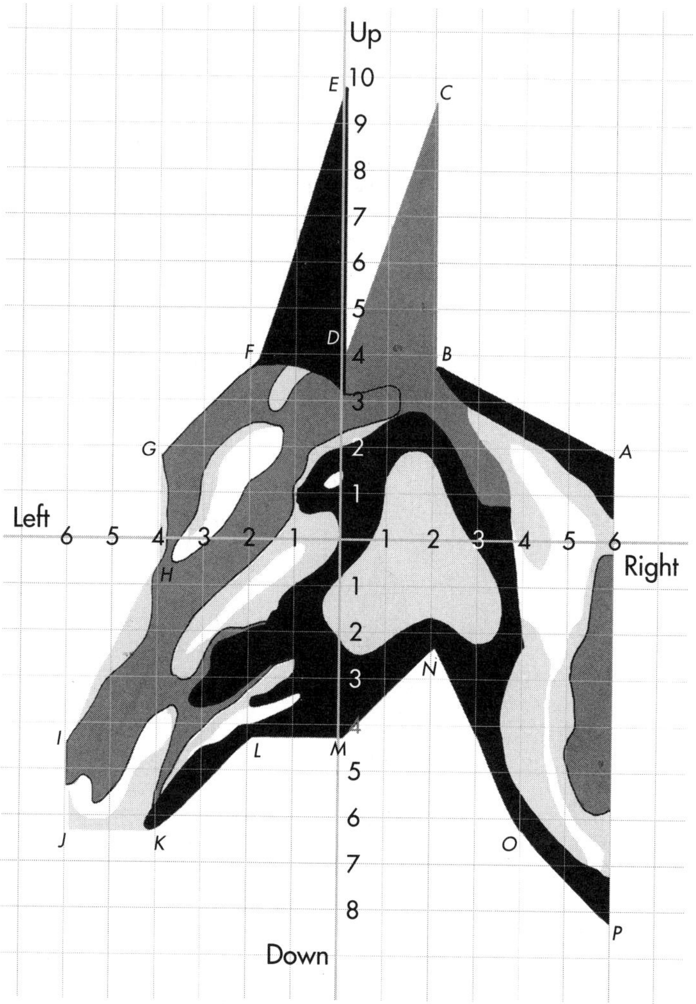

Almost everyone enjoyed plotting the points. Pupils were particularly fascinated that mathematics could be used to construct figures. They began to use colored pencils to create distinctive work.

Suddenly, my slow learners' interest increased markedly. For the first time some students were actually self-motivated. I had them create more coordinate pictures with more points. The figures became an astronaut, a Native American, a polygon, and an eagle.

Mike Terc is an eighth-grade mathematics teacher at Mineola Junior High School in Mineola, NY 11501. He recently received a professional diploma in educational administration and leadership from C. W. Post College, Long Island, New York.

Fig. 1. One of our first designs using fifteen points

As students' involvement increased, their personal pride began to flourish. Their pictures were really looking quite good! Students with active imaginations began to add their own backgrounds to the figures. A plain whale became Moby Dick with an appropriate seascape, complete with lighthouse and seagulls (fig. 2). Students whose attentions normally were prone to wander when working in an individual setting were transformed into high-powered students concerned with their work and eager to see their pictures materialize.

To capitalize on this enthusiasm, I decided to hold a contest. The rules were simple; students could enter as many figures as they wished. All were encouraged to submit at least one of their best pictures employing their most imaginative skills. Most students

Fig. 2. "Moby Dick" with an appropriate seascape

Second, when would the actual work be done? Could it be accomplished without interrupting everyone's schedule? Again the answer was yes! We would map out designs before or after school, and we would paint during the regular school day.

Now all that was needed was a small group of interested students and agreement about the murals to be drawn. Five student volunteers were selected according to neatness, dependability, and some mathematical or artistic ability. After the selection process was completed, we met and decided on the murals to be drawn. We agreed on a complete color scheme with accompanying diagrams.

Next, the walls were marked lightly in pencil so that they resembled giant graph boards with the lines spaced one inch apart. To ensure that the lines were vertical and horizontal, we used a level that we obtained from the wood shop. Scaffolds were used to reach those areas above normal height. The next phase involved plotting the figures by using the appropriate coordinates. The points were then connected to produce the desired figure. The third phase was the most exciting. A penciled figure became a beautifully painted whale. Bare walls were transformed into a series of polygons. A once drab corner became a showcase for a majestic eagle (fig. 3). Best of all, these transformations were achieved with mathematics. For the first time, many students realized that mathematics is practical—it can be seen, used, and appreciated as a part of our world!

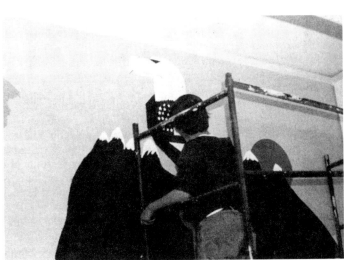

Fig. 3. A drab corner becomes a showcase for a majestic eagle.

enhanced the figures with colored pencils and felt-tipped markers. Some used glitter, and one student added real feathers. Out of 120 students, ninety entries were received. The classes then selected the top twenty entries, which were then attractively displayed on the bulletin board. The entry of each finalist was assigned a number, and all the students were asked to select their top five choices. The votes were tallied, and the five winners were announced the next day. Winners were awarded extra-credit points on their semester grade averages. As a final touch, the winning pictures were displayed around the room with the outstanding selections from previous years, creating a "mathematics hall of fame."

It was not until last year that I extended the topic on an even grander scale. Our principal challenged the faculty to improve the visual appeal of the building. Teachers were encouraged to consider special displays, bulletin boards, and other aesthetic projects. It occurred to me that we might use our knowledge of coordinate geometry to help draw murals on our classroom walls.

Our first consideration dealt with supplies. Could we obtain brushes, paints, and, more important, sturdy and safe scaffolds on which our students could work? The answer was yes! The art department and custodial staff would supply us with whatever materials we would need.

This lesson had additional positive side effects. For example, a parent called to say that his son had changed their basement wall into a beautiful sailboat scene. Another youngster used a piece of plywood, some string, nails, and his imagination to create a coordinate figure.

All in all, the coordinate geometry unit has been an exciting and worthwhile adventure through the wonderland of thought that we call mathematics. ▲

From the File:
Taste That Graph

by

Joy Glicksberg

Taste That Graph!

An attention-invoking introduction to graphs is one in which students put the raw material directly on the paper and eat it afterward. Popular sweet-and-sour tart candies furnish just such raw material. Each individual roll contains small circular candies of various colors. From roll to roll the number of colors varies, and not all colors are necessarily present in each roll.

Our graph paper consisted of a grid of one-inch squares arranged in columns, one for each color. Students first labeled the vertical axis starting with zero. Next, they labeled the horizontal axis with the colors. Finally, they literally placed the candy on the graph, one to a square in the appropriate column. Presto, a graph that was a cinch to read! Students found it easy to color the graph, eating as they went from the concrete to the representational.

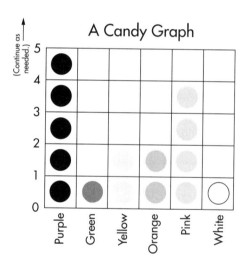

A Candy Graph

The data generated from our eatable graphs supplied a natural basis for word problems. How many pinks altogether? How many more yellows than oranges? What is the average number of purples? And ah, yes, how long on the average does it take a candy to melt in your mouth?

From the file of Joy Glicksberg, Broward County Schools, Coral Springs, FL 33065 ▲

Cemetery Mathematics

by

Ernest Woodward

Sandra Frost

Anita Smith

A student collects information from a tombstone.

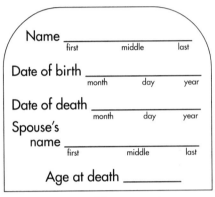

Name _____
first   middle   last

Date of birth _____
month   day   year

Date of death _____
month   day   year

Spouse's name _____
first   middle   last

Age at death _____

Fig. 1. A card for one tombstone

We planned and taught an eight-day graphing unit using data we collected from a local cemetery. This approach helped us make graphing concepts and procedures meaningful to students in a Chapter 1 mathematics program. Students in this federally funded program generally perform about one year below grade level in mathematics and are released from the classroom for forty to fifty minutes daily of remedial instruction. The unit was originally taught to Chapter 1 students at Burt Elementary School in Clarksville, Tennessee. Minor revisions were made in the unit, and it was then taught to Chapter 1 students at Cumberland Heights Elementary School, a small rural school located about two miles from Clarksville. This article reports only on the experiences we had at Cumberland Heights. A total of twenty-seven students in grades 4, 5, and 6 participated. The following is a day-by-day description of what happened.

Day 1

We took all twenty-seven students to Pleasant View Baptist Church Cemetery. The cemetery was divided into four sections. A parent volunteer and six or seven students were assigned to each section, and eventually each student was assigned to about a dozen tombstones. Students were given cards shaped like a tombstone (fig. 1) and told to complete the first four lines on a card for each stone. An easy-to-remove paper sticker was placed on a tombstone when the data had been collected from that stone. A red mark was placed on all cards corresponding to graves of females, and a blue mark was placed on all cards corresponding to graves of males.

Adult volunteers were available to assist students when necessary. These volunteers also checked to see that the information on each tombstone had been recorded, and then they removed the paper sticker from each grave just before we left the cemetery. Students were given calculators and directed to use the information on the cards to determine the age at the time of death for each person by subtracting the year of birth from the year of death. We decided not to address the subtlety of what happens when a person is born late in one year and dies early in another year. The students spent about two hours in the cemetery.

Day 2

The activities completed on this day and on all succeeding days were done during Chapter 1 mathematics class time. This period was a standard forty- or fifty-minute one in which the lesson was done with five subgroups from the original group of twenty-seven.

Ernest Woodward teaches mathematics and mathematics education at Austin Peay State University in Clarksville, TN 37044. He is particularly interested in problem solving in elementary school mathematics. Sandra Frost is employed by the Clarksville-Montgomery County School System, Clarksville, TN 37040, as a classroom teacher and a program specialist K–6. She is especially interested in activities that motivate remedial mathematics students. Anita Smith teaches Chapter 1 remedial mathematics to grades 2–6 at Cumberland Heights Elementary School in Clarksville, TN 37040. She is especially interested in creative teaching methods that foster underachievers' increased confidence in themselves and their mathematical capabilities.

The students divided the cards into groups by decades of age at death and then placed the cards end to end on the floor to form a bar graph. Next the students counted the cards corresponding to individuals whose age at the time of death was from zero to ten years, thirty-seven in all. Then, at the direction of the teacher, one student drew a segment across the 0–10-years-old column corresponding to thirty-seven on a previously labeled and laminated blank bar graph. Others in the group checked to see that this procedure was done correctly. The numbers of individuals in other age at-the-time-of-death categories were recorded in a similar manner. Finally the students completed the graph by shading in the bars. We mentioned the importance of including on the graph the name of the cemetery. One student said, "Let's don't forget the date because our information could change another time." A copy of the graph is shown in figure 2.

In each class the teacher initiated the discussion about the graph with the direction "Tell me what the graph shows at a glance." In one class one student noted that the most deaths occurred in the 71–80 age group. Another student noted that the 0–10 group had

the next greatest number of deaths, and the students proceeded to rank the groups by the number of deaths. When that kind of information did not come directly from the students, the teacher asked questions like the following:

1. During which period of ten years did the most deaths occur?
2. During which period of ten years did the fewest deaths occur?
3. How many more deaths occurred from ages 61–70 years than from 31–40 years?
4. Do any periods of ten years have the same number of deaths?

Most students were able to answer these questions correctly.

Finally the teacher presented the following situation. "Let's pretend that we could go to another cemetery in another town and that this cemetery has exactly the same number of graves as the one we visited. Do you think the graph would look exactly like this one?" Here are some students' responses.

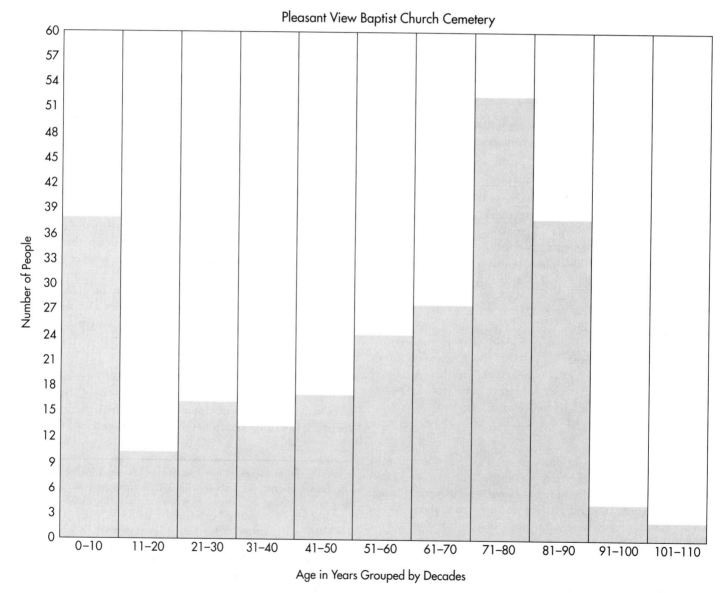

Fig. 2. Age at time of death (total population)

Two students work on a bar graph.

Students construct a bar graph.

1. "No, there might be more people dying in other years."
2. "There could have been a nuclear disaster which wiped out a bunch of young people."
3. "Different locations will change our information."

In one class a boy remarked that men live longer than women. When questioned about why he believed this assertion, he responded, "We had one man over one hundred and no women." (He had remembered this fact as a result of handling the cards,

not from the graph.) After a significant discussion that recalled a previous conversation about different locations, the class concluded that this one example did not constitute a proof.

Day 3

The students separated the cards into two groups by the sex of the person and completed from prelabeled charts individual graphs for age at the time of death for males and females. This task was done with only minimal assistance from the teacher because the students had previously constructed a comparable graph in large-group format on day 2. Copies of the two graphs appear in figures 3 and 4.

Day 4

The fourth day was spent discussing the graphs that had been constructed the previous day. Questions like those from day 2 were asked, except that this time they concerned males and females rather than the entire group.

Days 5 and 6

The students were asked in what month they thought the most deaths occurred. Many students speculated that more people would die during the winter months because of weather-related

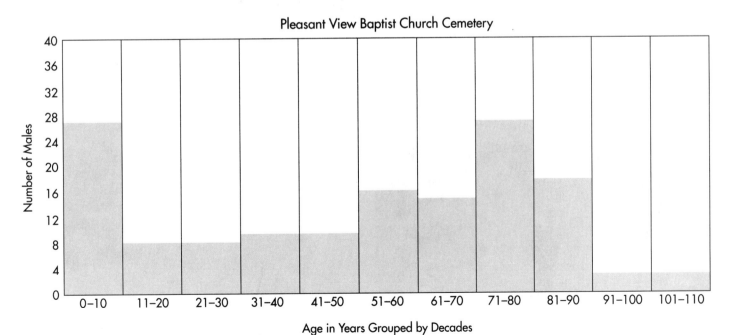

Fig. 3. Ages of males at time of death

Pleasant View Baptist Church Cemetery

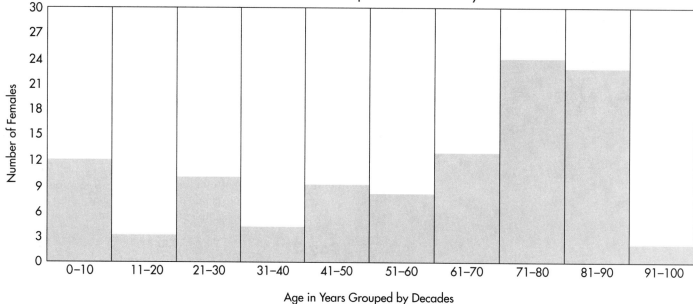

Fig. 4. Ages of females at time of death

problems. When questioned about the greatest-birth month, several students said they thought that it would be the same as the greatest-death month. They finally decided that the way to find out was to go back to the cards and separate them first into death months and construct a graph and then into birth months and construct a graph. At the direction of the teacher, one student put a dot corresponding to 12 over January on a previously labeled and laminated blank graph to represent the twelve people who had died in January. Other students checked to see that the dot was placed in the appropriate position. Then dots were placed on the

other lines representing the numbers of individuals who had died in those months. A similar process using a red pen was followed for graphing birth months. A copy of this graph appears in figure 5.

The following sequence of questions was asked by the teacher:

1. During which month did the most deaths (births) occur? Why?

2. During which month did the fewest deaths (births) occur? Why?

Two students construct a birth-month graph.

A student creates an individual graph.

3. Between which two months do we see the greatest increase (decrease) in deaths (births)?

These questions led to a spirited discussion. In general, most students were able to use the graph to answer all these questions except those that asked why. They had no explanation for why January was the greatest birth month, but several students suggested that July might be the greatest death month because of health problems related to hot weather and because of accidents that occur during summer activities. One girl said, "It looks like every time the birth line goes up, the death line goes down and every time the birth line goes down, the death line goes up." After a careful inspection of the graph, the class decided that this correlation did not always occur.

Day 7

The teacher asked, "If we have thirty people, how likely do you think it is that at least two people will have the same birthday?" A similar question was asked concerning a group of forty people.

The teacher suggested that students might investigate these questions by using the cards that had come from tombstones. Random selections of groups of thirty and forty cards were made. Thirty-five of thirty-six random samples of forty cards included two people with the same birthday and twenty-one out of twenty-five of the random samples of thirty cards revealed two people with the same birthday. This lesson served as a nice follow-up to probability lessons that had previously been taught.

Day 8

Each student constructed a decades-of-death graph. The students found this task quite easy, since they had already constructed a comparable graph in large-group format on day 6. One student's graph is shown in figure 6. The student has connected the points to show the pattern even though the data are not continuous and do not warrant this treatment. This graph sparked significant discussion concerning why more deaths occurred in certain decades than in others.

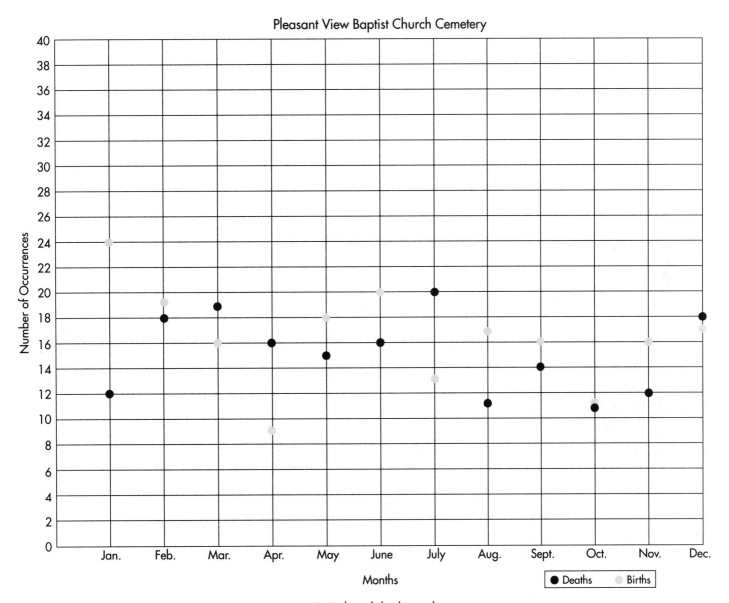

Fig. 5. Birth and death months

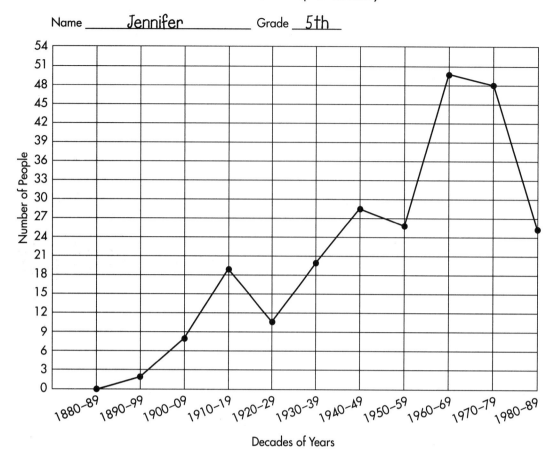

Decades of Death in the
Pleasant View Baptist Cemetery

Name _____ Jennifer _____ Grade __5th__

Decades of Years

Fig. 6. A student's graph of the findings

CONCLUSION

We asked students what they had learned from this activity. Here are some of their written responses:

- "When people died and when people alive"
- "How to classify people that have died"
- "A lot"
- "How to problem solf and how to graph"
- "How many died in a certain year"
- "A lot of people were siner citizens"

As a result of these responses and the observations that were made as the unit was taught, we are convinced that our students learned to construct bar graphs and scatterplots; more important, they learned how to analyze and interpret information presented in graphs. We believe that as a result of the students' working with real data—data they had collected themselves—the graphs that they constructed were important to them. The first version of several bar graphs came from placing the cards in a particular category end to end. Thus, in some sense these graphs were concrete

(pictographs) in the initial stage and progressed to a more abstract (bar graph) level. Both the bar graph and the scatterplots were initially constructed in a large-group format, and then each student constructed a graph individually. Having the raw data in card format was a distinct advantage in classifying data because it facilitated separating the information into categories.

As noted earlier, our students, in general, are performing about a year below grade level in mathematics. In some situations their ability limited what we could do in this unit. In one sixth-grade class we did calculate the average age of death for men (51) and for women (58). We felt the students in the fourth and fifth grades were not able to deal with the concept of averaging in this setting. We decided to include both bar graphs and scatterplots in this unit because we believe that students should have a variety of graphing experiences. However, we did not think that our students were ready to consider the advantages of one type of graph over another.

In our opinion, the unit could be studied more effectively in a standard self-contained classroom. During the field trip to the cemetery, we worked with the students for half a day, but on all the other days we were limited to a forty- or fifty-minute class. Thus, some of our time was spent getting out and putting back materials and reminding the students of what had happened on the previous day. The entire unit could probably have been completed in about two days in a self-contained classroom. Of course, other areas of the curriculum, such as language arts and social studies, could easily have been incorporated into the unit. Although we did not ask our students to write about the graphs, such an approach might be desirable, particularly in a self-contained-classroom situation.

The aspect of the project that pleased us most was the fact that our students learned at the same time that they enjoyed themselves. We had several spirited discussions, and in a number of instances, students made very insightful observations. ▲

Chapter 5

Probability and Statistics

Sampling Treats from a School of Fish

by

Jeanne Vissa

New York State Plans Fish Census" read the title of the newspaper article. The tagging method of doing an animal or fish census provided an interesting idea for a lesson with my seventh and eighth graders on estimation, proportions, central tendencies, and structured sampling. It was also an occasion for using food in a mathematics lesson, which was always a welcome treat.

I purchased a bag of miniature "goldfish" crackers and emptied them into a glass bowl, which became our lake. Each student was asked to estimate the number of fish in the bowl in two ways. First, the students guessed the whole number visually. Second, I counted 24 fish into a small flour scoop and asked the students to compare the scooped fish to all the fish originally in the bowl. If the students thought the fish in the scoop represented one-half the original number of fish in the bowl, then it would be appropriate to think that 48 fish had been in the bowl; if the students thought the scooped fish to be one-tenth of the bowl, then the estimate of fish in the bowl should be about 240. To simulate the tagging process, the single scoop of 24 fish was placed in a paper bag to which food coloring was added. Excess food coloring is usually absorbed by the bag, but blotting the fish with a paper napkin will also absorb any excess dye. Finally, these dyed fish were replaced in the bowl with the "untagged" fish, and all were mixed well.

What to do next? I wanted to establish the rationale for the sampling technique. The students knew one part-to-whole ratio: 24 tagged fish were part of the unknown number of total fish. Suppose that I were to catch samples of 10 fish in my scoop and that each time I did so, 2 of the 10 were always dyed. What could I then say about the probable size of the whole school of fish? We answered this question by setting up a part-to-whole proportion, as shown in table 1.

Students then proposed that the school would contain 120 fish on the basis of one of three relationships. Some students were immediately aware that the number of fish in the sample (10) was five times the number dyed in the sample (2), so the total number in the bowl (x) should be five times the number dyed in the bowl (24). Other students compared the

number of dyed fish in the scoop (2) to the number of dyed fish in the bowl (24). These students reasoned that the fish in the entire bowl must be twelve times the fish in the entire scoop (10). Still other students had to be helped to solve a formal proportion where the product of the mean terms equals the product of the extreme terms—hence, $2x = 240$ and $x = 120$. We also examined

Table 1. Setting Up a Proportion Using Number of Fish

Sample		Bowl
Number dyed	2	24
Total number	10	x

Jeanne Vissa is a classroom teacher and mathematics staff developer at White Plains Middle School, White Plains, NY 10601. She has given in-service courses on new curriculum strands, calculator use, and remediation of learning disabilities.

how the predicted size of the school would be affected if our samples had given us a different ratio of the number of dyed fish in the scoop to the total number in the scoop. Ratios of 4/10, 6/10, or 8/10 would have altered our predictions for total fish in the bowl to 60, 40, or 30, respectively.

Next we looked at what would happen if the ratios of dyed fish to the total number in the sample were inconsistent, that is, if we got successive samplings of 2/10, 4/10, 6/10, and then 8/10. It would be necessary to average the samplings before using the proportion method to predict the size of the school. This average can be calculated with fractions or decimal equivalents at this point, that is,

$$\frac{(0.2 + 0.4 + 0.6 + 0.8)}{4} = \frac{2.0}{4} = 0.5.$$

Using two of the methods used to solve the proportion given in table 1, students then solved the proportion shown in table 2 and found it to be 48.

In real life, not only would the ratio of part to whole in the samples be inconsistent, but the sample sizes themselves— the netted catch—would vary, instead of always being 10. To address this issue, the students were then told that they would have the opportunity to "net" their own samples of goldfish. Each student in turn was to net a sample of goldfish with the flour scoop and report the ratio of tagged fish to total fish. The goldfish were replaced in the bowl before the next sampling was done. In large classes the teacher can supply two identical bowls to facilitate the sampling process.

Because it would have been cumbersome for us to average fractions with different denominators, we reported our ratios in decimal equivalents that we obtained with a calculator (i.e., in the case of 2 dyed fish in a scoop of 15, we used the calculator sequence 2/15 to obtain the decimal $0.13\overline{3}$, which we then rounded to 0.133). Possible outcomes as charted on a chalkboard

or overhead projector are shown in table 3. Note that the decimal equivalents have been rounded to thousandths where necessary.

When each student had reported a ratio, we averaged the decimal equivalents, set up a proportion using this mean, and predicted the size of the whole school of fish. For the sample represented in table 3, we would use the ratio obtained by

$$\frac{(0.133 + 0.04 + 0.1)}{3} = 0.091.$$

Using 91/1000 as the average ratio of dyed fish to scoop size for the sample, we set up and solved the proportion shown in table 4. The prediction of the number of goldfish in this instance was 264.

Table 3. Ratios of Number of Dyed Fish in the Sample (Expressed as Decimals) to Total Number of Fish in the Sample

| 2/15 = 0.133 |
| 1/25 = 0.04 |
| 3/30 = 0.1 |

Table 2. Setting Up a Proportion Based on Averages of Dyed Fish to the Total Number of Fish in the Sample

	Average of samples	Bowl
Number dyed	5	24
Total number	10	x

Table 4. Setting Up a Proportion Based on Averages of Dyed Fish to the Total Number of Fish in the Sample

	Netted sample	School in the bowl
Part dyed	91	24
Whole number	1000	x

At the end of the experiment, students can eat the goldfish. In any event, they should count the goldfish to be able to compare the actual total to the estimated total. Where unacceptable discrepancies occur, a discussion can follow as to the large number of samplings necessary to ensure an unbiased experiment.

Bibliography

Organizing Data and Dealing with Uncertainty. Reston, Va.: National Council of Teachers of Mathematics, 1979.

Shulte, Albert P., ed. *Teaching Statistics and Probability.* 1981 Yearbook of the National Council of Teachers of Mathematics. Reston, Va.: The Council, 1981.

Souviney, Randall. "Problem Solving: Tips for Teachers." *Arithmetic Teacher* 33 (February 1986): 56–57. ▲

From the File: Using Plastic Recycling Numbers

by

Jean M. Shaw

Debby A. Chessin

Statistics

Using Plastic Recycling Numbers

Most plastic products are now voluntarily marked by manufacturers with numbers from 1 to 7 to indicate the ease with which they can be recycled. Items marked "1" are made of PETE—polyethylene terephthalate—and are easiest to recycle. Items marked "7," made of mixed plastics, are the most difficult to recycle.

Integrate the following data-handling investigation into an environmental studies unit. Ask each student to donate five to ten empty plastic items. Discuss possible ways to organize the data as the containers are categorized as "unmarked" and "1" through "7." Will students record the number of items in each category or measure the weight of plastic in each category? What type of graph will best communicate the fraction or percent of items that are marked with each number? Who might be interested in seeing or hearing about these data? What items could students substitute to make the recycling of their family purchases easier? Add a gentle reminder: even recyclable items cannot be used unless they are taken to a recycling center!

From the file of Jean M. Shaw and Debby A. Chessin, University of Mississippi, University, MS 38677 ▲

Gummy Bears in the White House

by

Martin Vern Bonsangue

David L. Pagni

Representation is an essential issue in statistical sampling. Policy in educational, scientific, and political arenas is driven by results based on samples that ideally reflect the characteristics of the larger group from which they are drawn. Biased samples can lead to unfortunate situations when they are used as a basis for reporting results or making decisions. The central question is this: Do the characteristics of a sample occur in approximately the same proportion as in the general population from which the sample was taken? Obtaining a representational sample for a diverse population can be a difficult task.

This article describes a one-week lesson in which gummy-bears candy was used to illustrate sampling procedures and to generate discussion and questions. The lesson models the "exploration of statistics in real-world situations" essential for the development of "an appreciation for statistical methods as powerful means for decision making," as recommended in the *Curriculum and Evaluation Standards for School Mathematics* (NCTM 1989, 105). The lesson is described, the data results are reported, and the students' reactions to problems of representation after holding an election are discussed. The data reported were taken from a lesson done with a class of fifth- and sixth-grade students at a large, diverse public elementary school. The lesson was based on "Gummy Bear Graphs" in Book 2 of the *Santa Ana-Fullerton Elementary Mathematics Project* (SAFEMAP 1991).

GUMMY-BEAR GRAPHS

To investigate the idea of sampling, the class looked at the distribution of gummy bears of different colors in packages from the same manufacturer. The class was divided into eight four-student teams. Each team was given a bag of gummy bears and was told to treat its bag of bears with care. After opening the bag, the team counted the bears and sorted them by color: red, yellow, green, white, orange, and purple.

Martin Bonsangue, mbonsangue@fullerton.edu, and David Pagni, dpagni@fullerton.edu, teach at California State University, Fullerton, CA 92634. Bonsangue teaches mathematics to prospective teachers K–12 and teaches around the country as part of the National Faculty. Pagni teaches similar courses and directs a National Science Foundation Teacher Enhancement Project for elementary teachers in the Santa Ana Unified School District.

Each team constructed a bar graph using the actual gummy bears as counting units. Then each team made a frequency table and colored a bar graph to display their data (fig. 1). One member of each team then colored the team's results on the whole-class gummy-bear chart (fig. 2).

The data for the individual bags and for the whole class are summarized in table 1. No two bags had the same color distribution, but some similarities among the distributions could be seen. For

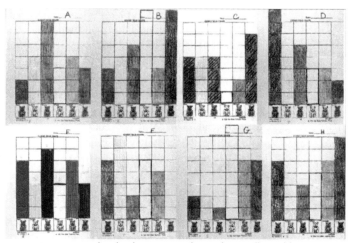

Fig. 1. Bar graphs display gummy-bear data collected by teams.

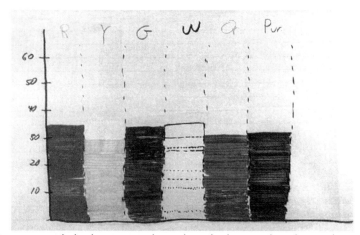

Fig. 2. Whole-class gummy-bear chart displays combined team data.

Table 1. Distribution of Gummy Bears by Color

	Red	Yellow	Green	White	Orange	Purple	Total
Team A	2	4	7	3	4	3	23
Team B	3	4	5	8	3	8	31
Team C	4	4	4	1	2	6	21
Team D	8	4	5	3	3	2	25
Team E	5	3	6	3	5	3	25
Team F	5	7	2	5	4	0	23
Team G	2	2	1	8	5	5	23
Team H	5	1	3	4	5	7	25
Total	34	29	33	35	31	34	196

example, six of the eight bags had at least seven bears of one color, although not necessarily of the same color. Similarly, all but one bag had at least one bear of each color. Several students observed that when the data from all the teams were combined, each color appeared about the same number of times.

INTERDISCIPLINARY CONNECTIONS: GUMMY-BEAR GOVERNMENT

To foster a connection between mathematics and social studies, the students next applied their data to elections in the gummy bears' world. Quantitative methods and proportional reasoning were applied in a social-sciences context. This part of the activity required the students to analyze and describe both the mathematical and social aspects of the lesson.

Voting for group interests

The students entered the world of gummy-bear government. Each student pretended to be a gummy bear and was asked to look at the distribution of colors in each bag and vote on which bag of gummy bears should be elected to the Gummy-Bear White House. That is, which bag of gummy bears best represented the world of gummy bears on the basis of the cumulative distribution?

The students who had earlier observed that the total numbers of bears of each color were approximately the same explained their observation in terms of the frequency distribution shown on the whole-class bar graph. Each bar was of about the same height (fig. 2). Before voting, the class discussed the pros and cons of each bag of gummy bears. Some students preferred bag B, which had at least three bears of each color. Opponents warned that if bag B was selected, white and purple bears would dominate the rest, especially the red and orange bears. One student observed that bags C, G, and H were not good choices, since each bag had only one bear of one color, and that bag F was the worst choice because it had no purple bears. After a secret ballot, bag E was overwhelmingly elected to the Gummy-Bear White House. The class decided that bag E would most fairly represent all the gummy bears because its color distribution closely resembled the distribution among all the gummy bears in the class.

Voting for personal interests

On the following day, a new voting scheme was presented. Each student was randomly assigned a gummy-bear color; the actual distribution was six red, six yellow, five green, five white, five orange, and five purple. Each student was then directed to vote for the bag of gummy bears that would best represent the interests of his or her own color. Which bag of gummy bears would be elected, given this new instruction? The students needed a few minutes to comprehend the new situation. An animated discussion ensued.

"Red" students clearly favored bag D. Some "purple" students wanted bag B, whereas others preferred bag H to ensure dominance by the purple gummy bears. "Orange" students saw no good choices, since they were outnumbered by at least one other color in each bag. One "orange" student simply said, "I'm voting for bag C, against white." In this election, bag D won the Gummy-Bear White House by a narrow margin.

The students compared the bar graph for bag D with the cumulative graph. The "red" students were delighted with the outcome, but most other students—especially the "white," "orange," and "purple" students—were not pleased. Although the contour of the cumulative graph was fairly flat, the bar graph for the newly elected Gummy-Bear White House was not. The red bar was the tallest and was more than twice as high as every other color except green. When asked what this situation meant, the students replied as follows:

- "It isn't fair. The red bears will control everything."
- "Even though there are more white bears in the gummy-bear world, they will have no control over what happens."
- "It could have been worse for purple. Bag F could have won."
- "How could this have happened?"

The class discussed why the vote had changed from the previous day. The first vote had seemed fair because the students made their choices on the basis of the good of the whole class. The second vote was based on individual interests.

If the gummy-bear lesson was repeated, students would probably find the color distribution to be different. On the basis of their first experience, they should expect the distributions to be different; therefore, different gummy-bear bags would likely be elected to the Gummy-Bear White House. Thus, the concept of variability was also conveyed by the activity.

A TIME FOR REFLECTION

On the third day, students wrote about their experiences of the previous two days, thus incorporating a language-arts experience into their mathematics lesson. How did they feel about the first day's result, which was based on a "group interests" approach to government? How did they feel about the vote on the second day, which resulted from a "personal interests" view of government?

Which method of voting was better? Why? Which situation was more likely to occur in real-world elections for government leaders? The students also drew a colored picture showing the gummy-bears' world and the two types of governments.

Which method of voting was better?

Almost all the students, including the "red" students, believed that being governed on the basis of group interests was the better situation, even if their own interests were not better served. One insightful student said, "If others are being treated fairly, it will probably be better for me in the end anyway." More than half the students thought that real-world governments were based on group interests. Some students, however, questioned this belief; if group interests were dominant, why were war and fighting going on in so many places in the world?

The gummy-bear activity described herein can easily be adapted to any grade level. Younger students can use gummy bears to learn about and produce pictographs or bar graphs. Older students can explore the concepts of sampling, representation, and variability. Students at all levels should see the connections among mathematics, social sciences, and language arts. The gummy-bears activity offers the opportunity to create a rich classroom experience in which mathematics serves as a link among disciplines.

Bibliography

Browning, Christine, Dwayne E. Channell, and Ruth A. Meyer. "Professional Development: Preparing Teachers to Present Techniques of Exploratory Data Analysis." *Mathematics Teaching in the Middle School* 1 (September-October 1994): 166–72.

National Council of Teachers of Mathematics. *Curriculum and Evaluation Standards for School Mathematics.* Reston, Va.: The Council, 1989.

Pagni, David, ed. *Santa Ana-Fullerton Elementary Mathematics Project: SAFEMAP Book 2.* Fullerton, Calif.: California State–Fullerton Press, 1991.

Zawojewski, Judith S. *Dealing with Data and Chance.* Addenda Series, Grades 5–8. Reston, Va.: National Council of Teachers of Mathematics, 1991. ▲

Hamster Math: Authentic Experiences in Data Collection

by

Beth Jorgensen

Students enjoy finding and recording physical data for the hamsters in their care.

Wanted: Houdini II, missing hamstr. Bigger then a mous, smaller then a ginny pig. She waes 126 grams. Woword is a caedy cane and a pansle. She is bron. And she has babys that arnt gron up. So you ned to find her fast. If you find her bring her to Mrs. Jorgensen class and you will get it.

These words adorn one of many posters decorating the halls of our school from time to time, alerting visitors to the class project dubbed "hamster math" by the children who helped create it. This article describes some of the data collection and interpretation engaged in throughout this project by the six- to eight-year-olds involved.

As educators, we are reminded that children construct their own understandings and that this process is facilitated when children are engaged in meaningful activities. As facilitators, teachers should offer such opportunities to help students confront and further develop current understandings. My search for a context that would furnish authentic problem-solving situations led to the use of classroom pets as a vehicle for such learning. Through this project, students develop their mathematical literacy in an authentic context.

Hamster math presents real-life problem-solving situations that put learning in context. It serves as a vehicle for developing strategies and learning concepts and skills. Through data collection and subsequent interpretation during problem-solving activities, students develop an ability to communicate and reason mathematically; refine their number sense and concepts of whole-number operations; develop computational abilities; estimate, compare, and apply units of measurement in determining mass; and develop concepts of statistics and probability. A discussion of some of the activities follows. The activities are ongoing but have been arranged in the order in which they have been implemented.

PREDICTING AND GRAPHING

Students use counters to graph their predictions of how many hamsters will be in a litter and when they will be born. These graphs are converted to bar graphs by aligning squares of colored paper (fig. 1), then graphs are read and interpreted during small-group and whole-class activities. Students' graph readings are written and pasted onto the graph, such as the one seen in the background of the photograph in figure 2. In addition to the large class graph, students keep personal copies of these graphs in their hamster-math and science journals. Students' observations of the general consistency of the graphs' shapes have led to discussions that introduce such terms as *bell-shaped curve, mean,* and *mode.* Students use these data to make future predictions.

As another prediction activity, students weigh the mother hamster by using a balance and gram cubes and chart changes in her weight. Students collaborate using that pattern of data to predict future birth dates and litter sizes. A few of the students have projected

---

Beth Jorgensen teaches at Weber Elementary School in Iowa City, IA 52245. She is particularly interested in curriculum integration. Jorgensen was a 1993 Presidential Awardee in Mathematics.

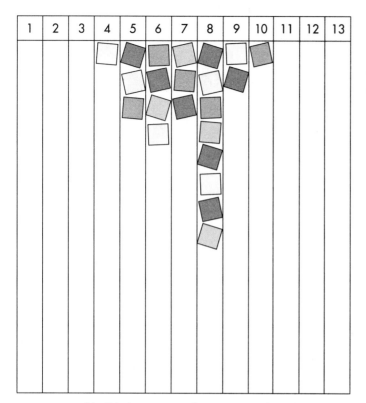

| 1 | 2 | 3 | 4 | 5 | 6 | 7 | 8 | 9 | 10 | 11 | 12 | 13 |

Fig. 1. Pearl had babies on Monday, 11 September. The construction-paper squares denote students' guesses of how many babies she would have.

populations by using information about how many babies a hamster usually has in a litter, the duration of a pregnancy, elapsed time between pregnancies, and weeks left in the school year.

ESTIMATING AND MEASURING

When the baby hamsters are big enough to handle, small groups of students weigh them, using the balance and gram cubes. Gram cubes constructed in units of ten present a context for understanding place value. Students estimate how much they think the hamsters will weigh and compare their estimate with the result. Students have become adept at using previous weights to make their predictions. When the hamsters have been weighed, students chart the growth of the babies (fig. 3). Small groups of students are usually involved in the weighing-and-charting activity, which occurs two or three times a week. A class chart and journal are kept, but, again, students also have personal copies.

FOSTERING NUMBER SENSE

Students develop basic number concepts using manipulatives as they solve relevant and contextualized problems. The ordinal aspects of number can be further developed by solving such problems as constructing sets of objects to represent the number of hamsters in a litter if hamsters have from one to fifteen babies. Odd and even numbers are introduced with such questions as these: "Could half be males and half be females?" "Can one more female than male occur?" Part and whole relations of operational numbers are also placed in context as students use manipulatives

Fig. 2. The graph shown in the background explains students' data.

to find all the possible combinations of male and female baby hamsters in a litter of a given number. Sets of possible male and female combinations are constructed, with two colors of manipulatives representing sexes. These sets are then represented in drawings, in words, and later in symbols. Part of this continuum of understanding is represented in figure 4.

CONSTRUCTING AUTHENTIC NUMBER PROBLEMS THROUGH DATA INTERPRETATION

Students interpret the information on the growth charts as they determine solutions to relevant questions: "Have any of the hamsters doubled their weight?" "Which hamster gained the most weight?" "Did a particular hamster gain as much weight this week as last week?" "How much more does a particular hamster weigh compared with another?" "How do the weights of this litter at eighteen days compare with the weights of the last litter at eighteen days?" "The hamsters were twenty-four days old on February 12, so how old are they today?" Although some of these questions are generated by the teacher, others arise from student collaboration.

	2 March (11 days)	4 March (13 days)	9 March (18 days)	11 March (20 days)	16 March (25 days)	18 March (27 days)	23 March (32 days)	25 March (34 days)
Mittens	12	14	19	38	41	46	53	54
Chocolate	12	13	18	22	32	35	42	50
Looney Tunes	10	12	15	18	24	27	33	40
Peaches	10	12	13	17	25	27	34	42
Cream Puff	10	11	11	13	16	19	23	27
Tippy	11	12	12	15	19	22	28	35
Brownie	11	13	13	22	34	38	44	51
Cocoa	11	13	13	21	29	34	40	47

Fig. 3. Hamster growth chart for Houdini II's babies

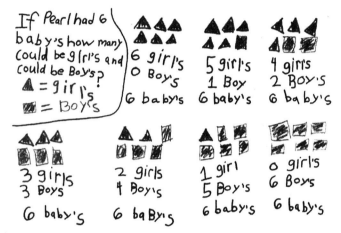

Fig. 4. Possible combinations of male and female hamsters in a litter of four

The problems that students generate also present insight into their misinterpretations of data, such as in the example in figure 5 in which a student treated the series of weights additively instead of cumulatively. Such embedded-assessment situations can inform decisions about instructional planning.

As students collaborate in constructing and solving these problems, they learn the language of mathematics through an active, developmental approach. Manipulatives and student's representations play important roles as students discuss, describe, solve, and validate their work with peers.

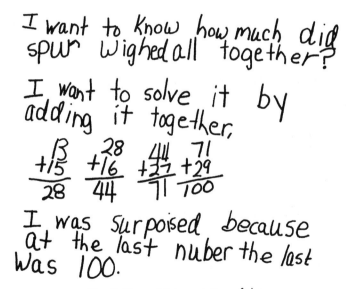

Fig. 5. One misinterpretation of data

Still other problems arise in a genuine problem situation as students apply their knowledge of hamsters and initiate their own questions: "How accurate is this weight when the hamster's cheek is stuffed with seeds? How can we get a more accurate weight?" One student-generated problem follows.

I want to now if one of Houdini's baby's doubled its weight betwen Mar. 2 and Mar. 11.

I plan to soulve the problem bey counting the weight two times and compier it to the number of the grafh.

Mittens 12 + 12 = 24 Mittens more than doubled his weight because 38 is more than 24.

Chocolate didnt double his weight because 22 is less than 24 by 2.

Tippy 11 and 11 = 10 + 10 + 2 = 22 15 is less than 22 so he did not double.

Brownie did double his weight because 11 + 11 = 22.

Cocoa would have doubled his weight if you aded 1.

Cream Puff didnt double his weight Because 10 + 10 = 20 But he weighed 13.

Looney [T]unes almost doubled his weight but 18 is 2 less then 20.

Peaches didnt double his weight Because 17 is less than 20.

PROBLEM SOLVING FOR REAL-WORLD APPLICATION

Our class has entered into a business partnership with a local pet store. As the baby hamsters mature, they are exchanged for store credit. Students keep track of credit earned by using student-designed "hamster bucks" and use this credit to buy supplies. Parental involvement makes field trips to the store possible so that supplies can be priced. Charts depicting the costs of various items, money earned, and money spent are used for students' reference. Decisions about how the money will be spent are made during class meetings, for which students prepare individually or in collaborative groups. Students use miniature hamster bucks to record how they would spend the money; these recordings then help explain their reasoning during our meetings. In addition, students estimate future earnings on the basis of projected populations and knowing that we receive two dollars for each hamster.

PROBABILITY

Students initially worked with the offspring of two albino parents whose offspring were also albino. Recently, a multicolored female and a brown male have been added, and students have begun recording color combinations of new offspring as an early exploration in genetics. This exploration serves as an informal introduction to probability, and we intend to use the information to predict color combinations of future litters.

I have found hamster math to be especially beneficial for my students because they have encountered learning in an engaging, real-life context. They have been immersed in situations that have enabled them to make connections in meaningful and relevant ways. And as for Houdini, the missing hamster? She was flushed out, amidst much excitement, from her hideout behind the cabinets and safely returned to her eager babies. ▲

Problem Solving with Combinations

by

Lyn English

This student adopted a pattern in his item selection, thereby avoiding duplication of outfits.

When you're trying to choose from a selection of sandwich fillings at a lunch canteen or trying to decide which shirt will best match a pair of pants, you're dealing with combinations. Defined simply, the topic of combinations involves the selection and arrangement of objects in a finite set where the order of selection does not matter (Jacobs 1982).

Because of its real-world applications, the combinatorial domain supplies a particularly rich source of problem-solving activities for both the lower and the middle grades. Furthermore, combinatorial problems allow—

- hands-on experiences,
- different solution strategies,
- nonnumber as well as number situations,
- variety in problem settings and structures,
- individual and group work, and
- a range of ability and age levels.

This article highlights combinatorial problems that the author has used with students aged four to twelve years and examines some of their responses. Such responses lend valuable insights into students' ability to generate their own strategies and to monitor their progress during novel problem solving.

COMBINATIONS FOR THE LOWER GRADES

An enjoyable series of problems for four- to nine-year-olds involves the dressing of toy bears in all possible different combinations of tops and pants, as shown in figure 1. The original bears are made of plywood but could easily be made from cardboard or copied onto paper for individual, group, or whole-class use. The clothes are constructed from colored poster board and are backed with self-adhesive material so that students can easily attach them to the bears. The problems include a surplus of items so that students won't rely on the depletion of materials as an indication of a problem's completion. A template for constructing these materials is given in figure 2.

Various materials were helpful.

The variations of problems listed in figure 1 are easily constructed by changing the number and type of clothing items and by placing additional constraints on the problem's goal. For example, in problems 4 and 5, color combinations have been replaced with numbers by using clothing items having varying numbers of buttons.

Lyn English teaches at Queensland University of Technology, P.O. Box 284, Zillmere, Brisbane 4034, Australia. She is particularly interested in mathematical thinking and novel problem solving in the lower and middle grades.

The author wishes to express her appreciation to Peter Hibble, who made the bears and their clothing items for this activity.

Problem 1

Materials
- Set of 8 bears
- Sets of clothing items as follows:

  4 green tops   4 yellow tops

  4 blue pants   4 pink pants   4 orange pants

Goal

Dress as many bears as you can so that each bear is wearing a different outfit. [6 possible outfits]

This problem can be repeated with three sets of tops and two sets of pants.

Problem 2

Materials
- Set of 11 bears
- Sets of clothing items as follows:

  4 blue tops   4 green tops   4 yellow tops

  4 blue pants   4 pink pants   4 orange pants

Goal

Dress as many bears as you can so that each bear is wearing a different outfit. [9 possible outfits]

Problem 3

Materials
- Set of 8 bears
- Sets of clothing items as follows:

  4 blue tops   4 yellow tops

  4 blue pants   4 pink pants   4 orange pants

Goal

Dress as many bears as you can so that each bear is wearing a different outfit, but this time, give the third bear a blue top. [6 possible outfits]

Problem 4

Materials
- Set of 8 bears
- Sets of clothing items as follows:

  4 one-button tops   4 two-button tops

  4 one-button pants   4 three-button pants   4 five-button pants

Goal

Dress as many bears as you can so that each bear is wearing a different *total number* of buttons. [6 possible outfits]

Problem 5

Materials
- Set of 8 bears
- Sets of clothing items as follows:

  4 one-button tops   4 two-button tops

  4 two-button pants   4 three-button pants   4 five-button pants

Goal

Dress as many bears as you can so that each bear is wearing a different *total number* of buttons. [5 possible outfits]

This problem involves a hidden constraint. Two outfits formed from different items have identical totals; hence, one of these outfits must be discarded.

Fig. 1. Combinations of clothing items

Fig. 2. Template for bear and clothing items

Before attempting the problems in figure 1, students must have a firm understanding of the terms *same outfits* and *different outfits*. It is important to let students initially experiment with the materials so that they become familiar with these terms. Questions such as the following should be asked: "Look at the bears you've dressed. Do they all have *different* outfits? How do you know? Do any bears have the *same* outfits? How can you tell whether they have the same outfits?"

Such questioning is particularly important when different outfits have common items, for example, a blue top with red pants versus a yellow top with red pants. Several of the four- and five-year-olds with whom I worked considered these outfits to be the same. Other four- and five-year-olds had difficulty distinguishing *difference across outfits* from *difference between outfits*. For example, they would state that the outfits of blue top with blue pants and yellow top with yellow pants are not different because each comprises identically colored tops and pants.

Some students decided to form outfits with pants only. They explained that because the day was hot, the bears could go without tops. A few four-year-olds tried to made additional outfits by reversing the position of the tops and pants on the bears and took great delight in doing so. They clearly realized that this option was not viable; however, they were determined to give it a try. These last two observations were particularly interesting because they showed a creative side to the preschool children's responses that was not seen in the responses of the schoolchildren.

This student makes a trial combination in her hand prior to attaching clothing to the bear.

Figure 3 displays other combinatorial problems involving hands-on materials that can easily be stored in the mathematics corner for individual or group use. Problems 1 and 2 are well within the grasp of lower-grade students, whereas problem 3 presents a challenge for the more able of these students.

COMBINATIONS FOR THE MIDDLE GRADES

The problems shown in figure 1 can be extended by including additional types of items (e.g., sets of tennis rackets), as shown in figure 4. These problems can be used with students in the middle grades, as well as with the more competent students in the earlier grades. When I presented these problems to seventy-two students aged seven to twelve years, I found that even the twelve-year-olds got immense pleasure from working with these materials, even if they were dealing with teddy bears!

Even older students enjoyed working with teddy bears.

Drawing a diagram and making a list are effective strategies for assisting students in their transition from hands-on combinatorial problems to those in written form. The first problem in figure 5 can initially be modeled with cutouts of the clothing items or with simple drawings of the items and the resultant outfits. The responses of two nine-year-olds, Amelia and Sarah, to a simpler version of this first problem are shown in figure 6. Although these girls attended the same class, they chose different solution strategies. A more sophisticated method was used by ten-year-old Michael (fig. 6), who used an array format to generate the combinations.

Tree diagrams also assist students in solving written combinatorial problems. Students can be guided in the drawing of these diagrams as indicated in figure 5. The tree diagram for the first problem commences with two branches to denote Marianne's yellow blouse and white blouse. Since Marianne can wear three different

These problems can be placed within a party context. Colored counters can be used to represent the cookies and the candies.

Problem 1

Materials
- Sets of cookies and candies as follows:
    - 4 chocolate cookies
    - 4 banana cookies
    - 4 lime candies
    - 4 raspberry candies
    - 4 strawberry candies

Goal
Make as many different cookie-candy pairs as you can.
[6 possible pairs]

Ensure that the students understand that a pair must comprise one cookie and one piece of candy. The term different pairs *should be explained prior to working the problems.*

Problem 2

Materials
- Sets of cookies and candies as follows:
    - 4 ginger cookies
    - 4 oatmeal cookies
    - 4 banana cookies
    - 4 peppermint candies
    - 4 chocolate candies
    - 4 orange candies

Goal
Make as many different cookie-candy pairs as you can.
[9 possible pairs]

Problem 3

Materials
- Sets of cookies, candies, and baskets as follows:
    - 5 carrot cookies
    - 5 raisin cookies
    - 5 raspberry candies
    - 5 strawberry candies
    - 5 pink baskets
    - 5 blue baskets

Goal
Make as many different party baskets as you can.
[8 possible baskets]

Ensure that the students understand that a party basket comprises one of the baskets, one cookie, and one piece of candy.

Fig. 3. Cookie and candy combinations

skirts with each blouse, three new branches are added to each of the initial branches. Finally, since Marianne can complete her outfit by wearing pink or black sneakers, two further branches are extended from each of the previous ones. This approach gives a total of twelve different outfits.

Examples of other problems that can be solved by tree diagrams are given in figure 5. A worthwhile follow-up activity is to have students create their own combinatorial problems for their friends to solve. These original problems can be kept in a class problem-solving book. Experience in constructing their own examples helps students appreciate the structure of combinatorial problems.

LEARNING FROM STUDENTS' APPROACHES

Students are surprisingly adept at solving hands-on combinatorial problems. In a series of three studies, I presented the problems listed in figures 1, 3, and 4 to 200 students aged four to twelve

Problem 1

Materials
- Set of 10 bears
- Sets of clothing items:
  - 5 blue tops   5 green tops
  - 5 orange pants   5 red pants
  - 5 blue tennis rackets   5 yellow tennis rackets

Goal

Dress as many bears as you can so that each bear has a different outfit. [8 possible outfits]

Ensure that students understand that in this problem, an outfit includes a top, a pair of pants, and a tennis racket.

Problem 2

Materials
- Set of 10 bears
- Sets of clothing items:
  - 7 red tops   7 yellow tops
  - 7 blue pants   7 orange pants   7 green pants
  - 7 blue tennis rackets   7 red tennis rackets

Goal

Dress as many bears as you can so that each bear has a different outfit. [12 possible outfits—1 for each of the 10 bears and 2 extra outfits]

Fig. 4. Extending combinations of clothing items

years. The students were administered the problems individually and were not given any assistance in solving them. Their responses alerted me to the range of strategies that students are able to invent and also to the number of different checking actions they spontaneously use to monitor their progress. These findings, summarized in the remainder of this article, have a number of implications for our teaching of problem solving.

Students invent their own strategies

These problems were novel to the students, that is, they didn't have a ready-made solution procedure. The majority of them initially used a trial-and-error approach, which required them to monitor their actions carefully, as discussed shortly. As I observed the students work through the problems, I noticed a distinct improvement in their solution strategies. However, this improvement was confined largely to students aged seven years and older. These students adopted a pattern in their item selection, as can be seen in the responses of Danny, a very vocal eight-year-old.

Danny used a trial-and-error approach to solve the first problem in figure 1. When he was given the repeated example (3 sets of tops and 2 sets of pants), Danny adopted a pattern in his selection of tops (blue top, red top, green top, blue top, …). However he lost his pattern toward the end of this problem. In so doing, he stated that he was becoming "a bit mixed up" because "I'm trying to follow a pattern in my mind and I'm getting stuck." When he approached problem 2, involving nine combinations, Danny quickly generated the solution by using an "odometer" pattern to select the items. This pattern works like the odometer in a car. That is, to form all the possible outfits, an item of one type (e.g., a red top) is held "constant" while items of the other type (e.g., each of the pants) are varied. This process is repeated with each "constant item."

Problem 1

Marianne has a yellow blouse and a white blouse. She also has a green skirt, a red skirt, and a blue skirt. With these outfits, she wears either pink sneakers or black sneakers. How many different outfits can she wear? [12 possible outfits]

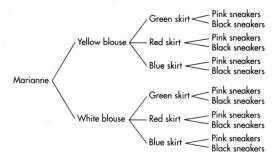

Problem 2

When he makes sandwiches, Sam sometimes uses white bread and sometimes uses brown bread. He chooses one or more fillings from those listed. How many different types of sandwiches can Sam make? [14 possible types]

Ham   Tomato   Cheese

Problem 3

In a box of greeting cards, some are white, some are pink, and some are blue; some have get-well greetings; some, graduation greetings; and some, anniversary greetings. How many cards are in each box if every combination is included and no two cards are exactly alike? [9 cards]

Problem 4

The Sunshine Furniture Company manufactures deck chairs that are made from either timber or plastic or metal and that have either red cushions or green cushions or blue cushions. From how many different deck chairs can a customer choose? [9]

Fig. 5. Use of tree diagrams

Through working these problems, Danny developed the skill of combinatorial reasoning and discovered an important mathematical principle of counting. The fundamental counting principle asserts that if one task can be performed in *m* ways and a second task in *n* ways, then the number of ways of performing the two tasks is *mn* (DeGuire 1991). It was evident that Danny understood how this principle worked. As he was solving the second problem of figure 1, I noticed that I had inadvertently omitted an item. When I proceeded to add it to his existing items, Danny claimed, "Oh, I don't need that pink top. I only need three of them." When he had finished the problem, I asked Danny how he knew he had solved it. He replied, "Because I have used all the different colored pants with all the different colored tops and I know that will give me nine outfits."

Students engage in self-monitoring

As the students worked through the problems, they spontaneously monitored their progress. Some were very thorough in their checking and were thus able to solve the problems even if their solution methods were not the most efficient. Others were rather careless and were thus prone to errors. In all, the students displayed four broad types of checking:

Little or no checking

Some children, mainly the four- and five-year-olds, either failed to do any checking whatsoever or checked only the unused items in front of them. They didn't bother to check the outfits they had made.

Doing then checking

Other children checked their combinations only after they had made them. They did not check to see whether a combination was possible before making it. Once again, this type of checking was observed mainly in the four- and five-year-olds.

Checking then doing

Many of the six- to twelve-year-old students checked the feasibility of a combination before forming it. They frequently did so by making trial combinations in their hands prior to attaching them to the bears.

Checking constantly

Many six- to twelve-year-olds also used constant checking. They checked before, during, and after forming a combination.

As indicated in the next section, the quality of the students' monitoring was a crucial factor in their ability to solve the problems.

Effective monitoring + adequate strategies = successful problem solving

Students' discovery of the efficient combinatorial procedure did not necessarily guarantee a problem's correct solution, particularly when the problem contained a hidden constraint, as in problem 5 of figure 1. Here, students who relied on their efficient procedures and didn't bother to monitor their actions failed to detect the two identical totals. As one student explained, "My method worked for the other problems. I thought it would work for this one…. I suppose that's why I didn't check." Danny, however, did solve this problem. As he applied his combinatorial procedure, he rehearsed aloud the totals he had made. When he came to the second total of four, he stated, "I can't have this one (outfit), as I've already got four." Several other students who were thorough checkers solved this problem without applying the combinatorial procedure.

> ## Students flourished when exploring without my offering rules.

Marianne has a yellow T-shirt, a white T-shirt, and a blue T-shirt. She also has a green skirt, a red skirt, and a blue skirt. How many different outfits can she make with these clothes?

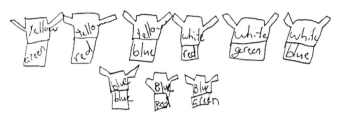

Amelia

Sarah

Michael

Fig. 6. Samples of students' responses

CONCLUSION

The topic of combinations is eminently suitable for students in the lower and middle grades. It is very much a part of the real world, lends itself readily to manipulative activity, and doesn't demand a prior knowledge of abstract concepts (Varga 1969).

Combinatorial reasoning is a useful mathematical tool in students' collection of representation schemes (Johnson 1991; NCTM 1989). It is essential, though, that students be given the opportunity to discover combinatorial ideas themselves rather then blindly follow rules given to them.

Once students discover efficient problem-solving methods, such as the combinatorial procedure, it is important that they continue to monitor their progress during solution attempts. Students need to be reminded that the pattern or rule they have discovered might have the potential for solving a problem but does not guarantee that a correct solution will result.

Bibliography

DeGuire, Linda J. "Permutations and Combinations: A Problem-solving Approach for Middle School Students." In *Discrete Mathematics across the Curriculum, K–12,* 1991 Yearbook of the National Council of Teachers of Mathematics, edited by Margaret J. Kenney and Christian R. Hirsch, 59–66. Reston, Va.: The Council, 1991.

Jacobs, Harold. *Mathematics: A Human Endeavor.* 2d ed. New York: W. H. Freeman & Co., 1982.

Johnson, Jerry. "Using Dominoes to Introduce Combinatorial Reasoning." In *Discrete Mathematics across the Curriculum, K–12,* 1991 Yearbook of the National Council of Teachers of Mathematics, edited by Margaret J. Kenney and Christian R. Hirsch, 128–36. Reston, Va.: The Council, 1991.

Maher, Carolyn A., and Amy M. Martino. "Implementing the *Professional Standards for Teaching Mathematics:* Teachers Building on Students' Thinking." *Arithmetic Teacher* 39 (March 1992): 32–37.

National Council of Teachers of Mathematics. *Curriculum and Evaluation Standards for School Mathematics.* Reston, Va.: The Council, 1989.

Varga, Tamas. "Combinatorials and Probability for Young Children: Part 1." *Journal of Structural Learning* 1 (February 1969): 49–99. ▲

Investigations: It's the Berries

by Martha H. Hopkins

The "Investigations" department recognizes the importance of children's exploring hands-on and minds-on mathematics and, therefore, presents teachers with open-ended explorations to enhance mathematical instruction. These meaningful tasks are designed to evolve as they are conducted. They invoke problem solving and reasoning, require communication skills, and encourage the identification of connections among various mathematical concepts and principles. To ensure usability, the activities presented in this column have been tested in various classroom settings.

A mathematical investigation is defined as a collection of worthwhile problem-solving tasks that—

- has multidimensional content;
- is open-ended, permitting several acceptable solutions;
- is an exploration requiring a full period or several classes to complete;
- is centered on a theme or event; and
- is often embedded in a focus question.

In addition, a mathematical investigation involves a number of processes, which include—

- researching outside sources to gather information;
- collecting data through such means as surveying, observing, or measuring;
- collaborating with peers in small learning groups; and
- using multiple strategies for reaching solutions and conclusions.

This month's investigation is centered on the collection and analysis of data in a scientific setting. Students conduct experiments to answer two research questions. After collecting, organizing, displaying, and analyzing data, they draw conclusions about the research questions as well as the scientific process. After completing the first experiment, children should have a basic understanding of data collection and be able to identify variables that might have affected the results of their experiment. The second activity extends the learning to include the design of an experiment that controls for these variables as well as an exploration of criteria appropriate for choosing various data displays. Although these activities are most appropriate for children in grades 5 and 6, teachers of grades 3 and 4 may wish to have their students complete the first part of the investigation.

LEVELS 5 AND 6

Objectives

The students will—

- design and conduct an experiment to answer a research question;
- collect data from experimentation;
- organize, display, and analyze data;
- apply the problem-solving strategy of organizing information in a table, chart, or graph;
- use averages as a summary of data;
- draw conclusions on the basis of collected data;
- explore the concept of a percent;
- identify variables that may affect data collection; and
- explore characteristics of data displays.

Materials

Students will need—

- a copy of the reproducible page for each student,
- four bags of fresh cranberries,
- a ruler for each group of four students, and
- one container large enough to hold a bag of cranberries.

Note: because the students will be designing their own experiments, a complete listing of materials is not possible here. Teachers whose classes tested the activities reported that students used thermometers, metersticks, snack baggies, plastic wrap, paper clips, masking tape, small plastic bowls, ice, a lamp, an overhead projector, and the school's refrigerator/freezer and microwave oven. All teachers reported, however, that they had restricted the materials list to things they thought were easily obtained and that many of the children redesigned their experiments accordingly.

Marty Hopkins, marthah@Ppegasus.cc.ucf.edu, is on the faculty at the University of Central Florida. Her present teaching assignment is in the fifth grade at Dommerich Elementary School in Maitland, Florida. Her main interests include critical thinking and authentic integration of mathematics into other curriculum areas.

The first portion of this investigation is an adaptation of part of the AIMS (Activities Integrating Mathematics and Science) activity titled Crazy over Cranberries (Miller 1984).

Preparing for the Investigation

Ask the children if they or their families have ever purchased something at the store that was not fresh. Discuss how they knew that the items were not absolutely fresh (e.g., dents in a pear, dark-brown color of a banana, bread that crumbled easily, gum that was brittle or hard to chew).

Hold up a bag of cranberries and ask the children how they would know if the berries in the bag were fresh. You might wish to pass a few around the room for the children to inspect.

Encourage the children to brainstorm ways to test for freshness. As ideas are presented, record them on the chalkboard. As the discussion evolves, ask the students to compare and contrast the ideas on the chalkboard, telling the advantages and disadvantages of each method listed. Be careful to stress that no one method is "best" for testing the freshness of cranberries. As part of this investigation, they will test freshness by seeing how high cranberries bounce, but some of the ideas they brainstorm might be even better. In fact, it might be fun to test the berries by using more than one method and compare the results! (See the "Extensions" section.)

After the students share their ideas, tell them that they are going to conduct an experiment to answer the research question "What percent of the cranberries in this bag are fresh?" After writing the question on the chalkboard, ask the children to explain the question to you. This is a good time to discuss percent as "per 100." If you are interested in the percent of fresh berries, you actually want to know how many cranberries out of every 100 are fresh.

Structuring the Investigation

First experiment

The method they will use to test freshness involves taking measurements in teams of four. Assign each team the following jobs: ruler holder, cranberry dropper 1, cranberry dropper 2, and recorder. Tell the students that they are going to place a ruler on edge so that the long edge is resting on the table or desk (see the drawing on the reproducible page). They will then drop a cranberry next to the ruler one at a time. A cranberry will be considered fresh if it bounces higher than the ruler.

Use only one bag of cranberries for this portion of the investigation. Distribute one ruler and ten cranberries to each group, along with a reproducible sheet for each student. Ask the groups to record their results under "Trial 1" in the "First Experiment" section of the reproducible sheet. Collect the cranberries and set them aside in a container.

Allow each group to share its results with the rest of the class. How did they record the data? (Some students will make tallies for the number of fresh cranberries; some will record both "fresh" and "not fresh"; others will merely write a number representing "fresh.") Make a chart on the chalkboard to show all of the raw data collected. Discuss the data. Did all groups get the same result? Were the data of one group quite different from the data of the other groups? If so, what might account for that difference? Did the students notice any characteristics of cranberries that did not bounce very well? How about those that bounced really high?

Have the students perform four more trials of the experiment, each time recording the data on their reproducible sheets. After each trial, collect the cranberries in the container and then redistribute ten of them to each group. Have students share the data collected in the trials; add the new data to the chart on the chalkboard. Do the data seem to change over time? Are individual groups consistently getting the same data even though the cranberries dropped differ each time?

After five trials the amount of data should be considerable; each group will have dropped 50 cranberries. Remind the students about the research question. Ask them how they can use the collected information to decide what percent of the cranberries in the bag are fresh. Do they need to test 100 cranberries to get this information? This number is an option. However, each group bounced only 50 cranberries. Can they determine the percent of fresh cranberries with only 50 pieces of data? How? Engage the class in a discussion of percents and remind them that percent means 'per 100." Allow each group to discuss how they think the percent of fresh berries can be found. The following are two responses from students during the field tests: "If I know how many fresh berries there are in 50 trials, then there is likely to be twice as many in 100 trials." "If 50 berries represent 100 percent of the berries tested, then each berry has a value of 2 percent. I found 38 fresh berries, and 38 times 2 is 76, so 76 percent of my berries were fresh."

Ask groups to use their data to determine the percent of fresh berries they bounced. Direct them to record this information on their reproducible sheets, along with an explanation of how they determined it. Allow ample time for groups to share their procedures and solutions with the rest of the class.

Using all the data recorded on the chalkboard, determine the percent of fresh berries overall. Use whatever method your students understand best. Does the percent differ from that recorded on their sheets? If so, how can they account for this difference? The amount of data may be one explanation.

Conclude this portion of the investigation with a discussion of variables that might have affected the data collected by each group. Some variables identified by previous classes include the height from which the cranberry is dropped; the number of times a particular cranberry is dropped (Does bouncing make it lose freshness?); the way the cranberry is dropped (Was it dropped or thrown?); and the width of the ruler (plastic rulers were wider than wooden ones).

Second experiment

Draw the students' attention to the research question in the "Second Experiment" section of the reproducible sheet: Does temperature affect the "bounceability" of a cranberry? Encourage discussion to clarify their understanding of the question. The interpretation of "temperature" used in the field tests was the temperature of the berry, not the room temperature. How does this research question differ from the first one? Brainstorm the types of data the groups might need to collect to answer this question. Call their attention to the fact that the experiment has two parts—they need to record the temperature information as well as the height of bounce. Ask the students to predict the kind of representation (table, chart, or graph) they might use to display their data. Be sure to ask them to explain their reasoning. Most students who completed this activity in our test sites thought that line graphs would probably be needed to display these data. When asked to justify their reasoning, they indicated that they would be looking for the relationship between two things, or variables—temperature and bounce.

Remind the students about the variables that might have affected the results of the freshness test. Could these same variables affect the new experiment? Should others be considered? Ask each group to design an experiment that they could perform to answer the new question, keeping in mind that they will need to control for these variables. As they design the experiment, direct them to complete the "Research Design" section of the reproducible sheet. What materials will they need? What specific procedures will they follow? How will they control for the variables? What data will they collect? How will they record the data? What is their hypothesis (i.e., what they think the result will be)?

It is recommended that students *not* conduct their experiments on the same day they design them. First, unless students are restricted to using materials already present in the classroom, they will need time to gather materials. Second, experience has shown that students may require more time to rethink and revise their designs. They may also wish to discuss their designs with family members.

Encourage the students to conduct their experiments and to record all data carefully on their reproducible sheets.

As individual groups complete the experiments, they will most likely have questions about what to do with the data and how best to display them on a chart or graph. After discussing the need for more than one trial in the freshness test, most groups will probably design their experiments to include several trials at each temperature. Consequently, they will have an abundance of data. The following questions can facilitate their decision-making process at this point:

• What kind of data do you have? For example, students might have recorded temperatures and the number of berries that bounced high enough at each temperature to meet their criteria, or temperature and how high berries bounced at each temperature.

• What kind of display were you thinking about making?

• Do you want to show on your graph every single piece of data that you have collected?

• How can you "collapse" the data without losing too much information?

At this point you might want to initiate a discussion about averaging as one method of collapsing the data. You can ask students whether averages would be a useful statistic to use on their graphs. Ask them to explain their reasoning.

Another opportunity to facilitate discussion naturally arises if the students use graphs to represent their data. Typically asked questions include the following:

• What label should we place on each axis?

• How do we choose the numbers to put on each axis?

• In what order should we present the data? In the order you conducted the experiment? From high temperature to low temperature?

Their tables, charts, or graphs should present their findings in the most logical and least complicated manner possible. Depending on the experiment, most students will likely display temperatures along one axis and the average height of bounce along the other.

After all students have recorded their findings, allow each group to share its procedures and findings with the class. Discuss them freely, encouraging students to ask questions about all phases of the experience. How well were variables controlled? Was it important to test more than one cranberry at each temperature? Why or why not? Did the groups vary in this regard? Did all groups collect the same kind of data? Are all of the data collected included on the graph? Where? Compare results. Did all groups reach the same conclusion? If not, what might account for the differences?

Extensions

1. Encourage the children to test the freshness of the cranberries by using one of the methods brainstormed at the beginning of the investigation. Compare the results with those from the "bounceability" test. If percents differ, encourage the children to identify the variables in the experiments that might have caused the variation.

2. Discuss the steps in the scientific method. (Identify a question or define a problem; guess the answer or form a hypothesis; design an experiment; carry out the experiment; draw conclusions.) How was each step applied to the freshness test? What kinds of questions might be studied using the scientific method? Encourage the children to use the scientific method to answer a question of their choice.

3. Ask the students to investigate the shelf life of different food items in the supermarket. How do store managers determine how long to keep food on their shelves? How does shelf life affect their ordering process? Students could compare different supermarket chains in this regard and display their results in a suitable graph or chart.

4. Other research questions students can answer using the scientific method are listed here. Each question has a set of interesting variables that the children will need to discuss when designing their experiments.

   • What percent of consumers spend less than thirty dollars when shopping at the supermarket? (Variables might include gender, age, time of day, season, etc.)

   • What is the busiest time of day along the street in front of our school?

   • Do plants grow better in artificial light or sunlight?

Concluding Comments

The NCTM's *Curriculum and Evaluation Standards for School Mathematics* (1989) emphasizes that collecting, organizing, describing, displaying, and interpreting data are skills that are increasingly important in a technical society. "Children need to recognize that many kinds of data come in many forms and that collecting, organizing, displaying, and thinking about them can be done in many ways" (p. 54). When we pose questions and allow children to develop their own methods of answering them, we are giving them the tools necessary to construct their own understanding of the world in which they live.

References

Miller, M. L. *Crazy over Cranberries*. Fresno, Calif.: AIMS Education Foundation, 1984.

National Council of Teachers of Mathematics (NCTM). *Curriculum and Evaluation Standards for School Mathematics*. Reston, Va.: NCTM, 1989.

IT'S THE BERRIES

Name _____

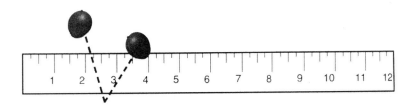

Our freshness test data:

Trial 1	Trial 2	Trial 3	Trial 4	Trial 5

_____ percent of the berries we tested were fresh. Here is how we found this percent: _____

_____

Second Experiment

Does the temperature affect the "bounceability" of a cranberry? _____

Research Design
We will need these supplies: _____

This is the procedure we plan to follow: _____

_____

_____

Variables we have identified: _____

How we are controlling for them: _____

_____

This is our hypothesis: _____

Results
Our data display is attached to this sheet. We chose this display because _____

_____

_____

These are our conclusions: _____

_____

Investigations: Truth or Coincidence?

by

Daniel J. Brahier

The "Investigations" department recognizes the importance of children's exploring hands-on and minds-on mathematics and, therefore, presents teachers with open-ended explorations to enhance mathematical instruction. These meaningful tasks are designed to evolve as they are conducted. They invoke problem solving and reasoning, require communication skills, and encourage identification of connections among various mathematical concepts and principles. To ensure usability, the ideas presented in this column have been tested in various classroom settings.

A mathematical investigation is defined as a collection of worthwhile problem-solving tasks that—

• has multidimensional content;

• is open-ended, permitting several acceptable solutions;

• is an exploration requiring a full period or several classes to complete;

• is centered on a theme or event; and

• is often embedded in a focus question.

In addition, a mathematical investigation involves a number of processes, which include—

• researching outside sources to gather information;

• collecting data through such means as surveying, observing, or measuring;

• collaborating, with each team member taking on specific jobs; and

• using multiple strategies for reaching solutions and conclusions.

This month's investigation focuses on mathematical situations that often have surprising results. Research has shown that children become curious when the outcome of a problem is differ-

ent from what they might have expected, and this curiosity can lead to increased excitement when engaging in mathematical problem solving. The investigation, applicable for grades 3–6, encourages children to hypothesize and to conduct experiments that verify or contradict their intuitions. Through hands-on explorations, children collect data and draw conclusions on the basis of the information.

A HEADS-OR-TAILS TOSS
LEVELS 3–6
Student Activity Goals
Students will—

• make conjectures on the basis of intuition;

• collect data from experimentation;

• draw conclusions on the basis of collected data;

• recognize and extend numerical patterns; and

• apply the problem-solving strategies of looking for patterns, organizing information in a table, and solving simpler problems.

Materials
The materials needed for each child are—

• a copy of the "A Heads-or-Tails Toss" reproducible page,

• a calculator,

• scissors,

• a coin or two-color counter, and

• paper and pencil.

Planning for Instruction
Begin the investigation by explaining to the students that they will be taking a five-question, true-or-false quiz. Distribute the reproducible page to each child and show him or her where to place "answers" to the five questions. Then tell the students that you have forgotten to bring the questions along, so that they will have to "guess" whether each answer is true or false. After guessing each of the five answers, have them exchange and grade each other's papers, reading the solutions as (*a*) true, (*b*) true, (*c*) false, (*d*) true,

Daniel Brainier teaches at Bowling Green State University, Bowling Green, OH 43403-0252. In addition to teaching university-level courses, he also teaches an eighth-grade-algebra course.

Edited by William R. Speer, 529 Education Building, Bowling Green State University, Bowling Green, OH 43403.

(e) false. After students have given their papers back to the original owners, ask how many students got all five questions correct and record the results on an overhead projector or chalkboard. Ask and record similar information for four, three, two, one, or none of the questions correct. Ask students if they are surprised at the results—most children believe that if a quiz has only five true-or-false questions, they can "guess" and still obtain a good grade.

Structuring the Investigation

1. Show the students several answer keys that could be made for different tests. Discuss why having an answer key makes the work a lot easier if many papers need to be checked. Engage the class in a discussion about the quiz discussed earlier. Explore the number of possible "answer keys" for quizzes of various lengths. Have the children use a separate piece of paper to trace and then cut out the true-false boxes on the reproducible sheet to help them determine the various possibilities. They should then write "true" on five boxes and "false" on the other five. By completing the table on the reproducible page, children should determine the number of answer keys for a five-question quiz and extend the pattern to conjecture the number of keys that are possible for longer quizzes. Note: They should discover that each time a question is added to the quiz, the number of keys doubles. The five-question quiz, therefore, has thirty-two possible answer keys. That means that the child only has one chance in thirty-two of obtaining 100 percent when guessing on a five-question quiz.

2. Tell the students that since you were aware of the existence of the thirty-two possible keys before administering the quiz, you had guessed that no more than one paper was likely to be entirely correct. Point out that your knowledge of the mathematics allowed you to predict the outcome. Explain that you are about to pose another problem and will use your knowledge of mathematics to "read the students' minds."

3. Ask students to use a separate piece of paper to trace and cut out the empty box on their copies of the reproducible page. Explain to them that later you will give each child a coin and ask him or her to toss it twenty times, each time recording a result of heads (H) or tails (T) in the box. Before receiving a coin, however, they are to predict the outcome of those twenty tosses of the coin and record it on one side of the box. Make sure to give students an example of how to record their prediction, such as "HHTHT," since children often initially interpret the directions to mean predict the *number* of heads and tails rather than the *sequence* of twenty tosses of the coin. It is important that they *not* indicate on the sheet which side represents the prediction and which side represents the actual results from the next step.

4. After recording their predictions, children should turn their boxes over. Distribute a coin to each student and ask him or her to toss the coin twenty times and record the string of heads or tails on the box as an actual result. Experience with this activity has shown that (a) you may want to have students work in pairs, with one person tossing the coin and the other recording the results, then reverse the roles; and (b) younger students may find it helpful to use a cup in which to shake and spill the coin.

5. As each child completes his or her coin tossing, walk up to the desk and look at the two sides of the box. You are very likely to see one sequence of results that includes "strings" of four or more heads or four or more tails on one side and much less likely to see this arrangement on the other side. The reason is that although a coin tossed many times will eventually result in roughly equal distributions of heads and tails, most actual results of several tosses contain strings of four or more of the same result in a row. However, most people—even adults—believe that a toss of a head is likely to be followed by a toss of a tail and will seldom predict strings of four or more. Place a check on the side containing the longest string and move to the next student.

6. After all slips of paper have been inspected and checked, tell the students that you predict that the checked side is their actual result. Count the number of students for which you were correct and incorrect and record the result on the chalkboard. Students are likely to be amazed at how accurately you selected the actual versus the predicted results!

Adults seldom predict strings of four or more heads.

7. In pairs, ask children to look at their boxes and try to determine how you might have known the predicted versus the actual results. Field-tests with this activity have shown that children will generally recognize that the streaks in their actual results went against their intuition when making predictions. Discuss the difference between intuition and actual results. Ask the class to give an example of how this discovery can be applied to real-life situations. They might, for example, point out that a basketball player with a 50 percent foul-shooting record is likely to have a fourth-quarter streak and sink five foul shots in a row to win a game, even though the opponents may deliberately foul him or her, expecting the player to make only every other shot. You may also want to explore the lengths of typical strings of heads or tails and conjecture as to the length of a typical string when the coin is tossed thirty or forty times.

Extensions

1. In the activity, students explored a five-question, true-false quiz. Conduct a similar experiment with a five-question, multiple-choice quiz in which each question has four possible responses of (a), (b), (c), and (d). Again, students can reduce the problem to a one-question quiz, a two-question quiz, and so on, to develop a numerical pattern and predict the likelihood of guessing to achieve 100 percent accuracy. They will likely be amazed to find that the chances of guessing to achieve 100 percent accuracy on a ten-question multiple-choice quiz are less than one in a million!

2. In athletics, as suggested earlier in this investigation, the issue of streaks is quite common. Even a goalie with a very low goals-against average may give up several goals in one game. Have students identify, for example, a popular basketball player and find his or her foul-shooting or field-goal-shooting average. Then observe a game in person or on television and record the results of shots taken. Use the data to determine if the player tends to have streaks, as observed with the coin-tossing example. Watch the newspaper or observe a baseball game and record winning streaks or losing streaks of teams or hitting streaks of individual players. Students should notice that wins or losses typically clump together rather than alternate.

Can an event be influenced by an independent observer's presence?

---

3. When a person is dealt a black card from a shuffled deck, he or she might incorrectly assume that it is likely to be followed by a red card. In reality, as was shown in this investigation, it is not unusual to have several cards of the same color in a row, even though the colors are randomly distributed throughout the deck. Students should shuffle a deck of cards and examine them, one-by-one, recording the string of colors to see if streaks are common and, if so, how long is a typical streak. In Las Vegas or Atlantic City, some people fall victim to a similar set of assumptions, known as the "gambler's fallacy," in which a string of twenty reds on a roulette wheel seems to indicate that the next one must be a black. Imagine that a person walked up to the table and was unaware of this string of twenty reds. This person would likely believe that he or she had an approximately fifty-fifty chance of having black come up on the next spin. The word *approximately* is used because most roulette wheels in the United States have two green slots as well as the eighteen black and eighteen red ones. Everyone else watching might believe that a black had a much better chance than fifty-fifty of appearing. But how can the probability of an event be influenced simply by an independent observer?

4. The investigation can be used to make a connection to social studies. Analysts promote long-term investments in the stock market, often noting that downward trends in stock prices have historically been temporary and that, in the long run, prices increase and constitute a sound investment. Students can investigate stock-market-price trends over the past fifty years and explore the difference between temporary downward streaks and long-term gains in market values.

5. Another connection for this investigation can be made to science. The issue of global warming has become a much-debated issue in recent years. Those who believe strongly that the depletion of the ozone layer is causing climatic changes are quick to note, for example, three unusually warm winters in a row or two consecutive summer droughts. Yet a closer look at weather records may suggest that these types of streaks of warm or wet weather have occurred for a hundred years or more. Does sufficient evidence suggest that global warming is occurring? If it is, is it directly attributable to the ozone layer or is it another streak? Students can collect data on their local weather conditions over several years' time and look for streaks of warm winters, cool summers, and so on, and compare these findings with long-term climatic trends.

Closing Comments

A homeowner recently recounted the misfortune that he had encountered within a two-week period of time: the dishwasher began to leak, the lawn mower's wheels fell off, the dehumidifier's motor burned out, the bathroom pipes started to leak, ants invaded the house, the car had a flat tire, and the garage-door opener broke. He remarked, "How can all these things go wrong in two weeks?" However, with some further thought, he recognized that he had gone through several months without any major incidents occurring and that, perhaps, bad luck had caught up with him.

Rather than to have one unfortunate event occur each month or every few weeks, several events happened within a short period of time. Mathematics helps us to collect data over extended periods of time and to predict the future on the basis of evidence over time. Most people would not predict that a die will always land on a "6" after one roll of a "6," and, similarly, experience suggests that some truth resides in the warning not to jump to conclusions on the basis of short-term trends.

A HEADS-OR-TAILS TOSS

Name _____

1. Answer these quiz questions: *(a)* _____ *(b)* _____ *(c)* _____ *(d)* _____ *(e)* _____

2. Using a separate sheet of paper, trace around the boxes and cut out each box. Write "true" in five boxes and "false" in the other five boxes.

TRUE	TRUE	TRUE	TRUE	TRUE
FALSE	FALSE	FALSE	FALSE	FALSE

3. Using your paper strips, complete the table of quizzes for different numbers of questions.

No. of questions	Possible Answer Keys	No. of Answer Keys
1	T or F	2
2	TT, TF, FT, or FF	4
3	_____	_____
4	_____	_____
5	_____	_____
6	(Do not list these combinations.)	_____
7	(Do not list these combinations.)	_____
8	(Do not list these combinations.)	_____
9	(Do not list these combinations.)	_____
10	(Do not list these combinations.)	_____

Explain the pattern that you see. _____

_____

4. Trace over the empty box below on a separate sheet of paper and cut it out. On one side, write down your prediction about the sequence of heads and tails for twenty tosses of a coin, and on the other side, record the actual results.

[empty box]

5. What do you believe will be the longest streak of heads or tails if you toss the coin forty times? _____
   Conduct the experiment and record the results on another sheet of paper. How long was your longest streak? _____

Investigations: Nuts about Mathematics

by

Daniel J. Brahier

William R. Speer

The "Investigations" department recognizes the importance of children's exploring hands-on and minds-on mathematics and, therefore, presents teachers with open-ended explorations to enhance mathematical instruction. These meaningful tasks are designed to evolve as they are conducted. They invoke problem solving and reasoning, require communication skills, and encourage identification of connections among various mathematical concepts and principles. To ensure usability, the ideas presented in this column have been field-tested in various classroom settings in grades 3–6.

A mathematical investigation is defined as a collection of worthwhile problem-solving tasks that—

- has multidimensional content;

- is open-ended, containing several acceptable solutions;

- is an exploration requiring a full period or several classes to complete; and

- is centered on a theme or event and is often embedded in a focus question.

In addition, a mathematical investigation involves a number of processes, which include—

- researching outside sources to gather information;

- collecting data through such means as surveying, observing, or measuring;

- collaborating, with each team member taking on specific jobs; and

- using multiple strategies for reaching solutions and conclusions.

This month features an upper-elementary investigation that encourages children to define a problem centered on purchasing peanuts and to determine the relevant data required to solve the problem. While finding a solution, children develop their problem-solving skills; collect, graph, and analyze data; and apply computational skills.

Edited by Daniel J. Brahier and William R. Speer, Bowling Green State University, Bowling Green, OH 43403

LEVELS 3–6

Objectives

- To determine missing information and relevant information in a problem-solving task

- To use estimation in an authentic context

- To collect data and make a bar graph based on the data

- To find the mean and the mode for a collected set of data

- To determine whether the use of mean or mode is more appropriate in a given situation

- To apply computational skills

Materials

- A can of dog food

- Twenty unshelled peanuts for each group of three or four students

- A bag of any uniform size of unshelled peanuts for each group of students

- A calculator for each student

- A copy of the reproducible pages for each student

- A sheet of butcher paper or poster board

- Glue for each group of students (optional)

Introduction

Begin by describing the following scenario: "The neighbors have left for vacation and have asked me to take care of their dogs." Hold up a can of dog food and ask the open-ended question, "How much dog food will I need?" This question by itself will probably catch students offguard and may not yield immediate responses. Its deliberate vagueness, however, will begin to focus students' attention on the need for more information. Since the reason for needing dog food has been established, students should begin to engage in a discussion about other important information required to answer the question. For example, the students need to determine how many dogs need food. They may also want to find out about the size of the dogs and the length of time that the neighbors will be gone. They might discuss, for example, that knowing whether the dog is a German shepherd or a cocker spaniel is not necessary for solving the problem, but knowing whether it eats one can or seven cans of food a day will greatly affect the solution. Numerous other factors can be incorporated into the answer. However, the point is not to solve the problem but to help students become aware that in real-life problem-solving situations, it is important to decide what information is relevant for finding solutions. Explain to students that they will be solving a similar problem involving people and food in this investigation.

Description

1. Organize the class into groups of three or four students. Explain that they will be working in teams to conduct this investigation. Assign jobs to each member of the team to facilitate the active involvement of each student. For example, each team should have a discussion leader, a secretary, a materials person, and a reporter. Distribute a copy of the reproducible pages to each student.

2. Hold up a handful of unshelled peanuts and pose the following problem: "I need to make a dessert. How many peanuts will I need?" Identifying why peanuts are needed leads to asking other important questions about the problem. Ask each team to brainstorm a short list of questions it would like to ask to define the problem better. Students should record these questions in the appropriate space on their reproducible pages and discuss their responses as a team so that a single report can be given to the class.

3. Ask each team to report its list of questions to the class. Record the questions on a blank overhead transparency or on the chalkboard. Students might ask such questions as "How many people will be having dessert?" "Will everyone be eating peanuts?" "How hungry are the people eating them?" "Are the peanuts only a topping, or are they the main part of the dessert?"

4. After collecting a list of questions from the students, explain that the peanuts are being purchased for a birthday party. Each person at the party will be offered a bowl of ice cream and may choose to put peanuts on the ice cream. Determine how many peanuts will need to be purchased for the party. This additional information may prompt students to identify other questions. Ask each team to prepare a second list of questions by first working individually and then combining results.

5. Ask each team to report its list of additional questions to the class. Record these questions as before. Students should now be able to ask more focused questions, such as "How many people will be attending the party?" "Will everyone want to eat the ice cream offered to them?" "Does everyone put peanuts on ice cream? " "How many peanuts does a person usually put on a bowl of ice cream?"

6. As a class, allow the students to decide from experience how many children will be attending the party, and record this number on the reproducible page. Then ask, "How can we determine the number of people that will want peanuts on their ice cream?" One way that the students may answer this question is to poll the class and to use the same proportion. For example, if twelve out of twenty-four children in a fourth-grade class prefer to have peanuts on their ice cream,

then it might be reasonable to assume that about half the children at a birthday party would want peanuts on their ice cream as well. The class can also discuss party situations in which a higher proportion might want peanuts and about other groups of people in which no one would want peanuts, but the idea is to estimate the number so as to plan the party. Once the students have estimated the number of individuals at the party that would want peanuts on their ice cream, they should record this number on their reproducible pages.

7. Discuss that to decide how many peanuts are needed, we also need to know how many peanuts a child is likely to put on ice cream. Poll the class and agree on a reasonable number of peanuts to put on ice cream as a topping. Make a round paper cutout representing a bowl of ice cream and draw some peanuts on it to help students visualize the topping and to make an informed estimate.

8. Ask the students, "What else do we still need to I find out to help solve the problem?" Eventually, they should realize that they need to know how many peanuts are typically found in a shell. To make an estimate, each team should be given approximately twenty unshelled peanuts. Before they crack the shells, ask students to guess how many peanuts each shell would typically hold. What is the largest and smallest number of peanuts that could be found? Demonstrate how to break open a shell into two halves to expose the peanuts, rather than crush the shell. Each team should crack open its shells, count the number of peanuts found, and tally them on the reproducible pages. Ask teams to report the total number of shells that contained zero, one, two, three, or possibly even four peanuts in each.

9. After the teams have completed their work, compile the data from the class and have students place these numbers on their reproducible pages. From these data, each student should draw a bar graph and answer the questions on the page. The graph and questions will help students focus on analyzing the data. As an optional activity, students can take their peanut shells and make a concrete graph by gluing the shells to a piece of butcher paper or poster board as shown in figure 1. It will be easier to construct the graph in figure 1 if the students have carefully separated the two halves of the shell.

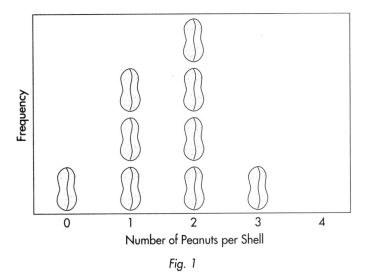

Fig. 1

10. When all students have completed the work on the reproducible pages, discuss their answers. Where appropriate, compare the mean of the class data with the mode. Ask the students, "If I pick up another shell and wonder how many peanuts it contains, will the mean or the mode be a more accurate predictor? Why?" Students should realize that a shell is not likely to contain, for example, 2.3 peanuts, so the mode is a more appropriate measure to use. Most shells contain two peanuts. In the event that students would find that all their shells contain two peanuts, conduct a further investigation to explore whether this scenario always occurs by purchasing additional peanuts and repeating the procedure on another day.

11. Return to the original problem and summarize the results for the class. Remind the students that they now know how many people are attending the party, how many are likely to want peanuts on their ice cream, how many peanuts are typically added to top ice cream, and the average number of peanuts found in each shell. Ask each team to use this information to determine how many unshelled peanuts would need to be purchased for the party. Students can calculate the number on the reproducible pages.

12. Using a uniformly sized bag, such as a brown-paper luncheon bag, fill it with unshelled peanuts for each team. Do not use the same number of peanuts in each bag. Have teams determine the number of unshelled peanuts that are in their bag and, consequently, the number of bags that they would need to purchase to serve the dessert.

13. Share team solutions with the class. Ask each team to report its answer and to explain how it obtained the solution. Note:

Answers may vary among teams, depending on whether they use the mean or the mode, how they round their answers, and how many peanuts were in their bag.

Extension

Peanuts are often purchased by the pound or kilogram. Students might visit a local grocery store to find out the cost of purchasing a pound or kilogram of peanuts. By weighing the number of peanuts needed for the birthday party, students can calculate their cost. In addition, they might estimate the quantity of peanuts that weighs approximately one pound or kilogram and develop a visual sense for the size of a pile of peanuts with this weight. Students could also investigate whether it is more economical to purchase shelled or unshelled peanuts and why. Finally, other ice-cream toppings, such as chocolate syrup or marshmallows, might be considered. The price of ice cream could be investigated in a grocery store so that the total cost of the dessert could be determined.

Conclusion

Discuss with students that real-life problem solving involves as much time posing questions and determining relevant information as actually calculating a solution. Students often hear radio or television advertisements that make such claims as, "We make so many different sandwiches that you could lay them end to end from New York to California." How often do students ask, "How do they know that?" "What would I have to know to figure it out?" Encourage students to bring similar problems to class in the future for similar investigation.

NUTS ABOUT MATHEMATICS

Name _____

1. List questions that you would like to ask about "How many peanuts will I need?"

_____

_____

_____

_____

_____

The Party

2. List additional questions that you would like to ask, knowing that the peanuts will be needed for topping ice cream at a birthday party.

_____

_____

_____

_____

_____

3. How many children will be attending the party? (Estimate a number from your own experience attending such parties.) _____

4. Estimate the number of children who will want peanuts on their ice cream._____

5. Estimate the number of peanuts each child will put on his or her ice cream._____

Our Peanuts

6. Record tallies for the number of peanuts found in each shell for your team.

     0 _____ 1 _____ 2 _____ 3 _____ 4 _____

7. Record the number of peanuts found in each shell for the whole class.

     0 _____ 1 _____ 2 _____ 3 _____ 4 _____

NUTS ABOUT MATHEMATICS

Name _____

8. Draw and label a bar graph using data from the class.

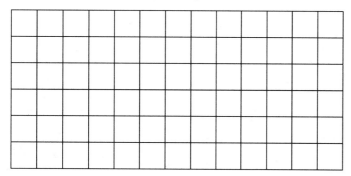

9. What was the largest number of peanuts found in any shell? _____

10. What was the smallest number of peanuts found in any shell? _____

11. Calculate the average number of peanuts in each shell (the *mean*). How did you find your answer?

_____

The average is _____.

12. What was the most common number of peanuts in each shell? _____ This number is called the *mode*.

Final Questions

13. In predicting how many peanuts would be found in a shell picked at random from a bag, which measure—the mean or the mode—seems the most appropriate and why?

_____

_____

14. Determine the total number of unshelled peanuts that would need to be purchased for the birthday party. Write your calculations and show your reasoning.

The total number of shelled peanuts is _____.

15. Determine the total number of bags of peanuts that would need to be purchased for the birthday party. Write your calculations and show your reasoning.

The total number of bags of peanuts is _____.

From *Teacher-Made Aids for Elementary School Mathematics, Vol. 3*

Chapter 6
Problem Solving

Multiple Strategies: Product of Reasoning and Communication

by

Alice J. Gill

Students communicate their thinking to classmates through verbal explanation and visual demonstration.

© Cleveland Public Schools

The NCTM's *Curriculum and Evaluation Standards* (1989) supports the idea that problems can be solved in more than one correct way. This multiple-strategy approach contains the seeds of motivation, success, and mind stretching. The curriculum standards that focus on reasoning and communication skills are integral to delivering mathematics education that generates the creative, problem-solving, divergent thinker that the business community would like to employ. For students to be comfortable in learning multiple strategies of solution, the following must be present:

1. A recognition by the teacher that students bring knowledge and perspective to situations and can apply this knowledge to solve problems

2. A chance for students to communicate their thinking to other students

3. A teacher able to formulate the mathematical context for students' thinking and translate that thinking into mathematical symbols

INTRODUCTION

Research has disclosed that children are able to think and operate mathematically before they have memorized the so-called "basics." They come to school with substantial intuitive sense about mathematical processes (Carpenter, Hiebert, and Moser 1981; Cobb, Yackel, and Wood 1988; Fuson, in press; Resnick 1986). Given objects with which to work and a context familiar to them, students, even at the kindergarten level, can solve problems we never dreamed they could. And they solve them not by using traditional algorithms but through a variety of strategies designed and understood by students (Lampert 1986; Resnick 1986). Their success with interesting high-level tasks breeds confidence, and they begin to look forward to doing more mathematics. Research

has shown that allowing and encouraging students to work in this manner rather than focusing on drill and practice of facts and computation has not adversely affected the ability of students to compute (Resnick, Bill, and Lesgold, in press; Carpenter and Fennema 1990).

As part of a collaboration funded by the National Science Foundation on how elementary and middle school students learn mathematics, I saw these findings come to life in a group of urban students. They reached a dimension of thinking and liked mathematics to an extent that I had never imagined in my twenty-two years of teaching. The collaboration's partners were the American Federation of Teachers and the Learning Research and Development Center of the University of Pittsburgh. I was privileged to be part of a team of five teachers who worked directly with eminent researchers. We worked as peers, with a common goal and belief that mathematics instruction built on research findings could improve mathematics achievement. Reaching the goal required mutual inquiry and exchange. The teachers—who came from places as diverse as Chippewa Falls, Wisconsin, and Cleveland, Ohio—had to become comfortable not only in a cross-community teacher-researcher collaboration but with an intracommunity teacher-teacher collaboration. The teachers who were experienced in the classroom played the central role in discovering the research's implications for the classroom. They initially piloted the ideas in schools ranging from inner-city neighborhoods to middle-class small towns and developed training activities that they thought were essential for enabling other teachers to apply the research findings. While the teachers worked through the interpretation and writing process together, their diverse backgrounds and viewpoints challenged them to rethink their individual ideas and reach a consensus.

Alice Gill was a primary-level teacher in the Cleveland Public Schools for twenty-four years. She is now an assistant director in the American Federation of Teachers' Educational Issues Department and coordinates the Thinking Mathematics Project out of Washington, DC 20001.

The author thanks Barbara W. Grover of LRDC, who furnished invaluable suggestions and editorial assistance for this article. The other project development teachers are Judith Bodenhausen (Berkeley, Calif.), Nancy Denhart (Pittsburgh, Pa.), Margaret Kaduce (Chippewa Falls, Wis.), and Marcy Miller (Rochester, N.Y.).

For me and many others, a traditional mathematics education entailed one correct way to solve problems, which always resulted in one correct answer. The basis for our knowledge was to memorize facts and formulas. Working with students from my new perspective that recognizes mathematics as a rich discipline with many paths has been an absolute joy. Doors have been opened to an exciting new world of instruction and interaction for me as a teacher and for my students as learners. Allowing students to invent and use different strategies for solving problems has challenged me to be a better listener, has made me an explorer of diverse paths, and has prodded expansion of my own mathematical knowledge.

MULTIPLE STRATEGIES

Multiple strategies are approached easily through the use of story problems that give a context for thinking. The lack of connections between school mathematics and students' intuitions has been identified as a cause of difficulty with school mathematics (Resnick 1987). Studies around the world have attested to the development of mathematical intuitions in natural life situations (Carpenter, Hiebert, and Moser 1981; Cobb, Yackel, and Wood 1988; De Corte and Verschaffel 1987; Fuson, in press; Resnick 1986; Schliemann 1990). Intuitions are most likely to surface around situations familiar to the student. Stories set within students' experiences lend themselves to intuitive understandings and are a natural vehicle for the development of multiple reasoning and solution strategies. Therefore, familiar situations become a reasonable starting point.

> # The teacher writes the student's verbal explanation in mathematical form.

From the outset, it is necessary for the teacher to be disposed to be a careful listener, as well as to encourage students to share their thoughts and listen to others. "[C]lass discussion is a rich environment for mathematics learning" (Lo, Wheatley, and Smith 1991). At first, the conversation may be limited. It becomes broader as three things happen:

1. The teacher continues to probe rather than give answers or tell the students that they are wrong. The fear of giving a wrong answer is blunted, and students do not need to fear being humiliated. Students also learn to reevaluate their own thinking on the basis of new information and recognize such reappraisal as a normal process.

2. The teacher writes the student's verbal explanation in mathematical form—a process that validates students' thinking as worthwhile and also enables them eventually to write their own thoughts mathematically.

3. Nonthreatening public sharing of students' thinking makes having something to share a desired social goal for the students.

KINDERGARTEN AND FIRST GRADE

Understanding that numbers can be decomposed and recomposed in many ways is a powerful concept that enables students to use different strategies to solve problems. This concept, as well as the notion that sometimes more than one answer can be correct, is the basis of the following lesson. "The Bears" is suitable for K–1 students. It was used with kindergartners and first graders in demonstration lessons for teachers involved in the Thinking Mathematics project in Anderson and Hammond, Indiana. Part 1 was presented to the class.

> The Bears: Part 1
> Michelle had a teddy bear collection. She played with her teddy bears often and kept them on two shelves in her room. One night when she went to bed, she had eight bears on the bottom shelf and four bears on the top shelf. How many teddy bears were on Michelle's shelves?

Each student had a small plastic bag of teddy-bear graham crackers and a workspace with two shelves drawn on it (see fig. 1). I asked the students what the story was about, and the following discussion ensued among the teacher (*T*) and various students (*S*):

S: Teddy bears.

T: What does the story say about teddy bears?

S: Michelle likes teddy bears. She kept them on her shelves.

T: What must you find out?

S: How many teddy bears Michelle has.

T: How can you find out how many bears Michelle has?

S: Count them.

> # Fear of giving a wrong answer is blunted.

I guided the discussion to the use of manipulatives by asking what they could count. The students suggested counting the bears in their bags.

T: How many should we take out?

S: Eight.

T: [To ensure that the students understood why they were putting out eight bears] Why are we taking out eight bears?

S: Because that's how many are on the bottom.

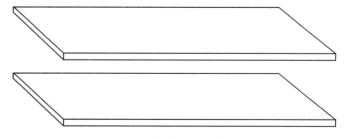

Fig. 1. Teddy bears workspace

T: Where should we put these eight bears?

S: On the bottom shelf.

Similar questioning led to the decision to place four bears on the top shelf. The students arranged their own bears, and I modeled the scene on the overhead projector as they told me what to place on the workspace (see fig. 2).

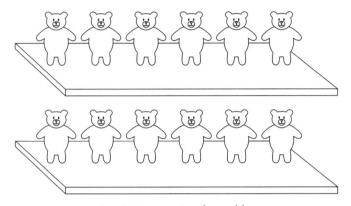

Fig. 2. Representing the problem

With all bears placed on the shelves, I next asked, "Now what should we do?" which brought the students back to their own suggestion to count the bears. All students counted their own teddy bears. I observed as they counted. Some counted every bear again after putting it on the shelf, but one student pointed only to the bears on the top shelf as she counted, indicating that she was counting on.

Students model the story with small teddy bears.

I asked if the students now knew how many bears Michelle had on her shelves. They responded that she had twelve teddy bears. The link to the story is important. Good problem solvers keep connecting their computation to the situation and the question (Silver, Mukhopadhyay, and Gabriele 1989). If this linking becomes a habit when students are young, in later years they may avoid making such errors as that "2 3/5" buses are needed to transport soldiers (Silver 1989).

At this point, the students were asked to demonstrate how they counted. I asked a student whom I had observed counting all to show us on the overhead projector how he counted the bears. He pointed to each bear and counted all.

T: So what did we find out about Michelle's bears? How many were on each shelf?

S: Eight bears on the bottom and four bears on the top.

T: [Writing "8 + 4" on the chalkboard] And how many bears is that?

S: Twelve.

T: So you're saying that eight bears plus four bears is twelve bears.

I finished the equation "8 + 4 = 12" and asked the students to write that equation on bear-shaped paper. (Had the students told

me that four bears were on the top and eight on the bottom, I would have recorded "4 + 8 = 12" to mirror what they said.)

I then asked if the bears could be counted in another way. One student responded by counting them all again. I called on the student whom I had observed counting on, told the class I saw her count in a different way, and asked her to demonstrate her method on the overhead projector.

S: I know there are eight here [pointing to the bottom shelf] and nine, ten, eleven, twelve.

T: How do you know there are eight there?

S: We put eight on the bottom shelf.

When I asked the class which way was faster, they indicated that counting on was faster. I affirmed that both ways were correct. (It is possible that students may suggest such other strategies as counting by twos or fives. The students in this demonstration did not.) This counting exercise is purposeful: it helps show that even counting can be done in more than one way, and it displays a counting-on model for students who are still counting all.

I continued the story by presenting part 2.

> The Bears: Part II
> Michelle didn't know it, but her teddy bears were magical. Sometimes during the night, they would chat and play. When they were having so much fun that they forgot what time it was, they sometimes had to hurry back to the shelves and didn't have time to get back to the places where Michelle had put them. How could they have arranged themselves differently on the shelves so no longer were four bears on the top shelf and eight bears on the bottom one?

The students used their teddy-bear crackers and workspaces to rearrange the bears. They were asked to record their new arrangement on the bear-shaped paper. The arrangements were then shared. As each student reported a different arrangement, I recorded it on the chalkboard and asked students to do the same on their papers (see fig.3).

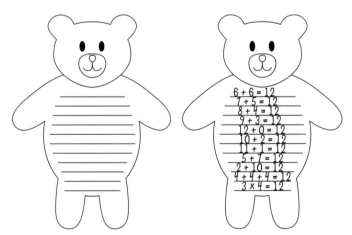

Fig. 3. Recording students' discoveries

When the question "Could we use any more ways to arrange the bears on the shelves?" elicited no more ways, I asked the students to look at the pairs of numbers that showed how they arranged the bears.

T: What can you tell me about the numbers?

The first respondents simply mentioned a pair of numbers, such as 7 and 5. I repeated some of the students' pairs: 7 and 5, 8 and 4, 9 and 3.

T: What happens to the number of bears on the top shelf as we put more bears on the bottom shelf?

S: [After some thought] The number gets smaller.

T: [Elaborating] As the number of bears on one shelf increases, or gets larger, the number of bears on the other shelf gets smaller, or decreases.

I purposely used more than one term to indicate increase and decrease to link those terms to the familiar, well-understood words of young students.

Extensions

1. Present the following situations:
   (a) Three of the bears are loaned to a friend. How many bears are left on the shelves?
   (b) Michelle gets three new bears for her birthday. How many teddy bears does she have now? How can she arrange them?
   (c) Michelle has so many bears that her father builds another shelf. How can she arrange her bears on three shelves? (See the activity sheet in fig. 4.)

2. Ask how many students like stuffed animals and why. The answers I have received range from cuteness to softness to hugability. Ask whether Michelle has enough bears so everyone in the class can hold one. If not, decide how each student could get a turn at holding one. (Many solutions are possible, e.g., make up a game, share, bring in additional bears.)

Fig. 4. Activity sheet for the extension of the problem to three shelves

THIRD GRADE

By third grade, multiple strategies are available to students for addition and subtraction situations. Students can decompose numbers in various ways that facilitate problem solving. They can find easy numbers, use compensation, or just count on. They can also draw on their intuitive ways of thinking to use nontraditional strategies for solving problems. It is important for students to listen to other students explain their strategies so as to expose them to new ways of looking at problems (Lo, Wheatley, and Smith 1991). Other students' language may furnish a key that the teacher's language has not. The sharing of different ways of solving problems became an

exciting part of my class, as students were eager to have their ways of thinking accepted and showcased. Valuing different strategies led to increased self-esteem. It wasn't necessary to have the most sophisticated strategy to be accepted. Although all the foregoing capabilities were developed while students were using manipulatives, they eventually could mentally explore strategies without them. The following problem was used with my third-grade class.

The Field Trip
Of 5 third-grade classes, 4 have 26 students and 1 has 27 students. On 20 March, the third graders went to the art museum. The teachers counted 109 students as they boarded the buses. How many third-grade students were absent from Woodland Hills School on 20 March?

In our discussion of the problem, a student identified the question as how many third-grade students were absent on 20 March. I asked how we could find out.

S: Who didn't come?

I asked whether we knew how many third-grade students *should* have come to school. One boy read the first sentence of the story in response.

T: Does that information tell us how many third-grade students should have been in school?

S: There were twenty-six students in four classes and twenty-seven in the other class.

I then asked the students to figure out how many were in all the third grades and then to continue working to find out how many third graders were absent. When the students finished, we first examined how they found out the total number of third-grade students. The first student to share wrote the number for each class in a column and added.

Traditional column addition

$$
\begin{array}{r}
26 \\
26 \\
26 \\
26 \\
+\ 27 \\
\hline
131
\end{array}
$$

Mental mathematics: Counting strategy

The next student wrote the number of students in each class and counted the tens and then the ones as he pointed to each number:

$$20, 40, 60, 80, 100$$

for the tens and

$$6, 12, 18, 24, 31$$

for the ones. He then totaled the sums of the tens and ones:

$$100 + 31 = 131 \text{ students}$$

Mental mathematics: Written-equations-with-decomposition strategy

Another student added using a mental-mathematics strategy involving decomposition (see fig. 5).

She explained her thinking.

$$26 + 26 + 26 + 26 + 27$$
$$\left.\begin{array}{l} 20 + 20 + 20 = 60 \\ 20 + 20 = 40 \\ 6 + 6 + 6 + 6 = 24 \quad 24 + 7 = \ 31 \end{array}\right\} \begin{array}{l} 60 + 40 = 100 \\ \end{array} \right\} 100 + 31 = 131$$

Fig. 5

S: I added the twenties—first three because it was too much to do all of them—and then the other twenties, and that was sixty and forty—one hundred. Then I added the four sixes and that was twenty-four, and then I added the seven. I put all the tens and ones together and that was one hundred thirty-one.

Other strategies are possible but were not used on this day; for instance, students could also have thought about connecting the solution to their knowledge of quarters. Knowing that $4 \times 25 = 100$, think that 4×26 is 4 more, making 104 in four classes. Then add the last class of 27; $104 + 27 = 131$.

We concluded that 131 third graders were enrolled in school and moved on to the second step of the problem—determining how many students were absent.

Traditional teachers would instruct students that the correct way to solve the problem is by subtracting. Yet research has found that students almost universally invent counting on and counting up to solve problems (Fuson, in press). The strategies that the students chose are illustrated here.

Subtraction

One boy explained his method of subtraction this way: "I took one hundred minus one hundred is zero. Thirty minus zero is thirty. One minus nine—there aren't enough, so minus eight. Then thirty minus eight—twenty-nine, twenty-eight, twenty-seven, twenty-six, twenty-five, twenty-four, twenty-three, twenty-two." He wrote the following as he explained:

$$131 - 109$$
$$100 - 100 = 0,$$
$$\left.\begin{array}{l} 30 - 0 = 30 \\ 1 - 9 = -8 \end{array}\right\} 30 - 8 = 22$$

Discussion: Although the student used the traditional strategy and subtracted, the subtraction was not traditional. He used left-to-right mental strategy. He avoided regrouping or trading by employing negative numbers. The last step involved counting backward.

Subtraction using recomposition and counting

Another student also subtracted. She also began with $100 - 100$ equals 0. Then she subtracted 9 from 31 and counted backward.

$$131 - 109$$
$$100 - 100 = 0,$$
$$31 - 9 = 22$$

Discussion: This student was sophisticated enough to recognize that she could subtract. Understanding of place value also enabled her to recognize that once the hundreds were removed, thirty minus zero would still leave thirty, so she just needed to count backward to nine from thirty-one; she did not need to subtract the tens and ones separately.

Additive strategy 1: Count on

One student decided to start with the number of students on the buses and count on until she reached the whole number of third graders. She said, "I added one to get to one hundred ten." I asked, "Why did you want to get to one hundred ten?" "Because it's an easy number. Then I had one hundred ten, so I added twenty, and that's one hundred thirty. Then I needed one more. So twenty and one and one is twenty-two." Her procedure can be written thus:

$$109 + \underline{\hspace{1cm}} = 131$$
$$\left.\begin{array}{l} 109 + 1 = 110 \\ 110 + 20 = 130 \\ 130 + 1 = 131 \end{array}\right\} 1 + 20 + 1 = 22$$

Discussion: Starting with a known part and adding to the whole number is often a more intuitive method of solution than subtraction (Fuson, in press; Riley, Greeno, and Heller 1983). A 1 was first added to 109 to get 110, a number ending in 0, which is easy to use mentally. Adding a 20 yielded 130; thus only a 1 was needed to sum to 131. The add-ons were then totaled. Students who have had frequent experiences with mental mathematics could have added 21 all at once after reaching 110.

Additive strategy II: Larger chunks

Another student also added, explaining, "I wanted the most first, so I put twenty and had one hundred twenty-nine. Then just two more and it's one hundred thirty-one. So twenty and two is twenty-two."

$$109 + \underline{\hspace{1cm}} = 131$$
$$\left.\begin{array}{l} 109 + 20 = 129 \\ 129 + 2 = 131 \end{array}\right\} 20 + 2 = 22$$

Discussion: Although in both additive strategies students are adding on to find the answer, the thought processes for reaching 131 differ. The first student could proceed more easily once she reached a number ending in 0; the second one was more comfortable finding first the largest number he could add.

Additive strategy III: Overshooting the mark

Still another student added on. "I started with the biggest I could, and one hundred nine plus thirty is one hundred thirty-nine. That was over, so I went back eight. I had added thirty, but I had to take eight back, so it's twenty-two."

$$109 + \underline{\hspace{1cm}} = 131$$
$$\left.\begin{array}{l} 109 + 30 = 139 \\ 139 - 8 = 131 \end{array}\right\} 30 - 8 = 22$$

Discussion: This student wanted to get to 131 as quickly as possible but had added on too much. He had no problem reversing gears and getting back to the target number. No more steps were involved than in other solution procedures, and he demonstrated a knowledge of how to use operations to move within the number system.

Compensation

Finally, a student employed compensation. "I used easy numbers. I took away one hundred ten and that's twenty-one. Took away one too many, so put it back. Answer is twenty-two."

$$131 - 109$$
$$131 - 110 = 21$$
$$21 + 1 = 22$$

Discussion: No trading was necessary because this student used the principle of compensation. Adding 1 to 109 results in a number that is easy to use mentally; but having subtracted 1 too many, the student must add it at the end. A more sophisticated understanding would lead the student to add 1 to each number initially and think "132 – 110."

The field-trip problem can be solved by two different operations that can each be performed differently.

Extensions

1. How many buses will be needed if each bus holds 60 people? (Note: If the students do not account for chaperones in their computations, the teacher should guide them to realize that the students must be accompanied on the field trip.)

2. If each student must pay $2 and each adult $4, how much will the field trip cost?

3. How much will gas for the trip cost? The bus uses one gallon of gas each five miles, and the museum is twelve miles from the school.

4. One of the second-grade classes, with 24 students, decides to go on the field trip, too. How many buses will be needed?

5. The school doesn't have enough money to pay for a third bus. What can be done to ensure that all those who wish to can go to the museum? (Solutions range from fund raising [introducing another whole group of problems to solve!] to leaving some students behind to parents' driving their own children to an assessment for the trip.)

6. Of the 155 students, estimate the number that might be absent on any day. Research third-grade attendance records and graph a month's absences. As well as indicating an average absentee rate, a graph might reveal patterns of higher absenteeism on Mondays or around holidays.

SUMMARY

The NCTM's curriculum standards seek to de-emphasize the notion that only one correct path can lead to a problem's solution. The lessons presented in this article illustrate that multiple solutions are available even at the beginning levels to students who are learning "the basics." The new standards also emphasize developing problem situations that require the application of several mathematical ideas. The preceding situations illustrate how such problems can be developed. The field-trip problem, for example, is a vehicle for counting, decomposition of numbers, addition, subtraction, multiplication, division, estimation, and open-ended problem solving.

> # Children don't think the way adults think.

To elicit the multiple solutions used by the students in the preceding lessons, the teacher had to understand that children do not always think the way adults think. Thus, it is necessary to encourage students to explain or demonstrate what they are thinking. The teacher can then assist in putting those thoughts into mathematical terms or notation. This endeavor requires serious listening. The entire sharing process is also a vehicle for students to learn to communicate mathematically and, in so doing, strengthen their own understandings. The teacher introduces other strategies as they are appropriate.

References

Carpenter, Thomas P., and Elizabeth Fennema. "Cognitively Guided Instruction: Multiplication and Division." Unpublished manuscript, 1990.

Carpenter, Thomas P., James Hiebert, and James M. Moser. "Problem Structure and First-Grade Children's Initial Solution Processes for Simple Addition and Subtraction Problems." *Journal for Research in Mathematics Education* 12 (January 1981): 27–39.

Cobb, Paul, Erma Yackel, and Terry Wood. "Curriculum and Teacher Development: Psychological and Anthropological Perspectives." In *Integrating Research on Teaching and Learning Mathematics,* edited by Thomas P. Carpenter, Elizabeth Fennema, and Susan J. Lamon, 92–130. Madison, Wis.: Wisconsin Center for Education Research, 1988.

De Corte, Erik, and Lieven Verschaffel. "The Effect of Semantic Structure on First Graders' Strategies for Solving Addition and Subtraction Word Problems." *Journal for Research in Mathematics Education* 18 (November 1987): 363–81.

Fuson, Karen. "Research on Learning and Teaching Addition and Subtraction of Whole Numbers." In *Analysis of Arithmetic for Mathematics,* edited by R. Hattrup, G. Leinhardt, and T. Putnam. Hillsdale, N.J.: Lawrence Erlbaum Associates. In press.

Lampert, Magdalene. "Knowing, Doing, and Teaching Multiplication." *Cognition and Instruction* 3 (1986): 305–42.

Lo, Jane-Jane, Grayson H. Wheatley, and A. C. Smith. "Learning to Talk Mathematics." Paper presented at the annual meeting of the American Educational Research Association, Chicago, 1991.

National Council of Teachers of Mathematics. *Curriculum and Evaluation Standards for School Mathematics.* Reston, Va.: The Council, 1989.

Resnick, Lauren B. "The Development of Mathematical Intuition." In *Perspective for Intellectual Development: Minnesota Symposium on Child Psychology,* edited by Marion Perlmutter, 159–94. Hillsdale, N.J.: Lawrence Erlbaum Associates, 1986.

———. *Education and Learning to Think.* Washington, D.C.: National Academy Press, 1987.

Resnick, Lauren B., Victoria Bill, and Sharon Lesgold. "Developing Thinking Abilities in Arithmetic Class." In *The Modern Theories of Cognitive Development Go to School,* edited by A. Demetriou, A. Efkides, and M. Shayer. London: Routledge. In press.

Riley, Mary S., James G. Greeno, and Joan I. Heller. "Development of Children's Problem Solving Ability in Arithmetic." In *The Development of Mathematical Thinking,* edited by Herbert P. Ginsburg, 153–96. New York: Academic Press, 1983.

Schliemann, Analucia, and Veronica Magalhaes. "Proportional Reasoning: From Shopping to Kitchens, Laboratories, and, Hopefully, Schools." Paper presented at the Fourteenth International Conference for the Psychology of Mathematics Education, Oaxtepec, Mexico, July 1990.

Silver, Edward A., Swapna Mukhopadbyay, and Anthony J. Gabriele. "Referential Mappings and the Solution of Division Story Problems Involving Remainders." Paper presented at the annual meeting of the American Educational Research Association, San Francisco, 1989. ▲

Let's Do It: Promoting Mathematical Thinking

by

John Van de Walle
Virginia Commonwealth University

Charles S. Thompson
University of Louisville

As we begin the fifth year since *An Agenda for Action* was published by NCTM (1980), few will argue that children's ability to think through a new and unusual situation—to reason through a problem and express their own conclusions—is a skill that is beginning to take on paramount importance in the curriculum. Today's students are clearly in an era where thinking is a more important goal of mathematics than the computational skills that we require them to practice again and again.

Many activities can be done with children, beginning in kindergarten and continuing through the grades, that are stimulating and fun and that require them to think. We believe that having children complete these types of activities contributes to the development of their general problem-solving skills.

THINKING THROUGH PATTERNS

Patterns can be explored, extended, and created using a wide variety of manipulative materials.

Toothpicks

On an overhead projector, place some flat toothpicks in a row to make a pattern. A few ideas are suggested in figure 1; however, the possibilities are limitless. After you have placed enough toothpicks to establish a pattern, allow children to suggest how to place each additional toothpick in the pattern. Try several different patterns in this manner. To give additional assistance to children having difficulty, try "reading" a pattern to give it a verbal form: "Up, flat, slant, slant, up, flat, slant, slant,...."

Next, provide children with toothpicks and sheets of dark-colored construction paper. Encourage the children to create their own patterns and extend them across the paper. Share ideas by displaying some patterns on the overhead projector. Eventually have children glue their toothpick patterns on the paper to make them permanent. The children should hold each toothpick in the center and dip only the ends into white glue. This technique is neat and tidy, and the toothpicks will still be firmly glued to the paper.

Paper strips

A significant advantage of having children make their own patterns is the internal reinforcement they receive from extending their

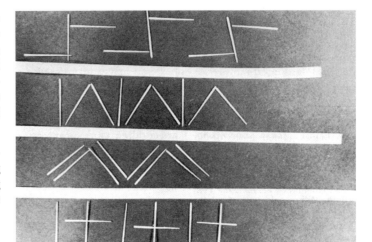

Fig. 1. How can you continue the pattern?

patterns as far as they wish, repeating an idea over and over. Simple color patterns made from rectangles of colored construction paper permit these extensions to be quite dramatic. Give students an ample supply of colored rectangles (about 4 cm × 8 cm) and let them create such patterns as red, yellow, yellow, green, red, yellow, yellow, green,.... To enable the children to extend their patterns, build the patterns on a long table or on the floor. If the pattern pieces are overlapped slightly, they can easily be stapled together and extended for several meters or even farther. Colorful patterns can then be displayed around your room—across the tops of chalkboards and around doorways and windows. In spare moments, the patterns can be "read" aloud by the children as a group. This activity will reinforce the patterning concept.

Wooden cubes

Stacks of wooden cubes can be used to make several kinds of patterns. Younger children can use short and tall stacks to create a pattern such as short, short, tall, short, short, tall,.... Primary-grade children can focus on the number of cubes in a stack to create a numeric pattern: 4, 1, 3, 1, 4, 1, 3, 1,.... These same stacks can be thought of as little "buildings" and lined up to form a patterned "street." Older children can be encouraged to develop progressive patterns with stacks or designs of cubes, as illustrated in figure 2.

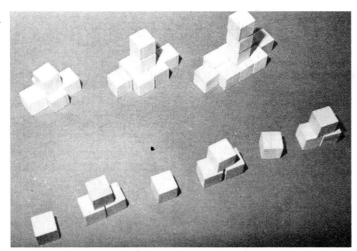

Fig. 2. What comes next in each row?

The ideas for cube patterns can be developed with a group of children or with the whole class in the same manner used to make the toothpick patterns. However, since your classroom may only have a limited number of cubes, you may want to set up a table or an area in the room for small groups of children to make and explore cube patterns. Most patterns can be recorded on paper by gluing down small squares of construction paper. For an even more realistic recording, have children glue sugar cubes together and then glue the resulting configurations on sheets of construction paper.

People patterns

Children enjoy making patterns with their own bodies. Have the class line up outside or around the room. Help the children make the line into a pattern, for example, arms up, arms down, arms out, arms up, arms down, arms out,…. Besides patterns made by positioning arms, suggest patterns made by arranging boys and girls, standing or sitting, or positioning bodies (e.g., one student bends over, another stands straight up, another squats down, one faces left or right, and one faces forward or backward).

With the children in a long line, oral or action patterns can also be developed: have each child say a word or perform some action, such as clapping or hopping in place.

More patterns

Patterning is catching. You and the students are limited only by your inventiveness. Patterns can be made with many items in the classroom or with items that can easily be collected. Here are some materials that can be used: Cuisenaire rods, shapes cut from colored paper, letters of the alphabet drawn on small squares of paper, bottle caps, buttons, Styrofoam packing pieces, fringe with colored balls, tags from plastic bread wrappers, leaves, links of plastic chain, Unifix cubes, or even paper clips.

THINKING WITH ATTRIBUTE ITEMS

Another problem-solving skill is classification. The process of looking for objects in a set and discovering how they are alike and different is both challenging and productive.

The activities in this section can be done with any standard set of attribute "blocks," that is, objects with the obvious attributes of size, shape, color, and, perhaps, thickness. However, three other sets of attribute materials can be used. The wide variety of properties, or attributes, of these three sets of materials makes them particularly appealing. Furthermore, these materials can easily be made or collected by your students.

Geocards

Geocards are simply squares made from tagboard or construction paper, each about 8 cm wide with a 4-by-4 grid of dots (like the pegs on a small geoboard). On each card draw a very simple shape or design using only straight lines to connect some of the dots on the card. Figure 3 shows some ideas. Keep the geocards very simple but make them differ from one another. A set of fifty or more cards is appropriate. The dot grids can easily be made on a photocopier or with a template made by punching sixteen holes in a square of poster board the same size as the geocards.

Fig. 3. Choose an attribute, then sort the cards.

Geocards can be sorted by shape; number of straight lines or sides; symmetry (and the number of lines of symmetry); the number of dots inside, outside, or touching the figures; concavity or convexity; open or closed figures; resemblance to an object; size; or the properties of parallel sides, square corners (right angles), and so on.

Name strips

Reproduce some graph paper with 2 cm × 2 cm squares and give each child a strip that has two rows and ten columns. See figure 4. Then have children print their names on the paper, with one letter in each square and the first name above the last name, as shown in figure 4. Each child's strip can then be pasted to a piece of tagboard, or it can be laminated.

The name strips can then be sorted by length, number of vowels, number of syllables, first letter, length of first name compared to length of last name, last letter, rhyming names, girls' or boys' names, names with double letters, and so on.

Treasures

In this activity, boxes are assembled from simple materials that have a wide variety of attributes. (We call these boxes "treasure

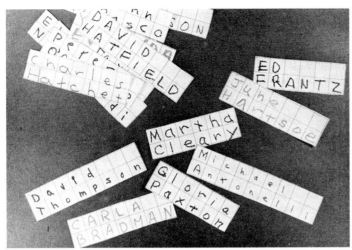

Fig. 4. Sort the names by length, number of vowels, and so on.

boxes." In *Mathematics Their Way*, Baratta-Lorton [1976] called them junk boxes.) The most common treasure boxes contain sets of buttons or small seashells. It is easy to create treasure boxes containing sets of any one of the following items: discarded keys, tags from plastic bread wrappers, lids from small jars, canceled stamps, or small swatches of material. Parents may have access to unusual materials discarded by a factory or collected as part of a hobby; these items would make unique treasure boxes. The requirements are that the materials have many different attributes and that not too many materials are duplicated.

The following activities can be done with each of three materials—geocards, name strips, or treasures—and each time an activity is completed with a new material, the activity takes on a new flavor,

spirit, and focus. Generally, the activities work best if small groups of children are seated at a table or on the floor. Different groups of children can work with different materials at the same time. It is not necessary to have sets of any particular materials, and since the activities can be done with any of the materials, directions can be given to the entire class at one time.

Activity 1: How many ways

You can design a variety of sorting tasks for the children. For example, challenge them to find as many ways as possible to sort their materials into exactly two sets or exactly three sets. With one set of twenty keys, we have seen children sort them in more than ten ways.

Another idea is to start with at least twenty different objects and have children sort them into two or more sets. Then they can sort each of these sets into smaller subsets, using the same criteria for each set. If possible, children can find a third way to sort each resulting subset into even smaller sets. Figure 5 illustrates how this activity might be done.

Activity 2: Secret sorting

These games involve one person sorting materials without revealing the attribute or combination of attributes used as the "sorting rule." For example, the child who is the Secret Sorter begins to select items for a group, one item at a time. All the items selected have some attribute in common, but only the sorter knows what it is. The rest of the children try to guess the common attribute. If a child thinks he or she knows the attribute, he or she says "stop" and then guesses the "sorting rule." If the guess is correct, this child becomes the Secret Sorter and begins with a

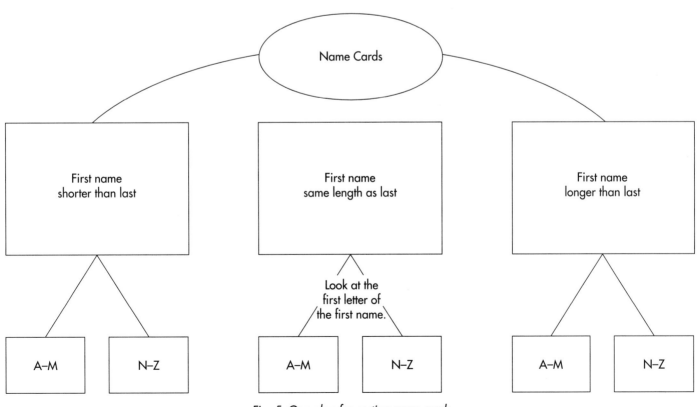

Fig. 5. One plan for sorting name cards

new secret sorting idea. If the guess is incorrect, then that child is out of that round and the sorter continues to sort the materials until the sorting method is discovered.

A similar game is modeled after the "Sesame Street" activity, "One of these things is not like the others." The Secret Sorter (or the teacher) sets out four or five objects, all but one of which have something in common. The rest of the group try to guess which object does not fit and then tell why. When guessing which one does not belong, the player must also say what the rest of the objects have in common. For example, one child might say, "Alexander Dietz doesn't belong in this group because the rest of the name strips all have first names that are shorter than the last names." Note that a guess may be a perfectly valid observation, but it may not be the rule that the Secret Sorter has in mind. Points can be awarded for good observations and extra points given for finding the rule used by the sorter.

Activity 3: String sorts

Two large loops of yarn can be overlapped to form three regions. Then objects with a common attribute are placed inside one loop. Objects placed in the other loop have a different attribute. The overlapping section contains objects with both attributes. Index cards can be used to label the attributes of each loop.

For a group activity, select two labels and place them beside the two overlapping strings. In turn, children close their eyes and select an object from the set of treasures being used. This object must then be correctly placed in one of the three sections, or outside both strings if it has neither attribute. For example, in figure 6, geocards were being sorted into "four sided" and "square corner" sets. In this case, geocards were available for all three sections and the outside. Sometimes, one or more of the sections will have no pieces in it, as would be the case with the labels "open regions" and "triangles." This sorting activity can become quite challenging if three loops are used, creating seven different regions, or if a combination of attributes is used (e.g., "four sides *and* symmetrical" *or* "triangle or square").

THINKING WITH GEOMETRIC MATERIALS

Many problem-solving situations involve spatial reasoning with geometric materials. In this section we shall develop a collection of problem-solving activities that are geometric in nature, challenging, and fun.

Geoboards and dot paper

Geoboards with 5 × 5 arrays of pegs provide an excellent vehicle for children to explore geometric problems. If dot paper is available, children can also record the ideas developed when they use rubber bands on the geoboards. Kindergartners will need paper with full-sized reproductions of the geoboards. Older children can use standard 8 1/2-by-11-inch paper with four geoboards (later sixteen) drawn on each sheet. To record designs, teach children to identify the dot corresponding to each corner of their designs. If these dots are circled first, children will find it much easier to draw lines from one dot to another.

Fig. 6. Using string to group the polygons

The following are just a few challenges that you can use to get children thinking geometrically with a geoboard. Each can be modified to suit the ability and maturity levels of the children. The children's lack of familiarity with an open-ended task may require that the initial tasks ask for more specific or well-defined results.

After the first few challenges we have suggested easier versions. Similar variations are possible with all the tasks.

1. How many different shapes can you make that have five sides?

   (a) Can you make a shape with five sides? Good! Now, copy that shape on paper and see if you can make a shape that is different but still has five sides.

2. How many triangles can you make with exactly one peg inside?

   (a) See if you can make a shape on your board that has only one peg inside. Look at the triangle I made. See this peg? It is the only one inside.

   (b) Can you make two different triangles on your board so that each has just one peg inside? Now copy those triangles on your dot paper and try to make some others that are different.

3. How many different rectangles can you make?

   (a) On your board make one shape that has exactly four sides. Good! Some of you have special shapes. They have square corners, just like the corner of a piece of paper. See if you can make your four-sided shape have square corners. These shapes are called rectangles.

4. Make some shapes that have two square corners. Can you find five different ones?

5. What is the smallest square you can make? What is the largest? How many different-sized squares are possible?

6. Try question 5 with triangles, right triangles, rectangles, and so on.

7. Can you make five shapes that have a line of symmetry?

8. Can you make a shape with seven sides that is symmetrical?

9. Make the biggest square you can on the geoboard. Can you cut it into two equal parts? How many ways can you do it?

10. Make some shapes with all corners square. What is the area of each square? What is the perimeter of each? Make an all-square-corner shape with a large perimeter but a small area.

11. Can you make shapes with larger and larger perimeters but all with the same area?

12. Choose two pegs on the geoboard that are in different rows and columns. How many different paths can you make from one peg to the other without going backward or away from the target peg?

13. Make a rectangle on the geoboard. Can you divide it into two regions that are exactly the same size and shape? How many different ways can you do it? Can you divide it into three congruent shapes?

The first six challenges can be adapted in some manner even for preschool children. With the teacher's guidance, all these challenges can be explored by third- or fourth-grade children. Working in groups, discussing different ideas, demonstrating new ones with examples, and gradually building the elements of a new concept or exploration are all ways that these ideas can be suited to even the youngest child.

The most difficult idea for children initially is that of the open-ended task. But with careful guidance, children will accept more open-ended activities and may even gravitate toward such tasks, since they provide the most challenge, freedom, and room for creative thought.

If other concepts are being developed in your class, create challenges involving them. For example, none of the previous questions involve rotational symmetry, similarity, concavity or convexity, open or closed ideas, or rotations and reflections. These concepts can also be explored on a geoboard.

Cubes

Wooden cubes can be stacked in many different configurations, and this feature yields a number of possible activities. More explorations are possible with plastic cubes that snap together on any face. Consider having children do the following activities with cubes:

1. Take five cubes and build a shape. Take five more and build a different shape. How many different shapes can you build with five cubes?

2. Build a shape with eight cubes. Its volume is eight cubes. What is its surface area in square units? (Remember, to determine surface area, all a child needs to do is count the exposed faces of the shape, including those on the bottom.) What other shapes can you build with the same volume and surface area?

3. With twelve cubes, what is the shape with the largest surface area that you can build? The smallest surface area? Can you make shapes with all the possible surface areas in between?

4. Choose a number less than 30. Can you make a shape with that surface area? What is its volume? Can you make a larger or smaller shape with the same surface area?

5. Build a 2 × 3 × 4 box. Notice that it can be sliced into two identical parts, one the mirror image of the other. The slice is a plane of symmetry. Can you make other shapes that have a plane of symmetry?

Simple puzzle pieces

From squares of tagboard or poster board, some simple shapes can be cut that provide opportunities for interesting explorations and endless puzzle possibilities. Three possible patterns for cutting the squares are shown in figure 7. The idea is to have a set of pieces that are "compatible," that is, that fit together nicely or that have several pieces with edges of the same length. The exact size of the initial square is not important. If the square is about 15 cm on each edge, the resulting pieces will be large enough for kindergarten and first-grade children. After cutting one square into pieces according to the pattern, you may find it easier then to draw and cut multiple copies of the individual pieces rather than cut them from an initial square.

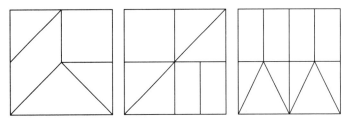

Fig. 7. Some suggestions for cutting shapes from a square

The following activities or challenges can be completed by children using any of the three sets of pieces shown in figure 7. Another variation is to combine pieces from two or more squares or to use standard tangram pieces.

1. With the pieces from one square, how many different shapes can you make if the edges of individual pieces must match?

2. Make any shape with all the pieces from one set. Make an outline of your shape. Now try to fill in the outline but arrange the pieces differently. See figure 8.

3. Make any shape using any number of pieces. Draw the outline of the shape. See if a classmate can fill the shape. Don't tell the classmate which pieces you used.

4. Once a shape has been made, its perimeter, or the distance around it, can be measured by referring to the edges of the pieces themselves. For example, a shape can have a perimeter of two short sides plus three medium sides plus one long

Fig. 8. How many different pieces can be used to fill in the shape?

side. Once this idea has been established, see how many shapes the children can make that have that same perimeter.

5. The symmetry of any piece (or of any shape) can be checked with a mirror. Place the mirror on what you think is a line of symmetry. If what you see in the mirror is exactly the same as what you see when the mirror is removed, then the line where the mirror rested is a line of symmetry. First find the pieces that have a line of symmetry. Next use those pieces to make a larger shape that has a line of symmetry. Then try to make a shape that has two lines of symmetry.

6. What familiar shapes can you make from two or more smaller shapes? Can you make a triangle? A square? A rectangle? Can you make a long skinny shape?

7. A convex shape has no "dents." Using a given set of pieces, how many convex shapes can you make?

These ideas are intended to be sketchy and open-ended. You may want to modify the directions to match the age levels of your students. If a small number of pieces are used, most of the activities can be explored even by kindergartners. By using more pieces and continually challenging students to make more shapes with a given property, you can also engage older children in geometric problem solving.

An overhead projector is an easy way to show the pieces to an entire class. If students each have a set of pieces at their desks, they can follow an idea as you model it on the overhead projector. Once a concept, such as symmetry, perimeter, or the alignment of two edges, is established, children will be able to follow up on these projects with only occasional encouragement from you.

The solutions to most of the challenges described can be copied on paper by tracing around the pieces. Doing so allows you to check the ideas that have been developed in your absence, to create bulletin boards that use the children's ideas, and to send "geometric think tasks" home so that parents can get involved in these problem-solving activities with their children.

CONCLUSION

In this article we have presented a few ways to involve children in mathematical tasks that require creative thinking. The intent is to reveal to children aspects of mathematics in which creative thinking is not only possible and valuable but also necessary.

Although these activities have been restricted to patterns, classification, and geometric tasks, these areas are certainly not the only ones where children can or should be encouraged to think on their own. The youngest children can and should solve simple word problems presented to them orally. Counters can be used to help them model and think through the situations. Children in the first and second grades can solve oral word problems involving multiplication and division. Children in the fourth grade and up can work on the nonstandard process-oriented problems frequently discussed in recent mathematics-education literature.

Another context for creative thinking is computer programming, either in BASIC or Logo. Both languages require and promote creative thought in a problem-solving context. Further, logic games, such as Mastermind, abound and many have been translated into computer software.

In summary, many activities are available to involve students in creative thought. We hope the ideas in this article will get you started toward promoting creative thinking in your classroom.

Bibliography

Baratta-Lorton, Mary. *Mathematics Their Way.* Menlo Park, Calif: Addison-Wesley Publishing Co., 1976.

Bruni, James V., and Helene Silverman. "Let's Do It: Making and Using Attribute Materials." *Arithmetic Teacher* 22 (February 1975): 88–95.

Brydegaard, Marguerite, and James E. Inskeep, eds. *Readings in Geometry from the Arithmetic Teacher.* Reston, Va.: National Council of Teachers of Mathematics, 1970.

Burton, Grace M. "Patterning: Powerful Play." *School Science and Mathematics* 82 (January 1982): 39–44.

Elementary Science Study. *Teacher's Guide for Attribute Games and Problems.* New York: McGraw Hill Book Co., 1966.

Fuys, David J., and Rosamond W. Tischler. *Teaching Mathematics in the Elementary School.* Boston: Little, Brown & Co., 1979.

Grimm, Leslie. *Moptown Parade.* Menlo Park, Calif.: Learning Co. Computer software package.

National Council of Teachers of Mathematics. *An Agenda for Action.* Reston, Va.: The Council, 1980. ▲

Station Break: A Mathematics Game Using Cooperative Learning and Role Playing

by

Rebecca D. Rees

"Station break" is a teacher-made game that incorporates role playing and cooperative learning as a way to help learners solve practical mathematical problems. It is intended for elementary and junior high school students, especially those who have limited interest or ability in mathematics. By writing problems that integrate current topics of study with learners' interests and ability levels, teachers can make the subject more interesting to students. Students learn to develop both social and collaborative skills while they improve their skills in mathematics. Students and the teacher work cooperatively to make preparation for the game easy.

"STATION BREAK" GAME

Object

The object of the game is for students, organized into teams, cooperatively to solve a mathematical word problem from each of four stations.

Teams

Sixteen students are divided into four teams composed of students with mixed mathematical ability levels. For example, a team might consist of one student with fourth-grade skills, two students with fifth-grade skills, and one student with sixth-grade skills. Team members select their team leader.

Stations

Stations are simply cardboard boxes containing manipulatives that can be used to solve mathematical problems about a particular area of interest. At a station, each team finds a card with one mathematical problem containing four or more interrelated tasks. The team leader reads the problem aloud. Team members role-play the situation and determine a strategy for solving the problem. Members decide how to allocate the individual tasks required by the problem. Each member solves one part of the problem, and the team collectively reaches the final solution.

Solution

When the team is satisfied with the answer, the leader checks the solution against an answer key; if more than one solution is correct, the teacher checks the team's answer. If correct, the team

earns a token from that station and attaches it to the team's certificate. Tokens are either purchased stickers or small pictures cut out from gift-wrapping paper representing the theme of the station. A team certificate is a paper plate labeled "Station Break: Certificate of Cooperation." A token from each station is placed on the paper-plate certificate. On completion of the game, team members sign their names on the paper-plate certificate. Certificates of cooperation can be displayed from the classroom ceiling by brightly colored gift ribbon (see fig. 1).

Fig. 1. Fast-food station and a certificate of cooperation

If the answer to the problem is incorrect, the team works together to arrive at the correct solution. Team members refer to "helpful hints" cards for assistance with mathematical concepts. As a last resort, teams can request assistance from the teacher. "Role playing" cards offer assistance in assigning characters, as well as mathematical tasks. At the end of a specified time period, teams move to the next station and solve the problem found there.

Success

When each team has solved the problems at all four stations, the game has been completed successfully.

Rebecca Rees, a former mathematics specialist at Park Century School, Los Angeles, CA 90025, is interested in integrating mathematical concepts with practical situations in the curriculum.

Group processing

When all four teams have solved a problem at each of the four stations, or when time has been called, all sixteen students sit together and analyze their group interaction. One team at a time, members discuss how well they were able to work together to assign interrelated tasks, to determine a strategy for solving the problem, to assist each other, to help each other correct errors, to share leadership, and to use the aids available in the station box. As members of a team analyze their interaction, members of other teams offer suggestions and comments.

THE TEACHER'S ROLE

The teacher's role involves identifying the students' interests and ability levels, working with the students to develop the stations, writing the four-part problems, and helping teams to analyze their collaborative skills.

Student interests and ability levels

The teacher identifies the mathematical abilities and personal interests of the students. Mathematical abilities are identified by examining such records as achievement tests and classwork. Students' interests can be determined by talking with the students and asking them such questions as the following:

- What is your favorite sport to play?
- What is your favorite sport to watch?
- What is your favorite pastime with friends?
- What is your favorite activity when alone?
- Where is your favorite place to travel?
- What is your favorite type of restaurant?
- What is your favorite food?

Stations

A cardboard box is needed for each of the four stations; shoe boxes are ideal. On the basis of the information obtained from the students about their interests, the teacher identifies four areas of interest. Or, students and teachers can decide on the four areas cooperatively. For example, if students like to (1) go to fast-food restaurants, (2) bicycle, (3) go to amusement parks, and (4) cook, the stations could be (1) fast-food station, (2) sports station, (3) amusement-park station, and (4) cooks' station. To decorate the stations, students divide into groups, choose a station, and draw or glue pictures cut from magazines on the sides of the cardboard boxes. During preparation for the game, students, directed by the teacher, discuss mathematical problems that might be solved at each of the stations and identify the types of manipulatives to be placed in the boxes. Working cooperatively in this way involves the students and makes preparation less work for the teacher.

Problems

The teacher is responsible for writing the mathematical problems with the appropriate level of difficulty for the students. Three index cards are used at each station; one for the problem, one for

role-playing, and one for helpful hints. On the problem card, the teacher writes a four-part problem corresponding to the ability level of the students. On the role-playing card, characters that might act out the problem are listed, and the mathematical tasks are distributed among those characters. Problems could have more than one correct solution, so helpful hints are written on a third index card. Students refer to the helpful hints when they cannot help each other. Helpful hints can include such procedures as the sequence of steps necessary to solve the problem and a list of the steps for a particular mathematical task, such as finding the percentage of a number or the procedure for dividing fractions. Many commercial texts list steps for particular mathematical concepts. These steps can be photocopied, thus reducing game-preparation time. Problem cards, role-playing cards, and helpful-hints cards are placed in library pockets in the station box. Teams are encouraged to devise their own problem-solving strategy, but if they require some help, they can refer to the cards.

Group processing

After the game is over, each team returns to a designated meeting place and analyzes their collaboration. The teacher guides the discussion by asking such questions as these:

- Did group members encourage others to do their best?
- If problems arose, did individuals offer or receive assistance?
- How were problems handled?
- Did each person complete his or her task?
- Did team members need to refer to the role-playing cards, or did they divide the tasks themselves?
- Did team members refer to the helpful-hints cards, or were they able to help one another without the aids?
- What suggestions could improve the next game?

The following types of stations and cards are representative of those I have developed for my students. The mathematical skills of these students ranged from fourth through sixth grade.

THE STATIONS

Fast-food station

The fast-food station consists of a cardboard box containing a menu, an order pad, play money, and a calculator or cash register. Students use these manipulatives when role-playing the problem and figuring out the solution. The box is decorated with a picture of people at a fast-food restaurant. The token for successful problem completion is a picture of an ice-cream soda cut out from gift-wrapping paper (see fig. l).

Problem card

Suppose you and your friends are having a party for 20 people. You want to buy your food at the fast-food restaurant. You have $100 to spend. The fast-food restaurant gives a discount of 15 percent on the entire bill for bills over $75. What do you serve your guests? How much does it cost? How much money do you have left (if any)? How much money do you save with the discount? Does everyone have enough food?

Role-playing card

Character 1: Fast-food restaurant manager: Explains and calculates discount

Character 2: Fast-food order clerk: Takes order, totals amount

Character 3: Party planner: Decides what to order, totals amount

Character 4: Party planner: Places order, pays totaled amount, and finds appropriate discount on amount over $75

Helpful-hints card

1. Lists steps for finding a percentage of a number

2. Lists steps for calculating sales tax

Sports station

The sports station is set up by filling the cardboard box with the following items: a newspaper advertisement from a local sporting-goods shop offering a variety of bicycles, helmets, cycling suits, and so on; a calculator; scratch paper; a simple teacher-made chart listing features, functions, and prices of bicycles, helmets, and bicycle equipment for the items advertised; a scaled street map; and a ruler (fig. 2). The box is decorated with pictures of cyclists cut from magazines. The token for successful completion of the problem is a purchased sticker of a cyclist.

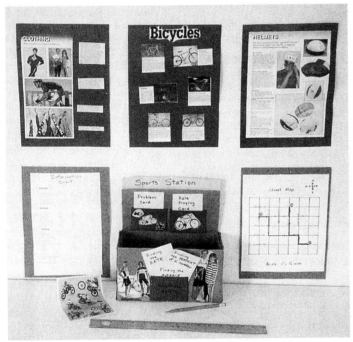

Fig. 2. Sports station

Problem card

1. You have $400 and you wish to purchase a bicycle, helmet, and cycling suit shown in the advertisement in the station box. Which items do you choose so as not to go over this amount?

2. You are traveling from point A on your map to point B, on to point C, and then back to point A. How many miles is the round trip? (Map is labeled with points A, B, and C.)

3. You average 15 miles per hour. How long does it take to complete a round trip that includes a two-hour break at point B?

4. You leave at 9:00 A.M. and average 15 miles per hour. At what time do you reach point C? If your friend leaves at 10:00 A.M., how many miles per hour must she average in order to reach you at point C by 11:00 A.M.?

Role-playing card

Character 1: Customer: Using information from the ad, selects bicycle, helmet, and suit, all for less than $400 (total amount must include tax)

Character 2: Map reader: Determines distance of the trip using a map

Character 3: Time keeper: Calculates length of time necessary for trip

Character 4: Speed engineer: Determines average speed that friend must cycle to meet at 11:00 A.M.

Helpful-hints card

1. Lists steps for finding the percentage of a number (for sales tax)

2. Lists steps for finding rate of speed

3. Lists steps for finding an average

Amusement-park station

The amusement-park station contains a scaled map of the park, a ruler, and some play money (fig. 3). Two charts are prepared by the teacher. One chart lists the prices of admission. The second chart lists various rides, their average length, and the approximate time it takes to wait in line. A luncheon menu is available, and a simple price sheet lists souvenirs. The station box is decorated with pictures of people at amusement parks or with theme park characters, such as Mickey Mouse or Snoopy. The token for successful completion of this station is a purchased balloon sticker.

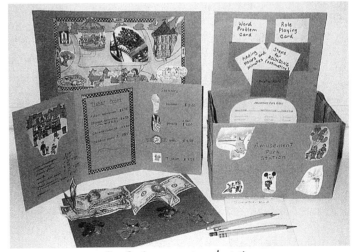

Fig. 3. Amusement-park station

Problem card

1. Suppose you and your friends are going to the amusement park. Using table 1, choose 6 rides. Add the time of the ride and the time you must wait in line to determine the total time for all 6 rides.

2. From the information in table 1, write a ratio comparing the time on each ride you selected to the time you must spend in line. Then write a ratio comparing the total time on the rides you selected to the total time you must wait in line. Reduce this ratio, written in fractional form, if possible.

3. You have $10 each to spend on souvenirs and lunch. Use the menu and the souvenir price sheet in the station box to determine what each of you buys with your money. Remember to include sales tax.

4. Using a map of the park, plan the most efficient route to each of the rides you selected in question 1. On the map, highlight your route with a yellow marker.

Table 1

Name of ride	Time in line	Time on ride
Castle of Mirrors	15 min	8 min
Haunted House	24 min	13 min
White-Water Roller Coaster	12 min	9 min
Jungle-Boat Adventure	14 min	11 min
Safari Train	7 min	12 min
Space Blast	23 min	14 min
Tree House	6 min	7 min
Wild-Horses Merry-Go-Round	8 min	8 min

Role-playing card

Character 1: Time keeper: With others, chooses 6 mutually agreeable rides, then using the chart, adds times

Character 2: Ratio writer: Writes ratio of time on ride to time in line for both individual rides and total of rides

Character 3: Spending-money organizer: Asks others what they plan to eat and what souvenirs they plan to buy, estimates to determine that totals do not exceed $10, totals the prices, and adds sales tax

Character 4: Route specialist: Plans the most efficient route for all team members to follow from ride to ride

Helpful-hints card

1. Lists steps in rounding for estimating
2. Lists suggestions for adding hours and minutes

Cooks' station

Inside the cardboard box of the cooks' station (fig. 4) are placed a pad of paper, a set of measuring cups, measuring spoons, a container for either sand or water (for measuring), and the following recipe. The box is decorated with pictures cut from magazines of people cooking and eating. The token for successful completion of the problem is a picture of a baking-powder can cut from gift-wrapping paper.

Fig. 4. Cooks' station

Recipe (*Better Homes and Gardens New Cookbook* 1953)

Butterscotch Thins
  1/4 cup butter or margarine
  1/4 cup shortening
  1/3 cup granulated sugar
  1/3 cup brown sugar
  1 egg
  1 1/3 cups sifted enriched flour
  3/4 teaspoon baking soda
  3/4 teaspoon vanilla
  1/3 cup chopped walnuts

Melt butter and shortening. Add sugars; mix well. Add egg; beat until light colored. Sift together flour and soda; stir into shortening mixture. Add vanilla and nuts.

Shape into rolls, one and one-half inches in diameter. Roll in waxed paper; chill thoroughly. Slice thin.

Bake on an ungreased cookie sheet in a moderate oven (375°) for ten minutes. Makes four dozen cookies.

Problem card

Suppose you and your friends are going to use this recipe to bake cookies for 24 people, including you and your friends. You want to have 4 cookies for each person. (1) How must you adjust the recipe so that you have enough cookies for 24 people? (2) How much of each ingredient in the recipe do you need? (3) Suppose your oven heats 25° higher than the temperature on the oven-temperature dial; for example, if you set your oven to 325°, it is actually heating to 350°. On what number do you have to set your oven-temperature dial for it actually to bake at the suggested 375°? (4) If you can fit two cookie sheets in the oven at one time and each cookie sheet holds 12 cookies, how long does it take to bake all the cookies?

Role-playing card

Character 1: Hostess: Determines how to adjust the recipe so that it yields enough cookies

Character 2: Chef: Determines how much of each ingredient is necessary

Character 3: Engineer: Determines on what number to set the oven-temperature dial

Character 4: Organizer: Determines how much time is necessary to bake the cookies

Helpful-hints card

1. Lists steps for multiplying fractions
2. Includes equivalence chart for liquid and dry measurement

CONCLUDING COMMENTS

These stations offer an opportunity for students to work with mathematical concepts using fractions, decimals, and percents; taking averages; and using time and money. Students solve problems together in a variety of practical situations on the basis of their interests. Several comments about the preparation and management of the game follow:

1. Although fifteen minutes at each station is suggested, teachers who wish to make their own station-break games will need to determine the appropriate length of time for their students to solve the problems. If students are having difficulty identifying and deciding among themselves how to distribute the mathematical tasks in the four-part problems, perhaps assigning the tasks could be the goal of the stations instead of actually solving the problems. As students become more adept at the cooperative nature of the game, solving the problems can become the goal of the activity.

2. We suggest that the problems be easier at the beginning when the students are learning how to play the game. After students have played "station break" and are consistently able to solve the problems cooperatively, the degree of mathematical difficulty can be increased.

3. Perhaps teachers would prefer developing *one* station instead of four and having several students try to solve the mathematical problem in the station box as a free-time activity, not as an organized game. Using this adaptation of "station break," the teacher can gradually develop new stations.

4. Finally, to save time in preparing the game, we suggest that teachers use readily available materials, such as purchased stickers, gift-wrapping paper, commercial maps, take-out menus, recipes photocopied from cookbooks, pictures from catalogs or newspaper advertisements, and so on. The teacher's time can be most efficiently spent working out the four-part mathematical problems.

Bibliography

Better Homes and Gardens New Cookbook. 1st ed. Des Moines, Iowa: Meredith Corp., 1953.

Brant, Ron. "On Cooperation in Schools: A Conversation with David and Roger Johnson." *Educational Leadership* 45 (November 1987): 14–19.

California State Department of Education. *Mathematics Framework for California Public Schools, Kindergarten through Grade Twelve.* Sacramento, Calif.: California State Department of Education, 1985.

Fennell, Francis M. *Focus on Problem Solving, Level F.* Elizabethtown, Penn.: Continental Press, 1985.

Joyce, Bruce, and Marsha Weil. *Models of Teaching.* 3d ed. Englewood Cliffs, N.J.: Prentice-Hall, 1986.

National Council of Teachers of Mathematics. *An Agenda for Action: Recommendations for School Mathematics of the 1980s.* Reston, Va.: The Council, 1980.

Rucker, Walter E., Clyde A. Dilley, and David W. Lowry. *Heath Mathematics Teacher's Edition, Level 5.* Lexington, Mass.: D.C. Heath & Co., 1985.

Slavin, Robert E. "Cooperative Learning and the Cooperative School." *Educational Leadership* 45 (November 1987): 7–13. ▲

Creative Problem Solving and Red Yarn

by

Barbara Wilmot

This activity is one of the more stimulating and enlightening I have discovered. It has worked well and with similar results in classes of mathematically gifted students in grades 2–10, in a class of advanced high school seniors, and in in-service workshops for teachers! A wide range? Yes, and I feel certain that it would work in almost any situation. Using colored yarn, participants are asked to create geometric figures. Since yarn is not a familiar "output device," it always supplies an ample number of problems.

The only materials required are loops of string or yarn approximately six to nine meters in length. (I use red yarn so that I can see it easily as I oversee the activity.) Each group of four to six participants needs a loop and enough space in which to stand and move around freely. One group is all that is necessary; however, as the number of groups increases, so does the variety of solutions and the level of competition. The only "rule" is that at all times, every person has to have both hands touching the yarn.

My task is to provide challenges for each group. The participants' task is to use the yarn to make the geometric figures suggested. Your task, as you read this, is to visualize and think, "How would *I* attack this challenge?"

I begin with a very simple instruction: "Make a triangle." Then we progress through a sequence of shapes like the following:

1. An isosceles triangle
2. A square
3. A parallelogram that is not a rhombus
4. A trapezoid
5. A hexagon
6. A decagon
7. A fifteen-sided polygon

Somewhere in this sequence is a term with which at least one person in each group is unfamiliar. This is the time when the participants first realize the value of teamwork. If no one in the group can help, I give the geometric definition of the unknown term. And they are off!

Barbara Wilmot teaches elementary mathematics content and methods courses at Illinois State University, Normal, IL 61761. Her special interest is in gifted education.

I circulate continually but only communicate when the team indicates that the final product is ready. I try not to approve or disapprove but to ask questions such as these: "How do you know it is isosceles?" "What is a trapezoid?" "How can you be sure that the sides are parallel?" Figure 1 shows students trying to decide how to prove that their triangle is equilateral. (Figs. 1–3 feature fifth and sixth graders at Tri-Valley Unit District Elementary School in Downs, Illinois.) As I leave for another group, I present the next challenge, which is always more difficult.

Fig. 1. These three fifth graders are trying to decide how to "prove" that they have formed an equilateral triangle.

Once they have reached the fifteen-sided polygon, they are using teeth, feet, elbows, chairs, or whatever is available. Usually they are also beginning to work as a team, with one or more leaders emerging. It is not unusual for the leader of the group to change from one task to the next. Sometimes the leader is the person who was familiar with the term; other times it is the one who can best visualize the required product or the one with the most aggressive personality. When the photograph in figure 2 was taken, Ryan was full of ideas and directions.

On completion of this activity, excellent group discussions can be pursued about cooperation and leadership, as well as passivity, risk taking, ranges of comfort, qualities of a good follower or leader, and so on. Because the activity calls for new or little-used

Fig. 2. Ryan (far left) readily assumed the leadership role as this group formed three congruent triangles.

skills, participants often find their self-concept challenged, which can provide a fertile environment for in-depth sharing.

Next I might ask for the following shapes:

1. Three equilateral triangles
2. Four congruent triangles
3. Five noncongruent triangles
4. Six similar triangles
5. Three parallelograms that are not rectangles
6. Three hexagons with the maximal number of shared sides

Because the students' definition of congruent figures states that the figures can be matched by putting one on top of the other, sometimes a group will use three hands to make one triangle and then wrap the yarn around the same hands several times. This procedure is correct, but for the next task I increase the number of congruent triangles and stipulate that only one side of each can coincide (fig. 3).

If a group makes the three triangles with a common vertex, I might specify that no more than two triangles can share a common vertex. I do not wish to spoil your fun and amazement by elaborating

Fig. 3. Create some triangles that have sides that coincide.

on other frequently recurring situations. Just continually ask each group to vary their product so that they have to think divergently.

As I circulate, I continue to be impressed by the diversity of solutions. Sometimes I ask for everyone's attention to allow one group to "show off" a particularly interesting solution. Other times I decide not to interrupt but save the discussion until the end. Either way, I let the praise flow freely. Students soon realize that it is not only the product with which I am so pleased but the creative, efficient, or cooperative means of attaining the result.

When asked to make four congruent triangles, most groups will stay with plane figures. Occasionally a group will produce a tetrahedron. For some, therefore, the next sequence seems quite logical, whereas other groups cannot believe that I now ask for a cube (fig. 4) followed by a triangular prism, and then possibly a hexagonal pyramid. These, of course, are much more complex but not necessarily more difficult. Some groups actually seem to function better when working with three-dimensional shapes.

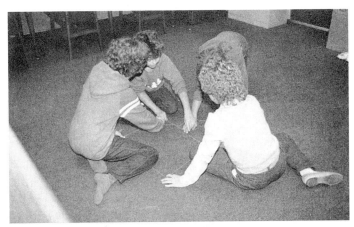

Fig. 4. When challenged to make a cube, the girls (a) used the floor and their legs, whereas the boys (b) requested an additional pair of hands once they decided that they needed eight vertices.

Leading students through activities of this type can be challenging and fun. Using the yarn gives students an opportunity to sharpen spatial perceptions, enlarge their vocabulary, stretch their thinking skills, and discover relationships. It also allows an onlooker to evaluate the participants' knowledge, spatial perceptions, and problem-solving abilities. In addition, it promotes leadership qualities, a high degree of cooperation, and a healthy spirit of competition.

Now with your red yarn, please make a.... ▲

Celebrate with Mathematics

by

Winnie J. Peterson

PATTERN CHAINS

Creating colorful holiday chains constitutes an excellent activity for a mathematics class. Using red and green construction paper, rulers, scissors, and glue sticks, students enjoy making pattern chains. In my fifth-grade class, two groups came up with simple chains: red, green, red, green, red, green, and so on; one red, two green, three red, four green, and so on. A third group created a chain of triangular numbers: one green, three red, six green, ten red, and so on. The completed chains were displayed around the room at the conclusion of each class, and the patterns became more intricate as the days progressed.

To make the chains, most students used rulers to draw straight lines but many worked freehand. A few students measured the width of their links. Seven chains with interesting patterns were hung at the front of the room. (See fig. 1.) On successive days, students worked with a partner to decode the seven chains and explain how each was made and how the patterns could be continued. Students recorded the patterns, using both numbers and colors. Later, several chains were displayed in the hall, and teachers and students from other classes were invited to identify and explain the patterns.

1	green	1	red	1	green	2	green
2	red	1	green	1	red	3	red
3	green	2	red	2	green	5	green
4	red	2	green	2	red	8	red
5	green	2	red	3	green	⋮	
6	red	2	green	3	red		
7	green	3	red			1	green
⋮		3	green	⋮		3	red
		3	red			6	green
2	green	3	red	1	green	10	red
4	red	3	green	4	red		
6	green	3	red	9	green	⋮	
⋮		3	green	16	red		
		⋮		⋮			

Fig. 1. Student patterns using two colors

TRIANGLE TREES

To continue the chain pattern of triangular numbers, I designed a mathematical holiday card, using the triangular-number pattern to create trees. (See fig. 2.) To draw attention to the card and how it was made, a balloon tree constructed from ten green balloons in a triangular pattern was placed on the bulletin board as shown in figure 3.

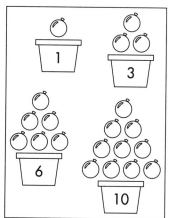
Cover of the greeting card

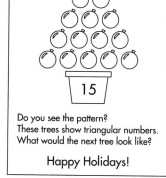
Inside the greeting card

Do you see the pattern?
These trees show triangular numbers.
What would the next tree look like?

Happy Holidays!

Fig. 2

Students first asked if it was a dartboard, but later they made the connections among the board display, the cards, and the chains. Next year, different representations to expand the pattern will include the song "The Twelve Days of Christmas" and the book *Emma's Christmas* by Irene Trivas (New York: Orchard Books Watts, 1988). Both use the triangular-number pattern. ▲

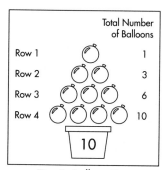

Fig. 3. Balloon Tree

Winnie Peterson teaches at Colonial School District, Plymouth Meeting, PA 37051. She is a doctoral student at Temple University and teaches at St. Joseph's University in Philadelphia.

Strategy Spotlight: Determining the Correct Operation with the Slow or Handicapped Learner

by

Carol A. Thornton
Illinois State University, Normal, Illinois

An extension of patterning underlies a student's ability to decide which of the four basic operations apply in solving a simple oral or written word problem. Many learning-handicapped and slower students cannot "see" what is set forth by the words of a problem—that a situation really fits the pattern of addition, or division.

> *Problem:* Randy has 26 dog biscuits. He wants to give them to his 3 dogs—the same number to each. How many biscuits will each dog get? How many extras will be left?

Miscued by the phrase "how many will be left," a typical response of slow or handicapped students is to subtract. An approach to building students' success in problem-solving situations like this is outlined in the following small steps:

- Use countable objects (or another appropriate model) to analyze and discuss the word problem. Use vocabulary that emphasizes the basic concept of the operation. (In this problem, we share among, or divide the biscuits.) The students themselves should move or group the objects. Encourage them to verbalize what they are doing: "sharing 26 among 3."

- Select the best arithmetic expression from a presented list (e.g., 26 – 3, 26 ÷ 3, 26 + 3) to represent the action in the problem. Use objects to verify that rejected expressions "don't work." When possible, help students "see" how the chosen expression simulates the action in the problem:

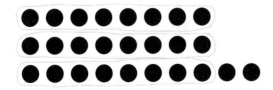

- Reverse the foregoing procedures. (This is a very important step!) Direct students to read the problem, write from a presented list the arithmetic expression they think "fits" the problem, and then use an appropriate model to check their answer.

- Have students change the numbers in given, similar problems to form new problems. Then ask them independently to write an expression they think "fits" the action of the problem and use an appropriate model to check the expression.

- Have students identify which problems among those given involve the specified operation (e.g., division) and use an appropriate model to check their thinking.

The basic thrust of the instructional sequence just outlined is to highlight the operation embedded in the basic structure or action of a problem. Parallel examples are then provided so that basic similarities between problems begin to emerge. Identifying just those problems that involve a given operation is a final step. Note that hands-on involvement by the child and modeling of appropriate language by the teacher, are integral to the interaction between teacher and student.

This sequence has been extended successfully and applied to multistep problems.

PROBLEM CORNER: SPECIAL HELP

Many students with learning difficulties "go blank" when they see problems with troublesome fractions, decimals, or larger whole numbers. Teach these students to help themselves. Help them learn to substitute small whole numbers for difficult numbers until they decide what operations to carry out.

CLASSROOM CLIMATE

Many handicapped and slower students have reading difficulties that interfere with success in problem solving. To help:

- Rely more on small, cooperative groups (watch for "Organizing the Classroom for Problem Solving" by Marilyn Burns in a forthcoming "Problem Solving Tips").

- Create a "buddy" system. Ask a student to be Johnny's or Mary's buddy for a while. This buddy can read and interpret difficult words. Allow the system to function even during tests. If the child with the learning difficulty becomes too dependent on the helper or is too easily drawn off task, the buddy assignment can be changed without issue.

TAKE A LOOK

John Cawley has specialized in developing problem-solving materials for mildly handicapped students. Refer to "Selected Views on Metacognition, Arithmetic Problem Solving, and Learning Disability" by John F. Cawley and James H. Miller in *Learning Disabilities Focus* 2 (Fall 1986): 36–48; or write to him: Department of Special Education and Habilitative Service, University of New Orleans, Lake Front, New Orleans, LA 70148.

LOOK AHEAD

Provide activities that build prerequisites to small successes in problem solving:

- Include a basic-fact review as part of a daily assignment. Present the review in a way that forces decision making, which is the heart of problem solving. For example, "Find and do five problems that have an answer of 7."

- Once every two weeks observe slower or handicapped learners as each uses countable objects, base-ten blocks, or other appropriate materials to check a written answer. Interact to help students use appropriate language to describe what they are doing. ("Start with 35; share among 4"; or "517 is the whole. We'll take away part, the 231....")

- Provide numeric problems with answers, but without signs. Help students develop reasoning skills by asking them to decide which sign "fits" and to tell *why* it does. As mentioned previously, emphasize appropriate language.

From time to time have students use appropriate models to check their thinking.

$$8 \square 2 = 6$$

$$\begin{array}{r} 42 \\ 38 \\ \hline 1596 \end{array} \qquad \begin{array}{r} 4387 \\ 2155 \\ \hline 6542 \end{array}$$

$$8 \square 2 = 4$$

SPONGE ACTIVITIES

Routinely provide occasions that force students to think about the basic structure of a problem situation. Fill otherwise wasted gaps during transition periods with short sponge activities that invite on-task behavior from even the slowest, most affected learner.

- Put thumbs up if you think I should divide to solve the problem. Otherwise, put thumbs down.

- Use fingers, chest high, to form +, −, ×, or ÷ to show me what you think I should do first to solve this problem.

Alternatively:

- Create bulletin-board displays or furnish individual cards and invite students to sort problems according to the arithmetic operation needed to solve them. Make an answer key available for self-checking.

- Structure assignments specifically to include sorting by problem type. For example, "Just do the division word problems on this page." Before students begin work, call on individuals to tell, in their own words, how they sort out division problems as opposed to other types of problems. ▲

Chapter 7
Everyday Applications

"Reality Math"

by

Linda K. Moniuszko

Junior high school and middle school students are a rare breed. They can be utterly charming one minute and yet extremely difficult to reach the next. Their minds seem to be everywhere but in the classroom. The far-off goal of high school graduation is too remote to entice some to hard work, and to others it must seem the impossible dream.

Students in special education and remedial classes are even more difficult to motivate. School achievement is often the last thing on their minds. Many have already failed one or more grades, resulting in differences in age and interest that put them "out of sync" with other junior high school students.

Motivation is the biggest challenge in instruction.

My students are reluctant even to try to achieve in a subject area in which they have already failed, and most see no purpose for, or practical application of, mathematics in their lives. Motivation is my most important goal and the biggest challenge in instruction.

Since my class is predominantly male, I decided to approach the teaching of mathematical principles through a young man's heart. It seems that every teenaged male thinks, eats, sleeps, and dreams about having his own car. I knew that a multitude of mathematical processes could be taught through the "purchase" of an automobile, so I transformed my classroom into an automobile dealer's showroom. I assumed that the automobiles would be more interesting and appealing to the boys than to the girls in my class. I was

wrong. The girls loved the racy sports cars and eagerly participated in choosing their vehicle. Bright, glossy photos of new cars and trucks adorned the walls, along with lists of base prices, down payments, finance charges, and accessories and their costs and insurance advertisements. All the photos and pertinent information were generously furnished by a local car dealer (see fig. 1).

Nissan Model	MSRP*	
2-door SE Pathfinder	$21 814	
SE Maxima	$19 149	
Sentra SE Sport Coupe	$12 229	
GXE Stanza	$14 975	
SE King Cab Hardbody Truck 4 × 2	$12 599	
300 ZX	$27 900	

*Manufacturer's suggested retail price as of 1 January 1990; does not reflect any options, freight, or taxes

Fig. 1. Selected cars and their cost

Linda Moniuszko is a teacher of special education at Boiling Springs Junior High School, Spartanburg, SC 29303. She is particularly interested in practical problem-solving strategies and motivational techniques for reluctant learners.

After tempting the students with these beautiful vehicles, I presented each one with a checkbook and his or her first mock paycheck. Sample checkbooks and record books were obtained from a local bank. I began "paying" my students the minimum wage for attending mathematics class. Raises were awarded for improved behavior, outstanding performance on tests and assignments, and cooperation and enthusiasm. Students were given a worksheet on which to record all important information about the car of their choice. We began by identifying the sales price, which varied for each student because each had decided to purchase a different model of car. Next we calculated the state sales tax and decided on a down payment. I advised the class that their down payment had to be at least $300. We then calculated monthly payment schedules over various amounts of time (see fig. 2).

Name _____

1. What is the price of the car you want to buy? _____
2. What is 5% of the price of your car? _____
3. Add the 5% sales tax to the price of your car. Total: _____
4. Your down payment will be _____.
5. What amount will you need to borrow? _____
6. Monthly payments over 12 months would be _____.
7. Monthly payments over 24 months would be _____.
8. Monthly payments over 36 months would be _____.
9. Monthly payments over 48 months would be _____.
10. Monthly payments over 60 months would be _____.
11. Monthly payments over 72 months would be _____.
12. At a 4.9% annual percentage rate (APR), what would be the finance charges on your car? _____
13. At a 7.9% annual percentage rate (APR), what would be the finance charges on your car? _____

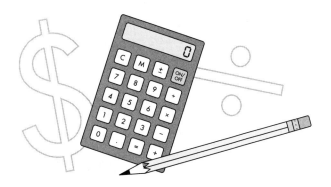

Fig. 2. Steps for calculating monthly payments

The long division turned out to be extremely stressful. My students had received instruction in this skill many times in previous years; however, they claimed it was too difficult. So while the class worked independently, I assisted each individual in completing the division. They did the mathematics; I just talked them through each step. I also rewarded each with a small treat after the worksheet had been completed successfully. Students who had not yet finished begged for me to work with them next. This year we will use newly purchased calculators for the more tedious calculations.

They do the math; I talk them through it.

Students deposited their paycheck weekly, saving enough money to make a down payment on the car of their choice. The first check they wrote was to a mock loan company for the down payment on their car. Monthly payment schedules were determined on the basis of their income and the number of months required to finance the cost of their chosen car. Finance charges were added, as well as insurance fees. Students were responsible for maintaining their own check record book, making "deposits" on payday and "deductions" when monthly checks were written to the Boiling Springs Junior High Loan Company or insurance companies.

Probably the most challenging task facing each student was to determine whether the car of their dreams could be purchased on a minimum-wage income. Students calculated their first weekly paycheck on the basis of the current minimum wage. I was surprised to observe the shocked expressions on their faces. Minimum wage for seven hours of school, five days a week, came to just a little over one hundred dollars. They thought their income was going to be a lot more than that. One major benefit of this teaching approach was to impress on remedial students the importance of staying in school. Too many of my students were counting the days until they could drop out. I am hopeful that "reality math" will help to keep some of them in school. The buying power of a minimum-wage job can be viewed more realistically in light of this experience.

Reality math stresses the importance of staying in school.

Reality-math pursuits continue throughout the school year and include ordinary daily consumer activities, such as eating out, purchasing groceries, and holiday shopping. I often supply a menu or catalog for each student and then allow them to make up problems for the class to solve. Each student determines which items to purchase. The class then totals the bill, adds sales tax, and computes change from large-denomination bills.

Often the problems my students come up with are more difficult to solve than the ones I write. They furtively grin and compete with each other in trying to devise the longest and most involved calculations.

One morning my students ordered lunch for the class from our favorite drive-in restaurant (see fig. 3). On another occasion, I developed the problems and students employed all the basic mathematical processes necessary to solve them (see fig. 4). Around Thanksgiving, students shopped for groceries from newspaper

BEACON DRIVE-IN

. . . there is only one Beacon!

PLENTIES

(with Potatoes and Onions)

Beef-A-Plenty	4.00	Hamburger Steak-A-Plenty	4.50
Beef and Cheese-A-Plenty	4.50	Chili Cheese w/Bacon-A-Plenty	4.50
Hash-A-Plenty	4.00	Cheeseburger-A-Plenty	4.00
Hash and Cheese-A-Plenty	4.50	Sliced Chicken-A-Plenty	4.00
Sliced Pork-A-Plenty	4.00	Breast on a Bun-A-Plenty	4.00
Ham-A-Plenty	4.00	Country Ham and Cheese-A-Plenty	4.50
Ham and Cheese-A-Plenty	4.50	Filet of Chicken-A-Plenty	4.00
Steak-A-Plenty	4.00	Country Ham-A-Plenty	4.00
World's Fair-A-Plenty	5.00	Bacon, Lettuce and Tomato-A-Plenty	4.00
Beacon Burger-A-Plenty	5.00	Club-A-Plenty	5.00
Burger-A-Plenty	4.00	Hot Dog-A-Plenty	4.50
Chili Burger-A-Plenty	4.00	Catfish Sandwich-A-Plenty	4.00
Chili Cheese-A-Plenty	4.00	Perch Sandwich-A-Plenty	4.00
Double Chili Cheese w/Bacon-A-Plenty	5.50	Flounder Sandwich-A-Plenty	4.00
Double Chili Cheese-A-Plenty	5.00	1/4 Fry-A-Plenty	4.00
Double Cheeseburger-A-Plenty	5.00	1/2 Fry-A-Plenty	5.00

BREAKFAST BISCUITS

Ham Biscuit	1.25	Steak & Egg Biscuit	2.00
Sausage Biscuit	1.00	Jelly Biscuit	.50
Bacon Biscuit	1.00	Ham & Egg Biscuit	1.50
Cheese & Egg Biscuit	1.00	Sausage & Egg Biscuit	1.50
Egg Biscuit	.80	Bacon & Egg Biscuit	1.50
Steak Biscuit	1.50	Bacon, Egg & Cheese Biscuit	1.75

DRINKS

Iced Tea	.70	Lemonade	.80
Hot Tea	.50	Cherry Lemonade	.90
Coffee	.50	Coke	.50 & .70
Large Coffee	.80	Vanilla Coke	.60 & .80
Sanka	.50	Chocolate Coke	.60 & .80
Hot Chocolate	.50 & .80	Cherry Coke	.60 & .80
Sweet Milk	.50 & .80	Lemon Coke	.60 & .80
Chocolate Milk	.80	Diet Coke	.50 &.70
Chocolate Milk with Ice Cream	1.00 & 1.50	Cherry Sprite	.60 & 80
Buttermilk	.80	Tea, 1/2 gallon	1.50
Milk Shakes	1.50	Tea, gallon	2.25
Malt-A-Plenty	1.75	Lemonade, gallon	3.00
Orange Juice	.50 & 80	Lemonade, 1/2 gallon	2.00
		Coffee, gallon w/cups, cream & sugar	3.00

DESSERTS

Banana Split	3.50	Fried Pies	.70
Nut Sundae	2.25	Strawberry Shortcake	2.25
Hot Fudge Sundae	2.25	Super Star	4.50
Hot Fudge Nut Sundae	2.25	Pig's Dinner	7.50
Strawberry Sundae	2.25	Whole Pecan Pies	5.00
Pineapple Sundae	2.25	Slice	.85

Fig. 3

Permission to publish given by John White, owner of Beacon Drive-In

Terrell Photography

Name ________________________

Lunch at the Beacon

1. You and three friends are going to share a banana split. How much will each of you pay? __________
2. You order ten small cherry Cokes. How much will you have to pay? __________
3. Two people share the 1/2 fried chicken. How much will each person pay? __________
4. Eight people each want one egg biscuit and one large coffee for breakfast. How much will their bill be? __________
5. Mr. Mullinax, our principal, orders five shrimp baskets. How much will he pay? __________ Mr. Mullinax leaves a tip of 15%. How much is his tip? __________
6. Coach Green offers to split the cost of the shrimp baskets with Mr. Mullinax. How much will each pay? __________
7. You order Double Chili Cheese-A-Plenty, a chocolate milk shake, and a slice of apple pie. How much will the meal cost? __________ You give Mr. White $15.00. How much change will you get back? __________
8. Six people are going to share a gallon of tea. How much will each one pay? __________
9. Ms. Moniuszko buys a small order of french fries for each student in the class. She has twenty students. How much will the fries cost? __________

Fig. 4. Problems based on the Beacon Drive-In menu (fig. 3)

advertisements. A turkey and all the trimmings were "bought" in quantity, so practice in multiplication was required, as well as computing sales tax and making change. The holidays afforded the opportunity to shop by catalog, and the New Year presented the perfect occasion to make a resolution to go on a class diet. Students figured the caloric intake of meals and then "reduced" by calculating calories burned through various forms of exercise. I began by preparing a list of foods, in alphabetical order, along with the corresponding caloric value of each per serving (table 1). I then listed different kinds of exercise with the number of calories each expends per minute (table 2). The students worked on some problems that challenged and amused them (see fig. 5).

Table 1. Calories of Popular Foods

Food	Calories
Apple	90
Bacon (1 strip)	50
Banana	130
Beans (green—1 cup)	30
Beef (roast—3 oz.)	165
Biscuit	130
Bread (1 slice)	70
Cake (chocolate—1 slice)	300
Candy (chocolate bar)	300
(jelly beans)	65
(lollipop)	215
Carrot	40
Catsup	20
Cereal (unsweetened—1 cup)	100
Cheese (American)	105
Chicken (fried)	465
Cookies (chocolate chip)	50
(marshmallow)	30
(oatmeal)	85
(Oreo)	40
Corn (1 ear)	100
Doughnut	150
Egg	80
Ice cream (1 cup)	130
Juice (apple—6 oz.)	115
(orange—6 oz.)	110
Milk (white, skim—8 oz.)	81
(chocolate)	210
Pancakes (1)	55
Peanut butter (3 oz.)	540
Pies (apple—1 slice)	325
(cherry—1 slice)	420
(pecan—1 slice)	670
Pizza (1 slice)	245
Pork (3 oz.)	300
Potatoes (french fries)	140
(mashed)	95
Rice (1 cup)	185
Soft drinks (cola)	105
Soup (chicken noodle—1 cup)	50
(tomato—1 cup)	90
(vegetable—1 cup)	80
Tea with milk and sugar	30
Waffle (1)	210
Watermelon (1 slice)	115

Table 2. Number of Calories Burned per Minute by Activity

Activity	Number of calories
Reading	1
Sleeping	1
Gardening	3
Bicycling	4
Bowling	4
Golfing	4
Swimming	5
Walking	5
Dancing	6
Tennis	7
Running	15

Just before school let out for the summer, my students grew tired, hot, and distracted. I decided that we needed to look forward to a fabulous vacation. A local travel agent furnished beautiful cruise brochures featuring white-sand beaches, aqua-blue lagoons, and faraway-sounding names. The brochures were outdated and of no use to the travel agent, but my students didn't mind. Each student chose a destination of Cozumel, Jamaica, Martinique, Trinidad, or Tobago and then got to work. They calculated distances from Miami, fares based on double occupancy, discount prices for reservations made six months in advance, and how much money would be saved if they sailed during value season instead of peak season (see fig. 6). Although they couldn't actually go on the cruise, they enjoyed wishful thinking and were constructively engaged in mathematical problem solving during the last week of school.

The merchants in our community are of great assistance to me in developing reality-math activities. Wherever I go to shop, I look for price lists, advertisements, samples, codes, and menus. Most stores are very eager to share information with me and exceptionally generous in supplying anything they can to help. I also regularly use newspapers, catalogs, cookbooks, and magazines.

Name _____

New-Year Diet

Each New Year, thousands of people make a resolution to lose weight. Help these calorie counters with their diet.

1. Chuck awakens ravenous and eats a huge breakfast. How many calories will he consume if he eats these foods?

   2 strips of bacon   _____
   1 waffle   _____
   2 eggs   _____
   1 glass of orange juice   _____
   1 banana   _____
                   Total   _____

2. Chuck decides to get some exercise and work off his big breakfast. He plays golf for 30 minutes and tennis for 30 minutes. How many calories does he burn while exercising? _____

3. Olivia indulges her sweet tooth while out with her friends. How many calories will she take in if she eats the following?

   1 scoop of chocolate ice cream   _____
   3 chocolate-chip cookies   _____
   1 piece of pecan pie   _____
   1 chocolate candy bar   _____
                        Total   _____

4. Olivia gardens for an hour, then takes an hour's nap. How many calories will she burn? _____

5. Harry is starving. For supper he eats these foods. What is his caloric intake?

   3 helpings of roast beef   _____
   1 cup of corn   _____
   2 cups of green beans   _____
   1 bowl of tomato soup   _____
   1 glass of milk   _____
   1 biscuit   _____
                   Total   _____

6. Harry cuts an impressive figure on the dance floor. If he dances for four hours straight, how many calories will he burn? _____

Fig. 5. Questions for dieters

Name _____

1. On which ship are you going to sail? _____
2. How many days will you cruise? _____
3. At which islands will you stop? _____
4. How many miles will you travel while on your voyage? _____
5. During value season, how much will your cabin cost? _____
6. How much is 5% sales tax on your fare? _____
7. What is your total cost for the cruise? _____
8. If you paid your fare in four equal monthly installments, what would each payment be? _____
9. If you book your reservations early, you may deduct 20% off the fare. What is 20% of your fare? _____
10. How much would you pay for the cruise if you make your reservations six months in advance? _____
11. A rich uncle offers to pay for half your trip if you book early. How much will your uncle pay? _____

Fig. 6. Questions based on dream-cruise vacation

Reality-math activities present an opportunity to use whole numbers, decimals, and fractions. The activities involve a multitude of mathematical processes. Students are required to determine which process is the most appropriate one to use in a given situation. Often more than one step is required to solve a problem. Reality-math activities are used to augment the district's regular mathematics curriculum, not supplant it. Thus, by experiencing reality math, my students experience real-life problem-solving situations and prepare themselves as future consumers.

Bibliography

Bitner, Joe, and M. Elizabeth Partridge. "'Stocking Up' on Mathematics Skills." *Arithmetic Teacher* 38 (March 1991): 4–7.

Fay, Nancy, and Catherine Tsairides. "Metric Mall." *Arithmetic Teacher* 37 (September 1989): 6–11.

Gerver, Robert, and Richard J. Sgroi. "Sound Foundations: A Mathematical Game Simulation That 'Stanza Part' from the Rest." *Mathematics Teacher* 76 (December 1983): 660–63, 680.

Grocki, John M., and Irving A. Robbins. "Sharing Teaching Ideas: The Gymnasium—a Dynamic Classroom for Teaching Slope." *Mathematics Teacher* 83 (November 1990): 636–37.

Isaacs, Carol M., and Julie Fisher. "Princess Di, Spaghettios, and M&Ms." *Mathematics Teacher* 83 (October 1990): 545.

Moses, Barbara. "Developing Spatial Thinking in the Middle Grades: Designing a Space Station." *Arithmetic Teacher* 37 (February 1990): 59–63.

Rees, Rebecca D. "Station Break: A Mathematics Game Using Cooperative Learning and Role Playing." *Arithmetic Teacher* 37 (April 1990): 8–12.

Sanders, Hal. "When Are We Ever Gonna Have to Use This?" *Mathematics Teacher* 73 (January 1980): 7–16.

Spalt, Sandra. "Spalt Incorporated: An Applied Mathematics Simulation." *Mathematics Teacher* 79 (September 1986): 414–17.

Weathers, J. S. "Students Can Discover the Occupational Link with Mathematics." *Mathematics Teacher* 82 (November 1989): 588–94. ▲

Math around the Clock

by

Jeane M. Joyner

"Math around the Clock" was to begin as a regular school day, but many last-minute preparations were carried out to get ready for the after-school events (table 1). Language arts classes polished the scripts for skits and practiced stunts while the principal and school secretary stored the food donations that were brought for supper, breakfast, and snacks. Because the schedule for "Math around the Clock" was a busy one and the school staff was small, much planning and preparation of materials were necessary.

Good programs in elementary school mathematics should include activities for building enthusiasm for mathematics as well as teaching basic concepts. Special projects offer teachers opportunities to motivate their students while children practice computational skills. When a mathematics activity involves children in ways in which each individual can be successful and feel that his or her contribution is as valuable as the next child's, then the students feel good about themselves and about mathematics. Teachers can capture the interest of children who are not self-motivated and build enthusiasm for mathematics in the classroom through projects.

"Math around the Clock" was one elementary school's special project designed to enrich the mathematics program for third-grade students. Focusing on mathematics in settings that held little resemblance to regular school activities, the project involved field-day activities, workshops, a song and stunt program, movies, and lots of food. Applications of mathematics were demonstrated in a variety of events that kept the children busy until the lights were turned out at midnight.

The adventure began when the students arrived at school on a Friday morning in May with sleeping bags, pillows, and an assortment of stuffed animals for a giant slumber party that generated enthusiasm with a capital E. The biggest challenge for the teachers was containing the excitement of the third graders.

Math and Art: blending colors in different proportions for icing and drinks

Table 1. Overnight Schedule

Friday

9 A.M.–3 P.M.	Regular school day
3:15 P.M.	Snack
3:30 P.M.	Field day: new games
5:50 P.M.	Hot-dog supper
6:30–9:30 P.M.	Workshops
9:30 P.M.	Songs and stunts
10:15 P.M.	Snack
10:30 P.M.	Movies
11:30 P.M.	Ready for bed
Midnight	Lights out!

Saturday

7:00 A.M.	Rise and shine: clean-up duties
7:30 A.M.	Breakfast
8–9 A.M.	Complete projects, videotape, cartoons
9 A.M.	Parents pick up students

When students in other grades left on Friday afternoon, the third graders took their sleeping bags and bed rolls to their assigned classrooms. Sleeping areas were chosen by two main criteria: they were the only carpeted areas in the school and they had bathrooms inside the rooms so that middle-of-the-night forays into the halls were unnecessary.

Jeane Joyner is a mathematics resource teacher in the Wake County Schools, Raleigh, NC 27608. She has served as the chairman of North Carolina's Math Education Week and a member of the state's Mathematics Curriculum Improvement Project and likes to create mathematical games.

Refreshments were served to students before the afternoon field day began. The mathematics used in sports was emphasized as students measured lanes for dashes and relays and discussed scorekeeping before the actual events began. The geometry of tumbling became apparent when students were instructed to form triangles with their heads and arms in performing headstands. Balance was improved if elbows were kept at right angles. Bodies were tucked into ellipses or circles, and students bent to make prescribed angles in tumbling routines.

Among the favorite field-day activities were the parachute events. In one event students numbered themselves from one to ten around the circle. When the teacher called out "three," students whose number was one less than three changed places. In another event the students with numbers that were the difference between two other numbers called out by the teacher changed places. For example, if the teacher said "fifteen minus seven," all the students with number eight changed places.

Other field-day activities stressed sequencing, following two- and three-step directions, timing, and directionality. Parents volunteered to help with athletic events and serve frozen treats in late afternoon. Twelve treats to a box and seventy children—do you know how many boxes were needed?

The heart of "Math around the Clock" was the series of workshops that began immediately after the hot-dog supper (table 2). Led by teachers and volunteers from the community, the workshops illustrated mathematical applications in informative and creative activities. Early in the week, each child had chosen seven workshops of individual interest from the eighteen sessions that were offered. Teachers then scheduled the children for four of their seven choices, balancing the sessions and limiting the participants in each workshop. Rosters for each session were typed and posted as a means of accounting for all seventy children. The children received schedules with the names, locations, and times of the sessions they chose.

One of the most popular workshops was "Math Magic." Students learned some of the many surprises found in hands-on geometry and special tricks that can be performed with certain combinations of numbers. If two even numbers are combined, is the sum an odd or an even number? Is this result true in just one example or is it true all the time? What happens when an odd number and an even number are added together? What about adding two odd numbers?

In another "Math Magic" activity, ropes looped through each other and tied to the wrists of two children required physical

Math Magic: Is it possible to untangle ourselves?

problem solving to untangle. Led by a consultant from the North Carolina State Department of Public Instruction, the "Math Magic" session was one of the few that was repeated.

Aerobic dancing kept students busy counting beats and doing fancy footwork to their favorite records. Many children did not realize that rhythms were mathematical. This discovery led to a good discussion of how to take a pattern such as AABBA and translate it in many different ways. The same pattern was illustrated by body positions, clapping patterns, and dance steps, and it was repeated many times to the popular records.

The stitchery session and knots workshop required students to measure the yarn and rope used in their evening workshops. The knots section, led by a local scouting leader, included children who had never participated in scouting as well as those who had camping experiences to share. Students estimated and then folded to find halves, thirds, and fourths of their ropes. In the stitchery workshop most of the children stitched their initials; students first graphed the letters and used coordinates to locate starting points on needlework canvas.

"Colorful Math" was a hands-on experience conducted by the art teacher. Students mixed granulated soft-drink colors in different proportions for rainbow punch to match cookies that had been iced in shades created by the children from canned icing. If two parts of this shade are mixed with one part of that color, what color do you think will result?

The sustained enthusiasm that the sign language workshop created was surprising. Not only were students interested in learning to communicate with their hands, they also were intrigued with learning how a hearing child helps her deaf parents. The leaders of the workshop, a ten-year-old girl whose parents are deaf and a hearing adult who teaches sign language, taught the students words and phrases, numbers, and their own names. Students learned to count and perform computations in sign language. Later in the evening, "good nights" were given in sign language across the classrooms.

Table 2. Workshop Choices

Aerobic Dancing	Balloon Animals
Knots	Math Magic
Sign Language	Estimate with Calculators
Crime Prevention	Makeup
Colorful Math	String Art
Rubik's Cube	Making Fraction Bars
Environmental Math	Stitchery
Making Geoboards	Tinker Toy Construction
Badge and Chain Making	Math Board Games

As a part of the badge-and-chain workshop, children colored their own "Math around the Clock" name tags (fig. 1). They also linked paper clips together in patterns, which were carefully stored in milk cartons. The segments were to be part of the million-link paper-clip chain that was a schoolwide project. Nine small clips were linked with a tenth, larger paper clip to facilitate counting by tens. Yarn marked the large clips that designated 100 clips in a chain. Some children created patterns for younger students to copy in their regular mathematics classes (e.g., small, small, small, large or large, large, small, large).

Fig. 1

Evenly spacing and hammering the nails to make one's own geoboard was a noisy project. Third graders measured and marked places for each nail. Banged fingers aside, students found that driving twenty-five nails straight into the boards was not an easy task. Other frustrations occurred in the string-art class, when the students drove nails into 8 in. × 8 in. boards that had been donated by a local contractor. Frustrations turned to fascination, however, as the straight lines of string produced ovals and curves in the pictures.

In the session on Tinker Toys, the constructions involved a review of the geometric shapes students had been learning during the past year. Challenged to construct something with gears or moving parts, students worked in pairs to build elaborate designs. The large workspace and unlimited access to materials gave creative minds a stimulating atmosphere. During the workshop, students explained their structures to each other as well as to the visitors from the local newspaper. Stick-on labels with alphabet letters named the points of each construction.

The popular Rubik's cube workshop included instruction from several students and adult "experts." The middle school teacher who volunteered to lead the section surprised the group with homemade brownies decorated like the cubes. Different levels of

Cube Designs: Can everyone make a cross or get one side a solid color? Who can solve the cube?

expertise were exhibited as some students worked to get one side correct while others were completing the third and fourth sides.

Is it possible to compare the costs of makeup when bottles are of different sizes and shapes? Lively discussions of cost per ounce and gram occurred as girls cleansed and beautified their faces in the makeup workshop. Consumer education had a very real meaning to these eight- and nine-year-old students who were becoming aware of magazine and television advertisements for cosmetics. Should allowances be raised so that students could afford to buy makeup? Third graders thought they would need more money in the next few years for these necessities.

North Carolina's crime prevention van came to the school in the evening with facts and figures about crime in the state and displays about crime prevention. Being able to read graphs enabled students to understand much of the information presented in the display. McGruff, the crime-biting dog (a costumed adult), accompanied the workshop leader, who brought video equipment to record the activities. On Saturday morning the half-hour tape was almost as good as the original events had been. All the children were excited about seeing themselves on television.

Clay Pizzas for Fraction Fun: Which is greater, 1/2 a pizza or 1/4 of one?

Some workshops were unusual in character; the session involving balloon animals was unique. Other workshops were more familiar, such as the calculator section, but all the workshops offered the students a wide variety of choices and opportunities for success. The sessions were valuable to students for their affective as well as their cognitive gains.

The evening's entertainment was the stunt and talent show. Many children spend weeks in sumer camps, but others never have opportunities to sit around a campfire, perform stunts, and sing. Since the ninety-degree weather was too warm for a campfire, the song and stunt program was held in the air-conditioned learning center. Each class entertained the group with rowdy skits, tricks, and songs learned especially for the evening.

After a late snack, movies were shown to calm down the group. By midnight all students were tucked into sleeping bags or bed rolls, and soon the last whispers gave in to snores.

Clean-up, breakfast, last-minute work on projects, videotapes, and cartoons filled Saturday morning until parents arrived to pick up the children at 9:00 A.M. Within an hour the school was deserted, back to its usual Saturday morning stillness.

DOING IT AGAIN

Will there be another "Math around the Clock"? Certainly! Immediately after the weekend, the second graders began asking if they could have a mathematics overnight next year. Third-grade students and their parents many times expressed their enthusiasm for the workshops and the giant "sleep in." Fourth graders complained about being neglected! The teachers began a list of dos and don'ts for next year.

Organizing a mathematics overnight is not difficult, but it does require a willing staff and many volunteers. Classroom teachers should not be asked to go from a full day of teaching to leading workshops, cooking meals and snacks, and supervising an enormous pajama party. Twenty-four hours is a long work day.

Parental volunteers, teachers from other levels, and friends in the community can work for a few hours if one coordinator keeps a

String Art: Straight lines created designs with curves. Measuring and driving nails are not easy tasks.

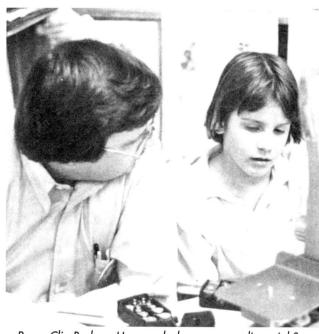

Paper Clip Badges: How much does a paper clip weigh? How much does a box of paper clips weigh? The North Carolina Bureau of Weights helped us decide.

Sign Language: Numbers are possible in sign language, too.

master schedule to ensure that all activities are covered. College students, grandparents, consultants from the state's education department, retired business people, local media personalities, craftspeople, and agricultural extension agents are among the resources for workshop leaders.

"Math around the Clock" was planned as a special project in mathematics, but many teachers in the school joined in the fun. Language arts classes were occupied with skit writing, public-speaking practices, and synonym drills. During the weeks following the project, children wrote thank-you letters to the volunteers who conducted the workshops and the parents who donated the food. Little snatches of sign language to friends across the room and moments of aerobic dance told of lasting effects of the workshops. Third-grade teachers felt that increased interest and enthusiasm for mathematics was definitely generated.

Whether a mathematics overnight will improve a student's knowledge of the number facts or provide insight needed to perform long division is doubtful, but among the purposes of projects, whether they are fairs or carnivals, contests or displays, are attempts to create enthusiasm for mathematics and to build positive feelings about oneself and school. "Math around the Clock" fulfilled all these purposes. ▲

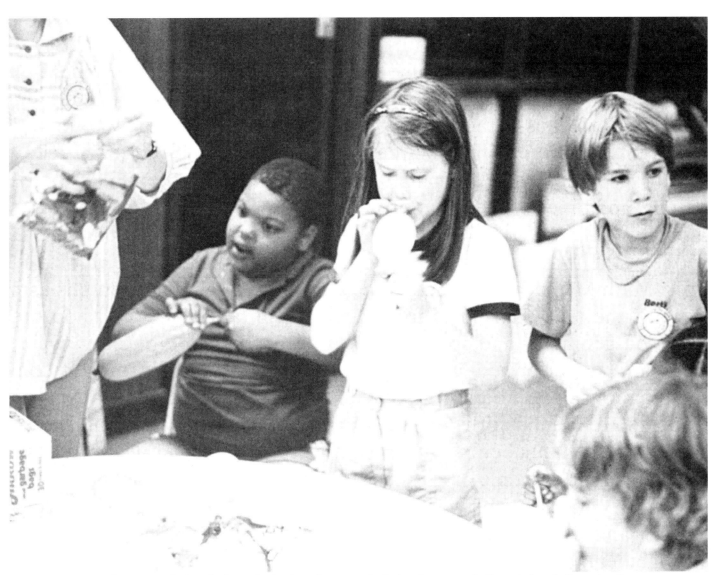

Balloon Animals: long balloons for bodies, short ones for limbs. How many balloons in four balloon dogs?

Newspapers: Connecting the Mathematics Classroom to the World

by

Susan R. O'Connell

Students need to see when and how mathematics can be used, rather than be promised that someday they will use it" (NCTM 1989, 35). The newspaper, as a classroom resource, allows a perfect opportunity to reveal to students the role of mathematics in their lives. When scanning a newspaper, students can find endless applications of classroom-taught skills. The use of money in advertising, the graphs of business profits, the data found in weather maps, the fractions in recipes, and the use of statistics in sports all show mathematics at work. A closer look through the newspaper reveals statements about the probability of events or current economic trends. Statistics appear in many articles, and graphics illustrate shapes, symmetry, and angles. Using the newspaper in the elementary classroom directly supports the NCTM's curriculum standards by connecting classroom-taught skills and the real world.

Measuring by column inch is one way to compute advertising costs.

The curriculum standards also view a problem-solving approach as being critical for effective mathematics instruction. Newspapers contain real information that can form the basis of classroom problem-solving activities. Classroom activities created from data from articles, graphics, or advertisements can motivate students because they contain real facts rather than the "made up" data in textbook exercises (fig 1). Sports, food, and entertainment are appealing topics that will interest students. The wide range of mathematics that is represented in the newspaper is a problem-solving opportunity just waiting to be tapped.

Newspaper activities also give students practice reading, thinking, discussing, and writing about mathematics tasks (fig. 2). These activities lend themselves to group work where students can collaborate to plan, execute, and evaluate the activity. Ask students to collect and organize data, set up tables or graphs to display their data, interpret data orally or in writing, or use the data to make decisions or justify arguments. These types of activities give students practice in communicating mathematically, which is another recommendation of the NCTM's curriculum standards (1989).

Activities lend themselves to group work.

Many newspapers sponsor Newspaper in Education (N.I.E.) programs to assist teachers in developing lessons. In addition, many independent teacher resources can be purchased through educational supply stores. Teachers, however, who begin to look to the newspaper as a source for real-life-mathematics problems will over time gain expertise and confidence in designing their own problems that relate specifically to their classroom lessons and render practical experience for almost any skill (fig. 3). The following are some sample newspaper activities and ideas for related or extension activities.

Susan O'Connell is the reading specialist at Glenn Dale Elementary School in Glenn Dale, MD 20769. She is also a consultant with the Educational Services Department of the Washington Post. *She has been involved in many projects that focus on integrating mathematics and language arts.*

Every 57 minutes in the United States, an underage drinker is involved in a traffic fatality. A recent federal report is urging a crackdown on teen-age drinking and driving.

(Excerpted from the Prince George's Sentinel, 13 May 1993, C-1)

Estimate the number of underage drinkers involved in traffic fatalities in one year. Describe how you got your answer.

> First I rounded 57 minutes to 1 hour. Then I said that there are 24 hours in a day. After that I said that there are 365 days in a year, so I multiplied 365 and 24 and got 8,760 teenagers.

Write one sentence that you think should be included in the federal report.

> 8,760 teenagers are in drunk driving accidents every year. This is too many people, parents, talk to your children about how dangerous alcohol is.

Fig. 1. Solving a problem involving underage drinking and driving

USING ADVERTISEMENTS

Elementary classroom teachers devote much time and effort to teaching such money-related skills as estimating costs, calculating exact costs, and finding correct change. Depending on the students' level of skill, many problem-solving opportunities can be presented using data from the newspaper. For example, using food advertisements, students can be asked to work in pairs or small groups to solve problems similar to the following.

Planning a Luncheon

Because your mathematics team has worked so well together, you have earned a special luncheon. Your team is responsible for planning the menu. Your group may not spend more than $25, and the food you select must feed 6 people. Decide together what your menu will be.

Students can select food items from advertisements that interest them. Students must decide about the quantity of items needed to feed six people. They might want to estimate the cost to get a rough idea of what they can afford to buy. Calculators can be used to determine the actual cost. Ask students to justify their choices in writing or to present them as a group. Unlike traditional textbook exercises, this type of open-ended situation allows students to approach the problem in their own unique way. Each group of students will likely have a very different solution to the problem.

Water Ways

[C]lean, fresh water isa precious resource worth thinking about. This area usually has plenty. But that's not true all over the world. If the Washington area experiences a drought, water used to wash clothes, flush toilets and sprinkle lawns may be restricted. But there is still plenty to drink. However, in some areas of the world including the Middle East, parts of Africa, much of central Asia and some of the American West, water is truly scarce. Every drop counts.

According to the National Geographic Society, which launched a freshwater awareness campaign last month, water covers 71 percent of Earth's surface. Of that amount, 97 percent is salty. Two percent is locked up in ice. Only 1 percent of all Earth's water is liquid fresh water. People depend on water. Along with the oxygen in the air they breath, they need it to survive. In fact, humans can live only a few days without water.

Water makes up 50 to 70 percent of a person's weight. It plays a vital role in chemical changes that keep the body functioning. It's a big part of blood, helps digest food and assists in lubricating joints so people can move easily. Water washes harmful waste products from the body in the form of urine. And as water evaporates through the skin's pores, it helps keep body temperature steady.

(Excerpted from a much larger article in the Washington Post, 7 December 1993)

Water Ways

The main idea of this article is __Water is precious, so don't waste any.__

Look back in the article to find out what percent of a person's weight is water weight. (It will be a *range*.)

> 50 to 70%

How much do you weigh? __70 lbs.__

Use what you know about percents to find out how much of your body weight is water weight. You may choose any value within the range for your calculations. Be sure to show your work.

50% of 70 = 35 lbs.

$$\begin{array}{r} 35 \\ 2\overline{)70} \\ -6 \\ \hline 10 \\ -10 \\ \hline 0 \end{array}$$

Are surprised at the answer? Why? __No, because I drink lots of water and other drinks but just about in every drink there's water.__

Fig. 2. Newspaper lessons include reading, writing, and discussing mathematics.

Select a restaurant that has an all-you-can-eat menu on Mother's Day. How much would it cost your family to eat in this restaurant? Explain who will be going and how you figured out the cost.

It will cost $35.80. I have two adults, and they will pay $10.95 each and I have no sisters and 1 brother that is 12 years old and will have to pay $6.95. I have to pay $6.95 because I am 10 years old. I am going to get the money from my allowance.

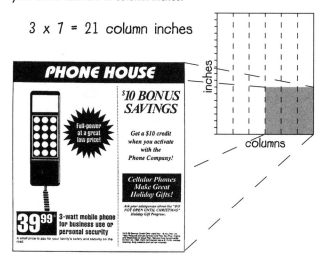

Fig. 3. An activity to reinforce column addition

As students learn about sales tax, problems similar to the following will offer practice.

Help!

It is your mother's birthday, and your father has asked you to help pick out a gift for her. He has given you $50 to spend. Look through the newspaper advertisements to find her gift. You may buy as many items as you want, but don't go over $50 and don't forget to include the 5 percent sales tax.

Students may choose to buy two blouses that cost $19.99 each, one bracelet costing $37.50, or a list of many smaller items. Estimation can be used to get an initial idea of how many items can be purchased, but an exact calculation, including sales tax, will be needed. Teachers might also like students to specify how much change Dad will be receiving when the shopping spree is over. A variation of this problem might include students' being notified that they have won a $25.00, $50.00, or $100.00 shopping spree, with materials being selected from the newspaper.

INTEGRATING SKILLS

Using the newspaper helps students to view mathematics as a series of related skills. Rather than viewing fractions, decimals, monetary amounts, and measurement as isolated topics, students can see how these mathematics skills appear together in real problem situations. Problems similar to the one in figure 4 require the

How Much Will It Cost?

Calculating the cost of a business advertisement requires finding the area of the advertisement, which is sold on the basis of how much space it occupies in the newspaper. Rather than calculate the area in square inches, newspapers calculate size in column inches.

A newspaper page is usually divided into six equal columns; rows are divided into one-inch-tall increments. An advertisement that is 2 columns wide and 8 inches tall has an area of 16 column inches. An advertisement that is 4 columns wide and 10 inches tall has an area of 40 column inches.

1. Glue your advertisement to this page, then calculate the area of your advertisement in column inches.

$3 \times 7 = 21$ column inches

2. An advertisement in the *Washington Post* costs about $160 per column inch. Calculate the cost of your ad. (Of course you may use a calculator!)

21 column inches x $160.00 = $3360.00

3. Find an ad with a similar area in the *Bowie Blade News*. An advertisement in this community newspaper costs about $18 per column inch. Calculate the cost of placing the advertisement.

The area of my ad __22 column inches__

The cost of my ad __$396.00__

4. Calculate the difference in cost between the two ads.

$2964.00

5. Explain why you think one newspaper charges so much more that the other for placing a business advertisement. Is the difference in cost justifiable?

I think the Washiton Post should be able to charge more than the Bowie Blade because more people see the Washinton Post. Also, Yes, the difference in cost is justifiable because, a lot more people see the Washinto Post. In fact, the hole country sees the Washiton Post. My question is how many people does the Washington Post deliver to?

Fig. 4. Some problems require using several mathematics skills.

knowledge of several mathematics skills. As students calculate the cost of a business advertisement, they are required to use a new formula first to determine the area and then to calculate the cost on the basis of the area of the advertisement. Students must apply what they have learned about measurement, monetary amounts, and arithmetic to find an effective way to solve the problem.

Once students have determined the cost of the advertisement, they might be asked to find one that they think is more or less expensive. To do so, students must predict which advertisements have smaller or larger areas. Teachers might want to select some examples with different rectangular dimensions to challenge students' predictions. This activity may generate discussion about the high cost of business advertising. Students might want to appoint a group representative to call a local newspaper to find out the exact cost for business advertisements in their area. Investigating the newspaper's circulation might enrich the discussion by furnishing information about the number of people reading each advertisement. Students might then want to discuss or investigate the relationship between the cost of the advertisement and the newspaper's circulation.

CALCULATING TRAVEL COSTS

Teachers can capitalize on students' interest in automobiles and, at the same time, reinforce geography skills through the following problem.

Away We Go

Plan a trip to a city of your choice in the continental United States. Using the automobile advertisements, decide on a car for your trip. use a map to determine the distance you will travel, and research the current cost of gasoline and the estimated miles per gallon for the car you chose. Using all of the data you have collected, determine how much you will spend on gasoline during your trip.

Students may find a map and scale in the newspaper, possibly as part of the national weather map, or they may need to use a classroom map or atlas to determine the distance. Finding the current cost of gasoline and the estimated MPG for the car can be a homework assignment, since a few telephone calls are needed to gather the information. Students may decide to take a scenic route to their destination, stopping at cities on the way, or to follow one route to their destination and a different route on the way home. Students might be asked to write about why they have chosen their destination city; why they selected a specific car—good MPG or a station wagon to allow more room for luggage; or how they planned their trip, for example, which stops they will make on their journey or why they chose to follow a different route on the way home. This activity can be integrated into a geography lesson on the United States with students learning facts about their destination. Students will enjoy sharing their trips with their classmates.

UNDERSTANDING TEMPERATURES

The weather map and world and local temperature charts present opportunities for children to investigate temperatures. Simple activities like the following can help students gain a greater understanding of temperatures and weather.

What Will I Do Today?

Look at the weather map. Based on the current forecast, plan an after-school activity. Explain why it would be a good day for that specific activity. Consider the temperature, chance of precipitation, and wind conditions.

Find a city in another part of the country or world that has a difference in temperature of at least 20 degrees from that of your city. Where is that city located? What kind of after-school activities might the students of that city be planning? Why?

Finding cities on a world map and discussing the cause of temperature differences around the world forge a strong mathematics-and-science link. Students might plan a trip around the country or world and be asked to decide the types of clothing they should pack for their trip. The daily weather reports also offer students the opportunity to compare weather predictions with actual reported temperatures. Each day for a week, students could record temperature predictions and the actual high and low temperatures for that day. Students can use tables and graphs to display their data. Discussions about the accuracy of weather predictions will allow teachers to integrate science concepts into the mathematics lesson.

STUDENT-DESIGNED PROBLEMS

Once students have experience using information from the newspaper to solve mathematics problems, they can be challenged to write their own problems. Groups or pairs of students can scan the newspaper for information to use to create mathematics problems, which can be exchanged with other teams or used for daily classroom warm-ups (fig. 5). Helping students recognize for themselves the ways in which mathematics is a part of their lives is an ultimate goal of the elementary mathematics program.

HOME CONNECTION

Newspapers offer a unique home-school connection. Children are able to discuss classroom activities with parents who have read the same newspaper article at home. Newspapers can be sent home by the classroom teacher for additional reading or home assignments, and parent-child activities can be developed to supplement classroom lessons. Students might be asked to use the data in a carpet advertisement to determine the cost of carpeting their bedroom or to use the most current basketball statistics to select players for a "dream team." In addition, newspapers are available in many homes every day of the year. Once students become familiar with its format, they can refer to the newspaper on their own, even when school is not in session.

CONCLUSION

Newspapers are authentic materials that are current and interesting and allow extensive opportunities to reinforce and extend mathematics classroom teaching. They contain real data to make problem-solving activities come alive, afford opportunities for students to communicate mathematically, and connect the classroom and the real world.

Newspaper use integrates mathematics skills. Fractions and measurement are combined when working with recipes in the food section. Percents and averages are blended in sports statistics. Time and money are factors in making selections from the movie

Read the article and then see if you can answer team 2's questions.

Bay Bridge Walk Set for May 2

If you have ever had a hankering to walk across the Chesapeake Bay, plan to be on the 19th Annual Bay Bridge Walk and Bayfest on May 2 from 9 a.m. to 4 p.m.

Each year, the state closes one of the twin spans of the William Preston Lane Bridge (the Chesapeake Bay Bridge) and allows walkers to stroll across. The walk is 4.3 miles long. Drinking water is provided half way across.

Parking sites provide access to buses that shuttle walkers to the Eastern Shore side of the bridge to start the walk.

The parking sites are the Navy/Marine Corps Stadium in Annapolis; Anne Arundel Community College in Arnold; and the Chesapeake Bay Business Park on the Eastern Shore.

The Bayfest at nearby Sandy Point Park will offer entertainment, environmental information, exhibits, refreshments and more.

Admission to the walk and the Bayfest is $1 for anyone over the age of 6. For more information call (800) 541-9595.

(Excerpted from the *Prince George's Sentinel*, 29 April 1993)

---

1. How much will it cost your family to walk across the bridge? (I'm sure team 2 would like you to explain how you got your answer.)

   It would cost my family $4.00 because there are 4 people in my family over 6 years old.

2. How many miles do you have to walk before you can get a drink of water? (Tell me how you figured out this answer.)

   You would have to walk 2.15 miles before getting a drink of water. I divided 4.3 by 2 since the water is halfway across the walk.

Fig. 5. Students write and share their questions with classmates.

listings. Students who are involved in newspaper activities begin to see the connection among various mathematics skills and between mathematics and other subject areas. Science, social studies, and health studies can be taught in combination with mathematics skills. Reading is an integral part of each lesson, whether the student is processing diagrams, tables, maps, or graphs, or needs to read an article for a related mathematics activity. Writing activities help students express their thoughts and opinions about mathematics problems and activities.

Newspapers contain real data for problem solving.

"Connections should occur frequently enough to influence students' beliefs about the value of mathematics in society and its contribution to other disciplines. Regardless of what mathematics is being studied, students should have the opportunity to apply the mathematics they have learned to real-world situations that go beyond the usual textbook word problems" (NCTM 1991, 89–90). Using the newspaper as a mathematics resource gives students varied opportunities to solve real-world problems and offers them a glimpse of the many ways in which mathematics is a part of their lives and their futures.

Bibliography

Apelman, Maja, and Julie King. *Exploring Everyday Math.* Portsmouth, N.H.: Heinemann Educational Books, 1993.

Boober, Becky Hayes, Jacqueline P. Mitchell, and Caroll Jordan Hatcher. *Measuring Up in Mathematics.* Chester Springs, Pa.: C. J. Hatcher & Assoc., 1990.

Czepiel, James, and Edward Esty. "Mathematics in the Newspaper." *Mathematics Teacher* 73 (November 1980): 582–86.

National Council of Teachers of Mathematics. *Curriculum and Evaluation Standards for School Mathematics.* Reston, Va.: The Council, 1989.

———. *Professional Standards for Teaching Mathematics.* Reston, Va.: The Council, 1991.

Additional Resources

Newspaper Association of America
529 14th Street, NW
Suite 440
Washington, DC 20045
(202) 638-4770

USA Today
Educational Development
1000 Wilson Boulevard
Arlington, VA 22229
(800) USA-0001

The *Washington Post*
Educational Services Department
1150 Fifteenth Street, NW
Washington, DC 20071-7300
(202) 334-4544 ▲

From the File: Record-Setting Word Problems

by

Robert J. Sovchik

Problem Solving

Record-Setting Word Problems

To help students learn to communicate about mathematics, my class of preservice teachers and I use a variety of interesting facts from the *Guinness Book of World Records* as stimulus material for elementary school students to create story problems.

The preservice teachers first locate fifteen interesting facts from the *Guinness Book of World Records*. They then present several of these unique, interesting facts to students in grades 4 through 7. Some sample word problems are also shown. The elementary school students then write story problems, with some revision work. Samples of the students' work follows:

- If Paul Lynch did 3857 one-arm pushups in five hours, how many could he do in seven hours?
- If Bill Cosby gets $92 million in two years, how much could he get in five years?
- If the largest pumpkin, weighing 671 pounds, was cut into seven equal pieces, how much would each piece weigh?
- If the heaviest dog in the world is 310 pounds and the next-heaviest is 14 pounds less, how much does the next-heaviest dog weigh?

Students enjoy the many strange and astounding facts that the *Guinness Book of World Records* contains and are motivated to approach this communication activity enthusiastically.

From the file of Robert J. Sovchik, University of Akron, Akron, OH 44325-4205 ▲

From the File:
If Only I Had a V-8

by

Winnie Peterson

Rational Numbers

If Only I Had a V-8

Assign students to cooperative groups and challenge them to list the eight vegetables found in Campbell's V-8 juice. When a group can list eight vegetables, tell how many choices are correct using a fraction, decimal, or percent equivalent. For example, if five of the eight are correct, respond that they have 5/8, 0.625, or 62 1/2 percent correct. Do not tell the students which ingredients are correct and do not translate the meaning of the fraction, decimal, or percent. The group then changes its original list of eight vegetables by taking away some vegetables and adding new ones. Each time a group presents a new list of eight vegetables, respond again with the appropriate fraction, decimal, or percent until the list is 100 percent correct. Treat the winners to a small can of V-8.

From the file of Winnie Peterson, Saint Joseph University, Philadelphia, PA 19131-1395 ▲

From the File:
Finding the Average with Frisbee Tosses

by

Mary E. Soles

Finding the Average with Frisbee Tosses

Each student throws a Frisbee six times. (This is a great activity for a warm day.) He or she counts the distance in "normal" walking steps. Each partner records the results, and then they switch roles.

Using a calculator students can then calculate the following: personal averages, partners' averages, girls' average, boys' average, and class average. Plot all data graphically.

Extension. Students could convert normal walking steps to meters, feet, or yards by measuring one normal step and multiplying.

From the file of Mary E. Soles, Northfield Elementary School, Ellicott City, MD 21043 ▲

A Practical Experience in Problem Solving: A "10 000" Display

by

Linda Bickerton-Ross

Recently, my third graders completed a project that involved estimating, problem solving, and counting as they explored number meaning. I discussed with them the third-grade mathematics curriculum requirement of understanding numbers up to 10 000. Acknowledging the difficulty of imagining numbers this large, I asked them what objects they might see together totaling this amount. They suggested such things as blades of grass, grains of sand, cornflakes, and pebbles. After listening to their suggestions I asked them if, as a class, they would like to bring 10 000 objects from home to the classroom. After an enthusiastic response, I asked them what we would need to consider in embarking on such a project. The students decided that the objects would have to be small and that we would have to decide how many objects each student would have to bring.

Since the students had recently worked with the "Guess and Check" (Lane County 1983) model of problem solving and their instincts told them they didn't have the skills to compute directly the amount each of them would have to bring, they quickly suggested the guess-and-check method to determine the amount. After they guessed their first number, I asked them how we could check to see if it was correct. They suggested that I add it fifteen times because we had fifteen third graders in the class. The resulting number was less than 10 000. After they suggested a higher number, I asked them if they would mind if I used multiplication to get the answer faster. They agreed we would get the same amount and that multiplication would save time. Gradually we worked up to 666, which totaled just below 10 000 when multiplied by 15. Next, they suggested 667, which totaled just over 10 000. Finally, they decided that each of them should bring 666 objects and that I should bring 10, in this way arriving at the total of 10 000.

The students' next question concerned whether each student should bring the same object or should be free to bring whatever he or she wanted. They thought it would be easier and more fun to bring whatever they wanted. We discussed the kinds of objects that might be suitable in terms of size and durability. We

Linda Bickerton-Ross teaches at the George Greenaway Elementary School in the Surrey School District, British Columbia. Her professional interests are in staff development and school improvement.

discussed how long we would need to complete this task and decided that four weeks would be sufficient. Each student's collection was to be brought in as soon as it was ready. After discussing criteria for containers, the group also decided that it would be important to have transparent containers if we were going to have a display.

During the final week, I asked the students how other people would be able to look at their displays and know for sure that they had each brought 666 objects. The students suggested grouping the objects by hundreds, tens, and ones. I then gave them class time to group their objects if they had not done so. After consulting with the class as to how we could share our project with other students, I divided a large bulletin-board space in the hall into fifteen sections using brightly colored wool as a divider. Each child was given a space for his or her display. At this point, one enterprising student decided to use plastic wrap as a container for the macaroni she had brought, and she proceeded to staple it to the wall. As others in the class followed suit, I put this first student in charge, along with the second student who had completed her individual display. They helped any other students who required assistance.

As the students completed their tasks, I gave them a 10 cm × 35 cm piece of colored tagboard on which to describe how they collected and grouped their objects (see table 1). I also asked for two volunteers to describe our class project on a large piece of tagboard stapled up beside the display. The "10 000 Display" consisted of a collection of beans, macaroni, rocks, paper dots punched by a hole puncher, dried peas, pencil stubs, rice, Lite Bright pegs, popcorn kernels, and even Sears catalog pages. The individuality of each section with its accompanying write-up aroused the curiosity of many passing students, causing animated discussions at recess and lunch time.

The students who took part in this project emerged with a more secure understanding of the value of 10 000 through the original guessing and checking; grouping into hundreds and tens; counting and recounting; discussion of choices, amounts, and procedures; and an awareness of the time it took to assemble 10 000 objects. A mysterious symbol had become a reality—a problem to solve through guessing, checking, counting, grouping, and finally observing the final product in its entirety.

Table 1. Sample of Children's Work

First I grouped the peas in hundreds then I counted 66 ^{more} peas then I got 666 peas. It took me a about an hour. When I was finished I could not believe that 666 pieces looked so small.

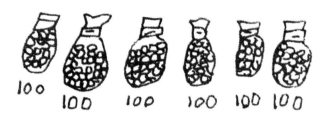

Jenna Carlson

I started counting on Oct. 28 and I finished in the afternoon I started counting with rice but that was too hard so I counted with macaroni.

by Laurie Archibald.

First I thought of something to count. Then I thought that holes would be so easy I did it. When I got 666 holes I grouped them in hundreds, tens, and ones. It took a long time, but it was fun!

By Jennifer Kadolija

Bibliography

Ellis, Glen. "Reader Reflections: How Large Is a Billion?" *Mathematics Teacher* 72 (May 1979): 324, 336.

Harrison, William B. "How to Make a Million." *Arithmetic Teacher* 32 (September 1985): 46–47.

Lane County Mathematics Project. *Problem Solving in Mathematics—Four,* pp. 5–10. Palo Alto, Calif.: Dale Seymour Publications, 1983.

O'Daffer, Phares. "Problem Solving: Tips for Teachers: Guess and Check." *Arithmetic Teacher* 32 (September 1984): 44–45.

Reese, Larry. "Reader Reflections: A Million Is …" *Mathematics Teacher* 74 (March 1981): 169. ▲

From the File: Bubble Gum Spheres

by

Gloria Sanok

Geometry

Bubble Gum Spheres

Object: To measure in metric units and to use the formula for the volume of a sphere,

$$V = \frac{4}{3}r^3$$

Materials: Sugarless gum, metric rulers, five to ten one-centimeter cubes

Students work in pairs to complete the following questions:

1. Blow a bubble (approximately a sphere). Have one partner estimate the volume of the sphere and make a stack of cubes that approximate its volume.

2. Have the same partner make an approximate measure of the diameter, then use the formula for finding the volume.

3. The students try this activity several times and complete a table with headings "Estimated Volume," "Calculated Volume," "Difference between Estimated and Calculated."

4. More able students can make sketches of the sphere and of the stack of cubes like those below.

$d = 2$ cm
$V \approx 4.19$ cm^3

$V = 4$ cm^3

From the file of Gloria Sanok, Packanack School, Wayne, NJ 07470 ▲

Food for Math

by

Mary Brickman

How many times have you thrown away empty containers or boxes not realizing that they would be useful in teaching mathematics? Stop! Start thinking differently. Save those boxes! What better way to involve children in problem-solving activities than to have them devise problems about items they have in their homes?

Begin by asking all students to bring in at least one food box or container that, if possible, still has the price on it. Second, have the students write four or five questions using the information that they have found on their boxes. Questions can deal with volume, measurement, prices, coupons, and recipes. Additional questions can count as a bonus or extra credit for students writing the questions as well as for those answering the questions later on. Students should provide the answers to their questions as well.

The questions should be edited so that they are appropriate for others in the class (fourth grade in my case). The revision of questions involves both the teacher and the student talking together.

Here are some sample questions based on the Bundt-cake and oatmeal boxes brought in by my students:

Bundt

1. We are having a party and need two Bundt cakes. How much will it cost to buy the mixes?
2. You hand the grocery clerk a $5 bill when you buy the two boxes. How much change will you get back?
3. How much water is needed to make batter for the two cakes? How much oil?

4. I can't believe I ate three slices of cake. How many calories will that be?
5. Each cake can serve sixteen slices. I need fifty slices for the school's bake sale. How many cakes do I have to bake? How many slices will I have left?

Oatmeal

1. You and three of your friends are making instant oatmeal for breakfast. How much water is needed to make the oatmeal for four servings?
2. I have $3 in my pocket. How many boxes of oatmeal can I buy? How much change will be left?
3. We are stocking up on oatmeal. How much would six boxes cost?
4. How heavy (in grams) would the parcel be if I carried eight boxes of oatmeal home?
5. We are having breakfast in class. How many boxes would we need for twenty-four students? How much would the oatmeal cost?
6. How much would each student pay for an individual oatmeal packet?

Mary Brickman is a fourth-grade teacher at Laura B. Sprague School, Lincolnshire, IL 60015, and is a member of her district's Mathematics Leadership Committee. Her major interest is in mathematics for elementary grades.

The boxes are fastened to the bulletin board with tacks. Students take down one box at a time and solve the questions in it. Since each child developed a set of questions for a box, all children can work on one box at the same time. A chart containing columns for the box codes, dates, and teachers initials (table 1) allows students to check which questions they have completed and which questions they need to select. This chart also allows the teacher to evaluate students' progress and accomplishments over a number of classroom sessions. I initial their work only when all the questions for one box are answered correctly; this determination is based on an answer key I've compiled. Completed answers are attached to the child's record sheet, and all papers are kept in a folder for future use.

Since students know that the problems have been written by their classmates, they have an incentive to solve them. If students have difficulty in answering questions, they are directed to the author to see what was intended. Students' names are included on the answer key, thus providing quick references. In this way students work with students.

The food boxes can be kept on a bulletin board for several months, or they can be placed in another classroom for mathematics lessons. A bulletin board in the hall can also be shared by many classrooms. The boxes themselves can be stored and used from year to year, thus permitting the collection to increase. ▲

Table 1

Name _____

Date began	Box code	Date completed	Teacher's initials

Chapter 8

Estimation and Approximation

From the File: Munchie Measurements

by

Barbara Disharoon

Estimation

Munchie Measurements

Materials

- Lunch bags
- Snacks (e.g., chocolate bars, packaged cheese crackers, granola bars, bananas, pretzel sticks)
- Centimeter rulers
- Scales

Procedure: Mark out or remove the weight information from each package or wrapper. Put one snack into each bag and fold over the top. Divide the class into groups of two to four students each and give each group a paper bag. Have students remove the snack from the bag and examine it. Then have them estimate its length and weight and record their estimates. Next, have them measure and record the snack's actual length and weight. Find error points (the difference between the estimates and the actual measurements) with a calculator. Compare the heaviest, lightest, longest, and shortest measurements. Finally, let students eat what they have measured!

From the file of Barbara Disharoon, Western Maryland College, Westminster, MD 21157 ▲

Readers' Dialogue: Popcorn and Mathematics

by

Kimberley Girard

The seventh-grade class at Nashua knows that popcorn and mathematics have something in common! Our investigation began one afternoon with our notes on volume. We use food a lot in our examples (and it makes us hungry). The food that day was popcorn! We wondered how much the volume changed when corn kernels were popped. Someone suggested popping some corn to find out, and we decided to give up our study hall period for this activity. Our classmates volunteered to bring in popping corn, bags, and air poppers and to get balance scales from the science teacher.

We wanted to answer three questions with our experiment:

1. How many kernels does one pound of popcorn contain?

2. Does one pound of popcorn still weigh one pound after popping?

3. How many cups of popped corn result from one pound of unpopped corn?

Before starting, we all guessed what the answers might be. The laboratory activity began with several minutes of counting kernels; one pound of popcorn contained 3577 kernels. To answer questions 2 and 3 we divided into groups and handed out equipment and jobs. Then we ran into a problem—the bag of popping corn was measured in pounds, but we had only gram weights for the scales. Luckily someone had a conversion table in a notebook. After that problem was solved, things went smoothly—students were doing their jobs, the poppers worked well, and no one was having a popcorn fight.

The volume of the popped corn was measured in cups when we collected it from the poppers. To weigh the popcorn, we put it in bags and then subtracted the weight of the empty bags. We also found the weight of the kernels that did not pop.

We discovered that 2 cups of unpopped corn turned into 53.5 cups of popped corn. The popped corn weighed 60 grams (about 2 ounces) less than the original kernels. We think that the lost weight resulted from the water in the kernels turning to steam—the process that causes the corn to pop.

The answers to our questions got us to thinking: If we counted another pound of popcorn, would we find the same number of kernels? If we used a different brand of popcorn, would the results be the same? (We used Jolly Time brand.) If we used oil poppers would the corn still lose two ounces during popping?

We challenge other seventh graders, or anyone who is interested, to try this experiment using oil and a pan or any method but air poppers. Send us your results.

The best part of this experiment was eating the popcorn!

Teacher's note: This laboratory activity was the students' idea. They did the planning, made up the questions, and did the work (except they called it fun). This letter is a compilation of the students' write-ups.

Kimberley Girard
Nashua Public Schools
Nashua, MT 59248 ▲

Estimation Is Mathematical Thinking

by

Sandra W. Harte

Matthew J. Glover

Hands-on activities prompt a rich variety of mathematical thinking.

D o I have enough money to buy the milk and the cereal, plus two cans of cat food?

Can all the milk left in the carton fit in my glass?

Will this fifty-foot hose be long enough to water the tomatoes at the back of the garden?

We need to have plenty of practice to cope with these real-life estimation problems. So do young students. The following is what happened one day in a first-grade classroom:

Teacher (holding plastic tub of golf balls): I would like you to estimate how many golf balls are in this tub. Here is one ball in my hand. How many balls are in this tub? Think about how many were in the tub yesterday; does this quantity look like more or less?

Students: More!

T: Would "5" be a good estimate?

S: No.

T: Why not?

S: Because "5" balls would fit in my hand, and all those would not.

T: Then would "500" be a good guess?

S: No, because I don't think "500" would even fit in the tub.

T: Those ideas show good thinking. I'll give you and your partner a minute now to decide on an estimate. Remember to explain your thinking and listen to your partner's ideas. Be ready to explain why you and your partner decided on that guess. (Allows thinking time)

T: Please write down your estimate. Who would like to share an estimate?

S: "45."

T: Why did you say "45"?

S: Because yesterday we had "30" and it looks like more than yesterday.

S: "90," because it looks like way more than "30."

S: "30"; I think it looks the same.

T: Those are all good estimates. How can we find out how many are really in the tub to see how close our estimates are?

S: Count them!

(Teacher begins counting them in the tub; starts to lose his place, counting some twice.)

S: No! You already counted that one!

T: Did I? How can I keep track as I count?

S: Take them out one at a time, and we'll count.

S: Give one to each person as we count them.

T: Do you think we might have too many for one for each person?

S: Oh, yes! Let's count them by "2's" instead.

(Teacher passes them out 2 at a time and the class counts. They count 41 balls; some students have 2 balls, and one has 1 ball.)

T: Raise your hand over your head if you have "1" ball; "2" balls.

T: Let's count backward as we put them back into the container…

Sandra Harte is a counselor and specialist in the education of the gifted in Indian Hill School District, Cincinnati, OH 45243. She has a special interest and experience in teaching mathematics. Matthew Glover teaches first grade at Indian Hill Primary School. He is interested in integrating mathematics into all areas of the curriculum.

In this first-grade classroom, the teacher effectively involved all the students in thinking about a reasonable estimate of the number of golf balls in the tub, justifying their thinking by expressing their ideas verbally, and verifying the actual number. In the process, concepts of number sense, one-to-one correspondence, skip-counting, and counting backward were reinforced.

Many situations involve estimation rather than precision.

In real life, problems and situations more often involve estimation than precise measurement or calculation. Until we are comfortable with approximation and have some experiences that give us confidence in approximating, we often either avoid it or work too hard to be precise.

Estimation is a process: it involves comprehending the problem, relating it to information that is already known, judging and verifying reasonableness, and revising as necessary. Two major themes of the NCTM's *Curriculum and Evaluation Standards for School Mathematics* (1989) are embedded in this process: (*a*) connections through linking mathematical ideas to the physical world and (*b*) communication through articulation of ideas.

The standards emphasize that mathematics is a way of thinking and communicating for everyone. Students must learn mathematics in ways that make them want to think mathematically. Technological advances in a world that is increasingly quantitative and complex make mathematics more and more important. Whether we teach mathematics better than we did in the past is not as important as teaching it increasingly better than we do today. The kind of mathematics that people will need in the future is changing; since symbol manipulation can be done so efficiently by machines, we need to emphasize the use of the uniquely human skills of higher-order thinking and the intelligent communication of mathematical ideas (Willoughby 1990).

Estimation is an effective and valuable way to integrate these ideas into the whole curriculum. In our first-grade classroom, a daily estimation activity has resulted in students' becoming actively involved in the exploration of number sense and spatial thinking in the process of solving the problem. Estimation can be integrated into any mathematics content and bridged into any curriculum area with a little creative planning. Students quickly become much more aware of mathematical relationships and more sophisticated in their thinking.

A wide variety of everyday materials and mathematics content can be planned. Here are some ideas:

- Estimate quantity using balls of different sizes (golf balls, tennis balls, marbles, and so on) so that meaningful estimates must include considering relative size. For example, after estimating the number of tennis balls in a bucket and in a plastic container, use the same containers to estimate the number of golf balls and marbles.

- Estimate length using nonstandard units (length of paper clips, hand span, paint stirrers, crayons, envelopes, a student, two or four students' combined heights) and standard units (centimeter cubes, metersticks, rulers). About how many paper clips wide is the student's desk? About how many hand spans? About how many inches?

- Estimate the effect of surface tension by verifying the number of drops of water that can be held on the surface of various coins. Using a penny and an eyedropper, carefully squeeze drops of water onto the penny; estimate how many drops the penny will hold before the water overflows. Use different coins and try both sides of the coins.

- Estimate the perimeter of books and desks using cubes; estimate the circumference of a bowl and a basketball. Let the students develop ways to verify perimeter and circumference, such as using a piece of string and then measuring it.

- Estimate the area of book covers of all different shapes and sizes; of lids of bowls; or of other small, flat objects with centimeter cubes, inch squares, and triangular patterning blocks. Allow students to explore the differences when different units of measurement are used on the same object.

- Estimate the volume of vases, jars, or boxes and check by counting the number of scoops of popcorn or rice needed to fill

Daily estimation activities can encompass a wide variety of everyday materials and mathematics content.

the various containers. Estimate the volume of such familiar containers as quart cartons, gallon jugs, and two-liter bottles and verify by filling them with water or sand.

- Estimate weight by using nonstandard (cubes, pencils, bricks, workbook) and standard (grams, ounces, pounds) units. Use a balance to determine the weight of smaller objects, such as an apple, a cup of water, or a pencil. Use a bathroom scale to determine the weight of larger or heavier objects.

Encourage students to justify their thinking.

Our experience suggests some instructional tips and strategies that will enhance estimation activities:

1. Establish an environment that allows and encourages risk taking; be sure it is a "safe" place to investigate ideas and try them out.

2. Integrate estimation with the curriculum in any way you find appropriate, for example, (a) estimate the number of gram weights necessary to sink an aluminum-foil boat in science or (b) estimate about how many caps the cap seller has in the book *Caps for Sale* (Slobodkina 1947).

3. Refrain from judging students' estimates and responses, but encourage them to justify their thinking.

4. Be sure everyone gets a turn. Every person's idea is important and can stimulate someone else's thinking.

5. Use a variety of instructional and managerial strategies: carry out some tasks as individuals, some as partners, some as small groups, and some as a whole class.

6. Through good use of questioning techniques, invite problem solving and exploration of strategies on the part of the students: How might we figure this out? In what ways could we come up with an estimate? Who thought about it in a different way? Tell us more about why you decided that.

7. Students need to generate the processes for solution; be sure not to tell them how to do it or how you would do it! They grow from trial and error and from the discussion that you facilitate through open-ended questions: the hows and whys and what-ifs and how-do-you-knows. It is important for students to realize that they can incorporate someone else's thinking into their own.

8. The exploration of thinking strategies for estimation is empowering for students; it motivates them and boosts their confidence in their own ideas.

9. Use materials with which the students are familiar and give them an opportunity to manipulate and explore the materials before using them for estimation.

10. Encourage students to use language in every step of their investigations and idea-generating activities; mathematical thinking must be articulated to be fully understood and meaningful.

11. Have fun with estimation! Not only will the students become more experienced, reasonable estimators, but you probably will, too!

How do these ideas translate into useful applications for the classroom? If we look back at our first-grade classroom, an estimating activity was part of the mathematics period every day; whenever possible, the estimating problem was integrated with the skill being addressed that day. The estimates to the actual measurement generated enthusiasm that carried over to the entire mathematics lesson. In the process of learning and practicing estimation skills, our first-grade students explored additional mathematics skills, such as counting, place value, measuring, and spatial reasoning; they actively and enthusiastically prepared for real-life problems.

Estimation activities generate enthusiasm that carries over to the entire mathematics lesson.

Bibliography

Heiman, Marcia, Ronald Narode, Joshua Slomianko, and Jack Lochhead. *Teaching Thinking Skills: Mathematics.* Washington, D.C.: National Education Association, 1987.

Mason, John, Leone Burton, and Kaye Stacey. *Thinking Mathematically.* Wokingham, England: Addison-Wesley Publishing Co., 1985.

National Council of Teachers of Mathematics. *Curriculum and Evaluation Standards for School Mathematics.* Reston, Va.: The Council, 1989.

National Research Council. Mathematical Sciences Education Board. *Everybody Counts: A Report to the Nation on the Future of Mathematics Education.* Washington, D.C.: National Academy Press, 1989.

Slobodkina, Esphyr. *Caps for Sale.* New York: William R. Scott, 1947.

Willoughby, Stephen S. *Mathematics Education for a Changing World.* Alexandria, Va.: Association for Supervision and Curriculum Development, 1990. ▲

Chapter 9

Calculators and Computers

Let Your Fingers Do the Counting

by

Charles D. Watson

Judy Trowell

Since many primary students have problems with fine-motor skills, one should be concerned that the keyboard be large enough for young children to use accurately when pressing keys. Since too many functions might be distracting to primary children, look for calculators with only the four basic operations (addition, subtraction, multiplication, and division). Also look for a calculator with a display that can be easily read. Solar-powered calculators are preferred, to eliminate the need for constant replacement of batteries.

What's more exciting than a fire drill for primary children? If you say doing mathematics with a hand-held calculator, you're correct! Suzanne McGee, a Chapter I mathematics teacher at Brady Elementary School in Little Rock, Arkansas, relayed this story in a recent interview:

> A few days ago my students were learning to use the calculator to count by 2s, 5s, and 10s. During the middle of my lesson, the bell sounded for a fire drill. My students were having so much fun that they did not want to leave the room. I told them that everyone must clear the building. They did ... carrying their calculators with them.

This story is just one illustration of the motivational impact that calculators can have for primary children. Carefully planned activities with the calculator can help primary students develop mathematical skills. The use of calculators also can provide stimulation to make learning mathematics fun and meaningful.

SELECTING THE CALCULATOR

Brands and models of calculators differ greatly. In selecting calculators for primary children, one should give careful consideration to the size of the calculator and its keys, sturdiness, readability of the display, power source, number of functions, and the order in which the keys must be struck (type of logic).

TEACHING ACTIVITIES

A one-to-one correspondence between students and calculators is ideal; however, many calculator activities can be effectively used by two students sharing one calculator. A good approach for introducing the calculator is to simply begin working with it. Students must be given plenty of time to explore on their own. Also, the first actual activity with the primary children is critical. Children will enjoy learning how calculator numerals are made. The first handout given students (fig. 1) shows each calculator numeral. Have each student point to a numeral on the sheet, then press that numeral key on the calculator. Discuss what was seen on the sheet and what was seen on the calculator. Using an overhead transparency of the calculator keyboard, introduce the

Charles Watson is a specialist in mathematics for the Arkansas Department of Education in Little Rock, AR 72201. He is serving as vice president of the Association of State Supervisors of Mathematics. Judy Trowell is a mathematics specialist (K–12) with the Little Rock School District, Little Rock, AR 72204. She is past president of the Arkansas Council of Teachers of Mathematics.

The activities described here were adapted and field-tested with primary children under a minigrant from the Arkansas Council of Teachers of Mathematics.

Fig. 1. Students need to recognize calulator numerals.

word "display." Although the vocabulary is not a major emphasis, the children will like using this special word. As the children press each numeral in order, they will discover that when they get to the "9," it will not show on the display. They actually "discovered" that the display will only hold eight places for numerals.

This is a perfect time to introduce the "clear" key and its meaning. Also discuss the "on" and "off" keys, and give oral activities for practicing with all three keys.

Construct a floor mat (fig. 2) to depict the calculator keyboard. Mat activities are designed to involve gross-motor skills and to furnish an active way for students to become totally involved in the learning process. Each student is given an opportunity to hop from one location to another as directed by the teacher or another student to become more familiar with the location of the number and function keys. Students then receive a handout of the calculator keyboard. With the mat and transparency as references, they are to fill in the symbols that appear on each key. This sheet will be kept in a folder for reference.

Fig. 2. This large floor mat was made from oil cloth, colored tape, and stick-on letters.

The floor mat is also used to help students learn the correct sequence for keying a problem into the calculator. For example, to enact the problem $2 + 4 = 6$, a student begins by hopping to the "on" key, then to the "2," to the " + ," to the "4," and finally to the "=" key. After this sequence the student states what was shown on the display, then hops to the "clear" key. (See fig. 3.)

To count by 2s, a student begins by hopping to the "on" or "clear" key, to the "0," to the "+," to the "2," and then to the "=." The student continues hopping on the "=" key while counting aloud by 2s. (This sequence requires a calculator with an automatic constant for addition.) While one student is on the floor mat, others use their calculators to perform each step with the action on the mat. It is recommended that this activity be used after students have been introduced to skip counting and have used manipulatives to develop and understand such counting patterns. The calculator allows students to explore this concept with much larger numbers than they would use otherwise. Students can immediately extend this activity to skip counting by 5s and 10s. Later on students may be able to relate skip counting by other numerals to the development of the multiplication concept.

A magnetic table and flannel board can also be constructed to reinforce the location of the keys. Figure 4 shows a learning

Fig. 3. Students hop on the floor mat to learn the locations of the number and function keys.

center with a student using these manipulatives. Activity sheets such as the one in figure 5 reinforce learning and guided work at the calculator center.

THE "PRESS, SAY, CLEAR" TECHNIQUE

For children who are still at the readiness level, the calculator is an exciting way to practice numeral recognition and number patterns. To develop these skills, use the "press, say, clear" technique. With this activity the teacher points to a numeral on a large poster or transparency or writes a numeral on the chalkboard. The children find that numeral key and then press it. Then they look at the display, say the numeral, and then press "clear." It is important to relate numeral recognition to concrete models. For example, the teacher can hold up four pencils, have each child press the number on the calculator, then say the number and press "clear." Move from desk to desk to see each display. In this way one can assess what the students are keying in. Another activity involves tapping on the table a number of times and then asking each child to press the key that matches that number. They should then say the number and press "clear."

The "press, say, clear" technique, balanced with concrete models and paper-pencil activities, can be extended to two-digit numerals. These exercises are particularly helpful for students who are having trouble changing the decade—from 19 to 20, 29 to 30, 39 to 40, and so on. Keying in the concept of "one more" is helpful for students. This sequence includes the following commands:

Press 2;
press 9;
say the number (twenty-nine);
press +;
press 1;
press =;
say the number (thirty).

This activity will help students recognize patterns in mathematics. Ask each child to press 131313. Next ask each child to enter the next two digits to complete the pattern. Each student should then write his or her two digits. Discuss the pattern and then press "clear." Repeat this activity several times and then give each child a chance to create his or her own pattern.

Another concept to explore with the calculator is estimation. Using the calculator to compare the exact answer gives students a new outlook.

OTHER ACTIVITIES

Extended teaching activities for primary children depend to a great extent on the creativity of the teacher and the willingness of the teacher, administrator, and school district to support the use of the calculator.

Fig. 4. Students use the magnetic table and flannel board to reinforce calculator skills.

Fig. 5. Activity sheets using the handheld calculator give a new twist to paper-and-pencil tasks.

In problem-solving situations, the use of the calculator allows the mathematical process to be stressed without the burden of excessive amounts of routine computation. It seems to change the entire mood of the children toward problem solving.

Consumer applications become possible for primary children when the calculator is used for computation. Advertisements from the newspaper and mail-order catalogs supply real-life data for projects and activities beyond the normal range of computational skills.

THE CHILDREN

What did the students say about using the calculator? When asked to complete this statement: "I like the calculator because…," many different responses were received. Here are a few of the responses. "It's fast." "It helps me check my work."

"I learn new things." "I do my work better." "It makes me think harder." "I can do harder problems." "It makes words when you turn it upside down."

SOME REMINDERS

The calculator is a tool that can make learning mathematical concepts more meaningful. It gives students new opportunities to apply concepts and new opportunities for discovery. And it motivates all students, even the most reluctant learners.

The calculator is not a replacement for the teacher nor for teaching. It does not replace the need to relate mathematical concepts to concrete models. It does not replace the need for students to know basic facts. It is not a one- or two-week isolated unit of instruction; rather, it becomes a part of the total mathematics program.

Bibliography

Beardslee, Edward. *Funtastic Calculator Math.* Sunnyvale, Calif.: Enrich, n.d.

DeMent, Gloria. *Calculator Capers Book 2.* Englewood Cliffs, N.J.: Prentice-Hall Learning Systems, 1977.

Engebricht, Victor. *Calculator Activities.* Wilkinsburg, Pa.: Hayes School Publishing Co., 1980.

Johnson, Barbara, and Kitty Scharf. *Menu Math for Beginners.* Scottsdale, Ariz.: Remedia Publications, 1982.

National Council of Teachers of Mathematics. *An Agenda for Action.* Reston, Va.: The Council, 1980.

Rudolph, William B., and A. D. Claassen. *The Calculator Book.* Boston, Mass.: Houghton Mifflin Co., 1976.

User's Guide to LCD Mickey Mouse Kiddy Calculator. Hong Kong: Tandy Corporation, 1985. ▲

Chapter 10
Multipurpose Aids

The Hundred-Board

by

Marvin C. Volpel
State Teachers College at Towson, Maryland

Every teacher of arithmetic should have a *hundred-board*. The writer believes it is one of the most efficient teaching aids for use in the development of understandings of concepts and operations with number quantities. If a teacher could select but one gadget for use in the arithmetic classroom he should choose the hundred-board because of its many uses with regard to both the scope and grade placement of material.

The hundred-board can take one of several forms. The simplest home-made board consists of a square of one-half-inch plywood large enough to be ruled off into 100 smaller squares each two inches by two inches, with a two-inch border around the outside. A finishing nail should be driven at the center of the top line of each small square. The finished product should then be stained and equipped with a handle to facilitate handling, hanging, and storing. In this form it can be used on a table, stand, easel, or tripod or in a chalk tray.

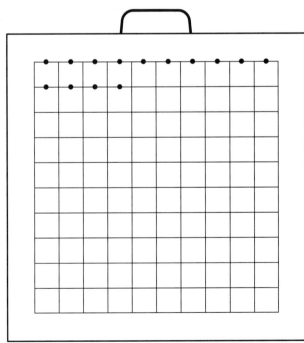

Variations of the above can be effected by using pegs or hooks placed at the exact center of each small square, by increasing its size so that it can be set on the floor for easy handling by small

children, or by constructing it with feet so that it can be used while resting in a horizontal position on a desk or table.

The teacher should have a set of numbers from 1 to 100 and a set of one hundred unnumbered objects which can be hung on the board. The numbers can be purchased commercially or prepared by numbering oaktag labels, department store price tags, or poker chips punched for hanging. The teacher should use objects that permit easy handling and which at the same time are attractive, such as spools, curtain rings, rubber washers, identification tags, one-inch pieces of plastic hose, and similar objects.

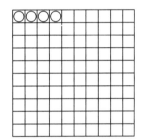 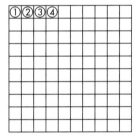

In the paragraphs that follow, the writer will show a few uses of the hundred-board.

NUMBER

The hundred-board, initially, can be used to show the cardinal aspect of numbers. To show that two represents 1 more than one, that three represents 1 more than two, and so on, we present the pictures of these objects. Thus when a child learns to say "4" he should associate that name with those things. This is "fourness." The meaning of the number expressions from one to ten should be shown on the board as follows:

O	1
O O	2
O O O	3
O O O O	4
O O O O O	5
O O O O O O	6
O O O O O O O	7
O O O O O O O O	8
O O O O O O O O O	9
O O O O O O O O O O	10

Now after a child has learned the meaning of "ten" he can count tens. Reference to a hundred-board filled with numbers clearly reveals groups of tens and the child should be taught to count them as tens. It should be as easy for him to comprehend 1 ten, 2 tens, 3 tens, 4 tens, and so on, as it is for him to learn to count 1 marble, 2 marbles, 3 marbles, … or 1 case, 2 cases, 3 cases, and so on.

Next we introduce the "teen" numbers with the help of a second hundred-board. Each row of the hundred-board represents a ten, so if a filled hundred-board is placed beside the one pictured above, the child ought to visualize number quantities like ten and 1, ten and 2, ten and 3 and the other numbers up to ten and 10 or 2 tens. If we encourage the child to continue to count in this manner, in terms of groups of tens and ones, he will readily learn and, we hope, comprehend the meaning of the numbers up to 10 tens or one hundred. In this way the child will learn to say expressions like "3 tens and 5," "3 tens and 6," "3 tens and 7" before he is told that such number expressions can be shortened to thirty-five (35), thirty-six (36), and thirty-seven (37).

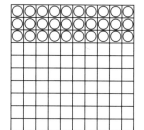
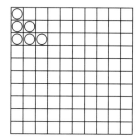

Ten and 1
Ten and 2
Ten and 3

When the child knows that four full rows of discs represent 4 groups of ten discs he can be shown how to express this quantity symbolically as 40. An extension of this concept should enable him to replace all the discs with others numbered to 100.

We can use the numbers on the hundred-board for teaching the child to count by twos. We begin by having all of the numbers turned over (face down). We ask the child to skip the first disc, number 1, and turn over the next disc. We skip one again and turn over the next one, we skip one again and "face-up" another. If we continue doing this until we reach 50 or 60 the child should observe the pattern of endings and should observe that full columns are turned down and full columns are exposed. Those numbers exposed are called "even" numbers and all of them end in either 2, 4, 6, 8, or 0.

The same procedure might be followed when teaching children to count by threes, fours, or fives. If all of the discs are turned down, then we skip two and turn over one, skip two and turn over one, and so on, when counting by threes. The numbers exposed will be 3, 6, 9, 12, 15, 18, 21, 24, 27, 30, and so on. The pattern of endings does not begin to repeat until after we have shown ten threes.

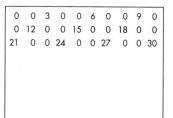

Another technique to follow in learning to count by twos or threes is to stack all the numbers in an ordered row or pile, take them one by one, place them in rows of 2 or 3 as the case may be. One does not have to replace all 100 numbers on the board but enough to enable him to understand the concept of counting by groups and to learn the respective patterns. The number board then will look like this:

1	2	21	22
3	4	23	24
5	6	25	26
7	8		
9	10	etc.	
11	12		
13	14		
15	16		
17	18		
19	20		

1	2	3	31	32	33
4	5	6	34	35	36
7	8	9	37	38	39
10	11	12			
13	14	15	etc.		
16	17	18			
19	20	21			
22	23	24			
25	26	27			
28	29	30			

The hundred-board is useful for picturing the various patterns of number quantities. The quantity 6, for instance, may be shown on the number board in several patterns. If children re-arrange discs (a constant number of discs) they will discover numerous facts concerning the given number. This activity develops insight into number quantities and number relationships.

Groups of different sizes may be pictured on the board and children challenged to determine the largest group. If they see groups containing 4, 6, and 7 spools they ought to be able to deduce that 6 contains (2) more than 4, that 7 contains (1) more than 6, and that 7 contains (3) more than 4. Conversely they will learn that 4 and 6 are smaller than 7 by 3 and by 1, respectively. The comparison phase of counting can be taught through the use of the hundred-board.

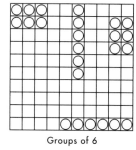
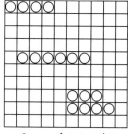

Groups of 6   Groups of 4, 6, and 7

ADDITION

The hundred-board is very useful in helping children discover basic addition facts. Since addition is a "putting together" operation we want to know how many we have altogether if we put 3 discs with a group of 4 discs. We show 4 discs on the top row and 3 discs on the second row and then combine them into one group. We discover that when we put 1 (of the 3) with 4 we will have 5, another 1 will make 6, and the last 1 will make 7. Thus 4 discs and 3 discs are 7 discs. Children will discover that there are many addition facts whose sums are less than 10—the combining of two small sets of discs will often leave the top row incomplete. Also, in learning the meanings of the numbers 1 to 10 they will have discovered how many more are needed to complete the row of 10. For instance, the last row of discs needs 0, the next to last row needs 1 so 9 + 1 = 10, the row containing 8 needs 2 so 8 + 2 = 10, and so on. In working with the complete set of 10, children ought to learn the subsets that add to 10. The board showing the sum of 4 discs and 3 discs should gradually have the following appearance:

0000 becomes 00000 then 000000 and then 0000000
000   00   0

Manipulations of this type suggest to the students that addition represents an increase, a movement to the right—a forward motion.

O x x x x x x x x x	1 + 9 = 10
O O x x x x x x x x	2 + 8 = 10
O O O x x x x x x x	3 + 7 = 10
O O O O x x x x x x	4 + 6 = 10
O O O O O x x x x x	5 + 5 = 10
O O O O O O x x x x	6 + 4 = 10
O O O O O O O x x x	7 + 3 = 10
O O O O O O O O x x	8 + 2 = 10
O O O O O O O O O x	9 + 1 = 10
O O O O O O O O O O	10 + 0 = 10

When children have mastered the combinations that total 10, they should have little difficulty recognizing sums that total more than 10. Since 7 + 3 = 10, then 7 + 4, 7 + 5, 7 + 6, and so on, must be greater than 10. Let us show the addition of 7 discs and 5 discs on the hundred-board. The first row should show 7 discs. The second row should show 5 discs. The discs from the set of 5 should be moved one by one until we have completed the first row. We need 3 of these, therefore there should be 2 left on the second row. Thus the sum of 7 discs and 5 discs is the same as the sum of 10 discs and 2 discs. Since 10 and 2 represent 12, then the sum of 7 discs and 5 discs is 12 discs.

In adding 6 + 7 (representing spools) children will visualize that they must take 4 of the 7 to put with the 6 to make a 10—therefore 6 + 7 is the same as 10 and 3. Addition with the hundred-board is similar to addition performed along a number line; the hundred-board is a number line decomposed into ten sections of ten where the concept of bridging is equally prominent. To add 6 to 7 on the number line one begins at the point marked 6 and moves forward (to the right) 4 places and then 3 more, arriving at 13. Thus 6 + 7 = 13.

When showing the addition of 3 or more quantities on the hundred-board children ought to sense the expediency of filling up groups of 10 so as to state the final sum as groups of tens plus ones. Thus 8 + 6 + 9 when combined on the hundred-board (fig. 1) becomes first 10 + 4 (2 discs have been moved from the group of 6 to the 8 group making a complete 10). Then 6 of the 9 are moved to the second row completing another 10. Since there are 3 left on the third row, the sum of 8 + 6 + 9 is 2 tens plus 3, or 23. A student might move 2 of the 9 into the top row and 4 of the 9 into the second row to obtain the same result.

The rationale of carrying is evident when one demonstrates the addition of 2 or more two-digit numbers with the aid of the hundred-board. To show the addition of 27 and 38 we set up 2 rows of tens and 7 ones and then 3 rows of tens and 8 ones. To find the composite sum we use some of the 8 ones to fill in the row containing the 7 ones. Since 3 are needed to complete the row the final result

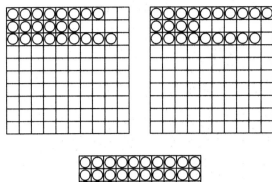

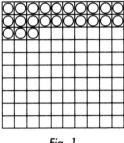

Fig. 1

shows 2 groups of ten, and 3 groups of ten (which we had in the beginning), and 1 more group of ten, and 5 ones. The sum, clearly visible on the hundred-board, is 65. There were enough ones to make another complete 10.

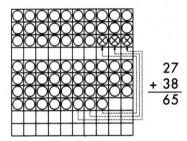

$$\begin{array}{r} 27 \\ + 38 \\ \hline 65 \end{array}$$

Two boards can be used effectively showing the tens on one board and the ones on the other. Then some of the ones can be used to make a ten. This procedure will enable children to "discover" that 2 tens and 7 plus 3 tens and 8 is the same as 6 tens and 5.

SUBTRACTION

Subtraction is an operation that separates a given group into 2 or more subgroups and is usually taught first as a "take away" operation, the opposite of the addition operation. If we wish to find the number of discs remaining after we have taken 3 discs from a group of 9 discs we first picture 9 discs on the hundred-board. When 3 of these are removed, one at a time, students should be encouraged to do so from right to left removing first the ninth one, then the eighth one, and then the seventh one. This backward operation will suggest a movement to the left along a number track … and that's the basic idea of "take-away subtraction."

Should we want to know the remainder when 5 things are taken from a group of 12 things we picture first the 12 things on the board. Children will see that the taking away operation (the 5 steps backward) will result in a remainder that is less than 10. They will first remove the 2 things on the second row and then move into the top row and take some from the group of 10. 12 − 5 = ?

The same reasoning is applicable when we perform compound subtraction. To illustrate further let us subtract 8 from 23. First we fill in 2 complete rows and place 3 items on the third row to make 23. We start removing 8 of these one-by-one—we take off the 3 and then move into the group of 10 to get 5 more (3 + 5 = 8). There will be only 15 left.

The solution of more difficult compound subtraction examples involving two digits illustrates the principle of reading and thinking from "left to right." Should we want to show the example

$$\begin{array}{r} 72 \\ -35 \end{array}$$

we would first show 72 items on the hundred-board. From these we are to remove 35. We will first take off 3 groups of 10 and then will take 5 ones. We take off the 2 single items and then take 3 more (enough to make 5) from one of the groups of 10. The final result is 37 and the algorism that will illustrate the thought pattern is as follows:

$$\begin{array}{r} 72 \\ -35 \end{array} \quad \begin{array}{|cccccc|c} 10 & 10 & 10 & 10 & 10 & 10 & \overline{10 + 2} \\ 10 & 10 & 10 & & & & -5 \\ & & & 10 & 10 & 10 & 7 \end{array}$$

MULTIPLICATION

If the addends of an addition example are equal, then the example can be solved by the operation called multiplication. Should we wish to add three groups of 2 we picture them as follows on the hundred-board:

X X
X X
X X

We discover that when we regroup these items they will fill up the first 6 places. Thus 3 twos equal 6. These can also be shown with numbers after the result has been obtained—the numbered discs can be placed two on each row so that the numbers show 1 and 2, 3 and 4, and 5 and 6 on the three rows.

① ②
③ ④
⑤ ⑥

To show that 4 threes are 12 we arrange four rows of three discs and then regroup them to form sets of 10, if possible. There will be one set of 10 with 2 remaining. Thus 4 × 3 = 12. When numbered discs are used to show the representation of 4 threes the numbers will form the following pattern:

① ② ③
④ ⑤ ⑥
⑦ ⑧ ⑨
⑩ ⑪ ⑫

Children should become aware of the fact that the numbers in the last column are the "threes' facts" representing the products in the table of threes.

To show that 3 sixes are 18 we first put 6 discs on each of the first 3 rows. Now we regroup them to form sets of 10. In doing this we discover that there will be one set of 10 with 8 remaining. Thus 3 × 6 = 18. When the single discs are moved to fill in rows there are many ways in which this can be done—there is no particular "best" procedure. Again, when these discs are shown as numbered discs, the numbers in the last column represent the products when 6 is the muliplicand. 1 × 6 = 6, 2 × 6 = 12, 3 × 6 = 18, and so on.

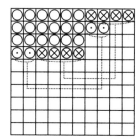 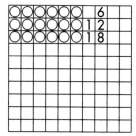

A hundred-board, with the addition of a few duplicate numbers, can be used to develop and display all of the multiplication facts and at the same time provide the opportunity for children to learn how to read tables. To do this, leave the first block of the hundred-board empty and hang all the numbers from 1 to 9 in the first row (9 will be in the place usually occupied by 10). Also, still leaving the first block empty, hang numbers from 1 to 9 in the first column. Now in the cells formed by the rows and columns hang numbers that represent the product of the two numbers which head the row and column. Thus in the cell of the row headed 4 and the column headed 7 put the number 28. Likewise in the cell of the row headed 7 and the column headed 4 put another 28. No other 28s are needed in the table. However, there are some numbers that appear more than twice as products within the table, namely, 8, 16, and 24.

	1	2	3	4	5	6	7	8	9
1									
2									
3									
4							28		
5									
6									
7			28						
8									
9									

DIVISION

Inasmuch as we have already shown ways to solve subtraction examples on the hundred-board, then division, which is also a separating or subtracting operation, can also be illustrated thereon. There are two concepts of the division process, the measurement concept and the part-taking concept. We will first illustrate the measurement concept, which asks one to find the number of groups when we know the size of the group (the multiplicand). An illustration of this idea is the question that asks how many groups of 2 can be formed from a group of 8. We begin with the dividend 8 and show that many things on the board. Now we remove 2 of these things and place them in a group elsewhere on the board. Then we repeat the operation with 2 more, and again 2 more until they have all been regrouped into sets of 2. We have discovered that 4 groups of 2 can be formed from a group of 8.

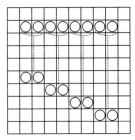

The example 16 ÷ 3 asks us to find the number of groups of 3 objects which can be formed from a group of 16 objects. We illustrate 16 objects on the board and then pick them off in sets of 3. We discover 5 sets of 3 objects with 1 object left over or remaining.

The example 97 ÷ 8 asks us to find the number of groups of 8 that can be formed from 97. Since the size of the subset is quite large and would require much tedious handling of objects we suggest the use of rubber bands, string, ribbons, and so on, to encircle the group. We circle 8, then circle 8 more, and so on, until all possible groups of 8 have been formed. We will discover that there are 12 groups of 8 in 97 and 1 item remaining.

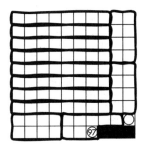

The partitioning aspect of division asks us to find the size of each subgroup when the number of groups is known. For instance, 6 ÷ 3 might ask us to find the number of items in each group if 6 items are divided into 3 equal groups. We show 6 items on the board and then remove 1 at a time, placing 1 in each of 3 different groups. "We put 1 here, 1 there, and 1 over there." Then we remove 1 more and 1 more and 1 more until they are all used up. Since we are trying to regroup into sets of the same size we must always put the same number in each of the subgroups. In 6 there are 2 in each of 3 groups.

17 ÷ 5 asks us to distribute 17 things equally among 5 people. We arrange 17 items on the hundred-board and then pick them off 1 at a time, putting one in each of 5 different places. Now we do the same thing again putting one in each of 5 different places, then we do it again. Now we see that there are not enough to go around again so we have learned that there will be 3 in each of the 5 groups with 2 items remaining.

After some experience with the simpler problems students will see that it is possible to remove more than 1 at a time—they could put 5 in each subgroup if they had to divide 37 by 6 and they could put as many as 10 in each subset if they were to divide 59 into 5 equal parts.

FRACTIONS

The relationships inherent in both common and decimal fractions can be exhibited on the hundred-board. By the use of elastic ribbons it is easy to show that 1/2 = 2/4, that 1/2 = 50/100, that 25/100 = 1/4, that 1/5 = 20/100, and so on. Also that 1/10 is equivalent to 10/100 and that 3/10 is equivalent to 30/100. If the whole board represents unity or 100% then each square represents 1 out of the 100 or 1% and is useful in showing the common fraction and percent equivalents. The board will be useful for revealing that 1/8 of 100 blocks represents 12 1/2 little blocks. Since each block represents 1 out of 100 or 1% of the whole, then 1/8 is equivalent to 12 1/2%.

One column represents 1/10 or .1 of the whole board and 6 rows or 6 columns represents 6/10 of the board or .6 of it. Forty-three of the little blocks represent 43 of the 100 blocks or 43 hundredths of the whole. Thus were we to compare .4 with .43 we see that the .43 is larger than .4 by 3 little blocks or by .03 (3 hundredths). The board is a helpful adjunct in teaching the meaning of and the relative sizes of common and decimal fractions whose values lie between 0 and 1.

There are numerous other uses for the hundred-board, which will be discovered by the teacher who uses one.

Editor's Note. Dr. Volpel's "hundred-board" has many uses. Many people have used such a device for percentage but have not explored all the ideas he has presented. Perhaps he is right when he says it is the most valuable piece of equipment for enhancing the teaching of arithmetic. As with other devices, it is the way in which an item is used to foster discovery, understanding, and learning that makes it valuable. Teachers will see possible variations of design and construction and more values will be discovered as the use of the board becomes more common. Devices are valuable in leading children to sense the objective background for the learnings which later should become more abstract. ▲

Cards, a Good Deal to Offer

by

Douglas H. Clements

Leroy G. Callahan

Activities with number cards can provide a wide variety of exploratory experiences in mathematics. In addition to being inexpensive and easy to make, these materials offer young children the opportunity to explore numbers without the frustration of writing them. Since the cards can be moved or rearranged, solutions can be changed easily. Children who are not confident in mathematics may find this attribute particularly attractive. Their anxiety about having teachers or peers see mistakes may be lessened.

The activities here include only explorations with the first twenty counting numbers, but the number cards can be extended or restricted depending on the students and the activities involved. Figure 1 illustrates the format of the cards.

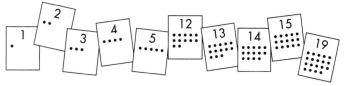

Fig. 1. Sample cards from a packet containing cards 1–20

EXPLORING SEQUENCES

The youngest children can rank a set of cards in order from least to greatest. The cards can then be turned facedown, and pairs of children can play "Superman." One child points to any card; the second "sees" it with "X-ray vision" and names it. The card is then turned over as "proof" of the child's super vision. It is left faceup as the second child indicates another card for the first to name, and so on. Strategies of counting, counting on, and counting back are involved, as well as the concepts of *before*, *after*, and *between*.

More advanced activities require the children to place the next three cards in a sequence begun by the teacher or another child and then give the rule they used in choosing these cards. Some examples are shown in figure 2.

Douglas Clements teaches courses for early childhood and elementary educators in mathematics, computing, and reading at Kent State University, Kent, OH 44242. Leroy Callahan teaches methods courses in elementary school mathematics, courses in diagnosis and remediation, and enrichment mathematicsfor elementary school teachers at the State University of New York at Buffalo, Amherst, NY 14260.

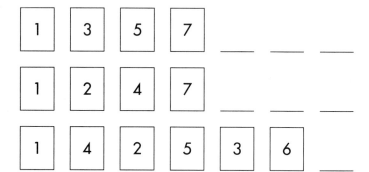

Fig. 2. Find the next three terms in the sequence.

Encourage the children to invent multiple solutions wherever they can. For example, the middle sequence in figure 2 could be extended as 1, 2, 4, 7, 11, 16, ..., using the rule +1, +2, +3, +4, +5, ...; or as 1, 2, 4, 7, 8, 16, 19, 20, 40, ... , using the rule +1, ×2, +3, +1, ×2, ..., and so on. Many other sequences and rules are possible. Challenge children to find solutions no one else has discovered. A "Sequences" bulletin board that is changed periodically can offer a simple yet stimulating challenge to children in exploring sequences with their number cards.

A spin-off of this activity is to have children transform the numerical sequences to another format. Figure 3 suggests a simple plotting of the sequences in figure 2 in a coordinate plane. The horizontal axis indicates the ordinal elements in the sequence (first, second, ...), and the vertical axis indicates the number property of the element. The children can discuss the path made by the plotted points in the plane.

ADDITION

Two children work together with two decks of cards, 1 to 20. Place the two sets of cards in order from least to greatest in two separate adjacent rows. Turn them facedown. Find card 10 in each row, turn it up, and determine the sum of the two 10s (see fig. 4). Now have the children turn up the card to the right of the 10 in one row and to the left of the 10 in the other row (9, 11). Determine that sum. Discuss how the "one more" and "one less" numbers compensate for one another and result in the constant sum of twenty. Next find the numbers that are "two more" and

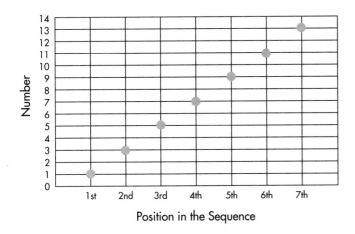

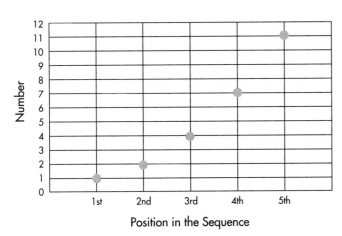

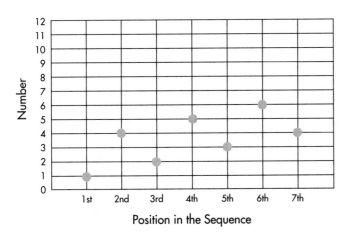

Fig. 3. Graphs of the sequences in figure 2

"two less" than ten and determine the sum. Have the children use their "X-ray vision" to find other numbers that result in a sum of twenty. Turn all the cards facedown again and explore other sums and the compensation idea.

SUBTRACTION

Practice with subtraction combinations can be carried out with a number-card game. Each student removes four cards from her or his deck of twenty to replicate a row presented by the teacher, such as that in figure 5a. The other cards are shuffled.

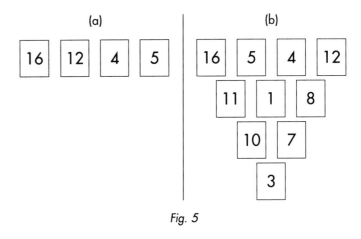

Fig. 5

The objective is to make a triangular arrangement of cards so that each card in the subsequent rows represents the difference between the two cards directly above it. A successfully completed arrangement is shown in figure 5b. Suppose the cards shown in figure 5a are presented as the top row. On the first turn students turn over the next card from their deck. They will find that either the number card can be placed below and between two of the faceup cards or it cannot. For instance, an 8 may be turned over and used between the 4 and the 12. But if a 3 is turned over, it cannot be correctly placed because none of the differences is three. In this situation, a student may rearrange any of the faceup cards in the top row so that the card drawn can be accommodated either in the next row or a subsequent one. Figure 5b shows a new arrangement in which three was found to be an answer for a lower row. Note that the top row shown in figure 5a must be rearranged because the difference between sixteen and twelve is four and the 4 card has already been used in the top row. It would be impossible to complete the triangular array without rearranging the row in figure 5a.

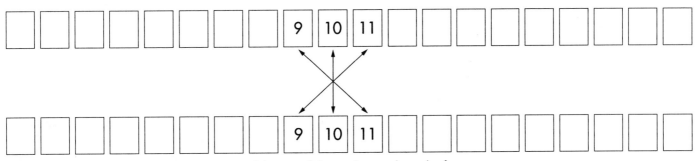

Fig. 4. Find the sum of the numbers at the ends of one arrow.

Often, rearrangements of the faceup cards to accommodate the card drawn during a turn will not be possible. At those turns the student will pass and place the unplayable card on the bottom of the pile. The child who successfully completes the triangular arrangement in the fewest number of turns wins the game. Once children are familiar with the game, they can shuffle the deck of twenty cards, place it facedown, and turn over the top four cards for row 1. This more random selection of the top row can create challenging situations.

COUNTING AND CHANCE

Keep track of the different combinations of the two cards that have a sum of twenty. Treat 9 + 11 as distinct from 11 + 9. Nineteen different combinations result in a sum of twenty. What is the range of sums you could expect when turning up one card from each row? (1 + 1 to 20 + 20) How many different combinations of two cards make a sum of twenty-one? Of twenty-two? Of nineteen? Of eighteen, … ? Figure 6 presents a graph of the results of the exploration. See Bestgen (1980) for other graphing ideas.

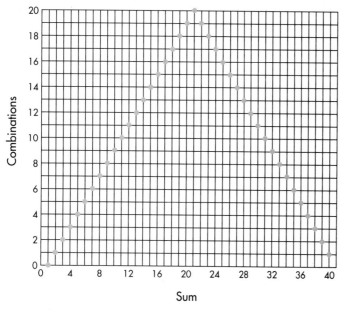

Fig. 6. There are twenty ways to get a sum of 21 with two addends.

Have each of two students pick up their twenty number cards, shuffle them, and place the piles facedown on the desk. If each student turned over the top card, which sum (2 to 40) would have the greatest chance of occurring? Which would have the least chance?

This activity can also be used as a bulletin-board idea. Place the graph in figure 6 on a bulletin board. Have the two piles of number cards available for use. Each day shuffle the two piles and turn over two combinations. Keep track of the frequency of occurrences of various sums by sticking a tack in the bulletin board or graph to represent each sum. How many samples are drawn before the "tack" graph begins to conform to the graph originally placed on the bulletin board? These results can give students a feel for taking a large number of samples before seeing a trend.

ARRAYS

With the cards in order from 1 to 20, have a child deal them facedown alternately in two columns, as in figure 7a. Have another child point to one of the columns and see if the other child can "see" all the cards in that column with his or her "X-ray vision." The column of cards could be turned over as "proof" of the child's super extended vision. Have children do the same activity after dealing the cards alternately in three piles; in four piles; in five piles; and so on.

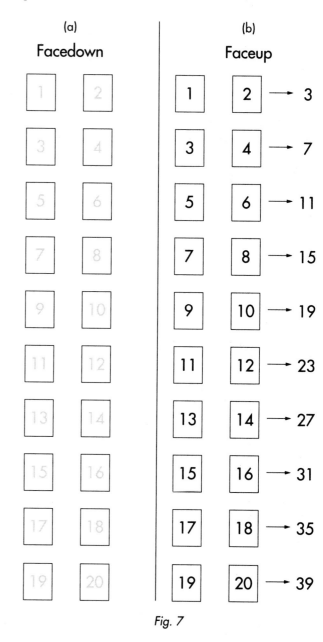

Fig. 7

Another activity with arrays of number cards involves a search for patterns. Have the children deal the ordered (1 to 20) cards faceup alternately into two columns. Have them find the sum of each horizontal row as in figure 7b. Can anyone find a pattern in the sums? Now have them deal the ordered cards faceup alternately into three columns and find the sum of each horizontal row. Do the same with four columns, then with five columns, each time searching for patterns in the sums of the horizontal rows.

CONCLUSION

Number cards can be used in exploratory activities like those suggested here, as well as in such simple games as war or concentration. They can also be used to explore various number puzzles or problems. For example, children may find it useful to explore a magic-square problem with moveable number cards before making a more permanent record of their solution in writing. Other ideas for using number cards can be found in Greenberg (1979), Lund (1977), Mort (1981), Nelson (1978), Reagan (1976), and Smith and Backman (1975, 61–63, 229–33).

The simple number card materials may not produce card sharks, but they do give children the opportunity to get their teeth into some interesting mathematical explorations.

References

Bestgen, Barbara J. "Making and Interpreting Graphs and Tables: Results and Implications from National Assessment." *Arithmetic Teacher* 28 (December 1980): 26–29.

Greenberg, Joanne Cecelia. "Your 'Ace in the Hole' for Teaching Mathematics." *Arithmetic Teacher* 26 (April 1979): 16–17.

Lund, Charles H. "Tricks of the Trade with Cards." *Arithmetic Teacher* 24 (February 1977): 104–11.

Mort, Janice K. "Odd Card." *Arithmetic Teacher* 28 (January 1981): 21.

Nelson, Rebecca S. "Variations on Rummy." *Arithmetic Teacher* 26 (September 1978): 40–41.

Reagan, Brenda Sue. "A Bonanza of Card Games." *Arithmetic Teacher* 23 (May 1976): 382–83.

Smith, Seaton E., Jr., and Carl A. Backman, eds. *Games and Puzzles for Elementary and Middle School Mathematics: Readings from the* Arithmetic Teacher. Reston, Va.: National Council of Teachers of Mathematics, 1975. ▲

Manipulatives for the Metal Chalkboard

by

Janet M. Sharp

Manipulatives represent one possible teaching tool for building a child's conceptual foundations. Once mathematical ideas are experienced at the concrete level, they must eventually be matched to a symbolic expression. In this way, conjectures can be explored and verified.

No teaching tools enable mathematics to jump magically into the child's mind and immediately enable him or her to reason mathematically and solve mathematics problems. The teacher must make decisions about the lesson and use the available materials in a manner beneficial to all children.

Generally, this goal means that the teacher must carefully plan and prepare the lesson. Manipulatives are not always the best approach—manipulatives do not teach. Manipulatives, however, offer the teacher a method to afford children opportunities to discover and explore various mathematical ideas.

When manipulatives are the best approach, the teacher must demonstrate to the students how they are expected to use—not abuse—the materials. While the children work at their desks with their desk-manipulatives, the teacher models with the demonstration materials a preferred method of use.

This process enables the child to see the teacher's suggestion before embarking on his or her own solution. For example, when creating patterns, the teacher might use pattern blocks for the overhead projector to demonstrate a particular pattern while the children use their desk-manipulatives to mimic and extend the pattern. Then, a child might model the extension of the pattern for the class using the demonstration materials. When the student shows his or her solution, the teacher-demonstration materials clarify the solution.

Overhead projector. The overhead projector offers an easy and efficient medium for demonstrating manipulatives. Many companies specializing in educational materials sell overhead manipulatives. Wiebe (1990) related an example of using transparencies or old report covers to create overhead manipulatives at a fraction of the commercial cost.

Janet Sharp teaches at Iowa State University, Ames, IA 50011-3190. She is interested in equipping her methods students with a wide range of teaching strategies.

Metal chalkboard. A chalkboard made of metal offers another medium for demonstrating manipulatives. The absence of a metal chalkboard can easily be overcome by purchasing a sheet of metal, such as an old television tray, or by using the side of a metal filing cabinet. Poster board and adhesive magnetic strips will be sufficient for creating these tools. By using a scaling factor of 5, teacher-demonstration manipulatives can be constructed. After the manipulatives are cut from the poster board, the magnetic pieces are secured to the back.

These large, magnetic teaching manipulatives have many advantages. They can easily be held up so that all students can see them. They slide around the chalkboard in the same way that the students' manipulatives move on their desks. They are inexpensive and simple to make. Finally, small hands can maneuver the demonstration materials more easily than the overhead-projector materials.

A word of caution: these manipulatives must be cut out perfectly. Precision must be exercised while cutting through the poster board. For example, a mathematics topic for which pattern blocks are useful is tiling the plane; the poster-board angles must be measured and cut with great care to ensure that the pieces exactly fit together. (See fig. 1.) To help children make the connection between the teacher-made manipulatives and their desk-manipulatives, match the color of the poster board with that of the corresponding commercial manipulative.

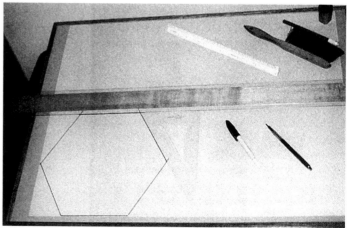

Fig. 1. *Drafting triangles and t-squares are more efficient than a protractor and a simple ruler.*

Any teacher-demonstration manipulatives can be created with this method. Pattern blocks, base-ten blocks, attribute blocks, Cuisenaire rods, teddy-bear counters, tangrams, and fraction circles are relatively simple to create. The teddy-bear counters can be cut with the Ellison Die Press. The students' desk-manipulatives are cut with the "tiny" die, and the teacher-demonstration manipulatives are cut with the larger die. The match is remarkable and effective. In fact, Ellison dies are available for all the aforementioned manipulatives.

We must be prepared to create demonstration manipulatives that are inexpensive and easy to make. The demonstration materials in figure 2 were cut from poster board. Foam board could also be used. Although these materials are not as sturdy as the commercial manipulatives, they are affordable.

Bibliography

Raphael, Dennis, and Merlin Wahlstrom. "The Influence of Instructional Aids on Mathematics Achievement." *Journal for Research in Mathematics Education* 20 (March 1989): 173–90.

Schultz, Karen A. "Representational Models from the Learners' Perspective." *Arithmetic Teacher* 33 (February 1986): 43–55.

Thompson, Patrick W. "Notations, Conventions, and Constraints: Contributions to Effective Uses of Concrete Materials in Elementary Mathematics." *Journal for Research in Mathematics Education* 23 (March 1992): 123–47.

Trueblood, Cecil R. "Hands On: Help for Teachers." *Arithmetic Teacher* 33 (February 1986): 48–51.

Wiebe, James H. "Teaching Mathematics with Technology: Teacher-Made Overhead Manipulatives." *Arithmetic Teacher* 37 (March 1990): 44–46. ▲

Fig. 2. The back side and front of a set of manipulatives for a metal chalkboard

IDEAS: Sneaker Tread Prints

by

Carne S. Barnett
Far West Laboratory for Educational Research and Development, San Francisco, California

LEVELS 1–4

Objective

Students compare and contrast the tread designs found on the soles of sneakers. They make their own sneaker tread prints, then sort, classify, and graph the prints according to their own criteria.

Materials

1. Sneakers
2. Lightweight paper
3. Dark crayons
4. A copy of "Sneaker Tread Prints" for each student

Directions

1. Conduct a whole-class discussion. Have students look at the sneaker tread prints at the top of the worksheet and talk about how they are alike or different. Students might focus on such attributes as geometric designs, words, left-right patterns, and the placement of designs.

2. Ask students to conjecture about why certain designs might be used. Older students might know that walking shoes or tennis shoes need less traction (or grab) than running shoes and that the texture of the sole is different for these shoes. They might also notice that some shoes have crease lines on the ball of the foot to ease walking or that some shoes have a circular shape where the joint of the big toe fits in the shoe. This design may indicate that a different material is used in this spot to furnish extra padding. Shoes having tread prints with basically horizontal patterns are usually used for running and walking because the foot is typically going in one direction and a horizontal pattern gives appropriate traction. Shoes with tread prints having more complex patterns are usually used for sporting activities in which the foot must change direction quickly.

3. Have students work in groups to collect fifteen or more sneaker prints. They might collect rubbings from other students in the class, from students on the playground, or from their family members and friends outside of school.

4. Each group should sort their sneaker tread prints in different ways. The following are some suggestions: (*a*) rough or smooth; (*b*) straight lines, no lines, curved lines, or both straight and curved lines; (*c*) words or no words; (*d*) circles or no circles; (*e*) long, medium, or short; and (*f*) left foot or right foot. Have students share some of the ways in which they sorted the prints.

5. Ask students to select one way to sort the tread prints into two groups and complete the pictograph on the worksheet. Students can then write and exchange questions about their graphs.

Answers

Answers will vary from group to group, depending on the different tread prints used and the different sortings. See figure 1 for a sample answer.

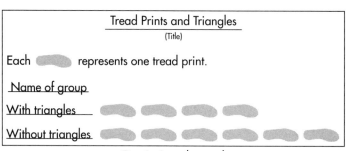

Fig. 1. Sample graph

Extensions

1. Have students estimate the length and width of a tread print in centimeters. Ask them to measure the length and width and then compare their estimates to the actual measure. Continue estimating and measuring. Ask students to describe their estimation strategies.

2. Students can take a survey to determine the class's favorite types of footwear. Ask them first to brainstorm various types of footwear, such as low-topped sneakers, high-topped sneakers,

Carne Barnett is director of the project Case Methods for Inservice Education in Mathematics, in which she is pioneering the development of cases (narratives about teaching experiences) for use in the professional development of teachers.

sandals, boots, other nonsneaker play shoes, and dress shoes. Each type can be listed on a large sheet of paper. Distribute small squares of paper to students, directing them to draw a picture of their face on the paper. Next, have students decide which is their favorite type of footwear and glue their paper square in the appropriate place on the graph, as shown in figure 2. After the graph is complete, discuss the results.

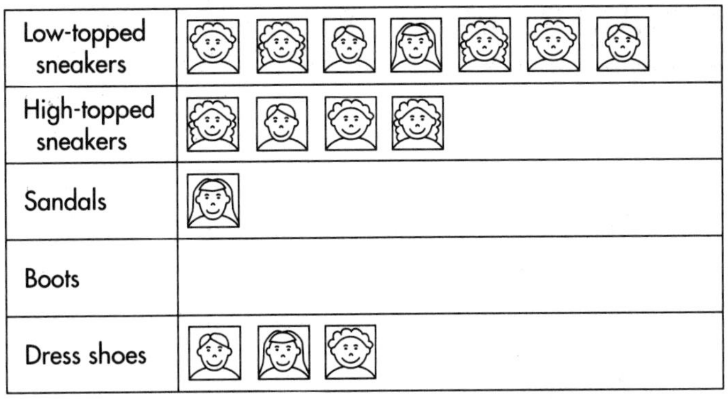

Low-topped sneakers							
High-topped sneakers				
Sandals	
Boots	
Dress shoes			

Fig. 2. A graph of the class's favorite footwear

SNEAKER TREAD PRINTS

Name _____

Student Worksheet

Work in a group.

1. Talk about these sneaker tread prints. How are they alike? How are they different?

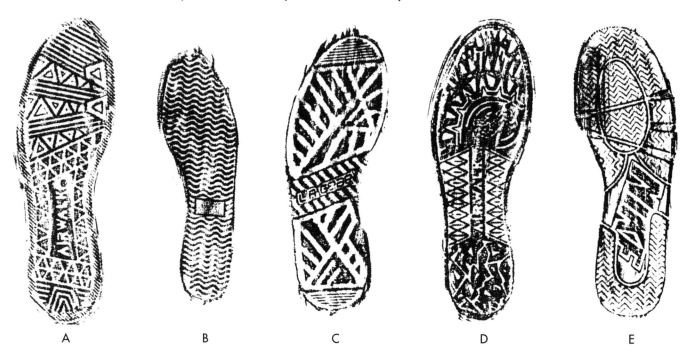

| A | B | C | D | E |

2. Make crayon rubbings of some sneaker treads. Sort the tread prints into two groups. Make a pictograph to show the number in each group.

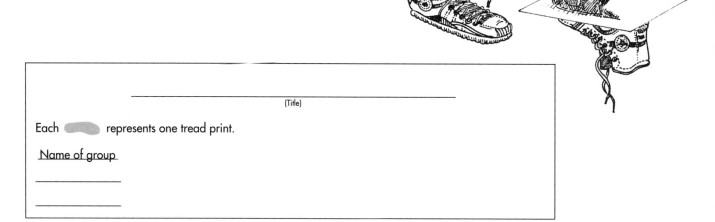

_____
(Title)

Each ⬭ represents one tread print.

 Name of group

_____

_____

3. Write a question that can be answered from your pictograph.

_____

_____

From the File: 31derful Ways to Use Math at Halloween

by

Cathy A. Barklay

Miscellaneous

31derful Ways to Use Math at Halloween

Teachers can use their imaginations to alter or extend the following activities for elementary school students. Some activities are particularly suitable for laboratories or work centers.

Pumpkin Activities

Materials: a pumpkin, tape measure, knife, and spoon. *Optional:* parent volunteer to help students roast pumpkin seeds

1. Measure the diameter of the pumpkin.
2. Measure the height of the pumpkin.
3. Count the ribs on the pumpkin.
4. Calculate the volume of the pumpkin by immersing it.
5. Describe geometrically the shape of the pumpkin.
6. Estimate the number of seeds inside the pumpkin.
7. Count the number of seeds from the pumpkin.
8. Divide the number of seeds evenly among the students.

Jelly-Bean Activities

Materials: a bag of orange and black jelly beans, glass jar, and scale

9. Estimate the number of jelly beans in a jar.
10. Estimate the fractional part of the beans that are orange.
11. Count the number of jelly beans in the jar.
12. State the ratio of orange beans to black beans.
13. State the ratio of orange beans to total beans.
14. Find the percent of orange beans to total beans.
15. Estimate the weight of a jelly bean.
16. Weigh a jelly bean on your scale (you may want to weigh ten candies and then divide the total weight by 10).
17. Find the total weight of all the jelly beans.

FOLD

Costumes

18. Poll your classmates to determine the types of costumes they will wear for Halloween, then decide on categories of costumes.
19. Make a frequency table for the types of costumes.
20. Construct a bar graph of costume choices.
21. Find the percent of each type of costume chosen.
22. Construct a circle graph of percents of costume choices.

Countdown

Materials: a calendar

23. Count the number of days until Halloween.
24. Name the last year that Halloween fell on the same day as it does this year.
25. List as many different sets of numbers as you can of which Halloween's date is a member.
26. On what day will Halloween fall during the next leap year?
27. Predict the temperature on Halloween night by using library resources.

Trick or Treat

28. Estimate the number of trick-or-treaters who will come to your house.
29. Decide how you will tally the exact number of trick-or-treaters who will come to your house.
30. Predict the number of pieces of candy YOU will get on Halloween.
31. Before you eat any of your candy on Halloween night, count the number of pieces you have collected. Tomorrow in mathematics class, find the average number of pieces collected by the students in your class.

From the file of Cathy A. Barkley, Mesa State College, De Beque, CO 81630 ▲

Young Students Investigate Number Cubes

by

Alex Friedlander

W orking with students in the first three grades is challenging for various reasons, among which are the following:

- The students' repertoire of concepts and skills is quite limited.

- Mathematics teachers tend to devote their attention and efforts to the processes of helping their students acquire basic skills. Developing appropriate activities for those who have already acquired these skills is relatively neglected.

- In many situations, working with these students on more advanced curricular skills or topics neither offers the desired intellectual challenges nor develops higher-level-thinking strategies.

As pointed out by both the *Curriculum and Evaluation Standards for School Mathematics* (NCTM 1989) and the *Professional Standards for Teaching Mathematics* (NCTM 1991), a strong need exists to develop activities that, in spite of the rather limited skills of these students, provide an informal encounter with some important concepts, develop problem-solving strategies, and offer a balanced and interesting approach to mathematics. One basic assumption is that primary students who have already mastered the basic skills and concepts included in the standard curriculum should deepen their understanding of these concepts as well as encounter—but not necessarily master—various new topics. The accumulated experience of many teachers and curriculum projects suggests that a sequence of mathematical investigations is more appealing and efficient if it is connected by a common

feature or topic (see, e.g., Lindquist [1989]). We decided to experiment with the first possibility and create units of eight to ten activities around a common theme. Thus, each unit is built around a manipulative, for example, number cubes (or dice), dominoes, and the calendar. Using a manipulative lends coherence to a wide variety of topics and concepts and allows students to become acquainted with many relatively new concepts in a concrete and informal way.

INVESTIGATING NUMBER CUBES

To illustrate this idea, we describe a ten-activity unit named "Dice," which is one of a sequence of short units we have developed at the Center for Educational Technology at Tel-Aviv, Israel, and implemented with groups of students in grades 1–3. The activities investigate some geometric and numerical properties of a regular number cube.

During the first two activities, the students get acquainted with the components and elementary properties of the cube and with the magic rule of seven—that the sum of the numbers on the opposite faces of any die is always seven. An entertaining use of this rule is

Alex Friedlander, ntfried@wiccmail.weizmann.ac.il, works at the Weizmann Institute of Science, Rehovot, Israel 76100. His main areas of interest are developing investigative activities for elementary and middle-grades students and student assessment.

The author expresses his thanks to the children of the School of Natural Sciences in Tel Aviv, Israel, who were the first to encounter the activities described in this article, and especially to Shelly Rota for her vital help in teaching and designing the unit.

playing Chutes and Ladders or any other board game using the hidden, rather than the visible, number on the die.

In the third activity—"the popular sum"—the students perform some experiments in intuitive probability by observing the frequency of each sum obtained by throwing a pair of dice. The data can be collected in pairs by students taking turns throwing twenty times and keeping a tally of the results. They then complete an addition table for the whole numbers from 1 through 6 (see fig. 1). Next the students are asked to make some *intuitive* comparisons, without using fractions, between the relative frequencies of sums in the table and their own experimental results and to draw some conclusions about the most and the least popular sums. Figure 1 also presents some of the questions that were posed toward the end of this activity.

1. Look at the sums that you can get when throwing two dice. Fill in the following addtion table. If you wish, you can record the sums in the table while you keep throwing your dice.

+	⚀	⚁	⚂	⚃	⚄	⚅
⚀						
⚁			5			
⚂						
⚃						
⚄						
⚅						

2. Look at your tallies and at this table. Try to find and explain which sums are more popular, or likely to turn up, and which are less so.

3. Galya and Ronen are playing games with two dice. Who has a better chance to win?
   Game 1: Galya wins if she gets a sum of 2; Ronen wins if he gets a sum of 7.
   Game 2: Galya wins if she gets a sum of 7; Ronen wins if he gets a sum of 12.
   Game 3: Galya wins if she gets a sum of 2; Ronen wins if he gets a sum of 12.
   Game 4: Galya wins if she gets a sum of 6; Ronen wins if he gets a sum of 7.
   Game 5: Galya wins if she gets a sum of 7; Ronen wins if he gets a sum of 8.

Fig. 1. "The popular sum"

In the fourth activity, called "odd or even," students investigate the result of adding odd and even numbers by throwing two dice rather than working through usual paper-and-pencil exercises. Figure 2 shows some interesting inequalities that our students were able to solve successfully as part of this activity.

The following three activities, titled "special pairs," introduce some basic concepts related to graphs in the plane coordinate system in a natural way by using two dice of different colors. First, students play an adaptation of tic-tac-toe (fig. 3) to familiarize themselves with the use of ordered pairs of numbers to locate points in the first, positive, quadrant. Then they investigate the relationship between a graph and the common property of its component points (fig. 4). This investigation is done in two directions by—

(a) translating into a graph a given property common to a set of results, obtained by throwing a pair of dice, and, conversely,

(b) translating a given graph into the common property of the set of its component points. For most students of this age, the reversed thinking can be performed only by making a written record of the corresponding pairs of numbers before a common numerical property is discovered.

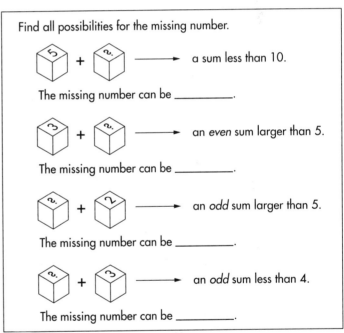

Find all possibilities for the missing number.

5 + ? ⟶ a sum less than 10.

The missing number can be _____.

3 + ? ⟶ an *even* sum larger than 5.

The missing number can be _____.

? + 2 ⟶ an *odd* sum larger than 5.

The missing number can be _____.

? + 3 ⟶ an *odd* sum less than 4.

The missing number can be _____.

Fig. 2. "Odd or even"

The final three activities are devoted to establishing number patterns, and students reached some surprising conclusions. Thus, in "towers," they investigated first the sum of all twenty of the numbers on the four walls of super towers—columns of five dice arranged so that on each "wall" all the dice show the same number; and the sum of all twenty "wall numbers" for regular towers—columns of five dice arranged randomly. See figure 5. The comparison of the two kinds of towers leads to the conclusion that the sum of the "wall numbers" for all towers of the same height is the same. The magic rule of seven provides the justification. Since

The game is for two players and consists of a board and two dice of different colors. Write these colors in the appropriate places on the board.

Rules:

1. Each player chooses a sign, say, X or O.
2. The players take turns throwing the dice and using their sign to mark the point on the board that corresponds to their throw.
3. If the point is already marked, the player loses the turn.

The winner is the first player to mark four adjacent points in a row, column, or diagonal. Or if the board is almost full, the player who has marked more points is the winner.

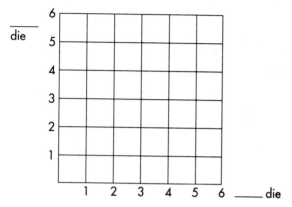

Fig. 3. An adaptation of tic-tac-toe

each pair of numbers on opposite walls on any floor always sums to seven, the total sum for the tower is always a multiple of fourteen, the multiple depending on the height.

The "towers" activity is followed by "trains," which is special in that it involves rows of three or four cubes showing consecutive numbers on their sides. From these special trains, children discover another consequence of the famous rule of seven: arranging consecutive numbers on a side creates a sequence of consecutive numbers on the opposite side as well. Therefore, taking care of one side and the "roof" ensures consecutive numbers on all four sides of the train. Employing the same rule and some spatial visualization, students can also guess the sequence of numbers on any train as viewed by a person sitting opposite a train (fig. 6). An interesting question that concludes this activity is "What kind of sequences look exactly the same from two opposite sides of a train?"

Finally, "super cubes" combines number operations, probability, and spatial visualization. Students are asked to use eight dice to make a larger cube with only ones on two of its faces and only twos and threes on the other four faces. What is the total number of dots on each side of a super cube? Can we predict the possible sums of dots that we get when rolling a pair of super cubes? What will the popular sum be in this situation?

CLASSROOM IMPLEMENTATION

These activities have been used with large groups of students selected from several classes and with small groups of four to seven within a regular class. Students were enthusiastic, as were their teachers, who expressed agreement with the approach and

Mark with an "O" all the points that fit the description.

The sum of the two numbers is less than 8.

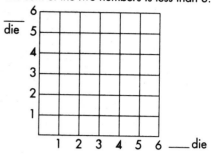

Both numbers are less than 4.

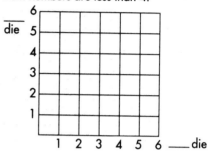

Write down the results marked by the points on the boards below. Next try to find a description for all the points marked.

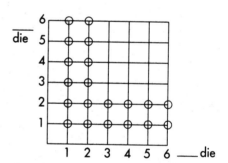

The marked points …

_____

_____

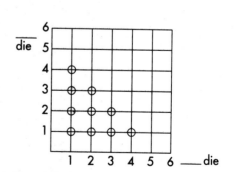

The marked points …

_____

_____

Fig. 4. "Special pairs"

Build a regular tower by piling up five dice in any arrangement of numbers.

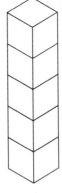

1. Find the sum of all twenty "wall numbers" on your tower.

2. Build some more regular towers, and find sum of all twenty "wall numbers" for each of them.

3. Explain what you found. _____
   _____
   _____
   _____
   _____

4. Predict the sum of the "wall numbers" on towers with
   7 floors _____, 10 floors _____, 20 floors _____.

Fig. 5. "Towers"

philosophy. Most activities allowed the students to discover patterns and rules according to their abilities and using their own methods, without having a particular approach or pace imposed on them.

The method of evaluation was chosen to fit the investigative nature of the unit. Thus, rather than assess performance on some traditional test items, the teacher monitored the processes of students' thinking and their ability to communicate their ideas to others. We believe that by synthesizing observations of a student while working through the unit, one can get a reliable assessment of mathematical ability in general and work on this unit in particular. As mentioned in the ample literature on assessment, written projects assigned as journal entries, portfolio items, or just plain homework can also be used to supplement student evaluation. We illustrate this philosophy by discussing examples of how we monitored students' thinking on two activities and suggesting further investigations that were assigned to supplement student evaluation.

Monitoring student thinking

Students found the sum of all twenty of the "wall numbers" of a super tower in various ways. Some did it the hard way, first finding the sum of the numbers on each wall or on each floor and adding, whereas others used the rule of seven right away. Some students detected the rule later when they compared their result with that of their classmates and realized that all three possible super towers have the same sum.

The following are some student responses to the "towers" activity:

I added up all the numbers on one wall, on the second wall, on the third wall, and on the fourth wall, all together.

6	+	2	+	3	+	5	+	3	=	19
2	+	1	+	2	+	3	+	4	=	12
1	+	5	+	4	+	2	+	4	=	16
5	+	6	+	5	+	4	+	3	=	23
19	+	12	+	16	+	23			=	70

I added the numbers on each die. On the first it came out 4 + 5 + 3 + 2 = 14; on the second, 1 + 5 + 6 + 2, also 14…. So I

Sarah and Dan are looking at the same train from opposite sides of a table. The drawing to the left shows Dan's side. The drawing to the right shows what Sarah sees. Write on this drawing the numbers that she sees.

In this drawing, Sarah and Dan are looking at another train. They notice that both of them are seeing *exactly* the same thing. Build his train and check whether the view from both sides is indeed the same.

Build two other trains that look the same from opposite sides. Use Example 1 to write the numbers from both sides of one train and Example 2 to write the numbers from the other.

Example 1

Example 2

Fig. 6. "Trains"

found that on each die the numbers add up to 14 ..., and then I remembered the magic rule. I added up 14 + 14 + 14 + 14 + 14 = 70.

I know that on each die the opposite numbers make 7. Then on each die I have twice 7 ... 14. Then 5 × 14 = 70.

On each die we have twice 7. We have 5 dice and that makes 10 magic rules ... 7 × 10 = 70.

These comments show that similar strategies were employed to find the sum of the "wall numbers" for the randomly arranged regular towers (fig. 5). However, as compared with the super towers, fewer students used the more sophisticated methods. With regular towers, most students first used simple addition and only then gave an explanation for the constant sum. A relatively small number of students were able to generalize for higher towers.

Similarly, to find the most popular sum when a pair of dice is thrown, students' strategies and responses varied in sophistication. At the experimental stage, many students attributed the results to chance or to the notion that some numbers are luckier than others. When confronted with the addition table of whole numbers from 1 through 6 (fig. 1), most students could relate their empirical results—some intuitively and others at a more "theoretical" level—to the patterns observed in the table. For example, one child noticed that "2 appears only once, because 1 + 1 = 2 and it doesn't matter on which die we get the 1, and the same goes for 12." Another remarked, "All the numbers are on diagonals, and 7 is on the longest one because you can get it from 1 + 6, 2 + 5, 3 + 4 and then the dice get changed."

Written assignments

The problem situations that we present to students as evaluation items must potentially have various solutions. On the one hand, they should give opportunities for creativity and expression to the talented; on the other hand, they should not close options and frustrate the less talented. Several examples follow:

• As a follow-up to the activity on the magic rule of seven, find the magic rules that correspond to dice that are numbered from 3 through 8 or from 25 through 30 instead of the regular numbering from 1 through 6. Do the numbers on the dice have to be consecutive to get a magic rule?

• As a follow-up to "the popular sum" (fig. 1), investigate some pairs of other than cubical dice, such as octahedral dice numbered from 1 through 8, and find their popular sum.

• As a follow-up to "special pairs" (fig. 4), invent some secret-number properties that can be outcomes of throwing a pair of dice then draw their graphs. Next show a classmate only the graphs and ask him or her to guess the secret properties.

CONCLUSION

The investigations described in this article do not have particularly new objectives, and they do not present a new approach to teaching mathematics. However, from our classroom experience, two characteristics previously mentioned are worth reemphasizing:

• Students can get involved in and enjoy relatively complex investigations in the early grades.

• Mathematical investigations can and should be organized and presented to students as coherent stories related to larger, comprehensive themes. This kind of activity seems to us more useful and enjoyable than puzzles or isolated challenge problems that promote some general and not always clearly defined thinking skills.

References

Lindquist, Mary Montgomery. "It's Time to Change." In *New Directions for Elementary School Mathematics*, 1989 Yearbook of the National Council of Teachers of Mathematics, edited by Paul R. Trafton, 1–13. Reston, Va.: The Council, 1989.

National Council of Teachers of Mathematics (NCTM). *Curriculum and Evaluation Standards for School Mathematics*. Reston, Va.: NCTM, 1989.

———. *Professional Standards for Teaching Mathematics*. Reston, Va.: NCTM, 1991. ▲

Seasonal Crafts: Discovering Mathematical Relationships and Solving Mathematical Problems

by

Sydney L. Schwartz

The goal of the math program is to enable children to use math through exploration, discovery and solving meaningful problems. (Bredekamp 1987, 71)

Every season poses a challenge for teachers as they select and implement craft activities. The image of four- and five-year-olds leaving school during the major holiday periods always includes a craft or art project, often identical except for the color, clutched in their hands. In response to this perceived need to produce a craft for every holiday and change of season, the publishing community offers books dedicated to the subject. These detailed, step-by-step instructions on how to produce each craft beckon to teachers, encouraging them to use these books as manuals. But such use relegates craft activities to a mechanistic view of learning, in direct contrast with what is known about how children make connections and construct their understandings about events and interactions. Further, the assembly-line approach to crafts in early childhood means that an important vehicle for children to discover mathematical relationships and solve mathematical problems in meaningful contexts is eliminated.

> ## The challenge is to tune into mathematical problems that children are seeking to solve.

More and more frequently, early childhood teachers are focusing on the ideas associated with developmentally appropriate practice, and whole-class craft productions are giving way to individualized products that evolve from children's experiences and that more accurately reflect children's design and constructive capabilities. As the approach to the crafts becomes more integrated, teachers can turn their attention to how to "build on the wholeness of their [the children's] perspective of the world and expand it to include more of the world of mathematics" (NCTM 1989, 32).

It is a given that children are always learning. In whatever activity they are engaged, they are physically or mentally interacting with the events while they make sense out of each experience. The challenge is to tune in to the nature and content of their processing to identify the logical and mathematical relationships that they are developing and using.

Craft activities depend so much on mathematical understandings and skills that they beg to be featured in an authentic and meaningful way. When children get caught up in thinking about the mathematical relationships, the teacher's role shifts from furnishing the opportunities to helping the children bring intuitive thinking to a conscious level for dialogue and expansion.

PROCESS-PRODUCT RELATIONSHIPS

Teachers of young children face a dilemma about so-called *production standards*. If a teacher values the process of developing the skills and understandings that craft activities evoke, then the products are likely to be unfinished, by adult standards. If a teacher values the product over the process, then children are denied the right to create and design, to learn through their own efforts, and to set their own standards. In the view of this author, the dilemma resolves itself when teachers more fully engage in planning for the teaching-learning potential of craft activities, especially in mathematics.

Sydney L. Schwartz, Queens College of the City University of New York, Flushing, NY 11367, is a professor of early childhood education who in her teaching and scholarly work has focused on mathematics and science for young children.

This department addresses the early childhood teacher's need to support young children's emerging mathematics understandings and skills in action-based prekindergarten and kindergarten classrooms in a context that conforms with current knowledge about the way young children learn mathematics. This issue describes how craft projects that emerge from the interests of children and are sparked by seasonal and holiday events offer a unique opportunity for children to discover mathematical relationships and solve problems.

The dilemma of production standards is resolved by planning.

Contrary to conventional wisdom, teaching plans that focus on children's thinking during the process of making a craft need not abandon a concern for the quality of the product. Instead, emphasizing to children the decisions that they make along the production route constitutes an important context for them to evaluate the product and secure some understandings of process-product relationships. For example, when in the process of creating a decorative place mat for a special event a child varies the length of the edging strips, a conversation about the length differences supplies a context for him or her to evaluate the final product in terms of how well he or she likes having full-length, or congruent, edges on some sides and shorter, noncongruent edges on the other sides. (See fig. 1.)

Fig. 1. In designing this place mat, the child must decide if she wants congruent or noncongruent side strips.

If the teacher wants to strengthen the measurement thinking that seems to be occurring, then some dialogue between teacher and child is needed at two points in the process: first, at the point when it becomes evident that the child is changing the edging pattern from congruency to noncongruency and, next, when the product is complete and the child is surveying the results. The initial dialogue can take the form of a teacher observation—"Oh, I see you are making this side-edge strip shorter than that side edge"—or an inquiry—"Are you planning to make the side strips a different length?" These remarks serve to ensure that the measurement thinking is dealt with at a conscious rather than intuitive level. The follow-up dialogue at the end of the task can then refer back to the midway conversation, focusing on an evaluation of the outcome: "You made these side strips shorter than the side edge of the mat. Did it turn out the way you wanted or expected it to look?" Depending on the child's response, a further discussion might ensue on how the place mat might look with decorative strips of different lengths or with more strips. Other children can join this final discussion.

In this way, the dilemma about process-product values resolves itself through the teacher's engaging actively in bringing the child's intuitive understandings to conscious awareness. This "sharing of ideas and thoughts, through oral rehearsal, not only helps the child to understand her own reasoning, but provides insight into conflicting and complementary perspectives" (Dunn and Larson 1990, 56). Further, it enhances the children's ability to use mathematical thinking to control outcomes and to set their own standards.

CRITERIA FOR DESIGNING CRAFT ACTIVITIES

Several criteria guide targeting children's meaningful use of mathematical thinking and problem solving during craft experiences. Essentially, mathematical thinking occurs when children *discover a relationship* or when they seek to *apply their understanding of a relationship* to a task. Between the discovery event and the final mastery, or "ownership," period occur various practice events, which, in essence, serve as a way to move from repeated discovery to ownership.

- *The discovery of mathematical relationships.* When young children manipulate materials and discover relationships, access to their thinking at this discovery point is not available unless the youngsters spontaneously talk as they think. This statement does not diminish the importance of the thinking that occurs during a discovery experience. However, if a teacher does not know what mathematical relationships a child is discovering, the opportunities for dialogue to stimulate further thinking is restricted. The natural teaching inclination is to ask questions; however, with such young children, this practice can be problematic for two reasons. First, catching the right moment is tricky. Asking questions too soon interrupts the thinking in progress. If the teacher waits too long, however, the child has moved on to another concern and the question fails to have relevance. Second, the children may not be able to express their intuitive understandings. Since observing and interviewing children about their mathematical strategies in the independent discovery activities is the only access, teachers must continue to probe, but with caution.

- *The application of mathematical understandings of relationships.* Probably the most significant mathematical thinking occurs during an application experience because the child is involved in selecting a mathematical route to a goal. If the route fails to achieve the goal, children are provoked to reexamine their understandings of relationships, be it number, geometry, patterns, or measurement. The teaching access here is also much more direct. The purpose of the application effort is more visible in a discovery situation, and children are considerably more interested in talking about their efforts to use mathematical procedures to produce an effect. The most difficult challenge for the teacher is finding ways to extend children's thinking about mathematical relationships without leading them or doing their thinking for them by supplying solutions.

- *The repeated use of mathematical skills in craft activities.* Some activities can be designed to feature children's repeated use of a skill, such as pasting one geometric form in each box of a class-produced lotto board. Such activities, although important in fostering necessary skill mastery—in this example, the discrimination of standard geometric forms—offer the least opportunity for either the discovery or application of understandings of mathematical relationships.

Craft activities involve all three forms of mathematical learning. The emphasis on application, discovery, or practice depends on the way the task is presented to the children or evolves from their ongoing interests. Irrespective of which aspect of mathematical development is featured in the craft activity, the most meaningful learning occurs when children build on their repertoire of understandings and skills toward ends that they care about.

> # Meaningful learning occurs when children build on their understandings toward ends that they care about.

DEVELOPMENTALLY APPROPRIATE DESIGNS FOR CRAFT PROJECTS

Developmentally appropriate craft projects emanate from the ongoing curriculum in response to topics of interest. Holidays, seasonal changes, and special events are major sources for craft projects, in addition to the daily program. The decision on how to organize a craft project grows out of a teacher's knowledge of the children's prior experience with the materials. If children are essentially unfamiliar with the materials, the context needs to feature *finding out,* or *discovering.* If the children are familiar with the properties of the materials and have had experience manipulating those properties, the context changes from *finding out* to *figuring out* or from *discovery* to *application.* The frame for each of these two approaches is distinctively different.

The finding-out model

In the *finding-out* model, unfamiliar materials are supplied for the craft project, which offers children opportunities to find out the mathematical relationships within the materials. Because the materials are unfamiliar, the final product *emerges* rather than follows a preset plan. An example of a finding-out activity follows.

Materials: a collection of small cardboard boxes of various sizes and sheets of cardboard that the children have never used before in craft projects

Prior experience: extensive work with diverse materials in collage collections, including the construction of three-dimensional collages, mobiles, and decorative table-top items; daily block-building experiences in which size, shape, and purpose of structures have been discussed

The task: to create a craft product that can be used at the class party for Halloween. The possibilities children might generate include a

"goblin" house centerpiece for the table, a mobile, or a storage container for Halloween cookies. The mathematical discoveries that are likely to occur primarily deal with measurement and geometry:

• Some sides and surfaces match whereas others do not.

• One large box may be attached on one side to two smaller boxes.

• All rectangular boxes have the same number of sides and surfaces.

• The height of the chain of boxes affects how well it "stands up."

• A horizontal chain of boxes looks different from a vertical chain with the same number of items.

• The same number of connected boxes does not always produce the same length of boxes.

If Styrofoam or other rounded materials are included in the collection, additional discoveries might revolve around the relationship between curved and straight edges. For example, curved edges do nd have aufficient surface to attach easily to straight edges.

As noted earlier, the kinds of mathematical discoveries that children are making in this process are not always visible. Listening to children's conversations frequently reveals information that allows the teacher to participate in the dialogue. Also, when a teacher sits near the action in the role of observer, some children invariably include her or him in the conversation. As children share their discoveries and talk about how they are proceeding with what they are making, the context emerges for understanding their own reasoning.

The figuring-out model

In the *figuring-out* model, the reverse situation is created: the product is identified instead of the materials, and the child chooses the materials and the process instead of the product. This kind of activity presupposes that the children have had considerable experience with the materials from which they will choose to make the craft project. Therefore, they can plan the task and engage in solving various mathematical problems that arise as they work at completing their plan.

The task: to make packaging materials for the "Parent Day" gifts the children have made

Prior experience: decorating paper and cardboard with graphic and collage materials; working with fabric and yarn; stringing assorted materials

Materials: various kinds of paper, graphic, and plastic materials; collage collections; fabric, yarn, and rope collections; cardboard containers in various sizes

One major set of mathematical problems embedded in this task involves measurement, both linear and weight. The size of the wrapping is measured and compared with the item to be wrapped, and the strength of the wrapping is considered in terms of the weight of the item. In addition, children create their own mathematical challenges within the decorative-design process.

TEACHING MATHEMATICS THROUGH CRAFTS

To capitalize on the mathematical learning embedded in a craft activity, it is necessary to plan for possibilities, that is, to identify the mathematical relationships and important ideas with which the children will be dealing. The following example illustrates the kind of teaching analysis that exposes the possibilities for highlighting mathematical relationships and inviting dialogue.

Specialty cooking is a craft activity that accompanies most holiday celebrations. It is especially dominant during the fall holidays, culminating in the multiple religious and cultural holidays that occur in December. The rich well of possible foods that can be cooked in class flows from the eating patterns of the children's families and the program activities being featured. For purposes of illustration, the analysis in table 1 looks at the use of ginger-cookie mix. Note that the *science* of the changing properties of food materials is often featured in cooking activities. This illustration focuses solely on the *mathematics* possibilities.

Creating a Thanksgiving design involved number, geometry, and patterning concepts.

Many, many craft activities are associated with seasonal and holiday events. A few of these are listed in table 2 to illustrate the variety of mathematical ideas that might engage children's thinking. One sample for each event is analyzed.

SUMMARY

Seasonal and holiday crafts offer a unique opportunity for children to discover and use their understandings of mathematical relationships in a context that is authentic for them. If the projects (1) relate to children's experiences, understandings, and interests and (2) allow for individual discovery, experimentation, and decision making, the motivation to solve the mathematical problems that are confronted in these projects is strong. The challenges to teachers are to tune in to the mathematical problems that children are identifying and seeking to solve and to offer a climate for discussion that enhances the problem-solving effort.

Table 1. Analysis of a Cooking Activity

Group Activity: The Sequence of Tasks in the Project	Mathematical Relationships: Discovery, Practice, and Problem Solving	Teacher Inputs
1. Assembling and organizing the ingredients and the measuring and cooking tools	• One-to-one matching of the items • Organizing the set of ingredients and the set of tools in order of use	• "Let's check to make sure we have everything we need. List all the ingredients and tools. Now let's line them up in the order we'll use them."
2. Measuring and mixing the ingredients	• Examining the meaning of *full volume measures* and *partial volume measures* • Practicing measuring volume • Associating whole-number and fraction words with measured amounts	• "We measured one full cup of mix and it's here in this plate. For the sugar, we need to measure one-half of a cup. Let's look at the difference in the amounts of sugar and mix."
3. After mixing ingredients, making cookie shapes. (Each child receives an equal amount of dough, enough to make a number of cookies. Children make cookies in different shapes, using plastic cutting utensils.)	• Creating standard and nonstandard geometric shapes • Matching identical and similar shapes • Comparing sizes of cookie shapes in terms of surface area and thickness • Comparing shapes, number of sides, rounded edges, and straight edges • Matching sides of different shapes	• As variations in shapes begin to appear, focus attention on similarities and differences in attributes of shape and size. "Look at the different shapes you are making." Encourage children to compare, finding identical, similar, and different shapes. Repeat the teaching strategy for comparing size and thickness. Repeat the teaching strategy for comparing combinations of shapes, for example, a gingerbread figure or building.
4. Decorating cookies with raisins, nuts, and dried fruit	• Making patterns with materials added as decoration • Repeating patterns, varying patterns, and comparing patterns	• With an individual child, focus attention on the sequence or pattern of use, such as a repeated pattern or a changing pattern: "Let's look at the different ways you put the raisins on the cookies." With several children, focus attention on describing and comparing the different ways of organizing the raisins, nuts, and dried fruit on the cookies. Look for repeated patterns and spatial order.

Table 2. An Analysis of Mathematics Learning Possibilities

Season/Holiday	Craft	Mathematics Learning
Fall season in temperate climates	• Pinecones: stringing, constructing sculptures and mobiles	• Comparing size and shape of cone and cone parts • Comparing weight of completed sculptures and mobiles
Halloween	• Pumpkin seeds: making a seed collage; gluing on seeds as a decorative coating for a bottle or can	• Comparing size, weight, and number in the craft projects • Creating patterns
Thanksgiving	• Using dried corn kernels to make collages and jewelry and to decorate containers and mobile items	• Comparing size, weight, and number under varying conditions • Identifying and comparing standard and nonstandard geometric shapes created on the collages
December holidays	• Modeling artifacts used in the family home celebrations	• Solving construction problems, such as matching lengths and sides of geometric shapes, comparing sizes, creating new shapes by joining nonidentical shapes (e.g., a square and a triangle to create a house with a slanted roof) • Developing a full range of mathematics ideas and content in number, geometry, measurement, and patterning for four- and five-year-olds • Estimating sizes and amounts
Valentine's Day	• Creating collages and patterns with hearts, diamonds, and other familiar environmental shapes	• Discovering relationships between nonstandard shapes • Comparing the number of items in the product and the size of the product

References

Bredekamp, Sue, ed. *Developmentally Appropriate Practice in Early Childhood Programs Serving Children from Birth through Age 8*, exp. ed. Washington, D.C.: National Association for the Education of Young Children, 1987.

Dunn, Susan, and Rob Larson. *Design Technology: Children's Engineering.* New York: Falmer Press, 1990.

National Council of Teachers of Mathematics. *Curriculum and Evaluation Standards for School Mathematics.* Reston, Va.: The Council, 1989. ▲

Jar Lids—an Unusual Math Manipulative

by

Carol R. Langbort

For the past fifteen years, many educators have made an effort to incorporate the use of concrete materials into the elementary school mathematics curriculum. These manipulatives are, in fact, useful with students at all levels; however, some teachers still reject using them. The authors of both the 1985 *Math Framework for California Public Schools* and the 1987 *Mathematics Model Curriculum Guide, K–8* recommend the use of concrete materials for all learners, including high school students and adults. Certainly, manipulative materials should be used without question in the elementary grades.

This article describes some activities that use an easy-to-collect, noncommercial item—jar lids. The activities were designed by

Carol Langbort is an associate professor of education at San Francisco State University, San Francisco, CA 94132. She teaches mathematics methods courses to preservice and in-service teachers, directs the San Francisco Math Leadership Project, and is coauthor of several books for teachers.

Special thanks to the following students at San Francisco State University for their contributions to this article. The number of the particular activity to which each contributed is given in parentheses.

Hilda Faziols (1)	Mary Heinemann (5)
Barbara Francis (7)	Michelle Kale (4)
Mitch Genser (3)	Barbara Mandel (9)
Susan Hatfield (2)	Pat Reynolds (6)

in-service teachers as part of a course. Many jar lids can be collected in a short time. Children can easily bring them in from home, and they are virtually free.

The following activities involve concepts from different content areas and grade levels. The activities involving sorting, classifying, and graphing are appropriate for both primary and intermediate grades. Several ordering activities are included for young children. The activities measuring circumference and diameter are suited to children in the intermediate grades.

SORTING, CLASSIFYING, AND GRAPHING

Activity 1: Sorting and graphing
Grade level: K–6

Materials: A variety of lids (about 20) for each pair of students; graph paper

Directions: The collection of lids can be sorted according to a variety of attributes. In addition to the more common characteristics of size and color, several other attributes are unique to the lids: solid color or mixed color; price printed on lid or no price; food product or nonfood product; words printed on lid or no words; smooth or ridged; snap-on or screw-on; metal or plastic; and flat or deep. Children can devise other categories.

Children can use loops of colored string or yarn on the floor to sort the lids into different sets. They can then discover each other's rules for sorting. The sorting activity can easily be extended to making a graph with the lids. First have the children decide on the categories, then place the lids in the appropriate columns on large graph paper. To help children interpret their graphs, they might use questions such as these:

Which category has the *most* lids?

Which has the *least*?

How many *more* ___ do we have *than* ___?

How many ___ and ___ do we have *in all*?

How many more lids do we need so that we will have just *as many as* ___?

Activity 2: Peanut butter graphs

Grade level: 3–6

Materials: Lids from different brands of peanut butter jars; graph made with push pins (see fig. 1)

Directions: Children work on this activity individually or in pairs at a learning station. The children can hang the lids directly on the push pins on the graph. Label the columns of the graph with the different brand names, such as Jif, Skippy, Numade, or Brand X. Then direct the children to hang their lids in the correct columns according to "which brand." After making statements and asking questions about the results, the children then place the same lids on a second graph labeled according to "which texture": chunky, extra chunky, smooth, or creamy. When all class members have completed the task and discussed the results, direct them to make up word problems using the information found on the graphs.

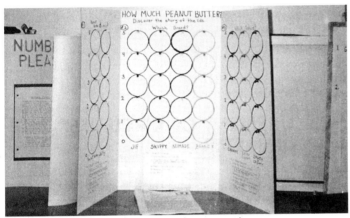

Fig. 1. Peanut butter graph

Activity 3: The lid data collection activity

Grade level: 4–6

Materials: A variety of lids for each child; a chart with questions about the lids as in figure 2; graph paper

Directions: Direct the children to examine each of their lids and record by tallying on their chart which categories describe them. Have them make a bar graph using the information from their charts. Then have them write a paragraph about their particular collection of lids.

A variety of benefits are derived from this activity, including increasing powers of observation; recognizing the varying forms that something as common as a lid can take; measuring in metric; noticing volume and weight labeling; discovering ways to categorize; noticing that the same lid may be in several categories at the same time; practicing making a bar graph; and generalizing from information on a graph and writing about it.

ORDERING ACTIVITIES

Young children need many experiences in ordering a variety of materials. The jar lids lend themselves well to this type of activity, and the following are four different activities on this topic.

How many lids—

1. are made of plastic?
2. have no writing on them?
3. are made of metal?
4. have the colors of blue and red?
5. have information about volume or net weight?
6. have information about refrigeration?
7. tell you what's inside?
8. have prices on them?
9. tell you who packaged the container?
10. have at least fifty words?
11. have a *diameter* of more than ten centimeters?
12. have a *circumference* of less than ten centimeters?
13. have little ridges around their circumference?
14. have a rubber ring on the underside?
15. Make up your own category and use it on all the lids.

Fig. 2

Activity 4: Ordering lids

Grade level: K–3

Materials: About fifteen different jar lids for each group of children; glue, strips of cardboard or heavy paper about fifteen centimeters wide

Directions: Give each group of children about fifteen jar lids of various sizes. Have them order the lids from smallest to largest and then glue them on a long strip of cardboard. See figure 3.

Activity 5: Matching lids

Grade level: K–3

Materials: Ten different lids for each pair of children; a long strip of paper; a paper bag

Directions: Direct each pair of children to arrange their lids in a row from smallest to largest according to the size of the diameter. Next, have them trace the lids in order on a long strip of paper and number the traced circles from 1 to 10. Finally, have them put the lids into a paper bag and take turns choosing a lid from the bag and guessing which circle it matches. If the lid correctly matches the circle, it is left on the paper. If it doesn't match, it is returned to the bag. This process continues until all the lids have been matched.

Activity 6: Filling and weighing lids

Grade level: 2–4

Materials: Six lids for each child; a strip of drawing paper; beans; a pan balance

Directions: Have the children order their six lids by size and trace them on a strip of paper. Next, they are to guess the number of beans that would fill one layer in the smallest lid and then fill the lid and count the beans. Below the circle have them record the estimate, the number counted, and the difference. After they repeat this process for each lid, have them write inside each circle

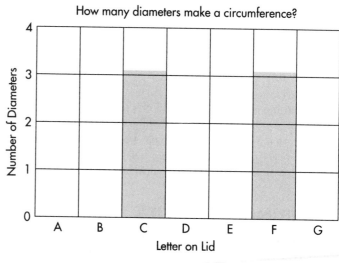

the number counted for the corresponding lid. Let them discover that the numbers are in order as are the lids.

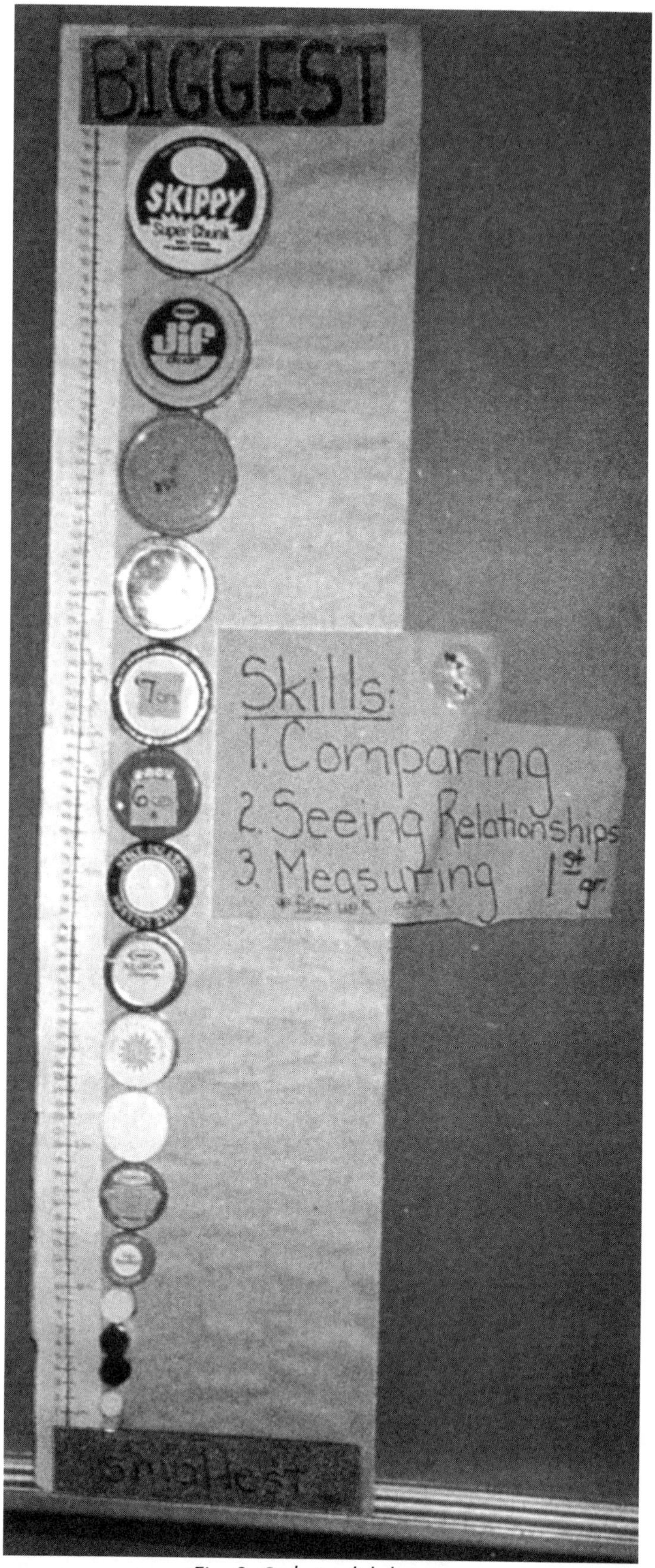

An alternative way of ordering the lids requires a pan balance along with the lids. After the children have ordered and traced the lids on a strip of paper, have them place each lid on the pan balance to determine how many units balance it; any nonstandard unit will work. Have them then write the number of units inside the circle. Depending on the material of the lids, it is possible that the weights may not always be in the same order as the lids. This possibility would be a good point for discussion.

Activity 7: A game called "slize"
Grade level: K–3

Materials: Fifteen lids for each pair of pupils

Directions: The two players distribute fifteen lids between them. The extra lid becomes the first lid of the game and is placed on the table. The first player chooses any lid to place next to the first lid. The next player chooses a lid to play, either larger than the largest or smaller than the smallest lid on the table. A lid cannot be placed between lids already played. The game continues until each player can play no more lids. The winner is the player with the fewest number of lids left.

MEASUREMENT OF CIRCUMFERENCE AND DIAMETER

One of the most useful concepts that can be developed using the lids is the relationship between the circumference and diameter of a circle, or pi (π). Many inexperienced students have heard of pi but, having learned it in a rote fashion without understanding, have no idea what it relates to or what it means. The following activities are examples of ways to develop this concept at various levels.

Activity 8: Discovering pi
Grade level: 4–6

Materials: Twenty-six lids, each labeled with a letter of the alphabet; a class graph as shown in figure 4; string

Fig. 3. Ordering lids by size

Fig. 4. Discovering pi

Chart A (table)

Lid	Circumference	Diameter	Circumference ÷ diameter
G	12.5	4	3.125
M	7.5	2.5	3.0

Chart B (graph)

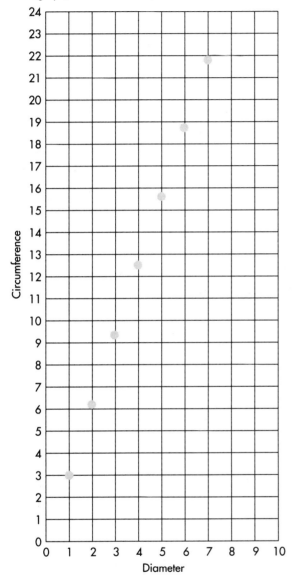

Fig. 5. Recording charts for activity 9

Directions: The students can find out how many diameters are needed to approximately equal a circumference by using the string to measure their lids. Have them cut a piece of string the length of the circumference by wrapping the string around the lid. Have them cut a piece of string for the diameter by measuring the string across the center of the lid. Then have them compare their strings and mark their results on the class bar graph like the one pictured in figure 4. When the graph is completed the relationship will be clear to the students. No matter what the size of the lids, the relationship is constant. Ribbon or paper strips can be used instead of string and may be easier for younger children to handle.

Activity 9: Round things

Grade level: 4–6

Materials: String, ruler, five lids for each child

Directions: This activity is similar to activity 8, but this time standard units are used to measure the circumference and diameter of the lids. Have the students cut two pieces of string—one the length of the circumference and the other the length of the diameter. Have them use a ruler to measure both pieces of string and record their results on charts A and B as shown in figure 5. They should measure five different lids. Encourage the students to use a calculator to find the result of circumference ÷ diameter when filling in the third column in chart A. Naturally, they won't all get exactly 3.14 units, but you can then have the students take the average of all five lids and perhaps even a class average of all the lids; the result will probably be close to 3.14 units.

Jar lids are useful manipulatives adaptable to activities for a variety of mathematical concepts for many grade levels. I'm sure that you'll be able to think of ways to use jar lids to help teach other mathematical concepts, thereby enhancing your mathematics program.

References

California State Department of Education. *Mathematics Framework for California Public Schools: Kindergarten through Grade Twelve.* Sacramento, Calif.: The Department, 1985.

———. *The Mathematics Model Curriculum Guide, Kindergarten through Grade Eight.* Sacramento, Calif.: The Department, 1987.

Szetela, Walter, and Douglas T. Owens. "Finding the Area of a Circle: Use a Cake Pan and Leave Out the Pi." *Arithmetic Teacher* 33 (May 1986): 12–18. ▲

Teaching Mathematics with Technology: Teacher-Made Overhead Manipulatives

by

James H. Wiebe
California State University, Los Angeles, Los Angeles, California

We all have experienced the frustration of trying to use manipulatives to model some mathematics concept to an entire classroom of pupils. Pupil-sized manipulatives are too small for most of the class to see, and besides, how do you hold them up for all to see while manipulating them? Chalkboard drawings cannot be manipulated. Felt-board manipulatives are a little better, but they, too, may be difficult for students to see, can be difficult to manipulate, and require special materials.

To the rescue, your trusty overhead projector on which transparent models can be manipulated and projected for all to see! A limited number of transparent manipulative materials are available commercially, but they are expensive and limited to a few models (e.g., Cuisenaire rods). The alternative is to make transparent models yourself. These manipulatives are easy to make with readily available materials, are easy to manipulate, and are highly visible to everyone in the class. Furthermore, some evidence indicates that students can benefit just as much from watching the teacher manipulate models as from performing their own manipulations (Knaupp 1970).

The general steps for making overhead manipulatives are as follows:

1. Draw the desired shapes in black ink on white paper or use the shapes in the figures in this article.
2. Make a photocopy of the drawings (note: better transparencies result from photocopied drawings than from the original ink or pencil drawings).
3. Copy the photocopied drawings onto transparencies using a heat-transfer copy machine (e.g., Thermofax machine).
4. Cut out the transparent shapes.
5. Color the shapes, if needed, with permanent colored marking pens (e.g., Sharpie permanent markers).
6. You may wish to slightly curl up one or more corners of your manipulatives so that they can be easily picked up and moved on the overhead projector.

What kinds of overhead manipulatives should you make? Of course, that choice depends on the type of manipulatives you use in your class. Descriptions of some of the more useful manipulatives and suggestions for making them follow.

Base-ten blocks

Materials: The shapes in figure 1, heat-transfer transparencies, scissors

Uses: Numeration, whole-number operations, decimal operations, metric measurement concepts

Procedure: Make two copies of the shapes in figure 1 on transparencies and cut them out.

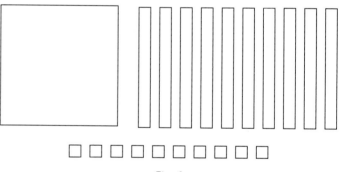

Fig. 1

Colored chips

Materials: A nickel or other object to assist in drawing circles, a black flow pen, paper, transparencies, permanent colored markers, scissors

Uses: Numeration, whole-number operations, other bases (base five, etc.)

Procedure: Draw circles on paper, copy them onto transparencies, and color them using marking pens. An alternative is to copy the circles on colored transparencies.

Place-value charts

Materials: Permanent marker, a transparency, dried beans or similar objects to be used as markers

Uses: Whole-number operations, numeration, decimal operations

Procedure: Draw the place-value chart directly on the transparency or draw it on paper and copy it onto the transparency. Use the beans as markers on the place-value chart.

Number lines

Materials: Black pen and paper, a transparency, one-half-inch-wide strips of paper or one-half-inch-wide strips of colored transparencies, scissors

Uses: Numeration (e.g., rounding), whole-number operations, meaning of fractions, operations on fractions (see Wiebe [1988]), integers, decimal numeration, decimal operations, and so on

Procedure: On paper, draw number lines for wholes, halves, thirds, and so on, as shown in figure 2. The number lines should be parallel and to the same scale. Cut strips of appropriate length from colored transparencies or cut them from clear transparencies and color them with permanent markers. Use these strips to represent fractions, find equivalent fractions, and do operations on fractions. For a more detailed discussion of the use of number lines and strips to represent fractions and operations on fractions, see Wiebe (1985).

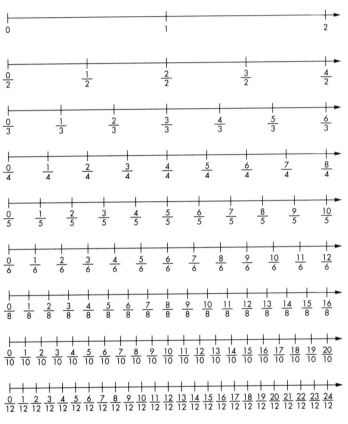

Fig. 2

Grids

Materials: A black pen, paper, a transparency, colored permanent markers, scissors

Uses: Fractions, decimals, and percentages

Procedure: Draw and shade shapes to represent fractions, decimals (e.g., a rectangle with 10 or 100 squares to represent tenths

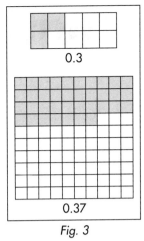

Fig. 3

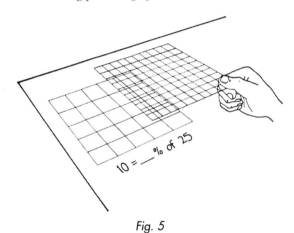

Fig. 4

and hundredths, respectively [see fig. 3]), and percentages. Congruent squares can be shaded in different colors to represent equivalent fractions then superimposed to develop this concept (see fig. 4) (Wiebe 1988). Squares (10 cm by 10 cm) divided into 100 congruent squares and superimposed over other squares can be used to represent percentage problems (see fig. 5) (Wiebe 1986). For a detailed description of the use of transparencies in solving percentage problems, see Wiebe (1986).

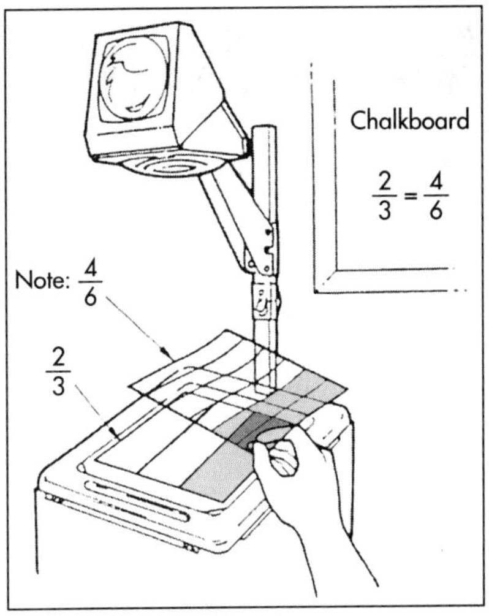

Fig. 5

References

Knaupp, Jonathan Elmer. "A Study of Achievement and Attitude of Second-Grade Students Using Two Modes of Instruction and Two Manipulative Models for the Numeration System." Ph.D. diss., University of Illinois at Urbana–Champaign, 1970. *Dissertation Abstracts International* 31 (1971), no. 6471A. (University Microfilms no. 71-14832)

Wiebe, James H. "Discovering Fractions on a 'Fraction Table.'" *Arithmetic Teacher* 33 (December 1985): 49–51.

———. "Manipulating Percentages." *Mathematics Teacher* 79 (January 1986): 23–26.

———. *Teaching Elementary Mathematics in a Technological Age.* Scottsdale, Ariz.: Gorsuch Scarisbrick Publishers, 1988. ▲

Landmark Mathematics

by

Trudy B. Cunningham

The classroom teacher is frequently caught between the students' lament, "We hate word problems," and the need to teach problem solving. This article suggests an exciting project that will tempt your students to pose questions, state hypotheses, measure, estimate, compute, and evaluate their answers in terms of a problem they can see and manipulate. It is based on the sequence of events that occurred in the Selinsgrove, Pennsylvania, classroom of Sylvia Glant after one of her fourth graders asked her to let the class adopt the four-by-four-by-nine-foot model of the Joseph Priestley House, which had been discarded after a parade (fig. 1). Be forewarned that this is not a lesson that will be given on Monday, tested on Wednesday, and stored in long-term memory on Friday. Moreover, this is a project likely to generate interest in the community and coverage by the local media, because it is one in which mathematics will rub elbows with history, architecture, and common sense.

How would your class respond to the invitation to plan, build, and furnish a scale model of a local historical landmark? Would they be willing to organize their classroom time and energy in such a way that two hours on each of six Thursday afternoons could be devoted to such a project? If so, then the following activities and variations could prove productive as well as interesting.

SELECTION AND ORGANIZATION

Bring to class available literature concerning three or four local landmarks. Allow groups of students to develop a rationale for choosing a particular landmark, to estimate the time needed to build a model of that landmark, and to guess what such a project might cost (fig. 2). After oral presentations and discussion, ask the group to select by secret ballot the best landmark for the project. Create a project log book (fig. 3) in which students record these presentations, a summary of the discussion, and the final vote. Construct a bar graph depicting the votes cast and discuss

A visiting assistant professor of mathematics at Bucknell University (Lewisburg, PA 17837), Trudy Cunningham has taught mathematics in Oregon, Kentucky, and Tennessee. Her daughter, Nancy, participated in a landmark project directed by Sylvia Glant in the public schools of Selinsgrove, Pennsylvania.

Part of the material in this article was presented at the 30th annual meeting of the PCTM in March 1981.

Young carpenters
(Daily Item—Harold Raker)

Fourth graders in the Selinsgrove Area School District's enrichment class in the Freeburg elementary school work to rebuild and remodel a scale model of Northumberland's Joseph Priestley House. The model will be displayed this summer in the Priestley House Museum, Northumberland.

Fig. 1

with the class the most appropriate finished size for the model, given available space and ease of construction.

COLLECTION OF DATA

Invite a local architect to talk to the class about the changes in architecture since the time the chosen landmark was constructed. Plan and make a field trip to the project site during which students are equipped with measuring tapes, clipboards, graph paper for

1. Structural Information:

_____ rooms	_____ windows	_____ available for tour
_____ hallways	_____ fireplaces	_____ furnished
_____ staircases	_____	_____
_____ outside doors	_____	_____

2.

Jobs to be done	No. of students	Time	Cost

Fig. 2. Estimating the cost of a class project

The selection process
- Literature on the three or four landmarks
- Outline of oral presentations
- Summary of the discussion
- Bar graph indicating the vote

Planning the model
- History of the landmark
- Survey sheets
- Scale drawing of each area
- Floor plan
- Pattern and specifications for cutting
- List of materials
- Students' comments on the ongoing project

Sharing the resulting model
- List of visitors
- Outline of presentations
- Clippings from local newspapers

Fig. 3. Suggested Content for Project Log Book

sketches (fig. 4), and a list of needed information (fig. 5). Assign small groups of students to each room in the building, including hallways and staircases. Make other groups responsible for the external features of the structure and the dimensions of the landscape. During the survey trip, ask each student to be responsible for a sketch of the assigned area and a record of its actual dimensions.

Scale drawing of _____ Date _____
By _____
Scale ⬜⬜ =

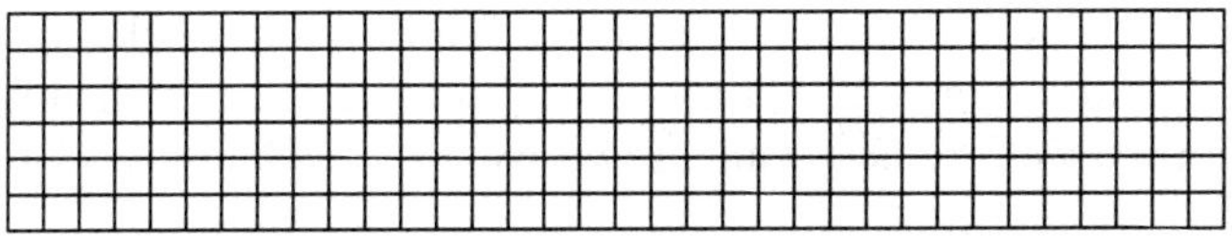

Fig. 4. Graph paper helps keep a record of room sizes.

Survey of _____ by _____
date _____ width _____ length _____ height _____ _____
Special features: _____

Inventory:
number   description   dimensions   suggested materials for model

Fig. 5. A form for information

DEVELOPING A BLUEPRINT

Give students classroom time to make a careful scale drawing of the assigned area. Have students mount the best drawing of each area on the bulletin board and later in the log book. Give committees of students the responsibility of developing a total floor plan and a pattern, complete with exact specifications, from which the sections of frame, walls, floors, and roof will be cut (fig. 6). This process must involve careful translation from the scale of the actual landmark to that of the model. Invite a local contractor or carpenter to help the class develop a careful list of materials. To reduce chaos and increase the need for concise measurement and communication, ask a group of parents or the high school wood shop teacher to build the frame and shell according to the students' specifications, using two-by-fours and masonite. If possible, establish a fund of perhaps fifty dollars from which the class must budget for the project. Use newspaper ads and comparison shopping for the necessary building materials and to gain experience with related problems (see fig. 7). Act surprised when eager students suggest that the class apply for a loan at the local bank, and be prepared for other students to react creatively in scavenging and recycling.

INTERIOR DECORATION

Ask the students to determine the amount of material needed to wallpaper, drape, carpet, and build scaled reproductions of the fixtures and furnishings of the landmark. Invite a furniture salesperson to describe the details appropriate to the period. Use the master list of materials to compare and compute the perimeter and area. The mouldings for the ceilings, baseboards, and door frames require linear measure, whereas carpet, paint, and materials for quilts and curtains must be computed in square units.

FABRICATION

Assign particular furnishings to individual students to design in class and build at home, but do not be surprised when an unassigned grandfather clock and a dining room table with golf-tee legs appear days ahead of schedule. Allow one or more classroom sessions in which to close in the frame of two-by-fours with precut sides of masonite, to install floors, walls, windows, and doors, and to deal with the realities of misfit. Questions like "How could we have measured more accurately?" and "Now, what can we do?" will arise spontaneously. Because too many cooks spoil even the largest pot of stew, have students rotate through the activities of fabricating, finishing, and furnishing. The log book should be brought up to date to include the history of both the landmark and the model.

PUBLICITY

Interest in the project within the school and the community at large will develop early and should be cultivated. Ask your students to prepare oral presentations and invite other classes, teachers, and the principal to attend. Arrange to have the finished model on display at the library or in the landmark itself. If reporters from the local newspapers do not appear, have a student issue written invitations. For several reasons, the finished model is not likely to be suitable for permanent exhibition. Plan,

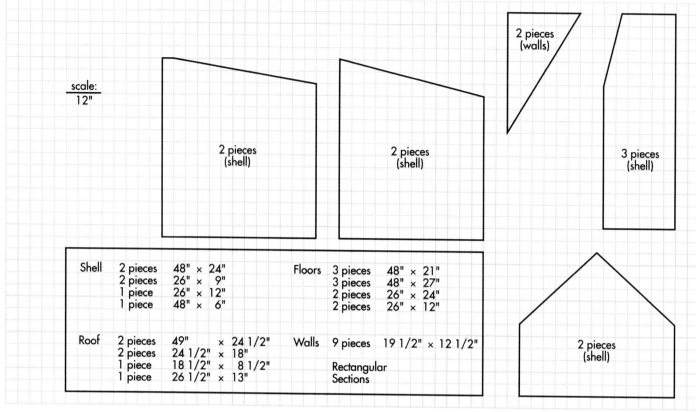

Shell	2 pieces	48" × 24"		Floors	3 pieces	48" × 21"
	2 pieces	26" × 9"			3 pieces	48" × 27"
	1 piece	26" × 12"			2 pieces	26" × 24"
	1 piece	48" × 6"			2 pieces	26" × 12"
Roof	2 pieces	49" × 24 1/2"		Walls	9 pieces	19 1/2" × 12 1/2"
	2 pieces	24 1/2" × 18"				
	1 piece	18 1/2" × 8 1/2"		Rectangular		
	1 piece	26 1/2" × 13"		Sections		

Fig. 6. Cutting plan for Priestley House model

instead, to draw one student's parental permission slip from a box and to send the model, all its furnishings, and a copy of the log book home with that student. Long after the model has gone the way of all creative playthings, the students will reflect with delight on the year it was built in your classroom.

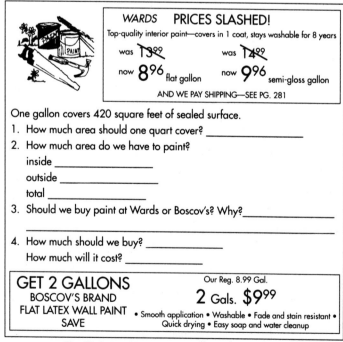

One gallon covers 420 square feet of sealed surface.

1. How much area should one quart cover? _____

2. How much area do we have to paint?

   inside _____

   outside _____

   total _____

3. Should we buy paint at Wards or Boscov's? Why?_____
   _____

4. How much should we buy? _____
   How much will it cost? _____

Fig. 7. Paint: How many gallons do we need?

VARIATIONS

Students and their parents will offer more suggestions than you can incorporate into a finite project. Perhaps a banker could come and compare the cost of borrowing the necessary fifty dollars over six weeks to that of borrowing fifty thousand dollars over thirty years to finance the construction of a new house. Likewise, a consultant from the local power company could explore with the students the energy requirements of the landmark in terms of cubic yards of space to be heated and the relative merits of the heat sources and types of insulation available then and now.

One class might explore the process of determining the areas of irregular figures in computing total surface area or pose the interesting question, "What percent of the roof must be considered in ordering shingles?" Another class might prepare an audiotape for a public service announcement on local radio or television and estimate the cost of equal time if the station charged advertising rates for such announcements. Or, with the school's permission, the class might prepare a simple questionnaire to be given to other students and parents before and after the project.

You will no doubt think of other, more interesting possibilities. Two bits of advice: Keep it simple, and never allow enthusiastic parents and visitors to take over the students' responsibility for planning and construction. The finished model need not be perfect to be a valuable learning experience. ▲

Cooking Up Mathematics in the Kindergarten

by

Elizabeth Partridge

Sue Austin

Elizabeth Wadlington

Joe Bitner

Cooking in the classroom requires hands-on use of measuring tools. Estimation and mental mathematics are integral parts of the process.

How can the NCTM's *Standards* be incorporated into cooking activities? Through cooking, mathematical skills and concepts are connected to each other (e.g., fractions, measurement, estimation), other subjects (e.g., reading, writing, health, science, social studies), and everyday life. Reading and talking about a recipe involve the children in communicating mathematics. Such thoughtful questions as "What do you think will happen if we heat the milk?" encourage children to reason logically, and follow-up experiences allow them to check their conclusions. Naturally occurring conflicts—How can we serve ten banana pops to twenty classmates?—involve children in resolving real-life problems and help them realize the importance of mathematics in practical situations.

Cooking in the kindergarten classroom also allows children to be successful in the use of mental mathematics. The finished product, or completed recipe, rather than a grade, reinforces the accuracy of computations and the importance of cooperation with others. In addition, it presents an alternative to paper-and-pencil tasks that are often overwhelming to young children, particularly those with learning disabilities or different learning styles. Thus, children can begin to form positive beliefs about their mathematical abilities that are not being developed by more traditional teaching methods. Creativity can be fostered as children invent their own recipes for such snacks as punch, salads, or trail mix. They can make their own recipe charts and teach the class how to prepare their foods.

Although cooking activities have been an integral part of kindergarten classes for years, teachers and administrators often do not perceive these experiences as being a springboard for integrating mathematics with other areas of the curriculum. Nutrition, health, and safety, as well as motor, sensory, and social skills, are often emphasized during these activities, with little or no thought given to the academic skills or concepts that can be taught (Cosgrove 1991; Maxim 1993). Science, social studies, reading readiness, language, and especially mathematics can be broadened and enriched through young children's cooking experiences.

Look carefully at all the skills involved in following a recipe.

How can the curriculum be integrated through snack preparation? First, the science-related processes of observing, making inferences, classifying, hypothesizing, and experimenting can occur as teachers lead cooking activities. Language is expanded as new terms are introduced and used. Recipe charts are a natural tool for teaching such reading-readiness skills as left-to-right tracking and top-to-bottom progression, as well as letter, word, and numeral recognition. Various cultures, food sources, customs, and geography can be integrated into lessons as recipes from around the world are tried. Finally, multiple aspects of the *Curriculum and Evaluation Standards for School Mathematics* (NCTM 1989) can be taught in a natural, motivating way.

The authors are on the faculty at Southeastern Louisiana University, Hammond, LA 70402. Elizabeth Partridge's main interest is teaching children through integrating subject matter at the early childhood and elementary levels. Sue Austin is interested in math anxiety as well as in blending affective education in content areas. Elizabeth Wadlington's interests include the diagnosis and remediation of reading and mathematics disabilities. Joe Bitner likes to help teachers use computers and realize the value of employing them for students' use.

Many other mathematical skills and concepts can be learned effectively through cooking activities. Number sense, numeration concepts, and measurement skills are developed as children read recipe charts and count or measure ingredients. Fraction concepts become meaningful as children halve or quarter fruits or vegetables and use measuring cups to determine one-half cup of milk or three-fourths cup of flour. Geometric properties are learned in a natural way as children slice bread diagonally to form triangles or observe the shapes of certain fruits, crackers, or cookies.

Cooking involves communicating about mathematics.

Technology can be incorporated by using calculators and computers. Recipes designating specific serving amounts allow children to estimate quantities for the whole class. Calculators or computers can be used to check the estimations. A database file can be created in which children can enter their recipes.

How are mathematics concepts and skills taught and learned through cooking activities? Teachers can prepare purposeful, hands-on mathematical experiences by (a) carefully choosing those recipes that are conducive to teaching mathematics; (b) thinking through the possibilities for developing number sense, measuring, and reading numerals on charts; and (c) devising questions that will help children develop problem-solving skills. Because all the senses are involved in preparing and eating food, children are totally immersed in the activities and learning is real and has meaning.

MAKING BASIC PREPARATIONS

Before any classroom cooking occurs, check children's health records for food allergies. Next, choose nutritious recipes whose preparation involves specific mathematics concepts and skills. Ask parents to send simple recipes for healthy snacks or check out children's cookbooks from the library. Examine recipes to determine their suitability for teaching such concepts as number sense, fractions, metric use, seriation, or quantity and such skills as counting, numeral recognition, and measuring. Begin with simple recipes that do not require many steps and build to more complicated ones.

Next, make large recipe charts containing amounts, picture clues, and directions. Metric or standard measurement can be used, depending on the objectives of the lesson. For example, if teaching fractions, standard measurement would be more appropriate. Equipment, such as bowls, measuring cups, spoons, plastic serrated knives, pots, pans, wooden spoons, and a hot plate, can be brought from home or donated by parents. Paper plates and aluminum foil can sometimes be donated by the school cafeteria or purchased with snack or supply money. Cleaning supplies should also be available.

Finally, think through the process to anticipate any potential problems, such as spills, measurement errors, or improper use of tools, and determine a solution in advance. Devise appropriate questions that promote creative and critical thinking so as to maximize the learning experience.

GETTING STARTED

Cooking activities are most successful when they are experienced by a small group of children at a learning center. The recipe can be made several times, with children rotating in and out of the center, or several children can be designated as "chefs of the week" who prepare the food for the rest of the class. Simple, self-checking activities can be set up at the remaining centers so that the teacher can concentrate on the cooking activity, or volunteers can supervise the children involved in other centers.

Ask children to wash their hands before the activity and to remember not to put their fingers in their mouths until they have finished. Discuss safety procedures around knives, heat, or electricity. Teach students to respect tools and electricity, not to fear them. Hot plates and popcorn poppers should be strategically placed near the teacher, and wires or extension cords must be taped to the floor to prevent tripping. Position a trash can near the table to help with cleanup.

LEARNING BY DOING

After children are seated, read the recipe chart aloud with them. Go over the chart again, encouraging individual children to point out numerals, fractions, or familiar words or letters. Then let them count cups or ingredients pictured on the chart. (See fig. 1.) Next ask the children to count out or measure the ingredients. If solid ingredients, such as fruits or vegetables, are part of the recipe, have students practice seriation and size by lining up the items from largest to smallest. Discuss fractions as they halve or quarter ingredients or use standard measuring cups. Let them describe food sources, color, and texture as they handle the ingredients. Use new words, such as *dice, puree,* and *grate,* to expand their language. Consider having extra ingredients so that the children can sample them as they are cooking, since sampling will probably occur anyway. While the food is cooking, review the chart, listing the steps taken in the preparation. Ask students to recall the various amounts that went into the recipe and to find these amounts on the chart. Review new fraction concepts and clear up any misconceptions that children might have.

FINISHING UP

Make sure that children understand that cleaning up is an important part of the cooking process and give them sponges to wipe the table. They can also wash the utensils if a sink is located nearby. Peelings, apple cores, celery tips, and other biodegradable matter can be taken to a compost heap. As the children prepare to serve their creation to their classmates, they can count out napkins, cups, or spoons and use one-to-one correspondence as they set the tables. Finally, it is time to eat!

Banana Crepes

Ingredients
350 ml, or 1 1/2 cups, self-rising flour
2 eggs
450 ml, or 2 cups, milk
2 bananas
Confectioners' sugar
Vegetable spray

Equipment
Blender
Electric frying pan
Spoons
Spatula
Bowl
Forks
Napkins
Paper plates

Directions
Mix flour, eggs, milk, and bananas in a blender. (Batter will be thin.) Spray electric frying pan with vegetable spray and heat to 300 degrees. Drop 2 tablespoons of batter per crepe into pan. Cook until underside is golden brown and top is covered with bubbles. Turn and brown on other side. Serve on paper plates and sprinkle with confectioners' sugar. Enjoy!

Apple Corn

Ingredients
4.5 l, or 5 quarts, popped popcorn
100 ml, or 1 stick, margarine
250 ml, or 1 cup, chopped dried apples
125 ml, or 1/2 cup, brown sugar
5 ml, or 1 teaspoon, cinnamon

Equipment
Popcorn popper
Large bowl
Large spoons
Plastic knives
Small saucepan
Hot plate
Paper towels
Paper plates

Directions
Pop popcorn and place in large bowl. While it is popping, chop dried apples. Melt margarine in saucepan. Add chopped apples, brown sugar, and cinnamon. Cook and stir until apples are puffy and start to turn brown. Carefully pour mixture over popcorn. Toss until corn is evenly coated. Let cool and enjoy!

Fig. 1. Sample recipes

All the senses are involved in preparing and eating food.

CONCLUSION

Cooking in the classroom does not have to be limited to health or nutrition lessons. It can foster the development of motor, emotional, social, and intellectual skills at any time. Cutting, stirring, and kneading ingredients develop fine and large muscles and strengthen eye-to-hand coordination. Children learn about success and feel empowered when they complete tasks usually considered to be adults' work. They also learn to cooperate with each other as they share and take turns to achieve a common goal.

Most important, cooking is a wonderful opportunity to integrate mathematics with many areas of the curriculum. So go for it—cook up a little mathematics!

References

Cosgrove, Maryellen S. "Cooking in the Classroom: The Doorway to Nutrition." *Young Children* 46 (March 1991): 43–45.

Maxim, George W. *The Very Young.* New York: Macmillan Publishing Co., 1993.

National Council of Teachers of Mathematics. *Curriculum and Evaluation Standards for School Mathematics.* Reston, Va.: The Council, 1989. ▲

DATE DUE

NOV 09 1999		
NOV 18 1999		
FEB 21 2000		
FEB 21 2000		
MAR 20 2000		
MAR 20 2000		
MAR 05 2002		
FEB 08 2002		
JUN 20 2002		
JUN 08 2002		
MAR 09 2007		
APR 07 2009		
NOV 20 2009		
GAYLORD		PRINTED IN U.S.A.